8, 13

CUSTOMS IN COMMON

Customs in Common

E. P. Thompson

THE MERLIN PRESS
LONDON

Copyright © E. P. Thompson, 1991

Published by The Merlin Press Ltd.,
10 Malden Road, London N. W. 5

set by Heather Hems, Gillingham, Dorset
and printed by Whitstable Litho, Whitstable, Kent

British Library Cataloguing in Publication Data

Thompson, E. P. (Edward Palmer), *1924–*
 Customs in common
 I. Title
 941.07

 ISBN 0-85036-411-6

Cover design by Louis Mackay

Contents

to Martin Eve
uncommon customer

List of Illustrations

Preface and Acknowledgements

The studies in this book were intended as a single closely-related argument. This argument is rehearsed in the Introduction. It has, however, taken much longer to complete than I could ever have intended. It commenced — the work on "time" and on "the moral economy" — soon after I published *The Making of the English Working Class* over twenty years ago. Then it was delayed by work on eighteenth-century crime, which resulted in *Whigs and Hunters* and (with colleagues in the University of Warwick's Centre for the Study of Social History) *Albion's Fatal Tree*. Then, in the early eighties, I was turned aside once again, by the emergency of the "second cold war" and by the heavy demands of the peace movement. I do not regret this: I am convinced that the peace movement made a major contribution to dispersing the cold war, which had descended like a polluting cloud on every field of political and intellectual life. These difficulties (as well as ill health) seriously delayed the completion of *Customs in Common*.

I should explain now what I have done to make a consecutive argument. Two chapters are reproduced with no change from earlier publication. These are "Time, Work-Discipline and Industrial Capitalism", first published in *Past and Present*, no. 38, December 1967, and "The Moral Economy of the English Crowd in the Eighteenth Century", *Past and Present*, no. 50, 1971. In the first case, while interesting new work has been done on the question of time, none of it seemed to call for any major revisions to my article. I have left "the moral economy" to stand for a different reason. The thesis has been much discussed, criticised and developed, and

at some points overtaken by subsequent research. At first I
laboured to revise and to up-date it. But this proved to be a
hopeless task. It was a kind of retrospective moving of the
goal-posts. I found that I was modifying a text upon which
much commentary by other scholars had been hung. I have
therefore republished the original study and have written a
quite new study, of greater length, "The Moral Economy
Reviewed", in which I respond to some critics and reflect
upon the issues raised by others.

The other studies in the book have either been extensively
revised or appear here for the first time. The "Introduction"
and "Patricians and Plebs" include passages which first
appeared in "Patrician Society, Plebeian Culture", *Journal
of Social History*, Vol. 7, no. 4, summer 1974, and
"Eighteenth-century English society: class struggle without
class?", *Social History*, Vol. 3, no. 2, May 1978. A shorter
version of "Rough Music" appeared as " 'Rough Music': Le
Charivari anglais" in *Annales: Économies, Sociétés, Civilisa-
tions*, 27e Année, no. 2, Mars-Avril 1972. I am grateful to the
editors and journals concerned for allowing me to draw upon
this material.

I am grateful also to those institutions and those colleagues
who have afforded me hospitality and the opportunity to
teach and to keep in touch with the historical profession over
this long period. These include several American universities
(Pittsburgh, Rutgers, Brown, Dartmouth College), as well as
a circuit of Indian universities and the Sir Douglas Robb
lectures at the University of Auckland, New Zealand. More
recently I am especially grateful to three universities which
took the risk of inviting me as a visitor — rusty as I was —
and enabled me to rehabilitate myself as a scholar, after the
long diversion of the peace movement years. These were,
first, Queen's University, Kingston, Ontario (1988); the
University of Manchester, which awarded me a Simon Senior
Research Fellowship in 1988-89; and Rutgers University,
which appointed me as Raoul Wallenberg Distinguished
Visiting Professor in 1989-90, working with the Center for
Historical Analysis. Without this generous assistance, and
the stimulus of congenial colleagues, I might have lost touch
with my trade. Finally, my warm thanks are due to the
University of Birmingham, for affording to me library and

research facilities as a Fellow of the Institute for Advanced
Research in the Humanities.

If I were to thank everyone who has sent me references (for
example of rough music or of wife sales) this preface would
be several pages longer. In some cases I have acknowledged
donors in my footnotes. I must beg forgiveness for over-
looking others. Among those who have passed on informa-
tion or who have exchanged views are: John Beattie, the late
Kathleen Bumstead, Andrew Charlesworth, Robin Clifton,
Penelope Corfield, Anna Davin, Natalie Davis, Isabel
Emmett, the late G. Ewart Evans, John Fine, John Fletcher,
Vic Gammon, John Gillis, Inge Goodwin, Jack Goody, the
late Herbert Gutman, Julian Harber, Brian Harrison,
J. F. C. Harrison, Martin Ingram, Joan Lane, Louis
Mackay, the late David Morgan, Polly Morris, Bryan
Palmer, Alfred Peacock, Iorwerth Prothero, Arnold
Rattenbury, Ruth Richardson, John Rule, Raphael Samuel,
Peter Searby, Robert Shenton, Paul Slack, Len Smith,
Michael Sonenscher, Joan Thirsk, Keith Thomas, Dror
Wahrman, John Walsh, E. R. Yarham, Eileen and Stephen
Yeo. Very particular thanks are due to the late E. E. Dodd,
who undertook many searches for me in the Public Record
Office, and to Malcolm Thomas (now Librarian at Friends
House, Euston Road) whose gifted services I was once for-
tunate to have as a research assistant; to Adrian Randall,
Wendy Thwaites and John Walter, for acute commentary on
my "moral economy" texts; to Douglas Hay and Peter
Linebaugh, formerly co-editors of *Albion's Fatal Tree*, for
advice on the law, on crime, and on many other matters; to
Robert Malcolmson and to Rex Russell, for their generosity
in passing on references as to wife sales and agrarian matters;
to Roy Palmer, for sharing his inexhaustible and expert
knowledge of ballad and broadside literature; to Nicholas
Rogers, for keeping me in touch with his outstanding work-
in-progress on the London and provincial crowd; and to
Jeanette Neeson, whose work on eighteenth-century *Commoners* — soon to be published — will transform the
understanding of that century's agrarian and social history,
and to whose insights I am deeply indebted. Further
particular thanks are due to Eveline King, who has skilfully

deciphered and typed my much-corrected manuscript; to two
friends over many years, who are also my publishers — in the
United States, André Schiffrin, until recently the directing
inspiration of Pantheon Books, before this was made impossible by the philistine policies of Random House — and in
Britain, Martin Eve of Merlin Press, who has come to my aid
in every difficulty. Both have been extraordinarily patient
and encouraging in the face of my long delays. Finally,
Dorothy Thompson, who has been my fellow-worker and
who has shared my interests for more than four decades, has
commented on each chapter as it came from the typewriter.
Without her help, of many kinds, this book would not have
been completed.

My thanks are also due to the libraries and county record
offices acknowledged in my footnotes. These include, of
course, the British Library, the British Museum Print Room,
and the Public Record Office. Transcripts of Crown-
Copyright records in the Public Record Office appear by
permission of the Controller of H. M. Stationery Office, and
my thanks are due for permission to reproduce Plates V and
VI. My thanks are also due to the Librarian of Cecil Sharp
house; to the marquess of Cholmondeley (for permission to
draw upon the Cholmondeley (Houghton) papers, now in the
Cambridge University Library); to the Librarian, the William
L. Clement Library, Ann Arbor, Michigan, for permission to
consult the Shelburne Papers; to the Rt. Hon. the Earl St.
Aldwyn (for the papers of Charles Withers); to His Grace,
the duke of Marlborough (for the papers of the earl of
Sunderland at Blenheim Palace); to Lord Crawford, for
permission to reproduce Plates XXIX and XXX, and to all
other sources acknowledged in the footnotes and text. The
passage (see p. 127) from A. W. B. Simpson, *A History of the
Land Law* (Oxford, 2nd edn., 1986) is cited by permission of
Oxford University Press. My thanks also go to the British
Library and British Museum Print Room for permission to
reproduce materials in their collections as illustrations.

Worcester, December 1990

Chapter One

Introduction: Custom and Culture

All the studies in this book are connected by different paths with the theme of custom as it was expressed within the culture of working people in the eighteenth century and into the nineteenth. It is my thesis that customary consciousness and customary usages were especially robust in the eighteenth century: indeed, some "customs" were of recent invention, and were in truth claims to new "rights". Historians of the sixteenth and seventeenth centuries have tended to see the eighteenth century as a time when these customary usages were in decline, along with magic, witchcraft and kindred superstitions. The people were subject to pressures to "reform" popular culture from above, literacy was displacing oral transmission, and enlightenment (it is supposed) was seeping down from the superior to the subordinate orders.

But the pressures of "reform" were stubbornly resisted, and the eighteenth century saw a profound distance opened, a profound alienation between the culture of patricians and plebs. Peter Burke, in his illuminating study of *Popular Culture in Early Modern Europe* (1978) suggests that this distance was a European-wide phenomenon, and that one consequence was the emergence of folklore, as sensitive (and insensitive) observers in the upper ranks of society sent out exploring parties to inspect the "Little Tradition" of the plebs, and to record their strange observances and rituals. Already, as the study of folklore emerged, these usages were coming to be seen as "antiquities" or survivals, and the great pioneer of folklore, John Brand, thought it necessary to preface his *Observations on Popular Antiquities* with an apology for attending to them at all:

... nothing can be foreign to our enquiry, much less beneath our notice, that concerns the smallest of the Vulgar; of those little Ones who occupy the lowest place, though by no means of the least importance in the political arrangement of human Beings.[1]

Thus folklore at its very origin carried this sense of patronising distance, of subordination (Brand noted that pride and the necessities of civil Polity had "portioned out the human Genus into. . . a variety of different and subordinate Species"), and of customs as survivals. For 150 years the preferred methodology of collectors was to group such survivals as "calendar customs", which found their last refuge in the deepest countryside. As one folklorist wrote at the end of the nineteenth century, his object was to describe:

The old customs which still linger on in the obscure nooks and corners of our native land, or which have survived the march of progress in our busy city's life.[2]

To such collectors we are indebted for careful descriptions of well-dressings or rush-bearings or harvest homes or, indeed, late examples of skimmington ridings. But what was lost, in considering (plural) customs as discrete survivals, was any strong sense of custom in the singular (although with many forms of expression), custom not as post-anything but as *sui generis* — as ambience, *mentalité*, and as a whole vocabulary of discourse, of legitimation and of expectation.

In earlier centuries the term "custom" was used to carry much of what is now carried by the word "culture". Custom was man's "second nature". Francis Bacon wrote of custom as induced and habitual inertial behaviour: "Men Profess, Protest, Engage, Give Great Words, and then Doe just as they have Done before. As if they were Dead Images, and Engines moved onely by the Wheeles of *Custome*." For Bacon, then, the problem was to induce better habits and as early in life as possible:

Since Custom is the principal Magistrate of Man's Life, let Men, by all Means, endeavour to obtain good Customs. . . Custom is most perfect

---

[1] John Brand and Henry Ellis, *Observations on Popular Antiquities* (1813), Vol. I, p. xxi. (Brand's Preface is dated 1795.)
[2] P. H. Ditchfield, *Old English Customs extant at the Present Time* (1896), Preface.

when it beginneth in young Years; This we call Education, which is, in Effect, but an early Custom.

Bacon was not thinking of the labouring people, but one hundred years later Bernard Mandeville, who was quite as convinced as was Bacon of the "Tyranny which Custom usurps over us",[1] was a great deal less well-disposed towards any universal provision of education. It was necessary that "great multitudes of People" should "inure their Bodies to Work" both for themselves and to support the more fortunate in Idleness, Ease and Pleasure:

> To make the Society Happy and People Easy under the meanest Circumstances, it is requisite that great numbers of them should be Ignorant as well as Poor. Knowledge both enlarges and multiplies our Desires. . . The Welfare and Felicity therefore of every State and Kingdom require that the Knowledge of the Working Poor should be confin'd within the Verge of their Occupations and never extended (as to things visible) beyond what relates to their Calling. The more a Shepherd, a Plowman or any other Peasant knows of the World, and the things that are Foreign to his Labour or Employment, the less fit he'll be to go through the Fatigues and Hardships of it with Chearfulness and Content.

Hence for Mandeville reading, writing and arithmetic "are very pernicious to the Poor".[2]

If many of the "poor" were denied education, what else did they have to fall back upon but oral transmission with its heavy freight of "custom". If nineteenth-century folklore, by separating survivals from their context, lost awareness of custom as ambience and *mentalité*, so also it lost sight of the rational functions of many customs within the routines of daily and weekly labour. Many customs were endorsed and sometimes enforced by popular pressure and protest. Custom was certainly a "good" word in the eighteenth century: England had long been priding herself on being Good and Old.[3] It was also an operative word. If, along one path, "custom" carried many of the meanings we assign now to

---

[1] Bernard Mandeville, *The Fable of the Bees* (Harmondsworth, 1970 edn.), p. 191: also p. 334.

[2] *Ibid.*, p. 294.

[3] For an excellent survey of custom, 1700-1880, see Bob Bushaway, *By Rite* (1982). Also R. W. Malcolmson, *Life and Labour in England, 1700-1780* (1981), Chapter 4, "Beliefs, customs and identities".

"culture", along another path custom had close affinities with the common law. This law was derived from the customs, or habitual usages, of the country: usages which might be reduced to rule and precedents, which in some circumstances were codified and might be enforceable at law.

This was the case, above all, with *lex loci*, the local customs of the manor. These customs, whose record was sometimes only preserved in the memories of the aged, had legal effect, unless directly voided by statute law.[1] This is discussed more fully in Chapter 3. There were some industrial groups for whom custom was claimed with equal legal force — the Cornish tinners, with their Stannary Court, the free miners of the Forest of Dean with their "Book of Dennis".[2] The rights claimed by the Dean miners could possibly have descended from the thirteenth century, but the "Laws and Customs of the Miners" were codified in an Inquisition of 1610, when 48 free miners recorded their usages (first printed in 1687). Frequently the invocation of the "custom" of a trade or occupation indicated a usage so long exercised that it had taken on the colour of a privilege or right.[3] Thus in 1718 when clothiers in the South-West attempted to lengthen the cloth piece by half a yard, the weavers complained that they were acting "contrary to law, usage and custom from time immemorial". And in 1805 London printers complained that employers were taking advantage of the ignorance of their journeymen by "disputing or denying custom, and by refusing to acknowledge precedents, which have been hitherto the only reference."[4] Many of the classic struggles at the entry to the

[1] "A custom or prescription against a statute is void": but an exception was made for local corn measures, where "it is said. . . the custom of the place is to be observed, if it be a custom beyond all memory, and used without any visible interruption": Richard Burn, *The Justice of the Peace and Parish Officer* (14th edition, 1780), vol. I, p. 408.

[2] For the breakdown of custom in the Forest of Dean, see C. Fisher, *Custom, Work and Market Capitalism* (1981). Is it possible that "Dennis" is a corruption of the Statute of De Donis (1285)?

[3] Several of the studies in E. J. Hobsbawm, *Labouring Men* (1964) bear centrally upon custom. See also John Rule, *The Experience of Labour in Eighteenth-Century Industry* (1981), esp. Chapter 8, "Custom, Culture and Consciousness".

[4] John Rule, *op. cit.*, pp. 194, 196.

industrial revolution turned as much on customs as upon wages or conditions of work.

Most of these customs may be described as "visible": they were codified in some form, or they can be accounted for with exactness. But as the plebeian culture became more opaque to gentry inspection, so other customs became less visible. The ceremonies and processionals of the trades, which had once been built into the calendar of the corporate year — under the patronage of Bishop Blaize for the woolcombers, St. Clement for the blacksmiths, St. Crispin for the shoemakers — might still be celebrated on special occasions, such as coronations or anniversaries, in the eighteenth century. But in the nineteenth century such processionals lost their consensual "trade" endorsement, they were feared by employers and corporations as occasions for high spirits and disorder (as indeed they sometimes were),[1] and St. Clement was honoured, not in the streets, but in the trades' club or friendly society meeting in the tavern.[2]

This is symptomatic of the disassociation between patrician and plebeian cultures in the eighteenth and early nineteenth centuries.[3] It is difficult not to see this division in terms of class. A perceptive folklorist, G. L. Gomme, saw folklore as customs, rites and beliefs belonging to the people —

[1] In 1837 a Woolwich shopkeeper complained that on St. Clements Day [November 23rd] "a procession got up by the Blacksmiths' apprentices passed through the principal streets of the Town, attended by a large Mob, some carrying Torches, others discharging fireworks in great abundance in the most reckless manner, by which the horses attached to one of Mr Wheatley's Omnibuses. . . were so terrified as to. . . run the Pole of the Omnibus through your Memorialist's shop window". Memorial of Robert Wollett of Woolwich, 27 November 1837, in PRO HO 73.2.

[2] William Hone, *Every-Day Book* (1826), vol. I, col. 1499; F. E. Sawyer, "Old Clem Celebrations and Blacksmiths Lore", *Folk Lore Journal*, II, 1884, p. 321; G. P. G. Hills, "Notes on Some Blacksmiths' Legends and the Observance of St. Clement's Day", *Proceedings of the Hampshire Field Club*, vol. VIII, 1917-19, pp. 65-82.

[3] For the polarisation of cultures in the seventeenth century, see the editors' introduction to Anthony Fletcher and John Stevenson (eds.), *Order and Disorder in Early Modern England* (Cambridge, 1985); and for the "momentous split" between patrician and plebeian cultures, see Patrick Curry, *Prophecy and Power: Astrology in Early Modern England* (Oxford, 1989), esp. ch. 7.

And oftentimes in definite antagonism to the accepted customs, rites and beliefs of the State or the nation to which the people and the groups of people belong. These customs, rites and beliefs are mostly kept alive by tradition. . . They owe their preservation partly to the fact that great masses of people do not belong to the civilisation which towers over them and which is never of their own creation.[1]

In the eighteenth century custom was the rhetoric of legitimation for almost any usage, practice, or demanded right. Hence uncodified custom — and even codified — was in continual flux. So far from having the steady permanence suggested by the word "tradition", custom was a field of change and of contest, an arena in which opposing interests made conflicting claims. This is one reason why one must be cautious as to generalisations as to "popular culture". This may suggest, in one anthropological inflexion which has been influential with social historians, an over-consensual view of this culture as "a system of shared meanings, attitudes and values, and the symbolic forms (performances, artifacts) in which they are embodied".[2] But a culture is also a pool of diverse resources, in which traffic passes between the literate and the oral, the superordinate and the subordinate, the village and the metropolis; it is an arena of conflictual elements, which requires some compelling pressure — as, for example, nationalism or prevalent religious orthodoxy or class consciousness — to take form as "system". And, indeed, the very term "culture", with its cosy invocation of consensus, may serve to distract attention from social and cultural contradictions, from the fractures and oppositions within the whole.

At this point generalisations as to the universals of "popular culture" become empty unless they are placed firmly within specific historical contexts. The plebeian culture which clothed itself in the rhetoric of "custom" and which is the central theme of this book was not self-defining or independent of external influences. It had taken form defensively, in opposition to the constraints and controls of

[1]G. L. Gomme, *Encyclopaedia of Religion and Ethics* (Edinburgh, 1913), entry on folklore, pp. 57-9, cited in Bushaway, *op. cit.*, pp. 10-11.
[2]P. Burke, *Popular Culture in Early Modern Europe* (1978), Preface, citing A. L. Kroeber and C. Kluckhohn, *Culture: a Critical Review of Concepts and Definitions* (New York, 1952).

the patrician rulers. The confrontations and negotiations between patricians and plebs are explored in Chapter 2, and case studies of the conflict between customary and innovative ("market") *mentalités* follow. In these studies I hope that plebeian culture becomes a more concrete and usable concept, no longer situated in the thin air of "meanings, attitudes and values", but located within a particular equilibrium of social relations, a working environment of exploitation and resistance to exploitation, of relations of power which are masked by the rituals of paternalism and deference. In this way (I hope) "popular culture" is situated within its proper material abode.

Let us resume the characteristic features of the eighteenth-century plebeian culture. As a matter of course it exhibits certain features commonly ascribed to "traditional" cultures. In rural society, but also in thickly populated manufacturing and mining areas (the West of England clothing regions, the Cornish tinners, the Black Country) there is a heavy inheritance of customary definitions and expectations. Apprenticeship as an initiation into adult skills is not confined to its formal industrial expression. It is also the mechanism of inter-generational transmission. The child serves her apprenticeship to household duties, first to her mother (or grandmother), then (often) as a domestic or farm servant. As a young mother, in the mysteries of child-rearing, she is apprentice to the matrons of the community. It is the same in the trades without formal apprenticeship. And with the induction into these particular skills comes an induction into the social experience or common wisdom of the community. Although social life is changing, and although there is much mobility, change has not yet reached that point at which it is assumed that the horizons of each successive generation will be different; nor has that engine of cultural acceleration (and estrangement), formal education, yet interpolated itself significantly into this generational transmission.[1]

[1] Two interesting studies of the restraint which custom may impose upon material expectations are: G. M. Foster, "Peasant Society and the Image of Limited Good", *American Anthropologist*, April 1965; Daniel Vickers, "Competency and Competition: Economic Culture in Early

Both practices and norms are reproduced down the generations within the slowly differentiating ambience of custom.
Traditions are perpetuated largely through oral transmission, with its repertoire of anecdote and of narrative
example; where oral tradition is supplemented by growing
literacy, the most widely circulated printed products, such as
chapbooks, almanacs, broadsides, "last dying speeches" and
anecdotal accounts of crime, tend to be subdued to the
expectations of the oral culture rather than challenging it with
alternatives.

This culture transmits vigorously — and perhaps it also
generates — ritualized or stylized performances, whether in
recreation or in forms of protest. It is even possible that
geographic mobility, together with growing literacy, actually
extends the range and distributes such forms more widely:
"setting the price", as the central action of a food riot, moves
across most of the country (Chapter 4); the ritual divorce
known as a "wife sale" appears to have distributed its
incidence throughout the country from some unknown point
of origin (Chapter 7). The evidence of rough music (Chapter
8) suggests that in the more traditional communities — and
these were by no means always ones with a rural profile —
quite powerful self-motivating forces of social and moral
regulation were at work. This evidence may show that while
deviant behaviour might be tolerated up to a point, beyond
that point the community sought to impose upon trans-
gressors its own inherited expectations as to approved marital
roles and sexual conduct. Even here, however, we have to
proceed with caution: this is not *just* "a traditional
culture". The norms so defended are not identical with those
proclaimed by Church or authority; they are defined within
the plebeian culture itself, and the same shaming rituals
which are used against a notorious sexual offender may be
used against the blackleg, or against the squire and his game-
keepers, the excise officer, the JP.

This, then, is a conservative culture in its forms, which
appeal to and seek to reinforce traditional usages. The forms

America", *William and Mary Quarterly*, 3rd series, vol. xlvii, no. 1,
January 1990.

are also non-rational; they do not appeal to "reason" through the pamphlet, sermon or platform; they impose the sanctions of force, ridicule, shame, intimidation. But the content or meanings of this culture cannot so easily be described as conservative. For in social reality labour is becoming, decade by decade, more "free" of traditional manorial, parochial, corporate and paternal controls, and more distanced from direct client dependence upon the gentry. Hence we have a customary culture which is not subject in its daily operations to the ideological domination of the rulers. The gentry's overarching hegemony may define the limits within which the plebeian culture is free to act and grow, but since this hegemony is secular rather than religious or magical it can do little to determine the character of this plebeian culture. The controlling instruments and images of hegemony are those of the Law and not those of the Church or of monarchical charisma. But the Law does not sow pious sisterhoods in cities nor extract the confessions of sinners; its subjects do not tell their rosaries nor go on pilgrimages to the shrines of saints — instead they read broadsides and carouse in taverns and at least some of the Law's victims are regarded, not with horror, but with an ambiguous admiration. The Law may punctuate the limits tolerated by the rulers; it does not, in eighteenth-century England, enter into the cottages, find mention in the widow's prayers, decorate the wall with icons, or inform a view of life.

Hence one characteristic paradox of the century: we have a *rebellious* traditional culture. The conservative culture of the plebs as often as not resists, in the name of custom, those economic rationalizations and innovations (such as enclosure, work-discipline, unregulated "free" markets in grain) which rulers, dealers, or employers seek to impose. Innovation is more evident at the top of society than below, but since this innovation is not some normless and neutral technological/sociological process ("modernization", "rationalization") but is the innovation of capitalist process, it is most often experienced by the plebs in the form of exploitation, or the expropriation of customary use-rights, or the violent disruption of valued patterns of work and leisure (Chapter 6). Hence the plebian culture is rebellious, but rebellious in defence of custom. The customs defended are the people's own, and some of them are in fact based upon rather recent assertions in practice. But when the people search for legitimations for protest, they often turn back to the paternalist regulations of a more authoritarian society, and select from among these those parts most calculated to defend their present interests — food rioters appeal back to the Book of Orders and to legislation against forestallers, etc., artisans appeal back to certain parts (e.g. apprenticeship regulation) of the Tudor labour code.

Nor is the social identity of many working people unambiguous. One can often detect within the same individual alternating identities, one deferential, the other rebellious.[1] This was a problem with which — using different terms — Gramsci concerned himself. He noted the contrast between the "popular morality" of folklore tradition and "official morality". His "man-in-the-mass" might have "two theoretical consciousnesses (or one contradictory consciousness)" — one of praxis, the other "inherited from the past and uncritically absorbed". When discussing ideology in his prison notebooks, Gramsci sees it as resting upon "the spontaneous philosophy which is proper to everybody". This philosophy (he concludes) derives from three sources: first, "language itself, which is a totality of determined notions and concepts, and not just of words, grammatically devoid of content"; second, "common sense"; and, third, popular religion and folklore.[2] Of these three, most Western intellectuals today would unhesitatingly award theoretical primacy to the first (language) as not only the carrier but as the constitutive influence upon consciousness. Indeed, while actual language — for example as dialect — has been little examined,[3] it has become fashionable to assume that the

[1] See Hans Medick, "Plebeian Culture in the Transition to Capitalism", in R. Samuel and G. Stedman Jones (eds.), *Culture, Ideology and Politics* (1982).

[2] See Antonio Gramsci, *Selections from the Prison Notebooks* (1971), pp. 419-25; Bushaway, *op. cit.*, pp. 11-12; T. J. Jackson Lears, "The Concept of Cultural Hegemony: Problems and Possibilities", *American Hist. Rev.*, 90, 1985.

[3] Social historians have made too little use of dialect studies, including Joseph Wright's in *English Dialect Dictionary*, 6 volumes (1898-1905), which is full of clues as to working usages.

plebs were in a sense "spoken" by their linguistic inheritance, which in turn is seen as a *bricolage* of disparate notions derivative from many sources but held in place by patrician categories. The plebs are even seen as captives within a linguistic prison, compelled even in moments of rebellion to move within the parameters of constitutionalism, of "Old England", of deference to patrician leaders and of patriarchy.

We can follow this argument some way. But what it over-looks are Gramsci's alternative sources of "spontaneous philosophy", and in particular "common sense" or praxis. For Gramsci also insisted that this philosophy was not simply the appropriation of an individual but was derived from shared experiences in labour and in social relations, and is "implicit in his activity and which in reality unites him with all his fellow-workers in the practical transformation of the real world. . ." Thus the "two theoretical consciousnesses" can be seen as derivative from two aspects of the same reality: on the one hand, the necessary conformity with the *status quo* if one is to survive, the need to get by in the world as it is in fact ordered, and to play the game according to the rules imposed by employers, overseers of the poor, etc.;[1] on the other hand the "common sense" derived from shared experience with fellow workers and with neighbours of exploitation, hardship and repression, which continually exposes the text of the paternalist theatre to ironic criticism and (less frequently) to revolt.

Another feature of this culture which is of special interest to me is the priority afforded, in certain areas, to "non-economic" over direct monetary sanctions, exchanges and motivations. This feature is now widely discussed as "the moral economy", and is the theme of Chapters 4 and 5. Again and again, when examining the behaviour of working people in the eighteenth century one finds it to be necessary to "de-code" this behaviour and its symbolic modes of expression and to disclose invisible rules unlike those which a historian of subsequent working-class movements has come to expect. In attending to the symbolism of protest, or in

[1] See my "Folklore, Anthropology, and Social History", *Indian Hist. Rev.*, vol. III, no. 2, Jan. 1977, p. 265.

decoding rough music or the sale of wives, one shares some of the preoccupations of historians of the sixteenth and seventeenth centuries of an anthropological orientation. In another sense the problems are different, and perhaps more acute, for capitalist process and non-economic customary behaviour are in active and conscious conflict, as in resistance to new patterns of consumption ("needs"), or in resistance to technical innovations or work-rationalizations which threaten to disrupt customary usage and, sometimes, the familial organization of productive roles.[1] Hence we can read much eighteenth-century social history as a succession of confrontations between an innovative market economy and the customary moral economy of the plebs.

In these confrontations it is possible to see prefigurements of subsequent class formations and consciousness; and the fragmented débris of older patterns are revivified and reintegrated within this emergent class consciousness. In one sense the plebeian culture is the people's own: it is a defence against the intrusions of gentry or clergy; it consolidates those customs which serve their own interests; the taverns are their own, the fairs are their own, rough music is among their own means of self-regulation. This is not *any* "traditional" culture but a rather peculiar one. It is not, for example, fatalistic, offering consolations and defences in the course of a lifetime which is utterly determined and constrained. It is, rather, picaresque, not only in the obvious sense that more people are mobile, go to sea, are carried off to wars, experience the hazards and adventures of the road.[2] In more settled ambiences — in the growing areas of manufacture and of "free" labour — life itself proceeds along a road whose hazards and accidents cannot be prescribed or avoided by forethought: fluctuations in the incidence of mortality, of prices, of unemployment, are experienced as external

[1] See, for example, Adrian J. Randall, "Work, Culture and Resistance to Machinery in the West of England Woollen Industry", in Pat Hudson (ed.), *Regions and Industries: a perspective on the Industrial Revolution in Britain* (Cambridge, 1989).
[2] Extreme examples of picaresque livelihoods are in Marcus Rediker, *Between the devil and the deep blue sea* (Cambridge, 1987), and Peter Linebaugh, *The London Hanged* (Harmondsworth, 1991).

accidents beyond any control; in general, the working population has little predictive notation of time — they do not plan "careers", or plan families, or see their lives in a given shape before them, or salt away weeks of high earnings in savings, or plan to buy cottages, or ever in their lives take a "vacation". (A young man, knowing that this will be so, may set off once in a lifetime, upon the road to "see the world".) Hence opportunity is grabbed as occasion arises, with little thought of the consequences, just as the crowd imposes its power in moments of insurgent direct action, knowing that its moment of triumph will last for only a week or a day.

I criticised earlier the term "culture", because of its tendency to nudge us towards over-consensual and holistic notions. And yet I have been driven back to an account of "plebeian culture" which may be open to the same criticisms. This may not much matter if we are using "culture" as a loosely descriptive term. After all, there are other descriptive terms in common currency, such as "society", "politics" and "economy": no doubt these deserve close interrogation from time to time, but if on every occasion that these were employed we had to engage in an exercise of rigorous definition the discourse of knowledge would indeed be cumbersome.

Even so we should not forget that "culture" is a clumpish term, which by gathering up so many activities and attributes into one common bundle may actually confuse or disguise discriminations that should be made between them. We need to take this bundle apart, and examine the components with more care: rites, symbolic modes, the cultural attributes of hegemony, the inter-generational transmission of custom and custom's evolution within historically specific forms of working and social relations. As the anthropologist Gerald Sider has shown in a group of astute studies of Newfoundland fishing villages:

> Customs do things — they are not abstract formulations of, or searches for, meanings, although they may convey meaning. Customs are clearly connected to, and rooted in, the material and social realities of life and work, although they are not simply derivative from, or reexpressions of these realities. Customs may provide a context in which people may do things it would be more difficult to do directly. . . they may keep the need for collective action, collective adjustment of interests, and

collective expression of feelings and emotions within the terrain and
domain of the coparticipants in a custom, serving as a boundary to
exclude outsiders.[1]

If I were to nominate those components of the bundle
which makes up "popular culture" which most require attention today, these would include "needs" and "expectations"
The industrial revolution and accompanying demographic
revolution were the backgrounds to the greatest transformation in history, in revolutionising "needs" and in
destroying the authority of customary expectations. This is
what most demarks the "pre-industrial" or the "traditional"
from the modern world. Successive generations no longer
stand in an apprentice relation to each other. If we need a
utilitarian apologia for our historical enquiry into custom —
but I think we do not — it might be found in the fact that this
transformation, this remodelling of "need" and this raising
of the threshold of material expectations (along with the
devaluation of traditional cultural satisfactions) continues
with irreversible pressure today, accelerated everywhere by
universally available means of communication. These
pressures are now felt among one billion Chinese, as well as
countless millions in Asian and African villages.

It is not simple to discuss these problems from our
comfortable perspective to the "North" of the global divide.
Any historian of labour is only too well aware of the self-
interest and the class-bound apologetics which can always
find reasons why the poor should stay poor. To cite Bernard
Mandeville once more:

> It is impossible that a Society can long subsist and suffer many of its
> Members to live in Idleness, and enjoy all the Ease and Pleasure they
> can invent, without having at the same time great multitudes of People
> that to make good this effect, will condescend to be quite the Reverse,
> and by use and patience inure their Bodies to Work for others and
> themselves besides.[2]

This text has not lost its force today: it is the hidden text of
the discourse between North and South. Yet we know also
that global expectations are rising like Noah's flood, and that

[1]Gerald M. Sider, *Culture and Class in Anthropology and History*
(Cambridge, 1986), p. 940.
[2]Mandeville, *op. cit.*, pp. 292-3.

the readiness of the human species to define its needs and satisfactions in material market terms — and to throw all the globe's resources onto the market — may threaten the species itself (both South and North) with ecological catastrophe. The engineer of this catastrophe will be economic man, whether in classically avaricious capitalist form or in the form of the rebellious economic man of the orthodox Marxist tradition.

As capitalism (or "the market") made over human nature and human need, so political economy and its revolutionary antagonist came to suppose that this economic man was for all time. We stand at the end of a century when this must now be called in doubt. We shall not ever return to pre-capitalist human nature, yet a reminder of its alternative needs, expectations and codes may renew our sense of our nature's range of possibilities. Could it even prepare us for a time when both capitalist and state communist needs and expectations may decompose, and human nature may be made over in a new form? This is, perhaps, to whistle into a typhoon. It is to invoke the rediscovery, in new forms, of a new kind of "customary consciousness", in which once again successive generations stand in apprentice relation to each other, in which material satisfactions remain stable (if more equally distributed) and only cultural satisfactions enlarge, and in which expectations level out into a customary steady state. I do not think that this is likely to happen. But I hope that the studies in this book may illuminate how custom is formed and how complex is its operation.

Chapter Two

The Patricians and the Plebs

"The miserable Circumstance of this Country is now such, that, in short, if it goes on, the Poor will be Rulers over the Rich, and the Servants be Governours of their Masters, the *Plebeij* have almost mobb'd the *Patricij*. . . in a Word, Order is inverted, Subordination ceases, and the World seems to stand with the Bottoim upward."

Daniel Defoe, *The Great Law of Subordination considered or, The Insolence and Insufirable Behaviour of SERVANTS in England duly enquired into* (1724).

I

The relationship which I wish to examine in this chapter is that between "the gentry" and "the labouring poor". Both terms are vague. But we have some notion as to what both stand for. In the first six decades of the eighteenth century one tends to associate the gentry with the land. Land remained the index of influence, the plinth on which power was erected. If one adds to direct landed wealth and status, that part of industry which either directly served the agricultural interest (transport, saddlery, wheelwrights, etc.) or which processed agricultural products (brewing, tanning, milling, the great woollen industry, etc.) one can see where the scales of wealth were tipped. So that, despite the immense growth of London and the growth of Liverpool, Manchester, Bristol, Birmingham, Norwich, Leeds etc., England retained until the 1760s an agrarian profile, and many who earned their wealth in urban, commercial occupations still sought to translate their wealth into gentry status by translating it into land. William Hutton, the Birmingham paper merchant, describes in his memoirs his first purchase of lands (1766): "ever since I was 8 years old, I had shewn a fondness for land. . . and wished to call some my own. This ardent desire after dirt never forsook me."[1]

Yet both "gentlemen" and "the poor" are "gentry-made terms"[2] and both carry a normative freight which can be taken on board uncritically by historians. We are told (for example) that "honour, dignity, integrity, considerateness, courtesy and chivalry were all virtues essential to the character of a gentleman, and they all derived in part from the nature of country life".[3] This suggests a somewhat distanced view of "country life", from which — just as from much eighteenth-century painting of the countryside[4] — the labourers have been subtracted. As for "the poor" this wholly indiscriminate term carries the suggestion that the bulk of the working population were deserving of gentry condescension, and perhaps of charity (and were somehow supported *by* the gentry instead of the direct opposite); and the term puts together paupers and fiercely-independent yeomen, small peasants, farm servants, rural artisans, and so on, in the same gentry-made category.

Vague as the two terms are, yet this chapter will turn upon these two poles and their relation to each other. I shall pass over a great deal of what lies in between: commerce, manufacture, London's luxury trades, overseas empire. And my emphases will not be those which are popular with most established historians. There is perhaps a reason for this. No-one is more susceptible to the charms of the gentry's life than the historian of the eighteenth century. His major sources are in the archives of the gentry or aristocracy. Perhaps he may even find some of his sources still in the muniments room at an ancient landed seat. The historian can easily identify with his sources: he sees himself riding to hounds, or attending Quarter Sessions, or (if he is less ambitious) he sees himself as at least seated at Parson Woodforde's groaning table. The "labouring poor" did not leave their workhouses stashed with documents for historians to work over nor do they invite

[1] *The Life of William Hutton* (1817), p. 177.
[2] Jeanette Neeson gave me the term "gentry-made" for "the poor".
[3] F. M. L. Thompson, *English Landed Society in the Nineteenth Century* (1963), p. 16.
[4] See John Barrell, *The Dark Side of the Landscape* (Cambridge, 1980).

identification with their back-breaking toil. Nevertheless for the majority of the population the view of life was not that of the gentry. I might phrase it more strongly, but we should attend to the quiet words of M. K. Ashby: "The great house seems to me to have kept its best things to itself, giving, with rare exceptions, neither grace nor leadership to villages, but indeed depressing their manhood and culture."[1]

When I and some colleagues offered, a few years ago, a somewhat sceptical view of the virtues of the Whig great gentry and of their lawyers some part of the historical profession was scandalised.[2] Our threat was beaten off, and a view of eighteenth-century England has been reconstituted which passes over, with a few words, the society's deep contradictions. We are told that it was a thriving "consumer society" (whatever that means) populated by "a polite and commercial people".[3] We are not reminded sharply that this was the century in which the commoners finally lost their land, in which the number of offences carrying the capital penalty multiplied, in which thousands of felons were transported, and in which thousands of lives were lost in imperial wars; a century which ended, despite the agricultural "revolution" and the swelling rent-rolls, in severe rural immiseration. Meanwhile the historical profession maintains a bland view of things: historical conferences on eighteenth-century questions tend to be places where the bland lead the bland. We will attempt a less reassuring reconstruction.

It has been a common complaint that the terms "feudal", "capitalist", or "bourgeois" are too imprecise, and cover phenomena too vast and disparate, to be of serious analytic service. We now, however, find constantly in service a new set of terms such as "pre-industrial", "traditional", "paternalism" and "modernization", which appear to be open to very much the same objections; and whose

[1] M. K. Ashby, *Joseph Ashby of Tysoe* (Cambridge 1961 and London, 1974).

[2] See my *Whigs and Hunters* (London and New York, 1975), and D. Hay, P. Linebaugh and E. P. Thompson (eds.), *Albion's Fatal Tree* (London and New York, 1975).

[3] P. Langford, *A Polite and Commercial People: England 1727-1783* (Oxford, 1989).

PATRICIANS AND PLEBS   19

theoretical paternity is less certain.

It may be of interest that whereas the first set of terms
direct attention to conflict or tension within the social
process, the second set appear to nudge one towards a view of
society in terms of a self-regulating sociological order. They
offer themselves, with a specious scientism, as if they were
value-free. They also have an eerie timelessness. My own
particular dislike is "pre-industrial", a tent within whose
spacious folds there sit beside each other West of England
clothiers, Persian silversmiths, Guatemalan shepherds, and
Corsican bandits.[1]

However, let us leave them happily in their bazaar,
exchanging their surprising cultural products, and look more
closely at "paternalism". In some writers the "patriarchal"
and the "paternal" appear as interchangeable terms, the one
carrying a sterner, the other a somewhat softened implication. The two may indeed run into each other in fact as well
as in theory. In Weber's description of "traditional" societies
the locus for analysis is posited in the familial relations of the
tribal unit or household, and from these are extrapolated
relations of domination and dependency which come to
characterise a "patriarchal" society as a whole — forms
which he relates specifically to ancient and feudal forms of
social order. Laslett, who has reminded us urgently as to the
social centrality of the economic "household" in the
seventeenth century, suggests that this contributed to the
reproduction of paternal or of patriarchal attitudes and relations which permeated the whole of society — and which
perhaps continued to do so until the moment of
"industrialization".[2] Marx, it is true, had tended to see
patriarchal attitudes as characteristic of the guild system of
the Middle Ages, when:

> The journeymen and apprentices were organised in each craft as it best
> suited the interest of the masters. The filial relationship in which they
> stood to their masters gave the latter a double power — on the one hand

[1] "Proto-industrial" introduces new difficulties, but it is a more
precise concept than "pre-industrial" and preferable for descriptive
purposes.
[2] This impression was given in Peter Laslett's *The World We Have
Lost* (1965). For a stricter view of theories of patriarchy, see G. Schochet,
Patriarchalism in Political Thought (New York, 1975).

because of their influence on the whole life of the journeymen, and on the other because, for the journeymen who worked with the same master, it was a real bond, which held them together against the journeymen of other masters and separated them from these.

Marx argued that in "manufacture" these relations were replaced by "the monetary relation between worker and capitalist"; but this relationship "in the countryside and in small towns retained a patriarchal tinge".[1] This is a large allowance, especially when we recall that at any time before about 1840 the bulk of the British population lived in such conditions.

And so for "a patriarchal tinge" we may substitute the weaker term, "paternalism". It may seem that this magical social quantum, every day refreshed from the innumerable springs of the small workshop, the economic household, the landed estate, was strong enough to inhibit (except here and there, for brief episodes) class confrontation, until industrialisation brought all that in its train. Before this occurred, there was no class-conscious working class; no class-conflict of that kind, but only fragments of proto-conflict; as an historical agent, the working class did not exist, and, since this is so, the exceedingly difficult business of attempting to find out what was the actual conscious-ness of the inarticulate labouring poor would be tedious and unnecessary. We are invited to think of the consciousness of a Trade rather than of a class, of vertical rather than horizontal divisions. We can even speak of a "one-class" society.

Examine the following accounts of the eighteenth-century landed gentleman. The first —

The life of a hamlet, a village, a parish, a market town and its hinterland, a whole county, might revolve around the big house in its park. Its reception rooms, gardens, stables and kennels were the centre of local social life; its estate office the exchange for farm tenancies, mining and building leases, and a bank for small savings and investments; its home farm a permanent exhibition of the best avail-able agricultural methods. . .; its law room. . . the first bulwark of law

---

[1] This is from a very general passage in *The German Ideology* (1845). See Marx and Engels, *Collected Works* (1976), V, pp. 65-7. For the difficulties arising from the appropriation to somewhat different meanings of "patriarchy" in feminist theory, see below, pp. 499-503.

and order; its portrait gallery, music-room and library the head-quarters of local culture; its dining-room the fulcrum of local politics.

And here is the second —

> In the course of running his property for his own interests, safety and convenience he performed many of the functions of the state. He was the judge: he settled disputes among his followers. He was the police: he kept order among a large number of people. . . He was the Church: he named the chaplain, usually some near relative with or without religious training, to care for his people. He was a welfare agency: he took care of the sick, the aged, the orphans. He was the army: in case of uprisings. . . he armed his kin and retainers as a private militia. Moreover, through what became an intricate system of marriages, kinship, and sponsorship. . . he could appeal for support if need be to a large number of relatives in the country or in the towns who possessed property and power similar to his own.

These are both acceptable descriptions of the eighteenth-century landed gentleman. However, it happens that one describes the aristocracy or great gentry of England, the other the slave-owners of Colonial Brazil.[1] Both might, equally, and with the smallest revision, describe a patrician in the *campagna* of ancient Rome, one of the landowners in Gogol's *Dead Souls*, a slave-holder in Virginia,[2] or the landowners in any society in which economic and social authority, summary judicial powers, etc., were united in a single place.

Some difficulties, however, remain. We may call a concentration of economic and cultural authority "paternalism" if we wish. But if we allow the term, then we must also allow that it is too large for discriminating analysis. It tells us little about the nature of power and of the State; about forms of property-ownership; about ideology and culture; and it is even too blunt to distinguish between modes of exploitation, between slave and free labour.

Moreover, it is a description of social relations as they may be seen from above. This does not invalidate it, but one should be aware that such a description may be too

[1] Harold Perkin, *The Origins of Modern English Society 1780-1800* (1969), p. 42; Alexander Marchant, "Colonial Brazil", in X. Livermore (ed.), *Portugal and Brazil: an Introduction* (Oxford, 1953), p. 297.

[2] See Eugene D. Genovese, *The World the Slaveholders Made* (New York, 1969), esp. p. 96.

persuasive. If the first description is the only one that we are offered, then it is only too easy to pass from this to some view of a "one-class society"; the great house is at the apex, and all lines of communication run to its dining-room, estate office or kennels. This is, indeed, an impression easily gained by the student who works among estate papers, quarter sessions records, or the duke of Newcastle's correspondence.

But there might be other ways of describing the society than the one offered by Harold Perkin in the first of our two extracts. The life of a parish might equally well revolve around the weekly market, the summer and winter festivals and fairs, the annual village feast, as about the occasions of the big house. The gossip of poaching, theft, sexual scandal and the behaviour of the overseers of the poor might occupy people's minds rather more than the remote comings and goings up at the park. The majority in the village would have little occasion for savings or investment or for agricultural improvement: they might be more bothered about access to firing, turves and grazing on the common than to crop rotations.[1] The law might appear not as a "bulwark" but as a bully. Above all, there might be a radical disassociation — and at times antagonism — between the culture and even the "politics" of the poor and those of the great.

Few would dispute this. But descriptions of the social order in the first sense, as seen from above, are far more common than are attempts to reconstruct the view from below. And whenever the notion of "paternalism" is introduced, it is the first model which it calls to mind. And the term cannot rid itself of normative implications: it suggests human warmth, in a mutually assenting relationship; the father is conscious of duties and responsibilities towards his son, the son is acquiescent or actively complaisant in his filial station. Even the model of the small economic household carries (despite disclaimers) some sense of emotional cosiness: "time was", Laslett once wrote, "when the whole of life went forward in the family, in a circle of loved, familiar faces, known and fondled objects, all to human size".[2] It

---

[1] They might have been surprised to learn that they belonged to a "consumer society".

[2] See Laslett, *ibid.*, p. 21.

would be unfair to meet this with the reminder that *Wuthering Heights* is presented in exactly such a familial situation. Laslett was reminding us of a relevant aspect of small-scale economic relations, even if the warmth could be of impotent revolt against abject dependency as often as it could be a warmth of mutual respect. In the early years of the industrial revolution workers often harked back to lost paternalist values, Cobbett and Oastler enlarged upon the sense of loss, and Engels endorsed the grievance.

But this raises a further problem. Paternalism as myth or as ideology is nearly always backward-looking. It offers itself in English history less as actuality than as a model of an antique, recently passed, golden age from which present modes and manners are a degeneration. Thus we have Langhorne's *Country Justice* (1774):

> When thy good father held this wide domain,
> The voice of sorrow never mourn'd in vain.
> Sooth'd by his pity, by his bounty fed,
> The sick found medecine, and the aged bread.
> He left their interest to no parish care,
> No bailiff urged his little empire there;
> No village tyrant starved them, or oppress'd;
> He learn'd their wants, and he those wants redress'd. . .
>
> The poor at hand their natural patrons saw,
> And lawgivers were supplements of law!

And so on, to the disclaimer that such relations have any present reality:

> . . . Fashion's boundless sway
> Has borne the guardian magistrate away.
> Save in Augusta's streets, on Gallia's shores,
> The rural patron is beheld no more. . .

But we may take our literary sources where we will. We may move back some sixty or seventy years to Sir Roger de Coverley, a late survivor, a quaint old-fashioned man, both ridiculous and lovable for being so. We may move back another hundred years to *King Lear*, or to Shakespeare's "good old man" Adam; once again, the paternalist values are seen as "antique", they are crumbling before the competitive individualism of the natural man of young capitalism, where "the bond [is] crack'd 'twixt son and father" and where the

gods stand up for bastards. Or we may move back another
hundred years to Sir Thomas More. Always paternalist
actuality appears to be receding into an ever more primitive
and idealized past.[1] And the term forces us into confusions
of actual and ideological attributes.

To resume: paternalism is a loose descriptive term. It has
considerably less historical specificity than such terms as
feudalism or capitalism; it tends to offer a model of the social
order as it is seen from above; it has implications of warmth
and of face-to-face relations which imply notions of value; it
confuses the actual and the ideal. This does not mean that the
term should be discharged as utterly unfit for service. It has
as much and as little value as other generalized terms —
authoritarian, democratic, egalitarian — which cannot in
themselves, and without substantial additions, be brought to
characterize a system of social relations. No thoughtful
historian should characterize a whole society as paternalist or
patriarchal. But paternalism can, as in Tsarist Russia, in
Meiji Japan, or in certain slave-holding societies, be a
profoundly important component not only of ideology but of
the actual institutional mediation of social relations. How do
matters stand in eighteenth-century England?

II

Let us put aside at once one tempting but wholly unprofitable
line of investigation: that of attempting to divine the specific
gravity of that mysterious fluid, the "patriarchal tinge", in
this or that context and at different moments in the century.
We commence with impressions: we ornament our hunches
with elegant or apt quotations; we end with impressions.

If we look, rather, at the institutional expression of social
relations, then this society appears to offer few genuine
paternalist features. What one notices about it first of all is
the importance of money. The landed gentry are graded less
by birth or other marks of status than by rentals: they are
worth so many thousand pounds a year. Among the
aristocracy and ambitious gentry, courtship is conducted by
fathers and by their lawyers, who guide it carefully towards

[1] See Raymond Williams, *The Country and the City* (Oxford, 1973),
passim.

its consummation, the well-drawn marriage settlement. Place and office could be bought and sold (provided that the sale did not seriously conflict with the lines of political interest); commissions in the Army; seats in parliament. Use-rights, privileges, liberties, services — all could be translated into an equivalent in money: votes, burgage-rights, immunities from parish office or militia service, the freedom of boroughs, gates on the common. This is the century in which money "beareth all the stroke", in which liberties become properties, and use-rights are reified. A dove-cot on the site of an ancient burgage may be sold, and with it is sold a right to vote; the rubble of an ancient messuage may be bought up in support of a claim for common right and, thereby, of an extra allocation of the common on enclosure.

If use-rights, services, etc., became properties to be marked up at so many £s value, they did not, however, always become commodities open to any purchaser on the free market. The property assumed its value, as often as not, only within a particular structure of political power, influence, interest and dependency, made familiar to us by Namier. Titular offices of prestige (such as Rangers, Keepers, Constables) and such perquisites as came with them might be bought and sold; but these could not be bought or sold by anyone (during Walpole's rule, no Tory or Jacobite peer was likely to succeed in this market); and the holder of an opulent office who incurred the disfavour of politicians or Court might find himself threatened with ejection by legal process.[1] Preferment to the highest and most lucrative offices in the Church, the Law and the Army were in a similar position. The offices came through political influence but, once gained, they normally carried life tenure, and the incumbent must milk them of all possible revenue while he could. The tenure of Court sinecures and of high political office was much more uncertain, although by no means less lucrative: the earl of Ranelagh, the duke of Chandos, Walpole and Henry Fox were among those who founded fortunes upon brief tenures of the office of Paymaster

[1] See the instructive cases of Walpole's entry into Richmond Park, and of General Pepper's eviction from Enfield Chase in my *Whigs and Hunters*, Chapter 8.

General. And on the other hand, the tenure of landed estates, as absolute property, was wholly secure and heritable. It was both the jumping-off point for power and office, and the point to which power and office returned. Rentals might be jacked up by keen stewardship and improving agriculture, but they offered no windfall gains as did sinecure, office, commercial speculation or fortunate marriage. Political influence could do more to maximize profits than could four-course rotations — as, for example, in smoothing the way for private acts, such as enclosure, or in bringing a wad of unearned sinecurist income back to mortgaged estates, in easing the way to a marriage uniting congenial interests, or in gaining preferential access to a new issue of stock.

This was a predatory phase of agrarian and commercial capitalism, and the State was itself among the prime objects of prey. Victory in high politics was followed by the spoils of war, just as victory in war was often followed by the spoils of politics. The successful commanders of Marlborough's wars gained not only public rewards but also huge sums out of military subcontracting, for fodder, transport, ordnance; for Marlborough there was Blenheim Palace, for Cobham and Cadogan the mini-palaces of Stowe and Caversham. The Hanoverian succession brought a new set of courtier-brigands in its train. But the great financial and commercial interests also required access to the State, for charters, privileges, contracts, and for the diplomatic, military and naval strength required to break open the way for trade.[1] Diplomacy gained for the South Sea Company the *assiento*, or licence to trade in slaves in Spanish America; and it was upon the expectations of massive profits from this concession that the South Sea Bubble was blown. Blowing a bubble cannot be done without spit, and the spit in this case took the form of bribes not only to the king's ministers and mistresses, but also (it is probable) to the king.

We are habituated to think of exploitation as something

[1] We should not forget that Namier's great enquiry into the character of the parliamentary system originated as a study of "The Imperial Problem during the American Revolution"; see *The Structure of Politics at the Accession of George III*, Preface to first edition (1928).

that occurs at ground level, at the point of production. In the early eighteenth century wealth was created at this lowly level, but it rose rapidly to higher regions, accumulated in great gobbets, and the real killings were to be made in the distribution, cornering and sale of goods or raw materials (wool, grain, meat, sugar, cloth, tea, tobacco, slaves), in the manipulation of credit, and in the seizure of the offices of State. A patrician banditti contested for the spoils of power, and this alone explains the great sums of money they were willing to expend on the purchase of parliamentary seats. Seen from this aspect, the State was less an effective organ of any class than a parasitism upon the backs of that very class (the gentry) who had gained the day in 1688. And it was seen as such, and seen to be intolerable, by many of the small Tory gentry during the first half of the century, whose land tax was transferred by the most patent means to the pockets of courtiers and Whig politicians — to that same aristocratic élite whose great estates were, during these years, being consolidated against the small. An attempt was even made by this oligarchy, in the time of the earl of Sunderland, to make itself institutionally confirmed and self-perpetuating, by the attempted Peerage Bill and by the Septennial Act. That constitutional defences against this oligarchy survived these decades at all is due largely to the stubborn resistance of the largely Tory, sometimes Jacobite, independent country gentry, supported again and again by the vociferous and turbulent crowd.

All this was done in the king's name. It was in the name of the king that successful ministers could purge even the most subordinate officer of State who was not wholly subordinate to their interest. "We have left nothing untry'd, to find out every malignant; and have dismiss'd all of whom we could have the least proof either from their present or pass'd behaviour," wrote the three grovelling Commissioners of Customs in Dublin to the earl of Sunderland in August 1715. It is "our duty not to suffer any subordinate to us to eat His Majesty's Bread, who have not all imaginable zeal & affection for his service & Government."[1] But it was a prime interest among the political predators to confine the

[1] Blenheim MSS (Sunderland), D II, 8.

influence of the king to that of *primus inter predatores.*
When George II at his accession seemed to be about to
dispense with Walpole, it turned out that he could be bought
like any Whig politician, but at a higher price:

> Walpole knew his duty. Never had a sovereign been more generously
> treated. The King — £800,000 a year down and the surplus of all taxes
> appropriated to the civil list, reckoned by Hervey at another £100,000:
> the Queen — £100,000 a year. The rumour ran that Pulteney offered
> more. If so, his political ineptitude was astounding. No one but Walpole
> could have hoped to get such grants through the Commons. . . a point
> which his Sovereign was not slow in grasping. . .
>
> "Consider, Sir Robert," said the King, purring with gratitude as his
> minister set out for the Commons, "what makes me easy in this
> matter will prove for your ease too; it is for my life it is to be fixed
> and it is for your life." [1]

So Walpole's "duty" turns out to be the mutual respect of
two safe-breakers raiding the vaults of the same bank. In
these decades the noted Whig "jealousy" of the Crown did
not rise from any fear that the Hanoverian monarchs would
effect a *coup d'état* and trample underfoot the liberties of the
subject in assuming absolute power — that rhetoric was
strictly for the hustings. It arose from the more realistic fear
that an enlightened monarch might find means to elevate
himself, as the personification of an "impartial", rationalizing, bureaucratic State power, above and outside the
predatory game. The appeal of such a patriot king would
have been immense, not only among the lesser gentry, but
among great ranges of the populace: it was exactly the appeal
of his image as an uncorrupted patriot which carried William
Pitt the elder on a flood of popular acclaim to power, despite
the hostility of politicians and of Court. [2]

---

[1] J. H. Plumb, *Sir Robert Walpole* (1960), II, pp. 168-9.
[2] See P. D. Langford, "William Pitt and public opinion, 1757",
English Historical Review, cccxlvi (1973). But when in power, Pitt's
"patriotism" was limited to the right hand of government only. The left
hand, Newcastle, "took the treasury, the civil and ecclesiastical patronage,
and the disposal of that part of the secret service money which was then
employed in bribing members of Parliament. Pitt was Secretary of State,
with the direction of war and of foreign affairs. Thus the filth of all the
noisome and pestilential sewers of government was poured into one
channel. Through the other passed only what was bright and stainless"
(T. B. Macaulay, *Critical and Historical Essays* (1880), p. 747.)

"The successors of the old Cavaliers had turned demagogues; the successors of the old Roundheads had turned courtiers." Thus Macaulay; and he continues:

> During many years, a generation of Whigs, whom Sidney would have spurned as slaves, continued to wage deadly war with a generation of Tories whom Jeffreys would have hanged for republicans.[1]

This characterization does not long survive the mid-century. The feud between Whigs and Tories had been greatly softened ten years before the accession of George III, and the ensuing "slaughter of the Pelhamite innocents". The Tory survivors among the great gentry re-entered the commission of peace, regained their political presence in the counties, had hopes of shares in the spoils of power. As manufacture moved up in the scales of wealth against merchanting and speculation, so certain forms of privilege and corruption became obnoxious to moneyed men, who became reconciled to the rationalized "impartial" arena of the free market: killings could now be made without some prior political purchase within the organs of State. The accession of George III changed in many ways the terms of the political game — the opposition got out its old libertarian rhetoric and dusted it, for some (as in the City of London) it assumed a real and revivified content. But the King sadly bungled any attempt to offer himself as an enlightened monarch, an imperial apex to a disinterested bureaucracy. The parasitic functions of the State came under increasing scrutiny and piecemeal attack (the reform of the Excise, attacks on the East India Company, upon places and sinecures, upon the misappropriation of public lands, etc.); but, despite an efficient revenue service, and a serviceable navy and army, the parasitic role of the State survived.

"Old Corruption" is a more serious term of political analysis than is often supposed; for political power throughout most of the eighteenth century may best be understood, not as a direct organ of any class or interest, but as a secondary political formation, a purchasing-point from which other kinds of economic and social power were gained or enhanced; in its primary functions it was costly, grossly

[1] *Ibid.*, p. 746.

inefficient, and it survived the century only because it did not seriously inhibit the actions of those with *de facto* economic or (local) political power. Its greatest source of strength lay precisely in the weakness of the State itself; in the desuetude of its paternal, bureaucratic and protectionist powers; in the licence which it afforded to agrarian, mercantile and manufacturing capitalism to get on with their own self-reproduction; in the fertile soil which it afforded to *laissez-faire*.[1]

It scarcely seems, however, to be a fertile soil for paternalism. We have become used to a rather different view of eighteenth-century politics, presented by historians who have become habituated to seeing this age in terms of the apologetics of its principal actors.[2] If corruption is noted, it can be passed off by noting a precedent; if Whigs were predators, then Tories were predators too. Nothing is out-of-the-way, all is subsumed in the "accepted standards of the age". But the alternative view which I have offered should come with no sense of surprise. It is, after all, the criticism of high politics offered in *Gulliver's Travels* and in *Jonathan Wilde*; in part in Pope's satires and in part in *Humphrey*

[1] I must emphasise that this is a view of the State as seen from "within". From "without", in its effective military, naval, fiscal, diplomatic and imperial presence, whether directly or indirectly (as in the para-State of the East India Company) it must be seen in a very much more aggressive aspect. John Brewer has helpfully analysed its military strength, and also the efficiency of its fiscal organisation and taxation bureaucracy — Treasury departments and the extensive excise service were comparatively free from the corruption and favours endemic in other government office — in *The Sinews of Power* (1989). This mixture of internal weakness and external strength, and the balance between the two (in "peace" and "war" policies) leads us to most of the real issues of principle thrown up in mid-eighteenth-century high politics. It was when the weaknesses inherent in the internal parasitism wreaked their revenges in external defeat (the loss of Minorca and the ritual sacrifice of Admiral Byng; the American disaster) that elements in the ruling class were shocked out of mere factionalism into a class politics of principle.

[2] But there has been a significant shift in recent historiography, to take more seriously into acccount relations between politicians and the political nation "without doors". See J. H. Plumb, "Political man", in James L. Clifford (ed.), *Man versus Society in Eighteenth-Century Britain* (Cambridge, 1968); John Brewer, *Party Ideology and Popular Politics at the Accession of George III* (Cambridge, 1976); and Linda Colley, *In Defence of Oligarchy: the Tory Party, 1714-1760* (Cambridge, 1982).

Clinker; in Johnson's "Vanity of Human Wishes" and "London" and in Goldsmith's "Traveller". It appears, as political theory, in Mandeville's *Fable of the Bees*, in the polemics of the "country party", with a Tory gloss in Bolingbroke's thought and it reappears, in more fragmentary form, and with a Whiggish gloss, in Burgh's *Political Disquisitions*.[1] In the early decades of the century, the comparison between high politics and the criminal under-world was a common figure of satire:

> I know that if one would be agreeable to men of dignity one must study to imitate them, and I know which way they get Money and places. I cannot wonder that the Talents requisite for a great Statesman are so scarce in the world since so many of those who possess them are every month cut off in the prime of their Age at the Old-Baily.

Thus John Gay, in a private letter, in 1723.[2] The thought was the germ for the *Beggar's Opera*. Historians have commonly dismissed this figure as hyperbole. They should not.

There are, of course, qualifications to be made. One qualification, however, which can *not* be made is that this parasitism was curbed, or jealously watched, by a purposive, cohesive, growing middle class of professional men and of the manufacturing middle class.[3] To be sure, all the elements of such a class were gathering, and recent historical research has emphasised the growth in the wealth, numbers and cultural presence of the commercial, professional, farming and trading sections of society;[4] the occasional assertion of independence in urban politics;[5] the vigorous growth of leisure centres and facilities mainly serving the "middling

---

[1] "In our time the opposition is between a corrupt Court joined by an innumerable multitude of all ranks and stations bought with public money. and the independent part of the nation" (*Political Disquisitions, or an Enquiry into Public Errors, Defects, and Abuses* (1774)). This, of course, is the critique of the old "country" opposition to Walpole also.

[2] C. F. Burgess (ed.), *Letters of John Gay* (Oxford, 1966), p. 45.

[3] But note the relevant discussion in John Cannon, *Parliamentary Reform, 1640-1832* (Cambridge, 1973), p. 49, note 1.

[4] This is a consistent and persuasive theme of Paul Langford, *A Polite and Commercial People, op. cit.*, esp. chapter two.

[5] See Nicholas Rogers, *Whigs and Cities* (Cambridge, 1989).

orders".[1] If in the first decades of the century such groups
could be held in place by palpable measures of clientage and
dependency,[2] by the mid-century they were numerous
enough — certainly in London and also in some large towns
— to be no longer dependent upon a few patrons, and to have
acquired the independence of the more anonymous market.
There is a sense in which a middle class was creating its own
shadowy civil society or public sphere.

Nevertheless, all this fell far short of a class with its own
institutions and objectives, self-confident enough to
challenge the managers of Old Corruption. Such a class did
not begin to discover itself (except, perhaps, in London) until
the last three decades of the century. For most of the century
its potential members were content to submit to a condition
of abject dependency. They made little effort (until the
Association Movement of the late 1770s) to shake off the
chains of electoral bribery and influence; they were consenting adults in their own corruption. After two decades of
servile attachment to Walpole, the Dissenters emerged with
their reward: £500 p.a. to be allocated to the widows of
deserving clergy. Fifty years later, and they had still failed to
secure the repeal of the Test and Corporation Acts. As
churchmen, the majority fawned for preferment, dined and
joked (upon suffrance) at the tables of their patrons, and,
like Parson Woodforde, were not above accepting a tip from
the squire at a wedding or a christening.[3] As surveyors,
attorneys, tutors, stewards, tradesmen, etc., they were
contained within the limits of dependency; their deferential
letters, soliciting place or favour, are stashed in the

[1] See especially P. Corfield, *The Impact of English Towns, 1700-1800*
(Oxford, 1982); P. Borsay, *The English Urban Renaissance* (Oxford,
1989); P. Clark (ed.), *The Transformation of English Provincial Towns,
1600-1800* (1984).
[2] Nicholas Rogers, "Aristocratic Clientage, Trade and Independency:
Popular Politics in Pre-Radical Westminster", *Past and Present*, 61, 1973.
[3] "April 11 1779. . . There were Coaches at Church. Mr Custance
immediately after the Ceremony came to me and desired me to accept a
small Present; it was wrapped up in a Piece of white Paper very neat, and
on opening of it, I found it contained nothing less than the sum of 4. 4. 0.
He gave the Clerk also 0. 10. 6." (*The Diary of a Country Parson* (1963),
p. 152).

manuscript collections of the great.[1] (As such, the sources give a historiographical bias to overemphasize the deferential element in eighteenth-century society — a man put, perforce, into the stance of soliciting favours will not reveal his true mind.) In general, the middle class submitted to a client relationship. Here and there men of character might break free, but even the arts remained coloured by dependency upon the liberality of patrons.[2] The aspirant professional man or tradesman sought to remedy his sense of grievance less by social organization than by social mobility (or geographical mobility to Bengal, or to that European "West" — the New World). He aimed to purchase immunity from deference by acquiring the wealth which would give him "independence", or land and gentry status.[3] The profound resentments generated by this client status, with its attendant humiliations and its impediments to the career open to talents, fuelled much of the intellectual radicalism of the early 1790s; its embers scorch the foot even in the cool rationalist periods of Godwin's prose.

Thus for at least the first seven decades of the century we can find no industrial or professional middle class which exercises an effective curb upon the operations of predatory oligarchic power. But if there had been no curbs at all, no qualifications of parasitic rule, the consequence must have been anarchy, one faction preying without restraint upon another. The major qualifications to this rule were four.

First, we have already noted the largely Tory "Country"

[1] "The letter-bag of every M.P. with the slightest pretensions to influence was stuffed with pleas and demands from voters for themselves, their relations or their dependents. Places in the Customs and Excise, in the Army and Navy, in the Church, in the East India, Africa and Levant Companies, in all the departments of state from door-keepers to clerks: jobs at Court for the real gentry or sinecures in Ireland, the diplomatic corps, or anywhere else where duties were light and salaries steady" (J. H. Plumb, "Political man", p. 6).

[2] Hence Blake's angry annotation to Sir Joshua Reynolds: "Liberality! we want not Liberality. We want a Fair Price & Proportionate Value & a General Demand for Art" (Geoffrey Keynes (ed.), *The Complete Writings of William Blake* (1957), p. 446).

[3] For Place's savage comments on deference and independence, see Mary Thale (ed.), *The Autobiography of Francis Place* (Cambridge, 1972), pp. 216-18, 250.

tradition of the independent lesser gentry. This tradition is
the only one to emerge with much honour from the first half
of the century; it re-emerges, in a Whig mantle, with the
Association Movement of the 1770s.[1] Secondly, there is the
Press: itself a kind of middle-class presence, in advance of
other articulated expression — a presence extending in range
as literacy extended, and as the Press itself learned how to
enlarge and sustain its freedoms.[2] Thirdly, there is "the
Law", elevated during this century to a role more prominent
than at any other period of our history, and serving as the
"impartial", arbitrating authority in place of a weak and
unenlightened monarchy, a corrupt bureaucracy and a
democracy which offered to the real intrusions of power little
more than rhetoric about its ancestry. The civil law afforded
to the competing interests both a set of defences to their
property and those rules of the game without which all would
have fallen into anarchy. The higher institutions of the law
were not free from influence and corruption, but they were
freer from these than was any other profession. To maintain
their credibility, the courts must sometimes find for the small
man against the great, the subject against the King. In terms
of style, the performance was superb: serene, untainted by
influence, remote from the hubbub of affairs, lucid,
combining a reverence for the precedents of antiquity with a

[1] Although the Country opposition to Walpole had central demands
which were democratic in form (annual parliaments, curbs on placemen
and corruption, no standing army, etc.), the democracy demanded was of
course limited, in general, to the landed gentry (as against the Court and
the moneyed interest) as is made clear by continued Tory support for
landed property qualifications for MPs. See Quentin Skinner's useful
discussion (which, however, neglects the dimension of the political nation
"without doors" to which Bolingbroke appealed). "The principles and
practice of opposition: the case of Bolingbroke versus Walpole", in Neil
McKendrick (ed.), *Historical Perspectives* (1974); H. T. Dickinson, "The
eighteenth-century debate on the 'Glorious Revolution'," *History*, vol. lxi,
201 (February 1976), pp. 36-40; and (for the continuity between the platform of old Country party and new radical Whigs), Brewer, *op. cit.*,
pp. 19, 253-5. The Hanoverian Whigs also endorsed the high property
qualifications for MPs: Cannon, *op. cit.*, p. 36.
[2] See Brewer, *op. cit.*, chapter 8; and, for one example of its
provincial extension, John Money, "Taverns, coffee houses and clubs local
politics and popular articulacy in the Birmingham area in the age of the
American Revolution", *Historical Journal*, (1971), vol. xiv, 1.

flexible assimilation of the present. Money, of course, could buy the best performers, and the longer purse could often exhaust the lesser; but money could never effect an outright purchase of judgement, and on occasion was visibly discomfited. The civil law provided a fair framework within which the predators could fight for some kinds of spoil: for tithes, for claims to timber and common land, over legacies and entails: on occasion their lesser victims could defend themselves in the same medium. But the criminal law, which faced in the main towards the loose and disorderly sort of people, wore an altogether different aspect. Moreover, eighteenth-century law was concerned less with relations between persons than with relations between property, or claims upon property, or what Blackstone called "the Rights of Things" (see below, p. 135).

Fourthly, and finally, there is the ever-present resistance of the crowd: a crowd which stretched at times from small gentry and professional men to the poor (and within whose numbers the first two groups sometimes sought to combine opposition to the system with anonymity), but which appeared to the great, through the haze of verdure surrounding their parks, to be made up of "the loose and disorderly sort". The relation between the gentry and the crowd is the particular concern of this argument.

III

One would not expect paternal responsibilities or filial deference to be vigorous in the predatory regime to which I have gestured. But it is of course possible for a society to be fissured and savagely factional at the top, but to preserve its cohesion below. The military juntas engage in coup and counter-coup, pretenders to the throne exchange places, warlords march and counter-march, but at the base of society the peasantry or plantation-workers remain passive, sometimes submitting to a change of masters, contained by the strength of local paternal institutions, made submissive by the absence of alternative social horizons. Whatever parasitism infested the eighteenth-century State, perhaps the gentry, secure in their counties, threw over the whole of society a paternalist net?

It would not be difficult to find instances of the great

estate or the closed manorial village where this might seem to be so. And we will return to such examples. It would be equally easy to find pasture and forest regions of expanding domestic industry where this is evidently false. The trading of instances will not get us very far. The question we should ask is: What were the institutions, in the eighteenth century, which enabled the rulers to obtain, directly or indirectly, a control over *the whole life* of the labourer, as opposed to the purchase, *seriatim*, of his labour power?

The most substantial fact lies on the other side of the question. This is the century which sees the erosion of half-free forms of labour, the decline of living-in, the final extinction of labour services and the advance of free, mobile, wage labour. This was not an easy or quick transition. Christopher Hill has reminded us of the long resistance made by the free-born Englishman against the pottage of free wage labour. One should note equally the long resistance made by their masters against some of its consequences. These wished devoutly to have the best of both the old world and the new, without the disadvantage of either. They clung to the image of the labourer as an *un*free man, a "servant": a servant in husbandry, in the workshop, in the house. (They clung simultaneously to the image of the free or masterless man as a vagabond, to be disciplined, whipped and compelled to work.) But crops could not be harvested, cloth could not be manufactured, goods could not be transported, houses could not be built and parks enlarged, without labour readily available and mobile, for whom it would be inconvenient or impossible to accept the reciprocities of the master-servant relationship. The masters disclaimed their paternal responsibilities; but they did not cease, for many decades, to complain at the breach of the "great law of subordination", the diminution of deference, that ensued upon their disclaimer:

> The Lab'ring Poor, in spight of double Pay,
> Are saucy, mutinous, and Beggarly.[1]

[1] Defoe, *The Great Law of Subordination Consider'd* (1724), p. 80. See Christopher Hill, "Pottage for Freeborn Englishmen: Attitudes to Wage Labour in Sixteenth and Seventeenth century England", in C. Feinstein (ed.), *Socialism, Capitalism and Economic Growth* (Cambridge, 1964).

The most characteristic complaint throughout the greater part of the century was as to the indiscipline of working people, their irregularity of employment, their lack of economic dependency and their social insubordination. Defoe, who was not a conventional "low wages" theorist, and who could on occasion see merit in higher wages which increased the consuming power of "manufacturers" or of "artificers", stated the full case in his *Great Law of Subordination Consider'd; or, the Insolence and Unsufferable Behaviour of Servants in England duly enquir'd into* (1724). He argued that through the insubordination of servants:

> Husbandmen are ruin'd, the Farmers disabled, Manufacturers and Artificers plung'd, to the Destruction of Trade. . . and that no Men who, in the Course of Business, employ Numbers of the Poor, can depend upon any Contracts they make, or perform any thing they undertake, having no Law, no Power. . . to oblige the Poor to perform honestly what they are hir'd to do.

> Under *a stop of Trade*, and a general want of Work, then they are clamorous and mutinous, run from their Families, load the Parishes with their Wives and Children. . . and. . . grow ripe for all manner of mischief, whether publick Insurrection, or private plunder.

> *In a Glut of Trade* they grow saucy, lazy, idle and debauch'd. . . they will Work but two or three Days in the Week.

Paternalist control over the whole life of the labourer was in fact being eroded; wage assessment fell into desuetude; the mobility of labour is manifest; the vigour of eighteenth-century hiring-fairs, "statutes" or "statties", proclaim the right of the rural (as well as urban) labourer to claim if he so wished, a change of master.[1] Moreover, there is evidence (in the very refusal of labourers to submit to the work-discipline demanded of them) of the growth of a newly-won psychology of the free labourer. In one of Defoe's moralistic anecdotes, the JP summons the cloth worker upon a complaint from his employer that his work was being neglected:

[1] See A. Kussmaul, *Servants in Husbandry in Early Modern England* (Cambridge, 1981); R. W. Malcolmson, *Life and Labour in England, 1700-1780* (1981), pp. 71-4; Michael Roberts, " 'Waiting upon Chance': English Hiring Fairs", *Journal of Historical Sociology*, vol. I (1988).

Justice.	Come in Edmund, I have talk'd with your Master.
Edmund.	Not *my Master*, and't please your Worship, I hop I am *my own Master.*
Justice.	Well, your Employer, Mr E —, the Clothier: will the word Employer do?
Edmund.	Yes, yes, and't please your Worship, any thing, but *Master.* [1]

This is a large change in the terms of relations: subordination is becoming (although between grossly unequal parties) negotiation.

The eighteenth century witnessed a qualitative change in labour relations whose nature is obscured if we see it only in terms of an increase in the scale and volume of manufacture and trade. This occurred, of course. But it occurred in such a way that a substantial proportion of the labour force actually became *more* free from discipline in their daily work, more free to choose between employers and between work and leisure, less situated in a position of dependence in their whole way of life, than they had been before or than they were to be in the first decades of the discipline of the factory and of the clock.

This was a transitory phase. One prominent feature was the loss of non-monetary usages or perquisites, or their translation into money payments. Such usages were still extraordinarily pervasive in the early eighteenth century. They favoured paternal social control because they appeared simultaneously as economic and as social relations, as relations between persons not as payments for services or things. Most evidently, to eat at one's employer's board, to lodge in his barn or above his workshop, was to submit to his supervision. In the great house, the servants who were dependent upon "vails" from visitors, the clothing of the mistress, the clandestine perquisites of the surplus of the larder, spent a lifetime ingratiating favours. Even the multiform perquisites within industry, increasingly being redefined as "theft", were more likely to survive where the workers accepted them as favours and submitted to a filial dependency.

On occasion, one catches a glimpse of the extinction of a perquisite or service which must have induced a shock to paternal control out of all proportion to the economic gain to

[1] Defoe, *op. cit.*, p. 97.

the employer. Thus when Sir Jonathan Trelawney, as Bishop of Winchester, was seeking to increase the revenue of his see, he employed as Steward one Heron, a man strongly committed to ruthless economic rationalization. Among accusations brought against Heron, in 1707, by tenants and subordinate officials of the Bishop's Courts were that:

> He breaks old Customes. . . in Minute and Small matters, which are of Small value to your Lordshipp. . . he has denied to Allow five Shillings at Waltham to the Jury att the Court. . . to drinke your Lordshipps health, a Custome that has beene used time out of Mind. . . he has denied your Lordshipp's Steward and Officers a small perquisite of haveing theire horses shoo'd att Waltham According to an Antient usage which never Exceeded above Six or Seven Shillings. . . he denied your Lordshipp's Tennants Timber for the repaire of Severall Bridges and Common pounds.

To this Heron replied, somewhat testily:

> I own, I affect sometimes to Intermit those minute Customs as he calls them because I observe that your Predecessor's favours are prescribed for against your Lordship & insisted on as Rights, & then your Lordship is not thanked for them; Besides though they are Minute, yet many Minute Expences. . . amount to a Sume at the end.[1]

In such ways economic rationalization nibbled (and had long been nibbling) through the bonds of paternalism. The other leading feature of this transitional period was of course the enlargement of that sector of the economy which was independent of a client relationship to the gentry. The "subject" economy remained huge: not only the direct retainers of the great house, the chambermaids and footmen, coachmen and grooms and gardeners, the gamekeepers and laundresses, but the further concentric rings of economic clientship — the equestrian trades and luxury trades, the dressmakers and pastry cooks and vintners, the coach makers, the innkeepers and ostlers.

But the century saw a growing area of independence within which the small employers and labourers felt their client relationship to the gentry very little or not at all. These were the people whom the gentry saw as "idle and disorderly", withdrawn from their social control; from among these — the

[1] Hants CRO, Eccles. II, 415809, E/B12. See also *Whigs and Hunters*, pp. 126-30.

clothing workers, urban artisans, colliers, bargees and porters, labourers and petty dealers in the food trades — the social rebels, the food or turnpike rioters, were likely to come. They retained many of the attributes commonly ascribed to "pre-industrial labour".[1] Working often in their own cottages, owning or hiring their own tools, usually working for small employers, frequently working irregular hours and at more than one job, they had escaped from the social controls of the manorial village and were not yet subject to the discipline of factory labour.

Many of their economic dealings might be with men and women little higher in the economic hierarchy than themselves. Their "shopping" was not done in emporiums but at market stalls. The poor state of the roads made necessary a multitude of local markets, at which exchanges of products between primary producers might still be unusually direct. In the 1760s,

> Hard-labouring colliers, men and women of Somersetshire and Gloucestershire, travelled to divers neighbouring towns with drifts of horses. . . laden with coals. . . It was common to see such colliers lade or fill a two bushel coal sack with articles of provisions. . . of beef, mutton, large half stript beef bones, stale loaves of bread, and pieces of cheese.[2]

Such markets and, even more, the seasonal fairs provided not only an economic but a cultural nexus, and a major centre for information and exchange of news and gossip.

In many regions, the people had not been shaken alto-

---

[1] Gwyn Williams in *Artisans and Sansculottes* (1968) writes of "the brief, bawdy, violent, colourful, kaleidoscopic, picaresque world of pre-industrial society, when anything from a third to a half of the population lived not only on the subsistence line but outside and sometimes against the law". That is one way of seeing a part of this population: and this is confirmed by several studies in P. Linebaugh, *The London Hanged* (1991). However, another part of this population should not be stereotyped as bawdy, colourful and criminal: upward revisions of the numbers engaged in industry (including rural industries) — see especially P. H. Lindert, "English Occupations, 1670-1811", *J. Econ. Hist.*, 40, (1980) — the rediscovery of the "cottage economy" and of an English peasantry — see David Levine, *Reproducing Families* (Cambridge, 1987) and below p. 176 — and the whole body of work and discussion around "proto-industrialization" have all served to emphasise the substantial and growing sector of the eighteenth-century economy independent of gentry control.

[2] J. Mathews, *Remarks on the Cause and Progress of the Scarcity and Dearness of Cattle* (1797), p. 33.

gether from some sketchy tenure of the land. Since much industrial growth took the form, not of concentration into large units of production, but of the dispersal of petty units and of by-employments (especially spinning) there were additional resources for "independence". This independence was for many never far from mere subsistence: a bountiful harvest might bring momentary affluence, a long wet season might throw people onto the poor rates. But it was possible for many to knit together this subsistence, from the common, from harvest and occasional manual earnings, from by-employments in the cottage, from daughters in service, from poor rates or charity. And undoubtedly some of the poor followed their own predatory economy, like "the abundance of loose, idle and disorderly persons" who were alleged, in the time of George II, to live on the margins of Enfield Chase, and who "infest the same, going in dark nights, with Axes, Saws, Bills, Carts and Horses, and in going and coming Rob honest people of their sheep, lambs and poultry. . ."[1] Such persons appear again and again in criminal records, estate correspondence, pamphlet and press; they appear still, in the 1790s, in the agricultural county surveys; they cannot have been wholly a ruling-class invention.

Thus the independence of labour (and small master) from clientage was fostered on the one hand by the translation of non-monetary "favours" into payments; and on the other by the extension of trade and industry on the basis of the multiplication of many small units of production, with much by-employment (especially spinning) coincident with many continuing forms of petty land tenure (or common right) and many casual demands for manual labour. This is an indiscriminate picture, and deliberately so. Economic historians have made many careful discriminations between different groups of labourers. But these are not relevant to our present enquiry. Nor were these discriminations commonly made by commentators from among the gentry when they considered the general problem of the "insubordination" of labour. Rather, they saw beyond the park gates, beyond the railings of the London mansion, a blur of indiscipline — the "idle

[1] Memorial of John Hale, Clerk of Enfield manor court, to George II n.d. Cambridge Univ. Lib., Cholmondeley (Houghton) MSS, 45/40.

and disorderly", "the mob", "the poor", the "populace" —
and they deplored —

> their open scoffings at all discipline, religious as well as civil: their
> contempt of all order, frequent menace to all justice, and extreme
> promptitude to tumultuous risings from the slightest motives.[1]

It is, as always, an indiscriminate complaint against the
populace as a whole. Free labour had brought with it a
weakening of the old means of social discipline. So far from a
confident patriarchal society, the eighteenth century sees the
old paternalism at a point of crisis.

IV

And yet one feels that "crisis" is too strong a term. If the
complaint continues throughout the century that the poor
were indisciplined, criminal, prone to tumult and riot, one
never feels, before the French Revolution, that the rulers of
England conceived that their whole social order might be
endangered. The insubordination of the poor was an inconvenience; it was not a menace. The styles of politics and
of architecture, the rhetoric of the gentry and their decorative
arts, all seem to proclaim stability, self-confidence, a habit of
managing all threats to their hegemony.

We may of course have overstated the crisis of paternalism. In directing attention to the parasitism of the State at
the top, and the erosion of traditional relations by free labour
and a monetary economy at the bottom, we have overlooked
intermediate levels where the older economic household
controls remained strong, and we have perhaps understated
the scale of the "subject" or "client" areas of the economy.
The control which men of power and money still exercised
over the whole life and expectations of those below them
remained enormous, and if paternalism was in crisis, the
industrial revolution was to show that its crisis must be taken
several stages further — as far as Peterloo and the Swing
Riots — before it lost all credibility.

[1] *Herald, or Patriot-Proclaimer*, 24 September 1757. Even *within* the
park gates the gentry complained of indiscipline. Thus, the servants in the
great house were accused of intimidating house-guests by lining the hall on
their departure and demanding tips or "vails": see *A Letter from a
Gentleman to his Friend, concerning the Custom of Giving and Taking
Vails* (1767).

Nevertheless, the analysis allows us to see that ruling-class control in the eighteenth century was located primarily in a cultural hegemony, and only secondarily in an expression of economic or physical (military) power. To say that it was "cultural" is not to say that it was immaterial, too fragile for analysis, insubstantial. To define control in terms of cultural hegemony is not to give up attempts at analysis, but to prepare for analysis at the points at which it should be made: into the images of power and authority, the popular mentalities of subordination.

Defoe's fictional cloth worker, called before the magistrate to account for default, offers a clue: "not *my Master*, and't please your Worship, I hope I am *my own Master*". The deference which he refuses to his employer overflows in the calculated obsequiousness to "your Worship". He wishes to struggle free from the immediate, daily, humiliations of dependency. But the larger outlines of power, station in life, political authority, appear to be as inevitable and irreversible as the earth and the sky. Cultural hegemony of this kind induces exactly such a state of mind in which the established structures of authority and modes of exploitation appear to be in the very course of nature. This does not preclude resentment or even surreptitious acts of protest or revenge; it does preclude affirmative rebellion.

The gentry in eighteenth-century England exercised this kind of hegemony. And they exercised it all the more effectively since the relation of ruler to ruled was very often not face-to-face but indirect. Absentee landowners, and the ever-present mediation of stewards and bailiffs apart, the emergence of the three-tier system of landowner, tenant farmer and landless labourer, meant that the rural labourers, in the mass, did not confront the gentry as employers nor were the gentry seen to be in any direct sense responsible for their conditions of life; for a son or daughter to be taken into service at the great house was seen to be, not a necessity, but a favour.

And in other ways they were withdrawn from the polarities of economic and social antagonism. When the price of food rose, the popular rage fell not on the landowners but upon middlemen, forestallers, millers. The gentry might profit from the sale of wool, but they were not seen to be in a direct exploitive relation to the clothing workers.[1]

In the growing industrial areas, the gentlemen JP frequently lived withdrawn from the main industrial centres, at his
country seat, and he was at pains to preserve some image of
himself as arbitrator, mediator or even protector of the poor.
It was a common view that "whenever a tradesman is made a
justice a tyrant is created".[2] The poor laws, if harsh, were
not administered directly by the gentry; where there was
blame it could fall upon the poor-rate-paring farmers
and tradesmen from among whom the overseers came.
Langhorne presents the idealized paternalist picture;
exhorting the country justice to —

> . . . bend the brow severe
> On the sly, pilfering, cruel overseer;
> The shuffling farmer, faithful to no trust,
> Ruthless as rocks, insatiate as the dust.
> When the poor hind, with length of years decay'd,
> Leans feebly on his once subduing spade,
> Forgot the service of his abler days,
> His profitable toil, and honest praise,
> This slave, whose board his former labours spread![3]

And, once again, at least a ghostly image of paternal
responsibilities could be maintained at very little real outlay
in effort. The same JP who in his own closed parish
aggravated the problems of poverty elsewhere, by refusing
settlements and by pulling down the cottages on the common,
could at quarter sessions, by granting the occasional appeal
against the overseers of other open parishes, or by calling to
order the corrupt workhouse master, place himself above the
lines of battle.

We have the paradox that the credibility of the gentry as

[1] Even in the West of England, where clothiers were becoming gentlemen, a strong sense of distinction was still felt in the first half of the
century. An "Englishman" wrote to Lord Harrington in 1738, to
complain of "the contrivances and pride of the clothiers, as living in
luxury, neglecting their business, trusting servants with the care of their
affairs", "beating down the wages of the poor", and paying them in truck.
The remedy (he suggested) lay in a commission of enquiry made up of
"men of great fortunes", who would be sufficiently independent to attend
to the evidence of poor weavers: PRO, SP 36.47.
[2] Ibid.
[3] Langhorne, The Country Justice (1774).

paternalists arose from the high visibility of certain of their functions, and the low visibility of others. A great part of the gentry's appropriation of the labour value of "the poor" was mediated by their tenantry, by trade or by taxation. Physically they withdrew increasingly from face-to-face relations with the people in village and town. The rage for deer parks and the threat of poachers led to the closure of rights of way across their parks and their encirclement with high palings or walls; landscape gardening, with ornamental waters and fish ponds, menageries and valuable statuary, accentuated their seclusion and the defences of their grounds, which might be entered only through the high wrought-iron gates, watched over by the lodge. The great gentry were defended by their bailiffs from their tenants, and by their coachmen from casual encounters. They met the lower sort of people mainly on their own terms, and when these were clients for their favours; in the formalities of the bench; or on calculated occasions of popular patronage.

But in performing such functions their visibility was formidable, just as their formidable mansions imposed their presence, apart from, but guarding over, the village or town. Their appearances have much of the studied self-consciousness of public theatre. The sword was discarded, except for ceremonial purposes; but the elaboration of wig and powder, ornamented clothing and canes, and even the rehearsed patrician gestures and the hauteur of bearing and expression, all were designed to exhibit authority to the plebs and to exact from them deference. And with this went certain significant ritual appearances: the ritual of the hunt; the pomp of assizes (and all the theatrical style of the law courts); the segregated pews, the late entries and early departures, at church. And from time to time there were occasions for an enlarged ceremonial, which had wholly paternalist functions: the celebration of a marriage, a coming-of-age, a national festival (coronation or jubilee or naval victory), the almsgiving to the poor at a funeral.[1]

---

[1] As one example, on the marriage of Sir William Blacket with Lady Barbara Vilers, in 1725, much of Northumberland was enlisted in the celebrations. At Newcastle there were bonfires for two days, and the sounding of bells and guns. The great bell at Hexham burst with the

We have here a studied and elaborate hegemonic style, a theatrical role in which the great were schooled in infancy and which they maintained until death. And if we speak of it as theatre, it is not to diminish its importance. A great part of politics and law is always theatre; once a social system has become "set", it does not need to be endorsed daily by exhibitions of power (although occasional punctuations of force will be made to define the limits of the system's tolerance); what matters more is a continuing theatrical style. What one remarks of the eighteenth century is the elaboration of this style and the self-consciousness with which it was deployed.

The gentry and (in matters of social intercourse) their ladies judged to a nicety the kinds of conspicuous display appropriate to each rank and station: what coach, how many footmen, what table, even what proper reputation for "liberality". The show was so convincing that it has even misled historians; one notices an increasing number of references to the "paternal responsibilities" of the aristocracy, upon which "the whole system rested". But we have so far noted gestures and postures rather than actual responsibilities. The theatre of the great depended not upon constant, day-by-day attention to responsibilities (except in the supreme offices of State, almost every function of the eighteenth-century aristocracy, and many of those of the higher gentry and clergy, was held as a quasi-sinecure, whose duties were farmed out to a subordinate) but upon occasional dramatic interventions: the roasted ox, the prizes offered for some race or sport, the liberal donation to charity in time of dearth, the application for mercy, the proclamation against forestallers. It is as if the illusion of paternalism was too fragile to be risked to more sustained exposure.

The occasions of aristocratic and gentry patronage certainly deserve attention: this social lubricant of gestures could only too easily make the mechanisms of power and exploitation revolve more sweetly. The poor, habituated to their

boisterous ringing. At Wellington the crags were illuminated, and a large punchbowl cut in the rock, and filled with liquor, &c, *Newcastle Weekly Courant*, 2 October, 1725.

irrevocable station, have often been made accessories, through their own good nature, to their own oppression: a year of short commons can be compensated for by a liberal Christmas dole. Their rulers were well aware of this. A contributor to the *London Magazine* commented: "Dancing on the Green at Wakes and merry Tides should not only be indulg'd but incourag'd: and little Prizes being allotted for the Maids who excel in a Jig or Hornpipe, would make them return to their daily Labour with a light Heart and grateful Obedience to their Superiors." [1]

But such gestures were calculated to receive a return in deference quite disproportionate to the outlay, and they certainly don't merit the description of "responsibilities". These great agrarian bourgeois evinced little sense of public, or even corporate, responsibility. The century is not noted for the scale of its public buildings but for that of its private mansions; and is as much noted for the misappropriation of the charities of previous centuries as for the founding of new ones.

One public function the gentry assumed wholly as their own: the administration of the law, the maintenance, at times of crisis, of public order. At this point they became magisterially and portentously visible. Responsibility this certainly was, although it was a responsibility, in the first and in the second place, to their own property and authority. With regularity and with awful solemnity the limits of tolerance of the social system were punctuated by London's hanging days; by the corpse rotting on the gibbet beside the highway; by the processional of Assizes. However undesirable the side-effects (the apprentices and servants playing truant from service, the festival of pickpockets, the acclamation of the condemned) the ritual of public execution was a necessary concomitant of a system of social discipline where a great deal depended upon theatre.

In the administration of justice there were gestures also, which partake of the general studied paternalist style. Notably, in the exercise of the prerogative of mercy the aristocracy and great gentry could make evident their degree

[1] *London Magazine*, viii, 1738, pp. 139-40. My thanks to Robert Malcolmson.

of interest by furthering or refusing to further intercession for the condemned. And, as Douglas Hay has shown, to share, even indirectly, in the powers of life and death greatly enlarged their hegemonic charisma.[1] The exercise of power of life and death could, on occasion, be arranged to the last detail. The duke of Montagu was writing in 1728 to the duke of Newcastle concerning "my man John Potter", who had been condemned to death for stealing the duke's hangings. Montagu desired that Potter might be transported for life instead of being executed: "I have talked with the Recorder about it, who when the Report is made tomorrow of the Condemned Malefactors at Council, will propose that he may be inserted in the dead warrant, but at the same tyme there may be a Repreeve for him, which he is to know nothing of till the Morning of Execution." Three days later Montagu wrote anxiously to make sure that the letter of reprieve would arrive in time, for if Newcastle were to forget it "he'll be hanged and if he is I had as good be hanged with him, for the Ladys of my famelly give me little rest to save him. . ." The king's role in this exercise of the prerogative of mercy seems to have been fictional.[2]

In any case, one is dubious as to how far it is useful to describe the function of protecting their own property and social order as "paternalist". Certainly, this function exacted little evidence of filial loyalty either from their victims or from the crowds around the gallows.[3] A century which

[1] Douglas Hay, "Property, Authority and the Criminal Law", in Hay et al., Albion's Fatal Tree (1975).
[2] Montagu to Newcastle, 19 & 22 March 1727/8, PRO, SP 36.5, fos. 218-9, 230-1.
[3] See Peter Linebaugh, The London Hanged, op. cit. Thomas Laquer's assertion that the authorities had no "authorial" control over the executions is supported by anecdotal evidence of the Newgate Calendar kind (examples of cock-ups at Tyburn, sedulously copied in popular chronicles) but not by research into the sources (state papers, legal and military papers, etc.) relevant to such a judgement. Executions were not, as Laquer supposes, "more risible than solemn", and to present the Tyburn crowd as a "carnival crowd" is both to misunderstand the crowd and to libel "carnival". Hanging days at Tyburn often enacted a conflict between alternative authorial scripts — that of the authorities and that of a resentful or brutalised Tyburn crowd. That sort of execution crowd was *an execution crowd* (and a carnival nothing). It was one of the most brutalised phenomena in history and historians ought to say so: see Laquer,

added more than one hundred new capital offences to the statute book had a stern (or flippant) view of fatherhood.

V

If the great were withdrawn so much, within their parks and mansions, from public view, it follows that the plebs, in many of their activities, were withdrawn also from them. Effective paternal sway requires not only temporal but also spiritual or psychic authority. It is here that we seem to find the system's weakest link.

It would not be difficult to find, in this parish or in that, eighteenth-century clergy fulfilling, with dedication, paternalist functions. But we know very well that these are not characteristic men. Parson Adams is drawn, not to exemplify the practices of the clergy, but to criticize them; he may be seen, at once, as the Don Quixote of the eighteenth-century Anglican Church. The Church was profoundly Erastian; had it performed an effective, a psychologically compelling paternalist role, the Methodist movement would have been neither necessary nor possible.

All this could no doubt be qualified. But what is central to our purpose is that the "magical" command of the Church and of its rituals over the populace, while still present, was becoming very weak. In the sixteenth and seventeenth centuries, Puritanism had set out to destroy the bonds of idolatry and superstition — the wayside shrines, the gaudy churches, the local miracle cults, the superstitious practices, the confessional priesthood — which, as one may still see in Ireland or in parts of southern Europe today, can hold the common people in awe. The Restoration could not restore a tissue of papist idolatry for which, in any case, England had never been notably disposed. But the Restoration did loosen the new bonds of discipline which Puritanism had brought in its place. There can be little doubt that the early eighteenth century witnessed a great recession in Puritanism, and the

"Crowds, carnival and the state in English executions, 1604-1868", in Beier *et al, The First Modern Society* (Cambridge, 1989). At times the crowd could express other kinds of solidarity with the condemned: see Linebaugh, "The Tyburn Riots against the Surgeons", in Hay *et al., op. cit.*

diminution in the size of the popular Puritan following even
in those artisan centres which had nourished the Civil War
sects. In the result, there was an accession of freedom,
although of a negative kind, to the poor — a freedom from
the psychic discipline and moral supervision of priesthood or
of presbyters.

A priesthood with active pastoral care has usually found
ways of co-existing with the pagan or heretical superstitions
of its flock. However deplorable such compromises may
appear to theologians, the priest learns that many of the
beliefs and practices of "folklore" are harmless; if attached
to the calendar year of the Church they can be to that degree
Christianized, and can serve to reinforce the Church's
authority. The forgers of the shackles of Holy Church, Brand
— the pioneer of folklore — remarked, "had artfully
enough contrived to make them sit easy, by twisting Flowers
around them. . . A profusion of childish Rites, Pageants, and
Ceremonies diverted the attention of the people from the
consideration of their real state, and kept them in
humour. . ."[1] What matters most is that the Church should,
in its rituals, command the rites of passage of personal life,
and attach the popular festivals to its own calendar.

The Anglican Church of the eighteenth century was not a
creature of this kind. It was served not by priests but by
parsons. It had, except in unusual instances, abandoned the
confessional. It recruited few sons of the poor into the
priesthood. When so many priests served as temporal
magistrates and officered the same law as the gentry, they
could scarcely present themselves convincingly as the agents
of an alternative spiritual authority. When bishops were
political appointments, and when the cousins of the gentry
were placed in country livings, where they enlarged their
vicarages and adopted the gentry's style of life, it was only
too evident from what source the Church's authority
was derived.

Above all, the Church lost command over the "leisure" of
the poor, their feasts and festivals, and, with this, over a large
area of plebeian culture. The term "leisure" is, of course,
itself anachronistic. In rural society where small farming and

[1] John Brand and Henry Ellis, *op. cit.*, Vol. I, p. xvii.

the cottage economy persisted, and in large areas of manufacturing industry, the organization of work was so varied
and irregular that it is false to make a sharp distinction
between "work" and "leisure". On the one hand, social
occasions were intermixed with labour — with marketing,
sheep shearing and harvesting, fetching and carrying the
materials of work, and so on, throughout the year. On the
other hand, enormous emotional capital was invested, not
piecemeal in a succession of Saturday nights and Sunday
mornings, but in the special feasts and festival occasions.
Many weeks of heavy labour and scanty diet were compensated for by the expectation (or reminiscence) of these
occasions, when food and drink were abundant, courtship
and every kind of social intercourse flourished, and the hardship of life was forgotten. For the young, the sexual cycle of
the year turned on these festivals. These occasions were, in an
important sense, what men and women lived for; and if the
Church had little significant part in their conduct, then it
had, to that degree, ceased to engage with the emotional
calendar of the poor.

One can see this in a literal sense. While the old saints' days
were scattered liberally across the calendar, the Church's
ritual calendar concentrated events into the months of light
demands upon labour, from the winter to the spring, from
Christmas to Easter. While the people still owed tribute to the
last two dates, which remained as days of maximum
communion, the eighteenth-century calendar of popular
festivity coincides closely with the agrarian calendar. The
village and town feasts for the dedication of churches — or
wakes — had not only moved from the saints' days to the
adjacent Sunday, but in most cases they had also been
removed (where necessary) from the winter to the summer
solstice. In about 1730, the antiquarian, Thomas Hearne,
made a note of the feast day of 132 villages or towns in
Oxfordshire or on its borders. All fell between May and
December; 84 (or more than three-fifths) fell in August and
September; no fewer than 43 (or almost one-third) fell in the
last week of August and the first week of September (old-
style calendar). Apart from a significant group of some
twenty, which fell between the end of June and the end of
July, and which in a normal year might be expected to fall

between the end of the hay harvest and the commencement of
the cereal harvest, the weight of the emotional festive
calendar fell in the weeks immediately after the harvest was
gathered in.[1]

Dr Malcolmson has reconstructed a calendar of feasts for
Northamptonshire in the later eighteenth century which
shows much the same incidence.[2] Along with the secularization of the calendar goes a secularization of the style and the
function of the occasions. If not pagan, then new secular
functions were added to old ritual; the publicans, hucksters
and entertainers encouraged, with their numerous stalls, the
feasts when their customers had uncustomary harvest earnings in their pockets; the village charity and benefit clubs
took over the old church ales of Whitsuntide. At Bampton
Whit-Monday's club feast included a procession with drum
and piper (or fiddler), morris dancers, a clown with a bladder
who carried the "treasury" (a money box for contributions),
a sword bearer with a cake. There was, of course, no crucifix,
no priest or nuns, no images of virgin or saints: their absence
is perhaps too little noticed. Not one of the 17 songs or
melodies recorded had the least religious association:

> Oh, my Billy, my constant Billy,
> When shall I see my Billy again?
> When the fishes fly over the mountain,
> Then you'll see your Billy again.[3]

Bampton, that living museum of folklore, was not an
isolated rural village, but a sturdy centre of the leather
industry; just as the Middleton and Ashton of Bamford's
boyhood were centres of domestic industry. What is
manifest, in many such districts, and in many rural regions
also in the eighteenth century, is that one could never for a
moment sustain the view which (for example) Paul Bois is
able to assert of the eighteenth-century French peasant of the
West, that "c'était l'église, a l'ombre de laquelle se nouaient
toutes les relations".[4] Of course, the religious and the

[1] Bodleian Library, MSS Hearne's diaries, p. 175.
[2] R. W. Malcolmson, "Popular Recreations in English Society,
1700-1850", (Ph. D. thesis, Univ. of Warwick, 1970), pp. 11-17.
[3] P. H. Ditchfield, *Old English Customs* (1896), p. 125.
[4] Paul Bois, *Paysans de l'Ouest* (Paris, 1960), p. 307.

secular (or pagan) had co-existed uneasily, or conflicted, for centuries: the Puritans were concerned to keep morris dancers out of the church, and huckster's stalls out of the church-yard. They complained that church ales were defiled by animal baiting, dancing, and all manner of "lewdness". But there remains a sense in which the Church was the hub around which the spokes of this popular tradition turned; and the Stuart Book of Sports sought to confirm this relationship against Puritan attack. In the eighteenth century, the agrarian seasonal calendar was the hub and the Church provided none of the moving force. It is a difficult change to define but without doubt it was a large one.

The dual experience of the Reformation and of the decline in Puritan presence left a remarkable disassociation between the polite and the plebeian culture in post-Restoration England. Nor should we underestimate the creative culture-forming process from below. Not only the obvious things — folk songs, trades clubs and corn dollies — were made from below, but also interpretations of life, satisfactions and ceremonials. The wife sale, in its crude and perhaps exotic way, performed a function of ritual divorce both more available and more civilized than anything the polite culture could offer. The rituals of rough music, cruel as they might sometimes be, were no more vengeful and really no more exotic than the rituals of a Special Commission of Oyer and Terminer.

The legend of the revival of "merry England" after the Restoration is one which historians have perhaps been too impatient to examine. Even if some of the more sensational claims are discounted (Defoe, as a good accountant, assures us that 6,325 maypoles were erected in the five years after the Restoration)[1] there is no doubt that there was a general and sometimes exuberant revival of popular sports, wakes, rush bearings and rituals. "Help Lord!" exclaimed the Rev. Oliver Heywood, the ejected minister, when recounting the cockfighting, horse racing and stool-ball endemic in the Halifax district in the 1680s: "Oh, what oaths sworn! What wickedness committed!" And recounting the May Day celebrations of 1680 he had lamented: "There never was such

[1] Defoe, *op. cit.*, p. 62.

work in Halifax above fifty years past. Hell is broke loose."[1]

We are more accustomed to analyse the age in terms of its intellectual history, and to think of the decline of hell. But the breaking loose of this hell of a plebeian culture quite beyond their control was the waking nightmare of surviving Puritans such as Heywood and Baxter. Pagan festivals which the Church had attached to its calendar in the middle ages (although with incomplete success) reverted to purely secular festivities in the eighteenth century. Wake nights came to an end; but the feasts of the following day or week became more robust with each decade. The ceremony of strewing rushes in the churches lingered here and there; but the feasts of rush bearings went from strength to strength. Near Halifax again, the incumbent (a Reverend Witter) attempted to prevent these feasts in 1682, at which festivals (Heywood complained) the people make great provision of flesh and ale, come from all parts, "and eat and drink and rant in a barbarous heathenish manner". Mr Witter's doors were broken down and he was abused as a "cobbler".[2] The rush-bearing ceremony continued in this district for at least a further one hundred and fifty years. But, as in most districts, it had lost any sacred significance. The symbols on the richly-decorated carts became bells and painted pots. The picturesque costumes of the men and the white dresses and garlands of the women appear more and more pagan. The pageants pay a mere passing obeisance to Christian symbolism: Adam and Eve, St George and the Dragon, the Virtues, the Vices, Robin Hood and Maid Marian, hobbyhorses, sweeps on pigs, morris dancers. The festivities ended with baitings, wrestling, dancing and drinking, and sometimes with the tour of the houses of the gentry and of wealthy householders for drink, food and money. "I could not suppress these Bacchanals," wrote the Rev. John William de La Flechere of the Shropshire Wakes: "the impotent dyke I opposed only made the torrent swell and foam, without stopping the course." Moreover, the people had found patrons outside the Church: if La Flechere preached against drunkenness, shows and

---

[1] J. Horsfall Turner (ed.), *The Rev. Oliver Heywood, B.A.* (Brighouse, 1881), Vol. II, pp. 294, 271.
[2] *Ibid.*, pp. 264, 294.

bullbaiting, "the publicans and malsters will not forgive me. They think that to preach against drunkenness and to cut their purse strings is the same thing." [1]

But the resurgence of this culture cannot be put down to the commercialization fostered by publicans alone. The gentry had means, through Quarter Sessions, to harry these in their licenses if they had wished. This efflorescence of festivities can scarcely have taken place without a permissive attitude on the part of many of the gentry. In one sense, this was no more than the logic of the times. The materialism of the eighteenth-century rich and the Erastianism of their Church were met by the materialism of the poor. The race meetings of the rich became the poor's popular holidays. The permissive tolerance of the gentry was solicited by the many taverns which — as inn signs still proclaim — sought to put themselves under the patronage of the great. The gentry could make no convincing missionary expeditions to reform the manners and morals of the poor if they were unwilling to reform their own ostentatious and pleasant vices.

But as explanation this is not finally convincing. Only a ruling class which feels itself to be threatened is afraid to flaunt a double standard. Mandeville is only unusual in pressing to the point of satire the argument that private vices were public benefits. In more softened form the same argument, as to the valuable function of luxury in providing employment and spectacle for the poor, was part of the economic cant of the time. Henry Fielding could make the same point without satirical intention:

> To be born for no other Purpose than to consume the Fruits of the Earth is the Privilege. . . of very few. The greater Part of Mankind must sweat hard to produce them, or Society will no longer answer the Purposes for which it was ordained. [2]

[1] J. Benson, *Life of the Reverend John William de la Flechere* (1805: 1835 edn.), p. 78, describing Madeley Wake in 1761. (My thanks to Barrie Trinder.)

[2] *An Enquiry into the Causes of the Late Increase of Robbers* (1751), in Henry Fielding, *Complete Works* (1967), Vol. xiii, p. 11. Cf. Bernard Mandeville, *The Fable of the Bees* (Penguin edn. 1970), pp. 257, 292-3.

Indeed, we have seen that the conspicuous display of luxury and "liberality" was part of the theatre of the great. In some areas (wages theory, the poor laws, the criminal code), the materialism of the rich consorted without difficulty with a disciplinary control of the poor. But in other areas — the permissive attitude to the robust, unchristian popular culture, a certain caution and even delicacy in the handling of popular disturbance, even a certain flattery extended to the poor as to their liberties and rights — in these areas we are presented with a problem which demands more subtle analysis. It suggests some reciprocity in the relations between rich and poor; an inhibition upon the use of force against indiscipline and disturbance; a caution (on the part of the rich) against taking measures which would alienate the poor too far, and (on the part of that section of the poor which from time to time rallied behind the cry of "Church and King") a sense that there were tangible advantages to be gained by soliciting the favour of the rich. There is some mutuality of relationship here which it is difficult not to analyse at the level of class relationship.

Of course, no one in the eighteenth century would have thought of describing their own as a "one-class society". There were the rulers and the ruled, the high and the low people, persons of substance and of independent estate and the loose and disorderly sort. In between, where the professional and middle classes, and the substantial yeomanry, should have been, relations of clientage and dependency were so strong that, at least until the 1760s, these groups appear to offer little deflection of the essential polarities. Only someone who was "independent" of the need to defer to patrons could be thought of as having full political identity: so much is a point in favour of the "one-class" view. But class does not define itself in political identity alone. For Fielding, the evident division between the high and the low people, the people of fashion and of no fashion, lay like a cultural fissure across the land:

> whilst the people of fashion seized several places to their own use, such as courts, assemblies, operas, balls, &c., the people of no fashion, besides one royal place, called his Majesty's Bear-Garden, have been in constant possession of all hops, fairs, revels, &c. . . . So far from

looking on each other as brethren in the Christian language, they seem
scarce to regard each other as of the same species. [1]

This is a world of patricians and of plebs; it is no accident
that the rulers turned back to ancient Rome for a model of
their own sociological order. But such a polarization of class
relations doesn't thereby deprive the plebs of all political
existence. They are at one side of the necessary equation of
the *res publica*.

A plebs is not, perhaps, a working class. The plebs may
lack a consistency of self-definition, in consciousness; clarity
of objectives; the structuring of class organization. But the
political presence of the plebs, or "mob", or "crowd", is
manifest; it impinged upon high politics at a score of critical
occasions — Sacheverell riots, excise agitation, cider tax,
the patriotic and chauvinistic ebullitions which supported the
career of the older Pitt, and on to Wilkes and the Gordon
Riots and beyond. Even when the beast seemed to be
sleeping, the tetchy sensibilities of a libertarian crowd
defined, in the largest sense, the limits of what was
politically possible. There is a sense in which rulers and
crowd needed each other, watched each other, performed
theatre and countertheatre to each other's auditorium,
moderated each other's political behaviour. This is a more
active and reciprocal relationship than the one normally
brought to mind under the formula "paternalism and
deference".

It is necessary also to go beyond the view that labouring
people, at this time, were confined within the fraternal
loyalties and the "vertical" consciousness of particular
trades; and that this inhibited wider solidarities and
"horizontal" consciousness of class. There is something in
this, certainly. The urban craftsman retained something of a
guild outlook; each trade had its songs (with the implements
of the trade minutely described), its chapbooks and legends.
So the shoemaker's apprentice might be given by his master
*The Delightful, Princely and Entertaining History of the
Gentle-Craft*, and there read:

---

[1] *Ibid.*, p. 164.

> . . . never yet did any know
> A Shooemaker a Begging go.
> Kind they are one to another,
> Using each Stranger as his Brother.

He read this in 1725, and he would have read much the same in the time of Dekker. At times the distinctions of trades were carried over into festival and social life. Bristol, in the early eighteenth century, saw an annual pugilistic combat on Ash Wednesday between the blacksmiths, and the coopers, carpenters and sailors, with the weavers sometimes joining in on the side of the smiths. And in more substantial ways, when defining their economic interests *as producers*, craftsmen and workers — Thames-side coal heavers, London porters, Spitalfields silk weavers, west of England clothing workers, Lancashire cotton weavers, Newcastle keelmen — organized themselves tightly within their trades, and petitioned the State or corporate authorities for their fading paternalist favours.

Indeed, there is substantial evidence on this side; and the degree to which a guild or "trade" outlook and even vestigial continuity of organization contributed to the early trade unions was understated by the Webbs. Brentano, in 1870, had explored the possibility of continuity of organization and of traditions between the guilds and companies and the early trade unions.[1] But the Webbs, in their weighty *History of Trade Unionism* (1894) decreed decisively against Brentano. They did this, partly by insisting on the distinctively new character of trade unionism (in consequence of a sharp split between the interests of masters and journeymen), and partly by imposing definitions which made much eighteenth-century evidence appear to be suspect or irrelevant — for example, the demand that organization must be continuous and must have national dimensions.[2] Such definitions for a long time discouraged further systematic enquiry, either into collective bargaining by direct action[3] or into local and

[1] L. Brentano, *On the History and Development of Guilds and the Origin of Trade Unions* (1870).

[2] Sidney and Beatrice Webb, *The History of Trade Unionism* (1894/ 1920), chapter 1.

[3] This question was re-opened by E. J. Hobsbawm, "The Machine Breakers", in *Labouring Men* (1964), first published in *Past and Present* in 1952.

regional organization, as of the Newcastle keelmen or west of England clothing workers.

Such studies have multiplied in recent years, and it is now clear that — if there is no record of continuous organization of national unions — there was certainly a continuous tradition of trade union activity throughout the century, and very probably (in clothing districts) continuous local organization and recognised leadership, for actions which sometimes disguised themselves as "rough musics"[1] and sometimes took on the protective masks of friendly societies. Such trade union traditions extend back into the seventeenth century, and I regret that several very helpful recent studies give a contrary impression.[2] Some years ago in the Public Record Office I came upon what may be one of the earliest membership cards of a trade union which has (as yet) been found: it comes from a branch of the journeymen woolcombers at the small town of Alton (Hants) in 1725, although the card is printed in London and the date of formation of the club or "Charity-Stock" is given as 1700. (See plate I.) The woolcombers were being prosecuted (in the court of King's Bench) in consequence of a long-standing dispute extending over several years. Edward and Richard Palmer, clothiers, employed 150 workers in the woollen manu-

[1] For local and community trade union organisation, see Adrian Randall, "The Industrial Moral Economy of the Gloucestershire Weavers in the Eighteenth Century", in John G. Rule (ed.), *British Trade Unionism, 1750-1850* (1988), esp. pp. 29-35.

[2] Thus John Rule's helpful collection on *British Trade Unionism: the Formative Years* takes 1750 as the starting date. C. R. Dobson, *Masters and Journeymen: A prehistory of industrial relations* (1980) covers the dates 1717-1800. See also R. W. Malcolmson's valuable essay, "Workers' combinations in eighteenth-century England", in M. and J. Jacobs (eds.), *The Origins of Anglo-American Radicalism* (1984), p. 160, note 38, gives a weavers' combination in Bristol in 1707. John Rule discusses the question more closely in *The Experience of Labour in Eighteenth-Century Industry* (1981), esp. pp. 151-4. None of these authors seems to mention the extensive organisation of the Essex weavers in Colchester and region which much preoccupied the Privy Council in 1715. When the mayor of Colchester arrested some of their spokesmen, their fellows effected a rescue and "many hundreds of them Marched into Town, all armed with Pistols, Swords, or Clubs. . ." and also with a clear statement of their grievances and demands: see extensive documentation in PRO, PC 1.14. 101 Parts II and III.

factory. Their woolcombers had formed into a Woolcombers Club, fifteen or twenty of whom met at a public house, the "Five Bells". A strike had been called (of seven combers) to enforce apprenticeship regulations and (in effect also) to enforce a "closed shop". Combers were imported to break the strike, and their workshop was twice broken into, their combs and materials burned. Shortly before these events the common seal which had hitherto been used was replaced by a card or "ticket" which entitled the member "to employment or to receive benefitt in all Clothing Towns where the Woolcombers had formed themselves into Clubbs". Strike pay or benefit for leaving an employer paying under rate (under the "By Laws and Orders" of the Club) was five shillings, with which the member must travel to another town. A blackleg woolcomber imported by the Palmers from Wokingham (Berks) deposed that as he passed along the street in Alton he was "often Affronted and Abused", until at length he left the Palmers' employment. Eight of the combers were duly convicted, and the case was given a little national publicity.[1]

This seems to push the date for trade unionism back at least as far as 1700, and all the recognised features of the craft society are already there — the attempt to make a closed shop, the control of apprenticeship, strike benefit, the tramping system. After all, the elaborate processional display of woolcombers, shoemakers, hatters, weavers, etc., on grand civic occasions (such as the Coronation of George III) did not spring out of nowhere. This was the Manchester order of procession:

The Procession of the Wool-Combers
Two Stewards with white wands. — A man on horseback in white, with a wool wig and sash, beating a pair of kettle drums. — A band of music. — The Arms of Bishop Blaize displayed on a banner. — The Treasurer and Secretary. — A Page Royal, with a white wand. — Bishop Blaze on horseback, attended by ten pages on foot. — The Members, two and two, with wool wigs, sashes, and cockades of the same. — Two Junior Stewards with each a white wand.

[1] Depositions and examinations in PRO, KB 1.3. The offenders, who must have spent some months in prison, were ordered to pay £80 to the prosecutor (their master): *British Journal*, 19 February 1726; *Newcastle Weekly Courant*, 19 February 1726; *Ipswich-Journal*, 7 August 1725, cited by Malcolmson, *op. cit.*, p. 160 (note 39), p. 157.

Bishop Blaize, the patron saint of woolcombers, was supposed to have invented wool-combing and to have been torn to pieces by the sharp-toothed wool "cards". The combers' society on this occasion recited the lines:

> Spectators all that on us now do gaze,
> Behold once more the sons of Bishop Blaze,
> Who here are met in this association,
> To celebrate the King and Queen's C'ronation. . .
> May happy Britain soon enjoy a peace:
> May joy and plenty and our trade increase;
> God save King George the Third; let virtue shine
> Through all the branches of his Royal line.[1]

The Bishop Blaize procession was still being celebrated vigorously in Bradford (Yorks) in 1825. Bishop Blaize is still at the centre of the Kidderminster ticket of 1838 (Plate III).

Such iconography emphasizes an appeal by the early trade unionists to tradition, and an attempt by the journeyman's club or union to take over from the masters' guild or company the representation of the interests of "the Trade". On occasion, the journeymen actually split from the masters' company, as did the hammermen of Glasgow in 1748, who formed their own society, levied contributions, and elected a dean and masters on the pattern of the Masters' Company. There are also several interesting cases of workers' organizations which emerged in close — if antagonistic — relationship to older companies. Perhaps the most consistently militant group of eighteenth-century workers — the Newcastle keelmen — were undoubtedly thoroughly cognisant with the forms of the Company of Hostmen, with whom, indeed, they wrestled for control of their own charitable institutions. The keelmen combined two features not usually found together: on the one hand, they were numerous, subject to a yearly bond, and well-placed to employ the tactics of mass action, strike and intimidation. On the other hand, since a high proportion of their numbers were Scottish, and since the bond did not entitle them to a settlement in Newcastle, it was

[1] *A Particular Account of the Processions of the different Trades, in Manchester, on the day of the Coronation of their Majesties, King George the Third and Queen Charlotte* (September 22, 1761), single sheet folio, Manchester Ref. Lib.

in their interests to provide systematically for sickness, injury and old age.[1]

The Webbs may have been right to have demolished some of the romantic myths abroad in the 1880s and 1890s — myths which were fostered by some trade unionists themselves — as to the origin of trade unions in guilds. But what they understated was the notion of "the Trade"; and also the way in which, from the late seventeenth century, the demand for the enforcement of the apprenticeship clauses of the Statute of Artificers became a demand which, increasingly, the journeymen sought to turn to their own advantage, and hence which served as a bridge between the old forms and the new. Brentano was perhaps right when he declared: "trade unions originated with the non-observance of 5 Eliz. c. 4." From the sixteenth century to the early nineteenth century there is evidence of the continuity of these craft and trade traditions in the pottery, friendly society insignia, the emblems and mottos of early unions, and in the chapbooks and verses designed for each trade. This appeal to legitimacy and to precedent (in the Statute of Artificers) can be found in some Essex verses of the late seventeenth century:

> From such as would our rights invade,
> Or would intrude into our trade,
> Or break the law Queen Betty made,
>   Libera nos Domine.[2]

They are also found in an "Ode to the Memory of Queen Elizabeth" which prefaces a report of a trial of a cause of apprenticeship involving the London saddlers in 1811:

> Her memory still is dear to journey men,
> For shelter'd by her laws, now they resist
> Infringements, which would else persist:
> Tyrannic masters, innovating fools
> Are check'd, and bounded by her glorious rules.
> Of workmen's rights she's still a guarantee. . .

---

[1] J. M. Fewster, "The Keelmen of Tyneside in the Eighteenth Century", *Durham University Journal*, n.s. Vol. 19, 1957-8.

[2] *HMC Var. Coll.* (1913), p. 581.

And rights of artizans, to fence and guard,
While we, poor helpless wretches, oft must go
And range this liberal nation to and fro.[1]

Indeed, we may have one record of the actual moment of transition from guild to union, in the diary of a Coggeshall weaver, which contains the rules of the Company of Clothiers, Fullers, Baymakers, and New Drapers of Coggeshall (?1659-1698), followed by those transmitted from the Company to a short-lived "Combers' Purse", clearly a local club, formed "that we may show that love we have to our trade, and one to another for trade sake".[2]

The sense of trade solidarities, thus, could be strong. But to suppose that such trade fraternity was necessarily at odds with larger objectives or solidarities is quite false. The trade consciousness of London craftsmen in the 1640s did not inhibit support for John Lilburne. What trade consciousness may inhibit is economic solidarities between different groups of producers as against their employers; but if we lay aside this anachronistic postulate, we will find among eighteenth-century working men and women abundant evidence of horizontal solidarities and consciousness. In the scores of occupational lists which I have examined of food rioters, turnpike rioters, riots over libertarian issues or enclosure of urban commons, it is clear that solidarities were not segregated by trade; in a region where clothing workers, tinners or colliers are predominant, these obviously predominate in the lists of offenders, but not to the exclusion of other working occupations. I hope to have shown, in another place, that all these groups, during food riots, shared a common consciousness — ideology and objectives — as petty consumers of the necessities of life. But these people were consumers also of cultural values, of libertarian rhetoric, of patriotic and xenophobic prejudice; and on these issues they could exhibit solidarities as well. When, in the quiet 1750s, Princess Amelia tried to close access to Richmond New Park, she was opposed by a vigorous horizontal consciousness

[1] *Report of the Trial of Alexander Wadsworth against Peter Laurie before Lord Ellenborough, 18 May 1811* (1811), in Columbia Univ. Lib., Seligman Collection, Place Vol. xii.
[2] *HMC Var. Coll.* VIII (1913), pp. 578-584.

which stretched from John Lewis, a wealthy local brewer, to Grub Street pamphleteers, and which embraced the whole local "populace" (pp. 111-114). When, in 1799, the magistrates attempted to put down Shrove Tuesday football in the streets of Kingston, it was "the populace" and "the mob" who assembled and triumphantly defied their orders.[1] The mob may not have been noted for an impeccable consciousness of class; but the rulers of England were in no doubt at all that it was a horizontal sort of beast.

VI

Let us take stock of the argument to this point. It is suggested that, in practice, paternalism was as much theatre and gesture as effective responsibility; that so far from a warm, household, face-to-face relationship we can observe a studied technique of rule. While there was no novelty in the existence of a distinct plebeian culture, with its own rituals, festivals, and superstitions, we have suggested that in the eighteenth century this culture was remarkably robust, greatly distanced from the polite culture, and that it no longer acknowledged, except in perfunctory ways, the hegemony of the Church. As dialect and polite speech drifted apart, so the distance widened.

This plebeian culture was not, to be sure, a revolutionary nor even a proto-revolutionary culture (in the sense of fostering ulterior objectives which called in question the social order); but one should not describe it as a deferential culture either. It bred riots but not rebellions: direct actions but not democratic organizations. One notices the swiftness of the crowd's changes in mood, from passivity to mutiny to cowed obedience. We have this in the satirical ballad of the "Brave Dudley Boys":

---

[1] Messrs Bytterwood, Cook, and Bradshaw to duke of Portland, 24 February 1799, PRO, HO 42.46. The magistrates complained that the military (at Hampton Court) failed to support them in suppressing the football or in enforcing the Riot Act, the officer-in-command absenting himself (despite prior notice). The duke of Portland annotated the complaint: "These Gent^n don't appear to have managed this business as well as they might but their credit, as Magistrates, makes it necessary that care sh^d be taken of them."

We bin marchin' up and deown
    Wo boys, wo
Fur to pull the Housen deown
And its O the brave Doodley boys
    Wo boys, Wo
It bin O the brave Doodley boys, Wo!

Some gotten sticks, some gotten steavs
    Wo boys, wo
Fur to beat all rogues and kne-avs. . .

But the riot reaches its appointed limit, and —

. . . the Dra-gunes they did come,
And twas devil take the hoindmost wum.

We all ran down our pits
    Wo boys, wo
We all ran down our pits
Frietened a' most out of our wits
And its O the brave Doodley boys. . .

And thence to the reassertion of deference:

God Bless Lord Dudley Ward
    Wo boys, wo
He know'd as times been hard

He called back the sojermen
    Wo boys, wo
And we'll never riot again. . .[1]

It is easy to characterise this behaviour as child-like. No doubt, if we insist upon looking at the eighteenth century only through the lens of the nineteenth-century labour movement, we will see only the immature, the pre-political, the infancy of class. And from one aspect, this is not untrue: repeatedly one sees pre-figurements of nineteenth-century class attitudes and organization; fleeting expressions of solidarities, in riots, in strikes, even before the gallows; it is tempting to see eighteenth-century workers as an immanent working class, whose evolution is retarded by a sense of the futility of transcending its situation. But the "to-fro lackeying" of the crowd itself has a history of great antiquity:

[1] I have improperly drawn lines from two different versions: Jon Raven, *The Urban and Industrial Songs of the Black Country and Birmingham* (Wolverhampton, 1977) version (b) p. 50, and Roy Palmer (ed.), *Songs of the Midlands* (Wakefield, 1972), p. 88.

the "primitive rebels" of one age might be seen, from an earlier age, to be the decadent inheritors of yet more primitive ancestors. Too much historical hindsight distracts us from seeing the crowd as it was, *sui generis*, with its own objectives, operating within the complex and delicate polarity of forces of its own context.

I have attempted in chapter 4 to reconstruct these crowd objectives, and the logic of the crowd's behaviour, in one particular case: the food riot. I believe that all other major types of crowd action will, after patient analysis, reveal a similar logic: it is only the short-sighted historian who finds the eruptions of the crowd to be "blind". Here I wish to discuss briefly three characteristics of popular action, and then return once again to the context of gentry-crowd relations in which all took place.

First is the anonymous tradition. The anonymous threat, or even the individual terrorist act, is often found in a society of total clientage and dependency, on the other side of the medal of simulated deference. It is exactly in a rural society, where any open, identified resistance to the ruling power may result in instant retaliation — loss of home, employment, tenancy, if not victimization at law — that one tends to find the acts of darkness: the anonymous letter, arson of the stack or outhouse, houghing of cattle, the shot or brick through the window, the gate off its hinges, the orchard felled, the fish-pond sluices opened at night. The same man who touches his forelock to the squire by day — and who goes down to history as an example of deference — may kill his sheep, snare his pheasants or poison his dogs at night.

I don't offer eighteenth-century England as a theatre of daily terror. But historians have scarcely begun to take the measure of the volume of anonymous violence, usually accompanied by anonymous threatening letters.

What these letters show is that eighteenth-century labouring men were quite capable, in the security of anonymity, of shattering any illusion of deference and of regarding their rulers in a wholly unsentimental and unfilial way. A writer from Witney, in 1767, urged the recipient: "do not suffer such damned wheesing fat guted Rogues to Starve the Poor by such Hellish ways on purpose that they may follow hunting horse racing &c and to maintain their familys in

Pride and extravagance". An inhabitant of Henley-on-Thames, who had seen the volunteers in action against the crowd, addressed himself to "you gentlemen as you are please to call Yourselves — Altho that is your Mistakes — for you are a sett of the most Damnable Rougs that Ever Existed". (An Odiham author, writing on a similar theme in 1800, remarked "we dont care a Dam for them fellows that Call Themselves Gentlemen Soldiers But in our opinion the[y] Look moore like Monkeys riding on Bears".) Sometimes the lack of proper deference comes through merely as a brisk aside: "Lord Buckingham," a handbill writer in Norwich remarked in 1793, "who died the other day had Thirty Thousand Pounds, yeerly For setting his Arse in the House of Lords and doing nothing." [1]

These letters show — and they are dispersed over most parts of England, as well as parts of Wales — that deference could be very brittle indeed, and made up of one part of self-interest, one part of dissimulation, and only one part of the awe of authority. They were part of the countertheatre of the poor. They were intended to chill the spine of gentry and magistrates and mayors, recall them to their duties, enforce from them charity in times of dearth.

This takes us to a second characteristic of popular action, which I have described as countertheatre. Just as the rulers asserted their hegemony by a studied theatrical style, so the plebs asserted their presence by a theatre of threat and sedition. From the time of Wilkes forward the language of crowd symbolism is comparatively "modern" and easy to read: effigy burning, the hanging of a boot from a gallows; the illumination of windows (or the breaking of those without illumination); the untiling of a house which, as Rudé notes, had an almost ritualistic significance. In London the unpopular minister, the popular politician, needed the aid of no pollsters to know their rating with the crowd; they might be pelted with obscenities or chaired in triumph through the streets. When the condemned trod the stage at Tyburn, the audience proclaimed vociferously their assent or disgust with the book.

But as we move backward from 1760 we enter a world of

[1] See my essay, "The Crime of Anonymity", in Hay *et al, op. cit.*

theatrical symbolism which is more difficult to interpret: popular political sympathies are expressed in a code quite different from that of the 1640s of of the 1790s. It is a language of ribbons, of bonfires, of oaths and of the refusal of oaths, of toasts, of seditious riddles and ancient prophecies, of oak leaves and of maypoles, of ballads with a political *double-entendre*, even of airs whistled in the streets.[1] We don't yet know enough about popular Jacobitism to assess how much of it was sentiment, how much was substance; but we can certainly say that the plebs on many occasions employed Jacobite symbolism success- fully as theatre, knowing well that it was the script most calculated to enrage and alarm their Hanoverian rulers.[2] In the 1720s, when an intimidated press veils rather than illuminates public opinion, one detects underground moods in the vigour with which rival Hanoverian and Stuart anniversaries were celebrated. The *Norwich Gazette* reported in May 1723 that Tuesday last, being the birthday of King George, was observed in the city "with all the usual demon- strations of joy and loyalty":

And Wednesday being the Anniversary of the Happy Restauration of King Charles II, and with him of the royal family, after a too long and successful usurpation of sanctified tyranny, it was celebrated in this city in an extraordinary manner; for besides ringing of bells, firing of guns, and bonfires, the streets were strown with seggs, oaken boughs set up at the doors, and in some streets garlands and pictures hung out, and

[1] For the calendar of popular poltical symbolism (Jacobite and Hanoverian) see especially Rogers, *Whigs and Cities*, pp. 354-8.

[2] Despite the substantial advances in Jacobite historical studies, the evidence as to the dimensions of popular support remains slippery. An excellent assessment is in Nicholas Rogers, "Riot and Popular Jacobitism in Early Hanoverian England", in Eveline Cruikshanks (ed.), *Ideology and Conspiracy: Aspects of Jacobitism, 1689-1759* (Edinburgh, 1982). Professor Rogers shows that the considerable volume of anti-Hanoverian and Jacobite manifestations (especially between 1714 and 1725) cannot be taken as an indication of organised commitment or of insurrectionary intent but should be considered as symbolic taunting of the Hanoverian rulers — "provocative, defiant, derisory" — and not the less important for that reason. Rogers has developed these insights in *Whigs and Cities, passim*, and he speculates (pp. 378-82) on the reasons for the marked decline in the Jacobite sympathies of English urban crowds between 1715 and 1745.

variety of antick and comick dances. . . (with) bumpers to the
Glorious Memory of Charles II.

Manifestly disloyal as this was, not only to the King but also
to the Great Man in his own county, it provided no handle to
the law officers of the Crown.

This was a war of nerves, now satirical, now menacing.
The arrows sometimes found their mark. In 1724 the king's
ministers were poring over depositions from Harwich where
the loyal Hanoverian caucus had been insulted by a most
unsavoury rough music:

while the Mayor and other Members of the Corporation were
assembled in the Town Hall to Commemorate His Majesty's Most
happy accession to the Throne by drinking His Majesty's and other
most Loyal Healths, he this Deponent. . . did see from a Window. . . a
person dressed up with horns on his head attended by a mob.

This "said Infamous Person", John Hart, a fisherman, was
being chaired about the town by one or two hundred others
of equal infamy. They were "drumming a ridiculous Tune of
Roundheaded Cuckolds &c, and [Hart] came to the Mayor's
and this Deponent's door and made signs with his hands
intimating that We might kiss his Arse".[1]

If some of the crowd's actions can be seen as countertheatre, this is by no means true of all. For a third
characteristic of popular action was the crowd's capacity for
swift direct action. To be one of a crowd, or a mob, was
another way of being anonymous, whereas to be a member of
a continuing organization was bound to expose one to
detection and victimization. The eighteenth-century crowd
well understood its capacities for action, and its own art of
the possible. Its successes must be immediate, or not at all. It
must destroy these machines, intimidate these employers or
dealers, damage that mill, enforce from their masters a
subsidy of bread, untile that house, before troops came on
the scene. The mode is so familiar that I need only recall it to
mind with one or two citations from the state papers. At
Coventry, 1772:

On Tuesday evening. . . a great Mob to the Number of near 1,000 of
the. . . lower class of People. . . assembled by Fife and Beat of Drum on

[1] Examinations and depositions in PRO, SP 44.124, fos. 116-132.

Account, as they pretended, of a Reduction of Wages by. . . one of the principal Ribbon Manufacturers. . . They declared their intention to. . . pull down his House, & to demolish him, if they could meet with him. . . Every gentle Means was made use of. . . to disperse them, but without Effect, and by throwing Stones and breaking his Windows, they began to carry their Purpose into Execution.[1]

In Newcastle-upon-Tyne in 1740, during the triumphant phase of a food riot:

About two on Thursday morning a great number of Colliers and Waggoners, Smiths and other common workmen [the horizontal beast again] came along the Bridge, released the prisoners, and proceeded in great Order through the Town with Bagpipes playing, Drum beating, and Dirty Clothes fixed upon sticks by way of Colours flying. They then increased to some thousands and were in possession of the principal Streets of the Town. The Magistrates met at the Guild Hall and scarce knew what to do.

In the result they panicked, scuffled with the crowd on the Guildhall steps, and fired a volley into it, killing more than one. In retaliation:

Stones flew in among us. . . through the windows like cannon shot. . . at length the mob broke in upon us in the most terrible outrage. They spared our lives indeed but obliged us to quit the place, then fell to plundering and destroying all about 'em. The several benches of justice were immediately and entirely demolished, the Town Clerk's Office was broke open, and all the books, deeds, and records of the town and its courts thrown out of the window.[2]

They broke into the Hutch and took out fifteen hundred pounds, they. . . broke down everything that was ornamental, two very fine capital Pictures of King Charles second and James second. . . they tore, all but the faces. . . and afterwards conducted the Magistrates to their own houses in a kind of Mock Triumph.[3]

Once again, one notes the sense of theatre even in the full flush of rage: the symbolic destruction of the benches of justice, the Clerk's books, the Tory corporation's Stuart portraits, the mock triumph to the magistrates' homes; and

[1] Mayor and Corporation to "My Lord", 7 July, 1772, PRO, WO 40.17.
[2] Mayor of Newcastle-upon-Tyne to duke of Newcastle, 27 June, 1740, PRO, SP 36.51.
[3] Alderman Ridley, "Account of the Riots", Northumberland CRO, 2 RI 27/8.

yet, with this, the order of their processions and the restraint which withheld them (even after they had been fired upon) from taking life.

Of course, the crowd lost its head as often as the magistrates did. But the interesting point is that neither side did this often. So far from being "blind" the crowd was often disciplined, had clear objectives, knew how to negotiate with authority, and above all brought its strength swiftly to bear. The authorities often felt themselves to be faced, literally, with an anonymous multitude. "These men are all tinners," a customs officer wrote from St. Austell in 1766 of local smuggling gangs, "seldom seen above ground in the daytime, and are under no apprehensions of being known by us".[1] Where "ringleaders" were detected, it was often impossible to secure sworn depositions. But solidarity rarely went further than this. If taken, the leaders of the crowd might hope for an immediate rescue, within twenty-four hours; if this moment passed, they could expect to be abandoned.

Other features might be noted: but these three — the anonymous tradition; countertheatre; and swift, evanescent direct action — seem of importance. All direct attention to the unitary context of class relationship. There is a sense in which rulers and crowd needed each other, watched each other, performed theatre and countertheatre in each other's auditorium, moderated each other's political behaviour. Intolerant of the insubordination of free labour, nevertheless the rulers of England showed in practice a surprising degree of licence towards the turbulence of the crowd. Is there some deeply embedded, "structural" reciprocity here?

I find the notion of gentry-crowd reciprocity, of the "paternalism-deference equilibrium" in which both parties to the equation were, in some degree, the prisoners of each other, more helpful than notions of a "one-class society" or of consensus or of a plurality of classes and interests. What must concern us is the polarization of antagonistic interests and the corresponding dialectics of culture. There is very articulate resistance to the ruling ideas and institutions of society in the seventeenth and nineteenth centuries: hence historians expect to analyse these societies in some terms of

[1] PRO, WO 1.989.

social conflict. In the eighteenth century resistance is less articulate, although often very specific, direct and turbulent. One must therefore supply the articulation, in part by decoding the evidence of behaviour, and in part by turning over the bland concepts of the ruling authorities and looking at their undersides. If we do not do this we are in danger of becoming prisoners of the assumptions and self-image of the rulers: free labourers are seen as the "loose and disorderly sort", riot is seen as spontaneous and "blind", and important kinds of social protest become lost in the category of "crime". But there are few social phenomena which do not reveal a new significance when exposed to this dialectical examination. The ostentatious display, the powdered wigs and the dress of the great must be seen also — as they were intended to be seen — from below, in the auditorium of the theatre of class hegemony and control. Even "liberality" and "charity" may be seen as calculated acts of class appeasement in time of dearth and calculated extortions (under threat of riot) by the crowd: what is (from above) an "act of giving" is (from below) an "act of getting". So simple a category as "theft" may turn out to be, in certain circumstances, evidence of protracted attempts by villagers to defend ancient common right usages, or by labourers to defend customary perquisites. And following each of these clues to the point where they intersect, it becomes possible to reconstruct a customary popular culture, nurtured by experiences quite distinct from those of the polite culture, conveyed by oral traditions, reproduced by example (perhaps, as the century goes on, increasingly by literate means), expressed by symbolism and in ritual, and at a very great distance from the culture of England's rulers.

I would hesitate before I described this as a *class* culture, in the sense that one can speak of a working-class culture, within which children were socialized into a value-system with distinct class notations, in the nineteenth century. But one cannot understand this culture, in its experiential ground, in its resistance to religious homily, in its picaresque flouting of the provident bourgeois virtues, in its ready recourse to disorder, and in its ironic attitudes towards the law, unless one employs the concept of the dialectical antagonisms, adjustments, and (sometimes) reconciliations, of class.

When analysing gentry-plebs relations one finds not so much an uncompromising ding-dong battle between irreconcilable antagonists as a societal "field-of-force". I am thinking of a school experiment (which no doubt I have got wrong) in which an electrical current magnetized a plate covered with iron filings. The filings, which were evenly distributed, arranged themselves at one pole or the other, while in between those filings which remained in place aligned themselves sketchily as if directed towards opposing attractive poles. This is very much how I see eighteenth-century society, with, for many purposes, the crowd at one pole, the aristocracy and gentry at the other, and until late in the century, the professional and trading groups bound down by lines of magnetic dependency to the rulers, or on occasion hiding their faces in common action with the crowd. This metaphor allows one to understand not only the very frequent riot situation (and its management) but also much of what was possible and also the limits of the possible beyond which power did not dare to go.

I am therefore employing the terminology of class conflict while resisting the attribution of identity to *a* class. It seems to me that the metaphor of a field-of-force can co-exist fruitfully with Marx's comment in the *Grundrisse*, that:

> In all forms of society it is a determinate production and its relations which assign every other production and its relations their rank and influence. It is a general illumination in which all other colours are plunged and which modifies their specific tonalities. It is a special ether which defines the specific gravity of everything found in it. [1]

This plebeian culture is, in the end, constrained within the parameters of gentry hegemony: the plebs are ever-conscious of this constraint, aware of the reciprocity of gentry-crowd relations, watchful for points to exert their own advantage. The plebs also take over to their own use some of the gentry's rhetoric. For, once again, this is the century of the advance of "free" labour. And the distinctive feature of the manufacturing system was that, in many kinds of work,

[1] For a slightly different translation, see *Grundrisse* (Penguin, 1973), pp. 106-7. Even here, however, Marx's metaphor relates not to class or social forms, but to co-existent dominant and subordinate economic relations.

labourers (taking petty masters, journeymen and their families together) still controlled in some degree their own immediate relations and modes of work, while having very little control over the market for their products or over the prices of raw materials or food. This explains something of the structure of industrial relations and of protest, as well as something of the culture's artefacts and of its cohesiveness and independence of control.[1] It also explains much of the consciousness of the "free-born Englishman", who took to himself some part of the constitutionalist rhetoric of his rulers, and defended stubbornly his rights at law and his rights to white bread and cheap ale. The plebs were aware that a ruling-class that rested its claim to legitimacy upon prescription and law had little authority to over-rule their own customs and rights.

The reciprocity of these relations underlies the importance of the symbolic expressions of hegemony and of protest in the eighteenth century. That is why I have directed so much attention to the notion of theatre. Of course, every society has its own kind of theatre; much in the political life of contemporary societies can be understood only as a contest for symbolic authority. But I am saying more than that the symbolic contests of the eighteenth century were particular to that century and require more study. I think that symbolism, in that century, had a peculiar importance, owing to the weakness of other organs of control: the authority of the Church is departing, and the authority of the schools and the mass media have not yet arrived. The gentry had four major resources of control — a system of influence and preferment which could scarcely contain the unpreferred poor; the majesty and terror of law; the local exercise of favours and charity; and the symbolism of their hegemony. This was, at times, a delicate social equilibrium, in which the rulers were forced to make concessions. Hence the contest for symbolic authority may be seen, not as a way of acting out ulterior "real" contests, but as a real contest in its own right. Plebeian protest, on occasion, had no further objective than to

---

[1] I am supporting here the argument of Gerald M. Sider, "Christmas mumming and the New Year in Outport Newfoundland", *Past and Present* (May, 1976).

challenge the gentry's hegemonic assurance, strip power of its symbolic mystifications, or even just to blaspheme. It was a contest for "face", but the outcome of the contest might have material consequences — in the way the poor law was administered, in the measures felt by the gentry to be necessary in times of high prices, in whether Wilkes was imprisoned or freed.

At least we must return to the eighteenth century, giving as much attention to the symbolic contests in the streets as to the votes in the House of Commons. These contests appear in all kinds of odd ways and odd places. Sometimes it was a jocular employment of Jacobite or anti-Hanoverian symbolism, a twisting of the gentry's tail. Dr Stratford wrote from Berkshire in 1718:

> Our bumpkins in this country are very waggish and very insolent. Some honest justices met to keep the Coronation day at Wattleton, and towards the evening when their worships were mellow they would have a bonfire. Some bumpkins upon this got a huge turnip and stuck three candles just over Chetwynd's house. . . They came and told their worships that to honour King George's Coronation day a blazing star appeared above Mr Chetwynd's house. Their worships were wise enough to take horse and go and see this wonder, and found, to their no little disappointment, their star to end in a turnip.[1]

The turnip was of course the particular emblem of George I as selected by the Jacobite crowd, when they were in good humour; in ill-humour he was the cuckold king, and horns would do instead of turnips. But other symbolic confrontations in these years could become very angry indeed. In a Somerset village in 1724 an obscure confrontation (one of a number of such affairs) took place over the erection of a maypole. A local land-owner (William Churchey) seems to have taken down "the Old Maypole", newly dressed with flowers and garlands, and then to have sent two men to the bridewell for felling an elm for another pole. In response his apple and cherry orchard was cut down, an ox was killed and dogs poisoned. When the prisoners were released the pole was re-erected and "May Day" was celebrated with "seditious" ballads and derisory libels against the magistrate. Among those dressing the maypole were two labourers, a maltster, a

---

[1] HMC, *Portland MSS*, pp. vii, 245-6.

carpenter, a blacksmith, a linenweaver, a butcher, a miller, an inn-keeper, a groom and two gentlemen.[1]

As we pass the mid-century the Jacobite symbolism wanes and the occasional genteel offender (perhaps pushing his own interests under the cover of the crowd) disappears with it.[2] The symbolism of popular protest after 1760 sometimes challenges authority very directly. Nor was symbolism employed without calculation or careful forethought. In the great strike of seamen on the Thames in 1768, when some thousands marched upon parliament, the fortunate survival of a document enables us to see this taking place.[3] At the height of the strike (7 May 1768), when the seamen were getting no satisfaction, some of their leaders went into a dock-side pub and asked the publican to write out in a good hand and in proper form a proclamation which they intended posting on all the docks and river-stairs. The publican read their paper and found "many Treasonable & Rebellious Expressions" and at the bottom "No W-, no K-" (i.e. "No Wilkes, No King"). The publican (by his own account) remonstrated with them:

---

[1] PRO, KB 2 (1), Affidavits, Easter 10 G I, relating to Henstridge, Somerset, 1724. On George's accession the common people of Bedford "put the May-pole in mourning" and a military officer cut it down. In August 1725 there was an affray about a maypole in Barford (Wilts.), between the inhabitants and a gentleman who suspected the pole had been stolen from his woods (as it probably was). The gentleman summoned a posse to his aid, but the inhabitants won: for Bedford, *An Account of the Riots, Tumults and other Treasonable Practices since His Majesty's Accession to the Throne* (1715), p. 12; for Barford, *Mist's Weekly Journal*, 28 August, 1725.

[2] However, as the maypole episodes remind us, the Tory tradition of paternalism, which looks backward to the Stuart "Book of Sports", and which extends either patronage or a warm permissiveness to the recreations of the people, remains extremely vigorous even into the nineteenth century. This theme is too large to be taken into this chapter, but see R. W. Malcolmson, *Popular Recreations in English Society, 1700-1850* (Cambridge, 1973); Hugh Cunningham, *Leisure in the Industrial Revolution* (1980), chapters one and two.

[3] William L. Clement Library, Ann Arbor, Michigan, *Shelburne Papers*, vol. 133, "Memorials of Dialogues betwixt several Seamen, a certain Victualler, & a S--l Master in the late Riot".

Publican: "I beg Gentlemen you would not talk of compulsion or be guilty of the least Irregularity."

Seamen: "What do you mean Sir, if we are not speedily redressed there is Ships & Great Guns at Hand which we will use as Occasion shall require in Order to redress Ourselves besides we are determined to unmast every ship in the River & then bid you, & Old England adieu & steer for some other country. . ."

The seamen here were only playing the same game as the legislature with their repeated enactments of capital offences and legislative overkill; both sides to the relation tended to threaten more than they performed. Disappointed by the publican the seamen took their paper to a schoolmaster who undertook this kind of clerical business. Once again the sticking-point was the conclusion to the proclamation — on the right hand "Seamen", on the left hand "No W-, no K-". The schoolmaster had more respect for his own neck than to be the author of such a paper. The following dialogue, by his own account, then ensued, although it is a somewhat unlikely conversation-piece on Shadwell stairs:

Seamen: "You're not a Seaman's Friend."

Schoolmaster: "Gentlemen I am so much Your Friend that I would by no means be an Instrument of doing you the greatest Injury by Proclaiming you Traitors to our Dread Sovereign Lord the King & raisers of Rebellion & Sedition amongst your fellow subjects and this I humbly conceive to be the Contents of Your Paper. . ."

Seamen: "Most of us have ventured our lives in defence of His Majesty's Person, Crown and Dignity and for our native country and on all occasions have attacked the Enemy with courage & Resolution & have been Victorious. But since the conclusion of the War We Seamen have been slighted and our Wages reduced so low & Provisions so Dear that we have been rendered uncapable of procuring the common necessaries of Life for ourselves & Familys, and to be plain with you if our Grievances is not speedily redressed there is Ships & Great Guns enough at Deptford and Woolwich we will kick up such a Dust in the Pool as the Londoners never see before, so when we have given the Merchants a coup de grease [*sic*] we will steer for France where we are well assured we shall meet with a hearty welcome."

Once again the seamen were disappointed; they exeunt on the line, "do you think such a Body of British seamen is to be dictated by an old Fusty School Master?" Somewhere they found themselves a scribe, but even this scribe refused the full commission. The next morning the proclamation duly appeared on the river-stairs, signed at the bottom right "Seamen" and on the left. . . "Liberty & Wilkes for ever!".

The point of this anecdote is that at the very height of the seamen's strike the leaders of the movement spent several hours going from pub to schoolmaster to scribe, in search of a writer willing to set down the biggest affront to authority which they could imagine: "No King". The seamen may not have been in any reflective sense republicans; but this was the biggest symbolic "Great Gun" that they could fire off, and if fired with the seeming support of some thousands of British tars it would have been a great gun indeed.[1]

Contrary to cherished legends, England was of course never without a standing army in the eighteenth century.[2] The maintenance of this army, in Walpole's years, was a particular cause of the Hanoverian Whigs. But for purposes of internal control this was often a small and emergency force. It was, for example, seriously over-stretched and inadequate to the needs of the situation during the riot year 1766. The permanent quartering of troops in populous districts was always impolitic. There was always delay, and often delay for several days, between the onset of disturbance and the arrival of the military. The troops, and equally their officers (whose power to act against civilians could be challenged in the courts) found this service "odious".[3] Jealousy of the Crown, seconded by the avarice of the aristocracy, had led to the weakness of all the effective organs for the enforcement of order. The weakness of the State was expressed in an incapacity to use force swiftly, in an ideological tenderness towards the liberties of the subject,

[1] It is not clear whether the seamen who were preparing the handbill were authentic spokesmen for their fellows. Another eye witness of the seamen's demonstrations recorded that "they boasted that they were *for King and Parliament*": P. D. G. Thomas, "The St. George's Fields 'Massacre' on 10 May 1768", *London Journal*, Vol. 4, no. 2, 1978. See also G. Rudé, *Wilkes and Liberty* (Oxford, 1962), p. 50; Brewer, *op. cit.*, p. 190; W. J. Shelton, *English Hunger and Industrial Disorders* (1973), pp. 188, 190.

[2] See John Brewer, *The Sinews of Power, op. cit.*, pp. 44-55.

[3] See Tony Hayter, *The Army and the Crowd in Eighteenth-Century England* (1978), chapters 2 and 3: also pp. 52-3 *et passim*.

and in a sketchy bureaucracy so riddled with sinecurism, parasitism and clientage that it scarcely offered an independent presence.[1]

Thus the price which aristocracy and gentry paid for a limited monarchy and a weak State was, perforce, the licence of the crowd. This is the central structural context of the reciprocity of relations between rulers and ruled. The rulers were, of course, reluctant to pay this price. But it would have been possible to discipline the crowd only if there had been a unified, coherent ruling class, content to divide the spoils of power amicably among themselves, and to govern by means of their immense command over the means of life. Such cohesion did not, at any time before the 1790s, exist, as several generations of distinguished historical scholars have been at pains to show.

The tensions — between court and country, money and and land, factions and families — ran deep. Until 1750 or 1760 the term "gentry" is too undiscriminating for the purposes of our analysis. There is a marked divergence between the Whig and Tory traditions of relations with the crowd. The Whigs, in those decades, were never convincing paternalists.[2] But in the same decades there developed between some Tories and the crowd a more active, consenting alliance. Many small gentry, the victims of land tax and the losers in the consolidation of great estates against the small, hated the courtiers and the moneyed interest as ardently as did the plebs. And from this we see the consolidation of the specific traditions of Tory paternalism — for even in the nineteenth century, when we think of paternalism, it is Tory rather than Whig which we tend to couple with it. At its zenith, during the reigns of the first two Georges, this

[1] Despite his persuasive case for the strength of the English "fiscal-military state", John Brewer concedes that "armed force was of very limited value in enforcing authority in England": Brewer, *op. cit.*, p. 63.

[2] Although great care was exercised to limit confrontations with the crowd: see Townshend's correspondence with Vaughan, concerning the West of England weavers' riots in January 1726/7, in PRO, SP 44.81 fos. 454-58: "His Majesty is always desirous that the Mildest Ways shou'd be used to quiet these Disturbances"; the employment of soldiers against the weavers is "very much against the King's inclination", "the King wou'd have no gentle ways omitted. . . [to] bring People to temper" etc.

alliance achieved an ideological expression in the theatrical effects of popular Jacobitism.

By the 'fifties this moment is passing, and with the accession of George III we pass into a different climate. Certain kinds of conflict between court and country had so far softened that it is possible to talk of the calculated paternalist style of the gentry as a whole. In times of disturbance, in handling the crowd, one may now forget the distinction between Whig and Tory — at any rate at the level of the practising JP — and one may see the magistracy as a whole as acting within an established tradition. To maintain a hold over the poor they must show themselves to be neither papists nor puritans. They must, at least in gestures, offer themselves as mediators. During episodes of riot, most JPs, of whatever persuasion, hung back from confrontation, preferred to intervene by moral suasion before summoning force. Indeed, the role of the JP in times of riot might almost be reduced to formula: "I was sure that *one Firm* Magestrate could have any day put an end to the Riot," a Quaker merchant wrote to a friend about a sailors' riot in North Shields in 1792:

> By first speaking to the Sailors as a Majistrate ought to speak on such an Occasion, and, then put on the Man of feeling and Humanity and promise to lay all their grievances before Parliam'. . .[1]

This stance flowed sometimes from an element of active sympathy for the crowd, especially where the gentry felt themselves to be aggrieved at the profit which middlemen were making out of their own and their tenants' corn. A riot in Taunton in 1753 (Newcastle was informed) had been provoked by "one Burcher who has the town mills, & who instead of corn grinds the poor, in short he is generally thought to deserve punishment, in a legal way, for malpractices of this kind. . ."[2] Earl Poulett, the Lord Lieutenant of Somerset, clearly found men like Burcher to be a damned nuisance. They made work for him and for the bench; and, of course, order must be maintained. A general "rising" or state of riot brought other ill consequences in its

---

[1] Friends House Library, Gibson MSS, Vol. ii, p. 113. Henry Taylor to James Phillips, 27 November 1792. My thanks to Malcolm Thomas.

[2] British Library, Newcastle MSS, Add. MSS 32, 732, Poulett to Newcastle, 11 July 1753.

train — the crowd became unmannerly, the locus for disloyal speeches and seditious thoughts, "for they will all follow one another sooner than listen to gentlemen when they are once risen". Indeed, on this occasion "at last some of them came to talk a levelling language, viz. they did not see why some should be rich and others poor". (There were even obscure murmurings about aid from France.)

But the maintenance of order was not a simple matter:

> The Impunity of those Rioters encouraged. . . subsequent ones. Gentlemen in the Commission are affraid to act, nor is it safe for them as their are no troops at Taunton, Ilminster &c &c only a grass guard. . . at Crewkerne without any officer. But it seems to be in general the disposition of those towns & of these gentlemen to let the spirit subside & not to provoke them for fear of the consequences.

The consequences feared were immediate ones: more damage to property, more disorder, perhaps physical threats to the magistracy. Earl Poulett was clearly in two minds on the matter himself. He would, if so advised by your Grace "get some of the principle Ring leaders convicted," but "the disposition of the town, & neighbouring gentlemen (was) against it." There is in any case, neither here nor in hundreds of similar exchanges in 1740, 1753, 1756, the 1760s and later, any sense that the social order as a whole was endangered: what was feared was local "anarchy", the loss of prestige and hegemony in the locality, relaxing social discipline. It is usually assumed that the matter will, in the end, subside, and the degree of severity to be shown — whether a victim or two should or should not swing from the gallows — was a matter of calculated example and effect. We are back in a theatre once more. Poulett apologized to Newcastle for troubling him with these "little disturbances". A Harwich fisherman giving a lewd Jacobite gesture had worried the king's ministers more than many hundreds of men and women marching about the country thirty years later, demolishing mills and seizing grain.

In such situations there was a practised technique of crowd appeasement. The mob, Poulett wrote,

> was appeased. . . by gentlemen going out & desiring to know what they wanted & what they wd have, apprising them of the consequences, & promising them the millers & bakers shd be prosecuted, that they wd

buy up the corn & bring it to market themselves & that they shd have it in small quantitys as they wanted it.[1]

But where the crowd offered a more direct threat to the gentry themselves, then the reaction was more firm. In the same year, 1753, West Yorkshire was disturbed by turnpike riots. Henry Pelham wrote to his brother that Mr Lascelles and his turnpike had been directly attacked: "at the head of his own tenants and followers only". Lascelles had met the rioters and "gallantly thrashed them & took 10 prisoners". The Recorder of Leeds had been threatened, "and all the active part of the magistrates with pulling down their houses, and even taking away their lives". Against this, nothing but a maximum display of ruling-class solidarity would suffice:

> I have endeavoured to persuade the few gentlemen that I have seen to be themselves more active. . . This affair seems to me of such consequence that I am persuaded nothing can entirely get the better of it but the first persons in the country taking an active part in defence of the laws; for if these people see themselves only overpowered by troops, and not convinced that their behaviour is repugnant to the sense of the first people of this country, when the troops are gone, hostilitys will return.[2]

It is a text worth examination. In the first place, it is difficult to recall that it is the Prime Minister of England who is writing, and to the "Home Secretary". What is being discussed appears to be the requisite style of private men of great property in dealing with an offence to their order: the Prime Minister is endeavouring to persuade "the few gentlemen that I have seen" to be more "active". In the second place, the incident illustrates superbly the supremacy of cultural over physical hegemony. Troops afford less security than the reassertion of paternalist authority. Above all, the credibility of the gentry and magistracy must be maintained. At an early stage in disturbance, the plebs should be persuaded *above all* to abandon an insubordinate posture, to couch their demands in legitimate and deferential terms: they should learn that they were likely to get more from a loyal petition than from a riot. But if the authorities failed to persuade the crowd to drop their bludgeons and await redress, then they were willing on occasion to negotiate with

[1] *Ibid.*
[2] *Ibid.*, H. Pelham to Newcastle, 7 July 1753.

them under duress; but in such cases it became far more probable that the full and terrible theatre of the Law would later perform its ghastly matinées in the troubled district. Punitive examples must be made, in order to re-establish the credibility of order. Then, once again, the cultural hegemony of the gentry would resume.

VII

This symbolic contest acquires its significance only within a particular equilibrium of social relations. The plebeian culture cannot be analysed independently of this equilibrium; its definitions are, in some part, antitheses to the definitions of the polite culture. What I have been attempting to show, perhaps repetitiously, is that each element of this society, taken separately, may have precedents and successors, but that when all are taken together they add up to a sum which is more than the sum of the parts: it is a structured set of relations, in which the state, the law, the libertarian ideology, the ebullitions and direct actions of the crowd, all perform roles intrinsic to that system, and within limits assigned by that system, which limits are at the same time the limits of what is politically "possible"; and, to a remarkable degree, the limits of what is intellectually and culturally "possible" also. The crowd, at its most advanced, can rarely transcend the libertarian rhetoric of the radical Whig tradition; the poets cannot transcend the sensibility of the humane and generous paternalist.[1] The furious anonymous letters which spring up from society's lower depths blaspheme against the gentry's hegemony but offer no strategy to replace it.

In one sense this is a rather conservative conclusion, for I am endorsing eighteenth-century society's rhetorical self-image — that the Settlement of 1688 defined its form and its characteristic relations. Given that that Settlement

---

[1] I do not doubt that there was a genuine and significant paternalist tradition among the gentry and professional groups. But that is a different theme. My theme here is to define the limits of paternalism, and to present objections to the notion that eighteenth-century social (or class) relations were mediated by paternalism, on paternalism's own terms.

established the form of rule for an agrarian bourgeoisie[1] it
seems that it was as much that form of State power as it was
that mode of production and productive relations which
determined the political and cultural expressions of the next
hundred years. Indeed that State, weak as it was in some of
its bureaucratic and rationalizing functions, was immensely
strong and effective as an auxiliary instrument of production
in its own right: in breaking open the paths for commercial
imperialism, in imposing enclosure upon the countryside, and
in facilitating the accumulation and movement of capital,
both through its taxing, banking and funding functions and,
more bluntly, through the parasitic extractions of its own
officers. It is this specific combination of weakness and of
strength which provides the "general illumination" in which
all colours of that century are plunged; which assigned to the
judges and the magistracy their roles; which made necessary
the theatre of cultural hegemony and which wrote its paternalist and libertarian script; which afforded to the crowd its
opportunity for protest and for pressures; which laid down
the terms of negotiation between authority and plebs, and

[1] Professor J. H. Hexter was astonished when I uttered this
improper copulation ("agrarian bourgeoisie") at the Davis Center seminar
in Princeton in 1976. Perry Anderson was also astonished ten years earlier:
"Socialism and pseudo-empiricism", *New Left Review*, xxxv (January-
February 1966), p. 8, "A bourgeoisie is based on *towns*; that is what the
word means." See also (on my side of the argument), Genovese, *The World
the Slaveholders Made*, p. 249; and a judicious commentary on the argument by Richard Johnson, *Working Papers in Cultural Studies*, xi
(Birmingham, Spring 1976). My re-statement of this (somewhat conventional) Marxist argument was made in "The peculiarities of the English",
Socialist Register (1965), esp. p. 318. Here I emphasise not only the
economic logic of agrarian capitalism, but the specific amalgam of urban
and rural attributes in the life-style of the eighteenth-century gentry: the
watering-places; the London or town season; the periodic urban pasage-
rites, in education or in the various marriage markets; and other specific attributes of a mixed agrarian-urban culture. The economic arguments
(already ably presented by Dobb) have been reinforced by
Brenner, "Agrarian class structure and economic development in pre-
industrial Europe", *Past and Present*, lxx, February 1976, esp. pp. 62-8.
Additional evidence as to the urban facilities available to the gentry is in
Peter Borsay, "The English urban renaissance: the development of
provincial urban culture, *c*. 1680–*c*. 1760", *Social History*, v (May 1977).

which established the limits beyond which negotiation might not go.

Finally, how far and in what sense do I use the concept of "cultural hegemony"? This can be answered at a practical or at a theoretical level. At a practical level it is evident that the gentry's hegemony over the political life of the nation was effectively imposed until the 1790s. Neither blasphemy nor sporadic episodes of arson call this in question; these do not offer to displace the gentry's rule but only to punish them. The limits of what was politically possible (until the French Revolution) were expressed externally in constitutional forms and, internally, within men's minds, as taboos, limited expectations, and a disposition towards traditional forms of protest, aimed often at recalling the gentry to their paternalist duties.

But it is necessary also to say what this hegemony does *not* entail. It does not entail any acceptance by the poor of the gentry's paternalism upon the gentry's own terms or in their approved self-image. The poor might be willing to award their deference to the gentry, but only for a price. The price was substantial. And the deference was often without the least illusion: it could be seen from below as being one part necessary self-preservation, one part the calculated extraction of whatever could be extracted. Seen in this way, the poor imposed upon the rich some of the duties and functions of paternalism just as much as deference was in turn imposed upon them. Both parties to the question were constrained within a common field-of-force.

In the second place, we must recall once more the immense distance between polite and plebeian cultures, and the vigour of the authentic self-activity of the latter. Whatever this hegemony may have been, it did not develop the lives of the poor and it did not prevent them from defending their own modes of work and leisure, and forming their own rituals, their own satisfactions and view of life. So that we are warned from this against pressing the notion of hegemony too far and into improper areas.[1] Such

[1] In a relevant criticism of certain uses of the concept of hegemony, R. J. Morris notes that it can imply "the near impossibility of the working class or organized sections of that class being able to generate radical. . .

hegemony may have defined the outside limits of what was politically, socially, practicable, and hence influenced the forms of what was practised: it offered the bare architecture of a structure of relations of domination and subordination, but within that architectural tracery many different scenes could be set and different dramas enacted.

Eventually an independent plebeian culture as robust as this might even have nurtured alternative expectations, challenging this hegemony. This is not my reading of what took place, for when the ideological break with paternalism came, in the 1790s, it came in the first place less from the plebeian culture than from the intellectual culture of the dissenting middle class, and from thence it was carried to the urban artisans. But Painite ideas, carried through by such artisans to an ever wider plebeian culture, instantly struck root there; and perhaps the shelter provided by this robust and independent culture enabled them to flourish and propagate themselves, until they gave rise to the great and undeferential popular agitations at the end of the French Wars.

Theoretically I am saying this. The concept of hegemony is immensely valuable, and without it we would be at a loss to understand how eighteenth-century social relations were structured. But while such cultural hegemony may define the limits of what is possible, and inhibit the growth of alternative horizons and expectations, there is nothing determined or automatic about this process. Such hegemony can be sustained by the rulers only by the constant exercise of skill, of theatre and of concession. Second, such hegemony, even when imposed successfully, does not impose an all-embracing view of life; rather, it imposes blinkers, which inhibit vision in certain directions while leaving it clear in others. It can

---

ideas independent of the dominant ideology". The concept implies the need to look to intellectuals for this, while the dominant value system is seen as "an exogenous variable generated independently" of subordinate groups or classes ("Bargaining with hegemony", *Bulletin of the Society for the Study of Labour History*, (Autumn 1977), pp. 62-3). See also Genovese's sharp response to criticisms on this point in *Radical History Review*, Winter 1976-7, p. 98; and T. J. Jackson Lears, "The Concept of Cultural Hegemony", *American Hist. Rev.* xc, 1985.

co-exist (as it did co-exist in eighteenth-century England) with a very vigorous self-activating culture of the people, derived from their own experience and resources. This culture, which may be resistant at many points to any form of exterior domination, constitutes an ever-present threat to official descriptions of reality; given the sharp jostle of experience, the intrusion of "seditious" propagandists, the Church-and-King crowd can become Jacobin or Luddite, the loyal Tsarist navy can become an insurrectionary Bolshevik fleet.

It follows that I cannot accept the view, popular in some structuralist and Marxist circles in Western Europe, that hegemony imposes an all-embracing domination upon the ruled — or upon all those who are not intellectuals — reaching down to the very threshold of their experience, and implanting within their minds at birth categories of subordination which they are powerless to shed and which their experience is powerless to correct. This may perhaps have happened here and there, but not in England, not in the eighteenth century.

VIII

It may now be helpful to restate, and also to qualify, some parts of this argument. When I first proposed it, in the nineteen-seventies, it was taken by some to have set up a more absolute dichotomy between patricians and plebs, with no intermediate forces of any serious influence, than I had intended. And criticism has turned upon the absence, in my analysis, of any role for the middle class. In such a reading, the emergence of a middle-class presence in the 1790s, and the radicalisation of a large section of the intelligentsia, appears as inexplicable, a *deus ex machina*.[1] And critics have complained of the "dualism" and bleak polarisation which ensues, of my failure to admit the middling orders as historical actors and "the neglect of the role of urban

[1] See Geoff Eley's helpful critique, "Re-Thinking the Political: Social History and Political Culture in 18th and 19th Century Britain", *Archiv für Sozialgeschichte* (Bonn), Band xxi, 1981. Also Eley, "Edward Thompson, Social History and Political Culture", in Harvey J. Kaye and Keith McClelland (eds.), *E. P. Thompson: Critical Perspectives* (Oxford, 1990).

culture and bourgeois dissidence".[1]

I can agree that my bi-polar model may have more relevance to rural, small town and, especially, manufacturing districts expanding beyond any corporate controls (the locus of "proto-industrialisation") than it does to the larger corporate towns and, certainly, to London. It was no part of my intention to diminish the significance of the growth throughout the century, in numbers, wealth and cultural presence, of the middling orders who came (in the terms of Jürgen Habermas[2]) to create and occupy a "public sphere". These include the groups described by John Brewer:

. . . lawyers, land agents, apothecaries, and doctors: middlemen in the coal, textile, and grain trades: carters, carriers, and innkeepers: booksellers, printers, schoolteachers, entertainers, and clerks: drapers, grocers, druggists, stationers, ironmongers, shopkeepers of every sort: the small masters in cutlery and toy making, or in all the various luxury trades of the metropolis.[3]

The list could be much extended, and should certainly include the comfortable freeholders and substantial tenant farmers. And it is from such middling groups that Eley sees "the emergence and consolidation of a new and self-conscious bourgeois public":

Ultimately related to processes of capitalist development and social transformation. . . processes of urban cultural formation, tendentially supportive of an emergent political identity and eventually linked to regional political networks; a new infra-structure of communications, including the press and other forms of literary production. . . and a new universe of voluntary association; and finally, a regenerate parliamentarism. . .[4]

I can assent to all this. But this emergence and consolidation was a complex process, and a very slow one, eventuating over a hundred years and more. As Professor Cannon has noted:

[1] Linda Colley, "The Politics of Eighteenth-Century British History", *Journal of British Studies*, 24, 1986, O. 366.
[2] Jürgen Habermas, "The Public Sphere", *New German Critique*, 3, Fall 1974.
[3] John Brewer, "English Radicalism in the Age of George III", in J. G. A. Pocock (ed.), *Three British Revolutions* (Princeton, N.J., 1980), p. 333.
[4] Eley, "Re-Thinking the Political", *op. cit.*, p. 438.

Though there is much evidence that merchants and financiers, teachers and journalists, lawyers and architects, shopkeepers and industrialists prospered in Hanoverian England, the questions to be explained seem to me to be almost the opposite of Marxist historiography — not how did they come to control government, but why did they not challenge aristocratic domination until towards the end of the century?[1]

The questions seem to me to be located in the actual historical record and not in any variety of historiography. And they continue to perplex historians of many persuasions. Certainly there were many prefigurements of middle-class "emergence" in urban politics. But, as John Brewer argues, middle-class independence was constantly constrained and brought back within the channels of dependency by the powerful controls of clientage:

The producers of luxury goods — of furniture, carriages, and clothing — retailers of all sorts, those, from prostitutes to dancing masters, who provided services for the rich, all these people (and they constituted a sizeable proportion of the metropolitan workforce) relied for their living on a culture centred upon the Court, Parliament and the London season.[2]

This situation need not induce deference: it could generate resentment and hostility. What it could not do, until the arena of the market became more anonymous, was generate independence.

If we consider the ever-present controls of clientage, of patronage and "interest", we are drawn back to the model of a bi-polar field of force, just as such bi-polar vocabulary was continually in the mouths of the historical actors themselves. Indeed, such a model of the social and political order was an ideological force in its own right. One of the ways in which patricians repelled the admission of the middle class to any share in real power was to refuse their admission to the vocabulary of political discourse. Patrician culture stubbornly resisted any allowance of vitality to the notion of "middle

[1] John Cannon, *Aristocratic Century: the Peerage of Eighteenth-Century England* (Cambridge, 1984), p. ix.

[2] Brewer, *op. cit.*, p. 339. See also Brewer, "Commercialization and Politics", in N. McKendrick, John Brewer, and J. Plumb, *The Birth of a Consumer Society* (Bloomington, 1982).

class" until the end of the century.[1] Moreover, it is an error to suppose that the growth in numbers and wealth of the "middling orders" necessarily modified and softened class polarisation in the society as a whole. In some circumstances it diverted hostilities; as we have seen (above pp. 43-46) the middling groups could serve to screen the landowner or great clothier. But so long as so many of the routes to office, preferment and contracts were controlled by the old and corrupt means of patronage, the growth in the numbers of the middling groups could only intensify the competition between them.[2]

Hence my argument has not been about the numbers, wealth or even cultural presence of the middle class, but about its identity as an autonomous, self-motivated political actor, its effective influence upon power, its modification in any serious way of the patrician-plebs equilibrium. I do not wish to retreat from the propositions in this chapter, although I salute the significance of current research into middle-class institutions and into urban political life.

The argument is in part about power, and in part about cultural alienation. (See above, p. 5.) Critics have suggested that I and others of the older generation of "crowd historians", by attending mainly to riots and protests, have excluded from view many other popular manifestations, including loyalist and patriotic ebullience, electoral partisanship, and uglier evidences of xenophobia or religious bigotry.[3] I am very willing to grant that these questions have

[1] Paul Langford, *op. cit.*, p. 653 notes the delay in the admission of "middle class" to general usage, and he comments that the middle class "was united in nothing more than in its members' determination to make themselves gentlemen and ladies, thereby identifying themselves with the upper class". I am indebted to Dror Wahrman of Princeton University for a sight of some of his unpublished research into the explicit and politically-motivated resistance to the admission of "middle class" to general usage.

[2] See Linda Colley, *op. cit.*, p. 371: "If sociopolitical antagonisms were becoming sharper in the late eighteenth century (as I believe they were), one would expect to see both an increase in plebeian consciousness and bitterness, and a ruling group that was more avid for office, honors, wealth, and a discrete cultural identity."

[3] For one excellent study see John Walsh, "Methodism and the Mob in the Eighteenth Century", in G. J. Cuming and D. Baker, *Studies in Church History* (Cambridge, 1971), Vol. 8.

not preoccupied me, and I am happy to see these absences being repaired by others.[1] Certainly, a more rounded view of the crowd is becoming available. But one hopes that the view does not become too round. Few generalisations as to the dominant political attitudes of the "plebs" across the eighteenth century are likely to stand, except that the crowd was highly volatile. Eighteenth-century crowds come in great variety, in every shape and size. In the early years of the century there were mughouse gangs, to be turned loose by politicians against their opponents. "I love a mob," said the duke of Newcastle in his later years: "I headed a mob once myself. We owe the Hanoverian succession to a mob."[2] At no time is this volatility more manifest than at the end of the century. Generalisations as to the crowd's political disposition will tell us one thing at the time of the Priestley Riots (1791); another at the height of the popularity of Tom Paine and Reform two or three years later. Revolutionary sentiments can be found in alehouse rhetoric and in anonymous threatening letters between 1797 and 1801 (years of the naval mutinies, the Irish insurrection, years of resistance to taxation and of fierce bread riots) and fervent popular loyalism and anti-Gallicanism can be found between 1803 and 1805 (years of invasion threat, of anger at Napoleon's imperial expansion, which aroused the hostility even of former English "Jacobins", years of mass enlistment in the Volunteers and of Nelson's bitter-sweet victory at Trafalgar).

These swift transitions took place, of course, within individuals as well as within the mood of crowds. Allen Davenport, who came from a labouring family on the Gloucestershire-Wiltshire border, described how he came to Bristol in 1794, at the age of 19:

> I was a bit of a patriot, and thought, at that time, that every thing that was undertaken by England was right, just, and proper; and that every other nation that opposed her was wrong and deserved chastisement. And that France who had just killed her king, exiled her nobles, and

[1] For example, Linda Colley, "The Apotheosis of George III: Loyalty, Royalty and the British Nation, 1760-1820", *Past and Present*, 102, February 1984.

[2] James L. Fitts, "Newcastle's Mob", *Albion*, Vol. 5, no. 1, Spring 1973.

reviled and desecrated the Christian religion, was very wicked indeed; and I shouted "Church and King" as loud and as long as any priest or lord in the kingdom. And believed that England was not only justified, but that it was her bounden duty to put down, and if possible to exterminate such a desperate nation of levellers, blasphemers, and regicides! And that was the feeling of nine tenths of the people of England [in] 1794.[1]

Davenport was to become a leading Spencean, a republican and a Chartist.

The eighteenth-century crowd was protean: now it employed Jacobite symbolism, now it gave full-throated endorsement to Wilkes, now it attacked Dissenting meetinghouses, now it set the price of bread. It is true that certain themes repeat themselves: xenophobia (especially anti-Gallicanism) as well as a fondness for anti-papist and libertarian ("free-born Englishman") rhetoric. But easy generalisations should stop at that point. Perhaps in reaction to overmuch sympathy and defensiveness which was shown by crowd historians of my generation, some younger historians are willing to tell us what the crowd believed, and (it seems) it was always nationalistic and usually loyalist and imperialist in disposition. But not all of these historians have spent much time in searching the archives where the enigmatic and ambivalent evidence will be found, and those of us who have done so are more cautious. Nor can one read off "public opinion" in a direct way from the press, since this was written by and for the middling orders; an enthusiasm for commercial expansion among these readers was not necessarily shared by those who served by land or sea in the wars which promoted this expansion. In contrast to the populist tone of the 1960s it is very much the fashion of our own time for intellectuals to discover that working people were (and are) bigoted, racist, sexist, but/and at heart deeply conservative and loyal to Church and King. But a traditional ("conservative") customary consciousness may in certain conjunctures appear as a rebellious one; it may have its own logic and its own solidarities which cannot be typed in a simple-minded way. "Patriotism" itself may be a rhetorical stratagem which the crowd employs to mount an assault upon

[1] *Life of Allen Davenport* (1845), pp. 18-19.

the corruption of the ruling Hanoverian powers, just as in the next century the Queen Caroline agitation was a stratagem to assault King George IV and his court. When the crowd acclaimed popular admirals it might be a way of getting at Walpole or at Pitt.[1]

We cannot even say how far explicit republican ideas were abroad, especially during the turbulent 1760s. It is a question more often turned aside with a negative than investigated. But we have the *caveat* of Sir John Plumb: "Historians, I feel, never give sufficient emphasis to the prevalence of bitter anti-monarchical, pro-republican sentiment of the 1760s and 1770s."[2] A similar thought has strayed across the mind of a more excitable historian, Mr J. C. D. Clark, who has quoted John Wesley in 1775, writing to the earl of Dartmouth about the "dangerously dissatisfied" state of the people "all over the nation" "in every city, town, and village where I have been". The people "aim at" the king himself: "they heartily despise His Majesty and hate him with a perfect hatred. They wish to imbrue their hands in his blood; they are full of the spirit of murder and rebellion. . ."[3] One suspects that there are times during the 1760s and 1770s when a part of the English people were more ready to secede from the Crown than were the American colonists, but they had the misfortune not to be protected from it by the Atlantic ocean.

I stand, then, by the patrician/plebs model and the field-of-force metaphor, both for the structuring of power and for the dialectical tug-of-war of ideology. Yet it should not be supposed that these formulae supply an instant analytical resource to unpick the meaning of every action of the crowd. Each crowd action took place in a specific context, was influenced by the local balance of forces, and often found its

---

[1] Gerald Jordan and Nicholas Rogers, "Admirals as Heroes: Patriotism and Liberty in Hanoverian England", *Journal of British Studies*, Vol. 28, no. 3, July 1989; Kathleen Wilson, "Empire, Trade and Popular Politics in Mid-Hanoverian Britain: the Case of Admiral Vernon", *Past and Present*, 121, 1988.

[2] Plumb, "Political Man", *op. cit.*, p. 15.

[3] J. Telford (ed.), *Letters to the Rev. John Wesley* (1931), Vol. vi, p. 178, cited in J. C. D. Clark, *English Society, 1688-1832* (Cambridge, 1985), p. 236. It is not clear how far Mr Clark endorses Wesley's alarmism.

opportunity and its script from the factional divisions within ruling groups or from issues thrown up in national political discourse. This question has been discussed cogently by Nicholas Rogers in *Whigs and Cities*; he (perhaps unfairly) suspects me of "essentialist" analytical procedures. If so, then Rogers is right and I am wrong, since his command of the material is superb, and his findings are supported by years of research and analysis of the urban crowd.[1] In Rogers's view most urban crowd actions should be seen as taking place on "a terrain in which ideology, culture and power intersect". In the early eighteenth century the rulers themselves, for their own reasons, opened this space for the crowd, allocating to it a client and subaltern role. High-church clergy and civic factionalists enlarged this space. The calendar of political aniversaries and celebrations — processions, illuminations, elections, effigy burnings, carnivalesque ebullitions — all allocated roles to the crowd and enlisted its participation. In this way in the four decades after 1680 "wide sections of the labouring populace" were drawn into the national political discourse:

> Years of acute party strife, in a social context which allowed the common people greater cultural space, had created a dynamic and contentious political culture, centred around royal and national anniversaries, in which the populace itself was a vigorous participant.

It was only under this tutelage that the crowd learned to assert its own autonomy and, on occasion, select its own objectives. The crowd was now a phenomenon that "had to be cultivated, nurtured, and contained", lest it should break out of its subaltern role.[2]

I can accept and applaud Professor Rogers's approach and its execution in his urban studies. It is preferable to a simple reduction to a dual patrician/plebs polarity, and — while it allows to the crowd less autonomy than I find (for example, in provincial food or turnpike or industrial or press-gang or

[1] One looks forward eagerly to his forthcoming volume, *Crowds, Politics, and Culture in Eighteenth-Century England*, which promises to replace all previous studies. One also looks forward to Kathleen Wilson's forthcoming, *"The Sense of the People": Urban Political Culture in England, 1715-1785.*

[2] Rogers, *Whigs and Cities*, esp. pp. 351, 368-72.

anti-militia actions) — it replaces urban crowd actions within
a more complex political and cultural context. But through
all these complexities I still must posit the underlying polarity
of power — the forces which pressed to enter upon and
occupy any spaces which fell open when ruling groups came
into conflict. Even where crowds were clearly managed and
subaltern, they were never regarded by the rulers without
anxiety. They might always exceed their permit, and the
unlicensed crowd would fall back into the "essentialist"
polarity, "transforming the official calendar into a carnival
of sedition and riot".[1] Underlying all crowd actions one can
sense the formation which has been my object of analysis, the
patrician/plebs equilibrium.

One component of this, the old pretences of paternalism
and deference, were losing force even before the French
Revolution, although they saw a temporary revival in the
Church-and-King mobs of the early nineties, the military
display and anti-Gallicanism of the wars. The Gordon Riots
had seen the climax, and also the apotheosis, of plebeian
licence; and inflicted a trauma upon the rulers which was
registered in a growing disciplinary tone in the eighties. But
by then the reciprocal relation between gentry and plebs,
tipping now one way, now the other, had lasted for a century.
Grossly unequal as this relationship was, the gentry nevertheless needed *some* kind of support from "the poor", and
the poor sensed that they were needed. For a hundred years
they were not altogether the losers. They maintained their
traditional culture; they secured a partial arrest of the work-
discipline of early industrialism; they perhaps enlarged the
scope of the poor laws; they enforced charities which may
have prevented years of dearth from escalating into crises of
subsistence; and they enjoyed liberties of pushing about the
streets and jostling, gaping and huzzaing, pulling down the
houses of obnoxious bakers or Dissenters, and a generally
riotous and unpoliced disposition which astonished foreign
visitors, and which almost misled them themselves into
believing that they were "free". The 1790s expelled that
illusion, and in the wake of the experiences of those years the
relationship of reciprocity snapped. As it snapped, so, in the

[1] *Ibid.*, p. 372.

same moment, the gentry lost their self-assured cultural hegemony. It suddenly appeared that the world was not, after all, bounded at every point by their rules and overwatched by their power. A man was a man, "for a' that". We move out of the eighteenth-century field-of-force and enter a period in which there is a structural reordering of class relations and of ideology. It is possible, for the first time, to analyse the historical process in terms of nineteenth-century notations of class.

Chapter Three

Custom, Law and Common Right

I

At the interface between law and agrarian practice we find
custom. Custom itself *is* the interface, since it may be
considered both as praxis and as law. Custom's original lies
in praxis; in a treatise on copyhold at the end of the seventeenth century we learn that "customs are to be construed
according to vulgar apprehension, because Customs grow
generally, and are bred up and brought up amongst the Lay-
gents, therefore are called *Vulgares Consuetudines'*. For
Sir Edward Coke (1641) there were "two pillars" for customs
— common usage, and time out of mind. For Carter in *Lex
Custumaria* (1696) the pillars had become four: antiquity,
continuance, certainty and reason:

> For a Custom taketh beginning and groweth to perfection in this
> manner. When a reasonable Act once done is found to be good, and
> beneficial to the People, and agreeable to their nature and disposition,
> then do they use it and practise it again and again, and so by often
> iteration and multiplication of the Act, it becomes a Custom; and being
> continued without interruption time out of mind, it obtaineth the force
> of a Law.

Custom is local, *lex loci*, and may except the locality from
common law, as, for example, in "Borough-English"
whereby the younger son might inherit. It is "alleged not in
the person, but in the manor" (Fisher): "So Custom lies upon

the Land" and "binds the Land" (Carter).[1]

The land upon which custom lay might be a manor, a parish, a stretch of river, oyster beds in an estuary, a park, mountain grazing, or a larger administrative unity like a forest. At one extreme custom was sharply defined, enforceable at law, and (as at enclosure) was a property: this is the business of the court roll, the manorial courts, the recitations of customs, the survey and of village by-laws. In the middle custom was less exact: it depended on the continual renewal of oral traditions, as in the annual or regular perambulation of the bounds of the parish:

> Gervas Knight. . . aged sixty seven yeares and upwards Maketh Oath that ever since he can remember. . . he has known Farming Woods Walk within the Forest of Rockingham. . . and says that ever since he was big enough. . . viz. from about the yeare 1664 until about the yeare 1720 he yearly or every two yeares. . . went with the Vicar and Parishioners of Brigstock to perambulate publickly for the same Parish and thereby make clayme of the Lands thereto belonging and to set forth their bounds. . .[2]

The perambulation followed the ancient watercourses, the hedges of closes, and at each boundary point a cross or mark was made in the ground.[3]

Not only the lord's court but also the church was trustee of the parish memory, and in the early eighteenth century one can still find examples where this trust was vigorously upheld. I have described in *Whigs and Hunters* the remarkable role as

---

[1] Sir Edward Coke, *The Complete Copy-holder* (1641); S.C. [S. Carter], *Lex Custumaria: or, A Treatise of Copy-hold Estates*, 2nd edn. 1701), ch. 4, which usefully summarises law *c.* 1700. Law relating to custom was of course modified by eighteenth-century judgements, and is usefully summarised *c.* 1800 in R. B. Fisher, *A Practical Treatise on Copyhold Tenure* (1794; 2nd edn. 1803), ch. 6. An authoritative treatise on customary law in the nineteenth century is John Scriven, *A Treatise on the Law of Copy-holds*, (7th edn., 1896). For the later nineteenth century, J. H. Balfour Browne, *The Law of Usages and Customs* (1875), ch. 1.

[2] Deposition of Jarvis Knight, PRO, KB 1.2 Part 2, Trinity 10 Geo. I.

[3] Small boys were sometimes ducked in the ditch or given a clout to imprint the spot upon their memories. Such practices are found everywhere. In Shetland "at a perambulation of the scattald marches of Uist in the year 1818. . . Mr Mowat to make it to be the better remembrd that Tonga was the march, gave Fredman Stickle. . . a crack over the back with his horse-whip": Brian Smith, "What is a Scattald?", in Barbara Crawford (ed.), *Essays in Shetland History* (Lerwick, 1984), p. 104.

recorder of Will Waterson, the vicar of Winkfield in Windsor Forest.[1] The vicar of Richmond led his parishioners in a perambulation which broke down the wall of Richmond Park.[2] An equally active part was played by Mr Henry Goode, the rector of Weldon, a parish which intercommoned with several others in the forest of Rockingham and whose rights were disputed by the parish of Brigstock. In 1724 in one of those disputes over timber rights and lops and tops which can be found in all forest areas, there was a formidable encounter in the forest. In Whitsun week the servants of Lord Gowran of Brigstock felled some trees in Farming Woods Walk and the Gowrans sent their tenants with wagons to carry the timber away. "You are very merry", said a Weldon man: "We will be merry with you." Shortly afterwards more than two hundred Weldon men and women surged into the forest, armed with hatchets, woodbills, pick hafts and staves, "hallowing. . . in a violent riotous and threatning manner and crying out 'Cutt the Waggons, Overthrow the Waggons'. . .", scaring the horses, and carrying off some of the lops and tops. Behind this affray lay further grievances about grazing rights and the impounding by Lord Gowran's orders of Weldon cattle. A deponent said that the rector of Weldon "did on a Sunday in his desk in Church there preach or read something to his Parishioners there that instigated or encouraged the said Riot, and that on the same day that Riot was committed the Bells in the Steeple there were rung backwards or jangled in order to raise or incite the people. . ."[3] Mr Goode continued his campaign twenty years later, with a "Commoner's Letter to his Brethren in Rockingham Forest", in which their precedents and rights were rehearsed. The notion of church guardianship was emphasised by a postscript:

[1] E. P. Thompson, *Whigs and Hunters* (1975), esp. pp. 298-300.
[2] Anon., *Two Historical Accounts of the Making of the New Forest and of Richmond New Park* (1751). In 1748 the rector of Bainton (Yorkshire) led his parishioners in breaking down enclosures made by the lord of the manor; the rector, William Territt, ended up at York Assizes: W. E. Tate, *The English Village Community and the Enclosure Movements* (1967), p. 152.
[3] Depositions of Charles Gray and of Richard Collyer in PRO, KB 1.2 Part 2 (1724).

N.B. I desire every Parish, that has any Right of Common in the Forest of Rockingham, to lay up two of these Letters in the Parish Chest, which may be a means of instructing their Children, and their Childrens Children, how to preserve their Right in the Forrest for Ages to come.[1]

Perhaps Henry Goode and Will Waterson strayed a little beyond a perambulation of the bounds of duty. A recommended Exhortation to be preached in Rogation Week had a good deal to say about avoiding contention with neighbouring parishes and turning the other cheek. Nevertheless, explicit commination is visited upon offenders against parish or common rights: "Accursed be he, said Almighty God by Moses, who removeth his neighbour's doles and marks":

They do much provoke the wrath of God upon themselves, which use to grind up the doles and marks, which of ancient time were laid for the division of meers and balks in the fields, to bring the owners to their right. They do wickedly, which do turn up the ancient terries of the fields, that old men beforetime[s] with great pains did tread out; whereby the lords' records (which be the tenants' evidence) be perverted and translated sometimes to the disheriting of the right owner, to the oppression of the poor fatherless, or the poor widow.

And if these exhortations are directed mainly at the petty malefactor, moving boundary marks in the night or shaving with his plough a foot off the common balks and walks, yet the sentence of commination was visited also on the rich and the great: "So witnesseth Solomon. The Lord will destroy the house of the proud man: but he will stablish the borders of the widow." And all farmers were exhorted "to leave behind some ears of corn for the poor gleaners".[2]

If the memories of the old, perambulation and exhortation lay towards the centre of custom's interface between law and praxis, custom passes at the other extreme into areas altogether indistinct — into unwritten beliefs, sociological norms, and usages asserted in practice but never enrolled in any by-law. This area is the most difficult to recover, precisely because it belongs only to practice and to oral tradition. It

[1] "A Commoner" [the Rev. Good of Weldon], *A Letter to the Commoners in Rockingham Forest* (Stamford, 1744), p. 18.
[2] "An Exhortation to be spoken to such Parishes where they use their Perambulation in Rogation Week", *Certain Sermons and Homilies appointed to be read in Churches in the Time of Queen Elizabeth* (1851), pp. 529-30.

may by the area most significant for the livelihood of the poor and the marginal people in the village community. Custumals and by-laws should not be taken to be an exhaustive accounting of the actual practice of common right usages, especially where these bear upon the fringe benefits of common, waste, the herbage of lanesides, to the landless inhabitants or the cottager. For these documentary sources are often partisan briefs drawn up by the lord's steward, or by the substantial landholders on the in-coming of a new lord; or they are the outcome of bargaining and compromise between several propertied parties in the manorial court, in which the cottager or the landless had no voice on the homage. As one learned legal antiquary noted,

> The Entries which are found in the manorial Books or on Manorial Court Rolls, kept in the hands of the Lord's Steward, and purporting to set out the bounds of manors are liable to great suspicion. . . They are always made by Parties having a positive interest in gaining the greatest extent of property possible.[1]

Other rights were of a nature that could never be brought to trial or proved. For example, a King's Bench affidavit of 1721 concerns a woman gleaner who was beaten and driven from the field in Hope-under-Dynemore, Herefordshire. The farmer, in defence, said he "would not suffer her to lease there because she had cursed him".[2] This might indicate only a neighbourhood quarrel, but — the evidence is too scanty for confidence — it might hint at further unwritten custom. A curse, of course, registered something more than a curse would normally register today. Both slander and assault were constant objects of social control. But a curse was more than slander. The Herefordshire case might suggest that a curse was strong enough to unloose the farmer (at least in his own eyes) from the acknowledged bond laid upon the land by custom.

I am suggesting that custom took effect within a context of sociological norms and tolerances. It also took effect within a

---

[1] Stacey Grimaldi, "Report upon the Rights of the Crown in the Forest of Whichwood", 2 vols. (MS in my possession, 1838), i, no pagination, section on "timber and saplings within manors".

[2] PRO, KB 2.1 Part 2, Rex v John Stallard. Elizabeth Blusk miscarried as a result of being beaten by Stallard.

workaday routine of livelihood. It was possible to acknowledge the customary rights of the poor, but place obstacles in the way of their exercise. A petition of the poor inhabitants of Loughton, adjoining Waltham Forest in Essex, claimed the liberty of lopping their firewood from the trees. The lord and lady of the manor had not disputed the right but had limited its exercise to Mondays only, "and if this day prove fair 'tis a loss to them because 'tis the day they generally lett themselves to work with the farmers that employ them for the whole week", whereas formerly they had gathered wood on any wet days when there was no work. Meanwhile (they complained) the lord and lady were felling timber, selling logs, overstocking the forest with cattle, ploughing up the greensward, and setting coney warrens whose rabbits were "eating up their green corn and poysoning their meadows".[1]

Agrarian custom was never fact. It was ambience. It may best be understood with the aid of Bourdieu's concept of "habitus" — a lived environment comprised of practices, inherited expectations, rules which both determined limits to usages and disclosed possibilities, norms and sanctions both of law and neighbourhood pressures.[2] The profile of common right usages will vary from parish to parish according to innumerable variables: the economy of crop and stock, the extent of common and waste, demographic pressures, by-employments, vigilant or absentee landowners, the role of the church, strict or lax court-keeping, the contiguity of forest, fen or chase, the balance of greater and lesser landholders. Within this habitus all parties strove to maximise their own advantages. Each encroached upon the usages of the others. The rich employed their riches, and all the institutions and awe of local authority. The middling farmers, or yeoman sort, influenced local courts and sought to write stricter by-laws as hedges against both large and petty encroachments; they could also employ the discipline of the poor laws against those beneath them, and on occasion they

---

[1] PRO, C 104.113 Part 1, *c.* 1720? For the unusually tenacious and ritualised customs of wood in Loughton, see Lord Eversley, *Commons, Forests and Footpaths* (1910), pp. 86ff, 106-8; and below pp. 142-3.

[2] Pierre Bourdieu, *Outline of a Theory of Practice* (Cambridge, 1977), Chap. 4. This is my own gloss upon Bourdieu's stricter concept.

defended their rights against the rich and powerful at law.[1] The peasantry and the poor employed stealth, a knowledge of every bush and by-way, and the force of numbers. It is sentimental to suppose that, until the point of enclosure, the poor were always losers. It is deferential to suppose that the rich and great might not act as law-breakers and predators. A reading of the successive reports on royal forests of the Land Revenue Commissioners will quickly disabuse us on both points.

Forests, chases, great parks and some fisheries were notable arenas, in the eighteenth century, of conflicting claims (and appropriations) of common rights. After a revival in the first decades, the forest courts fell back into disuse, so that the direct invigilation by "the Crown" declined. But the hierarchy of grantees, managers, keepers, forest officers, under-keepers, remained in being, as avaricious as ever, and most of them engaged in the rip-offs which their rank or opportunities of office favoured. The great encroached on the walks, fenced in new hunting lodges, felled acres of timber, or obtained little sweeteners, like the earl of Westmorland who was granted four hundred acres of Whittlewood Forest at one farthing an acre in 1718.[2] In the middle of the hierarchy forest officers and under-keepers, who had long supplemented their petty salaries with perquisites, made inroads into the venison, sold off the brushwood and furze, made private agreements with inn-keepers and pastry-cooks, butchers and tanners.[3] Early in the century Charles Withers, Surveyor-General for Woods and Forests, kept a diary of a tour of several forests. At Wychwood —

This Forest egregiously abused. The timber shrouded and browsed: none coming on in the Knipes or Coppices; cut by Keepers, without assignment, sold to the neighbourhood: especially Burford Town supplied thence. Landlord Nash at the Bull bought this year Ten Load; in short, 'tis scandalous!

[1] This was especially the case where copyhold and customary tenures survived strongly: see C. E. Searle, "Custom, Class Conflict and Agrarian Capitalism: the Cumbrian Customary Economy in the Eighteenth Century", *Past and Present*, 110 (1986), esp. pp. 121-132.
[2] *Commons Journals*, xlvii (1792), p. 193.
[3] P. A. J. Pettit, *The Royal Forests of Northamptonshire, 1558-1714* (Northants. Record Society, 1968), pp. 48-9.

Much the same was found in the New Forest. But, equally, Withers found that the working inhabitants of forest villages and purlieus were continually pressing and enlarging their claims. In the Forest of Dean the colliers were "cutting thriving Timber for their Pits, without assignment. They pretend a custom to demand it, but are now so lawless that they even take it without".[1] And in a Memorial to the Treasury Commissioners in 1729 Withers represented that —

> It is very observable that the Country people everywhere think they have a sort of right to the Wood, & timber in the Forests, and whether the Notion may have been delivered down to them by tradition, from the times these Forests were declared to be such by the Crown, when there were great Struggles and contests about them, he is not able to determine. But it is certain they carefully conceal the Spoyls committed by each other, and are always jealous of everything that is done under the Authority of the Crown.[2]

Disputes over common right in such contexts were not exceptional. They were normal. Already in the thirteenth century common rights were exercised according to "time-hallowed custom",[3] but they were also being disputed in time-hallowed ways. Conflict over "botes" or "estover" (small wood for fencing, repair of buildings, fuel) or "turbary" (turves and peats for fuel) was never-ending; only occasionally did it arise to the high visibility of legal action, or (as with Weldon and Brigstock (p. 99)) to a punch-up between contiguous parishes, or to a confrontation between the powerful rich and the numerous "poor", as in the disputed carrying-away of "lops and tops".[4] But there cannot be a forest or chase in the country which did not have some dramatic episode of conflict over common right in the eighteenth century. It was not only the deer which enraged farmers, by spilling out of the forests and eating their corn. There were also the coney warrens, which became a craze in

[1] Earl St Aldwyn's MSS, PPD/7, extracts from journals and diaries, c. 1722, copied in 1830.
[2] Camb. Univ. Lib., C(H) MSS, 62/38/1, Memorial of Charles Withers to Treasury Commissioners, 10 April 1729.
[3] Jean Birrell, "Common Rights in the Medieval Forest", *Past and Present*, 117 (1987), pp. 29ff.
[4] See Alice Holt Forest, for example, in my *Whigs and Hunters*, p. 244.

the early eighteenth century with lords of the manor anxious to improve, not their pastures but their income. In one robust complaint from Charnwood in North Leicestershire, rabbit warrens were identified with Stuart tyranny:

> When Popish Jemmy rul'd this Land
>   He rul'd it like a King.
> And bloody Jeffreys went about
>   Hanging & Gibbeting.
>
> The Warreners prick'd up their Ears
>   That was a Time of Grace,
> Game Laws & Justices were made
>   And Rabbets bred apace.
>
> They cover'd all our Common Ground
>   Or soon would do, no doubt
> But now, whilst George the Second reigns
>   We'l pull the Vermin out. . .

The lines of this "Charnwood Opera" (performed in "The Holly Bush" in the forest) may date from 1753, and refer to episodes three or four years earlier. Lord Stamford, Lord Huntingdon, and three great gentry had planted copious warrens on the commons:

> The Turf is short bitten by Rabbits, And now
> No milk can be stroak'd from ye Old Womans Cow
> Tom Threshers poor Children look sadly, And say
> They must eat Waterporridge, three times in a Day
>   Derry down.

In 1749 a great number of inhabitants, men, women and boys of neighbouring villages, including a party of colliers from Cole Orton, converged upon the warrens, marching over the plain "with rustick Noise & laughter. . . the Mobile Clamour mix'd with Threats & Jokes":

> On yonder Hill, See, How They stand
> — with Dogs — and Picks, and Spades in Hand.
> By Mars! A formidable Band!
>   Were they enclin'd to fight
> See! How they troop from ev'ry Town
> To pull these Upstart Warrens down,
> All praying for the Church & Crown
>   And for their Common Right.

In the ensuing encounter the warrens were thrown open. The "rioters" clashed with the Warrener and his party, and one of the rioters was killed. There followed troops of dragoons, wholesale arrests, trials. Right of common was proved for twenty-six neighbouring towns and villages, and Charnwood Forest remained unenclosed for a further half-century.[1]

This serves to remind us that high feeling around common rights, and episodes of disturbance, need not wait upon enclosure. Perhaps enclosure had been the most visible occasion of grievance in the sixteenth and seventeenth centuries.[2] And perhaps in the first six decades of the eighteenth century disputes about deer and other game,[3] about fishing rights, about timber, about the exploitation of quarries, sand-pits and peat, became more frequent and more angry. The notional economy of coincidental use-rights of greater and lesser substance was coming under greater strain. Demographic pressure, together with the growth of by-employments, had made the marginal benefits of turbary, estover etc. of more significance in the package that made up a subsistence-economy for "the poor"; while at the same time the growth of towns and, with this, the growing demand for fuel and building materials enhanced the marketable value of such assets as quarries, gravel- and sand-pits, peat bogs, for the larger landholders and lords of the manor. In a parallel movement, the law was conforming with an age of agri-cultural "improvement" and was finding claims to coincident use-rights to be untidy. So also did the modernising administrative mind. A survey of Salcey Forest in 1783

[1] The late W. E. Tate was given "The Charnwood Opera" in a mid eighteenth-century hand by a Nottingham bookseller: see Tate, *op. cit.*, plate XIII and p. 214; he kindly sent me a transcript many years ago. The original has been found among Tate's papers in the Reading University Library. See Roy Palmer, *A Ballad History of England* (1979), pp. 59-61; John Nichols, *History and Antiquities of the County of Leicester* (1800), iii, p. 131. The Act to enclose Charnwood Forest was passed in 1808 but not carried into effect until 1829. For other examples of opposition to warrens, see Douglas Hay, "Poaching and the Game Laws on Cannock Chase", in Douglas Hay, Peter Linebaugh and E. P. Thompson, *Albion's Fatal Tree* (1975); Fifth Report of Land Revenue Commissioners (New Forest), *Commons Journals*, xliv (1789), pp. 561, 565. An edition of "The Charnwood Opera" is being prepared for the press by Roy Palmer and John Goodacre.
[2] See Roger Manning, *Village Revolts* (Oxford, 1988).
[3] See my *Whigs and Hunters*, and also John Broad, "Whigs, Deer-Stealers and the Origins of the Black Act", *Past and Present*, 119 (1988).

noted "the ruinous Effects of a Mixture of opposite Interests in the same Property".[1]

If all the agricultural lands of England and Wales had been as open to rip-offs as the royal forests or as beset with disputes as Charnwood, then they might have served as illustrative proofs for the glum theses of Garret Hardin in "The Tragedy of the Commons".[2] It has been Professor Hardin's argument that since resources held in common are not owned and protected by anyone, there is an inexorable economic logic which dooms them to over-exploitation. The argument, in fact, is derived from the English propagandists of parliamentary enclosure, and from a specific Malthusian variant.[3] Despite its commonsense air, what it overlooks is that the commoners themselves were not without commonsense. Over time and over space the users of commons have developed a rich variety of institutions and community sanctions which have effected restraints and stints upon use.[4] If there were signs of ecological crisis in some English forests in the eighteenth century, this was as much for political and legal reasons as for economic or demographic. As the old forest institutions lapsed, so they fell into a vacuum in which political influence, market forces, and popular assertion contested with each other without common rules:

> The present state of the New Forest is little less than absolute anarchy [it was lamented in 1851]. The records are insufficient to ascertain who are entitled to rights; there is no certainty what law, forest or common law, is current; and, consequently, what officers have power, and under what authority to interfere.

At present the forest "has not, and cannot have, an owner. We seem reverting to Eastern and primeval manners". The

---

[1] *Commons Journals*, xlvi (1790-1), p. 101.

[2] *Science*, 162 (1968), pp. 1343-8.

[3] W. F. Lloyd, *Two Lectures on the Checks to Population* (1833), extracts reprinted in G. Hardin and J. Baden (eds.), *Managing the Commons* (San Francisco, 1977).

[4] See Bonnie M. McCoy and James M. Acheson (eds.), *The Question of the Commons* (Tucson, 1987). These studies on the culture and ecology of communal resources turn upon fishing, grazing and forest resources, and do not address the English agrarian context of the eighteenth century, from which W. F. Lloyd's argument is derived.

foresters (including many squatters) supposed, however, that *they* were the owners, improvising rules in informal ways. When a government inspector was sent down to examine the state of the forest in 1848-9, he was burned in effigy off Lyndhurst, the Deputy Warden supplying fuel from the forest for this meritorious purpose.[1]

These were dark places, however, possessed by "savage ignorance and barbarism". Over the rest of agricultural England there was a much stricter governance of common rights, both at common law and in *lex loci*. Common of pasture was stinted by the regulation of the lord's court or by village by-laws, regulations which had sometimes been in continuous evolution for centuries. The orderly village agricultural practices of medieval England disclosed by Warren Ault[2] are far from Garret Hardin's notions of common free-for-all.[3] But stinting could breed its own disputes. The court of Chancery decided, in a case in 1689, that the greater part of the landholders might regulate and stint a common (on grounds of "proper and natural equity") even if "one or two humoursome tenants stand out and will not agree".[4] But "one or two humoursome tenants" was too uncertain a legal term. In 1706 a new case arose from Bishop's Cleeve in Gloucestershire, where the landholders had agreed to stint five thousand acres of common, but the defendant (the rector of the parish) and nine others stood out. Evidently this was more than one or two humoursome fellows, for the court decided that "a right of common cannot be altered without the consent of all parties concerned therein".[5]

[1] "The Office of Woods and Forests, Land Revenue, Works and Buildings", *Law Magazine and Quarterly Review of Jurisprudence*, n.s. 14/o.s. 45 (1851), pp. 31-3.

[2] W. O. Ault, *Open-Field Farming in Medieval England: A Study of Village By-Laws* (1972).

[3] Hardin's "Tragedy of the Commons", in Hardin & Baden, *op. cit.*, is historically uninformed and assumes that commons were "pasture open to all. It is to be expected that each herdsman will try to keep as many cattle as possible on the commons".

[4] *Delabeere v Beddingfield* (1689), 2 Vern 103, ER 23, p. 676.

[5] *Bruges et Al' v Curwin et Al'* (1706), 2 Vern 575, ER 23, p. 974. This was revised by 13 Geo. III, c. 81, in 1772, when open field parishes were

One wonders if this might have been at the origin of the parliamentary process of enclosure, which is something of a mystery? For "the first private bill of enclosure ever passed" came up to parliament in February 1710. It concerned Ropley Commons and the old disparked park of Farnham, within the bishopric of Winchester. It was a decidedly unpopular and vigorously contested measure, and it contributed to the ill-will which led to raids on the bishop's deer and eventually to "blacking". It could scarcely have been pushed through in any other way.[1]

Once the private act of enclosure became possible, it was clear that *enclosure* might not take place unless by due parliamentary process if even one humoursome landholder dissented.[2] Until the 1760s (and in some cases later) this could act as a serious disincentive to the landowners. A young gentleman was writing on behalf of his mother to some noble

---

empowered to regulate their agriculture if three-quarters in number and value of the occupiers agreed: Sir W. S. Holdsworth, *A History of English Law*, xi, pp. 454-5. Sheila Lambert, *Bills and Acts* (Cambridge, 1971), p. 143 thinks the act may have been "a dead letter", although Withern-with-Woodthrope (Lincolnshire) was vigorously exercising its provisions in the 1790s (information from Rex Russell).

[1] For Ropley Commons and Farnham Park enclosure (and disturbance) see my *Whigs and Hunters*, pp. 133-41; *Lords Journals*, xix, pp. 50, 65-6, 77, 80, 83, 108, 111; *Commons Journals*, xvi, pp. 374, 381, 385-6, 476, 509. The "first ever private bill" is the description in *Annals of Agriculture*, xxxvii (1801), pp. 226-31, where the Act was reprinted. Lambert, *op. cit.*, pp. 129-30 says that "in 1706 inclosure bills had been almost unknown"; see also E. C. K. Gonner, *Common Land and Inclosure*, 2nd edn. (1966), p. 58. Joan Thirsk (ed.), *The Agrarian History of England and Wales* (Cambridge, 1985), v, pt. 2, p. 380 expresses puzzlement at the reasons for the resort to private act. The Bill passed through the Lords without contest (25 Feb. to 17 Mar. 1710) but ran into opposition in the Commons, with a petition from freeholders, copyholders and leaseholders against it (23 Mar. 1710), and with renewed petitioning next year to repeal the Act, on the grounds of the partial allotment of portions, and the obstruction of highways (3 Feb. 1711). The House referred this and a counter-petition (21 Feb. 1711) to committee, where the matter seems to disappear.

[2] Arthur Young was still complaining in 1798: "what a gross absurdity to bind down in the fetters of custom ten intelligent men willing to adopt the improvements adapted to inclosures, because one stupid fellow is obstinate for the practice of his grandfather": "Of Inclosures", *Annals of Agriculture*, xxi (1798), p. 546.

patron in 1742 about her predicament in the parish of Church
Oakley, Hampshire —

> My Mama has the largest farm there upon her hands, and she finds it a
> very difficult thing to get a Tennant for it, no Person caring to take it
> unless the Parish was inclosed, there being so great a dis-
> agreement amongst the Farmers at Oakly, that in mere spite to each
> other they will not manage the Common Fields so as to make the best
> advantage of them. . .

Enclosure would especially benefit his mother "as she has the
greatest Common there; there are but three freeholders and
the Parsonage, besides herself, they all consent to enclose,
except one person who in crossness sticks out. . .". His
mother begged to ask if the thing could be done, one man not
agreeing to it, without an Act of Parliament "which she
would be sorry to have, not only as it will be a great
Expense, but as she has not any friends in the House. . .".[1]
Historians have noted that the great age of parliamentary
enclosure, between 1760 and 1820, is testimony not only to
the rage for improvement but also to the tenacity with which
"humoursome" or "spiteful" fellows blocked the way to
enclosure by agreement, holding out to the last for the old
customary economy.

So that custom may also be seen as a place of class
conflict, at the interface between agrarian practice and
political power. The customary tenants of Sir William
Lowther in the Cumberland manor of Askham complained in
1803 that "violations of our Antient Custom has always felt
very painfull to us, and embittered many hours of our lives".
And Dr Searle comments:

> Custom, then, was not something fixed and immutable, carrying the
> same body of meaning for both social classes. On the contrary, its
> definition was highly variable in relation to class position, and
> accordingly it became a vehicle for conflict not consensus.[2]

Unequal as were the terms of power in this conflict, yet power
must submit to some constraints, not only because custom

---

[1] Henry Worsley to "Honoured Sir", 8 July 1742, typescript copy in
Earl St Aldwyn MSS. West Oakley was enclosed by agreement, but not
until April 1773.
[2] Searle, *op. cit.*, p. 120.

had juridical endorsement and could itself be a "property", but also because power might bring itself into danger if abuse of customary rights outraged the populace. Charles I's high-handed pursuit of revenue in the royal forests had weakened his throne. Even the most predatory of the Hanoverian Whigs had not forgotten the lesson. George II's consort, Queen Caroline, had "wished to shut up St. James' Park, and asked Sir Robert Walpole what it would cost her to do it. He replied, 'Only a *crown*, Madam' ".[1]

King Charles also set in motion one of the most politically-sensitive contests around common rights, when he enclosed and threw a high wall around Richmond Park. Several parishes were shut out from rights of common, and (Clarendon wrote) "the murmur and noise of the people. . . was too near London not to be the common discourse". The murmur continued in the eighteenth century, and was at its loudest during the rangership of Sir Robert Walpole (through his son), when gates were locked, ladders over the wall were removed, and passengers or carriages were admitted only by ticket. Since the tickets (made of base metal) were easy to counterfeit, they were replaced by paper tickets stamped at the stamp office (6d.) (and the counterfeiting of stamps was then a capital felony). Although the parishioners pulled down the park wall two or three times on their perambulations of parish bounds (see Plate IX), Walpole "pocketed the affront, and built up the wall again".

Walpole's successor as Ranger was Princess Amelia, who was loved no more than Walpole but was more easy to challenge than the great man. The grievances concerned chiefly rights of way through the park, and loss of access to gravel, underwood, furze, and also water rights. In this prosperous neighbourhood those concerned were not only farmers but also gentry, merchants, tradespeople and artisans. Champions of local rights included a stonemason, a brewer, and Timothy Bennett, a shoemaker, whose motto it was that he was "unwilling to leave the world worse than he found it". John Lewis, the brewer, led an agitation in the 1750s which prefigures some of the stratagems of John

---

[1] Horace Walpole, *Memoirs of the Reign of King George the Second* (1847), ii, pp. 220-1.

Wilkes: there were public meetings, memorials in the press (*London Evening Post*), a widely-signed petition presented to the King, and finally a series of actions at law.[1] From such episodes as this one may see the growing confidence of "civil society".

Cases came up at Surrey Assizes (Kingston) every summer from 1753 to 1758. Right of highway between Richmond and Croydon (through the park) was lost (1754), but right of footway (over stiles or ladders) from Richmond to Wimbledon was won. John Lewis then (1755) forced his way through a park gate, and sued the gatekeeper (Martha Gray) who pushed him out, for obstructing three ancient footways, one between East Sheene and Kingston. Trial was postponed to the next summer Assizes. At that time supporters of common right had published and circulated a pamphlet[2] on their side of the case, and Lord Mansfield — on the grounds that this could influence the jurors — used this as an excuse to put off the trial to a subsequent Assizes.

The trial finally came up at Surrey Lent Assizes, 1758, before Sir Michael Foster, then in his seventieth year. So many of the forty-eight special jurors who had been summoned to the panel were nervous about trying a cause against the Princess Amelia that it was necessary to put a talesman on the jury. Sir Michael promptly fined the absentees £20 a head. When the prosecution had got through some part of their evidence, the counsel for the Crown (Sir Richard Lloyd) said it was "needless for them to go on upon the right, as the Crown was not prepared to try that", since the obstruction was charged in the parish of Wimbledon whereas it was in truth in Mortlake:

[1] Anon., *A Tract on the National Interest, and Depravity of the Times* (1757); E. E. Dodd, "Richmond Park" (typescript, 1963); C. L. Collenette, *A History of Richmond Park* (1937); my *Whigs and Hunters*, pp. 181-4; Michael Dodson, *The Life of Sir Michael Foster* (1811), pp. 84-8; Rev. Gilbert Wakefield, *Memoirs* (1792), who has a good description of John Lewis's campaign, pp. 243-53; Walpole, *op. cit.*, i, pp. 401-2, ii, pp. 220-1.

[2] *A Tract on the National Interest*. A copy of this, and also of *German Cruelty: a Fair Warning to the People of Great-Britain* (1756) is in PRO, TS 11.347.1083, together with the Crown's brief against Joseph Shepheard, a Chancery Lane printer.

The judge turned to the jury, and said, he thought they were come there to try a right, which the subject claimed to a way through Richmond Park, and not to cavil about little low objections, which have no relation to that right. . . He thought it below the honour of the Crown, after this business had been depending three assizes, to send one of their select counsel, not to try the right, but to hinge upon so small a point as this.

The judge summed up in favour of the prosecution, and John Lewis won his case. Offered a gate or step-ladders, he chose the latter, as the freer mode of access. (With deer in the park, the gates would be kept closed, and might easily be locked.) When Lewis returned to the court with the complaint that the rungs on the ladders had been set too far apart for children and old men, Sir Michael Foster replied: "I have observed it myself, and I desire, Mr Lewis, that you would see it so constructed, that not only *children and old men*, but OLD WOMEN too, may get up."[1]

The case was a small sensation. For a while it gave the keepers real trouble, since triumphant citizens were clambering the ladders and did not confine themselves to the paths but "ranged & went at their pleasure over the greensward", declaring that "the park was a common & that they had a right to go anywhere. . . they liked". This was to the prejudice of the deer and game and "will greatly interrupt the Royal Family in the use & enjoyment" of the park.[2] Princess Amelia abandoned her Rangership in a paddy. These matters also became part of the discourse of London: the free-born old Englishwoman had triumphed over the royal lady. Such victories, of the humble citizen over the great or the royal, were decidedly infrequent. But even one or two went a long way to give popular legitimacy to the law and to endorse the rhetoric of constitutionalism upon which the

[1] Dodson, *op. cit.*, pp. 86-7; Wakefield, *op. cit.*, pp. 247-8; *Rex v Benjamin Burgess* (1760), 2 Burr. 908, ER 97, pp. 627-8.
[2] Various papers in PRO, TS 11.444.1415, especially "An Historical Account of the Inclosing Richmond New Park", an MS drawn up to brief Crown counsel. Richmond citizens were uncommonly tenacious of their rights of way (or uncommonly obstructed by royalty and aristocracy). In 1806 the iron rails in front of the duke of Queensberry's villa on the Thames were broken down in a "trespass committed by agreement in order to try the right". The jury found a verdict in support of the right and against the duke: *London Chronicle*, 1-3 Apr. 1806.

security of landed property was founded.[1] Even so, we should not forget that the Richmond victory was, in a sense, a victory of bourgeois commoners, who commanded money and resources which the rural commoners rarely did.

II

This chapter is not about enclosure nor about the decline of the peasantry. A novice in agricultural history caught loitering in those areas with intent would quickly be despatched. This is a tangential study of common right usages, and also of law and notions of property-right. But one cannot altogether avoid brushing against the other problems. And one must note that we still have little firm evidence as to the number of landholders who held by copyhold or other forms of customary tenure (such as beneficial leases from the church or from colleges) in the eighteenth century. A scholar with much expertise allows that the question of the proportion of landholders by customary tenures in the late seventeenth century is "almost entirely obscure", but it might have been "as many as one-third".[2] And it remained substantial at the end of the eighteenth — although falling away more rapidly in the last decades. The vigorous operation of the lord's court in the eighteenth century (as many county record offices can testify) is often coincident with some survival of copyhold tenures. There was certainly a substantial peasantry in England in the eighteenth and early nineteenth centuries,[3] and optimistic agricultural historians have sometimes told their story in such a way as to confuse two different totals:

[1] See my comments on "The Rule of Law" in *Whigs and Hunters*, pp. 258-69.

[2] Christopher Clay, in Thirsk (ed.), *Agrarian History*, V, p. 199, and pp. 198-208, and the same author's "Life-leasehold in the Western Counties of England 1650-1750", *Agric. Hist. Rev.*, xxix, 2 (1981).

[3] I welcome Mick Reed's "The Peasantry of Nineteenth-Century England: a Neglected Class", *History Workshop*, 18 (1984), although I am rebuked as a culprit. But what I was arguing ("Land of Our Fathers", *TLS*, 16 Feb. 1967) was that J. D. Chambers and G. E. Mingay were guilty of "statistical dilution", by watering the totals of large employers with the peasantry, hence minimising capitalist agricultural process: "the assimilation of two extremes to provide an impressionistic average does not in fact illuminate either extremity".

the acres and the people.[1] As I remarked in an earlier study, "the economic historian may find that the clues to expanding agrarian process lie in the 'free' [i.e. freehold or rackrent] sector, while the social historian may find that the psychological horizons and expectations of the majority of the farming community lie still within the customary sector".[2]

Secondly, it is now becoming clear that in the long historiographical reaction against those fine historians, Barbara and J. L. Hammond and their classic *The Village Labourer*, there has been a tendency (and in some minds an ideological determination) to seriously undercount the amount of popular protest attending upon loss of common rights or the enclosure of commons (which, as we have already seen, were not the same thing). It is heartening to see that a substantial challenge to the triumphal picture of the social consequences of agricultural improvement is now being made.[3] Even so, we are not going to discover that the eighteenth century was vibrant with major episodes of enclosure protest which have been somehow overlooked. There were more episodes than have been noted, but few of them were major. Resistance was more often sullen than vibrant. For every commoner "Rioutously threatening to kill

[1] Christopher Clay, " 'The Greed of Whig Bishops'?: Church Landlords and their Lessees 1660-1760", *Past and Present*, 87 (1980), exemplifies this kind of confusion: (a) it assumes that the claim that church beneficial leases had equal customary security with copyhold "had no legal validity", although this was precisely the question which was at issue in the 1720s, and (b) by concentrating upon large lay tenants of church lands, the more numerous small customary tenants disappear from view, as they do so often in orthodox agricultural history.

[2] "The Grid of Inheritance", in J. Goody, J. Thirsk and E. P. Thompson (eds.), *Family and Inheritance* (Cambridge, 1976), pp. 328-9.

[3] In the area of common rights, especially J. M. Neeson, "Common Right and Enclosure in Eighteenth-Century Northamptonshire" (Univ. of Warwick Ph.D. thesis, 1978); C. E. Searle, "The Odd Corner of England: Cumbria, *c.* 1700-1914" (Univ. of Essex Ph.D. thesis, 1983). The cogent re-opening of arguments in K. D. M. Snell, *Annals of the Labouring Poor* (Cambridge, 1985), ch. 4, is also welcome. The most devastating critique of the assumptions and the methodology of the "optimists", insofar as these bear upon the small landholder at enclosure, is in J. M. Neeson, "The Disappearance of the English Peasantry, Revisited", in G. Grantham and Carol Leonard (eds.), *Agrarian Organization in the century of Industrialization: Europe, Russia and North America in the Nineteenth Century* (Research in Economic History, Supplement 5) (JAI Press, 1989).

or be killed, that he wd raise 500 people who wd assist in the cutting down & destroying the Mounds and fences. . ."[1] a dozen will be found throwing a gate off its hinges, uprooting some quicksets, or pulling down a notice of enclosure from the church porch.

Yet there was more opposition to enclosure than used to be supposed.[2] The problem of estimating its extent is, in part, one of the appropriate research techniques and the nature of the sources. Enclosure protests were rarely reported in central administrative archives or in London newspapers; they did not take the form of regional "uprisings", highly visible and tumultuous. They will be found (especially before 1760) more often in the exchanges of letters between estate stewards and their absent masters, treated as domestic concerns (like poaching) which could be dealt with by the magistrates' summary powers. Larger affrays might necessitate the aid of neighbours, the levying of loyal tenants and servants, or even the *posse comitatus*. In 1710, when Robert Walpole was Secretary-at-War, he received (in his private capacity) a letter from his steward, John Wrott, describing a major confrontation over common rights on Bedingfield Common. The High Sheriff of Northamptonshire, Lord Cardigan, and other gentry were there with mounted patrols. "The mob began to gather from all corners, some in disguise with masks, and in women's cloakes, and others with axes, spades, pickaxes etc." Even the men whom the Sheriff had summoned to serve in his *posse* sympathised with the mob and helped any prisoners to escape. The crowd was dispersed for the time being, but "they still persist to say the Right of Common is theirs, & next year they hope to see the Hedges demolish't".[3]

---

[1] Thomas Kemp of Leigh, labourer, charged with riot with twelve others unknown, in "obstructing hindring and preventing one John Andrews in marking out the Boundaries of certain. . . Inclosures", Worcs. Lent Assize, 1777, PRO, Assi 4.21. Kemp was imprisoned for six months. The enclosures were of Malvern Link Common, where three years later (Lent Assize, 1780) 21 labourers and one labourer's wife were charged with pulling down 1,100 yards of fence. See also Brian S. Smith, *A History of Malvern* (Leicester, 1964), p. 167.

[2] For a recent record of known disturbances see Andrew Charlesworth (ed.), *An Atlas of Rural Protest* (1983).

[3] Camb. Univ. Lib., C(H) MSS, correspondence, item 608, John Wrott to Walpole, dated Oundle, 31 May 1710; Sir J. H. Plumb, *Sir Robert*

The estate correspondence of one of Walpole's political allies, Lady Diana Fielding in North Wootton (Norfolk), in 1728-9 was much preoccupied with contests between labourers and tenants, on one side, and her steward and the parish constable, on the other, concerning the cutting of "whins and flags" on "the Priories", where her ladyship had made new enclosures. Rival parties converged on the common with carts to carry away the whins, "the Mobb" rescued their whins from the steward's carts, threw them about, locked the horses to the cart wheels, "barbrosly used" the steward "& broke 3 of his Ribbs & allmost kill'd him". The mob went on to "break & destroy all the Gates & fences" of the late enclosures. Labourers and tenants shared these actions, but it was easier to discipline the tenants with the threat of loss of their tenancies.[1]

One can turn up other affairs like this in collections of estate papers. Or they may turn up in the press. Three years before, at Stokesby (again in Norfolk), many poor people, men and women, "threw down a new Mill and divers Gates and Fences on the Marsh". Eight or ten of them were carried to Norwich where they were examined: they said they were acting for the "Recovery of their Right", since the Marsh was common until a certain gentleman had taken it away and fenced it in. "Such a beginning had Kett's rebellion", the reporter commented.[2] These offenders were committed to Assizes. And not infrequently Assize records show proceedings against offenders who had thrown down fences or demolished enclosures. But such actions need never come to the notice of the law, since commoners claimed (and law cautiously acknowledged) a right to throw down encroachments[3] and this "possessioning" was indeed one of the purposes of parish perambulations. There was a fine-drawn

---

Walpole (1972), pp. 157-8. I am not clear why Wrott was at Bedingfield (now Benefield) Common, but the letter suggests ("I hope to receive your orders") that Walpole was personally interested in the enclosure.

[1] Norwich and Norfolk RO, HOW 725, 734 (a).

[2] *Mist's Weekly Journal*, 24 July 1725. See also R. W. Malcolmson, *Life and Labour in England, 1700-1780* (1981), p. 127, and also pp. 23-35.

[3] Since judges did not easily condone direct action, the law on this was cautious and mainly negative: the proper course for aggrieved commoners

line between the assertion of "right" and "riot",[1] and the balance of evidence and also of power might be such as to settle the issue outside the courts. John Lewis, the Richmond brewer, whom we have already noted in his assertion of rights of access to Richmond Park, told a story about another pathway which he found blocked by a locked gate. He passed by with a friend and with some of his men from the

---

should be an action for novel disseisin: see Richard Burn, *The Justice of the Peace and Parish Officer*, 14th edn. (1780), ii, "Forcible Entry". But the right of commoners to take direct action in support of right rested upon ancient law and precedents too strong to over-rule: see the full discussion in *Arlett v Ellis* (1827), 7 B & C 347, ER 108, pp. 752-64, when the Year Book of 15 Henry 7, Brooke's Abridgement and Coke's Institutes were among authorities cited: "If the Lord doth inclose any part, and leave not sufficient common. . . the commoners may break down the whole inclosure". This was affirmed in several cases in the late seventeenth and eighteenth century (e.g. *Mason v Caesar* (Hilary 27/28 Car 2), 2 Mod 65, ER 86), although this did not prevent indictments for riot against commoners who pulled fences down. In the sixteenth and seventeenth centuries, enclosure *riot* could be treason, if more than forty were involved. In the eighteenth century the law supported (feebly) commoners' right to remove nuisances, to pull up fences, and to distrain supernumerary cattle on a stinted common (on which point see *Hall v Harding* (1769), 4 Burr 2425, ER 98, pp. 271ff.). They might not, however, cut down trees nor kill rabbits and dig up coney burrows: this contentious issue much preoccupied the judges in several cases, and the decisive judgement was in *Cooper v Marshall* (1757), 1 Burr 259, ER 97, pp. 303-8, for which see Hay, *op. cit.*, p. 234. Lord Mansfield pronounced that the real issue was not the legality or illegality of the coneys, but "whether the commoner can do himself justice", and it was his decided view that the commoner might not. It was perhaps fortunate for commoners' rights that Lord Mansfield never sat in judgement upon fences. See also Halsbury's *Laws of England*, vi, pp. 250-4, esp. para. 655. Fences might also be removed in pursuance of an order from a manorial court. See Roger B. Manning, *op. cit.*, pp. 40-2.

[1] In 1698 there was an attempt to strengthen and enforce statutes of Edward I and Edward VI against the burning and destroying of enclosures, and a bill was read for the first time: but it met with fierce counter-petitions from Lincolnshire parishes adjoining Epworth Common, and it seems to have been dropped: *Commons Journals*, xii, pp. 38, 47, 96. The Black Act (1723) had ample provisions which might be used against rioters, irrespective of the justice of their cause: see my *Whigs and Hunters, passim*. Parliamentary enclosure was given a new set of teeth, under 9 Geo. III, c. 29, whereby pulling down fences of lands enclosed "in pursuance of any act of parliament" was made felony, with penalty of seven years transportation. I do not recall finding any offender so sentenced under this Act.

brewery the day before "our annual parochial procession at Richmond" —

> 'My lads', says I; 'take care to bring your hatchets with you tomorrow to cut down this gate, for we must go through it to our bounds'. 'Don't speak so loud,' said my friend: 'or you will be heard by the people at the Princess Dowager's.' 'Oh,' I replied, raising my voice: 'I have no objection to be heard. I am John Lewis of Richmond, and mean to knock down this gate tomorrow for a passage according to custom.'

But on the next day "the processioners" found that the gate's lock had been taken off.[1]

In a parish perambulation, some labourers might carry "an axe, a mattock, and an iron crow. . . for the purpose of demolishing any building or fence which had been raised without permission" on the common or waste.[2] This was stubbornly maintained as a lawful assertion of right. But this is also exactly what some offenders are indicted for in Assize records: at Feckenham (Worcestershire) in 1789 for "pulling down, prostrating and destroying with bilhooks, spades, mattocks, axes, saws" etc. fourteen yards of quickset fences;[3] at Culmstock (Devon) in 1807 for coming into a garden and orchard with hatchets, saws, pickaxes, spades and shovels, throwing down the fences, digging up the ground, erecting a tent to keep the owner (or the pretended owner) out of possession;[4] at Porlock (Somerset) in 1774 for entering a garden, throwing down hedges and fences, spoiling and carrying off garden stuff.[5] These could have been little affrays or "riots"[6] or they could have been actions deliberately

---

[1] Wakefield, op. cit., p. 251.

[2] See Bob Bushaway, op. cit., p. 83.

[3] PRO, Assi 4.22, Worcester, Lent 1789. Those charged were a labourer, a husbandman, a butcher, a cordwainer, four yeomen and four needlemakers.

[4] PRO, Assi 24.43, Devon, Summer 1807. Those charged were a spinster ("left the kingdom"), four labourers, and a labourer's wife.

[5] PRO, Assi 24.42, Somerset, Summer 1774: a shopkeeper, a carpenter, a yeoman, and four labourers charged, all found not guilty.

[6] They certainly could stir up strong feeling. When a crowd in the nail-making village of Kingswinford broke down a nailer's fences, pulled up his posts and destroyed his potatoes and beans, one of the crowd (Elizabeth Stevens) threatened to kill two women and "wash her hands in their blood": PRO, Assi 4/22, Worcester, Lent 1789. Three nailers, one nailer's wife, one labourer, two labourers' wives charged.

intended to bring on a case which would try their "right".

Even when riots did occur these need not become visible to historians. Magistrates and gentry were expected to take care of episodes in their own neighbourhood without recourse to troops. When troops were sent to put down rioting "in the new inclosed fields of West Haddon" (Northamptonshire) in 1765, the magistrate was reminded that "until the utmost extent of legal authority shall have been tried, application should not be made for military assistance".[1] In the same year, when forty-odd Banbury rioters were pulling down the fences of a newly-enclosed estate at Warkworth, a company of gentlemen were informed of it at dinner; they instantly were willing to forego their port, mounted their horses, descended on the "levellers" and routed them.[2] Knowledge of a more substantial enclosure riot at Maulden, (Bedfordshire) in 1796, in which two hundred poor people were involved, survives only because a letter about it was preserved in a War Office file of precedents.[3]

But problems and techniques of recovering the evidence is the lesser part of the story. In a study which demands that we review not only our methods but the whole problem, Jeanette Neeson has shown that historians may have been looking in the wrong places and for the wrong things. She presents cogent reasons for supposing that "parliamentary opposition and riot were the least effective, and probably least common, means of opposing enclosure".[4] And re-directing attention to the full length of the enclosure process, from its first promotion to its often-long-delayed implementation, she shows an astonishing volume and a variety of forms of protest — hitherto hidden from view in local records — lobbying, letters, petitions, the mobbing of surveyors, the destruction of records, and on to arson, riot, and fence-breaking, which might continue for years after

[1] PRO, WO 4.172.

[2] *Gentleman's Magazine*, (1765), p. 441.

[3] James Webster, 2 August 1796, in PRO, WO 40.17. I am indebted to Patricia Bell, when Assistant Archivist at the Bedford CRO (in 1968), for discovering more about this riot at which, it seems, the duke of Bedford was present (not, I think, as a rioter): papers then in R box 341.

[4] J. M. Neeson, "The Opponents of Enclosure in Eighteenth-Century Northamptonshire", *Past and Present*, 105 (1984), p. 117.

enclosure was completed. Nor was this stubborn resistance without function. It can be shown to have delayed enclosures, on occasion for decades, and it may sometimes have modified their terms. "If landlords and farmers eventually won the battle for enclosure, rural artisans and agricultural labourers may have had some say in the terms of surrender."[1]

If Dr Neeson's findings for Northamptonshire should be supported by research into other counties, this will change our understanding of eighteenth-century enclosure, and the depth of hostility with which it was regarded by a large part of the rural community. Opposition was in general overcome in the end; open fields were almost without exception enclosed by 1850, and opposition rarely kept commons and wastes open for much longer, except in special circumstances which include large wastes upon which several villages intercommoned, forest and fenland regions, and commons contiguous to market towns or larger urban centres. Urban protests over common rights were often more formidable and more visible than rural, and while they clearly are not characteristic of agrarian custom they may still afford one point of entry into general questions of common right.

The most obvious reason for urban success is simply that of greater numbers, and the anonymity which numbers supplied to rioters. By no means all the effective urban enclosure riots arose from incorporated boroughs. But the question of incorporation is of real significance, since it distinguishes between prescriptive rights and rights established by custom. Custom is laid upon the land, but prescription "is alledged in the Person": "it is always made in the Name of a Person certain, and his Ancestors, or of those whose Estate he hath", and is normally established by the recitation of the original Grant or Charter.[2] Boroughs incorporated by Charter were legal personalities, whose freemen might therefore plead prescriptive rights more generous than those which law would recognise for custom. In the important decision in Gateward's Case (below, p. 130) it was ruled that

[1] Neeson, *op. cit.*, p. 131.
[2] Carter, *Lex Custumaria*, pp. 37-42; Sir W. Blackstone, *Commentaries on the Laws of England* (1765-9), ii, p. 33.

"inhabitants" cannot prescribe to have profit in another's soil, with the reservation "unless they be incorporated".[1] If prescriptive rights to the use of common were granted by charter to a corporation, then the exercise of these rights (and the persons entitled to exercise them) became a matter not for the courts to decide but for the intramural regulation of the corporation.

In fact the often-cited charters from which townsmen derived their rights to the use of town lands are often as ambiguous and as open to various interpretations as rights in manorial villages. We can see this in the case of Coventry. The right was claimed as derived in the first place from a grant of Sir Roger de Montealto (1249) reserving to the "communiariis" "reasonable pasture" for as many beasts "with which they may conveniently plough and carry their arable lands, and which, by reason of those lands, as well of right as of custom, they ought and were wont to have common". This was englished — I suspect by a popular sea-lawyer in the late seventeenth or early eighteenth century — as "saving to all Cottiers reasonable Pasture and Commons for soe many Beasts as they bin abel hereafter to keepe and which they ought and were wont to have as wel by Right as by Customs".[2] As both land and rights became more valuable, attempts to limit these rights or to enclose lands were met with riotous resistance in 1421, 1430, 1469, 1473, 1495, and 1509,[3] while further enclosure was successfully resisted in a

[1] *Smith and Gateward* (4 Jac. I), Cro Jac 152, ER 79, p. 133. This was tightened in *Grimstead v Marlowe* (1792), 4 TR 717, ER 100, p. 1263: a tenant or inhabitant claiming prescriptive right may plead only by virtue of an ancient messuage tenure or as a member of a corporation, not *in alieno solo*.

[2] W. Reader, *Some History and Account of the Commons and Lammas and Michaelmas Lands of the City of Coventry* (Coventry, 1879), pt. One, p. 8; Humphrey Wanley, *A Particular and Authentic Account of the Common Grounds of. . . the City of Coventry* (1778), p. 4.

[3] *Victoria County History, Warwickshire*, viii, pp. 202-3. The historian of medieval Coventry is perhaps too dismissive of these small extra-urban matters ("the details do not concern us"): Charles Phythian-Adams, *Desolation of a City* (Cambridge, 1979), p. 183. For Rogation-tide perambulation of the commons in Coventry's calendar, see his "Ceremony and the Citizen", in Peter Clark and Paul Slack (eds.), *Crisis and Order in English Towns, 1500-1700* (1972), pp. 77-8.

major riot in 1525.[1] The definition of who possessed commoners' rights may have hardened only in the seventeenth century. An entry in the Court Leet book in 1663 suggests that all who "inhabit and pay Scot and Lott" had common right (this being a narrower definition than earlier entries suggest).[2] A more popular notion was that the land belonged to the "Mayor, Bailiffs and Commonalty of the City. . . and one Million and others were seized of the said Manor".[3] In 1674 this was clearly defined as freemen enrolled in companies. Throughout the eighteenth century freemen's rights were jealously maintained, especially through the means of apprenticeship; and into the nineteenth century rights in the Lammas Lands were signalled annually (as they were in other towns) by the Lammas riding, when the corporation and freemen rode the boundaries of the fields, trampled any corn grown in them (unless propitiated by supplies of ale and food) and tore down gates and obstructions.[4]

Coventry now in the nineteenth century was hemmed in on all sides by Lammas Lands, which increased the density of the population, and meant that the potential value of the lands as building sites rose annually. Eventually the freemen, after much controversy and a long and crafty negotiation, sold out their rights in exchange for a considerable allocation of these lands. By this time the freeman right had fallen into the hands of a minority (although a large one). Joseph Gutteridge, a ribbon-weaver, felt that the mid-century contest concerned only the rights of a privileged group. But he still regretted the loss of lands which in his youth, in the 1820s, were a "veritable paradise. I would roam over them

[1] Phythian-Adams, *Desolation of a City*, pp. 254-7. The riot succeeded in re-opening the enclosures, p. 257. See also R. J. Tawney, *The Agrarian Problem in the Sixteenth Century* (1912; reprint 1967), p. 250 for the city's dispute with the Prior and Convent of St. Mary over sheep commons.

[2] Coventry Leet Book, transcript and summary (compiled by Levi Fox?), Coventry RO, shelf 16.

[3] This rhetorical claim was made by the defendant in *Bennet v Holbech* (22 Charles II), 2 Wms Saund 317, ER 85, pp. 1113-6.

[4] Benjamin Poole, *Coventry: its History and Antiquities* (1879), p. 354.

without let or hindrance. . .".[1]

We have here a mixture of prescriptive right, myth, and assertion by tumultuous numbers. The intramural contest over the exercise of rights arose when the alienation of urban common was undertaken by the Corporation itself, in the name of freeman rights which were themselves becoming more exclusive and corrupt. When the Leicester Corporation enclosed the South Fields in 1753, and let them to three lessees (including two aldermen) riots continued for at least three years, in which the "post and rails and Quick sette. . . set down for the fencing of the said fields" were "Cut Down pulled up and Distroyed by great Numbers. . . in a most riotous and tumultuous manner". The enclosure, first attempted in 1708, was not completed until 1803.[2] In Nottingham where six hundred acres of Lammas Lands and another three hundred and fifty acres of pasture with common right remained open into Victorian times, a witness before the Select Committee on Commons Enclosure (1844) found that this had a most prejudicial effect upon the morals of the people:

> It occasions very great disrespect to the laws of the country generally; as an instance. . . when the day upon which the lands become commonable arrives [usually August 12th]. . . the population issue out, destroy the fences, tear down the gates, and commit a great many other lawless acts, which they certainly have a right to do, in respect of the right of common to which they are entitled. . . the consequence is constant violence and abuse.

The witness explained that the freemen were "all voters, which is a great misfortune, and they are misled with respect to their rights, and the value of them, by parties who have recourse at the periods of election to courses of agitation". They had exercised rights over the Lammas Lands for many years, and "being a very numerous body, and many of the

---

[1] Joseph Gutteridge, *Lights and Shadows on the Life of an Artisan* (Coventry, 1893), pp. 5-6; P. Searby, "Chartists and Freemen in Coventry, 1838-60", *Social History*, 2 (1977).

[2] C. J. Billson, "Open Fields of Leicester", *Trans. Leics. Archaeol. Soc.*, (1925-6), IV, pp. 25-7; Eric Kerridge, *Agrarian Problems in the Sixteenth Century and After* (1969), p. 98; *Records of the Borough of Leicester* v and vi.; A. Temple Patterson, *Radical Leicester* (Leicester, 1953).

body being of a very low class of society, they are enabled to resort to acts of violence which could not be resorted to by an incorporated body. . .".[1] Rights by prescription and rights by the assertion of usage had become altogether indistinct.

Nottingham and other commoners were offered by the printers "No Inclosure!" ballads, perhaps more likely to be read than sung: "You Freemen all of Nottingham come listen to my Song":

> Your Rights and your Liberties I would have you to revere,
> And look unto Posterity I think them always dear;
> To us to our Children by the Charter that prevails,
> So now my Boys united be and have no Posts or Rails. . .
>
> Let's suffer no Encroachments upon our Lane to be,
> But to repel such Tyranny let's ever now agree;
> But let ev'ry brave Freeman enjoy his Right of Land.[2]

The more that one looks, the more that one finds such disputes to be normal, in great towns and in small. They could be massive and very violent, as was the dispute in Sheffield in 1791. A private act had been passed to enclose six thousand acres of common and waste adjacent to the town, compensating the poor with two acres only. This precipitated spectacular riots, which may have influenced the citizens to turn in a Paineite or "Jacobin" direction. The enclosure commissioners were mobbed; the debtors' gaol was broken open and the prisoners released; there were cries of "No King!" and "No Taxes!".[3] Or the affairs could be small and symbolic, as at Streatham Common in 1794 when six men in black drove up in a hackney coach and demolished the duke of Bedford's paled inclosure.[4] London and its environs would have no parks today if commoners had not asserted their rights, and as the nineteenth century drew on rights of

[1] *PP*, 1844, v, pp. 223-6.
[2] *A New Song, entitled No Inclosure! Or, the Twelfth of August* (Tupman, printer, n.d.), in Nottingham Univ. Lib.; my thanks to Roy Palmer.
[3] William Eyre, 30 July 1791, in PRO, HO 42.19; Albert Goodwin, *The Friends of Liberty* (1979), pp. 164-5; John Bohstedt, *Riots and Community Politics in England and Wales* (1983), pp. 199-200.
[4] *Gentleman's Magazine*, (1794), p. 571. At the same time a "mob of poor people" burned the furze on the common because the duke had been selling it for his own profit.

recreation became more important than rights of pasture, and were defended vigilantly by the Commons Preservation Society.[1] We owe to these premature "Greens" such urban lungs as we have.[2] More than that, if it had not been for the stubborn defence by Newbury commoners of their rights to Greenham Common, where on earth could NATO have parked its nukes?[3]

III

Yet we should not press the distinction between prescriptive rights and rights established by custom too far. Although urban commoners might appeal to "chartered rights", when they succeeded it was through the assertion of usage, sheer numbers, political muscle. And the law was open to manipulation. "Prescription" could be a legal fiction, a suppositious (but unrecorded) grant.[4] Perhaps we should

[1] A mass of information on the law of commons, with particular relevance to the environs of London, is in G. Shaw-Lefevre (ed.), *Six Essays on Commons Preservation* (1867). The Commons Preservation Society was founded in 1866. Much information on commons, especially surrounding London, is in G. Shaw-Lefevre, *English Commons and Forests* (1894), subsequently revised as Lord Eversley, *Commons, Forests and Footpaths* (1910).

[2] But this could be a double-sided process. Commons contiguous to towns could become marginal zones with "rough" and dubious reputations, and regulated public parks could be a way of extinguishing rights and imposing social discipline: see Raphael Samuel, "Quarry Roughs", in *Village Life and Labour* (1975), esp. pp. 207-27; N. MacMaster, "The Battle for Mousehold Heath", *Past and Present*, no. 127, May 1990.

[3] "A regularly organised mob of many hundreds of the most abandoned and dissolute characters" threw down an encloser's fences "with most terrific hooting and abuse" on Newbury's commons in 1842: "To the Inhabitants of Newbury", 4 page printed broadside, signed R. F. Graham, Greenham, 30 Sept. 1842, in Berks. CRO D/Ex 24123 I.

[4] Late medieval law required that user should be shown since 1189: the fictional doctrine of presumed grant appeared early in the seventeenth century, but was most strongly argued in terms of easements: by *Lewis v Price* (1761) only twenty years enjoyment of use could be evidence of a suppositious grant: see A. W. B. Simpson, *A History of the Land Law*, 2nd edn. (Oxford, 1986), pp. 107-10, 266-7. In the nineteenth century sixty years uncontested user could establish forestal commonage — "the law presumes a grant"; Lord Hobhouse commented, "In plain English, this presumption of grants is a legal fiction resorted to for the purposes of justice": Eversley, *op. cit.*, p. 107.

turn the problem around. In the towns commons were often defended with more success than in the countryside. Does this tell us anything about right, and about property and law?

The tone of some writing on agricultural history suggests that there is little we need to know about law. Even Professor Hoskins, in his sympathetic and informative study of common lands, allows himself to state that "contrary to widespread belief. . . all common land is private property. It belongs to someone, whether an individual or a corporation, and has done so from time immemorial".[1] That might find a legalistic justification — of course Hoskins was simplifying his account — but "belonging", private property in land, is itself a concept which has had a historical evolution. The central concept of feudal custom was not that of property but of reciprocal obligations.[2] An authority on land law suggests that common rights —

> arose as customary rights associated with the communal system of agriculture practised in the primitive village communities. At a very early period such villages would be surrounded with tracts of waste land. . . On such land the villagers as a community would pasture their beasts and from it they would gather wood and turf and so forth. In the course of time, when the increase of population and the reduction in the quantity of uncultivated land started to produce crowding and conflict, their rights would tend to become more clearly defined but would still be communal rights, principally over waste lands regarded as the lands of the community itself. The tenurial system converted the villagers into tenants, and *the theory of the law* placed the freehold of most of the lands of the manor in the lord. Some of his tenants, it is true, will be freeholders, but the majority hold unfreely in villeinage, and the pre-eminence of the lord makes it natural to treat him as the 'owner' of the waste lands. Thus *a theory of individual ownership* supplants earlier more egalitarian notions.[3] (My italics.)

That is not quite "belonging" from "time immemorial". One is reminded of the saying addressed by Russian serfs to their lords: "We are yours, but the land is ours."[4]

It was Tawney's view that, in such matters as common of pasture, "communal aspirations are a matter of feeling and

[1] Hoskins, *The Common Lands of England and Wales* (1963), p. 4.
[2] See S. F. C. Milsom, *The Legal Framework of English Feudalism* (Cambridge, 1976).
[3] Simpson, *op. cit.*, p. 108.
[4] J. Blum, *Lord and Peasant in Russia* (Princeton, 1971), p. 469.

custom, not of national law".[1] These "communal aspirations" persist into the eighteenth century where they co-exist with the most scrupulous regulation of common rights and stints by village by-laws (and *lex loci* of manorial courts) and by rigorous definitions of common rights (appendant, appurtenant, of gross, and by vicinage) at national law. Law and usages may often seem to be at odds with each other. Authorities agree that in many parts of England and Wales, the cottagers and the landless exercised use-rights — of turbary, estover, and often of pasturage on waste (and sometimes Lammas lands or grazing over the harvested common fields). Thus Gonner: "Throughout the country it may be said that often the poor living near the commons, wholly without question of the occupation of ancient cottages, came by usage to enjoy the minor rights of common", including grazing for pigs, geese and sometimes cows.[2] Most authorities go on to state flatly that these minor rights of common had no basis in law and were illegally exercised or usurped. And in a self-fulfilling argument the statement is confirmed by the evidence that they usually received no compensation for such rights at enclosure. Thus Kerridge: "Occupiers of poor law and other newly erected cottages, and generally all squatters on the waste, were not entitled to rights of common, so no allotment was due to them."[3] And thus Chambers and Mingay:

> The *occupiers* of common right cottages. . . who enjoyed common right by virtue of their *tenancy* of the cottage, received no compensation because they were not, of course, the owners of the rights. This was a perfectly proper distinction between owner and tenant, and involved no fraud or disregard for cottagers on the part of the commissioners.[4]

Yet this is to assume two things: first, the priority of "the theory of the law" over usages, and, second, the propriety of splitting off the rights from the user. But these are, precisely, the questions to be examined. If Coke's definition be followed — "Customs are defined to be a law or right not

[1] Tawney, *op. cit.*, p. 246.
[2] Gonner, *op. cit.*, p. 31.
[3] Kerridge, *op. cit.*, p. 80.
[4] J. D. Chambers and G. E. Mingay, *The Agricultural Revolution, 1750-1880* (1966), p. 97.

written; which, being established by long use and the consent of our ancestors, hath been and is daily practised"[1] — then in many parishes the exercise of minor rights of common might have been proved by antiquity, continuance, certainty and reason as well as those of the landholders and customary tenants. Custom (Coke explained) takes away the common law, yet the common law might correct on such grounds, and especially on the grounds of reason. Kerridge, in one of his intemperate attacks upon Tawney, writes:

> The common law could only allow and confirm customary laws that were reasonable, certain, on good consideration, compulsory, without prejudice to the king, and to the profit of the claimant. Tawney assumed that 'reasonable' in this context was used in a loose or general sense, and that the lord's interests were more likely to seem reasonable to the lawyers than were the customer's; but 'reasonable' and 'unreasonable' are legal terms of art and mean 'compatible', 'consonant', 'consistent', 'reconcilable', or their opposites. A reasonable custom was one that could be reconciled with the other customary laws of that manor and with the common law. Thus to disallow unreasonable customs was, in almost every instance, to reject fraudulent ones.[2]

I cannot in any way accept Kerridge's assurances as to the powers of the common law over custom, which confuse the essential and the trivial, omit the criteria of antiquity and continuous usage, and mistake the true relation between the two.[3] The common law did not sit on high to "only allow and confirm" those customs which it approved; on the contrary, it might only disallow custom if it could fault it on these (and certain other legal) grounds, and only then when a case was referred to the common law courts. Nor, as it happens, can I find that Tawney wrote the opinions which Kerridge puts into his mouth.

"Reasonable" and "unreasonable" may be "legal terms of art" but on a very brief view of case law they were gates through which a large flock of other considerations might

[1] Co. Coph. S. 33.

[2] Kerridge, op. cit., p. 67.

[3] Blackstone, Commentaries, i, pp. 76-8, lists as grounds for making custom good: (1) Antiquity ("so long that the memory of man runneth not to the contrary"); (2) Continuity; (3) Peaceable user; (4) Must not be unreasonable (at law); (5) Certainty; (6) Compulsory: i.e. not optional; and (7) Consistency.

come baaing and grunting onto the fields of the common law.
Perhaps no case was more often cited in its bearing upon
the marginal use-rights of the villager that Gateward's
Case (1607). This was both a terminus of precedent judgements and the ground upon which many subsequent judgements stood. Defendant had pleaded common right "ratione
commorantiae et residentiae suae" in the town of Stixwold
in Lincolnshire. This was disallowed because the defendant
was occupier of a house in which he had no interest —

> No certain time or estate, but during his inhabitancy, and such manner
> of interest the law will not suffer, for custom ought to extent to that
> which hath certainty and continuance.

These are "legal terms of art", although we slide along them
from the use-right to the user to his house: "For none can
have interest in a common in respect of a house in which he
hath no interest." But in disallowing all "inhabitants" or
"residents" from the further ground of reasonableness was
added that "no improvements can be made in any wastes, if
such common should be allowed".[1] The court could not
have known that in 350 years time, when the term "improvement" had acquired a new resonance, they had licensed a
motorway to carry political economy across the commons.

Gateward's Case was technically brought in restraint of a
gentleman who was grazing Stixwold commons, although it
seems that in fact Gateward had come forward as a champion
of the customary use-rights of the poorer inhabitants also.[2]
The cases which came up to the common law courts for a
hundred years or more rarely concerned the minor rights of
common. They concerned the regulation and adjustment of
more substantial landholding interests. Attention was paid to
the definition of common appendant and appurtenant:
appendant belonged to occupiers of arable land, and carried
right to place commonable beasts (those who plough and
manure the arable) on the lord's waste. Levancy and

[1] *Gateward's Case* (4 Jas I), 6 Co Rep 59b, ER 77, pp. 344-6;
Smith v Gateward (4 Jas I), Cro Jac 152, ER 79, p. 133. See also my
comments in *Family and Inheritance*, pp. 339-41.
[2] For the background to Gateward's Case, see Manning, *Village
Revolts*, pp. 83-6.

couchancy stinted the right to the number of beasts that could be wintered on the arable holding. Common appurtenant was attached not to land but to a dominant tenement, and it extended to other stock, such as hogs, goats, geese, and rested upon immemorial usage and prescription. Decisions did not go only one way. On occasion the lord's rights to waste the common, carry off soil, or warren the waste with "coney-boroughs" were restrained. There were even decisions where substantial landholders excluded the lord from parcels of his own waste, under the same levancy and couchancy rule which excluded cottagers. But at least one such judgement against a Suffolk lord of the manor, in 1654, proved ineffectual, not because it was bad law but because it was unenforceable. Sir Francis North, in a learned argument in King's Bench in 1675, observed that it had been —

> A case of small consequence that concerned the lord only for his costs, for he has enjoyed his feeding against that verdict ever since: I can say it upon my own knowledge, for I know the parties and I know the place. . . I may add that this was in popular times, when all things tended to the licentiousness of the common people.[1]

By the mid eighteenth century the law had clearly ruled that levancy and couchancy were incident to common appendant as well as common appurtenant. In 1740, in a case arising from Mark in Somerset concerning the overstocking of Somer Leaze, the court acknowledged that —

> There are indeed some cases in the old books. . . which speak of common sans nombre, and which seem to imply that levancy and couchancy is only necessary in the case of common appurtenant, and not in the case of common appendant. But the notion of common sans nombre, in the latitude in which it was formerly understood, has been long since exploded, and it can have no rational meaning but in contradistinction to stinted common, where a man has a right only to put in such a particular number of cattle.[2]

At the beginning of the century the courts had found a generous interpretation of common appurtenant. A claim of common for cattle levant and couchant on a cottage was

---

[1] *Polter v Sir Henry North* (26 Charles II), 1 Ventris 383, 397, ER 86, pp. 245-54; the place was Elinswell, near Bury St Edmunds.

[2] *Robert Bennett v Robert Reeve* (1740), Willes 227, ER 125, pp. 1144-7.

found good, even if it had no land, since "a cottage contain-
eth a curtilage, & so there may be levancy. . . We will suppose
that a cottage has at least a court to it".[1] The contest around
this swayed back and forth. Did a butcher who kept sheep in
his cellar have levancy and couchancy? The dispute was
finally concluded in the high enclosure years, in 1792, when it
was determined that the cottage must carry sufficient land
for levancy and couchancy.[2]

When minor rights of common acquired a new value,
either in the market (the sale of clay, peats, wood) or in
compensation at enclosure, the courts gave them more
serious attention. Now the decision in Gateward's Case came
into new effect. When it was claimed, in 1741, that the right
of turbary was a custom laid "not only in the tenants but the
occupants" of a Cambridgeshire village, the court found this
"a very great absurdity, for an occupant, who is no more
than a tenant at will, can never have a right to take away the
soil of the lord".[3] In 1772 King's Bench took a more liberal
view of the right to cut rushes, in a case that arose from
Theberton in Suffolk, accepting oral testimony that "everybody in the world may cut rushes on the common".[4] But
this was reversed only two years later in a case arising from
Ludham Waste in Norfolk. It was accepted that copyholders,
occupiers of lands and occupiers of ancient houses might set
up a custom to cut turfs or rushes, but "inhabitants cannot,
because inhabitancy is too vague a description. . .".[5] In
the same tradition the claim — arising from Whaddon,
Buckinghamshire — for "all and every the poor, necessitous
and indigend. . . householders" to gather and break with
woodhooks rotten boughs in two coppices was disallowed
because "there is no limitation. . . the description of poor
householder is too vague and uncertain".[6]

It is not suggested that these decisions were unreasonable,
nor that they denied the "legal terms of art". Most decisions

[1] *Emerton v Selby* (2 Anne), 2 Ld Raym. 1015, ER 92, p. 175.

[2] *Scholes v Hargreave* (1792), 5 Term Rep 46, ER 101, p. 26.

[3] *Dean and Chapter of Ely v Warren*, 2 Atk 189-90, ER 26, p. 518.

[4] *Rackham v Joseph and Thompson* (1772), 3 Wils KB 334, ER 95,
pp. 1084-7. A full and interesting report.

[5] *Bean v Bloom* (14 Geo. III), 2 Black W 926, ER 96, pp. 547-9.

[6] *Selby v Robinson* (1788), 2 T R 759, ER 100, p. 409.

arose — at least until the mid eighteenth century — not with the intention of cutting off the petty exercise of minor rights of common, but in disputes between larger operators, with the intention of restraining the exploitation of these rights by interlopers and entrepreneurs. Thus in *Bennett v Reeve*, in 1740, the complainant had taken a ninety-nine year lease of one yard parcel in Old Auster, which carried right of common appendant, and on the basis of this square yard had turned sixty-four sheep onto Somer Leaze. Other cases arose from the exploitation of supposititious rights to sell peats, timber, clay, or (in the case of Norfolk rushes) a blacksmith carrying off rushes by the wagon load. Gateward's Case itself was aimed, not against the poor parishioner's cow or geese, but against a gentleman interloper.

Yet within this rationality there was evolving — as Tawney rightly saw — the ulterior rationality of capitalist definitions of property rights. I will not court an action for trespass into the lands of medieval historians in an attempt to define what, in origin, was meant by "the lord's waste" or "the soil of the lord". But both agrarian and legal historians appear to agree that the notion of the origin of common rights in royal or feudal grants is a fiction. Dr Thirsk has suggested that rights of grazing over pasture and waste were perhaps "the oldest element" in the common field system, descended from "more extensive rights. . . enjoyed from time immemorial", which Anglo-Saxon and Norman monarchs and lords did not graciously institute but, rather, regulated and curtailed.[1] And we have seen that it was "the theory of the law" (above, p. 127) which placed the freehold of the manor in the lord. But this was not in terms of subsequent notions of exclusive "ownership" or property: it was, rather, "in fee simple" and in feudal terms of law. So long as wastes remained extensive and unstinted, landowners and commoners might co-exist without precise definitions of rights. As late as 1620 in a case concerning Holme-on-Spalding Moor a witness deposed that he knew not if a tenement built on the common sixty years before had common by right or "by sufferance or negligence of the freeholder", since

[1] Joan Thirsk, "The Common Fields", *Past and Present*, no. 29, December 1964.

at the time it was built "the freeholder made little reckoning of common for so small goods as was then put upon the said common by the said tenants".[1] In a survey of Chilvers Coton (Warwickshire) in 1682 there is a very specific itemisation of freehold and copyhold in the open fields, but the homage becomes vague when it comes to common rights in the waste:

> What beasts sheep or other cattle the Lord of this mannor as such or his ffarmour may keep in Coton or Nuneaton Outwood wee do not precisely know, but the present Lord. . . doth claim a right to keep all manner of cattle but so as not to oppress our Commons.

One notes the phrase "our Commons". As we shall see, in village by-laws common rights in waste land are often expressed in loose or uncertain terms — sometimes all tenants, or copyholders, sometimes "all within this manor", or "inhabitants", or "cottiers", or "parishioners" — *except* when they are referred to the courts. Legal definitions are generally more precise than actual usages, and they may become more so the higher they go up the ladder of law.

There were two occasions which dictated absolute precision: a trial at law and a process of enclosure. And both occasions favoured those with power and purses against the little users. In the late seventeenth century and certainly in the eighteenth the courts increasingly defined (or assumed without argument) that the lord's waste or soil was his personal property, albeit restrained or curtailed by the inconvenient usages of custom. If the lord's access to any part of "his" soil should be restricted "this will be a ready way to enable tenants to withstand all improvements".[2]

Gateward's Case, and successive decisions in this spirit of "improvement", drew an expert knife through the carcass of custom, cutting off the use-right from the user. In one single operation this restrained unlicensed large interlopers, graziers and the like, in the interests of the landholders and customary tenants, and it altogether disqualified indistinct categories of small users, who held neither land nor ancient cottage tenures. While this may not have affected actual village

[1] Joan Thirsk, *Tudor Enclosures* (Hist. Assn. 1967), p. 10.
[2] *Polter v Sir Henry North* (26 Charles II), 1 Ventris 397, ER 86, pp. 245-54.

usages much it could leave the landless commoner stripped of any rights if a case came to the courts, or at the point of enclosure. The right of use had been transferred from the user to the house or site of an ancient messuage. It became not a use but a property.

This did not happen instantly nor without ambiguities. The logic of capitalist rationality was delayed by deeply-rooted copyhold and customary tenures.[1] Common appendant could not be detached and sold away from land, although at enclosure it was of course the land's owner and not its user (if farmed by a tenant) who could cash the right. Common appurtenant could be sold with a cottage or with the site of an ancient messuage, carrying so many gates (or grazing rights for beasts) on the common. But this was not a novelty, and legal historians can press us back as far as the twelfth century when certain incorporeal rights (such as church advowsons) began to be treated as properties or "things". Yet this was construed as a right in the "things", not to "own" the thing itself — "a present right" to use or enjoy.

What was happening, from the time of Coke to that of Blackstone, was a hardening and concretion of the notion of property in land, and a re-ification of usages into properties which could be rented, sold or willed. For good reason Blackstone entitled volume two of his *Commentaries*, "Of the Rights of Things" — not because these rights were a novelty (they were an ancient chapter of the law) but because the market in these rights was never more active, or more prolific in tests at law than at this time. Moreover, one might notice that Blackstone referred, not to rights *to* things, but to the rights *of* things. The eighteenth century sees this strange period of mixed law in which usages and rights were attached

---

[1] The lord's right over copyholders' timber was strongly contested, and although it moved in favour of the lord in *Ashmead v Ranger*, decided finally in the House of Lords (1702) by a bare majority of 11 to 10, it was not a decisive victory: see Allan Greenbaum, "Timber Rights, Property Law, and the Twilight of Copyhold", (MS Osgoode Hall Law School, York University, Toronto).

[2] Simpson, *op. cit.*, pp. 103-6; C. B. Macpherson, "Capitalism and the Changing Concept of Property", in Kamenka and Neale (eds.), *Feudalism, Capitalism and Beyond* (1975), p. 110.

to office or to place and then were regarded as if they were things which commanded human rights in their turn. The Rangership of a forest or park could be sold, with the powers, perquisites and rights attached to the office.[1] An ancient messuage (or its site) commanded rights of common, and the thing could be transferred between owners. And in much the same way decisions of the House of Commons in disputed cases tended to re-ify the definition of those who might be electors in boroughs from indistinct categories such as "inhabitants" or the "Commonalty in general" to inhabitants paying scot and lot, and thence to persons inhabiting ancient houses or houses built on ancient foundations (Bridport, 1628 and 1762; Arundell, 1693 and 1715; Bramber, 1715). In Seaford in 1676 the Bailiffs, Jurors and Freemen "had not only voices. . . but also the Election was in the populacy" but in 1761 "the word *populacy*. . . extends only to Inhabitants Housekeepers paying scot and lot", a decision in the same tradition as Gateward's. In Hastings, 1715, electors were confined to "all with estate of inheritance or for life in Burgage Houses or Burgage Lands" within the borough.[2] This led on to the absurdities of the Unreformed House of Commons, where the right of election could lie in dove-cots, pig-styes, a thorn tree or a quarry, and was exercised by the owners of these things by various fictions and stratagems. "The custom of attaching Rights to *place*, or in other words to inanimate matter, instead of to the *person*, independently of place, is too absurd to make any part of a rational argument" — thus spake Tom Paine.[3]

The re-ification — and cashing — of usages as properties came always to a climax at the point of enclosure. The owners of land and not the tenants (unless customary) received land in exchange for the extinguishment of rights. But the law, which disallowed the usages of the many, might allow as properties extinct assets and superordinate rights and offices

[1] A good example is Enfield Chase in my *Whigs and Hunters*, pp. 175-81.

[2] These precedents (mostly from *Commons Journals*) were usefully collected in Shelburne Papers (Univ. of Michigan, Ann Arbor), vol. 167, W. Masterman, "Compendium of the Rights and Privileges of Election".

[3] Thomas Paine, *Letter Addressed to the Addressers on the Late Proclamation* (1792), p. 67.

of the few with "interest". When the forest of Delamere was enclosed (1812) half of the eight thousand acres went to the King, together with £200 per annum in rental from the other half. John Arden, as Chief Forester, Bowbearer and Bailiff, with his under-keepers, were amply compensated for their loss of perquisites (including the "pasturage of coneys"), as was Thomas Cholmondeley "as Owner of the dissolved Monastery of Vale Royal, and of divers Messuages, Lands, Tenements and Heriditaments, heretofore parcel of the Possessions of the Abbot and Convent of Vale Royal". All rights of common in the forest were extinguished, save for some "Moss Pits or Turbaries" too wet for pasture and impracticable to be drained: here peats might still be cut. Tenants at rack-rent received no land in lieu of lost rights, although the landowners (who did receive land for their tenants' loss of right of common) were instructed to make them compensation.[1] All of this was proper to law: it follows normal procedures. But it signals a wholesale trans-formation of agrarian practices, in which rights are assigned away from users and in which ancient feudal title is richly compensated in its translation into capitalist property-right.

When Kerridge writes that "to disallow unreasonable customs was, in almost every instance, to reject fraudulent ones" he astonishes one first of all by the claim to omni-science. (Even the great Sir Edward Coke said that "should I go about with a catalogue of several customs, I should with Sysiphus. . . undertake an endless piece of work".) Of course, once the law had detached the right from the user, it could find reasonable grounds for disallowing usages of the greatest antiquity and certainty. The common law allowed "reasons" to be considered which had more to do with the political economy of "improvement" than with a strict atten-tion to the terms of law. Many judges shared the mentalities of improving landowners (reasonable men) and they prided themselves on their intuition into the real intentions of their predecessors and of legislators. As Abbott, C.J. noted, in a case which disallowed (yet again) the claims of "inhabitants",

[1] *An Act for Inclosing the Forest of Delamere* (1812), pp. 23, 27-9, 33.

The meaning of particular words in Acts of Parliament, as well as other instruments, is to be found not so much in a strict etymological propriety of language, nor even in popular use, as in the subject or occasion on which they are used, and the object that is intended to be obtained.[1]

It was tough luck if language's "popular uses" of right seemed unreasonable to a judicial mind. What Kerridge (and other authorities on enclosure)[2] fail to examine is whether, by this re-ification of right and by this introduction of the reasons of "improvement", the law itself may not have been the instrument of class expropriation.

By disqualifying imprecise categories of users — occupiers, inhabitants, residents, "all persons" etc. — Gateward's and successive cases had left to the populace or to inhabitants only the exception of rights of way or easements, "as in a way or causey to church".[3] It was a large allowance. By raising to a reason at law the question of "improvement" it was possible to effect a marriage between "legal terms of art" and the imperatives of capitalist market economy. The decision in 1788 in the Court of Common Pleas against gleaning is familiar, yet it may be of interest to read it once again with an eye to the reasons of law.

Here was certainly a custom which had immemorial sanction and which continued with undiminished vigour into the nineteenth century. The practice was sanctioned by custom, but also regulated by village by-laws.[4] Such

[1] *Rex v G. W. Hall* (1822), 1 B & C 136, ER 107, p. 51.

[2] Sadly, W. E. Tate in that fine book, *The Parish Chest* (2nd edn. Cambridge, 1951), p. 289 offered an even more anachronistic imposition of subsequent property categories upon the evidence. He apologised for the lack of allotment of land to the poor at enclosure because "from the legalist point of view. . . any land given to them could only be at the expense of the other proprietors, its legal owners. Open fields and common pastures belonged to the public (so said the lawyers) no more than does say a Co-operative Society, or a limited company, and when the open-field village was liquidated its assets were divided, like those of any other business concern, after satisfying the creditors among the shareholders".

[3] *Smith v Gateward* (4 Jas I), Cro Jac 152, ER 79, p. 133. See also ER 82, p. 157.

[4] For gleaning generally, see David Morgan, *Harvesters and Harvesting* (1982); Bushaway, *op. cit.*, esp. pp. 138-48; P. J. King, "Gleaners, Farmers and the Failure of Legal Sanctions in England, 1780-1850", *Past and Present*, no. 125 (November, 1989).

regulation continues in the eighteenth century, as evidenced by some by-laws, although in other by-laws the practice is assumed, and passed over in silence. In Raunds (Northamptonshire) in 1740 there is a suggestion of tighter controls to exclude foreigners and paupers in receipt of relief: John Adams and family are presented for gleaning without a settlement (1s.), and the by-law is entered: "no certificate person shall either glean in the fields or cutt any furzes from the common".[1] A trial of the general question of right in 1766 in King's Bench was confused. Gleaners, gaoled in Berkshire, had gleaned in an only partly cut field of barley. Lord Mansfield ruled that "stealing, under the colour of leasing or gleaning, is not to be justified". But another learned judge remarked that "the right of leasing does appear in our books. . .".[2] The issue came up to Common Pleas in 1788 from an action for trespass against Mary Houghton, wife of John Houghton, for gleaning in closes at Timworth in Suffolk. The case does not appear to have been argued in terms of custom (perhaps because it would at once have fallen foul of the precedents established by Gateward's Case) but on grounds of the universal recognition of the right at common law. The defendants were "parishioners and inhabitants of the said parish of Timworth, legally settled therein, and being poor and necessitous, and indigent persons. . .". Lord Loughborough found the claim indefinite:

1st, I thought it inconsistent with the nature of property which imports exclusive enjoyment.
2dly, Destructive of the peace and good order of society, and amounting to a general vagracy.
3dly, Incapable of enjoyment, since nothing which is not inexhaustible, like a perennial stream, can be capable of universal promiscuous enjoyment.

By removing the claim from custom to common law the defence had not removed the difficulty, since "if this custom were part of the common law of the realm, it would prevail in every part of the kingdom, and be of general and uniform practice", whereas in some parts it was unknown and in

[1] Northants CRO, Box 1053/2, Manor of Raunds, Court book, 27 November 1740.
[2] *Rex v John Price* (1766), 4 Burr 1926, ER 98, pp. 1-2.

others variously modified and enjoyed. As for the defendant's efforts to enlist the law of Moses, "the political institutions of the Jews cannot be obligatory on us, since even under the Christian dispensation the relief of the poor is not a legal obligation, but a religious duty". From this Lord Loughborough passed to a homily drawn directly from political economy:

> The consequences which would arise from this custom being established as a right, would be injurious to the poor themselves. Their sustenance can only arise from the surplus of productive industry; whatever is a charge on industry, is a very improvident dimunition of the fund for that sustenance; for the profits of the farmer being lessened, he would be less able to contribute his share to the rates of the parish; and thus the poor, from the exercise of this supposed right in the autumn, would be liable to starve in the spring.

Mr Justice Gould gave a directly contrary opinion, with considerable learning and recitation of precedent. But Mr Justice Heath and Mr Justice Wilson came to the side of Lord Loughborough. Heath expressed himself with singular force: "To sanction this usage would introduce fraud and rapine, and entail a curse upon the country." He entered even more largely upon the reasons of political economy:

> The law of Moses is not obligatory on us. It is indeed agreeable to Christian charity and common humanity that the rich should provide for the impotent poor; but the mode of provision must be of positive institution. We have established a nobler fund. We have pledged all the landed property of the kingdom for the maintenance of the poor, who have in some instances exhausted the source. The inconvenience arising from this custom being considered as a right by the poor would be infinite. . . It would open the door to fraud, because the labourers would be tempted to scatter the corn in order to make a better gleaning for their wives, children and neighbours. . . It would raise the insolence of the poor. . .

Mr Justice Wilson concurred, but made a little more show of grounding his opinion in law:

> No right can exist at common law, unless both the subject of it, and they who claim it, are certain. In this case both are uncertain. The subject is the scattered corn which the farmer chooses to leave on the ground, the quantity depends entirely on his pleasure. The soil is his, the seed is his, and in natural justice his also are the profits.[1]

---

[1] *Steel v Houghton et Uxor* (1788), 1 H BL 51, ER 126, pp. 32-9.

It is difficult to think of a purer expression of capitalist rationality, in which both labour and human need have disappeared from view, and the "natural justice" of profits has become a reason at law. In the arguments of *Steele v Houghton et Uxor* we see exposed with unusual clarity the law's complicity with the ideology of political economy, its indifference to the claims of the poor, and its growing impatience with coincident use-rights over the same soil. As Loughborough had it, "the nature of property. . . imports exclusive enjoyment". And how could enjoyment be exclusive if it did not command the power to exclude from property's physical space the insolent lower orders?

In these last few pages we have given a little attention to the law. And we should add a few words to safeguard against possible misunderstanding. The *English Reports* are not packed with cases in which poor commoners challenged their lords or great landowners in the highest courts of the land. On occasion freeholders or customary tenants did so, pledging themselves to each other to share the costs.[1] But taking cases upwards to the courts of Common Pleas or King's Bench was not the cottagers' nor the labourers' "thing". Unless some party with a substantial interest was involved on their side, their rights were liable to be lost silently and without contest.

We may illustrate the point by noticing two cases where the rights of "the poor" were involved. The first is the case of gleaning. In a skilful piece of detective work Peter King has found out more about this case. There were in fact two cases, the first, *Worledge v Manning* (1786), coming up two years before the case of Mary Houghton (1788), but failing to decide the point of law. Both cases came up from the same West Suffolk parish, and the prosecutions were probably supported by subscription among local landholders. Benjamin Manning and John Houghton were both shoe makers, and Dr King suggests that it was only the support of a benevolent Suffolk landowner and magistrate, Capel Lloft, which enabled Houghton to fee counsel. The loss of the cases (and the damages and costs involved) certainly did not

---

[1] An example of such an agreement in Yate (Gloucestershire), 1745, is in Glos. CRO D 2272.

advance the career of either defendant. The Houghtons were
forced to mortgage and then to sell their small property.
Mary Houghton, the widow of John, is last found in the poor
law records, receiving some £6 per annum relief.[1]

For the smallholder, cottager or small commoner the law
was always something to avoid. But surely in the nineteenth
century — after 1860 at least — small commoners could
contest their rights in the courts with the help of powerful
philanthropists or the Commons Preservation Society? On
occasion this was true. But even in those enlightened years
there could be difficulties, which may be illustrated by the
case of Mr Willingale. We have already encountered (above,
p. 102) the claims to wood of the poor inhabitants of
Loughton, adjoining Waltham Forest (itself part of Epping
Forest). The right of lopping trees up to a certain height in the
winter months was a custom supposed to find its origin in a
grant from Queen Elizabeth. Considerable ritual had gathered around its assertion, which must commence on midnight
of November 10th, when inhabitants (usually warmed up
with ale) perambulated the forest. In the early 1860s the lord
of the manor of Loughton enclosed the forest, gave some
compensation to tenants, fenced out the public and started
felling the trees.

In 1866 "a labouring man named Willingale", with his two
sons, broke in upon the fences and made the customary
perambulation. All three were convicted of malicious trespass
and sentenced to two months hard labour. In prison one of
the sons caught pneumonia and died. When Willingale was
released the matter was becoming a *cause célèbre* among the
Radicals of East London. The Commons Preservation
Society had just been founded and it offered to contest the
issue, raising a fund of £1,000 for the purpose. A suit was
commenced in the name of Willingale, since it could only be
pleaded in an inhabitant of Loughton. There was a
supporting lobby of Liberal MPs, QCs, editors, and eminent
persons including Sir T. Fowell Buxton and John Stuart Mill.
Yet despite this support and despite the publicity,
Willingale was subjected to the inexorable social control of

[1] P. J. King, "The Origins of the Gleaning Judgement of 1788",
forthcoming.

the manorial village. No-one dared employ him in the parish, and it was only with great difficulty that he could find lodging in the village, which he must do to remain an inhabitant. He was privately offered bribes — perhaps as much as £500 — to abandon the suit, but he rejected all offers.

After four years of this, the old man died (1870), hence abating the suit. It was resumed in a new form by the Corporation of London (which had no need to find lodging or employment in the manor). When it gained a qualified victory in 1879, "the whole population of the district turned out at midnight to the number of 5,000 or 6,000" for a last torchlight perambulation. Willingale's surviving son was still championing the common rights of the small occupiers, and his widow was awarded by London Corporation a pension of five shillings a week. [1]

Lord Eversley who records this story, and the part played in it by several philanthropists, appears to have forgotten "old Willingale's" Christian name. What is clear is that, even in mid-Victorian England, it was no easy matter for a labouring man to tangle about common rights with lords or landowners through the forms of law. What chances were there of doing so one hundred years before?

IV

The decision in the Court of Common Pleas in 1788 did not of course extinguish the practice of gleaning, unless perhaps by Mary Houghton and her neighbours in Timworth. [2] Custom remained *lex loci*, and while case law now decided that gleaning could not be claimed as a right in common law, the right might still be claimed as local right, by the custom of the manor or by village by-law. The decision strengthened the

[1] Eversley, *op. cit.*, ch. 8. Descriptions of Epping Forest in 1895, with its pollarded hornbeams, are in two letters of William Morris to the *Daily Chronicle. Letters of William Morris*, ed. Philip Henderson (1950), pp. 363-7.

[2] A few years after the Common Pleas judgement an observer of the picturesque enthused about the hundred-acre fields covered with gleaners, "while innumerable groups of children are sporting or working around": this was within a few miles of Timworth: S. Pratt, *Gleanings in England* (1801), ii, p. 271.

hands of farmers who wished to check the custom, or to restrict it to the families of their own labourers after enclosure. And enclosure did endanger the right, by removing the harvest from the huge open fields over which the customs of the rural community were habitually exercised, into the severalty of hedged or fenced "closes" with their sense of controlled access and private space. Indeed the decision might have led on to a general repression of gleaning if attempts to do so had not encountered the most stubborn resistance, especially from labouring women who, as Peter King has shown, refused to surrender their "rights" in the face of physical and legal harassment.[1]

No decision in the common law courts had immediate impact on the local practice of custom, although such decisions could stack the hands of the landowners with aces to be cashed for acres when it came to the point of enclosure. Where copyhold and other forms of customary tenure survived — indeed wherever lands survived in a village over which rights of common existed — one may expect to find some form of regulation of use. Some years ago, in my simplicity, I supposed that I had discovered a key to open the door upon the actuality of common right usages in surviving eighteenth-century recitations of customs, and especially in village by-laws still being promulgated in Courts Leet, or in other kinds of parish meeting, with vigour throughout the century. I made a habit then, whenever visiting a County Record Office, to rifle the card index and to collect examples of local regulation. But, alas, when I first came to sketch the present essay and turned this sack of notes onto my study floor, I found myself regarding this promiscuous gleaning of ears from several counties with blank dismay.

I learned at least a little humility. For this *lex loci*, which itself is only a partial guide to *praxis loci*, acquires meaning only when placed within the disciplined study of the local context. One must know about the balance of arable and waste, the diffusion or concentration of landholding, about crops and stock, soil fertility, access to markets, population

[1] See P. King, "Gleaners, Farmers and the Failure of Legal Sanctions, 1750-1850", *Past and Present*, no. 125 (November 1989).

and poor rates, and all those other matters which the disciplined agricultural historian so patiently puts together.[1] Without this careful provision of context my sack of gleanings turns out to be a sack of chaff. It is not much use to cite the stint for beasts allowed to graze the common per yardland or per cottage unless one can shew who and how many owned or tenanted these cottages and acres.

I might say, in self-defence, that several of the optimistic agrarian historians in the anti-Hammond school appear to have passed over such sources unread. But one is no more entitled to generalise indiscriminately about common right usages over the whole country than about soil, crops, or patterns of landholding. Common right usage, and the oral traditions as to these rights, is as specific and as local as are the geographic features. Perhaps a little may be deduced from such materials, even without contextual discipline. One finds, as one would expect, the tendency to translate rights to pasture on the waste (or gates on the common) into monetary equivalents, a sort of village echo of the re-ification of usages going on all around. Ryton-upon-Dunsmore, Warwickshire, a firmly regulated manor with good records, stipulated in 1735 that "no commons shall be let to no ought tounes [out-town]. . . for no less than 5s a common", whereas parishioners paid only 4s. for the right. There was an attempt to regulate the minor rights of common with unusual tightness: "No parson that is not a parrisoner shall cut any turf upone the common", and furze from the common might be taken only on own backs and only serve firing in own homes.

[1]Works which I have found most valuable in their bearing upon the exercise of common rights include (in addition to work by J. M. Neeson) W. G. Hoskins, *The Midland Peasant* (1957); C. S. and C. S. Orwin, *The Open Fields* (1948); A. C. Chibnall, *Sherington: Fiefs and Fields of a Buckinghamshire Village* (Cambridge, 1965); M. K. Ashby, *The Changing English Village: Bledington* (Kineton, 1974); W. Cunningham, *Common Rights at Cottenham & Stretham in Cambridgeshire* (Royal Hist. Soc., 1910); Joan Thirsk, "Field Systems in the East Midlands", in A. R. H. Baker and R. A. Butlin (eds.), *Studies of Field Systems in the British Isles* (Cambridge, 1973), esp. pp. 246-62; H. E. Hallam, "The Fen Bylaws of Spalding and Pinchbeck", *Lincs. Architectural & Archaeological Society*, (1963), pp. 40-56; R. S. Dilley, "The Cumberland Court Leet and Use of Common Lands", *Trans. Cumberland & Westmorland Antiq. & Archaeological Soc.*, lxvii (1967), pp. 125-51.

Money had made big inroads here:

> The grass hereafter growing in the highways or roads within this manner
> shall be sold to be mowed and not grazed and the moneys arising
> annually therefrom to be divided amongst the inhabitants of the said
> manor according to the rents of their respective livings.

No fewer than forty-seven persons were fined for offences
against by-laws in 1735, and forty-eight in each year, 1741
and 1749, and one suspects that an annual exercise in
disciplinary control was going on.[1]

My collection (which comes mainly from the Midlands)
shows no other example of a manor whose rights had been
monetarised to this extent. In some places — East and West
Leake (Nottinghamshire) 1730 and Towcester, 1712 —
commoners or cottagers received a monetary compensation if
they did not exercise a common right.[2] In others the rent for
a cow's common is specified, and (as at Harpole,
Northamptonshire) the townsmen were permitted to let six
cow commons in the heath "to any of the poor inhabitants
of Harpole as they. . . shall see necessity or occasion for so
doing".[3] In Whilton in the same Hundred a more affirmative by-law is found in 1699: "If any poor person. . . not
holding lands or comon in the. . . fields shall at May Day. . .
want a cows comon", they can obtain it for 8s. from the
fieldsman.[4] Thus in some places rights to pasture could now
be hired (but rarely to out-townsmen), in others there was
compensation for the non-use of such rights, and sometimes
there is a mixture of right and cash. Money is sometimes set
aside to pay for the village officers, fieldsearchers, herds etc.
or the local improvements; sometimes is redistributed to

---

[1] Warwicks. CRO, MR 19.

[2] Sidney P. Potter, "East and West Leake", *Nottinghamshire
Guardian*, 1 Apr. 1933; Northants. CRO, YZ 4289.

[3] Northants. CRO, YZ 6a, Hundred of Norbottle Grove, Court Leet
and Baron, "By Laws, Rules and Orders", 12 Oct. 1743. The stint was four
cows and breeders for a yardland, but the townsmen could let further rights
to any who held only a quartern of land (and therefore right for only one
cow), at 8s. a right.

[4] Northants. CRO, YZ 1. M14, Norbottle Court, regulation for
Whilton common fields, 1699. See also Hampton-in-Arden, 22 October
1802: "Such poor persons that apply the 1st of March. . . shall have each a
Cows commoning", Warwicks. CRO, MR 20.

landholders; sometimes offsets the poor rates. In Hellidon, Northamptonshire, 1744, "any. . . persons that are parishioners and inhabitants of the Parish of Hellidon. . . have Liberty to turn a Horse in the Comonable Places in the ffields. . . at all comonable times. . . paying ten shillings a year to the overseer of the poor".[1]

A uniform concern of all regulations is to exclude interlopers from outside the parish from using the common. This is as old as regulation itself, but nevertheless is often repeated: "It is ordered that the Heardsmen and Shepherds shal not take to keepe any cattle of any other person. . . but onely those of the Inhabitants of this Towne."[2] In manorial villages with extensive copyhold and effective stewardship, rights were adjusted according to levancy and couchancy in a manner that would have satisfied the courts of common law. Rights on the stinted common were assessed in ratio to lands occupied in the open fields. Yet in other parishes indefinite terms abhorrent to the common law — "parishioners", "inhabitants", "any persons" — recur with frequency. Some by-laws pass over in silence usages on the common or waste, being wholly concerned with common of pasture and Lammas grazing; or they may signal practices which in other parishes are so well-known as to need no written rehearsal: "Any man shall have liberty to cut rushes at Xmas & not after Candlemas".[3] Pains are far more frequent upon trespasses in the common field than upon trespassers in the waste. Probably, in parishes with extensive common, the threat was seen as coming less from the cottager or labourer with the odd unlicensed beast than from graziers moving cattle on the hoof, butchers and dealers, or overmighty landholders exceeding their stint. Commons are stinted to establish *maximums* for men of substance.[4]

---

[1] Northants. CRO, D 5.5 (c), draft orders, court leet and baron of Manor of Hellidon, 27 October, 1744.

[2] Cunningham, *op. cit.*, p. 237.

[3] Northants. CRO, F (W.W.) 501/1/1, orders for Wollaston, 1721.

[4] For example, orders in Uphaven (Wiltshire), 1742, PRO, TS 19.3: "That all dealers and jobbers of sheep. . . ought not to keep any more sheep than their Leaze, and not to feed any sheep upon the Common. . . but with the other tenants according to the number of Leazes".

If there was a general place of contest between the farmers (of all shapes and sizes) on the one hand and the cottagers and landless commoners on the other, it can perhaps be detected in the continuing attempts to control the grazing on the marginal herbage in and around the common fields. Gonner tells us that "meers and balks were. . . sometimes fed off by cattle but often of little value", and substantiates this with a citation from an improving pamphleteer of 1773:

> They are literally of no benefit to either the occupier or the Poor; for they are too narrow either to mow, or to graze without a boy to attend each beast with a halter. . .[1]

In this he reports correctly the viewpoint of the improving farmers who have become, perhaps properly, the heroes of much agrarian history. Yet this marginal herbage was viewed very differently by the peasantry, among whom boys (and girls) able to attend on beasts with a halter were plentiful and cheap. In some pasture-hungry Midlands parishes in the early eighteenth century, very considerable efforts were being made by the farmers themselves to increase the acreage in the common fields under greensward by widening joint ways and balks for "flitting grass".[2] If the little people of the village are harassed — and if their stock harasses the large farmers in their turn — it is in this matter of marginal herbage; not only balks, but sykes, the banks of streams, headlands on the fields, tracks under greensward, laneside grazing. Persons are presented "that turne out beasts into the Lanes without a follower".[3] With this go pains against trespass and against

---

[1] Gonner, op. cit., p. 27.

[2] For an example, see Northants. CRO, YZ 6a, By Laws Rules and Orders for Hundred of Norbottle Grove, 12 October 1743. See also J. M. Neeson, "Common Right and Enclosure in Eighteenth Century Northamptonshire" (Univ. of Warwick Ph.D. thesis, 1978), esp. ch. 2; Baker and Butlin, op. cit., pp. 47-8, 131-2; H. Beecham, "A review of Balks as Strip Boundaries in the Open Fields", Agric. Hist. Rev., iv, (1956), pp. 22-44.

[3] Hants. CRO, 159, 641, Bishop Waltham (Hampshire) presentments, 25 March 1712, and (pain on cows in lanes "without a driver") 2 April 1717. Also Hambledon presentments (159, 613), 29 September 1721. (A readier remedy in most villages was to put such straying beasts in the pound.) A Suffolk phrase for grazing laneside verges was to "feed the Long Meadow", George Ewart Evans, The Days that We Have Seen (1975), pp. 50-1.

forking horses on the balks or feeding horses under pretence of making hay.[1] (Horses are great eaters, and once a horse had broken from its tether it could do untold damage to crops.) In tolerant parishes marginal herbage might be grazed provided the beast was not forked or tethered but was led by a halter. A few sheep might be tolerated along the lanes.[2] What Gonner and his pamphleteer see as wasted land use "of little value" was of central importance to the subsistence-economy of "the poor". A correspondent ("Apuleius") in the *Northampton Mercury* in 1726 wrote of —

Baulks and Borders, and Slades and Bottoms, and other waste Places, in these Common-Fields, which the Farmer is never able to appropriate to himself or his own sole using. . . for there are in most Countries a sort of Cottagers, that have Custom and Right of Commoning, tho' they Rent nothing but their Houses: And if it were a meer Hovel built upon the Waste, who would hinder a poor Man from keeping an Ewe and Lamb, or if he can compass one, a little Heifer? For these can run upon a Green, or among the Lanes and Highways, till the Crop be ended; and then away with them into the common Fields. . . and by this Advantage in some Places divers poor Families are in good Part sustained.

But with enclosure (the correspondent continued) these baulks and borders "become one Staple with the rest. . . in the sole Use and Occupation but of one Person".[3]

The beast led round the margins and along the ridges of a field, or up and down the lanes, by the children or the aged, can be seen in any poor peasant economy to this day. Wordsworth, encountering in his country walks with Beaupuy —

[1] "A pain made that no one shall flit with a Tether above Six yds long Excepting on his own Grass. . . A Pain that no one shall flit a Mare in the fields after the foal is a Month old": Atherstone Orders Bylaws and Pains, 1745, Warwicks. CRO, L 2/89. ("Flitting" was to graze a beast on a tether.)

[2] In Horbling (Lincolnshire) the cottagers "buy lambs in April, let them run in the lanes during Summer": *Annals of Agriculture*, xxxvii (1801), p. 522.

[3] *Northampton Mercury*, 17 Oct. 1726. See also Malcolmson, *op. cit.*, pp. 32-3.

> a hunger-bitten Girl,
> Who crept along, fitting her languid self
> Unto a Heifer's motion, by a cord
> Tied to her arm, and picking thus from the lane
> Its sustenance, while the Girl with her two hands
> Was busy knitting. . .

found the image of poverty to be a deep affront, and his friend Beaupuy "in agitation said, 'Tis against *that*/Which we are fighting' ". For Arthur Young, in the *Northern Tour*, it was no less of an affront, and an incitement to the virtues brought by dear times and improvement; when one who "in cheap times, used to bask himself all day in the sun, holding a cow by a line to feed on a balk, in dear ones betakes himself to the pickaxe and the spade".[1]

Levancy and couchancy supposed some land to be levant and couchant upon. The assumption is still there in 31 Eliz., c.7 (1589), prohibiting the erection of cottages without four acres of land. The socio-economic reality of many mid-eighteenth century unenclosed parishes was altogether different. While many small farmers were still to be found, as well as rural craftsmen and craftswomen and traders with a little land, there were in many places a growing number of landless commoners. Their customary rights, if scrutinised by national courts, were nil or — if they were tenants of old cottages — might be attached to the cottage (and its owner) not to the user. Yet it is my impression, from by-laws and literary evidence, that custom as praxis — village usages — generally afforded greater latitude for the exercise of minor rights than will be found in a formal view of the law.

I am not suggesting that poor people could get away with putting a cow or a few sheep on the common without anyone noticing. Everything that anyone did was noticed by someone in the village. Nor need we explain this latitude in terms of "theft", "fraud", or usurpation by the poor; or in terms of the tender paternalist sensibility of landowners. No doubt there are examples of both. But village regulation is often drawn by middle and small farmers, whose reputation for hardheadedness or even meanness is notorious. Yet even in

---

[1] Arthur Young, *A Six Months Tour through the North of England* (1771), i, p. 175.

hardheaded terms there are sound reasons for affording latitude in minor common rights. It is better that a labour force should remain resident and available for the heavy calls of hay and harvest and incidental calls for labour including the extensive women's service in hall, farmhouse and dairy. To afford to the poor subsistence rights, including firing and a cow for the pail, was at the same time a means of holding down poor rates.[1] And to these reasons may be added the reasons of custom and of neighbourhood. Some of those without land were the kin of the farmers; others long-standing neighbours, with skills — thatching, sheep-shearing, hurdle-making, building — involved in the continual exchange of services and favours (without any passage of money) which marks most peasant societies. It is even possible, without sentimentality, to suppose community norms, expectations and senses of neighbourhood obligation, which governed the actual usages of common; and such usages, practised "time out of mind", were fiercely held to be rights.[2]

But we must give way, at this point, before the expertise of the agrarian social historians. Common right is a subtle and sometimes complex vocabulary of usages, of claims to property, of hierarchy and of preferential access to resources, of the adjustment of needs, which, being *lex loci*, must be pursued in each locality and can never be taken as "typical". Alternative assertions of right could be fiercely divisive (for example, in the run-up to enclosure), not only between "rich" and "poor", but between small landholders and landless cottagers, or between cottagers with rights recognised at law and labourers without. I will note a wholly untypical case to conclude this section, not because it can stand for the general

[1] Arthur Young himself was of course a belated convert to the advantages of the poor's access to cow commons and cottage gardens, after the high price and dearth years of 1795 and 1800-1: see "An Inquiry into the Propriety of Applying Wastes to the Better Maintenance and Support of the Poor", *Annals of Agriculture*, xxxvi (1801), and also *General Report on Enclosures* (1808; reprinted 1971), esp. pp. 150-70. Snell, *op. cit.*, reviews this evidence, pp. 174-80.

[2] H. Homer, *An Essay upon the Inclosure of Common Fields* (Oxford, 1766), p. 23 speaks of the labourers' "immemorial custom" of enjoying privileges on the common.

case (if anything it is upside-down) but because it may illustrate the way in which various interests articulated their opposition through their claims to common right.

Atherstone in North Warwickshire at the start of the eighteenth century was a small market town. It was the site of a market, deriving from a grant in the time of Henry III, and also a horse fair (with annual races).[1] The town was situated in the midst of a large open field of about seven hundred acres, to which were added Outwoods (135 acres), and a cowpasture of fifteen acres. There are three major players in view in the first half of the century: the lord of the manor, who, in the 1730s, had only five acres in the open field: the landholders, most of whom held by copyhold tenure at the start of the century; and the cottagers, many of them also copyholders, who claimed right of common by prescription.

In 1719 disputes arose between the lord and the copyholders, on the familiar grounds of fines, herriots, and the soke rights of the mill, "to the continuall breach of Christian Amity and freindship". The customers accused the lord's steward of playing both ends against the middle in the Court Leet:

> The Steward. . . putts upon the Jury some poor men who are not Copyholders with whom he can doe what he pleaseth and allthough there is a Hall or Chamber on purpose to keep the Court in, yet the Court is kep in private places and the Jury kep in one Roome, and the Steward doth all his buissines privately in another, and by the antient Customes the Jury ought to be of the best Copyholders and all the buissines used to be done publickly in open Court.[2]

In 1735-8 attempts to enclose Atherstone open field were activated. The parties were now realigned. The copyholders in the field were now enfranchised (by purchase), the lord having been baulked in his efforts to screw up herriots and fines. Lands had been consolidated, and the moving spirit in the enclosure was the major freeholder, Mr Abraham

---

[1] I was first made aware of this case by J. M. Martin, "Warwickshire and the Parliamentary Enclosure Movement" (Birmingham Univ. Ph.D. thesis, 1966). Atherstone is also discussed in the same author's "Village Traders and the Emergence of a Proletariat in South Warwickshire, 1750-1851", *Agric. Hist. Rev.*, 37, pt. 2 (1984), pp. 179-88.

[2] Manorial papers in Warwicks. CRO, MR 9, undated but *c.* 1719.

Bracebridge (who, however, rented out his land and was "a tradesman & no great farmer").[1] He was now in alliance with the lord of the manor. The opposition was based on the cottagers, 160 of whom claimed rights of common by prescription for two horses and two beasts:

> Tho several of the antient grants & Charters relating to this Town have been search'd. . . the Cottagers have not been able to find there or in any other *writing* the original of this wright of common but can easily prove their wrights by prescription or parole evidence. The freeholders have the general words of wrights of common in their deeds. . .

> Note. Mr Bracebridge some years since, under pretence of his being engaged in a Law Suit relating to the town, obtained the Inspection & custody of all the town books & writings which he now refuses to deliver or shew to the townsmen.

But the town chest remained in the cottagers' possession.[2]

It was the large common field which was at issue, and the unusual feature of this case was that the cottagers claimed more rights to pasture over it than the landholders. They claimed right of common for two horses and two cows each, and the butchers claimed for ten sheep each,[3] for ten months in the year. (The stock was moved around different parts of the common field at different times, but was kept "plentifully supplied with Grass".)[4] The landholders were entitled to common at the rate of four horses and eight cows and twenty sheep per yardland, of which there were $24\frac{1}{4}$ in the open field. By one rough computation, we get:

[1] The Bracebridge family was involved in sugar-refining, banking and jewellery, and Abraham Bracebridge inherited a small estate in Atherstone in 1695. He and his son, Walter, were actively buying up lands in the open field between that time and the 1730s. "The Case of Atherstone concerning Inclosure of the Com. Fields as drawn by Mr. Baxter & Others in January 1738-9", in Warwicks. CRO, Compton Bracebridge MS, HR/35/25; various papers in Warwicks. CRO, MR 9; M. J. Kingman, "Landlord versus Community: the Bracebridge Family and the Enclosure of Atherstone Open Fields", *Warwickshire History*, vii, 4 (1988-9).

[2] Warwicks. CRO, HR/35/25.

[3] A married butcher was allowed ten sheep, a bachelor only five. Sheep placed on the common must be killed before new ones were added. See e.g. "Orders, Bylaws and Pains made by the Jury. . . for the Manor of Atherstone", 3 October 1745, in Warwicks. CRO, L 2/89.

[4] See Martin, "Village Traders", p. 183.

Landholders sheep	500	
Lord of the manor's sheep	20)	
Landholders' beasts	192)	= 74 gates
Landholders' horses	96)	
	808	
Cottiers' beasts	320)	
Cottiers' horses	320)	= 326 gates
Butchers' sheep	60)	
	700	

There were only six owners of the twenty-four yardlands in the open field, and of these Bracebridge owned nearly eighteen. On the side of the "cottiers" there were 160 who claimed (as "inhabitants", by prescription) "cottagers" rights.[1]

Bracebridge, together with the lord of the manor, the lay tithe-owner, and several landholders, attempted first to enclose the open fields "by agreement", without the assent of the cottagers. When this proved to be more than law would allow, several drafts of enclosure by parliamentary Act were drawn, and the small market town became the scene of covert negotiations and then of furious controversy.[2] Bracebridge offered to the cottagers eighty acres (subsequently raised to one hundred acres) in compensation for the loss of grazing rights over the whole field. One hundred and twenty cottagers and one or two small landholders petitioned against enclosure, on the grounds that it would lessen the value of their houses, diminish population, increase the poor, ruin the market and "lay a fondation for quarrells & contentions about the cottagers rights. . . & at the same time only agrandise & enrich one particular person. . .".[3]

It is evident that the term "cottager" covers several different categories of inhabitant. A few may have been

[1] The figures come from "The Case of Atherstone", drawn by opponents of enclosure, and from a paper drawn by supporters of enclosure in Warwicks. CRO, HR/35/7. There are variations in the count.

[2] It was alleged that a gentleman (Bracebridge?) had been threatened and was obliged to keep a guard on himself and his family. Opponents of enclosure were quick to declare that "we hate Mobs and Mobbish doings as much as he doth": Warwicks. CRO, HR/35/12.

[3] "The Case of Atherstone".

professional persons (from amng whom an eloquent pamphleteer may have come), others shopkeepers, tradesmen, inn-keepers, and butchers (for whom the extensive common rights were a convenience). Another manuscript protest — these sheets were copied in a clear hand and were obviously circulated around the town — suggests that tradesmen had been buying houses in Atherstone because of these rights. The tradesmen "of a lower rank" (it was argued) needed horses for their business, fetching coals, hiring out, or in connection with the local trade in tammy-weaving and felt-making. Other trades which might need horses included "smiths, carpenters, coopers, masons, joyners, wheelwrights".[1] An annotated list of 123 Atherstone copyholders (who may well be the "cottiers" in question) shows among them "the Toyshop", two inn-keepers, and a wheelwright, gardener, shoemaker, bricklayer, weaver, maltster, retired butler, plumber, barber, exciseman and carpenter.[2]

Other cottagers were small peasant farmers, but it seems that a large group were labourers without stock and without other resources. They therefore did not and could not exercise their grazing rights — although in theory the 160 cottiers had rights to graze 320 horses, in fact (the enclosers argued) only eighty horses were grazed, and the land would not carry more.[3] But those cottagers and open field farmers who could graze stock had passed a by-law in the Court Leet to prevent the cottagers who had no stock from letting their gates on the common to others. Although a little "covert" letting still went on, the right was now technically valueless to them, and this was a grievance which Bracebridge and the enclosers tried to exploit. They tried to buy over the poor cottiers by offering to each 20s. per annum compensation for the loss of rights which they could not use. If this attractive bribe could have brought enough poor cottagers to the side of enclosure, then an Act might pass through parliament.

This offer stimulated a reply from the most eloquent of the opposing pamphleteers. "I cannot but observe," he remarked

[1] "Some of the Grievances that will result from the Inclosure of the Fields of Atherstone", Warwicks. CRO, HR/35/10.

[2] List of copyholders, n.d., revised and annotated, Warwicks. CRO, HR/35/39.

[3] Warwicks. CRO, HR/35/7.

with heavy sarcasm, "how tender these Gentlemen now seem to be of the rights of the Poor". Bracebridge "seems to be courting the lower and meaner sort and playing them against those in better circumstances. . . Gentlemen become levellers to obtain their own ends". And he reflected upon the historic origin and present function of commons:

> When these Commons in the fields were allotted to the use of the cottagers it was not meant what we call paupers, for in that age their was no such, but different degrees of men superiour and inferiour occupying the Cottages, but it was more the design to prevent poor, or at least to be a security for those whom fortune shou'd frown on, to have recourse for relief, that all might be employ'd in some way or other.

Even if the poor cottagers were unable to buy stock, common usages were intrinsic to their economy:

> By the Harvest work, the men will get 6s p.w. and beer, the women will get 2s till corn harvest then 3s p.w. . . The gleaning of the fields computed 15s a family in a season. . .

Gleaning was —

> an Injury to no man, although those who make use of this advantage accruing to the Inferior from the beginning of the Harvest being known in the World are at this day by some as Mr [?] call'd thieves. I cannot see in what more than robbing the Fowls of the Air.

To this might be added cutting firewood in the Outwoods, both for use and for sale — 6s. or 8s. per week "hath been known" to be gained by families from this. The men could find occasional labour in husbandry, with the muck cart, trenching and threshing in winter. And this led on to a detailed estimate:

	£ s d
Inferiour Men not stocking their Commons, by their Work by a near Computation including their beer at 5s per week each, they get some weeks more, some less, this being a Medium. . .	13 00 00
Women by their Harvest work, weeding, clotting, Hay Harvest, Reaping which we will allow to employ them Ten Weeks at 2.6d p week	01 05 00
Admitting they have no other work or spining &c they will get by fetching wood 1s 6d p.w.	03 03 00
Allow each Cottager one Boy or Girl able to do anything. . . they will get as much as the Mother	04 03 00

Each Family by their Gleaning or Pikeing in
the Season   00 15 00
                                              ————
                                              22 06 00

All this does not take into account
spinning and carding.[1]

This forms (the pamphleteer argued) "the Oeconomy of
Life for these useful and inferiour people". They can support
themselves and live without the aid of "people moving in a
superiour sphere, better than the Superiour can without the
Inferiour". Since they are "essentially necessary" they should
be "indulg'd so far and after the best manner their circumstances will allow; not to be deem'd thieves & trick'd out of
their and their Posterity's rights". Enclosure not only would
deprive the poor cottager of maintenance, but it would discourage him from trying to gain a competency, and would
encourage indolence. The commons right was "a sure
foundation whereon he may work, and room for him to
advance his fortune as he gets able to buy stock". For these
reasons the pamphleteer urged the poor cottagers not to
surrender their (latent) rights:

> In case of Inclosure, the Inferiour will be made slaves and oblig'd for
> what little work will be found to work for what wages those Mercenaries
> who at present call them Thieves will please to give them.

As for the 20s. per annum offered in compensation, this
money will "like the weekly pay be piss'd against the Wall &
the Families no better. . .".

It seems that very few of the cottagers were persuaded to
accept this 20s. bribe. Nor were those who exercised their
grazing rights impressed. They perhaps suspected that the
hundred acres compensation offered would be the poorest
land in the parish, and they had good reason.[2] The

[1] Untitled paper ("We have before us a Paper entitled the Inclosure
Vindicated", etc.); the arithmetic seems to be faulty: Warwicks. CRO,
HR/35/15. See also HR/35/14. "Clotting" was breaking up clods with a
wooden mallet; "piking" could be gleaning, or cleaning the edges of a
harvest field: see Joseph Wright, *English Dialect Dictionary.*
[2] A clause drafted for the Act (Warwicks. CRO, HR/35/33) shows that
the proposed commons were "very much over run with Gorse Hollies &
Thorns and Briers and. . . other parts of it grow Mossey".

proposed Act was withdrawn. Agreement as to enclosure was reached with a majority of the cottagers of a subsequent generation, in 1764, and a letter survives in which a surveyor confided in Bracebridge's grandson details of the hundred acres recommended to be set aside for the cottagers:

> We fixt upon 2 parcels of land which I am sure fourscore Acres is the worst in the fields but as it must be in one piece or two it cannot be done without laying to it about 20 acres [of] as good land as is on the Lower flat.

The surveyor was busy with plans to lay together "Fludgate Nuke" and "Sorry Midsummer", but alas not every bog and quicksand could be included.[1]

The case of Atherstone is not, of course, characteristic of the unenclosed village, any more than was neighbouring Sutton Coldfield where attempts to enclose were rebuffed, to an output of broadsides and songs about "the people's charter'd rights" in 1778, and delayed again in 1805 in part by the opposition of the vicar, John Riland, on the grounds that the town's charter granted rights to —

> *inhabitants, householders*, that is Cottagers, Day Labourers, Shop-keepers, and other little Housekeepers, not Freeholders. The Charter means those, so do I. . .
> "I mean the great body of all lower classes of the parish, whose consent has not been obtain'd."[2]

Both Atherstone and Sutton Coldfield claimed their rights and privileges by prescription, from charter and "wright of common", as if the act of writing carried some mysterious power. Villagers in the fenlands in the seventeenth century, in a tithe dispute, paraded "black boxes with writinges with great seales. . . cominge, as they say, from the kinge. . ." In Haxey church a fourteenth-century deed in which the lord, John de Mowbray, pledged to preserve the commons from further improvement was kept in an iron-bound chest (to which the chief freeholders held keys); the chest stood under a window, wherein (icon-like) "was the portraiture of Mowbray set in ancient glass, holding in his hand a writing

[1] Thomas Merler to Bracebridge, 1764, Warwicks. CRO, HR/35.
[2] Rev. W. K. Riland Bedford, *Three Hundred Years of a Family Living, being a History of the Rilands of Sutton Coldfield* (Birmingham, 1889), pp. 131-3.

which was commonly reputed to be an emblem of the deed".[1]

We have seen the role of the church in other cases (above pp. 98-100), and since so much enclosure took place by agreement, or was enrolled in Chancery Decrees, and since it often took a form in which the lord or substantial freeholders surrendered their rights over common and waste in return for licence to enclose their own lands, the memory of these decisions was indeed a source of power.[2] Court books could be "lost" or access to them denied. Oral traditions as to rights might be founded upon some long-forgotten decree. As late as 1880 in a dispute over Wigley Common, near the New Forest, a meeting of the tenants discussed an "old paper" which declared their rights. A copyholder was found to have a heavy box with three locks in his possession, which was known by the tenants as "the monster". Within the box was found an exemplification, under the Great Seal, of a decree in Chancery of 1591, establishing the copyholders' customs. There was subsequently found in the court rolls of the manor some two hundred years later (1783) an order of the homage placing the decree in the custody of three tenants, who each had a key to a lock on the box. "The monster" was, no doubt, a corruption of the Latin *monstravi*. All that the owner recollected of the box was that his grandfather had brought it home after his admission as a tenant, saying: "See, I have brought home the monster!".[3]

V

It was always a problem to explain the commons within capitalist categories. There was something uncomfortable about them. Their very existence prompted questions about the origin of property and about historical title to land.

In the sixteenth and seventeenth centuries landowners had asserted their titles in land against the prerogative of the king,

[1] C. Holmes, "Drainers and Fenmen" in A. Fletcher and J. Stevenson (eds.), *Order and Disorder in Early Modern England* (Cambridge, 1985), pp. 192-3. See also Jack Goody, *The Logic of Writing and the Organization of Society* (Cambridge, 1986), pp. 163-5.

[2] See J. A. Yelling, *Common Field and Enclosure in England, 1450-1850* (1977), ch. 5, "Piecemeal and Partial Enclosures".

[3] Eversley, *op. cit.*, pp. 125-8.

and copyholders had asserted their titles and customs against their lords. They therefore had discarded theories of the origin to title in divine right. Yet if they fell back upon Hobbesian violence or on the right of conquest, how could they reply to the telling counter-argument of the Norman Yoke? When Locke sat down to offer an answer, all this was stewing around in his mind. In his First Treatise he dismissed notions of title by succession from Father Adam or from the donation of God. In the Second Treatise his chapter on property commences with an extended metaphor of common right usage. God granted the world to "mankind in common", and the fruits and beasts "are produced by the spontaneous hand of nature". But the common was seen as a negative, not a positive community: it belonged to nobody and was open to any taker.[1] Locke took as a paradigm of the origin of property the mixing of labour (which was man's only original "property", in himself and in his own hands) with the common:

> Whatsoever, then, he removes out of the state that nature hath provided and left it in, he hath mixed his labour with. . . and thereby makes it his property.

"It hath by this labour something annexed to it that excludes the common right of other men":

> Thus the grass my horse has bit, the turfs my servant has cut, and the ore I have dug in any place where I have a right to them in common with others, become my property. . .

It is not clear that Locke has overcome all difficulties — why are the turfs to be his, and not his servant's or, indeed, his horse's? Legal decisions in the eighteenth century introduced arguments from "labour" in terms of the general reasons of "improvement". More often they fell back in the question of custom or *lex loci* upon the legal fiction that customary usages must have been founded upon some original grant, from persons unknown, lost in the mists of antiquity. The law pretended that, somewhere in the year dot, the commons were granted by benevolent Saxon or Norman landowners, so that uses were less of right than by

---

[1] See Istvan Hont and Michael Ignatieff (eds.), *Wealth and Virtue* (Cambridge, 1983), p. 36.

grace. The fiction was purely ideological: it guarded against the danger that use-rights might be seen as inherent in the users, in which case the successors of Levellers or Diggers might arise and plead their original title.

Locke's property theory was written in terms which two scholars have sternly described as an English "vernacular", as against the stricter European tradition of natural jurisprudence. He "did not follow Grotius's and Pufendorf's restriction of the use of the term 'property' to its modern meaning of exclusive and absolute right of dominion".[1] In the flexible traditions of the English common law the meanings of property remained various — an absolute right, a coincident use-right, a claim to preference, a man's property in his own life or privileges. Undoubtedly C. B. Macpherson was right to show the increasingly absolute definition of property in the seventeenth century, and the triumph of the claim to the "virtually unlimited and saleable rights *to* things" in the eighteenth.[2] This process was not, perhaps, as univocal as Professor Macpherson proposed, and was, indeed, two-sided. For the landowners, landed property was "increasingly becoming subsumed to contract, that is. . . taking on the qualities and functions of capital", through the liquidity of mortgages and the complex forms of marriage settlements, trusts, entail etc. "Yet at the same time, in the name of absolute individual property, the common and use rights of the 'lower orders' were eroded."[3]

Sir William Blackstone had too precise a mind to linger long in speculations, although he endorsed, in passing, the Lockeian view that property in land allows an origin in which in prehistoric times the land "belonged generally to everybody, but particularly to nobody". But his concern was to define the rights to property as he now found them to be justified at law. And he asserted the right of property (and,

[1] *Ibid.*, p. 35.
[2] C. B. Macpherson, "Capitalism and the Changing Concept of Property", in E. Kamenka and R. S. Neate (eds.), *Feudalism, Capitalism and Beyond* (1975).
[3] See the overview by G. R. Rubin and David Sugarman (eds.), *Law, Economy and Society* (Abingdon, 1984), esp. pp. 23-42. Also P. S. Atiyah, *The Rise and Fall of Freedom of Contract* (Oxford, 1979), pp. 85-90.

in the case of land, the control of physical space) to be
exclusive and unqualified:

> . . . that sole and despotic dominion which one man claims and exercises
> over the external things of the world, in total exclusion of the right of
> any other individual in the universe. [1]

This bleak and absolutist definition he then (of course) did go
on to qualify. His account of customary rights and copyhold
is scrupulous, and on some matters (such as gleaning) he
leaned to a liberal view. Yet these customs also were
considered less as usages than as properties annexed to
things. Through the ill-management of history these things
were muddled up amongst each other on the land, and it was
the business of law to sort each exclusive property out.

Political economy aided and abetted the law. For Adam
Smith "property was either 'perfect' and absolute or it was
meaningless", [2] and it was the function of government to
protect property from the indignation of the poor. As he
wrote in *The Wealth of Nations* (1776),

> It is only under the shelter of the civil magistrate that the owner of that
> valuable property, which is acquired by the labour of many years, or
> perhaps of many successive generations, can sleep a single night in
> security.

Somehow the language summons to mind the substantial
property, the settled estate, the freehold, while the secure
sleep of commoners falls out of view. (After his change-of-
heart, Arthur Young reported that poor commoners in a
Cambridgeshire village regarded the approach of inclosure
"with a sort of terror".) [3] It was Adam Smith's achievement
to shift "the terms of analysis from a language of rights to a
language of markets", in a "constitutive move in the making
of classical political economy". [4]

By the 1780s both law and political economy regarded co-
existent properties in the same land with extreme impatience.

[1] Blackstone, *op. cit.*, ii, pp. 2, 8.
[2] Hont and Ignatieff, *op. cit.*, p. 25.
[3] *Annals of Agriculture*, xlii (1804), p. 497, describing Morden
Guildon, then under enclosure, where the cottagers had been in the habit of
keeping cows, wintering them in the farmers' yards at 6d. per week, in
summer leading them on balks, etc.
[4] Hont and Ignatieff, *op. cit.*, pp. 24-6.

We recall Lord Loughborough's judgement that "the nature of property. . . imports exclusive enjoyment" (above p. 139). And this was seconded by the immoderate ideological zeal of the propagandists of enclosure. Monotonously, in pamphlet, in the *Annals of Agriculture* and in agricultural surveys, the same impatient tone comes through. Opponents of Lincolnshire fenland enclosure wish to "live at large, and prey, like pikes, upon one another", or these commoners are "Buccaneers" who "sally out, and drive, or drown or steal, just as suits them".[1] "The appropriation of the forests", Vancouver remarked in the *General View of the Agriculture of Hampshire* (1810),

> Would. . . be the means of producing a number of additional useful hands for agricultural employment, by gradually cutting up and annihilating that nest and conservatory of sloth, idleness and misery, which is uniformly to be witnessed in the vicinity of all commons, waste lands and forests. . .

And the surveyor expressed his earnest wish that "old as he now is, he yet may live to see the day when every species of intercommonable and forest right may be extinguished". The vocabulary — "prey", "buccaneers", "cutting up and annihilating" — reveals a mind-set impervious to alternative definitions; and, as the high tide of enclosure coincided with the political polarisation of the 1790s, so arguments of property and improvement are joined to arguments of class discipline. Parliament and law imposed capitalist definitions to exclusive property in land.

If parliamentarians, landowners, judges and many enclosure commissioners did gross natural injustices in enclosures I do not mean that they were clearly aware of what they were doing. They observed the rules which they themselves had made. They were so profoundly imbued with preconceptions which translated the usages of the poor into the property-rights of the landowners that they really found it difficult to view the matter in any other way. (Although — it is important to note — there were always contrary voices, even among their own ranks.) What may give to this matter a

---

[1] W. Pennington, *Reflections on the various Advantages resulting from the Draining, Inclosing and Allotting of Large Commons and Common Fields* (1769), pp. 32, 37.

greater significance is that this law and this mind-set were not confined in place or in time. The concept of exclusive property in land, as a norm to which other practices must be adjusted, was now extending across the whole globe, like a coinage reducing all things to a common measure.

The concept was carried across the Atlantic, to the Indian sub-continent, and into the South Pacific, by British colonists, administrators, and lawyers, who, while not un-aware of the force of local customs and land systems, struggled to construe these within their own measure of property. It is an interesting inversion of the expected sequence of reciprocity between "social being" and "social consciousness" which, in the Marxist tradition, used to be rehearsed in terms of "basis and superstructure". To be sure, capitalist notations of property rights arose out of the long material processes of agrarian change, as land use became loosed from subsistence imperatives and the land was laid open to the market. But now these concepts and this law (or *lex loci* of that part called England of a European island) were transported and imposed upon distant economies in various phases of evolution. Now it was law (or "super-structure") which became the instrument of reorganising (or disorganising) alien agrarian modes of production and, on occasion, for revolutionising the material base.

A global ecological history might be written, one central episode of which turned upon the mis-match between English and alien notions of property in land and the imperialist essays in translation. Even within the main island of Britain, successive emigrations and clearances from the Scottish Highlands were testimony to the decisions of a law which afforded no shelter to a population evicted from lands which they had supposed to be communally owned, from time out of mind, by their clans. But the law could take no cognisance of such a communal personality. Nor could its categories match the communal usages of hunter-gatherer peoples. Locke had ruminated, in his chapter on property, on "the wild Indian. . . who knows no enclosure, and is still a tenant in common". This Indian served as a paradigm for an original state before property became individuated and secure: "In the beginning all the world was America". Locke decided that the American Indian was poor "for want of improving" the land by labour. Since labour (and improvement) constituted the right to property, this made it the more easy for Europeans to dispossess the Indians of their hunting grounds. The Puritan colonists were ready to moralise their appropriation of Indian lands by reference to God's commands, in *Genesis* 1, 28, to "replenish the earth, and subdue it".[1]

Hunting, fishing, and even planting some unfenced patches of corn and squash clearly fell far short of "subduing" the earth. (In any case, the work was left to the women.) It could not be said to be "improvement" and therefore its claim to establish rights of property was slender. The same improving mind-set, whether in Old England or in New, found reprehensible the lack of useful productive labour, whether on the ill-governed forest or waste or in the Indians' hunting grounds. In the English cottager and "the wild Indian" alike there was seen a degrading cultural submission to a picaresque, desultory or vagrant mode of livelihood. "Forests and great Commons", John Bellers wrote, "make the Poor that are upon them too much like the *Indians*. . .". Commons were "a hindrance to Industry, and. . . Nurseries of Idleness and Insolence".[2] Security of property is complete only when commons come to an end.

The same notions of property-right accompanied the earliest British colonists in the South Pacific. In 1770 Cook claimed the east coast of New South Wales for the Crown, not because it was empty of aborigines but because "we never saw one inch of cultivated land in the whole country". Title could therefore rest on "discovery", or *vacuum domicilium*. Title could not be claimed so easily in New Zealand lands, in which both settlement and cultivation was so evident. The trouble was that property rights among the Maori were insufficiently individuated and absolute. James Busby, the British Resident, allowed in 1835 that —

---

[1] An excellent study which brings legal and ecological themes together is William Cronon, *Changes in the Land: Indians, Colonists and the Ecology of New England* (New York, 1983). I am at work on a study of these issues, in relation to the Mohegans of Connecticut, which I hope to conclude shortly.

[2] A. Ruth Fry, *John Bellers, 1654-1725* (1935), p. 128.

As far as has been ascertained every acre of land in this country is appropriated among the different tribes; and every individual in the tribe has a distinct interest in the property; although his possession may not always be separately defined.[1]

As in New England, setting land loose onto the market was complicated by communal claims upon property. In comparison with their American forerunners, the Maoris were fortunate in that by the time of colonisation the procedures under which the "Pakeha" settlers appropriated land were a little more scrupulous. The Maoris were also numerous and formidable at war. The Treaty of Waitangi (1840) was the most serious attempt made to match capitalist and communal notions of property in land, and the complexity of this task is witnessed by the fact that arguments as to the treaty's interpretation occupy a central place in New Zealand's political life to this day.

But while it was possible for the colonial power to draw up treaties with native nations or tribes (as was done also in many North American cases), it was a different matter when rights to property in land came to be cashed in law. How could land be loosed for the market when even a *hupa*, or sub-tribe, might share among hundreds of persons communal rights in land? A solution must either be political and sociological or it must be legal. As to the first, it was necessary to bring about —

The detribalization of the Natives — to destroy, if it were possible, the principle of communism which ran through the whole of their institutions. . . and which stood as a barrier in the way of all attempts to amalgamate the Native race into our own social and political system.[2]

As to the second, New Zealand law attempted to deal with it under the Native Land Act of 1865 whose aim was to assimilate native rights to land "as nearly as possible to the ownership of land according to British law". Since British law could never recognise a communist legal personality, section 23 of the Act ordered that communal rights could not

[1] Claudia Orange, *The Treaty of Waitangi* (Wellington, 1987), p. 38.
[2] Henry Sewell in *New Zealand Parliamentary Debates*, 9 (1870), p. 361: see Keith Sorrenson, "Maori and Pakeha", in W. H. Oliver (ed.), *The Oxford History of New Zealand* (Oxford, 1981), p. 189.

be vested in more than ten persons. A Maori witness testified: "When the Crown agent was ordered, the Court told us to go outside to arrange whose names should be in. We went outside — perhaps one hundred of us. We picked those who were to be in the grant." This fraudulent device was then pleaded as "according to Maori custom".[1]

The notion of absolute property in land which triumphed in England in the late eighteenth century had both a legal and a political aspect. Property in land required a landowner, improving the land required labour, and therefore subduing the earth required also subduing the labouring poor. As Lord Goderich, the Colonial Secretary, remarked in 1831 (with reference to Upper Canada):

> Without some division of labour, without a class of persons willing to work for wages, how can society be prevented from falling into a state of almost primitive rudeness, and how are the comforts and refinements of civilized life to be procured?[2]

Hence property-plus-improvement required the model of the local property-owner in whose nexus were combined economic, social, and perhaps judicial authority over his labourers, on the model of the English country gentleman (and perhaps JP).

The most ambitious projects to transpose both the law of property and the sociological model of a landowner into an alien context were the succession of land settlements imposed by British administrators upon India. The earliest of these — the Permanent Settlement of Bengal — offers a paradigm of the mind-set which has been my theme. Although the Settlement finally took form in the proclamation of Lord Cornwallis, the Governor General (22 March 1793), it had, as Ranajit Guha has shown, a long prehistory.[3] Proposals of

---

[1] See D. Williams, "The Recognition of 'Native Custom' in Tanganyika and New Zealand — Legal Pluralism or Monocultural Imposition?" in Sack and Minchin (eds.), *Legal Pluralism* (Canberra Law Workshop, VII, ANV, 1985), pp. 139-54: a lucid and helpful study.

[2] Cited by Bryan D. Palmer, in "Social Formation and Class Formation in North America, 1800-1900", *Proletarianization and Family History* (1984).

[3] In the next page or two I have drawn heavily upon Ranajit Guha, *A Rule of Property for Bengal* (Paris, 1963), and also R. B. Ramsbotham, *Studies in the Land Revenue: History of Bengal 1769-87* (Oxford, 1926).

mercantilist, physiocrat and of Smithian political economists alike all agreed in the need to establish security of property, and all converged upon a solution which would vest these permanent property rights in the zemindars. Alexander Dow, the author of *The History of Hindostan* (1768) doubted the supposed zemindary title to property-rights. Land (in his view) was owned by the "Crown" or Moghul emperor, and while granted to the zemindars — who in effect were civil and administrative officers of the empire and collectors and guarantors of revenue — it could not be said to be owned, absolutely and exclusively, by them. In theory at least the grant could be revoked. Nevertheless Dow favoured the settlement of the land upon the zemindars, as an alternative to the corrupt and oppressive system of "farming" out the revenues (which many observers believed had contributed to the terrible famine of 1770). "An established idea of property is the source of all industry among individuals, and, of course, the foundation of public prosperity."

This argument derived title to land from the real or presumed grant from the Moghul power to the East India Company, along with the revenues attached to the land. Philip Francis — perhaps because he felt that this title was insecure — disputed the "erroneous opinion" that in the Moghul empire the governing power had been proprietor of the soil. He preferred to exalt zemindary proprietary rights, and cited as proof "the inheritable quality of the lands". In this he mistook the heritable character of zemindary *office* — to manage the lands and collect their revenue — for the *ownership* of the lands. And if Francis had reflected there were plenty of examples of heritable rights and claims over land, which fell far short of absolute property, acknowledged in English law: the most common being copyhold.

One need not be a specialist in the complexities of South Asian agrarian systems to see that these disputants were trying to compress their features into a modernising — or "improving" — English mask. With the English landowner and JP in his mind, Francis wrote that "zemindars are or ought to be the instruments of government in almost every branch of the civil administration". He even compared the zemindar to the Lord of the Manor. Once a Bengal gentry had been established, then the rest of the desired sociological model could hang from that — "those intermediate gradations of rank, authority and responsibility, by which all great civil societies are held together", and formed into "successive ranks of subordination".[1] This also was a part of the accepted rhetoric of all British parties. Amongst these voices, only that of Warren Hastings and his close circle — the very people whom the improvers indicted as bandits and parasites enriching themselves by farming out the Company's revenues — suggested settling the land upon the ryots, the actual cultivators. It is probable that Hastings was making a debating-point and was not serious.

Charles Cornwallis took up his duties in Bengal just before the French Revolution. It would be interesting to know in what ways he had assembled his notions as to what was proper to the ownership of land. His father had made a fortunate marriage into the Townshend-Walpole clan from whom, no doubt, young Charles had learned not only about turnips but about the patrician arrogation of superordinate rights. A short tenure of office as Chief Justice in Eyre south of the Trent may have taught him to abhor indistinct forest usages. His service in the American Wars will have given him adequate opportunity to meditate on the difference between improved and unimproved lands. "Improvement was a key word which frequently occurred in his minutes and correspondence."[2] In intervals from service his seat was at Culford in Suffolk. Two miles away was Timworth, where, in 1787 — the year after Cornwallis sailed for Bengal — Mary Houghton's flagrant contempt of property-rights occasioned the celebrated judgement against gleaning. Peter King has examined the Cornwallis estate papers, and he has established that the offending Houghtons were indeed within the Cornwallis lands and had given offence to his steward or estate manager, being petty proprietors of a cottage with common rights who had been able to block a cherished plan of enclosure and reorganisation on the Cornwallis lands. It is possible that this could have been the reason for the selection

---

[1] *Ibid.*, pp. 105-22. Philip Francis's plan (which was rejected) was presented in 1776, the same year as the publication of *The Wealth of Nations.*

[2] *Ibid.*, p. 172.

of Mary Houghton for prosecution for gleaning.[1]

Dr King has discovered no reference to the ferocious Mary Houghton in Cornwallis's surviving correspondence. But we need not suppose that the Governor General of Bengal followed every detail of rationalisation on his distant Suffolk estate. He was content to leave mundane decisions to his brother, the bishop of Lichfield. No doubt the brothers shared the same Whiggish, improving outlook. Professor Guha has shown one intellectual origin of the Permanent Settlement in physiocratic thought, but the less theoretical praxis of the Whig patricians was of equal significance.[2] As a historian of my father's generation — in point of fact, my own father — noted: "The same era that saw the English peasant expropriated from his common lands saw the Bengal peasant made a parasite in his own country",[3] and this was done by the same mind-set, the same legal dicta of absolute property-right, and sometimes by the same men.

The immediate motive of the Permanent Settlement was convenience in collecting the revenue and the need to check the abuses of collection. But behind this lay a Whiggish model of class relations, in which — as Locke had written — "subduing or cultivating the earth, and having dominion, we see are joined together". Dominion gave security to exclusive rights in property, and landed property was the proper station not only for planting turnips but also for planting

[1] I first suggested a connection between the Mary Houghton case at Timworth and the Cornwallis estates at Culford when I lectured at an Open Meeting of the Past and Present Society on "Law, Use-Rights and Property in Land" in March 1986. This was based on guesswork only. Dr Peter King has now established that there was such a connection, and his thorough examination of "The Origins of the Gleaning Judgement of 1788" is forthcoming.

[2] James Mill in *The History of British India* (1817) voiced the utilitarian reaction when he referred to Cornwallis's "aristocratical prejudices". It is not clear why Dr Guha (*op. cit.*, pp. 170-1) should reprove this as "exaggerated language". It is surely a correct description?

[3] Edward J. Thompson, *The Life of Charles, Lord Metcalfe* (1937), p. 268. "The Permanent Settlement was made in the face of substantial awareness of the facts, in order to clamp down everlasting quietness on these matters of revenue and land possession rights; and it was made by men who could not conceive any better arrangement than that under which England's innumerable Tolpuddles enjoyed such happiness".

political interest. Sir Henry Strachey wrote in 1802 that we
are anxious to secure the "assistance of the men of property
and influence in preserving the peace throughout the
country", but such rights of property should be invested
"only in estates of a certain extent":

> There are no gentlemen, in whose honour and probity, in whose spirit
> and activity, government can repose confidence. There exists not
> between the common people and the rulers, a middle order, who
> respect their rulers, or are by them respected; who. . . could. . . exert
> themselves heartily and effectually, each in his own sphere, for the
> public good. Such a set of men in the society, is here unknown.[1]

The intention of the Permanent Settlement was to establish
a Whig gentry, and the role was given to the greater zemindars, "for preserving order in civil society".[2] The measure
"was effected to naturalise the landed institutions of England
among the natives of Bengal".[3] It is inadequate to describe
the zemindars' true status as that of "hereditary rent-
collectors". Even this implies that some direct translation is
possible between two radically incompatible systems of landholding. There simply was no way of converting the practices
and customs of Bengal and Bihar or Orissa into a common
specie to be exchanged with English practice and common
law. As Sir William Hunter was later to write:

> My own investigations point to an infinite gradation in the rights of the
> various classes interested in the land. In some districts the landholder
> was almost independent of the Mussulman Viceroy. . . in others he was
> only a bailiff appointed to receive the rents. In some districts, again,
> peasant rights were acknowledged, and the old communal system
> survived as a distinct influence; in others the cultivators were mere serfs.
> This is the secret of the contradictory objections which were urged
> against Lord Cornwallis' interpretation of the land-law. . . Those
> collectors who had to deal with districts in which the landholders were
> the real owners of the soil, complained that the Permanent Settlement
> had stripped them of their rights and ruined them; while those who had

[1] *Fifth Report from the Select Committee of the House of Commons
on the Affairs of the East India Company* (1812), ed. W. K. Firminger
(Calcutta, 1917), ii, pp. 609-10.
[2] Cornwallis, cited in Eric Stokes, *The English Utilitarians and India*
(Oxford, 1959), p. 5.
[3] Sir Richard Temple, cited in Edward J. Thompson and G. T.
Garratt, *Rise and Fulfilment of British Rule in India* (1935), p. 191.

derived their experience from parts of the country in which the
Mussulman system had uprooted the ancient houses, objected that Lord
Cornwallis had sacrificed the claims of the Government and the rights
of the people to elevate a parcel of tax-gatherers and land-stewards into
a sham gentry.[1]

This referred to rural Bengal. When Hunter came to
consider the subsequent settlement of Orissa (1804),[2] his
account was even more nuanced. Taking as his theme
"Inchoate Proprietory Rights", he distinguished more clearly
between a right of "ownership" vested under the Hindu
dynasties in the prince, and a right of "occupancy" vested in
the village community or in the cultivators. In between there
was a complex hierarchy of tax collectors, land stewards,
accountants, down to village heads, whose status was
consolidated for the convenience of Moghul revenue and
rûle:

> A long chain of intermediate holders grew up between the Ruling Power
> which had the abstract ownership and the Cultivator who enjoyed the
> actual occupancy. Thus the superior Landholder (*zamindar*) received
> the rent from a subordinate Tenure-holder (*taluqdar*), who gathered it
> from the Village Heads, who often collected it by means of. . . Village
> Accountants, who levied it from the individual husbandmen. Each of
> these had his own separate set of proprietory rights. . . Their rights,
> from the highest to the lowest, consisted in a title to finger the land-tax
> and pass it on.[3]

But even this account (Hunter warned) was "clearer and
more systematic" than his evidence warranted, "for English
words referring to landed rights have acquired a fixity and
precision which they could not possess during a period of
inchoate growth". What the Permanent Settlement in Orissa
attempted to do (following upon the example of Bengal) was
to erect the zemindar's "*quasi*-hereditary, *quasi*-transferable
office of managing the land and transmitting the land-
revenue, into a full proprietary tenure". Yet this title to
property remained in some sense "abstract", since even

[1] W. W. Hunter, *The Annals of Rural Bengal* (1883), pp. 373-4.
[2] W. W. Hunter, *Orissa* (Calcutta, 1872), "being the second volume of
the *Annals of Rural Bengal*", notably ch. 9. The settlement of Orissa was
undertaken more scrupulously than that of Bengal, and was procrastinated
from 1804 to 1815 to 1836 to 1866 (p. 257).
[3] *Ibid.*, pp. 214, 221-7.

"ownership" could not give to the new "owners" possession
or occupancy of the land "as these belonged for the most part
to the actual cultivators".[1] In all the debates of the 1770s to
1790s, the Whiggish British mind had largely passed over
without consideration the rights of the *ryots* or real
possessors of the land.[2] British administrators "defined and
consolidated the title of the Landholders, and left the rights
of the Cultivators unascertained. The former received a
legislative *status*; the latter did not".[3]

Sir Charles Metcalfe saw the Permanent Settlement of
Bengal as "the most sweeping act of oppression ever
committed in any country, by which the whole landed
property of the country had been transferred from the class
of people entitled to it, to a set of Baboos, who have made
their wealth by bribery and corruption". Lord Cornwallis (he
said) was celebrated as "the great creator of private property
in land in India". "I should say. . . that he was the creator of
private property in the State revenue, and the great destroyer
of private property in India, destroying hundreds of
thousands of proprietors for every one that he gratuitiously
created. . ."[4]

Metcalfe argued that

> The real Proprietors of the Land are generally Individuals of the Village
> Communities who are also, for the most part, the natural occupiers and
> cultivators of the Land.

The injustice had been done by those who "wishing to
advocate the rights of private property, applied English ideas
and systems to India", and "classed the cultivators of India,
the poor but lawful hereditary possessors of the land, with
the labourers of England".[5] What Metcalfe did not see, or
say, was that the dispossession of the commoners of England,
and the English common law's insistence that "the nature

[1] *Ibid.*, pp. 227-8, 255-6, 260-1.
[2] An exception is in the Minutes of the able administrator, John
Shore, see Guha, *op. cit.*, pp. 192-4. Also Charles William Boughton Rous,
Dissertation Concerning the Landed Property of Bengal (1791).
[3] Hunter, *Orissa*, pp. 264-5. Even in the case of Bengal it became
belatedly necessary (Act X of 1859) to recognise the "Right of Occupancy"
(p. 228).
[4] Thompson, *Metcalfe*, pp. 267-8.
[5] *Ibid.*, esp. pp. 130-40.

of property. . . imports exclusive enjoyment" were the templates for the Settlement of Bengal.

Metcalfe was perhaps the most humane of those whom Eric Stokes described as mounting a paternalist or Burkean romantic reaction to Cornwallis's measures. (Since Burke was an advocate of political economy (below p. 252) and was not noted for defending the rights of commoners, the adjective may be misplaced.) The ideological battles within British ruling groups were fought out upon the Indian land. Subsequent Settlements withdrew from the simplistic Whig model. In Madras and Bombay Munro's *ryotwar* system sought to invest property rights in a yeomanry or middle peasantry.[1] Metcalfe sought even to sustain the communal property of the village. But the administration's inexorable demands for revenue, and its dispossession of defaulters, collapsed all intentions. After these came the utilitarians, a modernising urban liberalism of individualism, money and the market, contemptuous of the landed aristocracy and of "Gothic" or Hindu custom, and (with Bentham and James Mill) eager to impose administrative occidental despotism upon the East. Later again, commencing with Burma and extending in this century to West Africa, there was, in a remarkable series of reversals of Whig ideology, the settlement of extensive lands in the superordinate ownership of the State, combined with measures to inhibit the growth of private property in land.[2]

But all that belongs to a different epoch of imperialism, more preoccupied with the rights of money than with property in land. In Africa colonialism learned how to co-exist with tribal land usages and with customary law, indeed to invent customary law or to codify and institutionalise it in such ways as to create a new and more formal structure of rule.[3] One consequence might be the development of

[1] See Stokes, *op. cit.*, pp. 15, 18-22.
[2] See especially Robert Shenton, *The Development of Capitalism in Northern Nigeria* (Toronto, 1986), ch. 3, for an account of the interlocking pressures of bureaucracy (the expediency of taxation), merchant capital, and "Single Tax" socialist idealism which led to this reversal.
[3] See Terence Ranger, "The Invention of Tradition in Colonial Africa", in Eric Hobsbawm and Terence Ranger (eds.), *The Invention of Tradition* (Cambridge, 1983), esp. pp. 251-62. Even the act of writing

a dual economy and dual regimen, the one "modernised" and fully marketised, the other (indirect rule) sequestered within "custom", where the penetration of market forces was left to loosen labour more gently from the land, and to dissolve traditional forms of communal, or familial property-statute. The processes have not been (and are not) univocal, and there is a growing expert literature on customary law which should signal caution to a novice. Nor should we expect that the history of property in land could be written out in one single overarching theme, such as the triumph of possessive individualism, spanning the continents and centuries. The Permanent Settlement in Bengal was the zenith in the long ascent of the ideology of the patrician Whigs and the great gentry whom I still insist on seeing as an agrarian bourgeoisie. And by its very excess and doctrinaire impracticability it was also that ideology's *reductio ad absurdam.*

VI

This essay has been concerned to explore the interface between, on the one hand, law and ruling ideologies, and, on the other, common right usages and customary consciousness. It does not seek to revive in their old form certain debates, such as the effect of enclosure upon the creation of a proletariat. I am heartened to see that such issues are being addressed once more (in new forms) but my own evidence is not of such a kind as to add much to the discussion.[1]

Custom was a place in which many interests contested for advantage in the eighteenth century. Ultimately, at the point when commons were enclosed, it was a place of unqualified class conflict. The law was employed as an instrument of agrarian capitalism, furthering the "reasons" of

---

custom down could formalise it and expose it to new meanings and manipulation: see Goody, *op. cit.*, pp. 133-56; Don F. McKenzie, "The Sociology of a Text: Oral Culture, Literacy and Print in Early New Zealand", in P. Burke and R. Porter (eds.), *The Social History of Language* (Cambridge, 1987).

[1] The most substantial resistance to the triumphalism of the "agricultural revolution" historians came, not from an agricultural historian, but from Raymond Williams, *The Country and the City.*

improvement. If it is pretended that the law was impartial, deriving its rules from its own self-extrapolating logic, then we must reply that this pretence was class fraud.[1]

The zealous propagandists of enclosure cast as the villains and enemies of "progress" the stubborn cottagers, small-holders, the squatters and the "buccaneers" of forest and fen. But social classes can perform double roles, and these groups have been returning in recent years as the heroes and heroines of a different drama. For these villains can be seen as playing a revolutionary part in the growth of "proto-industrialisation" or of "the cottage economy". Their poverty and the marginality of their access to land was stimulating them to prodigious exertions in developing rural crafts and industrial by-employments on the edges of the commons. And they are flooding back into learned articles, triumphantly spinning or lace-making, carrying milk and poultry and butter and cheese to urban markets, grazing their pack-horses on the waste, introducing stocking-frames and looms, and going out on their depradations on the commons only in the intervals of making shoes or cloth or furniture or nails, and in general exercising every possible proto-industrial virtue.

I don't know what I am mocking — perhaps only the solemnity with which, every decade or two, the historical profession reverses its fashions. For undoubtedly the revision is helpful, and undoubtedly it is in the cottage economy that resources of common right were so important.[2] A Midlands pamphleteer in 1767 wrote that —

> There are some in almost all open parishes, who have houses, and little parcels of land in the field, with a right of common for a cow or three or four sheep, by the assistance of which, with the profits of a little trade or their daily labour, they procure a very comfortable living. Their land

[1] This was clearly expressed in the early working-class movement. The *Poor Man's Guardian* wrote, in 1835, "Property is but the creation of law. Whoever makes the law has the power of appropriating the national wealth. If they did not make the law, they would not have the property"; Malcolm Chase, *'The People's Farm'* (Oxford, 1988), p. 180.

[2] Especially helpful are David Levine, *Reproducing Families* (Cambridge, 1987), and Pat Hudson, "Proto-industrialisation: the Case of the West Riding Wool Textile Industry in the 18th and early 19th Centuries", *History Workshop*, 12 (1981), pp. 38-45.

furnished them with wheat and barley for bread, and, in many places, with beans or peas to feed a hog or two for meat; with the straw they thatch their cottage, and winter their cow, which gives a breakfast and supper of milk nine or ten months in the year for their families. These almost universally disapprove of inclosing.[1]

No doubt some of Atherstone's commoners were such. Others, were more fully occupied in trade: butchers, maltsters, alehouse-keepers, village traders of various kinds, blacksmiths, wheelwrights, masons and builders, those engaged in carpentry, tailoring, shoemaking. J. M. Martin has found such among the commoners disadvantaged by enclosure in South Warwickshire[2] and it was, exactly, in these "mixed agricultural and manufacturing villages" that Neeson has found, in her study of Northamptonshire, the strongest resistance to enclosure.[3]

Indeed, access to an extensive common could be critical to the livelihood of many villagers even if they had no common right, for they could rent upon it grazing for a cow, or parking and some fuel for their essential transport: i.e. grazing for a horse. In Maulden (Bedfordshire) whose extensive common was enclosed in 1797, to the accompaniment of riot (above p. 120) Young was told by a cottager in 1804 that "inclosing would ruin England; it was worse than ten wars. . . I kept four cows before the parish was inclosed, and now I do not keep so much as a goose". In Eaton (Bedfordshire) Arthur Young recorded that "the persons who were most affected and hurt" by the enclosure of 1796 were "higlers — fish, gingerbread, apples, carting for hire, &c; these kept horses, and turned without any right on the commons. . . they complain, but with no right to do it". In March (Cambridgeshire), enclosed in 1793, there were twenty families of dairy-men "who made an entire livelihood, —

[1] Anon. [S. Addington?], *An Enquiry into the Reasons for and against Inclosing the Common Fields* (Coventry, 1768). Cf. John Cowper, *An Essay Proving that Inclosing Commons and Common-field-Lands is Contrary to the Interest of the Nation* (1732), p. 8, referring to the loss from enclosure to "Carpenters, Wheelwrights, Millwrights, Smiths, Shoemakers, Taylors, and other Handicraftsmen, as well as to Shopkeepers".
[2] Martin, "Village Traders", *op. cit.*
[3] Neeson, "The Opponents of Enclosure", *op. cit.*

brought up their families decently; — after the enclosure they were reduced to day-labour, or to emigrate. These men were mere hirers and had no common rights themselves".[1] Such persons have eluded the attention of historians since they were neither agriculturalists nor emergent proletarians, and were of no importance to anyone except themselves.

When I first sketched this essay, more than twenty years ago, I rejected the triumphal accounts of improvers and modernisers, but I considered that radical historiography — and notably the Hammonds — had also been at fault in focussing too sharply on parliamentary enclosure, and hence in presenting us with a catastrophic paradigm. But such enclosure was only the last act of several centuries of agrarian capitalism, including extensive enclosure by agreement among the landholders. Relationships in most villages were already monetarised and subjected to market imperatives long before the act of enclosure struck. Common right usages clung by a thread to the customary tree, and many were over-ripe to fall. The wasp was already in them. Copyholders had become tenants at rack-rent, many cottagers had become day labourers, perhaps supplementing their wages with some spinning and a little stock. Grazing rights had been commercialised, and gates on the common could long have been hired. I remember teaching that, by the late eighteenth century, the communal forms of the unenclosed village were only a formal husk, whose kernel had been eaten by money from within.

Yet my own research and that of other scholars has persuaded me to look again. There were many villages where common right usages were a good deal more than form, not least those in which the resources of common and waste, Lammas and laneside grazing, wage-labour at harvest and in busy times, and crafts or by-employments each supplemented each other to make up a subsistence. The subsistence was not any more than meagre, the way of life might be desultory, but it was not subjected from early youth to death to an alien

---

[1] *Annals of Agriculture*, xlii (1804), pp. 27, 39, 323. But Young adds: "Their accounts of advantages, especially when they are gone, are not to be credited".

work-discipline.[1] In some part of their lives "the poor" still felt themselves to be self-determined, and in that sense "free". Indeed "the poor" was a gentry-made term which could sometimes disguise a sturdy peasantry. For John Clare the unenclosed moor was a symbol also of the poor's "freedom":

> Unbounded freedom ruled the wandering scene
> Nor fence of ownership crept in between
> To hide the prospect of the following eye
> Its only bondage was the circling sky. . .[2]

Moreover, even where the communal forms of the un-enclosed village were only an empty husk, form itself is not nothing. Form gave sanction to custom, that habitus, or field of play and possibility, in which interests knew how to co-exist and contend. And it reproduced an oral tradition, a customary consciousness, in which rights were asserted as "ours" rather than as mine or thine. To be sure, this was not some generous and universalistic communist spirit. "Natures wide and common sky"[3] is also the "circling sky": the bounded, circular, jealously possessive consciousness of the parish.[4] The communal economy was parochial and exclusive: if Weldon's rights were "ours", then Brigstock men and women must be kept out (above, p. 99). But for those who "belonged" to the parish, there remained some sense that they "owned" it and had a voice in its regula-tion.[5] In this sense, enclosure, as it came to each village, was experienced as catastrophic to the customary culture. Within the space of a year or two the labourers' world shrank suddenly, from "our" parish to a cottage which might not be their own:

[1] Where rural industries developed, they could also be the locus for intensive familial self-exploitation: see J. de Vries, "Labour/Leisure Trade Off", *Peasant Studies*, i (1972).

[2] John Clare, "The Mores".

[3] John Clare, "Emmonsales Heath".

[4] See John Barrell, *The Idea of Landscape and the Sense of Place, 1730-1840: an Approach to the Poetry of John Clare* (Cambridge, 1972).

[5] For the notion of the "real" owners — families with long local presence — see Marilyn Strathern, *Kinship at the Core* (Cambridge, 1981).

> Fence now meets fence in owners little bounds
> Of field and meadow large as garden grounds
> In little parcels little minds to please
> With men and flocks imprisoned ill at ease.[1]

Enclosure was announced with the "hated sign" of the private owner, which ordered labourers (like any strangers) not to "trespass" on their own commons.

Despite the long erosion of common right usages and the long pre-history of capitalist penetration into the peasant economy, parliamentary enclosure still "marked a turning-point in the social history of many English villages", a turning-point identified most clearly by Dr Neeson:

> It struck at the roots of the economy of multiple occupations and it taught the small peasantry the new reality of class relations. John Clare's hatred of its symbol — the newly prosperous, socially aspirant farmer — is illustration of the growing separation of classes that enclosure embodied. . . Perhaps this separation was a long time coming. But until enclosure it was masked by other relationships born of customary agricultural regulation and shared use-rights over land. The organization of work in the open field system encouraged co-operation; and defence of common rights required the protection of lesser rights as well as greater. Enclosure tore away the mask not only to reveal more clearly the different interests of small and large landowners but also to profit one at the expense of the other. . . Enclosure had a terrible but instructive visibility.[2]

We are fortunate to have in John Clare's writing a sensitive record of this customary consciousness as it came under agonising strain. It does not matter whether enclosure in Helpston resulted in more or fewer small farmers. The immiseration of the rural workers was not at the centre of Clare's poetic concern (although he did not forget it). What concerned him more was the new instrumental and exploitative stance, not only towards labour ("that necessary tool of wealth and pride") but also towards the natural world. It is not (as some critics suppose) that this peasant poet was more motivated by "aesthetic" than by social protest. Clare may be described, without hindsight, as a poet of ecological protest: he was not writing about man here and

---

[1] John Clare, "The Mores".
[2] Neeson, "Opponents of Enclosure".

nature there, but lamenting a threatened equilibrium in which both were involved:

> Ah cruel foes with plenty blest
> So ankering after more
> To lay the greens and pasture waste
> Which proffited before.[1]

The mutual profit of both greens and pasture and of their farmers is suggested "before"; now these are laid waste for the sole profit of the enclosers.

Helpston was enclosed during Clare's adolescence, and thereafter pre-enclosure Helpston was recalled as an Eden, a world of lost childhood innocence. No doubt his memories were sweetened by the contrast:

> I was never easy but when I was in the fields passing my sabbath and leisure with the shepherds & herdboys as fancys sometimes prompted playing at marbles on the smooth-beaten sheeptracks or leapfrog among the thymy molehills sometimes running among the corn to get the red & blue flowers for cockades to play at soldiers or running into the woods to hunt strawberries or stealing peas in churchtime. . .[2]

This conveys his sense of belonging, since childhood — perhaps especially in childhood — within a shared and "free" communal space, a space which shrank within the fenced bounds of private ownership with enclosure.

We do not have to ask for other evidence to support John Clare, since his poems *are* the evidence of a tormented customary consciousness. If Clare became known as a poet of locality, this also belongs to the customary consciousness. There is a set of customary norms and practices here which go together. There is an economy in which exchanges of services and favours remain significant, of which local features of the landscape are reminders. There is the local idiom of dialect — drawn upon so effectively in Clare's verse — which seems (deceptively) to be a more "social" product than standardised English, — dialect which was becoming in the eighteenth century, not the medium of local or regional speech but of regional *plebeian* speech, and which is itself the sign of a

---

[1] John Clare, "The Lamentations of Round-Oak Waters".
[2] *The Prose of John Clare*, ed. J. W. and Anne Tibble (1951), p. 12.

certain kind of customary consciousness.[1] There are local institutions for regulating the occasions of the community, including the poor laws, which might still, in pre-enclosure days be administered with a rough rule-of-thumb neighbourliness, but which in step with "improvement" acquired their end-of-century mix of indignity, dependency and discipline. "The parish", a term which once suggested home and security, was becoming a term ("on the parish") suggestive of meanness and shame. And, finally, there are the forms of customary pastimes and of ritual in which people "lose themselves in recreation in order to recreate themselves as a community".[2]

No doubt we will be warned against sentimentalising this customary pre-enclosure consciousness, which was the vector of its own kinds of narrowness, brutality and superstition. That is true, but it is sometimes the only part of the truth which is now remembered. The commons and wastes shrank, in the nineteenth century, to the village greens (if such survived) and communally-shared custom shrank to the "calendar customs" and survivals collected by the folklorists. I have been trying to recall customary consciousness in a larger sense, in which community was sustained by actual resources and usages. Young Clare was driven to fury by a farmer who actually locked up a public pump —

> To lock up Water — must undoubted stand
> Among the Customs of a Christian Land
> An Action quite Uncommon. . .[3]

No doubt he savoured the double resonance of "Uncommon". The private appropriation of the natural world which enclosure symbolised was (for Clare) an offence to both "nature" and human community, and he identified as

---

[1] I find especially helpful on many of these points Johanne Clare, *John Clare and the Bounds of Circumstance* (Kingston and Montreal, 1987).

[2] See *ibid.*, p. 99; Robert W. Malcolmson, *Popular Recreations in English Society* (Cambridge, 1973), esp. ch. 4 and Hugh Cunningham, *Leisure in the Industrial Revolution* (1980), ch. 2.

[3] John Clare, *The Parish*, ed. Eric Robinson and David Powell, notes p. 90.

enemy to both a logic which is with us still in factory farming and the privatisation of water.

Clare's remarkable enclosure elegies, "The Mores" and "Remembrances", take us back within that conceptual universe before "lawless laws enclosure came". After leading us through childhood memories of play upon the common he comes with startling suddenness upon the gamekeeper's gibbet:

> I see the little mouldiwarps hang sweeing to the wind
> On the only aged willow that in all the field remains
> And nature hides her face while theyre sweeing in their chains
> And in silent murmuring complains
> Here was commons for their hills where they seek for freedom still
> Though every commons gone and though traps are set to kill
> The little homeless miners. . .

These are real moles, but the image is also one of displaced commoners. So close is the mutual ecological imbrication of the human and the natural that each might stand for the other. And Clare strains to convey the strength of feeling of "a rhyming peasant"[1] for a locality whose landmarks are not privately possessed but still (in a shared sense) intensely *owned*!

> By Langley bush I roam but the bush hath left its hill
> On cowper green I stray tis a desert strange and chill
> And spreading lea close oak ere decay had penned its will
> To the axe of the spoiler and self interest fell a prey
> And crossberry way and old round oaks narrow lane
> With its hollow trees like pulpits I shall never see again
> Inclosure like a buonaparte let not a thing remain
> It levelled every bush and tree and levelled every hill
> And hung the moles for traitors — though the brook is running still
> It runs a naked stream cold and chill[2]

The old landmarks of the parish perambulation have gone and that whole universe of custom is now only a memory in the poet's head. The gentry had accomplished the final and most precipitate episode of enclosures during the French

[1] Clare wrote that "The Village Minstrel" dissatisfied him because "it does not describe the feelings of a rhyming peasant strongly or localy enough", *Selected Poems and Prose of John Clare*, ed. Eric Robinson and G. Summerfield (Oxford, 1967), p. 67.

[2] John Clare, "Remembrances".

Wars, with the cry that "Bony is coming!", and they had
harried their domestic opponents with their Associations for
the Protection of Property against Republicans and
Levellers. In the word "levelled" Clare turns their world
around and reveals its underside of greed and repression. As
the Maulden cottager told Arthur Young in 1804 "Inclosing
was worse than ten wars". And in the moles, hanged and
"sweeing to the wind" there is probably an allusion — for
"Remembrances" was written in 1832 — to the Swing riots of
1830 and the victims selected for the gallows.

It is not that John Clare — nor the commoners for whom
he spoke — were primitive communists. Viewed from their
standpoint, the communal forms expressed an alternative
notion of possession, in the petty and particular rights and
usages which were transmitted in custom as the *properties* of
the poor. Common right, which was in lax terms coterminous
with settlement, was *local* right, and hence was also a power
to exclude strangers. Enclosure, in taking the commons away
from the poor, made them strangers in their own land.

Chapter Four

The Moral Economy of the English Crowd in the Eighteenth Century

He that withholdeth Corn, the People shall curse him: but Blessing shall be upon the Head of him that selleth it.

Proverbs xi. 26

I

We have been warned in recent years, by George Rudé and others, against the loose employment of the term "mob". I wish in this chapter to extend the warning to the term "riot", especially where the food riot in eighteenth-century England is concerned.

This simple four-letter word can conceal what may be described as a spasmodic view of popular history. According to this view the common people can scarcely be taken as historical agents before the French Revolution. Before this period they intrude occasionally and spasmodically upon the historical canvas, in periods of sudden social disturbance. These intrusions are compulsive, rather than self-conscious or self-activating: they are simple responses to economic stimuli. It is sufficient to mention a bad harvest or a downturn in trade, and all requirements of historical explanation are satisfied.

Unfortunately, even among those few British historians who have added to our knowledge of such popular actions, several have lent support to the spasmodic view. They have reflected in only a cursory way upon the materials which they themselves disclose. Thus Beloff comments on the food riots of the early eighteenth century: "this resentment, when unemployment and high prices combined to make conditions unendurable, vented itself in attacks upon corn-dealers and

millers, attacks which often must have degenerated into mere
excuses for crime".[1] But we search his pages in vain for
evidence as to the frequency of this "degeneration".
Wearmouth, in his useful chronicle of disturbance, allows
himself one explanatory category: "distress".[2] Ashton, in his
study of food riots among the colliers, brings the support of
the paternalist: "the turbulence of the colliers is, of course, to
be accounted for by something more elementary than
politics: it was the instinctive reaction of virility to hunger".[3]
The riots were "rebellions of the belly", and there is a
suggestion that this is somehow a comforting explanation.
The line of analysis runs: elementary — instinctive — hunger.
Charles Wilson continues the tradition: "Spasmodic rises in
food prices provoked keelmen on the Tyne to riot in 1709, tin
miners to plunder granaries at Falmouth in 1727". One spasm
led to another: the outcome was "plunder".[4]

For decades systematic social history has lagged in the rear
of economic history, until the present day, when a qualification in the second discipline is assumed to confer, auto-
matically, proficiency in the first. One cannot therefore
complain that recent scholarship has tended to sophisticate
and quantify evidence which is only imperfectly understood.
The dean of the spasmodic school is of course Rostow, whose

[1] M. Beloff, *Public Order and Popular Disturbances, 1660-1714*
(Oxford, 1938), p. 75.
[2] R. F. Wearmouth, *Methodism and the Common People of the
Eighteenth Century* (1945), esp. chs. 1 and 2.
[3] T. S. Ashton and J. Sykes, *The Coal Industry of the Eighteenth
Century* (Manchester, 1929), p. 131.
[4] Charles Wilson, *England's Apprenticeship, 1603-1763* (1965), p. 345.
It is true that the Falmouth magistrates reported to the duke of
Newcastle (16 Nov. 1727) that "the unruly tinners" had "broke open and
plundered several cellars and granaries of corn". Their report concludes
with a comment which suggests that they were no more able than some
modern historians to understand the rationale of the direct action of the
tinners: "the occasion of these outrages was pretended by the rioters to be a
scarcity of corn in the county, but this suggestion is probably false, as most
of those who carried off the corn gave it away or sold it at quarter price".
PRO, SP 36/4/22.

crude "social tension chart" was first put forward in 1948.[1]
According to this, we need only bring together an index of
unemployment and one of high food prices to be able to chart
the course of social disturbance. This contains a self-evident
truth (people protest when they are hungry): and in much the
same way a "sexual tension chart" would show that the onset
of sexual maturity can be correlated with a greater frequency
of sexual activity. The objection is that such a chart, if used
unwisely, may conclude investigation at the exact point at
which it becomes of serious sociological or cultural interest:
being hungry (or being sexy), what do people do? How is
their behaviour modified by custom, culture, and reason?
And (having granted that the primary stimulus of "distress"
is present) does their behaviour contribute towards any more
complex, culturally-mediated function, which cannot be
reduced — however long it is stewed over the fires of
statistical analysis — back to stimulus once again?

Too many of our growth historians are guilty of a crass
economic reductionism, obliterating the complexities of
motive, behaviour, and function, which, if they noted it in
the work of their marxist analogues, would make them
protest. The weakness which these explanations share is an
abbreviated view of economic man. What is perhaps an
occasion for surprise is the schizoid intellectual climate,
which permits this quantitative historiography to co-exist (in
the same places and sometimes in the same minds) with a
social anthropology which derives from Durkheim, Weber,
or Malinowski. We know all about the delicate tissue of
social norms and reciprocities which regulates the life of
Trobriand islanders, and the psychic energies involved in the
cargo cults of Melanesia; but at some point this infinitely-
complex social creature, Melanesian man, becomes (in our
histories) the eighteenth-century English collier who claps his
hand spasmodically upon his stomach, and responds to
elementary economic stimuli.

[1] W. W. Rostow, *British Economy in the Nineteenth Century* (Oxford,
1948), esp. pp. 122-5. Among the more interesting studies which correlate
prices, harvests, and popular disturbance are: E. J. Hobsbawm,
"Economic Fluctuations and Some Social Movements", in *Labouring Men*
(1964) and T. S. Ashton, *Economic Fluctuations in England, 1700-1800*
(Oxford, 1959).

To the spasmodic I will oppose my own view.[1] It is possible to detect in almost every eighteenth-century crowd action some legitimising notion. By the notion of legitimation I mean that the men and women in the crowd were informed by the belief that they were defending traditional rights or customs; and, in general, that they were supported by the wider consensus of the community. On occasion this popular consensus was endorsed by some measure of licence afforded by the authorities. More commonly, the consensus was so strong that it overrode motives of fear or deference.

The food riot in eighteenth-century England was a highly complex form of direct popular action, disciplined and with clear objectives. How far these objectives were achieved — that is, how far the food riot was a "successful" form of action — is too intricate a question to tackle within the limits of a chapter; but the question can at least be posed (rather than, as is customary, being dismissed unexamined with a negative), and this cannot be done until the crowd's own objectives are identified. It is of course true that riots were triggered off by soaring prices, by malpractices among dealers, or by hunger. But these grievances operated within a popular consensus as to what were legitimate and what were illegitimate practices in marketing, milling, baking, etc. This in its turn was grounded upon a consistent traditional view of social norms and obligations, of the proper economic functions of several parties within the community, which, taken together, can be said to constitute the moral economy of the poor. An outrage to these moral assumptions, quite as much as actual deprivation, was the usual occasion for direct action.

While this moral economy cannot be described as "political" in any advanced sense, nevertheless it cannot be described as unpolitical either, since it supposed definite, and passionately held, notions of the common weal — notions which, indeed, found some support in the paternalist tradition of the authorities; notions which the people

---

[1] I have found most helpful the pioneering study by R. B. Rose, "Eighteenth Century Price Riots and Public Policy in England", *International Review of Social History*, vi (1961); and G. Rudé, *The Crowd in History* (New York, 1964).

re-echoed so loudly in their turn that the authorities were, in some measure, the prisoners of the people. Hence this moral economy impinged very generally upon eighteenth-century government and thought, and did not only intrude at moments of disturbance. The word "riot" is too small to encompass all this.

II

As we speak of the cash-nexus which emerged through the industrial revolution, so there is a sense in which we can speak of the eighteenth-century bread-nexus. The conflict between the countryside and the town was mediated by the price of bread. The conflict between traditionalism and the new political economy turned upon the Corn Laws. Economic class-conflict in nineteenth-century England found its characteristic expression in the matter of wages; in eighteenth-century England the working people were most quickly inflamed to action by rising prices.

This highly-sensitive consumer-consciousness co-existed with the great age of agricultural improvement, in the corn belt of the East and South. Those years which brought English agriculture to a new pitch of excellence were punctuated by the riots — or, as contemporaries often described them, the "insurrections" or "risings of the poor" — of 1709, 1740, 1756-7, 1766-7, 1773, 1782, and, above all, 1795 and 1800-1. This buoyant capitalist industry floated upon an irascible market which might at any time dissolve into marauding bands, who scoured the countryside with bludgeons, or rose in the market-place to "set the price" of provisions at the popular level. The fortunes of those most vigorous capitalist classes rested, in the final analysis, upon the sale of cereals, meat, wool; and the first two must be sold, with little intermediary processing, to the millions who were the consumers. Hence the frictions of the market-place take us into a central area of the nation's life.

The labouring people in the eighteenth century did not live by bread alone, but (as the budgets collected by Eden and David Davies show) many of them lived very largely on bread. This bread was not altogether wheaten, although wheaten bread gained ground steadily over other varieties until the early 1790s. In the 1760s Charles Smith estimated that of a supposed population of about six millions in England and Wales, 3,750,000 were wheat-eaters, 888,000 ate rye, 739,000 ate barley, and 623,000 oats.[1] By 1790 we may judge that at least two-thirds of the population were eating wheat.[2] The pattern of consumption reflected, in part, comparative degrees of poverty, and, in part, ecological conditions. Districts with poor soils and upland districts (like the Pennines) where wheat will not ripen, were the strongholds of other cereals. Still, in the 1790s, the Cornish tinners subsisted largely on barley bread. Much oatmeal was consumed in Lancashire and Yorkshire — and not only by the poor.[3] Accounts from Northumberland conflict, but it would seem that Newcastle and many of the surrounding pit villages had by then gone over to wheat, while the countryside and smaller towns subsisted on oatmeal, rye bread, maslin,[4] or a mixture of barley and "gray pease".[5]

Through the century, again, white bread was gaining upon darker wholemeal varieties. This was partly a matter of status-values which became attached to white bread, but by no means wholly so. The problem is most complex, but several aspects may be briefly mentioned. It was to the advantage of bakers and of millers to sell white bread or fine flour, since the profit which might be gained from such sales was, in general, larger. (Ironically, this was in part a consequence of paternalist consumer-protection, since the Assize of Bread was intended to prevent the bakers from taking their profit from the bread of the poor; hence it was in

[1] C. Smith, *Three Tracts on the Corn-Trade and Corn-Laws*, 2nd edn. (1766), pp. 140, 182-5.

[2] See Fitzjohn Brand, *A Determination of the Average Depression of Wheat in War below that of the Preceding Peace etc.* (1800), pp. 62-3, 96.

[3] These generalisations are supported by "replies from towns as to bread in use", returned to the Privy Council in 1796 in PRO, PC 1/33/A.87 and A.88.

[4] For maslin (a mixed bread of several cereals) see Sir William Ashley, *The Bread of our Forefathers* (Oxford, 1928), pp. 16-19.

[5] See Smith, *op. cit.*, p. 194 (for 1765). But the mayor of Newcastle reported (4 May 1796) that rye bread was "much used by the workmen employed in the Coal Trade", and a reporter from Hexham Abbey said that barley, barley and gray pease, or beans, "is the only bread of the labouring poor and farmers' servants and even of many farmers", with rye or maslin in the towns: PRO, PC 1/33/A.88.

the baker's interest to make as little "household" bread as possible, and that little nasty.[1]) In the cities, which were alert to the dangers of adulteration, dark bread was suspect as offering easy concealment for noxious additives. In the last decades of the century many millers adapted their machinery and bolting-cloths, so that they were not in fact able to dress the flour for the intermediary "household" loaf, producing only the finer qualities for the white loaf and the "offal" for a brown loaf which one observer found "so musty, griping, and pernicious as to endanger the constitution".[2] The attempts of the authorities, in times of scarcity, to impose the manufacture of coarser grades (or, as in 1795, the general use of the "household" loaf), were attended by many difficulties, and often resistance by both millers and bakers.[3]

By the end of the century feelings of status were profoundly involved wherever wheaten bread prevailed, and was threatened by a coarser mixture. There is a suggestion that labourers accustomed to wheaten bread actually could not work — suffered from weakness, indigestion, or nausea — if forced to change to rougher mixtures.[4] Even in the face of the outrageous prices of 1795 and 1800-1, the resistance of many of the working people was impermeable.[5] The Guild Stewards of Calne informed the Privy Council in 1796 that

[1] Nathaniel Forster, *An Enquiry into the Cause of the High Price of Provisions* (1767), pp. 144-7.

[2] J. S. Girdler, *Observations on the Pernicious Consequences of Forestalling, Regrating and Ingrossing* (1800), p. 88.

[3] The problem was discussed lucidly in [Governor] Pownall, *Considerations on the Scarcity and High Prices of Bread-corn and Bread* (Cambridge, 1795), esp. pp. 25-7. See also Lord John Sheffield, *Remarks on the Deficiency of Grain occasioned by the bad Harvest of 1799* (1800), esp. pp. 105-6 for the evidence that (1795) "there is no household bread made in London". A Honiton correspondent in 1766 described household bread as "a base mixture of fermented Bran ground down and bolted, to which is added the worst kind of meal not rang'd": HMC, *City of Exeter*, series lxxiii (1916), p. 255. On this very complex question see further S. and B. Webb, "The Assize of Bread", *Economic Journal*, xiv (1904), esp. pp. 203-6.

[4] See e.g. Lord Hawkesbury to the duke of Portland, 19 May 1797, in PRO, HO 42/34.

[5] See R. N. Salaman, *The History and Social Influence of the Potato* (Cambridge, 1949), esp. pp. 493-517. Resistance extended from the wheat-eating South and Midlands to the oatmeal-eating North; a correspondent

"creditable" people were using the barley-and-wheat mixture required by authority, and that the manufacturing and labouring poor with large families

> have in general used barley bread alone. The rest, making perhaps something about one-third of the poor manufactures and others, with smaller families (saying they could get nothing *but bread*) have, as before the scarcity, eat nothing but baker's bread, made of wheatmeal called seconds.[1]

The Bailiff of Reigate reported in similar terms:

> . . . as to the poor labourers who have scarce any sustenance but bread, & from the custom of the neighbourhood have always eaten bread made of wheat only; amongst these I have neither urged nor wished a mixture of bread, least they should not be nourished sufficiently to support their labour.

Those few labourers who had tried a mixture "found themselves feeble, hot, & unable to labour with any degree of vigor".[2] When, in December 1800, the government introduced an Act (popularly known as the Brown Bread Act or "Poison Act") which prohibited millers from making any other than wholemeal flour, the response of the people was immediate. At Horsham (Sussex),

> A number of women. . . proceeded to Gosden wind-mill, where, abusing the miller for having served them with brown flour, they seized on the cloth with which he was then dressing meal according to the directions of the Bread Act, and cut it into a thousand pieces; threatening at the same time to serve all similar utensils he might in future attempt to use in the same manner. The amazonian leader of this petticoated cavalcade afterwards regaled her associates with a guinea's worth of liquor at the Crab Tree public-house.

---

from Stockport in 1795 noted that "a very liberal subscription has been entered into for the purpose of distributing oatmeal & other provisions among the poor at reduced prices — This measure, I am sorry to say, gives little satisfaction to the common people, who are still clamorous & insist on having wheaten bread": PRO, WO 1/1094. See also J. L. and B. Hammond, *The Village Labourer* (1966), pp. 119-23.

[1] PRO, PC 1/33/A.88. Compare the return from J. Boucher, vicar of Epsom, 8 Nov. 1800 in HO 42/54: "Our Poor live not only on the finest wheaten bread, but almost on bread alone."

[2] PRO, PC 1/33/A.88.

As a result of such actions, the Act was repealed in less than two months.[1]

When prices were high, more than one-half of the weekly budget of a labourer's family might be spent on bread.[2] How did these cereals pass, from the crops growing in the field, to the labourers' homes? At first sight it appears simple. There is the corn: it is harvested, threshed, taken to market, ground at the mill, baked, and eaten. But at every point within this process there are radiating complexities, opportunities for extortion, flash-points around which riots could arise. And it is scarcely possible to proceed further without sketching out, in a schematic way, the paternalist model of the marketing and manufacturing process — the traditional platonic ideal appealed to in Statute, pamphlet, or protest movement — against which the awkward realities of commerce and consumption were in friction.

The paternalist model existed in an eroded body of Statute law, as well as common law and custom. It was the model which, very often, informed the actions of government in times of emergency until the 1770s; and to which many local magistrates continued to appeal. In this model, marketing should be, so far as possible, *direct*, from the farmer to the consumer. The farmers should bring their corn in bulk to the local pitching market; they should not sell it while standing in the field, nor should they withhold it in the hope of rising prices. The markets should be controlled; no sales should be made before stated times, when a bell would ring; the poor should have the opportunity to buy grain, flour, or meal first, in small parcels, with duly-supervised weights and measures.

---

[1] PRO, PC 1/33/;a.88; *Reading Mercury*, 16 Feb. 1801. Hostility to these changes in milling, which were imposed by an Act of 1800 (41 Geo. III, c.16) was especially strong in Surrey and Sussex. Complainants produced samples of the new bread to a Surrey JP: "They represented it as disagreeable to the taste (as indeed it was), as utterly incompetent to support them under their daily labour, & as productive of bowelly complaints to them and to their children in particular": Thomas Turton to Portland, 7 Feb. 1801, HO 42/61. The Act was repealed in 1801: 42 Geo. III, c.2.

[2] See especially the budgets in D. Davies, *The Case of Labourers in Husbandry* (Bath, 1795); and Sir Frederick Eden, *The State of the Poor* (1797). Also D. J. V. Jones, "The Corn Riots in Wales, 1793-1801", *Welsh Hist. Rev.*, ii, 4 (1965), App. I, p. 347.

At a certain hour, when their needs were satisfied, a second bell would ring, and larger dealers (duly licensed) might make their purchases. Dealers were hedged around with many restrictions, inscribed upon the musty parchments of the laws against forestalling, regrating and engrossing, codified in the reign of Edward VI. They must not buy (and farmers must not sell) by sample. They must not buy standing crops, nor might they purchase to sell again (within three months) in the same market at a profit, or in neighbouring markets, and so on. Indeed, for most of the eighteenth century the middle-man remained legally suspect, and his operations were, in theory, severely restricted.[1]

From market-supervision we pass to consumer-protection. Millers and — to a greater degree — bakers were considered as servants of the community, working not for a profit but for a fair allowance. Many of the poor would buy their grain direct in the market (or obtain it as supplement to wages or in gleaning); they would take it to the mill to be ground, where the miller might exact a customary toll, and then would bake their own bread. In London and those large towns where this had long ceased to be the rule, the baker's allowance or profit was calculated strictly according to the Assize of Bread, whereby either the price or the weight of the loaf was ordered in relation to the ruling price of wheat.[2]

This model, of course, parts company at many points with eighteenth-century realities. What is more surprising is to note how far parts of it were still operative. Thus Aikin in 1795 is able to describe the orderly regulation of Preston market:

[1] The best general study of eighteenth-century corn marketing remains R. B. Westerfield, *Middlemen in English Business, 1660-1760* (New Haven, 1915), ch. 2. Also see N. S. B. Gras, *The Evolution of the English Corn Market from the Twelfth to the Eighteenth Century* (Cambridge, Mass., 1915); D. G. Barnes, *A History of the English Corn Laws* (1930); C. R. Fay, *The Corn Laws and Social England* (Cambridge, 1932); E. Lipson, *Economic History of England*, 6th edn. (1956), ii, pp. 419-48; L. W. Moffitt, *England on the Eve of the Industrial Revolution* (1925), ch. 3; G. E. Fussell and C. Goodmen, "Traffic in Farm Produce in Eighteenth Century England", *Agricultural History*, xii, 2 (1938); Janet Blackman, "The Food Supply of an Industrial Town (Sheffield)", *Business History*, v (1963).

[2] S. and B. Webb, "The Assize of Bread".

The weekly markets. . . are extremely well regulated to prevent forestalling and regrating. None but the town's-people are permitted to buy during the first hour, which is from eight to nine in the morning: at nine others may purchase: but nothing unsold must be withdrawn from the market till one o'clock, fish excepted. . .[1]

In the same year in the South-West (another area noted for traditionalism) the city authorities at Exeter attempted to control "hucksters, higlers, and retailers" by excluding them from the market between 8 a.m. and noon, at which hours the Guildhall bell would be rung.[2] The Assize of Bread was still effective throughout the eighteenth century in London and in many market towns.[3] If we follow through the case of sale by sample we may observe how dangerous it is to assume prematurely the dissolution of the customary restrictions.

It is often supposed that sale of corn by sample was general by the middle of the seventeenth century, when Best describes the practice in East Yorkshire,[4] and certainly by 1725, when Defoe gave his famous account of the corn trade.[5] But, while many large farmers were no doubt selling by sample in

[1] J. Aikin, *A Description of the Country from thirty to forty Miles round Manchester* (1795), p. 286. One of the best surviving records of a well-regulated market in the eighteenth century is that of Manchester. Here market lookers for fish and flesh, for corn weights and measures, for white meats, for the Assize of Bread, aletasters, and officers to prevent "engrossing, forestalling and regretting" were appointed throughout the century, and fines for short weight and measure, unmarketable meat, etc. were frequent until the 1750s; supervision thereafter was somewhat more perfunctory (although continuing) with a revival of vigilance in the 1790s. Fines were imposed for selling loads of grain before the market bell in 1734, 1737, and 1748 (when William Wyat was fined 20s. "for selling before the Bell rung and declaring he would sell at any Time of the Day in Spite of either Lord of the Mannor or any person else"), and again in 1766. *The Court Leet Records of the Manor of Manchester*, ed. J. P. Earwaker (Manchester, 1888/9), vii, viii and ix, *passim*. For the regulation of forestalling at Manchester, see note 3 on p. 209.

[2] Proclamation by Exeter Town Clerk, 28 March 1795, PRO, HO 42/34.

[3] See S. and B. Webb, *op. cit., passim*; and J. Burnett, "The Baking Industry in the Nineteenth Century", *Business History*, v. (1963), pp. 98-9.

[4] *Rural Economy in Yorkshire in 1641* (Surtees Society, xxxiii, 1857), pp. 99-105.

[5] *The Complete English Tradesman* (1727), ii, pt. 2.

most counties by this date, the old pitching markets were still common, and even survived in the environs of London. In 1718 a pamphleteer described the decline of country markets as having taken place only in recent years:

> One can see little else besides toy-shops and stalls for bawbles and knick-knacks. . . The tolls are sunk to nothing; and where, in the memory of many inhabitants, there us'd to come to town upon a day, one, two, perhaps three, and in some boroughs, four hundred loads of corn, now grass grows in the market-place.

The farmers (he complained) had come to shun the market and to deal with jobbers and other "interlopers" at their doors. Other farmers still brought to market a single load "to make a show of a market, and to have a Price set", but the main business was done in "parcels of corn in a bag or handkerchief which are called *samples*".[1]

This was, indeed, the drift of things. But many smaller farmers continued to pitch their grain in the market as before; and the old model remained in men's minds as a source of resentment. Again and again the new marketing procedures were contested. In 1710 a petition on behalf of the poor people of Stony Stratford (Buckinghamshire) complains that the farmers and dealers were "buying and selling in the farmyards and att their Barne Doores soo that now the poor Inhabitants cannot have a Grist at reasonable rates for our money which is a Great Calamity".[2] In 1733 several boroughs petitioned the House of Commons against the practice: Haslemere (Surrey) complained of millers and meal-men engrossing the trade — they "secretly bought great quantities of corn by small samples, refusing to buy such as hath been pitch'd in open market".[3] There is a suggestion of something underhand in the practice, and of a loss of transparency in the marketing procedure.

As the century advances the complaints do not die down, although they tend to move northwards and westwards. In

[1] Anon., *An Essay to prove that Regrators, Engrossers, Forestallers, Hawkers, and Jobbers of Corn, Cattle, and other Marketable Goods are Destructive of Trade, Oppressors to the Poor, and a Common Nuisance to the Kingdom in General* (1719), pp. 13, 18-20.
[2] Bucks. CRO, Quarter Sessions, Michaelmas 1710.
[3] *Commons Journals*, 2 March 1733.

the dearth of 1756 the Privy Council, in addition to setting in motion the old laws against forestalling, issued a proclamation enjoining "all farmers, under severe penalties, to bring their corn to open market, and not to sell by sample at their own dwellings".[1] But the authorities did not like to be pressed on the point too closely: in 1766 (another year of scarcity) the Surrey magistrates enquired whether buying by sample in fact remained a punishable offence, and received a portentously evasive reply — H.M.'s Secretary is not by his office entitled to give interpretation to the Laws.[2]

Two letters give some insight into the spread of new practices towards the West. A correspondent writing to Lord Shelburne in 1766 accused the dealers and millers at Chippenham of "confederacy":

> He himself sent to market for a quarter of wheat, and though there were many loads there, and it soon after the market bell rang, wherever his agent applied, the answer was " 'Tis sold". So that, though. . . to avoid the penalty of the law, they bring it to market, yet the bargain is made before, and the market is but a farce. . .[3]

(Such practices could be the actual occasion of riot: in June 1757 it was reported that "the population rose at Oxford and in a few minutes seized and divided a load of corn that was suspected to have been bought by sample, and only brought to the market to save appearances".[4]) The second letter, from a correspondent in Dorchester in 1772, describes a different practice of market-fixing: he claimed that the great farmers got together to fix the price before the market,

> and many of these men won't sell less than forty bushels, which the poor can't purchase. Therefore the miller, who is no enemy to the farmer, gives the price he asks and the poor must come to his terms.[5]

Paternalists and the poor continued to complain at the extension of market practices which we, looking back, tend

---

[1] PRO, PC 1/6/63.
[2] *Calendar of Home Office Papers* (1879), 1766, pp. 92-4.
[3] *Ibid.*, pp. 91-2.
[4] *Gentleman's Magazine*, xxvii (1757), p. 286.
[5] Anonymous letter in PRO, SP 37/9.

to assume as inevitable and "natural".[1] But what may now appear as inevitable was not, in the eighteenth century necessarily a matter for approval. A characteristic pamphlet (of 1768) exclaimed indignantly against the supposed liberty of every farmer to do as he likes with his own. This would be a "natural", not a "civil" liberty.

> It cannot then be said to be the liberty of a citizen, or of one who lives under the protection of any community; it is rather the liberty of a savage; therefore he who avails himself thereof, deserves not that protection, the power of Society affords.

Attendance of the farmer at market is "a material part of his duty; he should not be suffered to secret or to dispose of his goods elsewhere".[2] But after the 1760s the pitching markets performed so little function in most parts of the South and the Midlands that, in these districts, the complaint against sample-sale is less often heard, although the complaint that the poor cannot buy in small parcels is still being made at the end of the century.[3] In parts of the North it was a different matter. A petition of Leeds labourers in 1795 complains of the "corn factors and the millers and a set of peopul which we call hucksters and mealmen who have got the corn into thare hands that they may hold it up and sell it at thare owne price or they will not sell it." "The farmers carry no corn to market but what they carre in thare pocket for thare sample. . . which cause the poore to groane very

---

[1] Examples, from an abundant literature, will be found in *Gentleman's Magazine*, xxvi (1756), p. 534; Anon. [Ralph Courteville], *The Cries of the Public* (1758), p. 25; Anon. ["C.L."], *A Letter to a Member of Parliament proposing Amendments to the Laws against Forestallers, Ingrossers, and Regraters* (1757), pp. 5-8; *Museum Rusticum et Commerciale*, iv (1765), p. 199; Forster, *op. cit.*, p. 97.

[2] Anon., *An Enquiry into the Price of Wheat, Malt, etc.* (1768), pp. 119-23.

[3] See e.g. Davies (below p. 216). It was reported from Cornwall in 1795 that "many farmers refuse to sell [barley] in small quantities to the poor, which causes a great murmuring": PRO, HO 42/34; and from Essex in 1800 that "in some places no sale takes place excepting at the ordinaries, where buyers and sellers (chiefly Millers and Factors) dine together. . . the benefit of the Market is almost lost to the neighbourhood"; such practices are mentioned "with great indignation by the lower orders": PRO, HO 42/54.

much."[1] So long it took for a process, which is often dated from at least one hundred years earlier, to work its way out.

This example has been followed to illustrate the density and particularity of the detail, the diversity of local practices, and the way in which popular resentment could arise as old market practices changed. The same density, the same diversity, exists throughout the scarcely-charted area of marketing. The paternalist model was, of course, breaking down at many other points. The Assize of Bread, although effective in checking the profits of bakers, simply reflected the ruling price of wheat or flour, and could in no way influence these. The millers were now, in Hertfordshire and the Thames Valley, very substantial entrepreneurs, and sometimes dealers in grain or malt as well as large-scale manufacturers of flour.[2] Outside the main corn-growing districts, urban markets simply could not be supplied without the operation of factors whose activities would have been nullified if legislation against forestallers had been strictly enforced.

How far did the authorities recognise that their model was drifting apart from reality? The answer must change with the authorities concerned and with the advance of the century. But a general answer can be offered: the paternalists did, in their normal practice, recognise much of the change, but they referred back to this model whenever emergency arose. In this they were in part the prisoners of the people, who adopted parts of the model as their right and heritage. There is even an impression that ambiguity was actually welcomed. It gave magistrates in disturbed districts, in time of dearth, some room for manoeuvre, and some endorsement to their attempts to reduce prices by suasion. When the Privy Council authorised (as it did in 1709, 1740, 1756 and 1766) the posting of proclamations in unreadable Gothic type threatening dire penalties against forestallers, badgers, laders, broggers, hucksters, etc., it helped the magistrates to put the fear of God into local millers and dealers. It is true that the legislation against forestallers was repealed in 1772; but the

[1] PRO, HO 42/35.
[2] See F. J. Fisher, "The Development of the London Food Market, 1540-1640", *Econ. Hist. Rev.*, v (1934-5).

repealing act was not well drawn, and during the next major scarcity in 1795 Lord Kenyon, the chief justice, took it upon himself to announce that forestalling remained an indictable offence at common law: "though the act of Edward VI be repealed (whether wisely or unwisely I take not upon me to say) yet it still remains an offence at common law, co-eval with the constitution. . .".[1] The trickle of prosecutions which can be observed throughout the century — usually for petty offences and only in years of scarcity — did not dry up: indeed, there were probably more in 1795 and 1800-1 than at any time in the previous twenty-five years.[2] But it is clear that they were designed for symbolic effect, as demonstrations to the poor that the authorities were acting vigilantly in their interests.

Hence the paternalist model had an ideal existence, and also a fragmentary real existence. In years of good harvests and moderate prices, the authorities lapsed into forgetfulness. But if prices rose and the poor became turbulent, it was revived, at least for symbolic effect.

III

Few intellectual victories have been more overwhelming than that which the proponents of the new political economy won in the matter of the regulation of the internal corn trade. Indeed, so absolute has the victory seemed to some historians that they can scarcely conceal their impatience with the

---

[1] Lord Kenyon's charge to the Grand Jury at Shropshire Assizes, *Annals of Agriculture*, xxv (1795), pp. 110-11. But he was not proclaiming a new view of the law: the 1780 edition of Burn's *Justice*, ii, pp. 213-4 had already stressed that (despite the Acts of 1663 and 1772) "at the common law, all endeavours whatsoever to enhance the common price of any merchandize. . . whether by spreading false rumours, or by buying things in a market before the accustomed hour, or by buying and selling again the same thing in the same market" remained offences.

[2] Girdler, *op. cit.*, pp. 212-60, lists a number of convictions in 1795 and 1800. Private associations were established in several counties to prosecute forestallers: see the Rev. J. Malham, *The Scarcity of Grain Considered* (Salisbury, 1800), pp. 35-44. Forestalling etc. remained offences at common law until 1844: W. Holdsworth, *History of English Law* (1938), xi, p. 472. See also note 2 on pp. 209-10.

defeated party.[1] The model of the new political economy may, with convenience, be taken as that of Adam Smith, although *The Wealth of Nations* may be seen not only as a point of departure but also as a grand central terminus to which many important lines of discussion in the middle of the eighteenth century (some of them, like Charles Smith's lucid *Tracts on the Corn Trade* (1758-9), specifically concerned to demolish the old paternalist market regulation) all run. The debate between 1767 and 1772 which culminated in the repeal of legislation against forestalling, signalled a victory, in this area, for *laissez-faire* four years before Adam Smith's work was published.

This signified less a new model than an anti-model — a direct negative to the disintegrating Tudor policies of "provision". "Let every act that regards the corn laws be repealed", wrote Arbuthnot in 1773; "Let corn flow like water, and it will find its level".[2] The "unlimited, unrestrained freedom of the corn trade" was also the demand of Adam Smith.[3] The new economy entailed a de-moralising of the theory of trade and consumption no less far-reaching than the more widely-debated dissolution of restrictions upon usury.[4] By "de-moralising" it is not suggested that Smith and his colleagues were immoral[5] or were unconcerned for

[1]See e.g. Gras, *op. cit.*, p. 241 (". . . as Adam Smith has shown. . ."); M. Olson, *Economics of the Wartime Shortage* (North Carolina, 1963), p. 53 ("People were quick to find a scapegoat").

[2]J. Arbuthnot ("A Farmer"), *An Inquiry into the Connection between the Present Price of Provisions and the Size of Farms* (1773), p. 88.

[3]Adam Smith's "digression concerning the Corn Trade and Corn Laws" is in Book IV, chapter 5 of *The Wealth of Nations*.

[4]R. H. Tawney takes in the question in *Religion and the Rise of Capitalism* (1926), but it is not central to his argument.

[5]The suggestion was made, however, by some of Smith's opponents. One pamphleteer, who claimed to have known him well, alleged that Adam Smith had said to him that "the Christian Religion debased the human mind", and that "Sodomy was a thing in itself indifferent". No wonder that he held heartless views on the corn trade: Anon, *Thoughts of an Old Man of Independent Mind though Dependent Fortune on the Present High Prices of Corn* (1800), p. 4.

the public good.[1] It is meant, rather, that the new political economy was disinfested of intrusive moral imperatives. The old pamphleteers were moralists first and economists second. In the new economic theory questions as to the moral polity of marketing do not enter, unless as preamble and peroration.

In practical terms, the new model worked in this way. The natural operation of supply and demand in the free market would maximise the satisfaction of all parties and establish the common good. The market was never better regulated than when it was left to regulate itself. In the course of a normal year, the price of corn would adjust itself through the market mechanism. Soon after harvest the small farmers, and all those with harvest wages and Michaelmas rents to pay, would thresh out their corn and bring it to market, or release what they had pre-contracted to sell. From September to Christmas low prices might be expected. The middling farmers would hold their corn, in the hope of a rising market, until the early spring; while the most opulent farmers and farming gentry would hold some of theirs until still later — from May to August — in expectation of catching the market at the top. In this way the nation's corn reserves were conveniently rationed, by the price mechanism, over fifty-two weeks, without any intervention by the State. Insofar as middlemen intervened and contracted for the farmers' crops in advance, they performed this service of rationing even more efficiently. In years of dearth the price of grain might advance to uncomfortable heights; but this was providential, since (apart from providing an incentive to the importer) it was again an effective form of rationing, without which all stocks would be consumed in the first nine months of the year, and in the remaining three months dearth would be exchanged for actual famine.

The only way in which this self-adjusting economy might break down was through the meddlesome interference of the

---

[1] On the level of *intention* I see no reason to disagree with Professor A. W. Coats, "The Classical Economists and the Labourer", in E. L. Jones and G. E. Mingay (eds.), *Land, Labour and Population* (1967). But intention is a bad measure of ideological interest and of historical consequences.

State and of popular prejudice.[1] Corn must be left to flow
freely from areas of surplus to areas of scarcity. Hence the
middleman played a necessary, productive, and laudable
role. The prejudices against forestallers Smith dismissed
curtly as superstitions on a level with witchcraft. Interference
with the natural pattern of trade might induce local famines
or discourage farmers from increasing their output. If
premature sales were forced, or prices restrained in times of
dearth, excessive stocks might be consumed. If farmers did
hold back their grain too long, they would be likely to suffer
when prices broke. As for the other popular culprits —
millers, mealmen, dealers, bakers — much the same logic
applied. Their trades were competitive. At the most they
could only distort prices from their natural level over short
periods, and often to their ultimate discomfiture. When
prices began to soar at the end of the century, the remedy was
seen not in a return to the regulation of trade, but in more
enclosure, tillage of waste lands, improvement.

It should not be necessary to argue that the model of a
natural and self-adjusting economy, working providentially
for the best good of all, is as much a superstition as the
notions which upheld the paternalist model — although,
curiously, it is a superstition which some economic historians
have been the last to abandon. In some respects Smith's
model conformed more closely to eighteenth-century realities
than did the paternalist; and in symmetry and scope of
intellectual construction it was superior. But one should not
overlook the specious air of empirical validation which the
model carries. Whereas the first appeals to a moral norm —
what *ought* to be men's reciprocal duties — the second
appears to say: "this is the way things work, or would work if
the State did not interfere". And yet if one considers these
sections of *The Wealth of Nations* they impress less as an
essay in empirical enquiry than as a superb, self-validating
essay in logic.

---

[1] Smith saw the two as going together: "The laws concerning corn may
everywhere be compared to the laws concerning religion. The people feel
themselves so much interested in what relates either to their subsistence in
this life, or to their happiness in a life to come, that government must yield
to their prejudices. . .".

When we consider the actual organisation of the eighteenth-century corn trade, empirical verification of neither model is to hand. There has been little detailed investigation of marketing;[1] no major study of that key figure, the miller.[2] Even the first letter of Smith's alphabet — the assumption that high prices were an effective form of rationing — remains no more than an assertion. It is notorious that the demand for corn, or bread, is highly inelastic. When bread is costly, the poor (as one highly-placed observer was once reminded) do not go over to cake. In the view of some observers, when prices rose labourers might eat the same quantity of bread, but cut out other items in their budgets; they might even eat *more* bread to compensate for the loss of other items. Out of one shilling, in a normal year, 6d. might go on bread, 6d. on "coarse meat and plenty of garden stuff"; but in a high-price year the whole shilling would go on bread.[3]

In any event, it is well known that the price movements of grain cannot be accounted for by simple supply-and-demand price mechanisms; and the bounty paid to encourage corn exports distorted matters further. Next to air and water, corn was a prime necessity of life, abnormally sensitive to any

[1] See, however, A. Everitt, "The Marketing of Agricultural Produce", in Joan Thirsk (ed.), *The Agrarian History of England and Wales, 1500-1600*, vol. iv (Cambridge, 1967) and D. Baker, "The Marketing of Corn in the first half of the Eighteenth Century: North-east Kent", *Agric. Hist. Rev.*, xviii (1970).

[2] There is some useful information in R. Bennett and J. Elton, *History of Corn Milling*, 4 vols. (Liverpool, 1898).

[3] Emanuel Collins, *Lying Detected* (Bristol, 1758), pp. 66-7. This seems to be confirmed by the budgets of Davies and Eden (see note 2 on p. 193), and of nineteenth-century observers: see *The Unknown Mayhew*, eds. E. P. Thompson and E. Yeo (1971), App. II. E. H. Phelps Brown and S. V. Hopkins, "Seven Centuries of the Prices of Consumables compared with Builders' Wages rates", *Economica*, xxii (1956), pp. 297-8 allow only 20% of the total household budget to farinaceous food, although the budgets of Davies and Eden (taken in high-price years) show an average of 53%. This again suggests that in such years bread consumption remained stable, but other items were cut out altogether. In London there may already have been a greater diversification of diet by the 1790s. P. Colquhoun wrote to Portland, 9 July 1795, that there was abundance of vegetables at Spitalfields market, especially potatoes, "the great substitute for Bread", carrots and turnips: PRO, PC 1/27/A.54.

deficiency in supply. In 1796 Arthur Young calculated that the overall crop deficiency in wheat was less than 25 per cent; but the price advance was 81 per cent: giving (by his calculation) a profit to the agricultural community of £20 millions over a normal year.[1] Traditionalist writers complained that the farmers and dealers acted from the strength of "monopoly"; they were rebutted in pamphlet after pamphlet, as "too absurd to be seriously treated: what! more than two hundred thousand people. . .!".[2] The point at issue, however, was not whether this farmer or that dealer could act as a "monopolist", but whether the producing and trading interests as a whole were able, with a long-continuing train of favourable circumstances, to take advantage of their command of a prime necessity of life and to enhance the price to the consumer, in much the same way as the advanced industrialised nations today have been able to enhance the price of certain manufactured goods to the less advanced nations.

As the century advanced marketing procedures became less transparent, as the corn passed through the hands of a more complex network of intermediaries. Farmers were selling, not in an open competitive market (which, in a local and regional

---

[1] *Annals of Agriculture*, xxvi (1796), pp. 470, 473. Davenant had estimated in 1699 that a deficiency in the harvest of one-tenth raised the price by three-tenths: Sir C. Whitworth, *The Political and Commercial Works of Charles Davenant* (1771), ii, p. 244. The problem is discussed in W. M. Stern, "The Bread Crisis in Britain, 1795-6", *Economica*, new series, xxxi (1964), and J. D. Gould, "Agricultural Fluctuations and the English Economy in the Eighteenth Century", *Jl. Econ. Hist.*, xxii (1926). Dr Gould puts weight on a point often mentioned in contemporary apologetics for high prices, e.g. *Farmer's Magazine*, ii (1801), p. 81, that the small growers, in a year of scarcity, required their entire crop for seed and for their own consumption: in such factors as this he finds the "chief theoretical explanation of the extreme volatility of grain prices in the early modern period". One would require more investigation of the actual operation of the market before such explanations carry conviction.

[2] Anon. ["A Country Farmer"], *Three Letters to a Member of the House of Commons. . . concerning the Prices of Provisions* (1766), pp. 18-19. For other examples see Lord John Sheffield, *Observations on the Corn Bill* (1791), p. 43; Anon., *Inquiry into the Causes and Remedies of the late and present Scarcity and high Price of Provisions* (1800), p. 33; J. S. Fry, *Letters on the Corn-Trade* (Bristol, 1816), pp. 10-11.

sense, was the aim of the paternalist rather than the *laissez-faire* model) but to dealers or millers who were in a better position to hold stocks and keep the market high. In the last decades of the century, as population rose, so consumption pressed continually upon production, and the producers could more generally command a seller's market. Wartime conditions, while not in fact inhibiting greatly the import of grain during conditions of scarcity, nevertheless accentuated psychological tensions in such years.[1] What mattered in setting the post-harvest price, was the expectation of the harvest yield: and there is evidence in the last decades of the century of the growth of a farming lobby, well aware of the psychological factors involved in post-harvest price levels, assiduously fostering an expectation of shortage.[2] Notoriously, in years of dearth the farmers' faces were wreathed in smiles,[3] while in years of abundant harvest Dame Nature's inconsiderate bounty called forth agricultural cries of "distress". And no matter how bountiful the yield might appear to the eye of the townsman, every harvest was accompanied by talk of mildew, floods, blighted ears which crumbled to powder when threshing commenced.

The free market model supposes a sequence of small to large farmers, bringing their corn to market over the year; but at the end of the century, as high-price year succeeded high-price year, so more small farmers were able to hold back supply until the market rose to their satisfaction. (It was, after all, for them not a matter of routine marketing but of intense, consuming interest: their profit for the year might depend very largely upon the price which three or four corn-stacks might fetch.) If rents had to be paid, the growth in country banking made it easier for the farmer to be

[1] See Olson, *Economics of the Wartime Shortage*, ch. 3; W. F. Galpin, *The Grain Supply of England during the Napoleonic Period* (New York, 1925).

[2] See e.g. Anon. ["A West Country Maltster"], *Considerations on the present High Prices of Provisions, and the Necessities of Life* (1764), p. 10.

[3] "I hope", a Yorkshire landowner wrote in 1708, "the dearth of corn which is likely to continue for several years to come will make husbandry very profitable to us, in breaking up and improving all our new land": cited by Beloff, *op. cit.*, p. 57.

accommodated.[1] The September or October riot was often precipitated by the failure of prices to fall after a seemingly plentiful harvest, and indicated a conscious confrontation between reluctant producer and angry consumer.

These comments are offered, not in refutation of Adam Smith, but simply to indicate places where caution should be exercised until our knowledge is greater. We need only say of the *laissez-faire* model that it is empirically unproven; inherently unlikely; and that there is some evidence on the other side. We have recently been reminded that "merchants made money in the eighteenth century", and that grain merchants may have made it "by operating the market".[2] Such operations are occasionally recorded, although rarely as frankly as was noted by a Whittlesford (Cambridgeshire) farmer and corn merchant in his diary in 1802:

> I bought Rey this Time Twelve Month at 50s per Qr. I could have sold it 122s per Qr. The poor had their flower, good rey, for 2s 6d per peck. Parish paid the difference to me, which was 1s 9d per peck. It was a Blessing to the Poor and good to me. I bought 320 Quarters.[3]

The profit on this transaction was above £1,000.

IV

If one can reconstruct clear alternative models behind the policies of traditionalists and of political economists, can one construct the same for the moral economy of the crowd? This is less easy. One is confronted by a complex of rational analysis, prejudice, and traditional patterns of response to dearth. Nor is it possible, at any given moment, clearly to identify the groups which endorsed the theories of the crowd. They comprise articulate and inarticulate, and include men of

[1] The point is noted in Anon., *A Letter to the Rt. Hon. William Pitt. . . on the Causes of the High Price of Provisions* (Hereford, 1795), p. 9; Anon. ["A Society of Practical Farmers"], *A Letter to the Rt. Hon. Lord Somerville* (1800), p. 49. Cf. L. S. Pressnell, *Country Banking in the Industrial Revolution* (Oxford, 1956), pp. 346-8.

[2] C. W. J. Grainger and C. M. Elliott, "A Fresh Look at Wheat Prices and Markets in the Eighteenth Century", *Econ. Hist. Rev.*, 2nd series, xx, (1967), p. 252.

[3] E. M. Hampson, *The Treatment of Poverty in Cambridgeshire, 1597-1834* (Cambridge, 1934), p. 211.

education and address. After 1750 each year of scarcity was accompanied by a spate of pamphlets and letters to the press, of unequal value. It was a common complaint of the protagonists of free trade in corn that misguided gentry added fuel to the flames of mob discontent.

There is truth in this. The crowd derived its sense of legitimation, in fact, from the paternalist model. Many gentlemen still resented the middleman as an interloper. Where lords of the manor retained market rights they resented the loss (through sample-sales etc.) of their market tolls. If they were landlord-farmers, who witnessed meat or flour being marketed at prices disproportionately high in relation to their own receipts from the dealers, they resented the profits of these common tradesmen the more. The essayist of 1718 has a title which is a précis of his matter: *An Essay to prove that Regrators, Engrossers, Forestallers, Hawkers and Jobbers of Corn, Cattle, and other Marketable Goods. . . are Destructive of Trade, Oppressors to the Poor, and a Common Nuisance to the Kingdom in General.* All dealers (unless simple drovers or carters, moving provisions from one point to the next) appeared to this not unobservant writer as a "vile and pernicious set of men"; and, in the classic terms of reproval adopted by men of settled estate to the bourgeois,

> they are a vagabond sort of people. . . They carry their all about them, and their. . . stock is no more than a plain riding habit, a good horse, a list of the fairs and markets, and a prodigious quantity of impudence. They have the mark of Cain, and like him wander from place to place, driving an interloping trade between the fair dealer and the honest consumer.[1]

[1] Adam Smith noted nearly sixty years later that the "popular odium. . . which attends the corn trade in years of scarcity, the only years in which it can be very profitable, renders people of character and fortune averse to enter into it. It is abandoned to an inferior set of dealers". Twenty-five years later again Earl Fitzwilliam was writing: "Dealers in corn are withdrawing from the trade, afraid to traffic in an article trafficking in which had render'd them liable to so much obloquy & calummy, and to be run at by an ignorant populace, without confidence in protection from those who ought to be more enlighten'd": Fitzwilliam to Portland, 3 Sept. 1800, PRO, HO 42/51. But an examination of the fortunes of such families as the Howards, Frys and Gurneys might call in question such literary evidence.

This hostility to the dealer existed even among many country magistrates, some of whom were noted to be inactive when popular disturbances swept through the areas under their jurisdiction. They were not displeased by attacks on dissenting or Quaker corn factors. A Bristol pamphleteer, who is clearly a corn factor, complained bitterly in 1758 to the JPs of "your law-giving mob", which prevented, in the previous year, the export of corn from the Severn and Wye valleys, and of "many fruitless applications to several Justices of the Peace".[1] Indeed, the conviction grows that a popular hubbub against forestallers was not unwelcome to some in authority. It distracted attention from the farmers and rentiers; while vague Quarter Sessional threats against fore-stallers gave to the poor a notion that the authorities were attending to their interests. The old laws against fore-stallers, a dealer complained in 1766,

> are printed in every newspaper, and stuck up in every corner, by order of the justices, to intimidate the engrossers, against whom many murmurings are propagated. The common people are taught to enter-tain a very high opinion and reverence for these laws. . .

Indeed, he accused the justices of encouraging "the extra-ordinary pretence, that the power and spirit of the mob is necessary to enforce the laws".[2] But if the laws were actually set in motion, they were directed almost without exception against petty culprits — local wide-boys or market-men, who pocketed small profits on trivial transactions — while the large dealers and millers were unaffected.[3]

[1] Collins, op. cit., pp. 67-74. In 1756 several Quaker meeting-houses were attacked during food riots in the Midlands: Gentleman's Magazine, xxvi (1756), p. 408.

[2] Anon., Reflections on the present High Price of Provisions, and the Complaints and Disturbances arising therefrom (1766), pp. 26-7, 31.

[3] Contrary to the common assumption, the forestalling legislation had not fallen into desuetude in the first half of the eighteenth century. Prosecutions were infrequent, but sufficiently evident to suggest that they had some effect upon regulating petty dealing in the open market. At Manchester (see note 1 on p. 195) fines for forestalling or regrating took place sometimes annually, sometimes every two or three years, from 1731 to 1759 (seven fines). Commodities involved included butter, cheese, milk, oysters, fish, meat, carrots, pease, potatoes, turnips, cucumbers, apples, beans, gooseberries, currants, cherries, pigeons, fowls, but very rarely oats and wheat. Fines are less frequent after 1760 but include 1766 (wheat and

Thus, to take a late example, an old-fashioned and crusty Middlesex JP, J. S. Girdler, instituted a general campaign of prosecutions against such offenders in 1796 and 1800, with handbills offering rewards for information, letters to the press, etc. Convictions were upheld at several Quarter Sessions, but the amount gained by the speculators amounted only to ten or fifteen shillings. We can guess at the kind of offender whom his prosecutions touched by the literary style of an anonymous letter which he received:

> We no you are an enemy to Farmers, Mealmen and Bakers and our Trade if it had not bene for me and another you you son of a bitch you wold have bene murdurd long ago by offering your blasted rewards and persecuting Our Trade God dam you and blast you you shall never live to see another harvest. . .[1]

---

butter), 1780 (oats and eels), 1785 (meat), and 1796, 1797 and 1799 (all potatoes). Symbolically, the Court Leet officers to prevent forestalling jumped from 3 to 4 appointed annually (1730-1795) to 7 in 1795, 15 in 1796, 16 in 1797. In addition offenders were prosecuted on occasion (as in 1757) at Quarter Sessions. See Earwaker, *Court Leet Records* (cited p. 195), vii, viii and ix and *Constables' Accounts* (p. 212), ii, p. 94. For other examples of offences, see Essex Quarter Sessions, indictments, 2 Sept. 1709, 9 July 1711 (engrossing oats), and also 1711 for cases involving forestallers of fish, wheat, rye, butter, and, again, 13 Jan. 1729/30: Essex CRO, Calendar and Indictments, Q/SR 541, Q/SR 548, Q/SPb b 3; Constables' presentments for forestalling hogs, Oct. 1735 and Oct. 1746: Bury St. Edmunds and West Suffolk CRO, DB/1/8 (5); ditto for forestalling of butter, Nottingham, 6 Jan. 1745/5, *Records of the Borough of Nottingham* (Nottingham, 1914), vi, p. 209; conviction for forestalling of fowls (fine 13s. 4d.) at Atherstone Court Leet and Court Baron, 18 Oct. 1748: Warwicks. CRO, L2/24 23; cautions against the forestalling of butter etc., Woodbridge market, 30 Aug. 1756: Ipswich and East Suffolk CRO, V 5/9/6-3. In most Quarter-Sessional or market records the odd prosecution is to be found, before 1757. The author of *Reflections* (cited p. 209) writing in 1766, says these "almost-forgotten and disregarded statutes" were employed for the prosecution of "some submissive hucksters and indigent or terrified jobbers", and implies that the "principal factors" have despised "these menaces", believing them to be bad law (p. 37). For 1795 and 1800 see note 2, p. 200: the most important cases of the prosecution of large dealers were those of Rushby, for regrating oats (1799): see Barnes, *op. cit.*, pp. 81-3; and of Waddington, convicted for forestalling hops at Worcester Assizes: see *Times*, 4 Aug. 1800 and (for conviction upheld on appeal) I East 143 in *ER*, cii, pp. 56-68.

[1] Girdler, op. cit., pp. 295-6.

Compassionate traditionalists like Girdler were joined by townsmen of various ranks. Most Londoners suspected everyone who had any part in handling grain, flour or bread of every kind of extortion. The urban lobby was, of course, especially powerful in the middle years of the century, pressing for an end to the export bounty, or for the prohibition of all exports in time of dearth. But London and the larger towns harboured inexhaustible reserves of resentment, and some of the wildest accusations came from this milieu. A certain Dr Manning, in the 1750s, published allegations that bread was adulterated not only with alum, chalk, whiting and beanmeal, but also with slaked lime and white lead. Most sensational was his claim that millers turned into their flour "sacks of old ground bones": "the charnel houses of the dead are raked, to add filthiness to the food of the living", or, as another pamphleteer commented, "the present age [is] making hearty meals on the bones of the last".

Manning's accusations went far beyond the bounds of credibility. (A critic computed that if lime was being used on the scale of his allegations, more would be consumed in the London baking than building industry.)[1] Apart from alum, which was widely used to whiten bread, the commonest form of adulteration was probably the admixture of old, spoiled flour with new flour.[2] But the urban population was quick to believe that far more noxious adulterations were practised, and such belief contributed to the "Shude-hill Fight" at Manchester in 1757, where one of the mills attacked was believed to mix "Accorns, Beans, Bones, Whiting, Chopt Straw, and even dried Horse Dung" with its flour, while at another mill the presence of suspicious adulterants near the hoppers (discovered by the crowd) led to the burning of bolters and sieves, and the destruction of

---

[1] Collins, *op. cit.*, pp. 16-37. P. Markham, *Syhoroc* (1758), i, pp. 11-31; *Poison Detected: or Frightful Truths. . . in a Treatise on Bread* (1757), esp. pp. 16-38.

[2] See e.g. John Smith, *An Impartial Relation of Facts Concerning the Malepractices of Bakers* (n.d. [1740?]).

mill-stones and wheels.[1]

There were other, equally sensitive, areas where the complaints of the crowd were fed by the complaints of traditionalists or by those of urban professional people. Indeed, one may suggest that if the rioting or price-setting crowd acted according to any consistent theoretical model, then this model was a selective reconstruction of the paternalist one, taking from it all those features which most favoured the poor and which offered a prospect of cheap corn. It was, however, less generalised than the outlook of the paternalists. The records of the poor show more particularity: it is this miller, this dealer, those farmers hoarding grain, who provoke indignation and action. This particularity was, however, informed by general notions of rights which disclose themselves most clearly only when one examines the crowd in action. For in one respect the moral economy of the crowd broke decisively with that of the paternalists: for the popular ethic sanctioned direct action by the crowd, whereas the values of order underpinning the paternalist model emphatically did not.

The economy of the poor was still local and regional, derivative from a subsistence-economy. Corn should be consumed in the region in which it was grown, especially in times of scarcity. Profound feeling was aroused, and over several centuries, by export in times of dearth. Of an export riot in Suffolk in 1631 a magistrate wrote: "to see their bread thus taken from them and sent to strangers has turned the impatience of the poor into licentious fury and desperation".[2] In a graphic account of a riot in the same county seventy-eight years later (1709), a dealer described how "the Mobb rose, he thinks several hundreds, and said that the corn should not be carried out of town": "of the Mobb some had halberds, some quarter staffs, and some clubbs. . .". When travelling to Norwich, at several places on the way:

---

[1] See J. P. Earwaker, *The Constables' Accounts of the Manor of Manchester* (Manchester, 1891), iii, pp. 359-61; F. Nicholson and E. Axon, "The Hatfield Family of Manchester, and the Food Riots of 1757 and 1812", *Trans. Lancs. and Chesh. Antiq. Soc.*, xxviii (1910/11), pp. 83-90.

[2] *Calendar State Papers, Domestic*, 1631, p. 545.

the Mobb hearing that he was to goe through with corn, told him that it should not go through the Towne, for that he was a Rogue, and Corn-Jobber, and some cry'd out Stone him, some Pull him off his horse, some Knock him down, and be sure you strike sure; that he. . . questioned them what made them rise in such an inhuman manner to the prejudice of themselves and the countrey, but that they still cryed out that he was a Rogue & was going to carry the corn into France. . .[1]

Except in Westminster, in the mountains, or in the great sheep-grazing districts, men were never far from the sight of corn. Manufacturing industry was dispersed in the countryside: the colliers went to their labour by the side of corn-fields; domestic workers left their looms and workshops for the harvest. Sensitivity was not confined to overseas export. Marginal exporting areas were especially sensitive, where little corn was exported in normal years, but where, in times of scarcity, dealers could hope for a windfall price in London, thereby aggravating local dearth.[2] The colliers — Kingswood, the Forest of Dean, Shropshire, the North-East — were especially prone to action at such times. Notoriously the Cornish tinners had an irascible consumer-consciousness, and a readiness to turn out in force. "We had the devil and all of a riot at Padstow", wrote a Bodmin gentleman in 1773, with scarcely-concealed admiration:

Some of the people have run to too great lengths in exporting of corn. . . Seven or eight hundred tinners went thither, who first offered the corn-factors seventeen shillings for 24 gallons of wheat; but being told they should have none, they immediately broke open the cellar doors, and took away all in the place without money or price.[3]

The worst resentment was provoked in the middle years of the century, by foreign exports upon which bounty was paid. The foreigner was seen as receiving corn at prices sometimes below those of the English market, with the aid of a bounty paid out of English taxes. Hence the extreme bitterness sometimes visited upon the exporter, who was seen as a man seeking private, and dishonourable, gain at the expense of his own people. A North Yorkshire factor, who was given a

[1] PRO, PC 1/2/165.
[2] See D. G. D. Isaac, "A Study of Popular Disturbance in Britain, 1714-54" (Edinburgh Univ. Ph.D. thesis, 1953), ch. I.
[3] *Calendar of Home Office Papers*, 1773, p. 30.

ducking in the river in 1740, was told that he was "no better than a rebel".[1] In 1783 a notice was affixed to the market-cross in Carlisle, commencing:

> Peter Clemeseson & Moses Luthart this is to give you Warning that you must Quit your unlawfull Dealing or Die and be Damed your buying the Corn to starve the Poor Inhabitants of the City and Soborbs of Carlisle to send to France and get the Bounty Given by the Law for taking the Corn out of the Country but by the Lord God Almighty we will give you Bounty at the Expence of your Lives you Damed Roagues. . .

"And if Eany Publick House in Carlisle [the notice continued] Lets you or Luthart put up. . . Corn at their Houses they shall suffer for it."[2] This feeling revived in the last years of the century, notably in 1795, when rumours flew around the country as to secret exports to France. Moreover, 1795 and 1800 saw the efflorescence of a regional consciousness once more, as vivid as that of one hundred years before. Roads were blockaded to prevent export from the parish. Wagons were intercepted and unloaded in the towns through which they passed. The movement of grain by night-convoy assumed the proportions of a military operation:

> Deep groan the waggons with their pond'rous loads,
> As their dark course they bend along the roads;
> Wheel following wheel, in dread procession slow,
> With half a harvest, to their points they go. . .
> The secret expedition, like the night
> That covers its intents, still shuns the light. . .
> While the poor ploughman, when he leaves his bed,
> Sees the huge barn as empty as his shed.[3]

Threats were made to destroy the canals.[4] Ships were stormed at the ports. The miners at Nook Colliery near Haverfordwest threatened to close the estuary at a narrow point. Even lighters on the Severn and Wye were not

[1] PRO, SP 36/50.
[2] *London Gazette*, March 1783, no. 12422.
[3] S. J. Pratt, *Sympathy and Other Poems* (1807), pp. 222-3.
[4] Some years before Wedgwood had heard it "threatened. . . to destroy our canals and let out the water", because provisions were passing through Staffordshire to Manchester from East Anglia: J. Wedgwood, *Address to the Young Inhabitants of the Pottery* (Newcastle, 1783).

immune from attack.[1]

Indignation might also be inflamed against a dealer whose commitment to an outside market disrupted the customary supplies of the local community. A substantial farmer and publican near Tiverton complained to the War Office in 1795 of riotous assemblies "threatening to pull down or fire his house because he takes in Butter of the neighbouring Farmers & Dairymen, to forward it by the common road waggon, that passes by his door to. . . London".[2] In Chudleigh (Devon) in the same year the crowd destroyed the machinery of a miller who had ceased to supply the local community with flour since he was under contract to the Victualling Department of the Navy for ship's biscuits: this had given rise (he says in a revealing phrase) "to an Idea that ive done much infimy to the Community".[3] Thirty years before a group of London merchants had found it necessary to seek the protection of the military for their cheese-warehouses along the river Trent:

> The warehouses. . . in danger from the riotous colliers are not the property of any monopolizers, but of a numerous body of cheese-mongers, and absolutely necessary for the reception of their cheese, for the conveyance to Hull, there to be ship'd for London.[4]

These grievances are related to the complaint, already noted, of the withdrawal of goods from the open market. As the dealers moved further from London and attended more frequently at provincial markets, so they were able to offer prices and buy in quantities which made the farmers impatient to serve the small orders of the poor. "Now it is out of the course of business", wrote Davies in 1795, "for the farmer to retail corn by the bushel to this or that poor man; except in some particular places, as a matter of favour, to his own labourers". And where the poor shifted their demand from grain to flour, the story was much the same:

---

[1] PRO, PC 1/27/A.54; A.55-7; HO 42/34; 42/35; 42/36; 42/37; see also Stern, *op. cit.*, and E. P. Thompson, *The Making of the English Working Class* (Penguin, 1968), pp. 70-3.

[2] PRO, WO I/1082, John Ashley, 24 June 1795.

[3] PRO, HO 42/34.

[4] PRO, WO I/986 fo. 69.

Neither the miller nor the mealman will sell the labourer a less quantity
than a *sack* of flour under the retail price at shops; and the poor man's
pocket will seldom allow of his buying a whole sack at once.[1]

Hence the labourer was driven to the petty retail shop, at
which prices were enhanced.[2] The old markets declined, or,
where they were kept up, they changed their functions. If a
customer attempted to buy a single cheese or half flitch of
bacon, Girdler wrote in 1800, "he is sure to be answered by
an insult, and he is told that the whole lot has been bought up
by some London contractor".[3]

We may take as expressive of these grievances, which
sometimes occasioned riot, an anonymous letter dropped in
1795 by the door of the mayor of Salisbury:

Gentlemen of the Corporation I pray you put a stop to that practice
which is made use of in our Markits by Rook and other carriers in your
giving them the Liberty to Scower the Market of every thing so as the
Inhabitance cannot buy a singel Artickel without going to the Dealers
for it and Pay what Extortionat price they think proper and even
Domineer over the Peopel as thow they was not Whorthy to Look on
them. But their time will soon be at an End as soon as the Solders ear
gon out of town.

The corporation is asked to order carriers out of the market
until the townspeople have been served, "and stop all the
Butchers from sending the meat away by a Carces at a time
But make them cut it up in the Markit and sarve the Town
first". The letter informs the mayor that upwards of three
hundred citizens have "posetively swor to be trow to each
other for the Distruction of the Carriers".[4]

Where the working people could buy cereals in small
parcels intense feeling could arise over weights and measures.
We are exhorted in Luke: "Give, and it shall be given unto
you, good measure pressed down, and shaken together, and
running over, shall men give unto your bosom." This was

[1] Davies, *op. cit.*, pp. 33-4.
[2] "The first principle laid down by a baker, when he comes into a
parish, is, to get all the poor in his debt; he then makes their bread of what
weight or goodness he pleases. . .": *Gentleman's Magazine*, xxvi (1756),
p. 557.
[3] Girdler, *op. cit.*, p. 147.
[4] PRO, HO 42/34.

not, alas, the practice of all farmers and dealers in protestant England. An enactment of Charles II had even given the poor the right to *shake* the measure, so valuable was the poor man's corn that a looseness in the measure might make the difference to him of a day without a loaf. The same Act had attempted, with total lack of success, to enforce the Winchester measure as the national standard. A great variety of measures, varying even within county boundaries from one market-town to the next, gave abundant opportunities for petty profiteering. The old measures were generally larger — sometimes very much larger — than the Winchester; sometimes they were favoured by farmers or dealers, more often they were favoured by the customers. One observer remarked that "the lower orders of people detest it [the Winchester measure], from the smallness of its contents, and the dealers. . . instigate them to this, it being their interest to retain every uncertainty in weights and measures".[1]

Attempts to change the measure often encountered resistance, occasionally riot. A letter from a Clee Hill (Shropshire) miner to a "Brother Sufferer" declared:

> The Parliament for our relief to help to Clem [starve] us Thay are going to lessen our Measure and Wait [weight] to the Lower Standard. We are about Ten Thousand sworn and ready at any time And we wou'd have you get Arms and Cutlasses and swear one another to be true. . . We have but one Life to Loose and we will not clem. . .[2]

Letters to farmers in Northiam (Sussex) warned:

> Gentlemen all ie hope you whill take this as a wharning to you all for you to put the little Bushels bie and take the oald measher [measure] again for if you dont there whill be a large company that shall borne [burn] the little measher when you are all abade and asleep and your cornehouses and cornstacks and you along with them. . .[3]

[1] *Annals of Agriculture*, xxvi (1796), p. 327; *Museum Rusticum et Commerciale*, iv (1765), p. 198. The difference in bushels could be very considerable: as against the Winchester bushel of 8 gallons, the Stamford had 16 gallons, the Carlisle 24, and the Chester 32: see J. Houghton, *A Collection for Improvement of Husbandry and Trade* (1727), no. xlvi, 23 June 1693.

[2] *London Gazette*, March 1767, no. 10710.

[3] November 1793, in PRO, HO 42/27. The measures concerned were for malt.

A Hampshire contributor to the *Annals of Agriculture* explained in 1795 that the poor "have erroneously conceived an idea that the price of grain is increased by the late alteration from a nine-gallon bushel to the Winchester, from its happening to take place at a moment of a rising market, by which, the same money was paid for eight as used to be paid for nine gallons". "I confess", he continues,

> I have a decided predeliction for the nine-gallon measure, for the reason that it is the measure which nearest yields a bushel of flour; whence, the poor man is enabled to judge of what he ought to pay for a bushel of flour, which, in the present measure, requires more arithmetic than comes to his share to ascertain.[1]

Even so, the arithmetical notions of the poor may not have been so erroneous. Changes in measures, like changes to decimal currency, tend by some magic to disadvantage the consumer.

If less corn was being bought (at the end of the century) in the open market by the poor, this also indicated the rise to greater importance of the miller. The miller occupies a place in popular folklore, over many centuries, which is both enviable and unenviable. On one hand he was noted as a fabulously successful lecher, whose prowess is still perhaps perpetuated in a vernacular meaning of the word "grinding". Perhaps the convenience of the village mill, tucked around a secluded corner of the stream, to which the village wives and maidens brought their corn for grinding; perhaps also his command over the means of life; perhaps his status in the village, which made him an eligible match — all may have contributed to the legend:

> A brisk young lass so brisk and gay
> She went unto the mill one day. . .
> There's a peck of corn all for to grind
> I can but stay a little time.
>
> Come sit you down my sweet pretty dear
> I cannot grind your corn I fear
> My stones is high and my water low
> I cannot grind for the mill won't go.

---

[1] *Annals of Agriculture*, xxiv (1795), pp. 51-2.

> Then she sat down all on a sack
> They talked of this and they talked of that
> They talked of love, of love proved kind
> She soon found out the mill would grind. . .[1]

On the other hand, the miller's repute was less enviable. "*Loving!*", exclaims Nellie Dean in *Wuthering Heights*: "*Loving!* Did anybody ever hear the like? I might as well talk of loving the miller who comes once a year to buy our corn". If we are to believe all that was written about him in these years, the miller's story had changed little since Chaucer's Reeve's Tale. But where the small country miller was accused of quaintly medieval customs — over-size toll dishes, flour concealed in the casing of the stones, etc. — his larger counterpart was accused of adding new, and greatly more enterprising, peculations:

> For ther-biforn he stal but curteisly,
> But now he was a thief outrageously.

At one extreme we still have the little country mill, exacting toll according to its own custom. The toll might be taken in flour (always from "the best of the meal and from the finer flour that is in the centre of the hopper"); and since the proportion remained the same with whatever fluctuation in price, it was to the miller's advantage if prices were high. Around the small toll-mills (even where toll had been commuted for money payments) grievances multiplied, and there were fitful attempts at their regulation.[2] Since the millers entered increasingly into dealing, and into grinding corn on their own account for the bakers, they had little time for the petty customers (with a sack or two of gleaned corn);

---

[1] James Reeves, *The Idiom of the People* (1958), p. 156. See also Brit. Lib. Place MSS, Add MSS 27825 for "A pretty maid she to the miller would go", verse 2:

> Then the miller he laid her against the mill hopper
> Merry a soul so wantonly
> He pulled up her cloaths, and he put in the stopper
> For says she I'll have my corn ground small and free.

[2] See Markham, *Syhoroc*, ii, p. 15; Bennett and Elton, *op. cit.*, iii, pp. 150-65; information of John Spyry against the Miller of Millbrig Mill, 1740, for taking sometimes 1/6th, sometimes 1/7th, and sometimes 1/8th part as mulcture: West Riding Sessions papers, County Hall, Wakefield.

hence endless delay; hence also, when the flour was returned it might be the product of other, inferior, grain. (It was complained that some millers purchased at half-price damaged corn which they then mixed with the corn of their customers.[1]) As the century wore on, the translation of many mills to industrial purposes gave to the surviving petty corn-mills a more advantageous position. In 1796 these grievances were sufficiently felt to enable Sir Francis Bassett to carry the Miller's Toll Bill, intended to regulate their practices, weights and measures, more strictly.[2]

But these petty millers were, of course, the small fry of the eighteenth century. The great millers of the Thames Valley and of the large towns were a different order of entrepreneurs, who traded extensively in flour and malt. Millers were quite outside the Assize of Bread, and they could immediately pass on any increase in the price of corn to the consumer. England also had its unsung *banalités* in the eighteenth century, including those extraordinary survivals, the soke mills, which exercised an absolute monopoly of the grinding of grain (and the sale of flour) in substantial manufacturing centres, among them Manchester, Bradford, Leeds.[3] In most cases the feoffees who owned the soke rights sold or leased these to private speculators. Most stormy was the history of the School Mills at Manchester, whose soke rights were intended as a charitable endowment to support the grammar school. Two unpopular lessees of the rights inspired, in 1737, Dr Byrom's rhyme:

> *Bone and Skin*, two millers thin,
>   Would starve the town, or near it;
> But be it known, to *Skin and Bone*,
>   That Flesh and Blood can't bear it.

When, in 1757, new lessees sought to prohibit the importation of flour to the growing town, while at the same time managing their mills (it was alleged) with extortion and delay,

---

[1] See Girdler, *op. cit.*, pp. 102-6, 212.

[2] *Annals of Agriculture*, xxiii (1795), pp. 179-91; Bennett and Elton, *op. cit.*, iii, p. 166; 36: Geo III, c.85.

[3] See Bennett and Elton, *op. cit.*, iii, pp. 204 ff; W. Cudworth, "The Bradford Soke", *The Bradford Antiquary* (Bradford, 1888), i, pp. 74ff.

flesh and blood could indeed bear it no longer. In the famous "Shude-hill Fight" of that year at least four men were killed by musketry, but the soke rights were finally broken.[1] But even where no actual soke right obtained, one mill might command a populous community, and could provoke the people to fury by a sudden advance in the price of flour or an evident deterioration in its quality. Mills were the visible, tangible targets of some of the most serious urban riots of the century. The Albion Mills at Blackfriars Bridge (London's first steam mills) were governed by a quasi-philanthropic syndicate; yet when they burned down in 1791 Londoners danced and sang ballads of rejoicing in the streets.[2] The first steam mill at Birmingham (Snow Hill) fared little better, being the target of a massive attack in 1795.

It may appear at first sight as curious that both dealers and millers should continue to be among the objectives of riot at the end of the century, by which time in many parts of the Midlands and South (and certainly in urban areas) working people had become accustomed to buying bread at the baker's shops rather than grain or flour in the market-place. We do not know enough to chart the change-over with accuracy, and certainly much home-baking survived.[3] But even where the change-over was complete, one should not underestimate the sophistication of the situation and of the crowd's objectives. There were, of course, scores of petty riots outside bread shops, and the crowd very often "set the price" of bread. But the baker (whose trade in times of high prices can sacrcely have been an enviable one) was, alone of all those who dealt in the people's necessities (landlord,

[1] See note 1, p. 212 and Bennett and Elton, *op. cit.*, pp. 274ff.

[2] *Ibid.*, iii, pp. 204-6.

[3] Replies from towns to Privy Council enquiry, 1796, in PRO, PC I/33/A.88: e.g. mayor of York, 16 April 1796, "the poor can get their bread baked at common ovens. . ."; mayor of Lancaster, 10 April, "each family buys their own flour and makes their own bread"; mayor of Leeds, 4 April, it is the custom "to buy corn or meal, and to mix up their own bread, and to bake it themselves or get it baked for hire". A survey of bakers in the hundred of Corby (Northamptonshire) in 1757 shows that out of 31 parishes, one parish (Wilbarston) had four bakers, one had three, three had two, eight had one, and fourteen had no resident baker (four gave no return): Northants. CRO, H (K) 170.

farmer, factor, carrier, miller), in daily contact with the consumer; and he was, more than any of the others, protected by the visible paraphernalia of paternalism. The Assize of Bread clearly and publicly limited their lawful profits (thereby also tending to leave the baking trade in the hands of numerous small traders with little capital), and thus protected them, to some degree, from popular wrath. Even Charles Smith, the able exponent of free trade, thought the continuation of the Assize to be expedient: "in large Towns and Cities it will always be necessary to set the Assize, in order to satisfy the people that the price which the Bakers demand is no more than that what is thought reasonable by the Magistrates".[1]

The psychological effect of the Assize was, therefore, considerable. The baker could hope to enhance his profit beyond the allowance calculated in the Assize only by small stratagems, some of which — short-weight bread, adulteration, the mixing in of cheap and spoiled flour — were subject either to legal redress or to instant crowd retaliation. Indeed, the baker had sometimes to attend to his own public relations, even to the extent of enlisting the crowd on his side: when Hannah Pain of Kettering complained to the justices of short-weight bread, the baker "raised a mob upon her. . . and said she deserved to be whipped, there were enough of such scambling scum of the earth".[2] Many corporations throughout the century, made a great show of supervising weights and measures, and of punishing offenders.[3] Ben Jonson's "Justice Overdo" was still busy in the streets of Reading, Coventry, or London:

[1] Smith, *Three Tracts on the Corn-Trade*, p. 30.
[2] Examination of Hannah Pain, 12 Aug. 1757, Northants. CRO, H (K) 167 (I).
[3] It is notable that punishments for these offences were most frequent in years of dearth, and doubtless these were intended to have symbolic force: thus 6 presentments for false or short weight at Bury St. Edmunds sessions, May 1740: Bury St. Edmunds and West Suffolk CRO, D8/I/8(5); 6 fined for deficient weight in Maidenhead, October 1766: Berks. CRO, M/JMI. At Reading, however, surveillance appears to be fairly constant, in good years as well as bad: Central Public Library, Reading, R/MJ Acc. 167, Court Leet and View of Frankpledge. At Manchester the market officials were vigilant until the 1750s, more casual thereafter, but very active in April 1796: Earwaker, *Court Leet Records*, ix, pp. 113-4.

Marry, go you into every alehouse, and down into every cellar; measure the length of puddings. . . weigh the loaves of bread on his middle finger. . . give the puddings to the poor, the bread to the hungry, the custards to his children.

In this tradition we find a London magistrate in 1795 who, coming on the scene of a riot in Seven Dials where the crowd was already in the act of demolishing the shop of a baker accused of selling light-weight bread, intervened, seized the baker's stock, weighed the loaves, and finding them indeed deficient, distributed the loaves among the crowd.[1]

No doubt the bakers, who knew their customers, sometimes complained of their powerlessness to reduce prices, and diverted the crowd to the mill or the corn-market. "After ransacking many bakers' shops", the miller of Snow Hill, Birmingham, related of the 1795 attack, "they came in great numbers against us. . .".[2] But in many cases the crowd clearly selected its own targets, deliberately by-passing the bakers. Thus in 1740 at Norwich the people "went to every Baker in the City, and affix'd a Note on his Door in these words, Wheat at *Sixteen Shillings a Comb*". In the same year at Wisbech they obliged "the Merchants to sell Wheat at 4d per Bushel. . . not only to them, but also to the Bakers, where they regulated the Weight & Price of Bread".[3]

But it is clear at this point that we are dealing with a far more complex pattern of action than one which can be satisfactorily explained by a face-to-face encounter between the populace and particular millers, dealers or bakers. It is necessary to take a larger view of the actions of the crowd.

[1] *Gentleman's Magazine*, lxv (1795), p. 697.

[2] MS notebook of Edward Pickering, Birmingham City Ref. Lib. M 22.11.

[3] *Ipswich Journal*, 12 and 26 July 1740. (I am indebted to Dr R. M. Malcolmson of Queen's University, Ontario, for these references.) The crowd by no means mistook the bakers for their main opponents, and forms of pressure were often of considerable complexity; thus "incendiary" papers set up around Tenterden (1768) incited people to rise and force the farmers to sell their wheat to the millers or the poor at £10 a load, and threatened to destroy the millers who gave to the farmers a higher price: Shelburne, 25 May 1768, PRO, SP 44/199.

V

It has been suggested that the term "riot" is a blunt tool of
analysis for so many particular grievances and occasions. It is
also an imprecise term for describing popular actions. If we
are looking for the characteristic form of direct action, we
should take, not squabbles outside London bakeries, nor
even the great affrays provoked by discontent with the large
millers, but the "risings of the people" (most notably in 1740,
1756, 1766, 1795 and 1800) in which colliers, tinners, weavers
and hosiery workers were prominent. What is remarkable
about these "insurrections" is, first, their discipline, and,
second, the fact that they exhibit a pattern of behaviour for
whose origin we must look back several hundreds of years:
which becomes more, rather than less, sophisticated in the
eighteenth century; which repeats itself, seemingly
spontaneously, in different parts of the country and after the
passage of many quiet years. The central action in this
pattern is not the sack of granaries and the pilfering of grain
or flour but the action of "setting the price".

What is extraordinary about this pattern is that it
reproduces, sometimes with great precision, the emergency
measures in time of scarcity whose operation, in the years
between 1580 and 1630, were codified in the *Book of Orders*.
These emergency measures were employed in times of scarcity
in the last years of Elizabeth, and put into effect, in a
somewhat revised form, in the reign of Charles I, in 1630. In
Elizabeth's reign the magistrates were required to attend the
local markets,

> and where you shall fynde that there is insufficiente quantities broughte
> to fill and serve the said marketts and speciallie the poorer sorte, you
> shall thereupon resorte to the houses of the Farmers and others using
> tyllage. . . and viewe what store and provision of graine theye have
> remayninge either thrashed or unthrashed. . .

They might then order the farmers to send "convenient
quantities" to market to be sold "and that at reasonable
price". The justices were further empowered to "sett downe a
certen price upon the bushell of everye kynde of graine".[1]

---

[1] "A Coppie of the Councells her[e] for graine delyvrd at Bodmyn the
xith of May 1586": Bodleian Library, Rawlinson MSS B 285, fos. 66-7.

The queen and her Council opined that high prices were in part due to engrossers, in part to the "greedie desier" of corn-growers who "bee not content wth anie moderate gayne, but seeke & devise waies to kepe up the prices to the manifest oppression of the poorer sort". The Orders were to be enforced "wth out all parciality in sparing anie man".[1]

In essence, then, the *Book of Orders* empowered magistrates (with the aid of local juries) to survey the corn stocks in barns and granaries;[2] to order quantities to be sent to market; and to enforce with severity every part of the marketing, licensing and forestalling legislation. No corn was to be sold except in open market, "unless the same be to some pore handicrafts Men, or Day-Labourers within the parish wherein you doe dwell, that cannot conveniently come to the Market Townes". The Orders of 1630 did not explicitly empower justices to set the price, but ordered them to attend the market and ensure that the poor were "provided of necessary Corne. . . with as much favour in the Prices, as by the earnest Perswasion of the Justices can be obtained". The power to set a price upon grain or flour rested, in emergency, half-way between enforcement and persuasion.[3]

---

[1] There is some account of the operation of the *Book of Orders* in E. M. Leonard, *Early History of English Poor Relief* (Cambridge, 1900); Gras, *op. cit.*, pp. 236-42; Lipson, *op. cit.*, iii, pp. 440-50; B. E. Supple, *Commercial Crisis and Change in England, 1600-42* (Cambridge, 1964), p. 117. Papers illustrative of their operation are in *Official Papers of Nathaniel Bacon of Stiffkey, Norfolk* (Camden Society, 3rd series, xxvi, 1915), pp. 130-57.

[2] For an example, see *Victoria County History, Oxfordshire*, ed. W. Page (1907), ii, pp. 193-4.

[3] By an Act of 1534 (25 Henry VIII, *c.* 2) the Privy Council had the power to set prices on corn in emergency. In a somewhat misleading note, Gras (*op. cit.*, pp. 132-3) opines that after 1550 the power was never used. It was in any case not forgotten: a proclamation of 1603 appears to set prices (Seligman Collection, Columbia Univ. Lib., Proclamations, James I, 1603); the *Book of Orders* of 1630 concludes with the warning that "if the Corne-masters and other Owners of Victuall. . . shall not willingly performe these Orders", His Majesty will "give Order that reasonable Prices shall be set"; the Privy Council attempted to restrain prices by Proclamation in 1709, Liverpool Papers, Brit. Mus., Add. MS. 38353, fo. 195; and the matter was actively canvassed in 1757 — see Smith, *Three Tracts on the Corn Trade*, pp. 29, 35. And (apart from the Assize of Bread) other price-fixing powers lingered on. In 1681 at Oxford market (controlled by the University) prices were set for butter, cheese, poultry,

This emergency legislation was falling into disrepair during the Civil Wars.[1] But the popular memory, especially in a pre-literate society, is extraordinarily long. There can be little doubt that a direct tradition extends from the *Book of Orders* of 1630 to the actions of clothing workers in East Anglia and the West in the eighteenth century. (The literate had long memories also: the *Book of Orders* itself was republished, unofficially in 1662, and again in 1758, with a prefatory address to the reader referring to the present "wicked combination to make scarcity".)[2]

The Orders were themselves in part a response to the pressure of the poor:

> The Corne is so dear
> I dout mani will starve this yeare —

So ran a doggerel notice affixed in the church porch in the parish of Wye (Kent) in 1630:

> If you see not to this
> Sum of you will speed amis.
> Our souls they are dear,
> For our bodys have sume ceare
> Before we arise
> Less will safise. . .
> You that are set in place
> See that youre profesion you doe not disgrace. . .[3]

---

meat, bacon, candles, oats, and beans: "The Oxford Market", *Collectanea* 2nd ser. (Oxford, 1890), pp. 127-8. It seems that the Assize of Ale lapsed in Middlesex in 1692 (Lipson, *op. cit.*, ii, p. 501), and in 1762 brewers were authorized (by 2 Geo. III, *c.* 14) to raise the price in a reasonable manner; but when in 1773 it was proposed to raise the price by $\frac{1}{2}$d. a quart Sir John Fielding wrote to the earl of Suffolk that the increase "cannot be thought reasonable; nor will the subject submit to it": *Calendar of Home Office Papers*, 1773, pp. 9-14; P. Mathias, *The Brewing Industry in England, 1700-1830* (Cambridge, 1959), p. 360.

[1] See G. D. Ramsay, "Industrial *Laisser-Faire* and the Policy of Cromwell", *Econ. Hist. Rev.*, 1st series, xvi (1946), esp. pp. 103-4; M. James, *Social Problems and Policy during the Puritan Revolution* (1930), pp. 264-71.

[2] *Seasonable Orders Offered from former Precedents Whereby the Price of Corn. . . may be much abated* (1662) — a reprint of the Elizabethan Orders; J. Massie, *Orders Appointed by His Majestie King Charles I* (1758).

[3] *Calendar State Papers, Domestic*, 1630, p. 387.

One hundred and thirty years later (1768) incendiary papers
were once again being nailed to church doors (as well as to
inn-signs) in parishes within the same lathe of Scray in Kent,
inciting the poor to rise.[1] Many similar continuities can be
observed, although undoubtedly the pattern of direct action
spread to new districts in the eighteenth century. In many
actions, especially in the old manufacturing regions of the
East and West, the crowd claimed that since the authorities
refused to enforce "the laws" they must enforce them for
themselves. In 1693 at Banbury and Chipping Norton the
crowd "took away the corne by force out of the waggons, as
it was carrying away by the ingrossers, saying that they were
resolved to put the law in execution, since the magistrates
neglected it".[2] During the extensive disorders in the West in
1766 the sheriff of Gloucestershire, a gentleman clothier,
could not disguise his respect for the rioters who

> went. . . to a farmhouse and civilly desired that they wou'd thresh out
> and bring to market their wheat and sell it for five shillings per bushel,
> which being promised, and some provisions given them unasked for,
> they departed without the least violence or offence.

If we follow other passages of the sheriff's accounts we
may encounter most of the features found in these actions:

> On Friday last a Mobb was rais'd in these parts by the blowing of Horns
> &c consisting entirely of the lowest of the people such as weavers,
> mecanicks, labourers, prentices, and boys, &c. . .

"They proceeded to a gristmill near the town. . . cutting open
Baggs of Flower and giving & carrying it away & destroying
corn &c." They then attended at the main markets, setting
the price of grain. Three days later he sent a further report:

> They visited Farmers, Millers, Bakers and Hucksters shops, selling corn,
> flower, bread, cheese, butter, and bacon, at their own prices. They
> returned in general the produce [i.e. the money] to the proprietors or in
> their absence left the money for them; and behaved with great
> regularity and decency where they were not opposed, with outrage and
> violence where they was: but pilferd very little, which to prevent, they
> will not now suffer Women and boys to go with them.

[1] *Calendar of Home Office Papers*, 1768, p. 342.
[2] Westerfield, *op. cit.*, p. 148.

After visiting the mills and markets around Gloucester, Stroud and Cirencester, they divided into parties of fifty and a hundred and visited the villages and farms, requesting that corn be brought at fair prices to market, and breaking in on granaries. A large party of them attended on the sheriff himself, downed their cudgels while he addressed them on their misdeameanours, listened with patience, "chearfully shouted God Save the King", and then picked up their cudgels and resumed the good work of setting the price. The movement partook of the character of a general strike of the whole clothing district: "the rioters come into our workshops. . . and force out all the men willing or unwilling to join them".[1]

This was an unusually large-scale and disciplined action. But the account directs us to features repeatedly encountered. Thus the movement of the crowd from the market-place outwards to the mills and thence (as in the *Book of Orders*) to farms, where stocks were inspected and the farmers ordered to send grain to market at the price dictated by the crowd — all this is commonly found. This was sometimes accompanied by the traditional round of visits to the houses of the great, for contributions, forced or voluntary. At Norwich in 1740 the crowd, after forcing down prices in the city, and seizing a keel loaded with wheat and rye on the river, solicited contributions from the rich of the city:

> Early on Thursday Morning, by Sound of Horns, they met again; and after a short Confabulation, divided into Parties, and march'd out of Town at different Gates, with a long Streamer carried before them, purposing to visit the Gentlemen and Farmers in the neighbouring Villages, in order to extort Money, Strong Ale, &c, from them. At many places, where the Generosity of People answer'd not their Expectation, 'tis said they shew'd their Resentment by treading down the Corn in the Fields. . .

Perambulating crowds were active in this year, notably in Durham and Northumberland, the West Riding, and several parts of North Wales. Anti-export demonstrators, commencing at Dewsbury (April 1740) were led by a drummer and "a sort of ensign or colours"; they performed a regular circuit of

[1] Letters of W. Dalloway, Brimscomb, 17 and 20 Sept. 1766, in PRO, PC 1/8/41.

the local mills, destroying machinery, cutting sacks, and carrying away grain and meal. In 1766 a perambulating crowd in the Thames Valley called themselves "the Regulators"; a terrified farmer allowed them to sleep in the straw in his yard, and "could hear from his Chamber that they were telling one another whom they had most frightened, & where they had the best success". The pattern continues in the 1790s: at Ellesmere (Shropshire) the crowd stopping the corn as it goes to the mills and threatening the farmers individually; in the Forest of Dean the miners visiting mills and farmers' houses, and exacting money "from persons they meet in the road"; in West Cornwall the tinners visiting farms with a noose in one hand and an agreement to bring corn at reduced prices to market in the other.[1]

It is the restraint, rather than the disorder, which is remarkable; and there can be no doubt that the actions were approved by an overwhelming popular consensus. There is a deeply-felt conviction that prices *ought*, in times of dearth, to be regulated, and that the profiteer put himself outside of society. On occasion the crowd attempted to enlist, by suasion or force a magistrate, parish constable, or some figure of authority to preside over the *taxation populaire*. In 1766 at Drayton (Oxfordshire) members of the crowd went to John Lyford's house "and asked him if he were a Constable — upon his saying 'yes' Cheer said he sho'd go with them to the Cross & receive the money for 3 sacks of flour which they had taken from one Betty Smith and which they w'd sell for 5s a Bushel"; the same crowd enlisted the constable of Abingdon for the same service. The constable of Handborough (also in Oxfordshire) was enlisted in a similar way, in 1795; the crowd set a price — and a substantial one — of 40s a sack upon a wagon of flour which had been inter-

---

[1] Norwich, 1740 — *Ipswich Journal*, 26 July 1740; Dewsbury, 1740 — J. L. Kaye and five magistrates, Wakefield, 30 Apr. 1740, in PRO, SP 36/50; Thames Valley, 1766 — testimony of Bartholomew Freeman of Bisham Farm, 2 Oct. 1766, in PRO, TS 11/995/3707; Ellesmere, 1795 — PRO, WO I/1089, fo. 359; Forest of Dean — John Turner, mayor of Gloucester, 24 June 1795, PRO, WO I/1087; Cornwall — see John G. Rule, "Some Social Aspects of the Cornish Industrial Revolution", in Roger Burt (ed.), *Industry and Society in the South-West* (Exeter, 1970), pp. 90-1.

cepted, and the money for no fewer than fifteen sacks was paid into his hands. In the Isle of Ely, in the same year, "the mob insisted upon buying meat at 4d per lb, & desired Mr Gardner a Magistrate to superintend the sale, as the Mayor had done at Cambridge on Saturday sennight". Again in 1795 there were a number of occasions when militia or regular troops supervised forced sales, sometimes at bayonet-point, their officers looking steadfastly the other way. A combined operation of soldiery and crowd forced the mayor of Chichester to accede in setting the price of bread. At Wells men of the 122nd Regiment began

> by hooting those they term'd forestallers or jobbers of butter, who they hunted in different parts of the town — seized the butter — collected it together — placed sentinels over it — then threw it, & mix't it together in a tub — & afterwards retail'd the same, weighing it in scales, selling it after the rate of 8d per lb. . . though the common price given by the jobbers was rather more than 10d.[1]

It would be foolish to suggest that, when so large a breach was made in the outworks of deference, many did not take the opportunity to carry off goods without payment. But there is abundant evidence the other way, and some of it is striking. There are the Honiton lace-workers, in 1766, who, having taken corn from the farmers and sold it at the popular price in the market, brought back to the farmers not only the money but also the sacks; the Oldham crowd, in 1800, which rationed each purchaser to two pecks a head; and the many occasions when carts were stopped on the roads, their contents sold, and the money entrusted to the carter.[2]

Moreover, in those cases where goods were taken without payment, or where violence was committed, it is wise to

---

[1] Drayton, Oxon — brief against Wm. Denley and three others, in PRO, TS 11/995/3707; Handborough — information of Robert Prior, constable, 6 Aug. 1795, PRO, Assizes 5/116; Isle of Ely — Lord Hardwicke, Wimpole, 27 July 1795, PRO, HO 42/35 and H. Gunning, *Reminiscences of Cambridge* (1854), ii, pp. 5-7; Chichester — duke of Richmond, Goodwood, 14 Apr. 1795, PRO, WO I/1092; Wells — "Verax", 28 Apr. 1795, PRO, WO I/1082 and the Rev. J. Turner, 28 Apr., HO 42/34. For an example of a constable who was executed for his part in a tinners' riot in St. Austell, 1729, see Rule, *op. cit.*, p. 90.

[2] See Rose, *op. cit.*, p. 435; Edwin Butterworth, *Historical Sketches of Oldham* (Oldham, 1856), pp. 137-9, 144-5.

enquire whether any particular aggravation of circumstances enters into the case. The distinction is made in an account of an action at Portsea (Hampshire) in 1795. The bakers and butchers were first offered by the crowd the popular price: "those that complied in those demands were paid with exactness". But those who refused had their shops rifled "without receiving any more money than the mob chose to leave". Again, the quarrymen at Port Isaac (Cornwall) in the same year seized barley warehoused for export, paying the reasonably high price of 11s. a bushel, at the same time warning the owner that "if he offer'd to ship the Remainder they would come & take it without making him any recompence". Very often the motive of punishment or revenge comes in. The great riot in Newcastle in 1740, when pitmen and keelmen swept into the Guildhall, destroyed the town books and shared out the town's hutch, and pelted aldermen with mud and stones, came only after two phases of aggravation: first, when an agreement between the pitmen's leaders and the merchants (with an alderman acting as arbitrator) setting the prices of grain had been broken; second, when panicky authorities had fired into the crowd from the Guildhall steps. At one house in Gloucestershire in 1766 shots were fired at the crowd which (writes the sheriff) —

> they highly resented by forceing into the house, and destroying all the furniture, windows, &c and partly untiled it; they have given out since that they greatly repented of this act because 'twas not the master of the house (he being from home) that fired upon them.

In 1795 the tinners mounted an attack upon a Penryn (Cornwall) merchant who was contracted to send them barley, but who had sent them spoiled and sprouting grain. When mills were attacked, and their machinery damaged, it was often in furtherance of a long-standing warning, or as punishment for some notorious practice.[1]

Indeed, if we wish to call in question the unilinear and

[1]Portsea — *Gentleman's Magazine*, lxv (1795), p. 343; Port Isaac — Sir W. Molesworth, 23 March 1795, PRO, HO 42/34; Newcastle — *Gentleman's Magazine*, x (1740), p. 355, and various sources in PRO, SP 36/51, in Northumberland CRO and Newcastle City Archives Office; Gloucestershire, 1766 — PRO, PC 1/8/41; Penryn, 1795 — PRO, HO 42/34.

spasmodic view of food riots, we need only point to this continuing motif of popular intimidation, when men and women near to starvation nevertheless attacked mills and granaries, not to steal the food, but to punish the proprietors. Repeatedly corn or flour was strewn along the roads and hedges; dumped into the river; mill machinery was damaged and mill-dams let off. To examples of such behaviour the authorities reacted both with indignation and astonishment. It was symptomatic (as it seemed to them) of the "frantic" and distempered humours of a people whose brain was inflamed by hunger. In 1795 both the Lord Chief Justice and Arthur Young delivered lectures to the poor, pointing out that the destruction of grain was not the best way to improve the supply of bread. Hannah More added a Half-penny Homily. An anonymous versifier of 1800 gives us a rather more lively example of these admonitions to the lower orders:

> When with your country Friends your hours you pass,
> And take, as oft you're wont, the copious glass,
> When all grow mellow, if perchance you hear
> "That 'tis th' Engrossers make the corn so dear;
> "They must and will have bread; they've had enough
> "Of Rice and Soup, and all such *squashy* stuff:
> "They'll help themselves: and strive by might and main
> "To be reveng'd on all such rogues in grain":
> John swears he'll fight as long as he has breath,
> "'Twere better to be hang'd than starv'd to death:
> "He'll burn Squire Hoardum's garner, so he will,
> "Tuck up old Filchbag, and pull down his mill".
> Now when the Prong and Pitchfork they prepare
> And all the implements of rustick war. . .
> Tell them what ills unlawful deeds attend,
> Deeds, which in wrath begun, and sorrow end,
> That burning barns, and pulling down a mill,
> Will neither corn produce, nor bellies fill.[1]

But were the poor really so silly? One suspects that the millers and dealers, who kept one wary eye on the people and the other on the maximisation of their profits, knew better than the poetasters at their *escritoires*. For the poor had their own sources of information. They worked on the docks. They moved the barges on the canals. They drove the carts

[1] Anon., *Contentment: or Hints to Servants, on the Present Scarcity* (broadsheet, 1800).

and manned the toll-gates. They worked in the granaries and the mills. They often knew the local facts far better than the gentry; in many actions they went unerringly to hidden supplies of grain whose existence the JPs, in good faith, denied. If rumours often grew beyond all bounds, they were always rooted in at least some shallow soil of fact. The poor knew the one way to make the rich yield was to twist their arms.

VI

Initiators of the riots were, very often, the women. In 1693 we learn of a great number of women going to Northampton market, "with knives stuck in their girdles to force corn at their own rates". In an export riot in 1737 at Poole (Dorset) it was reported: "The Numbers consist of so many Women, & the Men supporting them, & Swear, if any one offers to molest any of the Women in their Proceedings they will raise a Great Number of Men & destroy both Ships & Cargoes". The mob was raised in Stockton (Durham) in 1740 by a "Lady with a stick and a horn". At Haverfordwest (Pembroke) in 1795 an old-fashioned JP who attempted, with the help of his curate, to do battle with the colliers, complained that "the women were putting the Men on, & were perfect furies. I had some strokes from some of them on my Back. . .". A Birmingham paper described the Snow Hill riots as the work of "a rabble, urged on by furious women". In dozens of cases it is the same — the women pelting an unpopular dealer with his own potatoes, or cunningly combining fury with the calculation that they had slightly greater immunity than the men from the retaliation of the authorities: "the women told the common men", the Haverfordwest magistrate said of the soldiers, "that they knew they were in their Hearts for them & would do them no hurt".[1]

[1] Northampton — *Calendar State Papers, Domestic*, 1693, p. 397; Poole — memorial of Chitty and Lefebare, merchants, enclosed in Holles Newcastle, 26 May 1737, PRO, SP 41/10; Stockton — Edward Goddard, 24 May 1740, PRO, SP 36/50 ("We met a Lady with a Stick and a horn going towards Norton to raise the people. . . took the horn from her, She using very ill language all the while and followed into the Town, raising all the People she could. . . Ordered the Woman to be taken up. . .

These women appear to have belonged to some pre-history
of their sex before its Fall, and to have been unaware that
they should have waited for some two hundred years for their
Liberation. (Southey could write as a commonplace, in 1807:
"Women are more disposed to be mutinous; they stand less in
fear of law, partly from ignorance, partly because they
presume upon the privilege of their sex, and therefore in
all public tumults they are foremost in violence and
ferocity".[1]) They were also, of course, those most involved
in face-to-face marketing, most sensitive to price significancies, most experienced in detecting short-weight or inferior
quality. It is probable that the women most frequently
precipitated the spontaneous actions. But other actions were
more carefully prepared. Sometimes notices were nailed to
church or inn doors. In 1740 "a Mach of Futtball was Cried
at Ketring of five Hundred Men of a side, but the design was
to Pull Down Lady Betey Jesmaine's Mills". At the end of
the century the distribution of hand-written notices may have
become more common. From Wakefield (Yorkshire), 1795:

To Give Notice
To all Women & inhabitance of Wakefield they are desired to meet at
the New Church. . . on Friday next at Nine O'Clock. . . to state the price
of corn. . .
By desire of the inhabitants of Halifax
Who will meet them there

From Stratton (Cornwall), 1801:

To all the labouring Men and Tradesmen in the Hundred of Stratton
that are willing to save their Wifes and Children from the Dreadfull
condition of being STARVED to DEATH by the unfeeling and Griping
Farmer. . . Assemble all emeadiately and march in Dreadfull Array to

---

She all the way Crying out, Damn you all, Will You See me Suffer, or be
sent to Gaol?"); Haverfordwest — PRO, HO 42/35; Birmingham —
J. A. Langford, *A Century of Birmingham Life* (Birmingham, 1868),
ii, p. 52.
[1] *Letters from England* (1814), ii, p. 47. The women had other
resources than ferocity: a colonel of Volunteers lamented that "the Devil in
the shape of Women is now using all his influence to induce the Privates to
brake their attachments to their Officers": Lt.-Col. J. Entwisle,
Rochdale, 5 Aug. 1795, PRO, WO 1/1086.

the Habitations of the Griping Farmer, and Compell them to sell their Corn in the Market, at a fair and reasonable Price. . .[1]

The small-scale, spontaneous action might develop from a kind of ritualised hooting or groaning outside retailers' shops;[2] from the interception of a wagon of grain or flour passing through a populous centre; or from the mere gathering of a menacing crowd. Very quickly a bargaining-situation would develop: the owner of the provisions knew very well that if he did not comply voluntarily with the price imposed by the crowd (and his compliance made any subsequent prosecution very difficult) he stood in danger of losing his stock altogether. When a wagon with sacks of wheat and flour was intercepted at Handborough (Oxfordshire) in 1795, some women climbed aboard and pitched the sacks on the roadside. "Some of the persons assembled said they would give Forty Shillings a Sack for the Flour, and they would have it at that, and would not give more, and if that would not do, they would have it by force." The owner (a "yeoman") at length agreed: "If that must be the price, it must be the price". The procedure of forced bargaining can be seen equally clearly in the deposition of Thomas Smith, a baker, who rode into Hadstock (Essex) with bread on his panniers (1795). He was stopped in the village street by forty or more women and children. One of the women (a labourer's wife) held his horse

> and having asked whether he had fallen in his price of Bread, he told her, he had no Orders to fall from the Millers, & she then said, "By God if you don't fall you shall not leave any Bread in the Town". . .

Several in the crowd then offered 9d. a quartern loaf, while he demanded 19d. They then "swore that if he would not let them have it at 9d a Loaf, they would take it away, & before

---

[1] Kettering — PRO, SP 36/50: for other examples of the use of football to assemble a crowd, see R. M. Malcolmson, "Popular Recreations in English Society, 1700-1850" (Warwick, Univ. Ph.D. thesis, 1970); Wakefield — PRO, HO 42/35; Stratton — handwritten notice, dated 8 April and signed "Cato", in PRO, HO 42/61 fo. 718.

[2] A correspondent from Rosemary Lane (London), 2 July 1795, complained of being awoken at 5 a.m. "By a most dreadful Groaning (as the Mob call it) but what I should call Squealing": PRO, WO 1/1089 fo. 719.

he could give any other Answer, several Persons then about him took several of the Loaves off his Pads. . .". Only at this point did Smith agree to the sale at 9d. the loaf. The bargaining was well understood on both sides; and retailers, who had to hold on to their customers in the fat years as well as the lean, often capitulated at the first sign of crowd turbulence.[1]

In larger-scale disturbances, once the nucleus of a crowd had been formed, the remainder was often raised by horn or drums. "On Monday last," a letter from a Shropshire magistrate commences in 1756, "the colliers from Broseley &c assembled with horns blowing, & proceeded to Wenlock Market. . .". What was critical was the gathering of the determined nucleus. Not only the "virility" of the colliers, and their particular exposure to consumer-exploitation, explain their prominent role, but also their numbers and the natural discipline of the mining community. "On Thursday morning", John Todd, a pitman at Heaton Colliery, Gateshead, deposed (1740), "at the time of the night shift going on", his fellow pitmen, "about 60 or 80 in number stopped the gin at the pit. . . and it was proposed to come to Newcastle to settle the prices of corn. . .". When they came from Nook Colliery into Haverfordwest in 1795 (the magistrate relates that his curate said: "Doctor, here are the colliers coming. . . I looked up & saw a great crowd of men women & children with oaken bludgeons coming down the street bawling out, 'One & all — one & all' ") the colliers explained later that they had come at the request of the poor townspeople, who had not the morale to set the price on their own.[1]

The occupational make-up of the crowd provides few surprises. It was (it seems) fairly representative of the occupations of the "lower orders" in the rioting areas. At Witney (Oxfordshire) we find informations against a blanket-weaver, a tailor, the wife of a victualler, and a servant; at Saffron Walden (Essex) indictments against two collar-makers, a cordwainer, a bricklayer, a carpenter, a sawyer, a

[1] Broseley — T. Whitmore, 11 Nov. 1756, PRO, SP 36/136; Gateshead — information of John Todd in Newcastle City Archives; Haverfordwest — PRO, HO 42/35.

worsted-maker, and nine labourers; in several Devonshire villages (Sampford Peverell, Burlescomb, Culmstock) we find a spinster, two weavers, a woolcomber, a cordwainer, a thatcher, and ten labourers indicted; in the Handborough affair a carpenter, a mason, a sawyer, and seven labourers were mentioned in one information.[1] There were fewer accusations as to the alleged incitement by persons in a superior station in life than Rudé and others have noted in France,[2] although it was more often suggested that the labourers were encouraged by their superiors towards a tone hostile to farmers and middlemen. An observer in the South-West in 1801 argued that the riots were "certainly directed by inferior Tradesmen, Woolcombers, & Dissenters, who keep aloof but by their language & immediate influence govern the lower classes".[3] Occasionally, large employers of labour were alleged to have encouraged their own workers to act.[4]

Another important difference, as compared with France, was the relative inactivity of farm labourers in England as contrasted with the activity of the *vignerons* and petty peasantry. Many cereal farmers, of course, continued the custom of selling cheap grain to their own labourers, while the living-in hired farm servants shared the farmer's board. Rural labourers did participate in riots, when some other groups (like colliers) formed the original nucleus, or where

[1]Witney — information of Thomas Hudson, 10 Aug. 1795, PRO, Assizes 5/116; Saffron Walden — indictments for offences on 27 July 1795, PRO, Assizes 35/236; Devonshire — calendar for Summer Circuit, 1795, PRO, Assizes 24/43; Handborough — information of James Stevens, tythingman, 6 Aug. 1795, PRO, Assizes 5/116. All 13 of the Berkshire rioters of 1766 tried by Special Commission were described as "labourers"; of 66 persons brought before the Special Commission at Gloucester in 1766, 51 were described as "labourers", 10 were wives of "labourers", 3 were spinsters: the descriptions reveal little: *G. B. Deputy Keeper of Public Records, 5th Report* (1844), ii, pp. 198-9, 202-4. For Wales, 1793-1801, see Jones, "Corn Riots in Wales", App. III, p. 350. For Dundee, 1772, see S. G. E. Lythe, "The Tayside Meal Mobs", *Scot. Hist. Rev.*, xlvi (1967), p. 34: a porter, a quarryman, three weavers, and a sailor were indicted.
[2]See Rudé, *The Crowd in History*, p. 38.
[3]Lt.-Gen. J. G. Simcoe, 27 Mar. 1801, PRO, HO 42/61.
[4]Thus in an export riot in Flint (1740) there were allegations that the steward of Sir Thomas Mostyn had found arms for his own colliers: various depositions in PRO, SP 36/51.

some activity brought them together in sufficient numbers. When a large band of labourers toured the Thames Valley in 1766, the action had commenced with gangs at work on a turnpike-road, who said "with one Voice, Come one & all to Newbury in a Body to Make the Bread cheaper". Once in town, they raised further support by parading in the town square and giving three huzzas. In East Anglia in 1795 a similar nucleus was found from among the "bankers" (gangs "employed in cleansing out Drains & in embanking"). The bankers also were less subject to instant identification and punishment, or to the revenges of village paternalism, than were field labourers, being "for the most part strangers from different countries [who] are not so easily quieted as those who live on the spot".[1]

In truth, the food riot did not require a high degree of organisation. It required a consensus of support in the community, and an inherited pattern of action with its own objectives and restraints. And the persistence of this form of action raises an interesting question: how far was it, in any sense, successful? Would it have continued, over so many scores, indeed hundreds, of years, if it had consistently failed to achieve its objectives, and had left nothing but a few ruined mills and victims on the gallows? It is a question peculiarly difficult to answer; but one which must be asked.

VII

In the short-term it would seem probable that riot and price-setting defeated their own objects. Farmers were sometimes intimidated so far that they refused afterwards, for several weeks, to bring goods to market. The interdiction of the movement of grain within the country was likely only to aggravate shortage in other regions. Although instances can be found where riot appeared to result in a fall in prices, and instances can be found of the opposite, and, further, instances can be found where there appears to be little difference in the movement of prices in riot and non-riot markets, none of these instances — however aggregated or averaged — need necessarily disclose the effect of the

[1] Newbury — brief in PRO, TS 11/995/3707; East Anglia — B. Clayton, Boston, 11 Aug. 1795, PRO, HO 42/35.

expectation of riot upon the total market-situation. [1]

We may take an analogy from war. The actual immediate benefits of war are rarely significant, either to victor or defeated. But the benefits which may be gained by the *threat* of war may be considerable: and yet the threat carries no terrors if the sanction of war is never used. If the market-place was as much an arena of class war as the factory and mine became in the industrial revolution, then the threat of riot would affect the entire marketing situation, not only in years of dearth but also in years of moderate harvest, not only in towns notorious for their susceptibility to riot but also in towns where the authorities wished to preserve a tradition of peace. However carefully we quantify the available data these cannot show us to what level prices would have risen if the threat of riot had been altogether removed.

The authorities in riot-prone areas were often cool and competent in handling disturbance. This allows one sometimes to forget that riot was a calamity, often resulting in a profound dislocation of social relations in the community, whose results could linger on for years. The provincial magistracy were often in extreme isolation. Troops, if they were sent for, might take two, three or more days to arrive, and the crowd knew this very well. The sheriff of Gloucestershire could do nothing in the first days of the "rising" of 1766 but attend at Stroud market with his "javelin men". A Suffolk magistrate in 1709 refrained from imprisoning the leaders of the crowd because "the Mob threatened to pull both his house and the Bridewell down if he punished any of their fellows". Another magistrate who led a ragged and unmartial *posse comitatus* through North Yorkshire to Durham in 1740, capturing prisoners on the way, was dismayed to find the citizens of Durham turn out and release two of his prisoners at the gate of the gaol. (Such rescues were common). A Flint grain exporter had an even more unpleasant experience in the same year. Rioters entered his house, drank the beer and wine in his vaults, and stood —

---

[1] Undoubtedly detailed investigation of short-term price-movements in relation to riot will help to refine the question; but the variables are many, and evidence as to some (*anticipation* of riot, persuasion brought to bear on tenants, dealers, etc., charitable subscriptions, application of poor rates, etc.) if often elusive and difficult to quantify.

with a Drawn Sword pointed upon my Daughter in Laws breast. . . They
have a great many Fire Arms, Pikes and Broadswords. Five of the Pikes
they declare that four of them shall do to Carry my Four Quarters and
the other my head in triumph about with them. . .[1]

The question of order was by no means simple. The
inadequacy of civil forces was combined with a reluctance to
employ military force. The officers themselves had sufficient
humanity, and were surrounded by sufficient ambiguity as to
their powers in civil affrays, to show a marked lack of
enthusiasm for employment in this "Odious Service".[1] If
local magistrates called in the troops, or authorised the use of
fire-arms, they had to go on living in the district after the
troops had left, incurring the odium of the local population,
perhaps receiving threatening letters, and being the victims of
broken windows or even arson. Troops billeted in a town
quickly became unpopular, even with those who had first
called them in. With uncanny regularity requests for the aid
of troops are followed, in Home Office or War Office
papers, after an interval of five or six weeks, by petitions for
their removal. A pitiful petition from the inhabitants of
Sunderland in 1800, headed by their Rector, asked for the
withdrawal of the 68th Regiment:

Their principal aim is robbery. Several have been knocked down and
plundered of their watches, but always it has been done in the most
violent and brutal manner.

One young man had had his skull fractured, another his
upper lip cut off. Inhabitants of Wantage, Farringdon and
Abingdon petitioned

in the name of God. . . remove the part of Lord Landaff's regiment
from this place, or else Murder must be the consequence, for such a sett
of Villains never entered this Town before.

A local magistrate, supporting the petition, added that the
"savage behaviour of the military. . . exasperates the
populace to the highest degree. The usual intercourse of the
husbandmen at fairs and markets is much interrupted."[2]

[1] ". . . a most Odious Service which nothing but Necessity can
justify", Viscount Barrington to Weymouth, 18 Apr. 1768, PRO,
WO 4/83, fos. 316-7.
[2] Sunderland — petition in PRO, WO 40/17; Wantage and
Abingdon — petition to Sir G. Young and C. Dundas, 6 Apr. 1795, *ibid.*

Riot was a calamity. The "order" which might follow after riot could be an even greater calamity. Hence the anxiety of authorities, either to anticipate the event, or to cut it short in its early stages, by personal presence, by exhortation and concession. In a letter of 1773 the mayor of Penryn, besieged by angry tinners, writes that the town was visited by three hundred "of those Banditti, with whom we were forced to beat a Parley and come to an agreement to let them have the Corn for one-third less than the Prime Cost to the Proprietors". Such parleys, more or less reluctant, were common. An experienced Warwickshire magistrate, Sir Roger Newdigate, noted in his diary on 27 September 1766:

> At 11 rode to Nuneaton. . . and with the principal people of the town met the Bedworth colliers and mob who came hallowing and armed with sticks, demanded what they wanted, promised to satisfy all their reasonable demands if they would be peacable and throw away their sticks which all of them then did into the Meadow, then walked with them to all the houses which they expected had engrossed and let 5 or 6 go in search and persuaded the owners to sell what was found of cheese. . .

The colliers then left the town quietly, after Sir Roger Newdigate and two others had each given them half a guinea. They had, in effect, acted according to the *Book of Orders.* [1]

This kind of bargaining, in the first commencement of riot, often secured concessions for the crowd. But we should also note the exertions by magistrates and landowners in anticipation of riot. Thus a Shropshire magistrate in 1756 describes how the colliers "say if the farmers do not bring their corn to the markets, they will go to their houses & thresh for themselves":

> I have sent to my Tenants to order them to take each of them some corn to the market on Saturday as the only means I can think of to prevent greater outrages.

In the same year we may observe magistrates in Devon exerting themselves in a similar way. Riots had occurred at Ottery, farmers' corn seized and sold off at 5s. a bushel, and

---

[1] Penryn — PRO, WO 40/17; Warwickshire — H. C. Wood, "The Diaries of Sir Roger Newdigate, 1751-1806", *Trans. Birmingham Archaeological Soc.*, lxxviii (1962), p. 43.

several mills attacked. Sir George Yonge sent his servant to affix an admonitory and conciliatory paper in the market-place:

> The mob gather'd, insulted my Servant, and intimidated the Cryer. . . On reading [the paper] they declared It would not do, the Gentlemen need not trouble themselves, for *They* would fix the Price at 4s 9d next Market Day: upon this I rode into the Town yesterday, and told both the Common people and the better sort, that if things were not quiet the military must be sent for. . .

He and two neighbouring gentry had then sent their own corn into the local markets:

> I have ordered mine to be sold at 5s 3d and 5s 6d per bushell to the poorer sort, as we have resolved to keep rather above the Price dictated by the Mob. I shall send to the Millers to know if they can part with any Flour. . .

The mayor of Exeter replied to Yonge that the city authorities had ordered corn to be sold at 5s. 6d.: "Everything was quiet immediately the farmers fell the price. . .". Similar measures were still being taken in Devon in 1801, "some Gentlemen of the most respectable characters in the neighbourhood of Exeter. . . directing. . . their Tenantry to bring Corn to the Market, under the penalty of not having their leases renewed". In 1795 and 1800-1 such orders by traditionalist landowners to their farming tenants were frequent in other counties. The earl of Warwick (an arch-paternalist and an advocate of the legislation against forestallers in its fullest rigour) rode in person around his estates giving such directions to his tenants.[1]

Such pressures as these, in anticipation of riot, may have been more effective than has been proposed: in getting corn to market; in restraining rising prices; and in intimidating certain kinds of profiteering. Moreover, a disposition to riot was certainly effective as a signal to the rich to put the machinery of parish relief and of charity — subsidised corn and bread for the poor — into good repair. In January 1757

---

[1] Shropshire — T. Whitmore, 11 Nov. 1756, PRO, SP 36/136; Devon — HMC, *City of Exeter*, series lxxiii (1916), pp. 255-7; Devon, 1801 — Lt.-Gen. J. G. Simcoe, 27 Mar. 1801, PRO, HO 42/61; Warwick — T. W. Whitley, *The Parliamentary Representation of the City of Coventry* (Coventry, 1894), p. 214.

Reading Corporation agreed:

> that a Subscription be set on foot for Raising money to Buy Bread to be Distributed to the Poor. . . at a Price to be fixed much below the present price of Bread. . .

The Corporation itself donated £21.[1] Such measures were very commonly followed, the initiative coming sometimes from a corporation, sometimes from individual gentry, sometimes from Quarter Sessions, sometimes from parish authorities, sometimes from employers — especially those who employed a substantial labour-force (such as lead-miners) in isolated districts.

The measures taken in 1795 were especially extensive, various and well-documented. They ranged from direct sub-scriptions to reduce the price of bread (the parishes sometimes sending their own agents direct to the ports to purchase imported grain), through subsidies from the poor rates, to the Speenhamland system. The examination of such measures would take us farther into the history of the poor laws than we intend to go.[2] But the effects were sometimes curious. Subscriptions, while quieting one area, might provoke riot in an adjacent one, through arousing a sharp sense of inequality. An agreement in Newcastle in 1740 to reduce prices, reached between merchants and a deputation of demonstrating pitmen (with aldermen mediating), resulted in "country people" from outlying villages flooding into the city; an unsuccessful attempt was made to limit the sale to persons with a written certificate from "a Fitter, Staithman, Ton Tail Man, or Churchwarden". Participation by soldiers in price-setting riots in 1795 was explained, by the duke of Richmond, as arising from a similar inequality: it was alleged by the soldiers "that while the Country People are relieved by their Parishes and Subscriptions, the Soldiers receive no such Benefit". Moreover, such subscriptions,

---

[1] MS diary of Reading Corporation, Central Public Library, Reading: entry for 24 January 1757. £30 was disbursed "towards the present high price of Bread" on 12 July 1795.

[2] Especially useful are replies from correspondents in *Annals of Agriculture*, xxiv and xxv (1795). See also S. and B. Webb, "The Assize of Bread", *op. cit.*, pp. 208-9; J. L. and B. Hammond, *op. cit.*, ch. vi; W. M. Stern, *op. cit.*, pp. 181-6.

while being intended to buy off riot (actual or potential), might often have the effect of *raising* the price of bread to those outside the benefit of subscription.[1] In South Devon, where the authorities were still acting in 1801 in the tradition of 1757, the process can be seen. The Exeter crowd demonstrated in the market for wheat at 10s. a bushel:

> The Gentlemen and Farmers met, & the People waited their decision. . . They were informed that no Price they shou'd name or fix would be agreed to, & principally because the principle of fixing a Price wou'd be resisted. The Farmers then agreed at 12s and every Inhabitant to have it in proportion to their Families. . .
>
> The Arguments of the discontented at Exmouth are very cogent. "Give us whatever *quantity* the Stock in Hand will afford, & at a price by which we can attain it, & we shall be satisfied; we will not accept any Subscription from the Gentry because it enhances the Price, & is a hardship on them".[2]

The point here is not just that prices, in time of scarcity, were determined by many other factors than mere market-forces: anyone with even a scanty knowledge of much-maligned "literary" sources must be aware of that. It is more important to note the total socio-economic context within which the market operated, and the logic of crowd pressure. One other example, this time from a hitherto riot-free market, may show this logic at work. The account is that of a substantial farmer, John Toogood, in Sherborne (Dorset). The year 1757 commenced with "general complaint" at high prices, and frequent accounts of riots elsewhere:

> On the 30th of April, being Market-Day, many of our idle and insolent Poor Men and Women assembled and begun a Riot in the Market House, went to Oborn Mill and brought off several Bags of Flour and divided the Spoil here in Triumph.

On the next Monday an anonymous letter, directed to Toogood's brother (who had just sold ten bushels of wheat at 14s. 10d. — "a great price indeed" — to a miller), was found

[1] A point to be watched in any quantified analysis: the price officially returned from a market in the aftermath of riot might *rise*, although, as a consequence of riot or threat of riot, the poor might be receiving corn at subsidised rates.

[2] Newcastle — advertisement 24 June 1740 in City Archives Office; duke of Richmond, 13 Apr. 1795, PRO, WO 1/1092; Devon — James Coleridge, 29 Mar. 1801, HO 42/61.

in the abbey: "Sir, If you do not bring your Wheat into the Market, and sell it at a reasonable price, your Barns shall be pulled down. . .".

> As Rioting is quite a new Thing in Sherborne. . . and as the neighbour-ing Parishes seemed ripe for joining in this Sport, I thought there was no Time to be lost, and that it was proper to crush this Evil in it's Bud, in Order to which we took the following Measures.
>
> Having called a Meeting at the Almshouse, it was agreed that Mr. Jeffrey and I should take a Survey of all the most necessitous Families in the Town, this done, We raised about £100 by Subscriptions, and before the next Market Day, our Justice of the Peace and some of the principal Inhabitants made a Procession throughout the Town and published by the Cryer of the Town the following Notice.
>
> "That the Poor Families of this Town will be supplied with a Quantity of Wheat sufficient for their Support every Week 'till Harvest at the Rate of 8s p. Bushel and that if any person whatsoever after this public Notice shall use any threatening Expressions, or commit any Riot or Disorder in this Town, the Offender shall be forthwith committed to Prison."

They then contracted for wheat, at 10s. and 12s. the bushel, supplying it to a "List of the Poor" at 8s. until harvest. (Sixty bushels weekly over this period will have involved a subsidy of between £100 and £200.) "By these Means we restored Peace, and disappointed many loose, disorderly Fellows of the Neighbouring Parishes, who appeared in the Market with their empty Bags, expecting to have had Corn without Money." John Toogood, setting down this account for the guidance of his sons, concluded it with the advice:

> If the like Circumstances happen hereafter in your Time and either of you are engaged in Farmering Business, let not a covetous Eye tempt you to be foremost in advancing the Price of Corn, but rather let your Behaviour shew some Compassion and Charity towards the Condition of the Poor. . .[1]

It is within such a context as this that the function of riot may be disclosed. Riot may have been, in the short term, counter-productive, although this has not yet been proved. But, once again, riot was a social calamity, and one to be avoided, even at a high cost. The cost might be to achieve some medium, between a soaring "economic" price in the market, and a traditional "moral" price set by the crowd.

[1] MS diary of John Toogood, Dorset CRO, D 170/1.

That medium might be found by the intervention of
paternalists, by the prudential self-restraint of farmers and
dealers, or by buying-off a portion of the crowd through
charities and subsidies. As Hannah More carolled, in the
persona of the sententious Jack Anvil, when dissuading Tom
Hod from riot:

> So I'll work the whole day, and on Sundays I'll seek
> At Church how to bear all the wants of the week.
> The gentlefolks, too, will afford us supplies,
> They'll subscribe — and they'll give up their puddings and pies.
>
> *Derry down.*[1]

Derry down, indeed, and even Tra-la-dee-bum-deeay! However, the nature of gentlefolks being what it is, a thundering
good riot in the next parish was more likely to oil the wheels
of charity than the sight of Jack Anvil on his knees in church.
As the doggerel on the *out*side of the church door in Kent had
put it succinctly in 1630:

> Before we arise
> Less will safise.

VIII

We have been examining a pattern of social protest which
derives from a consensus as to the moral economy of the
commonweal in times of dearth. It is not usually helpful to
examine it for overt, articulate political intentions, although
these sometimes arose through chance coincidence. Rebellious
phrases can often be found, usually (one suspects) to chill the
blood of the rich with their theatrical effect. It was said that
the Newcastle pitmen, flushed with the success of their
capture of the Guildhall, "were for putting in practice the old
levelling principles"; they did at least tear down the portraits
of Charles II and James II and smash their frames. By
contrast, bargees at Henley (Oxfordshire) in 1743 called out
"Long Live the Pretender"; and someone in Woodbridge
(Suffolk) in 1766 nailed up a notice in the market-place which
the local magistrate found to be "peculiarly bold and
seditious and of high and delicate import": "We are wishing
[it said] that our exiled King could come over or send some

---

[1] "The Riot: or, half a loaf is better than no bread, &c", 1795, in
Hannah More, *Works* (1830), ii, pp. 86-8.

Officers." Perhaps the same menace was intended, in the South-West in 1753, by threats that "the French w'd be here soon".[1]

Most common are general "levelling" threats, imprecations against the rich. A letter at Witney (1767) assured the bailiffs of the town that the people would not suffer "such damned wheesing fat guted Rogues to Starve the Poor by such Hellish Ways on purpose that they may follow hunting horse-racing etc. and to maintain their familys in Pride and extravagance". A letter on the Gold Cross at Birmingham's Snow Hill (1766), signed "Kidderminster & Stourbridge", was perhaps in the mode of rhyming doggerel —

> . . . there is a small Army of us upwards of three thousand all ready to fight
> & I'll be dam'd if we don't make the King's Army to shite
> If so be the King & Parliament don't order better
> we will turn England into a Litter
> & if so be as things don't get cheaper
> I'll be damd if we don't burn down the Parliament House & make all better. . .

A letter in Colchester in 1772 addressed to all farmers, millers, butchers, shopkeepers and corn merchants, warned all the "damd Rogues" to take care,

> for this is november and we have about two or three hundred bum shells a getting in Readiness for the Mellers [millers] and all no king no parliment nothing but a powder plot all over the nation.

The gentlemen of Fareham (Hampshire) were warned in 1766 to prepare "for a Mob or Sivel war", which would "pull George from his throne beat down the house of rougs [rogues] and destroy the Sets [seats] of the Law makers". "Tis better to Undergo a forrieghn Yoke than to be used thus", wrote a villager near Hereford in the next year. And so on, and from most parts of Britain. It is, in the main, rhetoric, although rhetoric which qualifies in a devastating

---

[1] Newcastle — MS account of riots in City Archives; Henley — Isaac, *op. cit.*, p. 186; Woodbridge — PRO, WO 1/873: 1753 — Newcastle MSS, Brit. Lib. Add MS 32732, fo. 343. Earl Poulet, Lord Lieutenant of Somerset, reported in another letter to the duke of Newcastle that some of the mob "came to talk a Levelling language, viz. they did not see why some sh'd be rich & others poor": *ibid.*, fos. 214-5.

way the rhetoric of historians as to the deference and social solidarities of Georgian England.[1]

Only in 1795 and 1800-1, when a Jacobin tinge is frequent in such letters and handbills, do we have the impression of a genuine undercurrent of articulate political motivation. A trenchant example of these is some doggerel addressed to "the Broth Makers & Flower Risers" which gave a Maldon (Essex) magistrate cause for alarm:

> On Swill & Grains you wish the poor to be fed
> And underneath the Guillintine we could wish to see your heads
> For I think it is a great shame to serve the poor so —
> And I think a few of your heads will make a pretty show.

Scores upon scores of such letters circulated in these years. From Uley (Gloucestershire), "no King but a Constitution down down down O fatall down high caps and proud hats forever down down. . .". At Lewes (Sussex), after several militiamen had been executed for their part in price-setting, a notice was posted: "Soldiers to Arms!"

> Arise and revenge your cause
> On those bloody numskulls, Pitt and George,
> For since they no longer can send you to France
> To be murdered like Swine, or pierc'd by the Lance,
> You are sent for by Express to make a speedy Return
> To be shot like a Crow, or hang'd in your Turn. . .

At Ramsbury (Wiltshire) in 1800 a notice was affixed to a tree:

> Downe with Your Luxzuaras Government both spiratal & temperal Or you starve with Hunger. they have stripp you of bread Chees Meate &c &c &c &c &c. Nay even your Lives have they Taken thousands on their Expeditions let the Burbon Family defend their owne Cause and let us true Britons look to Our Selves let us banish Some to Hanover where they came from Downe with your Constitution Arect a republick Or you and your offsprings are to starve the Remainder of our Days dear Brothers will you lay down and die under Man eaters and Lave your

[1] Witney — *London Gazette*, Nov. 1767, no. 10779; Birmingham — PRO, WO 1/873; Colchester — *London Gazette*, Nov. 1772, no. 11304; Fareham — *ibid.*, Jan. 1767, no. 10690; Hereford — *ibid.*, Apr. 1767, no. 10717.

offspring under that Burden that Blackguard Government which is now eatain you up.

God Save the Poor & down with George III.[1]

But these crisis years of the wars (1800-1) would demand separate treatment. We are coming to the end of one tradition, and the new tradition has scarcely emerged. In these years the alternative form of economic pressure — pressure upon wages — is becoming more vigorous; there is also something more than rhetoric behind the language of sedition — underground union organisation, oaths, the shadowy "United Englishmen". In 1812 traditional food riots overlap with Luddism. In 1816 the East Anglian labourers do not only set the prices, they also demand a minimum wage and an end to Speenhamland relief. They look forward to the very different revolt of labourers in 1830. The older form of action lingers on into the 1840s and even later: it was especially deeply rooted in the South-West.[2] But in the new territories of the industrial revolution it passed by stages into other forms of action. The break in wheat prices after the wars eased the transition. In the northern towns the fight against the corn jobbers gave way to the fight against the Corn Laws.

There was another reason why 1795 and 1800-1 bring us into different historical territory. The forms of action which we have been examining depended upon a particular set of social relations, a particular equilibrium between paternalist authority and the crowd. This equilibrium was dislodged in the wars, for two reasons. First, the acute anti-Jacobinism of the gentry led to a new fear of any form of popular self-activity; magistrates were willing to see signs of sedition in price-setting actions even where no such sedition existed; the fear of invasion raised the Volunteers, and thus gave to the

[1] Maldon — PRO, WO 40/17; Uley — W. G. Baker, Oct. 1795, HO 42/36; Lewes — HO 42/35; Ramsbury — enclosure in the Rev. E. Meyrick, 12 June 1800, HO 42/50.

[2] See A. Rowe, "The Food Riots of the Forties in Cornwall", *Report of Royal Cornwall Polytechnic Society* (1942), pp. 51-67. There were food riots in the Scottish Highlands in 1847; in Teignmouth and Exeter in November 1867; and in Norwich a curious episode (the "Battle of Ham Run") as late as 1886.

civil powers much more immediate means for meeting the crowd, not with parley and concession, but with repression.[1] Second, such repression was legitimised, in the minds of central and of many local authorities, by the triumph of the new ideology of political economy.

Of this celestial triumph, the Home Secretary, the duke of Portland, served as Temporal Deputy. He displayed, in 1800-1, a quite new firmness, not only in handling disturbance, but in overruling and remonstrating with those local authorities who still espoused the old paternalism. In September 1800 a significant episode occurred in Oxford. There had been some affair of setting the price of butter in the market, and cavalry appeared in the town (at the request — as it transpired — of the Vice-Chancellor). The Town Clerk, on the direction of the mayor and magistrates, wrote to the Secretary at War, expressing their "surprise that a military body of horse soldiers should have made their appearance early this morning":

> It is with great pleasure I inform you that the people of Oxford have hitherto shewn no disposition to be riotous except the bringing into the market [of] some hampers of butter and selling it at a shilling a pound and accounting for the money to the owner of the butter be reckoned of that description. . .

"Notwithstanding the extreme pressure of the times", the City authorities were of "the decided opinion" that there was "no occasion in this City for the presence of a regular Soldiery", especially since the magistrates were being most active in suppressing "what they conceive to be one of the principal causes of the dearness, the offences of forestalling, ingrossing, and regrating. . .".

The Town Clerk's letter was passed over to the duke of Portland, and drew from him a weighty reproof:

> His Grace. . . desires you to inform the Mayor and Magistrates, that as his official situation enables him in a more particular manner to appreciate the extent of the publick mischief which must inevitably ensue from a continuance of the riotous proceedings which have taken place in several parts of the Kingdom in consequence of the present

---

[1] See J. R. Western, "The Volunteer Movement as an Anti-Revolutionary Force, 1793-1801", *Eng. Hist. Rev.*, lxxi (1956).

scarcity of Provisions, so he considers himself to be more immediately called upon to exercise his own judgement and discretion in directing adequate measures to be taken for the immediate and effectual suppression of such dangerous proceedings. For greatly as His Grace laments the cause of these Riots, nothing is more certain than that they can be productive of no other effect than to increase the evil beyond all power of calculation. His Grace, therefore, cannot allow himself to pass over in silence that part of your letter which states "that the People of Oxford have hitherto shewn no disposition to be riotous, except the bringing into Market some Hampers of Butter, and selling it at a Shilling a pound, and accounting for the money to the Owner of the Butter, can be reckoned of that description".

So far from considering this circumstance, in the trivial light in which it is represented in your letter (even supposing it to stand unconnected with others of a similar and a still more dangerous nature, which it is to be feared is not the case) His Grace sees it in the view of a violent and unjustifiable attack on property pregnant with the most fatal consequences to the City of Oxford and to it's Inhabitants of every description; and which His Grace takes it for granted the Mayor and Magistrates must have thought it their bounden duty to suppress and punish by the immediate apprehension and committal of the Offenders.[1]

Throughout 1800 and 1801 the duke of Portland busied himself enforcing the same doctrines. The remedy for disturbance was the military or Volunteers; even liberal subscriptions for cheap corn were to be discouraged, as exhausting stocks; persuasion upon farmers or dealers to lower prices was an offence against political economy. In April 1801 he wrote to Earl Mount Edgcumbe,

Your Lordship must excuse the liberty I take in not passing unnoticed the agreement you mention to have been voluntarily entered into by the Farmers in Cornwall to supply the Markets with Corn and other Articles of Provision at reduced Prices. . .

The duke had information that the farmers had been subjected to pressure by the county authorities:

. . . the experience I have. . . calls upon me to say that every undertaking of the kind cannot in the nature of things be justified and must unavoidably and shortly add to and aggravate the distress which it

[1] W. Taunton, 6 Sept. 1800; I. King to Taunton, 7 Sept. 1800: PRO, WO 40/17 and HO 43/12. In private letters Portland exerted himself even more forcefully, writing to Dr Hughes of Jesus College, Oxford (12 Sept.) of the "unjust & injudicious proceedings of your foolish Corporation": Univ. of Nottingham, Portland MSS, PwV III.

252   CUSTOMS IN COMMON

pretends to alleviate, and I will venture also to assert that the more
general it could be rendered the more injurious must be the consequences by which it could not fail to be attended because it necessarily
prevents the Employment of Capital in the Farming Line. . .[1]

The "nature of things" which had once made imperative,
in times of dearth, at least some symbolic solidarity between
the rulers and the poor, now dictated solidarity between the
rulers and "the Employment of Capital". It is, perhaps,
appropriate that it was the ideologist who synthesized an
hysteric anti-Jacobinism with the new political economy who
signed the death-warrant of that paternalism of which, in his
more specious passages of rhetoric, he was the celebrant.
"The Labouring *Poor*", exclaimed Burke: "Let compassion
be shewn in action",

. . . but let there be no lamentation of their condition. It is no relief to
their miserable circumstances; it is only an insult to their miserable
understandings. . . Patience, labour, sobriety, frugality, and religion,
should be recommended to them; all the rest is downright
fraud.[2]

Against that tone the notice at Ramsbury was the only
possible reply.

IX

I hope that a somewhat different picture has emerged from
this account than the customary one. I have tried to describe,
not an involuntary spasm, but a pattern of behaviour of
which a Trobriand islander need not have been ashamed.
It is difficult to re-imagine the moral assumptions of
another social configuration. It is not easy for us to conceive

[1] Portland, 25 Apr. 1801, PRO, HO 43/13, pp. 24-7. On 4 October
1800 Portland wrote to the Vice-Chancellor of Oxford University
(Dr Marlow) as to the dangers of the people "giving way to the notion of
their difficulties being imputable to the avarice and rapacity of those, who
instead of being denominated Engrossers are correctly speaking the
purveyors and provident Stewards of the Public": Univ. of Nottingham,
Portland MSS, PwV III.

[2] E. Burke, *Thoughts and Details on Scarcity, originally presented to
the Rt. Hon. William Pitt in. . . November, 1795* (1800), p. 4.
Undoubtedly this pamphlet was influential with both Pitt and Portland,
and may have contributed to the tougher policies of 1800.

that there may have been a time, within a smaller and more integrated community, when it appeared to be "unnatural" that any man should profit from the necessities of others, and when it was assumed that, in time of dearth, prices of "necessities" should remain at a customary level, even though there might be less all round.

"The economy of the mediaeval borough", wrote R. H. Tawney, "was one in which consumption held somewhat the same primacy in the public mind, as the undisputed arbiter of economic effort, as the nineteenth century attached to profits".[1] These assumptions were under strong challenge, of course, long before the eighteenth century. But too often in our histories we foreshorten the great transitions. We leave forestalling and the doctrine of a fair price in the seventeenth century. We take up the story of the free market economy in the nineteenth. But the death of the old moral economy of provision was as long-drawn-out as the death of paternalist intervention in industry and trade. The consumer defended his old notions of right as stubbornly as (perhaps the same man in another role) he defended his craft status as an artisan.

These notions of right were clearly articulated. They carried for a long time the church's imprimatur. The *Book of Orders* of 1630 envisaged moral precept and example as an integral part of emergency measures:

> That all good Means and Perswasions bee used by the Justices in their severall Divisions, and by Admonitions and Exhortations in Sermons in the Churches. . . that the Poore may bee served of Corne at convenient and charitable Prices. And to the furtherance thereof, that the richer Sort bee earnestly mooved by Christian Charitie, to cause their Graine to be sold under the common Prices of the Market to the poorer sort: A deed of mercy, that will doubtlesse be rewarded of Almighty God.

At least one such sermon, delivered at Bodmin and Fowey (Cornwall) before the Sessions in 1630 by the Rev. Charles Fitz-Geffrey, was still known to eighteenth-century readers. Hoarders of corn were denounced as

> these Man-haters, opposite to the Common good, as if the world were made onely for them, would appropriate the earth, and the fruits thereof, wholly to themselves. . . As Quailes grow fat with

[1] R. H. Tawney, *Religion and the Rise of Capitalism* (1926), p. 33.

Hemlocke, which is poison to other creatures, so these grow full by Dearth. . .

They were "enemies both to God and man, opposite both to Grace and Nature". As for the dealer, exporting corn in time of scarcity, "the savour of lucre is sweet to him, though raked out of the puddle of the most filthy profession in Europe. . .".[1]

As the seventeenth century drew on, this kind of exhortation became muted, especially among the Puritans. With Baxter one part of moral precept is diluted with one part of casuistry and one part of business prudence: "charity must be exercised as well as justice", and, while goods might be withheld in the expectation of rising prices, this must not be done "to the hurt of the Commonwealth, as if. . . keeping it in be the cause of the dearth".[2] The old moral teaching became, increasingly, divided between the paternalist gentry on one hand, and the rebellious plebs on the other. There is an epitaph in the church at Stoneleigh (Warwickshire) to Humphrey How, the porter to Lady Leigh, who died in 1688:

> Here Lyes a Faithful Friend unto the Poore
> Who dealt Large Almes out of his Lord[ps] Store
> Weepe Not Poore People Tho' Y[e] Servat's Dead
> The Lord himselfe Will Give You Dayly Breade
> If Markets Rise Raile Not Against Theire Rates
> The Price is Stil the Same at Stone Leigh Gates.[3]

The old precepts resounded throughout the eighteenth century. Occasionally they might still be heard from the pulpit:

Exaction of any kind is base; but this in the Matter of Corn is of the basest Kind. It falls heaviest upon the Poor, It is robbing them because they are so. . . It is murdering *them* outright whom they find half dead, and plundering the wreck'd Vessel. . . These are the Murderers accused by the Son of *Sirach*, where he saith, *The Bread of the Needy is their Life: he that defraudeth them thereof is a Man of Blood*. . . Justly may

[1] C. Fitz-Geffrey, *God's Blessing upon the Providers of Corne: and God's Curse upon the Hoarders* (1631; reprint 1648), pp. 7, 8, 13.
[2] Tawney, *op. cit.*, p. 222. See also C. Hill, *Society and Puritanism in Pre-Revolutionary England* (1964), esp. pp. 277-8.
[3] I am indebted to Professor David Montgomery for this evidence.

such Oppressors be called *'Men of Blood'*; and surely will the Blood of those, who thus perish by their means, be required at their Hands.[1]

More often they were heard in pamphlet or newspaper:

To keep up the Price of the very Staff of Life at such an extravagent Sale, as that the Poor. . . cannot purchase it, is the greatest Iniquity any Man can be guilty of; it is no less than Murder, nay, the most cruel Murder.[2]

Sometimes in broadsheet and ballad:

Go now you hard-hearted rich men,
In your miseries, weep and howl,
Your canker'd gold will rise against you,
And Witness be against your souls. . .[3]

and frequently in anonymous letters. "Donte make a god of your mony", the gentlemen of Newbury were warned in 1772:

but think of the por you great men do you think of gohing to heaven or hell. think of the Sarmon which preach on 15 of March for dam we if we dont make you do you think to starve the pore quite you dam sons of wors [whores]. . .[4]

"Averishes Woman!", a corn-hoarder in Cornwall was addressed in 1795 by Cornish tinners: "We are. . . determined to assemble and immediately to march till we come to your Idol, or your God or your Mows [Moses?], whome you esteem as such and pull it down and likewise your House. . .".[5]

Today we shrug off the extortionate mechanisms of an unregulated market economy because it causes most of us only inconvenience, unostentatious hardships. In the eighteenth century this was not the case. Dearths were real dearths. High prices meant swollen bellies and sick children whose food was

---

[1] Anon. ["A Clergyman in the Country"], *Artificial Dearth: or, the Iniquity and Danger of Withholding Corn* (1756), pp. 20-1.

[2] Letter to *Sherborne Mercury*, 5 Sept. 1757.

[3] "A Serious Call to the Gentlemen Farmers, on the present exorbitant Prices of Provisions", broadside, n.d., in Seligman Collection (Broadsides — Prices), Columbia Univ.

[4] *London Gazette*, Mar. 1772, no. 11233.

[5] Letter from "Captins Audacious, Fortitude, Presumption and dread not", dated 28 Dec. 1795, "Polgooth and other mines", and addressed to Mrs Herring, *ibid.*, 1796, p. 45.

coarse bread made up from stale flour. No evidence has yet been published to show anything like a classic *crise des subsistances* in England in the eighteenth century:[1] the mortality of 1795 certainly did not approach that in France in the same year. But there was what the gentry described as a distress that was "truly painful": rising prices (wrote one) "have stript the cloaths from their backs, torn the shoes and stockings from their feet, and snatched the food from their mouths".[2] The risings of the Cornish tinners were preceded by harrowing scenes: men fainted at their work and had to be carried home by their fellows in scarcely better state. The dearth was accompanied by an epidemic described as "Yellow Fever", very possibly the jaundice associated with near-starvation.[3] In such a year Wordsworth's "pedlar" wandered among the cottages and saw

> The hardships of that season; many rich
> Sank down as in a dream among the poor,
> And of the poor did many cease to be,
> And their place knew them not. . .[4]

But if the market was the point at which working people most often felt their exposure to exploitation, it was also the point — especially in rural or dispersed manufacturing districts — at which they could most easily become organised. Marketing (or "shopping") becomes in mature industrial society increasingly impersonal. In eighteenth-century Britain or France (and in parts of southern Italy or Haiti or rural India or Africa today) the market remained a social as well as an economic nexus. It was the place where one-hundred-and-one social and personal transactions went on; where news was passed, rumour and gossip flew around, politics was (if ever) discussed in the inns or wine-shops round the market-square. The market was the place where the people, because they

---

[1] This is *not* to argue that such evidence may not be soon forth-coming as to local or regional demographic crisis.

[2] *Annals of Agriculture*, xxiv (1795), p. 159 (evidence from Dunmow, Essex).

[3] Letter of 24 June 1795 in PRO, PC 1/27/A.54; various letters, esp. 29 Mar. 1795, HO 42/34.

[4] W. Wordsworth, *Poetical Works*, ed. E. de Selincourt and Helen Darbishire (Oxford, 1959), v, p. 391.

were numerous, felt for a moment that they were strong.[1]

The confrontations of the market in a "pre-industrial" society are of course more universal than any national experience. And the elementary moral precepts of the "reasonable price" are equally universal. Indeed, one may suggest in Britain the survival of a pagan imagery which reaches to levels more obscure than Christian symbolism. Few folk rituals survived with such vigour to the end of the eighteenth century as all the paraphernalia of the harvest-home, with its charms and suppers, its fairs and festivals. Even in manufacturing areas the year still turned to the rhythm of the seasons and not to that of the banks. Dearth always comes to such communities as a profound psychic shock. When it is accompanied by the knowledge of inequalities, and the suspicion of manipulated scarcity, shock passes into fury.

One is struck, as the new century opens, by the growing symbolism of blood, and by its assimilation to the demand for bread. In Nottingham in 1812 the women paraded with a loaf upon a pole, streaked with red and tied with black crepe, emblematic of "bleeding famine decked in Sackecloth". At Yeovil (Somerset) in 1816 there was an anonymous letter, "Blood and Blood and Blood, a General Revolution their mus be. . .", the letter signed with a crude heart dripping blood. In the East Anglian riots of the same year such phrases as, "We will have blood before dinner". In Plymouth "a *Loaf* which had been *dipped in blood*, with a heart by it, was found in the streets". In the great Merthyr riots of 1831 a calf was sacrificed and a loaf soaked in its blood, impaled on a flagpole, served as emblem of revolt.[2]

This fury for corn is a curious culmination of the age of agricultural improvement. In the 1790s the gentry themselves were somewhat perplexed. Sometimes crippled by

[1] See Sidney Mintz, "Internal Market Systems as Mechanisms of Social Articulation", *Intermediate Societies, Social Mobility and Communication* (American Ethnological Society, 1959); and the same author's "Peasant Markets", *Scientific American*, cciii (1960), pp. 112-22.

[2] Nottingham — J. F. Sutton, *The Date-book of Nottingham* (Nottingham 1880), p. 286; Yeovil — PRO, HO 42/150; East Anglia — A. J. Peacock, *Bread or Blood* (1965), *passim*; Merthyr — G. A. Williams, "The Insurrection at Merthyr Tydfil in 1831", *Trans. Hon. Soc. of Cymmrodorion*, 2, (Session 1965), pp. 227-8.

an excess of rich food,[1] the magistrates from time to time put aside their industrious compilation of archives for the disciples of Sir Lewis Namier, and peered down from their parklands at the corn-fields in which their labourers hungered. (More than one magistrate wrote in to the Home Office, at this critical juncture, describing the measures which he would take against the rioters if only he were not confined to his house by gout.) The country will not be secure at harvest, wrote the Lord Lieutenant of Cambridgeshire, "without some soldiers, as he had heard that the People intended to help themselves when the Corn was ripe". He found this "a very serious apprehension indeed" and "in this open country most likely to be effected, at least by stealth".[2]

"Thou shalt not muzzle the ox that treadeth out the corn." The breakthrough of the new political economy of the free market was also the breakdown of the old moral economy of provision. After the wars all that was left of it was charity — and Speenhamland. The moral economy of the crowd took longer to die: it is picked up by the early co-operative flour mills, by some Owenite socialists, and it lingered on for years somewhere in the bowels of the Co-operative Wholesale Society. One symptom of its final demise is that we have been able to accept for so long an abbreviated and "economistic" picture of the food riot, as a direct, spasmodic, irrational response to hunger — a picture which is itself a product of a political economy which diminished human reciprocities to the wages-nexus. More generous, but also more authoritative, was the assessment of the sheriff of Gloucestershire in 1766. The mobs of that year (he wrote) had committed many acts of violence,

> some of wantoness and excess; and in other instances some acts of courage, prudence, justice, and a consistency towards that which they profess to obtain.[3]

[1] In 1795, when subsidised brown bread was being given to the poor of his own parish, Parson Woodforde did not flinch before his continuing duty to his own dinner: March 6th, ". . . for Dinner a Couple of boiled Chicken and Pigs Face, very good Peas Soup, a boiled Rump of Beef very fine, a prodigious fine, large and very fat Cock-Turkey rosted, Maccaroni, Batter Custard Pudding", etc.: James Woodforde, *Diary of a Country Parson*, ed. J. Beresford (World's Classics, 1963), pp. 483, 485.

[2] Lord Hardwicke, 27 July 1795, PRO, HO 42/35.

[3] W. Dalloway, 20 Sept. 1766, PRO, PC 1/8/41.

Chapter Five

The Moral Economy
Reviewed

I

The foregoing chapter was first published as an article in *Past and Present* in 1971. I have republished it without revision. I see no reason to retreat from its findings. And it has now entered into the stream of subsequent historical scholarship — it has been criticised and extensions of its theses have been proposed. It would confuse the record if I were to alter a text upon which commentary depends.

But some comment on my commentators is required. And also upon significant work which approaches the same problems, with little or no reference to my own. This is not a simple matter. For the "market" turns out to be a junction-point between social, economic and intellectual histories, and a sensitive metaphor for many kinds of exchange. The "moral economy" leads us not into a single argument but into a concourse of arguments, and it will not be possible to do justice to every voice.

A word first about my essay. Although first published in 1971 I commenced work on it in 1963 while awaiting proofs of *The Making of the English Working Class*. The project started then, for a joint study of British and French grain riots in the 1790s, in collaboration with Richard Cobb whose fine *Terreur et Subsistances, 1793-1795* came out in 1964. He was then in Leeds and I was in Halifax and Gwyn A. Williams (then in Aberystwyth) was also enlisted as a collaborator in the project. I don't remember how or when the project fell through, except that each member of the triumvirate moved in a different direction, Richard Cobb to Oxford, Gwyn Williams to York and myself to the University of Warwick. By 1970, when Cobb published his *The Police and the People*, our plan had certainly been dropped. There need be no regret for the failure of my part in that project to come to a conclusion, since Roger Wells has now explored every aspect of food and its mediations in England in the 1790s in copious detail in his *Wretched Faces* (1988).

But this explanation serves to place my essay, which was an enterprise not marginal but central to my research interests for nearly ten years. My files bulge with material collected on mills and marketing and meal mobs, etc., but since much of this repeats the evidence adduced in my article, it need not now be deployed. But a lot of work underlay my findings, and I may be forgiven if I am impatient with trivial objections.

II

It may be necessary to restate what my essay was about. It was not about *all* kinds of crowd, and a reader would have to be unusually thick-headed who supposed so.[1] It was about the crowd's "moral economy" in a context which the article defines. Nor was it about English and Welsh food riots in the eighteenth century — their where, why and when? — although it was certainly concerned with these. My object of analysis was the *mentalité*, or, as I would prefer, the political culture, the expectations, traditions, and, indeed, superstitions of the working population most frequently involved in actions in the market; and the relations — sometimes negotiations — between crowd and rulers which go under the unsatisfactory term of "riot". My method was to reconstruct a paternalist model of food marketing, with protective institutional expression and with emergency

[1] Mark Harrison reprimands me for applying the term "crowd" to what was "a very specific category of mass formation": *Crowds and History: Mass Phenomena in English Towns, 1790-1835* (Cambridge, 1988), p. 13. I followed George Rudé and Eric Hobsbawm in preferring the term "crowd" to the pejorative "mob" which some previous historians had used. No-one ever supposed that all crowds were riotous, although Harrison's attention to their variety is helpful. Harrison also pronounces that my article "has a number of shortcomings, which will be examined more fully in chapter 6". Since chapter 6 does not mention my article, and the shortcomings are identified nowhere else in his book, I am still waiting for the blow to fall.

routines in time of dearth, which derived in part from earlier Edwardian and Tudor policies of provision and market-regulation; to contrast this with the new political economy of the free market in grain, associated above all with *The Wealth of Nations*; and to show how, in times of high prices and of hardship, the crowd might enforce, with a robust direct action, protective market-control and the regulation of prices, sometimes claiming a legitimacy derived from the paternalist model.

To understand the actions of any particular crowd may require attention to particular market-places and particular practices in dealing. But to understand the "political" space in which the crowd might act and might negotiate with the authorities must attend upon a larger analysis of the relations between the two. The findings in "The Moral Economy" cannot be taken straight across to any "peasant market" nor to all proto-industrial market-places nor to Revolutionary France in the Years II and II nor to nineteenth-century Madras. Some of the encounters between growers, dealers and consumers were markedly similar, but I have described them as they were worked out within the given field-of-force of eighteenth-century English relations.

My essay did not offer a comprehensive overview of food riots in England in that century; it did not (for example) correlate the incidence of riots with price movements, nor explain why riot was more common in some regions than in others, nor attempt to chart a dozen other variables. Abundant new evidence on such questions has been brought forward in recent years, and much of it has been helpfully brought under examination in Andrew Charlesworth's *An Atlas of Rural Protest in Britain, 1548-1900* (1983). Dr John Stevenson complains that "The Moral Economy" tells us "virtually nothing about why some places were almost perennially subject to disturbances, whilst others remained almost completely undisturbed",[1] but this was not the

[1] J. Stevenson, "Food Riots in England, 1792-1818", in R. Quinault and J. Stevenson (eds.), *Popular Protest and Public Order* (London, 1974), p. 67. Also J. Stevenson, "The 'Moral Economy' of the English Crowd: Myth and Reality", in Anthony Fletcher and J. Stevenson (eds.), *Order and Disorder in Early Modern England* (Cambridge, 1985) — an essay which adds little to the discussion.

essay's theme. Nor is there any sense in which the findings of scholars (such as Dr Stevenson) who have been addressing such themes must necessarily contradict or compete with my own. Economic and social historians are not engaged in rival party-political performances, although one might sometimes suppose so. The study of wages and prices and the study of norms and expectations can complement each other.

There are still a few ineducable positivists lingering about who do not so much disagree with the findings of social historians as they wish to disallow their questions. They propose that only one set of directly economic explanations of food riots — questions relating to the grain trade, harvests, market prices, etc., is needed or is even proper to be asked. An odd example is a short essay published by Dale Williams in 1976 entitled "Were 'Hunger' Rioters Really Hungry?".[1] In this he described my "moral economy" as intended as "a replacement" for an economic or quantitative approach. He had somehow got it into his head that riots must *either* be about hunger *or* about "social issues involving local usages and traditional rights". But it will be recalled that I warn against precisely this confusion at the outset of my essay, using the analogy of a sexual tension chart: "the objection is that such a chart, if used unwisely, may conclude investigation at the exact point at which it becomes of serious sociological or cultural interest: being hungry (or being sexy), what do people do?" (p. 187). *Of course* food rioters were hungry — and on occasion coming close to starvation. But this does not tell us how their behaviour is "modified by custom, culture and reason".

Nevertheless, this illustrates one point which we take far too easily for granted. Comparative study of food riots has been, inevitably, into the history of nations which *had* riots. There has been less comparative reflection upon national histories which afford evidence — and sometimes evidence sadly plentiful — of dearth passing into famine without passing through any phase in which riots of the West-European kind have been noted. Famines have been suffered in the past (as in Ireland and in India) and are suffered today

[1] *Past and Present*, no. 71, May 1976.

in several parts of Africa, as our television screens reveal, with a fatalism sometimes mistaken for apathy or resignation. It is not only that beyond a certain point the undernourished have no physical or emotional resources for riot. (For this reason riot must take place *before* people are so weakened, and it may presuppose a watchful estimate of future supply and of market prices.) It is also that riot is a group, community, or class response to crisis; it is not within the power of a few individuals to riot. Nor need it be the only or the most obvious form of collective action — there may be alternatives such as the mass-petitioning of the authorities, fast days, sacrifices and prayer; perambulation of the houses of the rich; or the migration of whole villages.

Riot need not be favoured within the culture of the poor. It might provoke the gods (who had already sent dearth as a "Judgement"), and it could certainly alienate the governors or the rich from whom alone some small relief might come. An oncoming harvest failure would be watched with fear and awe. "Hunger employs its own outriders. Those who have already experienced it can see it announced, not only in the sky, but in the fields, scrutinized each year with increasing anxiety, week by week during the hot summer months. . ."[1] In the eighteenth century Britain was only emerging from the "demographic *ancien régime*", with its periodical visitations of famine and of plague, and dearth revived age-old memories and fears. Famine could place the whole social order on the rack, and the rulers were tested by their response to it. Indeed, by visible and well-advertised exertions the rulers might actually strengthen their authority during dearth, as John Walter and Keith Wrightson have argued from seventeenth-century examples. Central government, by issuing proclamations, invoking the successive regulations which became known as the *Book of Orders*, and proclaiming national days of fast, and the local authorities by a flurry of highly-visible activity against petty offenders ranging from badgers, forestallers and regrators to drunkards, swearers, sabbath-breakers, gamblers and rogues, might actually gain

[1] R. C. Cobb, *The Police and the People* (Oxford, 1970), p. 323. For a comparative overview, see David Arnold, *Famine: Social Crisis and Historical Change* (Oxford, 1988).

credibility among that part of the population persuaded that dearth was a judgement of God.[1] At the least, the authorities made a public display of their concern. At the best, they might restrain rising prices or persuade farmers to release stocks to the open market.

Riot may even be a signal that the *ancien régime* is ending, since there is food in barns or granaries or barges to be seized or to be got to market, and some bargaining to be done about its price. True famine (where there really is no stock of food) is not often attended with riot, since there are few rational targets for the rioters. In the pastoral North-West of England as late as the 1590s and 1620s the population appears to have suffered from famine mortality. But "the poor. . . starved to death quietly, & created no problems of order for their governors".[2] In the Irish famine of 1845-7 there were a few anti-export riots in the early stages,[3] but the Irish people could be congratulated in the Queen's speech in 1847 for having suffered with "patience and resignation". Riot is

[1] John Walter and Keith Wrightson, "Dearth and the Social Order in Early Modern England", *Past and Present*, 71 (1976). See also (for a sharper assertion of authority) John Walter, "Grain Riots and Popular Attitudes to the Law: Maldon and the Crisis of 1629" in John Brewer and John Styles (eds.), *An Ungovernable People* (1980). For the *Book of Orders*, see A. Everitt, "The Marketing of Agricultural Produce", in J. Thirsk (ed.), *The Agrarian History of England and Wales*, vol. iv, *1500-1640* (Cambridge, 1967), pp. 581-6; P. Slack, "The Book of Orders: The Making of English Social Policy, 1577-1631", *TRHS*, xxx (1980); R. B. Outhwaite, "Food Crisis in Early Modern England: Patterns of Public Response", *Proceedings of the Seventh International Economic History Congress* (Edinburgh, 1978), pp. 367-74; R. B. Outhwaite, "Dearth and Government Intervention in English Grain Markets, 1590-1700", *Econ. Hist. Rev.*, xxxiii, 3 (1981); and Buchanan Sharp, "Popular Protest in 17th-Century England", in Barry Reay (ed.), *Popular Culture in 17th-Century England* (1985), esp. pp. 274-289. Sharp argues (p. 279) that seventeenth century food riots "were often attempts to enforce officially-sanctioned market regulations and can be regarded, in many instances, not as attacks upon established order but as efforts to reinforce it".

[2] Sharp, *op. cit.*, p. 275; A. B. Appleby, in the classic account of famine mortality in Cumberland and Westmorland in the late sixteenth and early seventeenth centuries, reports no disturbances: see *Famine in Tudor and Stuart England* (Liverpool, 1978).

[3] Cecil Woodham Smith, *The Great Hunger* (1970), pp. 120-1; James S. Donnelly, Jr., *The Land and the People of Nineteenth-Century Cork* (1975), pp. 89-91.

usually a rational response, and it takes place, not among helpless or hopeless people, but among those groups who sense that they have a little power to help themselves, as prices soar, employment fails, and they can see their staple food supply being exported from the district.

The passivity of the victims of famine is noted also in Asia. Under the *ancien régime* of famine in the East (as in the terrible Orissa famine of 1770) districts were depopulated by deaths and fugitives. The ryots fled the land to which they were tied. "Day and night a torrent of famished and disease-stricken wretches poured into the great cities." Those who stayed on the land

> Sold their cattle; they sold their implements of agriculture; they devoured their seed-grain; they sold their sons and daughters, till at length no buyer of children could be found; they ate the leaves of the trees and the grass of the field. . .

But they did not (in the sense that we have been using) riot. Nor did they riot in the Bengal famine of 1866, when "many a rural household starved slowly to death without uttering a complaint or making a sign", just as there are tales of the West of Ireland in 1847 where whole families walled themselves up in their cabins to die.[1]

In the Bengal famine of 1873-4, the people turned to government as the only possible provider. Over 400,000 settled down along the lines of relief roads, pleading for relief and work: "they dreaded quitting the road, which they imagined to be the only place where subsistence could be obtained". At one place the line of carts bringing in the famine-struck from the villages stretched for twenty miles. At first there was screaming from the women and children, and begging for coin or grain. Later, the people were "seated on the ground, row after row, thousand upon thousand, in silence. . .".[2]

[1] W. H. Hunter, *The Annals of Rural Bengal* (1883), i, pp. 26-27. Many of the poor in the western counties of Ireland were overcome by fever in their own homes: see Sir W. P. MacArthur, "Medical History of the Famine", in R. D. Edwards and T. D. Williams (eds.), *The Great Famine* (Dublin, 1956), esp. pp. 270-89.
[2] Sir Richard Temple, Lieutenant-Governor of Bengal, memorandum on the scarcity of 1873-4, *Extra Supplement of the Gazette of India*, 26 Feb. 1875, pp. 25, 56-7.

There is not one simple, "animal", response to hunger. Even in Bengal the evidence is contradictory and difficult to interpret. There is some evidence of the male heads of household abandoning their families (below p. 347), and other accounts of intense familial solidarities and of self-abnegation. A relief worker in rural Bengal in 1915 gives us a common story:

> At noon I sat down at the foot of a tree to eat my bit of lunch. . . The people spotted me and long before I had finished there was a crowd of starving people around me. I did not finish it. I had a loaf of bread with me and. . . I gave the rest to the children. One little chap took his share and immediately broke it up into four pieces for his mother, two sisters and himself, leaving by far the smallest portion for himself.[1]

This is a learned response to hunger, which even the small children know. Begging, in which the children again are assigned their roles, is another learned response, or strategy. So also may be threats to the wealthy, or the theft of foodstuffs.[2]

"Riot" — itself a clumsy term which may conceal more than it reveals — is not a "natural" or "obvious" response to hunger but a sophisticated pattern of collective behaviour, a collective alternative to individualistic and familial strategies of survival. Of course hunger rioters were hungry, but hunger does not dictate that they must riot nor does it determine riot's forms.

In 1984 Dale E. Williams launched a direct assault on "The Moral Economy" in an article in *Past and Present* under the title "Morals, Markets and the English Crowd in 1766".[3] The article draws a little upon his own substantial doctoral thesis on "English Hunger Riots in 1766" presented in 1978. But its intent is mainly polemical, and it is tedious to find that, after nearly two decades, one is invited to return to square one and to argue everything through again.

Andrew Charlesworth and Adrian Randall have been kind enough to correct the record and to point out Williams's

---

[1] J. Mitchell, *Bankura Wesleyan College Magazine*, January 1916.

[2] Much curious and contradictory evidence as to responses to famine is in Robert Dirks, "Social Response during Severe Food Shortages and Famines", *Current Anthropology*, xxi (1980), pp. 21-44.

[3] *Past and Present*, 104 (1984).

self-contradictions.[1] To their critique I will only add that several of his sallies appear to be directed against his own findings in his doctoral thesis. So far from refuting my account of norms and behaviour, the crowds in Williams's thesis conform to the account in "The Moral Economy". Given high prices and the advance signals of dearth, the West of England clothing workers inhibited further exports of grain from the district, regulated markets with unusual discipline, forcibly persuaded farmers to send supplies to market, made certain of the authorities — including Mr Dalloway, the High Sheriff of Gloucestershire — for a time the "prisoners" of their demands, stimulated local measures of charity and relief, and (if I read Dr Williams aright) may have prevented dearth from passing into famine. And if Dale Williams wants examples of the crowd being informed by concern for "local usages and traditional rights" he need only turn to Dale Williams's thesis where he will find sufficient examples, such as the crowd punishing millers by destroying their bolting machinery, as well as an Appendix of anonymous letters full of threats against broggers, forestallers, regrators, corn hoarders, sample sales, and the rest.[2]

Dr Williams has brought no issues of principle into debate, he is simply confused as to the questions which he is asking. There may also be a little ideological pressure behind his polemic. When I first published "The Moral Economy", "the market" was not flying as high in the ideological firmament as it is today. In the 1970s something called "modernisation theory" swept through some undefended minds in Western academies, and subsequently the celebration of "the market economy" has become triumphal and almost universal. This renewed confidence in "the market" can be found in

[1] A. Charlesworth and Adrian Randall, "Morals, Markets and the English Crowd in 1766", *Past and Present*, 114 (1987), pp. 200-13. On the 1766 riots see also A. J. Randall, "The Gloucestershire Food Riots in 1766", *Midland History*, x (1985); W. J. Shelton, *English Hunger & Industrial Disorder* (1973), and reviews of Shelton by myself in *Econ. Hist. Rev.*, 2nd series, xxvii (1974), pp. 480-4 and by Peter Linebaugh in *Bull. Soc. Lab. Hist.*, 28 (1974), pp. 57-61.

[2] Univ. of Wales Ph.D. thesis, 1978. Dale Williams's excellent article on "Midland Hunger Riots in 1766" in *Midland History*, iii, 4 (1976), might even have been written in illustration of the moral economy thesis. What happened between 1976 and 1984 to change the events of 1766?

Dr Williams's article, where I am rebuked for failing to pay "sufficient attention to the *systems* which produce wealth". "The riot groups of 1766 were. . . all participants in a capitalist market system which, by the 1760s, was developed to a pitch of refinement unmatched elsewhere in the world." "The Moral Economy" has become suspect because it explored with sympathy alternative economic imperatives to those of the capitalist market "system". . . and offered one or two sceptical comments as to the infallibility of Adam Smith.

Similar questions worried more courteous critics shortly after "The Moral Economy" was published: Professors A. W. Coats and Elizabeth Fox-Genovese. I did not reply to either comment, since the arrows flew past my ear. Professor Coats[1] devoted his comment to rehearsing Smithian doctrine on the internal trade in grain, in terms of its logical consistency (but without recourse to empirical confirmation), and he repeated uncritically the statement that "high prices resulted mainly from physical shortages", as if this explanation of price movements suffices for all cases. But, as we shall see (pp. 283-7), it does not. Then Coats debated my notion as to the "de-moralizing of the theory of trade and consumption" implicit in the model of the new political economy. What I say (above, pp. 201-2) is this:

> By 'de-moralising' it is not suggested that Smith and his colleagues were immoral or were unconcerned for the public good. It is meant, rather, that the new political economy was disinfested of intrusive moral imperatives. The old pamphleteers were moralists first and economists second. In the new economic theory questions as to the moral polity of marketing do not enter, unless as preamble and peroration.

Coats takes this to imply an acceptance on my part of the credentials of "positive" economics, as a science purged of norms, and he reminds me of the "moral background and implications of Smith's economic analysis". But I had not forgotten that Smith was also author of the *Theory of Moral Sentiments* (1759). I had supposed that Coats's point had been met in a footnote (above p. 202) in which I had allowed Smith's intention to serve the public good but had added that "intention is a bad measure of ideological interest and of

[1] A. W. Coats, "Contrary Moralities: Plebs, Paternalists and Political Economists", *Past and Present*, 54 (1972), pp. 130-3.

historical consequences". It is perfectly possible that *laissez-faire* doctrines as to the food trade could have been *both* normative in intent (i.e. Adam Smith believed they would encourage cheap and abundant food) *and* ideological in outcome (i.e. in the result their supposedly de-moralised scientism was used to mask and to apologise for other self-interested operations).

I would have thought that my views were commonplace. The Tudor policies of "provision" cannot be seen, in a modern sense, as an "economic" strategy only: they depended also on theories of the State, of the reciprocal obligations and duties of governors and governed in times of dearth, and of paternalist social control; they still, in the early seventeenth century, had strong religious or magical components. In the period 1700-1760, with the dominance of mercantilist theory, we are in a kind of middle passage of theory. The magical components of the Tudor theory became much weaker. And the social location of the theory became more ambiguous; while some traditionalist gentry and magistrates invoked it in times of dearth, the authority of the theory was fast eroding as any acceptable account of normal marketing practice. The paternal obligations of "provision" were at odds with the mercantilist imperative to maximise the export of grain. At the same time there was a certain migration of the theory from the rulers to the crowd.

Nevertheless, the form of much economic argument remained (on all sides) moralistic: it validated itself at most points with reference to moral imperatives (what obligations the state, or the landowners, or the dealers *ought* to obey). Such imperatives permeated economic thinking very generally, and this is familiar to any student of economic thought. One historian has written that

> Economic theory owes its present development to the fact that some men, in thinking of economic phenomena, forcefully suspended all judgments of theology, morality, and justice, were willing to consider the economy as nothing more than an intricate mechanism, refraining for the while from asking whether the mechanism worked for good or evil. [1]

[1] W. Letwin, *The Origins of Scientific Economics* (1963), pp. 147-8. See however Joyce Appleby, *Economic Thought and Ideology in Seventeenth-Century England* (Princeton, 1978), pp. 258-9 for qualifications.

Joyce Appleby has shown the moral economy "in retreat" in the mid-seventeenth century, but the tension between norms and "mechanism" once again became marked in the eighteenth. A *locus classicus* is the scandal provoked by Mandeville's *Fable of the Bees*, which, by its equation private vices = public benefits, sought exactly to divorce moral imperatives on the one hand and economic process on the other. This was felt by some to be an outrage to official morality; by demystifying economic process it would strip authority of its paternal legitimacy; and the book was presented, in 1723, by the Grand Jury of Middlesex as a public nuisance.

Thus the notion of "economics" as a non-normative object of study, with objective mechanism independent of moral imperatives, was separating itself off from traditionalist theory during the mercantilist period, and with great difficulty: in some areas it did this with less difficulty (national book-keeping, arguments about trade and bullion), but in areas which related to internal distribution of the prime necessities of life the difficulties were immense. For if the rulers were to deny their own duties and functions in protecting the poor in time of dearth, then they might devalue the legitimacy of their rule. So tenaciously and strongly was this view held that as late as 1800 the Lord Chief Justice, Lord Kenyon, pronounced that the fact that forestalling remained an offence at Common Law "is a thing most essential to the existence of the country". "When the people knew there was a law to resort to, it composed their minds" and removed the threat of "insurrection".[1] This is an argument, not from economics and not even from law, but from the highest reasons of State.

The "morality" of Adam Smith was never the matter at issue, but — in relation to the internal trade in grain — the terms and the vocabulary, indeed the problematic of that argument. "The market economy created new moral problems", Professor Atiyah has written, and "it may not have been so obvious then, as it became later, that this was not so much to separate morality and economics, as to adopt

[1] Douglas Hay, "The State and the Market: Lord Kenyon and Mr. Waddington", *Past and Present* (forthcoming).

MORAL ECONOMY REVIEWED

a particular type of morality in the interests of a particular type of economy".[1] Perhaps I might have made it more clear that "preamble and peroration" had real significance in the intentions of the classical political economists: these were something more than rhetorical devices. Professor Coats's reminder that Smithian economics "were securely grounded in the liberal-moral philosophy of the eighteenth-century enlightenment" has in recent years become a centre for intense academic interest and we will return to it.

Maybe the trouble lies with the word "moral". "Moral" is a signal which brings on a rush of polemical blood to the academic head. Nothing has made my critics angrier than the notion that a food rioter might have been more "moral" than a disciple of Dr Adam Smith. But that was not my meaning (whatever the judgement might have been in the eye of God). I was discriminating between two different sets of assumptions, two differing discourses, and the evidence for the difference is abundant. I wrote of "a consistent traditional view of social norms and obligations, of the proper economic functions of several parties within the community, which, taken together, can be said to constitute the moral economy of the poor" (above p. 188). To this were added a dense tissue of precedents and of practices in the sequence of food marketing. I could perhaps have called this "a sociological economy", and an economy in its original meaning (*oeconomy*) as the due organisation of a household, in which each part is related to the whole and each member acknowledges her/his several duties and obligations. That, indeed, is as much, or more, "political" than is "political economy", but by usage the classical economists have carried off the term.

Elizabeth Fox-Genovese's arrow flies past my ear for much the same reason.[2] She finds that both traditional and classical economics can be said to be "moral" (at least in their own self-image) and also that both were "part of larger ruling class ideologies". There is not much here that conflicts with,

[1] P. S. Atiyah, *The Rise and Fall of Freedom of Contract* (Oxford, 1979), p. 84.
[2] Elizabeth Fox-Genovese, "The Many Faces of Moral Economy", *Past and Present*, 58 (1973).

or even engages with, my arguments, and perhaps Fox-Genovese's real difference of emphasis lies in her feeling that I "lean towards a romantic view of the traditionalists". My tendency "to favour the paternalists" leads me to overlook that "if the rise of a market society brought indisputable horrors, it also brought an emphasis on individual freedom of choice, the right to self-betterment, eventually the opportunity to political participation".

That is also what we are assured — or used to be assured — by the modernisation theorists. And *of course* the rioters were already deeply involved, in some part of their lives, in a market economy's exchanges of labour, services, and of goods. (I will refrain from mentioning those critics who have put up the fat-headed notion that there has been proposed an absolute segregation between a moral and a market economy, to save their blushes.[1]) But before we go on to consider all these undoubted human goods we should delay with the market as dispenser of subsistence in time of dearth, which alone is relevant to my theme. For despite all the discourse that goes on about "the market" or "market relations", historiographical interest in the actual marketing of grain, flour or bread is little more evident today than it was in 1971.[2]

[1] One is reminded of David Thorner's wise caveat: "We are sure to go astray, if we try to conceive of peasant economies as exclusively 'subsistence' oriented and to suspect capitalism wherever the peasants show evidence of being 'market' oriented. It is much sounder to take it for granted, as a starting point, that for ages peasant economies have had a double orientation towards both. In this way, much fruitless discussion about the nature of so-called 'subsistence' economies can be avoided". Would that the same warning was borne in mind in discussions of "proto-industrial" economies! See "Peasant Economy as a Category in History", in Teodor Shanin (ed.), *Peasants and Peasant Societies*, 2nd ed. (Oxford, 1987), p. 65.

[2] The outstanding exception is Wendy Thwaites, "The Marketing of Agricultural Produce in Eighteenth Century Oxfordshire" (Univ. of Birmingham Ph.D. thesis, 1980). See also the same author's "Dearth and the Marketing of Agricultural Produce: Oxfordshire, c. 1750-1800", *Agric, Hist. Rev.*, xxxiii (1985), pt. ii; John Chartres, "Markets and Marketing in Metropolitan Western England in the late Seventeenth and Eighteenth Centuries", in Michael Havinden (ed.), *Husbandry and Marketing in the South-West* (Exeter, 1973), pp. 63-74, and John Chartres, "The Marketing of Agricultural Produce", in Joan Thirsk (ed.), *The Agrarian History of England and Wales*, vol. v, pt. 2 (Cambridge, 1985), ch. 17. The silence as

Is market *a* market or is market a metaphor? Of course it can be both, but too often discourse about "the market" conveys the sense of something definite — a space or institution of exchange (perhaps London's Corn Exchange at Mark Lane?) — when in fact, sometimes unknown to the term's user, it is being employed as a metaphor of economic process, or an idealisation or abstraction from that process. Perhaps to acknowledge this second usage, Burke sometimes employed the word without the definite article:

> Market is the meeting and conference of the *consumer* and *producer*, when they mutually discover each other's wants. Nobody, I believe, has observed with any reflection what market is, without being astonished at the truth, the correctness, the civility, the general equity, with which the balance of wants is settled. . . The moment that government appears at market, all the principles of market will be subverted.[1]

That is loop-language: it is wholly self-fulfilling. And much the same feedback loop-language is being used today in the higher theorising of market relations. Political economy has its sophisticated intellectual genealogies, and the history of political economy is a vigorous academic discourse with its own journals and its controversies and conferences, in which changes are rung on approved themes: Pufendorf, Virtue, natural law, Pocock, Grotius, the Physiocrats, Pocock, Adam Smith. These chimes have fascination, and for the bell-ringers it is an admirable mental exercise, but the peal can become so compelling that it drowns out other sounds. Intellectual history, like economic history before it, becomes imperialist and seeks to over-run all social life. It is necessary to pause, from time to time, to recall that how people thought their times need not have been the same as how those times eventuated. And how some people thought "market" does not prove that market took place in that way. Because Adam Smith offered "a clear analytical demonstration of

---

to corn milling has at last broken by John Orbell, "The Corn Milling Industry, 1750-1820", in C. H. Feinstein and S. Pollard (eds.), *Studies in Capital Formation in the United Kingdom* (Oxford, 1988), which shows (p. 162) the rapidly rising rate of annual capital investment in milling, from 1761 rising to a peak in the dearth (and riot) year of 1801.

[1] Edmund Burke, "Thoughts and Details on Scarcity" (1795), in *Works* (1801), vii, pp. 348-51.

how markets in subsistence goods and labour could balance themselves out in a manner consistent with strict justice and the natural law of humanity"[1] this does not show that any empirically observable market worked out in that way. Nor does it tell us how strict justice to the rights of property could balance with natural humanity to labouring people.

Messrs Hont and Ignatieff, in the course of a prestigious research project into "Political Economy and Society, 1750-1850" at King's College, Cambridge, have fallen across my "Moral Economy" article and they rebuke it for failing to conform to the parameters of Cambridge political thought:

> By recovering the moral economy of the poor and the regulatory system to which they made appeal, Thompson has set the iconoclasm of the Smithian position in sharp relief, crediting him with the first theory to revoke the traditional social responsibility attached to property. Yet the antinomy — moral economy versus political economy — caricatures both positions. The one becomes a vestigial, traditional moralism, the other a science 'disinfested of intrusive moral imperatives'. To the extent that favouring an adequate subsistence for the poor can be called a moral imperative, it was one shared by paternalists and political economists alike. . . On the other hand, to call the moral economy traditionalist is to portray it simply as a set of vestigial moral preferences innocent of substantive argument about the working of markets. In fact, so-called traditionalists were quite capable of arguing their position on the same terrain as their political economist opponents. Indeed, and this is the crucial point, debate over market or 'police' strategies for providing subsistence for the poor divided philosophers and political economists among themselves no less deeply than it divided the crowd for Smith. Indeed, it makes no sense to take Smith as typical of the range of opinion within the European Enlightenment camp. This becomes apparent if one moves beyond the English context, to which Thompson confines his discussion, and considers the debate in its full European setting. The crucial context for Smith's 'Digression on Grain' was not the encounter with the English or Scottish crowd, but the French debates over the liberalization of the internal trade in 1764-6, which occurred. . . when Smith himself was in France.[2]

There are some wilful confusions here. The first point to make about this passage is that, just as much as with the ineducable positivists, it is not so much offering to debate my

[1] Istvan Hont and Michael Ignatieff, "Needs and Justice in *The Wealth of Nations*", in I. Hont and M. Ignatieff (eds.), *Wealth and Virtue* (Cambridge, 1983), p. 43.
[2] *Ibid.*, pp. 14-15.

views as to disallow my questions. Hont and Ignatieff prefer to operate in a detached discipline of political ideas and rhetoric. They do not wish to know how ideas presented themselves as actors in the market-place, between producers, middlemen and consumers, and they imply that this is an improper light in which to view them. It may be "the crucial point" for Hont and Ignatieff that debate over market strategies divided philosophers among themselves no less deeply than it divided the crowd from Smith, but my essay is about the crowd and not about philosophers. Hont and Ignatieff are rebuking me for writing an essay in social history and in popular culture instead of in approved Cambridge themes. I ought to have grabbed a bell-rope and pealed out Quesnay along with Pufendorf, Pocock, Grotius, Hume and the rest.

Even so, Hont and Ignatieff's censures are sloppier than the case calls for. So far from "crediting" Adam Smith "with the first theory to revoke the traditional social responsibility attached to property" (their words, not mine) I am at pains to note the opposite, describing the *Wealth of Nations* "not only as a point of departure but also as a grand central terminus to which many important lines of discussion in the middle of the eighteenth century. . . all run". (Above p. 201.) It is in fact Hont and Ignatieff, and not Thompson, who write that "by 1776, Smith remained the only standard-bearer for 'natural liberty' in grain",[1] a spectacular mis-statement which they reach by confusing the British context with the French context in the aftermath of the *guerre des farines*. As for portraying the "moral economy" as "a set of vestigial moral preferences innocent of substantive argument about the working of markets", the trouble is, once again, the vulgarity of the crowd. They were not philosophers. They did, as my essay shows, have substantive and knowledgeable arguments about the working of markets, but about actual markets rather than theorised market relations. I am not persuaded that Hont and Ignatieff have read very far in the pamphlets and newspapers — let alone in the crowd relations — where these arguments will be found and I do not know what business they have to put me, or the crowd, down.

[1] *Ibid.*, p. 18.

I did not, of course, take Smith as "typical of the range of opinion within the European Enlightenment camp". I took Smith's "Digression Concerning the Corn Trade" in Book Four, Chapter 5, of *The Wealth of Nations* as being the most lucid expression in English of the standpoint of the new political economy upon market relations in subsistence foodstuffs. As such it was profoundly influential within British governmental circles, and few chapters can have had a more palpable influence upon policies or have been used more extensively to justify policies which were already being enacted. Pitt and Grenville read it together in the 1780s and became wholly converted; when Pitt wavered in the crisis year 1800 Grenville called him back to their old faith.[1] Burke was an ardent adherent and had reached similar positions independently; he had been, in 1772, a prime mover in the repeal of the ancient forestalling legislation, and he was to moralise the "laws" of political economy and nominate them to be divine.[2] In the nineteenth century class after class of administrators were sent out to India, fully indoctrinated at Haileybury College in Smith's "Digression", and ready to respond to the vast exigencies of Indian famine by resolutely resisting any improper interventions in the free operation of the market. T. R. Malthus, appointed Professor of Political Economy at Haileybury in 1805, was an early and apt instructor.

Hont and Ignatieff know that "the crucial context" for Smith's digression "was not the encounter with the English or Scottish crowd, but the French debates over the liberalization of the internal trade in 1764-6". I wonder how they know? A French philosophic influence is more reputable than an English or Scottish crowd, and of course Adam Smith was profoundly influenced by physiocratic thought. The influence of "the French debates" may be guessed at, but is not evident in the few pages of Smith's digression. The debate about the liberalisation of trade had proceeded in England

---

[1] See Roger Wells, *Wretched Faces* (Gloucester, 1988), p. 88.
[2] See Douglas Hay, "The State and the Market", *op. cit.*,; C. B. Macpherson, *Burke* (Oxford, 1980), *passim*; Burke, "Thoughts and Details on Scarcity", p. 354: "the laws of commerce, which are the laws of nature, and consequently the laws of God".

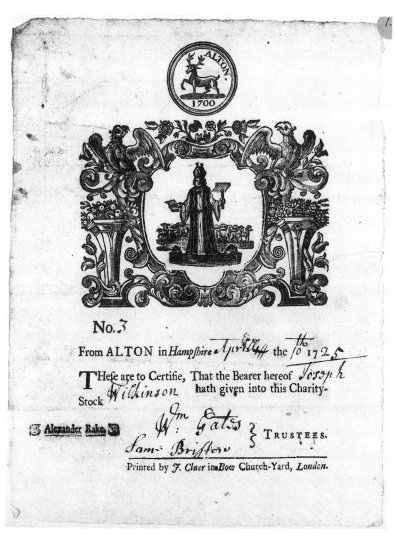

No. 3

From ALTON in *Hampshire* April the 10th 1725

THese are to Certifie, That the Bearer hereof *Joseph Wilkinson* hath given into this Charity-Stock

Alexander Rake *Wm Gates* } TRUSTEES.
Sam: Bristow

Printed by *J. Cluer in Bow* Church-Yard, *London.*

Plate I. One of the earliest surviving trade union cards, which was filed among the Crown's affidavits when woolcombers were prosecuted in 1725 in Alton, Hants. (See p. 59.) Note that the union (or "Charity") has a London printer and claims to have been founded in 1700. Bishop Blaize, the patron of the woolcombers, is in the centre.

AMICABLE SOCIETY OF WOOLSTAPLERS

WOOL 1785.

Be you to others KIND & TRUE,
As you'd have others be to you,
And neither DO nor SAY to men,
What you'd not like to take again.

BRETHREN
  This is to CERTIFY that the Bearer here
        is LEGAL, has an undoubte
Right to the Wool-stapling Trade, and to receive a
usual Benefits whatever.

(Signed)

Plate II. The ticket of the Amicable Society of Woolstaplers, 1785,
invokes associations with trade and with pastoral life rather than
with industry.

Plate III. This woolcombers' union card of 1838 still has the figure of Bishop Blaize at top centre.

THE
P I L L O R Y
IN ITS
G L O R Y,
With the Eloquent Speech it made soon after WILLIAMS had left it.
To which is added, an Antient Prophecy of MERLIN's
On the J A C K - B O O T.

We hear that WILLIAM's Pillory (fuppofed to be made of the Defcendants of the Oaks of Dodona, which formerly fpoke Prophetic) made a Speech as foon as he had left it to the following Purport:

GENTLEMEN,

" THE very favourable Treatment I have juft now met with from you calls immediate Thanks. I have been accuftomed to Ufage of a very different nature : for feldom have I fhewn 'my Face but Filth of every kind hath been thrown againft it.—But fuch is the prefent Occafion, and fuch your juft Opinion of it, that now you have been pleafed to decorate me with Laurels, and honour me with your Acclamations. Such univerfal Applaufe makes me fomething proud of myfelf and induces me to think I am not unwortny of having Perfons of higher Rank ftand upon me. Perhaps I foon may, as Matters go on ; And I muft own to you, I fhould be glad to experience your Behaviour towards me, when Criminals of a fuperior Station peep thro' my wooden Windows. Indeed I heartily wifh they foon may: fuch with Gentlemen is no Libel; nor can the DOUBLE FEED Advocate by all his Art in Inuendo's, make it fo. Why fhould not great Villains ftand upon me as well as little ones? If any Lawer, in that place I now look upon, fhould dare to attempt to pervert the Laws of this Land, and undermine the Liberties of the People, why fhould not I expofe him to your View and Contempt? or if any Perfon fhould take a private Bribe to betray a public Truft , why fhould not I lift up the Rafcal to your Refentment? I would haxe every Man meet with his due Reward: and he deferves Halters of Axes let them have them : or, if any fhall merit only a Poft upon me, your grateful Servant is very ready to exalt them, tho' loads of Dirt and rotten Eggs, inftead of Laurels and Acclamations fhould be my Lot."

An antient Prophecy of MERLIN's.

WHEN from the North a cruel Bird call'd ----,
   Shall fly o'er ENGLAND and devour its Fruit,
Shall o'er this Land his baneful Pinions fpread.
And from their Months fhall take the Children's Bread ;
Shall, Cuckoo-like, make other Nefts his own,
And caft his filthy Eggs behind the ----.-
Then Magna Charta to Excife fhall turn;
The Apple be caft off, the Merchant mourn ;
Then fhall pack'd Juries try the Fact alone,
And under J----- the Bench fhall groan,
Then Pillories into Repute fhall come,
And the Prefs, ENGLAND's Bulwark, be ftruck dumb,

Plate IV. This broadside combines visual and literary forms with the old oral form of rhyming "prophecies". Williams, a bookseller, was sentenced to the pillory for republishing Wilkes's *North Briton*, no. 45. He was cheered by the crowd, which "erected a gallows of ladders, on which they hung a jack-boot [symbol of the King's favourite, the Earl of Bute], an axe and a Scotch bonnet which articles, after a while, were taken down, the top of the boot cut off with the axe, and then both boot and bonnet thrown into a large bonfire". (Thomas Wright, *Caricature History of the Georges* London, 1867, p. 300).

ANTICIPATION
OF THE
Death-bed Confession.
OF A
NOTORIOUS SINNER.

MY Father was a celebrated Cocker, my Mother the Daughter of a Fiddler, and previous to her Marriage, had employed her Charms to fome advantage. By thefe laudible means my Parents were poffeffed of fome wealth : no expence was fpared to give me an Education, and the accomplifhment of a Gentleman; but alas, my fteril nature was never able to abide the firft rudiments of a fcholar, and all my attempts at gentility only ferved to make me rediculous.

How I have fulfilled the duties of the cloth, my Charity towards the poor Cottagers will evince, and having obtained the rank of a Magiftrate, I unblufhingly firft exercifed my authority in convicting and fending to prifon a poor honeft man, the father of a large family, for felling ale without a licence; though all my neighbours knew it was through my influence alone that a licence had been refufed him; I was induced to commit this act of meannefs and wanton cruelty, only becaufe he was the Tenant of a refpectable gentleman, richer and more refpectable than myfelf, whom I hated for obliging me ftrictly to obferve the pious duties I had undertaken, and was amply paid for, but had no inclination to perform.

Manifold have been my Sins, and at the awful moment of diffolution their horrid deformity prefents itfelf to my difturbed mind. I humbly afk forgivenefs of the numbers I have oppreffed, and hope thefe my laft words may be publifhed as a warning to thofe of mean extraction, who, like me, may become poffeffed of fome little power, and employ it to the injury of their fellow-creatures.

A Penitent SINNER.

Plate V. A lampoon on a clerical magistrate (see p. 519). Two Staffordshire gentlemen were feuding in 1796-1800, John Gough, Esq., and the Reverend Thomas Lane, JP, Rector of Handsworth, to whom are attributed these last dying words. John Gough was trying to enlist his tenants in the feud, and skilfully combined visual lampoon with the most popular literary form, the "last dying words" of the condemned.

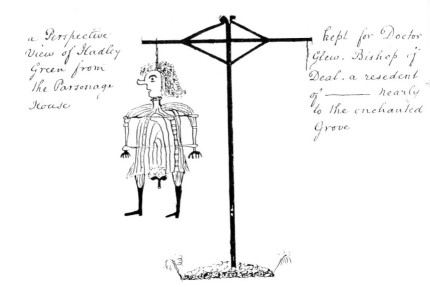

a Perspective View of Hadley Green from the Parsonage House

kept for Doctor Glew. Bishop of Deal. a resedent of ——— nearly to the enchanted Grove

Bretheren . Bretheren behold my exalted Station . Plante amongst elegant trees. Shrubs and sweet flowers, but all afre to me Pifs a beds. Nettles and Brambles . I feel the Sting of my Consience . O yea I repent from ever been Parson Just Afs and so forth . O what a miserable Shitting . Stinking Dogmatick Prig of an April fool I do appear , all over Filth . from such filth of Body and Consience Good Lord diliver Me . and from this high Promotion I beseech thee to encline my Heart to do Iestice that I may walk in Peace before all Men . Women and Children , Amen

Plate VI. Isaac Emmerton, a nurseryman, was prosecuted in 1800 for such lampoons and for erecting a ten-foot-high gibbet with an effigy ridiculing the Reverend C. J. Cottrell, JP., the Rector of Handley, Middlesex, the chairman of the local Commissioners of Tax (see p. 481).

Tom Bobbin Jun.ʳ et pinxt Lancashire.

Price 6ᵈ plain 1ˢ Colour'd

THE PLURALIST AND OLD SOLDIER

A Soldier once and in the Beggar's list
Did thus address a well-fed Pluralist.

Soldier.

At Guardalupe my Leg, and Thigh I lost;
No Pension have I, tho' its right I boast.
Your Rev.ᶜᵉ please, some Charity bestow.
Heav'n will pay double, when you're there, you know.

Pluralist.

Heav'n pay me double —! Vagrant; know that I
Ne'er give to Strolers, they're so apt to lie:
Your Parish, and some work woud you become,
So haste away — or Constables your doom.

Soldier.

May't please your Rev.ᶜᵉ hear my case, and then,
Youll say I'm poorer than the most of Men.
When Marlbro Sieged Lisle I first drew breath,
And there my father met untimely Death:
My Mother follow'd of a broken heart:
So I've no friend, or Parish, for my part.

Pluralist.

I say begone — with that he loudly knocks
And Timber-toe, begun to smell the Stocks:
Away he stumps - but in a Rood or two
Thrice clear'd his Wezon, and his tho.ᵗˢ broke thrṽ

Soldier.

Thus tis to beg of those who (Sometimes) Preach
Up Charity, and all the Virtues teach:
But their disguise, to Common-Sense is thin,
A Pocket button'd —. Hypocrite within _.
Send me kind Heav'n the well-tann'd Cap.ᵗˢ Face.
Who gives me Twelvepence, and a Curse with Grace
But let me not, in House, or Lane, or Street
These Treble-pensiond Parsons ever meet:
And when I die, may I still number'd be
With the rough Soldier to eternity.

Pub.ᵈ according to Act of Parl.ᵗ by M. Darly facing New Round Court the Strand 1766

Plate VII. This 1766 broadside by John Collier (or "Tim Bobbin"), the celebrated Lancashire caricaturist, combines the popular appeal to patriotism with popular hostility to pluralist clergy.

Plate VIII. J. Penkethman, *Artachthos: Authentic Accounts of the History and Price of Wheat, Bread, Malt &c* was published in 1638 and republished in 1765. This frontespiece carries below: "From the Original Tables, formerly in the Treasury, of the King's Exchequer at Westminster and late in the Possession of the Right Honourable Edward Earl of Oxford." This shows the careful regulation of weights and measures of wheat and the punishment in the stocks of forestallers and regrators.

Richmond Park.

Plate IX. Parishioners, led by their vicar, beat the bounds of their parish, and assert their right of way into Richmond Park by breaking down the wall (see p. 111).

Plate X. As prices began to fall in 1801, caricaturists mocked corn hoarders who had supplies left on their hands. The agricultural labourer is shown (right) as innocent.

Plate XI. Based on an incident in Bishop's-Clyst, Devon, in August 1800. There was a long tradition in Devon of crowds scouring the countryside and visiting farmers reputed to be hoarding corn, and threatening them with rope. Women are shown to be prominent in this action.

Plate XII. "A Legal Method of Thrashing Out Grain" — a tribute to Lord Chief Justice Kenyon, who had presided over the trial and conviction of Rusby, a corn factor, for regrating oats (July 1800), and who sought to revive the old laws against forestalling, &c., on the grounds that — despite their repeal — they remained recognised by the common law.

Plate XIII. During the grain crisis of 1800-01 the Home Secretary, the duke of Portland, actively supported *laissez-faire*, and in March 1801 he issued a circular letter to Lords Lieutenant deploring those local authorities who had been reviving the old laws against sale by sample.

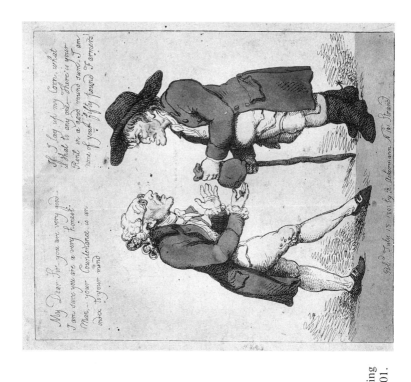

Plate XIV. An urban view of landlord and farmer conspiring with each other to raise prices during the grain crisis of 1801.

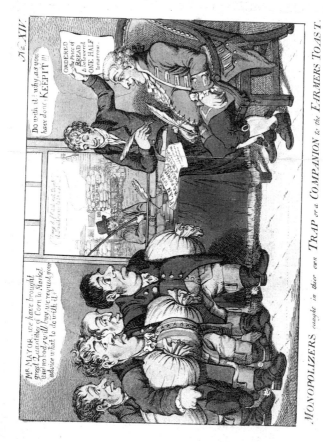

Plate XV. Monopolizers are left with unsold corn, May 1801. The Mayor is setting the Assize of Bread. The agricultural labourer looks through the window and says, "Dang I, if I did not think it would come to this at last!"

Woodward delin.

Etch'd by Roberts

OLD FRIENDS with NEW FACES, or WELCOME VISITORS to JOHN BULL.

London Pub'd by P. Roberts 28 Middle Row Holborn.

Plate XVI. Prices really do fall in the autumn of 1801.

Plate XVIIa (left). The Butter Cross at Witney, Oxon, was built in 1683 and repaired in 1811. Many market buildings were built in the seventeenth century and still provide evidence of the vigour of market controls. Plate XVIIb (right). The Corn Market at Ledbury, Herefordshire, was built shortly after 1617. Corn storage chambers were added above, some fifty years later, where any unsold grain was held until the next market day. As corn came to be sold by sample in the next century, the chambers were hired out, and a poultry and butter market continued below.

Plate XVIII. Time, work and mortality are invoked at the Neptune Yard, Walker, Newcastle-upon-Tyne.

Plate XIX. This plaster panel is in the Great Chamber at Montacute House, near Yeovil, Somerset, and dates from *circa* 1601. The husband, who had been left in charge of the baby, is surprised by his wife while he is surreptitiously drawing beer. She hits him over the head with a shoe, and this is witnessed by a neighbour (rear).

Plate XX. On the right of this Montacute panel, either the husband or a proxy is made to ride a pole. This is described often as riding Skimmington, but a "true" Skimmington has two riders, one impersonating the wife who belabours the husband, who rides facing the horse's or donkey's tail. (See Hogarth's Skimmington, plate XXII.) The Montacute riding might equally well be Riding the Stang (North of England) or cool-staffing in the West Country.

That pucary, Rabble that came down
From all the carrets in the Town
And Stalls & day hovents in next Session.

To cry the Cause up, bestirring
And bawl the Bishops out of Door
Are now drawn up in greater Shoals

And all ye Grandees of our members
In carbonading on the Embers
Knights Gitizens and Burgesses

That serve for Chanstock & Badges
To represent their privatedges
Each Bonfire is a funeral Pile

And as a Miracle we are not
Herself, burnts it Incarnate
For while we overtopds here and sat

Some on the Sign Post of an Ale House
Hang in Effigie on the Gallows
Made up of rags to personate

Plate XXI. Hogarth's illustration from "Hudibras" of burning the rumps at Temple Bar shows the street theatre of London politics, and the preparation of effigies for the bonfire.

Plate XXII. Hogarth's illustration from "Hudibras" of a Skimmington.

Dr SYNTAX WITH THE SKIMERTON RIDERS.

Plate XXIII. Rowlandson's "Skimerton" (from illustrations to "Dr. Syntax") shows all the symbolism and paraphernalia of a carnival of cuckoldry, and shows a more active participation by the women than does Hogarth.

A GENERAL SUMMONS

TO ALL THE HORNIFIED FUMBLERS,

To assemble at Horn Fair October 18,

Printed and sold by T. Batchelar, 115, Long Alley, Moorfields, London.

Plate XXIV. A summons to Horn Fair at Charlton (north of Blackheath). Claiming great antiquity, in the eighteenth century this carnival of cuckoldry was patronised by many genteel young people, masked and in drag, and with horns plentifully in evidence.

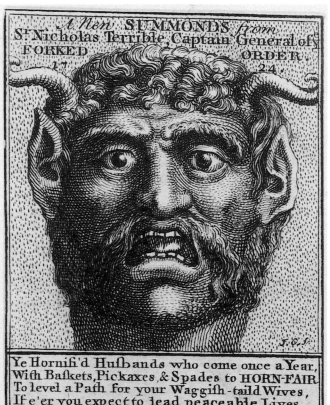

A New SUMMONS from St Nicholas Terrible, Captain General of FORKED ORDER 17 24

Ye Hornifi'd Husbands who come once a Year,
With Baskets, Pickaxes & Spades to HORN-FAIR
To level a Path for your Waggish-taild Wives,
If e'er you expect to lead peaceable Lives
Make the best of your Bargains, & think it no scorn
That Fortune has doom'd you to wearing the Horn,
For 'twas worn by OLD NICK, before you were begot
And will be so, after you're all dead and rotten, ten
Make him but ye Captain to fight for your Cause
And then you'll have nothing to fear, my brave Boys
Sold by the Printsellers &c. Price 6 Pence.

Plate XXV. The printer, T. Batchelar, used these premises between
1817 and 1828 (information from Roy Palmer) so that this
"Summons" extends the iconography of cuckoldry and skimmingtons
well into the nineteenth century.

Plate XXVI. This diabolic mask, known as the "Ooser", was held at a farm in Melbury Osmond, Dorset, but it is now lost. The lower jaw was moveable and was worked with a string; in its last years it was supposedly used to frighten unruly children.

CHAPTER VIII.

OLD SHOPS, OLD HOUSES, AND OLD INHABITANTS.

As a picture of the past, and one that had never been altered for many long years, I shall now endeavour to bring before the eye the trades and shops, odd characters, and old houses, ancient lanes, yards, and 'twitchells,' in some such order as they stood, and with the old names by which the trades were

Plate XXVII. This reconstruction of riding the stang comes from a local history of Grimsby, published in 1857. A proxy (or neighbour?) is being ridden, in some comfort, while the victim watches apprehensively out of the window.

Plate XXVIII. The last days of rough music: a "lewbelling" in a
Warwickshire village (Brailes) in 1909. The band parades before the
effigies of "the erring pair", which are set up in front of the woman's
house. After three nights the dummies are burned. Notice that this
band is wholly male, and the "historic instruments" have given way to
kettles, milk churns and corrugated iron.

JOHN HOBBS, JOHN HOBBS.

Sung by Mr. LOVEGROVE, with unbounded Applause, in " Any Thing New," at the Lyceum Theatre, Strand.

LY shoe-maker, John Hobbs, John Hobbs,
y shoe-maker, John Hobbs;
He married Jane Carter,
No damsel look'd smarter,
But he caught a Tartar,
Hobbs, John Hobbs,
he caught a Tartar, John Hobbs.

ed a rope to her, John Hobbs, John Hobbs,
ed a rope to her, John Hobbs:
To 'scape from hot water
To Smithfield he brought her,
But nobody bought her,
Hobbs, Jane Hobbs,
all were afraid of Jane Hobbs.

Oh, who'll buy a wife? says Hobbs, John Hobbs,
A sweet pretty wife, says Hobbs;
But somehow they tell us,
The wife-dealing fellows
Were all of them sellers,
John Hobbs, John Hobbs,
And none of 'em wanted Jane Hobbs.

The rope it was ready, John Hobbs, John Hobbs,
Come, give me the rope, says Hobbs,
I won't stand to wrangle,
Myself I will strangle,
And hang dingle dangle,
John Hobbs, John Hobbs,
He hung dingle dangle, John Hobbs.

But down his wife cut him, John Hobbs, John Hobbs,
But down his wife cut him, John Hobbs;
With a few hubble bubbles
They settled their troubles,
Like most married couples,
John Hobbs, John Hobbs,
Oh, happy shoe-maker John Hobbs.

Plate XXIX. John Hobbs: like much standard ballad-vendor's stock,
this is intended to amuse, and has no evidential value whatsoever.

A MAN
SELLING HIS WIFE
In the Market-place, Thetford,

17 Sept 1859.

On Saturday last, for the sum of £5. together with a true and laughable Dialogue which took place between the man & his wife after she was sold, when she was retiring with her new husband.

Simpson

k

On Saturday last the Market-place of Thetford was thrown into a state of excitement, seldom witnessed there, by a man about forty years of age, in a shabby-genteel dress; leading a smart-looking woman, with a handkerchief round her neck, and shouting with a loud voice, " who'll buy a wife ?" After arriving at the centre of the Market, he mounted a chair, and offered her for sale. " She was good looking, but that was all he could say for her." A young man of plausible appearance offered 10s. for her; but he was immediately opposed by an old gentleman bidding 5s. more. Afterwards the young man became the purchaser for £5. The money was paid down and the husband on handing over the handkerchief to the purchaser, began to dance and sing, declaring he had got rid of a troublesome noisy wife, which caused much merriment in the crowd. The young woman turned sharply round and said, you know you old rascal you are jealous—you are no man, and have no need of a young wife, and that is the reason you sold me, you useless old dog. Here the laugh was turned against him, and the women began to clap their hands at him. He then said she was a gormandizing woman, and would eat any man's substance up; and declared if he had kept her another year, she would have eaten him out of house and harbour. Here the woman looked blue, but soon turned round, nothing daunted, and said, "swallow your substance indeed, that might soon be swallowed by any lady present for what there is of it. Only think, he wished half a pound of sugar and one ounce of tea to serve us both the whole blessed week ; and as for dinners, fresh meat we never saw, but a half-penny worth of onions and a small quantity of bread & cheese were our dinners for days together." Here the women became uproarious, but he walked off singing, "I fairly got rid of her." The fortunate purchaser led her away in loud huzzas. The seller's name is John Simpson, of Brandenham, and the purchaser's name is John Hart, of whom he had been jealous, having lodged in his house.

You married men and women too,
  Of every degree,
If you wish to live contented,
  Pray be advis'd by me ;
Take caution from this man and wife,
  Who did in Brandenham dwell—
And what between them did take place
  I unto you will tell

CHORUS.

So men look out what you are about'
  For your wives do all you can,
For a woman is a blessing,
  And a comfort to a man.

It happened in that neighbourhood,
  Upon the other day,
A man resov'd to sell his wife,
  Through jealousy they say;
To part it was agreed it seems,
  To Thetford market they went.

And for five pounds he sold her,
  And half-a-crown was spent,

This man was worth some money.
  And a miser did appear,
He kept his wife on bread and cheese,
  With allowance of small beer ;
Besides he kept her from her tea,
  Woman's comfort and delight,
Likewise he was so jealous,
  He lay grunting every night.

Oh, jealousy is a cruel thing,
  I'd have you push it out,
It is worse than Itch, Stitch, Palsy,
  The Rheumatism or Gout;
So you that feel those cruel pains,
  Think on this man and wife,
Be sure you have convincing proof,
  Before you blame your wife.

Printed for, and Sold by Joseph Bamfylde, Thetford.

Plate XXX. This locally-printed Thetford wife sale broadside was probably based on a real incident, touched up for entertainment.

nerai à observer qu'une coutume aussi infâme s'est conservée sans interruption, qu'elle est mise chaque jour à exécution ; que si quelques magistrats des comtés, informés que de semblables marchés allaient se faire, ont cherché à les empêcher en envoyant sur les lieux des constables ou huissiers, la populace les a toujours dispersés, et qu'elle a maintenu ce qu'elle considère comme son droit.

Plate XXXI. This vignette concludes an account of the sale of wives in London in a French travel book which like many others exaggerates the prevalence of the custom ("qu'elle est mise chaque jour à exécution").

Plate XXXII. *Punch's* "physiology of courtship": it is intended to typify the English manner of courtship as conceived by the French and Germans. The scene is Smithfield market: on the right "Lord the Honourable Sir Brown (eldest son of the Lord Mayor) is making in the cold and formal fashion of his compatriots, a declaration of his sentiments to a young miss, daughter of a duke. . ." On the left "may be perceived a church dignitary in a fit of the spleen disposing of his wife, for ready cash, to a field-marshal — sad, but only too frequent Result, of our insular Incompatability of Temper".

and Scotland also, and had become more heated at the time of the dearth of 1756-7, when many English local authorities had symbolically enforced some of the old protective legislation.[1] As it happens the only authority cited by Smith in his digression is not a French physiocrat but Charles Smith, whose *Three Tracts on the Corn Trade* date from 1758 (above p. 201). Adam Smith is likely to have been influenced in his market theories by Scottish experience as well as French, but the digression is argued almost wholly in terms of English practices and laws.[2]

My essay was taken by some to be derogatory both to Adam Smith and to the "free market", which is a very great personage these days. But my comments were deferential, mild and agnostic. They were offered

> Not in refutation of Adam Smith, but simply to indicate places where caution should be exercised until our knowledge is greater. We need say only of the *laissez-faire* model that it is empirically unproven; inherently unlikely; and that there is some evidence on the other side (p. 207).

There is no final historical verdict after more than two hundred years, because Adam Smith theorised a state of perfect competition and the world is still waiting for this state to arrive.

But, even if we were to suppose market conditions more perfect, there are peculiarities in the market for the necessities of subsistence which raise their own theoretical

[1] Adam Smith's "real contact" with the French thinkers came during his visit to Paris, December 1765 to October 1766: see Adam Smith, *An Inquiry into the Nature and Causes of the Wealth of Nations*, ed. R. H. Campbell and A. S. Skinner (Oxford, 1976), i, pp. 22-3, note 8. He will therefore have been absent from Britain during the height of the 1766 rioting. But Smith himself insisted that his views of *laissez-faire* were already formed in 1749: see Jacob Viner, *The Long View and the Short* (Glencoe, Illinois, 1958), p. 215.

[2] Even Smith's famous comparison of the popular prejudices against forestallers to belief in "witchcraft" might have been borrowed from an earlier pamphleteer: see *Reflections on the Present High Price of Provisions; and the complaints and disturbances arising therefrom* (1766), p. 39, which refers also to witchcraft and notes that in the Commission for the appointment of magistrates "inchantments, sorceries, arts of magic, forestalling, regratings, and ingrossings are ranged together, as offences of a similar nature, because they were committed by wicked persons, in a manner both amazing and unknown".

problems. The question is not whether, in the long run, it is not advantageous to all parties for communications to be improved and for national and, in the end, international markets in grain or in rice to be formed. As soon as that question is proposed the answer is self-evident. . . and we are into a feedback loop. Direct obstruction of this flow, whether by local authorities or by the crowd, could be plainly reactionary. But dearth and famine are always in the short run and not the long. And Adam Smith has only long-run remedies (such as high prices encouraging the breaking-up of more acres for grain) for short-run crisis. By 1776, when *The Wealth of Nations* was published, the desirability of a more fluent national commerce in grain had become a truism. What were disputed (in France as in England), were the measures the authorities might or should take in times of high prices and dearth. Here there were wide disagreements, not only between traditionalists (and of course the crowd) and political economists, but also — as Hont and Ignatieff very helpfully show — within the ranks of the political economists.[1]

Adam Smith took a sterner and more doctrinaire position on the inviolability of *laissez-faire* even during times of dearth than did many of his colleagues. He insisted that the interests of dealers (inland) and the "great body of the people" were "exactly the same", "*even in years of the greatest scarcity*". "The unlimited, unrestricted freedom of the corn trade", as it is the only effectual preventive of the miseries of a famine so it is the best palliative of the inconvenience of a dearth."[2] Smith was not, "the only standard-bearer for 'natural liberty' in grain" but he was one of the more extreme standard-bearers for this liberty to remain uncontrolled even in times of great scarcity. And he must have known very well that it was exactly this point of emergency measures in time of dearth that was most controversial. His notable forerunner in developing *Political Oeconomy*, Sir James Steuart, had refused this fence, and

[1] Hont and Ignatieff, *op. cit.*, pp. 16-19.
[2] These passages are selected for emphasis by Salim Rashid in "The Policy of *Laissez-faire* during Scarcities", *Economic Journal*, 90 (1980), pp. 493-503.

was an advocate of the stockpiling of grain in public granaries for sale in time of dearth.[1] Smith's successor and biographer, Dugald Stewart, was a true executor when he lectured in unqualified terms on the "unlimited liberty of the corn trade" right through the crisis year of 1800.[2] On this question Adam Smith was neither "vulgarised" nor "misunderstood".

It is not (as some accounts imply) the total theoretical structure of *The Wealth of Nations* which is at issue, but the few pages of Smith's digression on the corn trade in that treatise. These pages acquired oracular authority, and in each episode of scarcity — in Britain in 1795 and 1800, in Ireland, India and the Colonial Empire through much of the nineteenth century — these were the arguments which politicians and administrators rehearsed. In Britain in the 1790s both Government and Foxite opposition endorsed these arguments, and when the Home Secretary, the duke of Portland, harried traditionalist Lords Lieutenant, magistrates and local authorities with homilies on political economy and instructions to preserve the freedom of markets, he was not vulgarising the views of Dr Smith but enforcing these strictly.

Thus when the Nottingham Corporation endorsed the crowd's imposition of price ceilings and brought pressure onto local farmers to supply the market at these rates, Portland insisted, in Smithian terms, that

> Whenever any reduction in the price of a Commodity has been effected by intimidation it has never been of any duration, and besides, by having things out of their natural and orderly courses, it almost necessarily happens that the evil, instead of being remedied returns with increased violence.[3]

To this Portland added, but with his own special vehemence, the Smithian theme of natural justice to the rights of property: there should be a "religious observance of the respect. . . due to private property", and the Lord

[1] Sir James Steuart, "A dissertation on the policy of grain", in *Works* (1805; reprint 1967), v, pp. 347-77. Steuart's proposal was first made in 1757, but was maintained in subsequent years.

[2] Dugald Stewart, *Lectures on Political Economy* (Edinburgh, 1855; reprint 1968), ii, p. 52.

[3] Wells, *Wretched Faces*, p. 238.

Lieutenant of Oxfordshire, the duke of Marlborough — a traditionalist and paternalist — was instructed that:

> If the employment of Property is not secure, if every Man does not feel that he has power to retain what he possesses so long as he pleases and dispense it at the time, in the manner and for the Price he chuses to fix upon it, there must be an end of Confidence in Industry and of all valuable and virtuous Exertions of all descriptions. . . the whole Order of things must be overturned and destroyed.

All must "maintain the Principle of perfect Freedom of Property".[1]

It was the same principle and the same authority that was appealed to during famine conditions in Western India in 1812. The judge and magistrate of Kaira had urged the government to intervene by importing grain and selling it to retailers at little over its cost price. The proposal was rejected:

> The Right Honourable the Governor in Council is disposed to think. . . that those approved and recognised principles. . . which prescribe an entire and unrestricted freedom in the grain trade, as best adapted to the relief of any existing scarcity and to the prevention of famine, are particularly applicable to the dealers in grain in the province of Goozerat. . . The digression of the celebrated author of the *Wealth of Nations* concerning the Corn-Trade. . . particularly as far as respects the *inland Trader*, is forcibly and irresistibly applicable to every state of society where merchants, or dealers, in grain may be established.[2]

Similar homilies were expressed in orders of the Madras Government in 1833 which argued that high prices constitute the best security against famine: "The interference of Government in such emergencies. . . disturbs the natural current (by which, where trade is free, the demands of any commodity is sure to meet, as far as circumstances will allow, with a corresponding supply) and has a tendency to convert a

---

[1] Roger Wells, "The Grain Crisis in England, 1794-96, 1799-1801" (Univ. of York Ph.D. thesis, 1978), pp. 472-3. Also Wells, *Wretched Faces*, pp. 238-9.

[2] Srinivasa Ambirajan, "Economic Ideas and Indian Economic Policies in the 19th Century" (Manchester Univ. Ph.D. thesis, 1964), pp. 363-4. A similar circular, quoting almost verbatim from *The Wealth of Nations*, originated from the Board of Revenue in Madras in 1811: Arnold, *Famine*, p. 113. See also Ambirajan, S., *Classical Political Economy and British Policy in India* (Cambridge, 1978).

season of scarcity into one of absolute famine".[1]

Despite the appalling example of the great Irish famine, Smithian imperatives continued to inform policies in India during the famines of the 1860s and 1870s. Baird Smith, reporting on the famine of 1860-1, applauded the non-interventionist principles of *The Wealth of Nations* and advised that the remedy for dearth be left to "the order of nature [which] if it occasionally produces dire sufferings, does also provide generally the most effective means for their mitigation".[2] (In Orissa alone, in 1860, famine deaths were estimated at 1,364,529.[3]) It has been suggested that some administrators were fortified in policies of non-interference by literal-minded assent to Malthusian doctrines.[4] The magistrate at Patna was advised by the Governor-General that, while it was "beyond the power. . . of the public authorities to remedy the unfortunate dearth of grain", yet the magistrates may "effect much to soften the distress and calm the irritation of the people":

[1] *Ibid.*, p. 366. The view that famines were always the consequence of well-intentioned interventions by the authorities which disrupted the "natural" flow of trade is one of Adam Smith's least well-supported assertions: "Whoever examines, with attention, the history of the dearths and famines which have afflicted any part of Europe during either the course of the present, or that of the two preceding centuries" will find that dearths arise in a few cases from the waste of war but in the greatest number of cases "by the fault of the seasons; and that *a famine has never arisen from any other cause but the violence of government attempting, by improper means, to remedy the inconvenience of dearth*". (My italics.) Upon this pretence to omniscience, Smith and his disciples could denounce protective measures as iniquitous. Smith also asserted that "the drought in Bengal, a few years ago, might probably have occasioned a very great dearth. Some improper regulations, some injudicious restraints, imposed by the servants of the East India Company upon the rice trade, contributed, perhaps, to turn that dearth into a famine." This assertion has been challenged by H. Sur, "The Bihar Famine of 1770", *Indian Econ. & Social Hist. Review*, xiii, 4 (1976), who finds a better explanation in the collapse of the traditional Moghul administration and the ensuing vacuum.

[2] B. M. Bhatia, *Famines in India* (Bombay, 1967), p. 105.

[3] Ambirajan, thesis, p. 367.

[4] See S. Ambirajan, "Malthusian Population Theory and Indian Famine Policy in the 19th Century", *Population Studies*, xxx, 1 (1976).

By manifesting a sympathy in their sufferings, by a humane, patient and indulgent hearing of their complaints, by encouraging them to look forward to the approaching harvest. . . they may be persuaded to bear with resignation the inevitable calamities under which they labour.[1]

This throws one back, not only to Smith and to Malthus, but also to Edmund Burke's *Thoughts on Scarcity*.

What political economy forbade was any "violent interferences with the course of trade", including the prosecution of profiteers or hoarders, the fixing of maximum prices, and government intervention in grain or rice dealing.[2] Relief exercises must take the form of distributing a pittance of purchase money (at whatever height "the order of nature" had brought prices to) to those whose need passed the examination of labour on public relief works.[3] These policies, or negatives in the place of policies, were based upon theories which — however elaborated by other authors — rested upon the few pages of Adam Smith's digression.

These pages, then, were among the most influential writings in history, with a global influence which was sometimes baneful. Their arguments discredited or disallowed traditional protective interventions in time of dearth, could be used to justify profiteering and hoarding, and could serve as apologetics to soothe the troubled consciences of the authorities by commending inactivity as correct political economy. Two Indian economists who have had the temerity to question their profession's habitual complacency about Smith's views on the grain trade receive a lofty rebuke from Hont and Ignatieff: they have "overlooked" "the traditional theory of justice framing Smith's discourse of free trade in subsistence goods during dearth and famines". And they cite this passage of the digression:

To hinder. . . the farmer from sending his goods at all times to the best market, is evidently to sacrifice the ordinary laws of justice to an idea of publick utility, to a sort of reasons of state — an act of legislative

---

[1] Ambirajan, thesis, pp. 366-7.

[2] See Bhatia, *op. cit.*, p. 105.

[3] The absolutes of political economy were modified by the Famine Code of 1880, although the general principle of non-intervention in the grain trade "remained inviolate until the Second World War": Arnold, *op. cit.*, p. 114.

authority which ought to be exercised only, which can be pardoned
only, in cases of the most urgent necessity.

And somehow or other Hont and Ignatieff find this passage
endorsement of their conclusion that "Smith's discourse was
not about the conditions of actual famines, which belonged
to the discourse on grave necessity which 'breaks all laws' ".
But one may search in vain in the digression or anywhere in
The Wealth of Nations for any such "discourse on grave
necessity". What is pretentiously named as a "discourse" is,
at most, a brief saving clause (measures "which can be
pardoned only in cases of the most urgent necessity") and a
prolonged silence as to what these measures might be.[1]

As for "the traditional theory of justice framing Smith's
discourse of free trade", the justice is to the rights of
property. As Hont and Ignatieff acknowledge elsewhere,
Smith "insisted on the all but absolute priority of the
property rights of grain merchants and farmers over the
claims of need made by poor labourers". This position was
more extreme than that of many contemporary political
economists and physiocrats; indeed, Diderot considered the
privileging of private property above need in times of famine
to be a "cannibal principle".[2]

My argument is not (as it happens) intended to show that
Dr Adam Smith was a cannibal. Smithian advocacy of free
trade in grain had evident virtues in the long run but had only
negative relevance in times of crisis, since his remedies —
such as increasing cereal production — were long-run
remedies or — such as very high prices — were not remedies
at all. Among the deficiencies of Smithian doctrine were
1) that it *was* doctrinaire and counter-empirical. It did not
want to know how actual markets worked, any more than its
disciples do today. As dogma it could serve as an apologia for
inactivity, as exemplified in several Irish and Indian disasters.
2) It promoted the notion that high prices were a (painful)
remedy for dearth, in drawing supplies to the afflicted region

[1] Hont and Ignatieff, *op. cit.*, p. 20. Adam Smith in *The Theory of
Moral Sentiments*, ed. D. D. Raphael and A. L. Macfie (Oxford, 1976),
p. 27, found "violent hunger" to be an offence against "propriety".
Though sometimes "unavoidable" it "is always indecent".
[2] *Ibid.*, p. 22.

of scarcity. But what draws supply are not high prices but people with sufficient money in their purses to pay high prices. A characteristic phenomenon in times of dearth is that it generates unemployment and empty purses; in purchasing necessities at inflated prices people cease to be able to buy inessentials, and the shoemaker, the weaver, the stockinger, the fisherman, the barber, the transport worker, and many others fall on hard times.[1] Hence the number of those able to pay the inflated prices declines in the afflicted regions, and food may be exported to neighbouring, less afflicted, regions where employment is holding up and consumers still have money with which to pay. In this sequence, high prices can actually withdraw supply from the most afflicted. A leading authority on recent famines, Dr Amartya Sen, notes that in a slump hunger and even starvation have "little market pull" and in many famines food was exported from the famine-stricken country or region. This was notoriously the case in Ireland in the 1840s and was observed in Indian famines also:

> Adam Smith's proposition is, in fact, concerned with efficiency in meeting a market demand, but it says nothing on meeting a need that has not been translated into effective demand because of lack of market-based entitlement and shortage of purchasing power.[2]

3) The most unhappy error flows from Smith's metaphor of price as a means of rationing. Smith argues that high prices discourage consumption, putting "everybody more or less, but particularly the inferior ranks of people, upon thrift and good management". By comparing the dealer who raises prices to the "prudent master of a vessel" rationing his crew, there is a persuasive suggestion of a fair distribution of limited resources. These resources will be rationed not only between individual consumers but also over time, dividing "the inconveniences" of scarcity "as equally as possible

---

[1] Thus in Bengal in 1873 the first to starve were "non-agricultural classes" — weavers, metal workers, carpenters, fishermen, menials. The field labourers and small cultivators followed: *Extra Supplement to the Gazette of India*, 26 Feb. 1875, p. 33.

[2] Amartya Sen, *Poverty and Famines* (Oxford, 1981), pp. 161-2. "Food being *exported* from famine-stricken areas may be a 'natural' characteristic of the market, which respects entitlement rather than needs."

through all the different months and weeks and days of the year.

However persuasive the metaphor, there is an elision of the real relationships assigned by price, which suggests — for the argument has been repeated ever since and may still be heard today — ideological sleight-of-mind. Rationing by price does not allocate resources equally among those in need; it reserves the supply to those who can pay the price and excludes those who can't. Perhaps one-fifth or one-quarter of the English population in the eighteenth century rubbed along on the edge of bare subsistence, and was in danger of falling below this whenever prices rose. In a recent authoritative study it is shown that

> In hard years perhaps 20 per cent of the population could not, unaided, have bought sufficient bread even if they had been able to eliminate all other expenditure; and. . . in a very hard year, 45 per cent of the entire population could be thrown into such destitution.[1]

What Hay finds for eighteenth-century England, Sir William Hunter and other observers found for nineteenth-century India. Even in normal years one-fifth of the population "went through life on insufficient food".[2] The raising of prices during dearth could "ration" them out of the market altogether.

This is something one must hold steadily in view. High prices of bread mattered little to the rich, were inconvenient to the middling sort, were painful to steadily-employed labourers, but could threaten the survival of the poor. That is why they were at once a matter of "politics". It was against this socially-unequal "rationing" by purse that the food riot was a protest and perhaps a remedy.

This may remind us that the world has not done yet with dearth or with famine. The problem occupies many able minds and, as one might expect, some of the most relevant work comes from Indian economists and historians, for whom famine is not so distant a problem and yet who share with Britain some common histories of administration, law, and ideology. One arresting approach is that of Amartya Sen,

[1] Douglas Hay, "War, Dearth and Theft in the Eighteenth Century", *Past and Present*, 95 (1982), p. 132.
[2] See Bhatia, *op. cit.*, p. 39.

in his *Poverty and Famines* (1981), which employs "entitle-ment theory" and also an advanced statistical apparatus. "Entitlement" indicates all the various means by which people gain access to essential food supply, whether this is through direct subsistence farming or through the provision by an employer or master (in his household) or by purchase in the market. A famine is triggered by the breakdown of such entitlements and the merit of this approach is that it does not only tell us that there has been a decline in the amount of food available but it also examines "why some groups had to starve while others could feed themselves. . . What allows one group rather than another to get hold of the food that is there?".[1]

Dr Sen examines twentieth-century famines in Asia and Africa, for which the statistical data is more reliable than any we have for the eighteenth century, and he concludes that, in the greater number of cases examined, famine cannot be simply attributed to "food availability decline". Where there had been a crop failure, "a moderate short-fall in *production*" was "translated into an exceptional short-fall in *market release*". The market cannot be isolated and abstracted from the network of political, social and legal relations in which it is situated. Once the downward spiral of famine is entered, the process can become cumulative, and "no matter how a famine is *caused*, methods of *breaking* it call for a large supply of food in the public distribution system".[2]

This approach is relevant to dearth in eighteenth-century Europe also,[3] and is preferable to the one most commonly adopted, which focuses on harvest failures as if these could supply not only necessary but also sufficient explanation of all that followed. Dr Sen argues that this "FAD" (food availability decline) approach

> Gives little clue to the causal mechanism of starvation, since it does not go into the *relationship* of people to food. Whatever may be the

[1] Sen, *op. cit.*, p. 154.
[2] *Ibid.*, pp. 75, 79.
[3] See Louise Tilly, "Food Entitlement, Famine, and Conflict", in R. I. Rotberg and Theodore K. Rabb (eds.), *Hunger and History* (Cambridge, 1985), pp. 135-152.

oracular power of the FAD view, it is certainly Delphic in its reticence.[1]

In general the eighteenth-century English poor were sheltered by poor laws and charity from outright starvation, but Dr Sen's argument remains valid. Smithian and Malthusian explanations of years of dearth rest heavily upon crop failures (FAD) and remain "Delphic" as to the relationship of people to food and the socially-differential entitlements that obtained.

The "relationship of people to food" involves systems of power, property and law. Conflict over entitlement to food in the market might be seen as a forum of class struggle, if most historians were not too prissy nowadays to use the term. It may also be seen as a forum for the conflict of interests, "Town" versus "Country", as manufacturing workers, woollen workers, or colliers, confronted farmers and dealers.

Both forms of conflict can be observed in England during the high-price years of the Napoleonic Wars, and as government intervened with doctrine and with armed force in support of the unfettered operation of agrarian capitalism there can be no doubt which classes and interests were winners. Professor Mingay has estimated that, in areas which he has investigated, rents rose between 40 per cent and 50 per cent between 1750 and 1790; and between 1790 and 1815 rents rose by a further 80 per cent to 90 per cent.[2] At the same time (as the substantial farm buildings of that period remain to witness) the middling and larger farmers were well able to pay these enhanced rentals and were rising in prosperity and in assumptions of social status. Rent was the means by which the landowners clawed back their share of farming profits. These rentals indicated a very considerable rise in the wealth of the agrarian capitalist classes (in which affluence the agricultural labourers had no share), and this was supported in its turn by the sale of food — and especially cereals — to the consumers of the "Town". The wealth of the landowners

[1] See Sen, *op. cit.*, p. 154. And see A. K. Ghose, "Food Supply and Starvation: a Study of Famines with reference to the Indian Sub-Continent", *Oxford Economic Papers*, xxxiv (1982).

[2] G. E. Mingay, "The Course of Rents in the Age of Malthus", in Michael Turner (ed.), *Malthus in his Time* (Basingstoke, 1986), pp. 90-1.

was further supported by enclosures, which reached a peak in the war years when three million acres, or 9 per cent of the land area of England, came under parliamentary enclosure, much of this coming under the plough for cereal crops. [1]

This prosperity did not pass unnoticed among the woollen workers, colliers and "proto-industrial" manufacturers who lived adjacent to prospering farming areas. It is in this context that the confrontations of 1795-96 and 1800-1 must be seen. Dr Roger Wells's *Wretched Faces* (1988) is the most copiously documented study of every aspect of these years of dearth that we have or are ever likely to have, and one must express gratitude to him for his archival industry and for the illumination that flows from many of his pages. Yet certain of his conclusions seem to be to be wrong-headed and to be contradicted by his own evidence, and this may be because even Dr Wells has been unduly influenced by the seeming common-sense of the Smithian (FAD) approach.

There were of course serious harvest short-falls in these years, and the country might have faced real famine conditions if there had not been considerable foreign imports. [2] But when Roger Wells writes that the implementation of "the moral economy" was "a recipe for disaster" [3] he is taking too narrow a view of the question. His case against "the moral economy" — a catch-all term which he uses throughout his major study to indicate *any* measures taken by the authorities or imposed by the crowd to protect the consumer, to regulate markets or to control price — is at times as alarmist as that of Edmund Burke or the duke of Portland. He argues that market disturbances "decimated

[1] Michael Turner, "Corn Crises in Britain in the Age of Malthus", in Turner, *op. cit.*, p. 120.

[2] Adam Smith's doctrine of non-interference in the grain trade was limited, in his digression, to the *inland* trader. Wells is mistaken when he supposes (e.g. *Wretched Faces*, p. 7) that vigorous governmental exercises in the import of corn during a time of shortage was in breach of Smithian precepts. But (in Smith's doctrine) government must not then intervene in the internal market by selling off imports beneath the self-regulating market rate, and this was generally avoided in the 1790s by selling off the cargo immediately at the port of arrival, at which sales representatives from inland towns and parishes often attended.

[3] Roger Wells, "The Revolt of the South-West, 1800-01", *Social History*, 6 (1977), p. 743; Wells, *Wretched Faces*, p. 230.

future supplies and then accelerated inflation", that "price controls aggravated the impact of violence", that "havoc followed where the Assize of Bread operated", and that the moral economy "directly stimulated violent populist intervention while simultaneously weakening community resolve to contain disorder".[1] And he conjures up visions of a vicious circle with "riot deterring supplies, empty markets stimulating renewed violence, and further disturbances annihilating commercial confidence":

> Ultimately, from a global perspective, the entire country would be affected. In this context the 'positive' aspects of popular intervention, discouraging mercantile malpractice, militating against maximum exploitation, rivetting public attention on the poor's plight and galvanising greater relief measures, pale in significance. For these latter characteristics of protest, however important, were essentially localised. The historian's assessment of riot must also adopt governmental criteria. Macro, as opposed to micro economic examination of the grain trade reveals the dangers of protest to national subsistence in general, and the consumption centres in particular. Staving off starvation in the most vulnerable locations necessitated the speediest suppression of riot.[2]

The trouble is that hunger is usually "localised" (in the stomach). Deaths from starvation appear as localised microdots. Roger Wells has been reading too many state papers of Pitt's war administration and has been drawn into their feedback loops. Moreover in his over-coloured language ("disaster", "decimated", "violence", "violent populist intervention", "annihilating") we have moved a long way from the self-disciplined and often bloodless direct actions of the crowd, with its "protocol" and "orderly disorder"[3] which recent historiography has disclosed and which Dr Wells's own researches confirm, and have moved back to the bad old school when every crowd was recorded as a violent gullible "mob".

There is something in Wells's case, and it is strongest when he cites — especially in the summer of 1795 — the widespread crowd blockades of the passage of grain by water or

[1] *Ibid.*, pp. 178-181, 230-6.
[2] *Ibid.*, p. 181.
[3] John Bohstedt, *Riots and Community Politics in England and Wales, 1790-1810* (Cambridge, Mass., 1983), p. 27.

by road. This embargo could have precipitated disaster in large centres of consumption such as Birmingham, Nottingham and Leicester, although it did not. In other matters Wells (uncharacteristically) offers thin and uncertain evidence. His few examples do not persuade that price regulation always "decimated" the future supply of those markets. Where towns or manufacturing districts depended upon a local food supply, the farmers also depended upon their local custom; and the crowd might visit the farmers with threats to requisition supplies. In the end the farmers must go back to the market and there was a complexity of influences upon their behaviour: relationships with the consumers, with their landlords, with their own consciences.

Roger Wells's assertion that "havoc" followed where the Assize of Bread operated" is supported by a single anecdote from Oxfordshire in 1800. But as it happens Oxford is the one centre for which we have a careful study of the operation of the Assize in the eighteenth century, and this by no means supports the ascription of "havoc". Dr Wendy Thwaites's research suggests that the operation of the Assize may have marginally raised the price of bread in Oxford in normal years but restrained the rise in years of dearth. It afforded to the market authorities, the bakers and the consumers "a sense of security in relation to each other",[1] and it should in any case be seen not in isolation but as part of a wider regulation which included weight and quality control. London also set an Assize of Bread throughout the eighteenth century, and so far from "havoc" food riots in the capital were rare.[2]

Roger Wells draws too one-sided a balance. It is true that Pickard, Birmingham's biggest merchant-miller, was forced out of business by the hostility of the crowd in September 1800.[3] But this did not leave Birmingham provisionless. There was another steam mill, the "Union Mill", although

[1] W. Thwaites, "The Assize of Bread in 18th-Century Oxfordshire", *Oxoniensia*, li (1986), pp. 171-81.

[2] Differing explanations for the rarity of food riots in London are to be found in George Rudé, *Paris and London in the 18th Century* (1970), pp. 55-7; John Stevenson, *Popular Disturbances in England, 1700-1870* (1979), pp. 99-100; Bohstedt, *op. cit.*, pp. 208-9. Undoubtedly securing the provisioning of London was a priority of State.

[3] See Wells, *Wretched Faces*, pp. 180-1.

this mainly supplied bread to its numerous tradesmen and operative subscribers, and at prime cost — perhaps a translation of "moral economy" principles into early co-operation.[1] And Pickard's mill was not closed: it was rented to a new company, as an emergency measure, to ensure the continued supply of the town. Pickard's son, Edward, recorded the erratic fluctuations in the fortunes of this emergency Company of "benevolent gentlemen":

One of the gentlemen was at Hull soon after the first term [of six month's rental] commenced, and having left Birmingham under a fearful impression that the town would be really without a supply of food, ventured to make a very large purchase of wheat. . . which had just arrived from the Baltic, and sent it to Birmingham on account of this new Company. How the wheat was paid for or by whom I know not: I presume their banker accomodated them with the money. . . Exorbitant as was the price of wheat at that time, it unexpectedly rose considerably higher: and although the Company was thus enabled to provide a large quantity of flour weekly to the poor at a lower rate than the general dealers, yet at the end of the first six months, they found their profits so large, that they feared some popular indignation on the exhibition of their accounts. They therefore applied to my father to prolong their term, which he did, to enable them, as they said, to make some diminution in their gains, and thus present to the public a more satisfactory statement. About the period of the renewal of the term, the price of wheat began to give way, and continued falling into the end of · it: in consequence of which, and also from losses sustained on other large purchases again made early in their last term, these benevolent men sunk not only all their first six months profits, but also lost all the capital they had advanced.[2]

This story conforms to the properties of neither Smithian nor "moral economy" doctrine. It suggests that in these eccentric wartime conditions all parties in the grain market were playing blind man's buff. In any case, generalisations as to the characteristics and functions of food riots are risky if taken only from these war years, since they are a special case:

[1] Anon., "A Record of the Staff of Life from 1796 to 1900: at the Old Mill of the City", *Birmingham Magazine of Arts and Industries*, iii (1899). See also J. Tann, "Co-operative Corn Milling; Self-help during the grain crises of the Napoleonic Wars", *Agric. Hist. Rev.*, 28 (1980), p. 52; the Union Mill was founded in 1796 with 1360 subscribers, principally labouring workmen.

[2] MS notebook of Edward Pickard, Birmingham Reference Library, MS 22/11.

both the climax and the terminus of the riot tradition, in a context of war and invasion fears, with the gentry and their retainers under arms (as Yeomanry) and in a state of anti-Jacobin panic. These last years of the eighteenth century were also a watershed in marketing constituencies and practices, mid-way between the locally-supplied markets where consumers and farmers, magistrates and dealers, all knew something of each other, might come face to face with each other, and could "negotiate" prices, even by "riot"; and the more impersonal relations of the large urban markets which farmers rarely visited, supplied by dealers who purchased in distant markets.[1] Moreover the 1790s experience is further complicated by the deep inner divisions within the ruling authorities, with central government imposing *laissez-faire* dogmas but with some local authorities and traditionalist landowners attempting to control prices by persuasion, and giving a nod and a wink to the crowd. In such confused conditions we are likely to come up with contradictory findings, and with some examples of "havoc".

It is over the long view through the seventeenth and eighteenth centuries that the strongest case can be made for riot's "success". Two historians of the seventeenth century conclude that riots were "invariably successful in stimulating authoritative actions to alleviate grievances".[2] This is true in general of the eighteenth century also. Price regulation might even succeed, and the most persuasive analysis of the crowd's success will be found in John Bohstedt's chapter on "Devon's Classic Food Riots" in his *Riots and Community Politics in England and Wales, 1790-1810* (1983). He shows the small or medium-sized market town to be the classic site of crowd direct action (supported by the visitation of farmers in the neighbourhood), and suggests that such actions were supported by both horizontal and vertical networks of relationship within communities which had their own traditions and remembered their own precedents. In the

---

[1] These points are developed by Bohstedt, *op. cit., passim*, especially in his contrast between Manchester and Devon's markets. Still in 1800 the Birmingham Union Mill normally obtained their supply in Birmingham market or within a radius of twenty miles: J. Tann, *op. cit.*, p. 54.

[2] Walter and Wrightson, *op. cit.*, p. 41.

vertical relationships he suggests that "social patronage" may be a more helpful term than "paternalism", a patronage which however entailed reciprocal duties and obligations. While riot, or direct action to bring down prices, was by no means legitimate, yet both the authorities and the crowd abided by a recognised "protocol". Rioters "did not challenge directly the whole system of property and power", and so long as this was so, and violence was avoided, the authorities were sometimes accomplices to price-fixing, recognising that "social peace was more important than absolute property rights or, rather, profit rights". Hence rioters "modified the property rights of farmers and food dealers. . . and their exertion of force at the margin of legitimacy and illegality was a real if limited exercise of political power". Indeed, "riots were a dynamic constituent moment in the system of property and power".[1]

John Bohstedt claims with confidence the Devon rioters' success: "riot would have been neither so frequent nor so orderly had there been no payoff". Food rioting of course appears in other national histories also, first in Europe and China,[2] subsequently in India and elsewhere. There is some suggestion that it marks a transitional phase between the

[1] Bohstedt, op. cit., esp. chs. 2 and 9 and pp. 54, 202, 220-1. Cf. Thwaites, thesis, pp. 522-7, for an estimate of riot's effectiveness in prompting consumer protection.

[2] China provides an example of successful bureaucratic management of food supplies, during the Qing dynasty in the eighteenth century. The Chinese state undertook far-reaching measures to feed the people during times of scarcity; these included public granaries, the provision of loans, discouragement of hoarders, encouragement of circulation by canals and roads. This was supported by a "Confucian" value-system which endorsed the imperative of "benevolence", and by the popular belief that any regime which presided over disasters such as famine and flood had "lost the mandate of heaven". Hence everything to do with the distribution of food in time of scarcity was of highly-sensitive political import. The Chinese peasant did not beg for charity, he demanded relief and saw the bureaucracy as bound by its office to provide this, and the rich as bound by duty. Many actions of Chinese food rioters closely resembled European riots — blockading transport, attacking hoarders, lobbying bureaucrats and the rich — and riot was a recognised way of putting the state measures of relief in motion: Lillian M. Li, "Introduction: Food, Famine and the Chinese State"; R. Bin Wong, "Food Riots in the Qing dynasty"; Paul R. Greenough, "Comment"; all in Journal of Asian Studies, August 1982.

locally-based demographic *ancien régime* of absolute subsistence crises and the "modern" national "free market"
regulated by price and by police alone.[1] Riot is unlikely to
have had so universal an emergence if there had not been
some "payoff", some space in which direct action was a
protection from the newly-liberated appetites of agrarian
interests, a warning to speculators and profiteers and an
alarm signal to the authorities to set emergency measures and
charities into motion. Such action could (and can) take many
forms, from humble petitions to threatening letters and
arson,[2] or to blockades and attacks on mills, but it was
always a profoundly political as well as economic event.

Riot, as "a dynamic constituent moment in the system of
property and power", has obviously taken different forms
and significance in different national histories, and in the
English case must be seen within the particular structure of
patrician/plebeian relations which we have examined (chapter
two), with its limits and its space for licence. But let us
read back from the Indian and Irish evidence to the English.
In a lucid study David Arnold has looked into the emergence
of a food riot tradition in India, perhaps commencing in the
Madras Presidency in 1876. Some 120 incidents swept South
India in 1918-19, with similar characteristics and objectives to
their counterparts in eighteenth-century England and France:
the prevention of exports, forcing down of prices, and pressing local officials to take measures to ensure provision. Just
as in England two centuries before, the "looting" of food
shops did not result usually in the theft but in the spoiling of
goods, and its intention was to humiliate dealers whom the
crowd held to be guilty of profiteering and hoarding at a time
of extreme hardship. Thus one function of riot was to
moderate the appetite for profit unleashed by the developing
"free market", and Arnold relates its assertiveness to the

[1] For the interplay of other factors in different national histories, see
Charles Tilly, "Food Supply and Public Order in Modern Europe", in
C. Tilly (ed.), *The Formation of National States in Europe* (Princeton,
1975), pp. 380-455; and Louise Tilly in Rotberg and Rabb (eds.), *Hunger
and History*, pp. 143-8.
[2] For threatening letters, see my "The Crime of Anonymity", in
Douglas Hay *et. al., Albion's Fatal Tree*, pp. 325-41. For arson, see Wells,
Wretched Faces, pp. 165-7.

transitional moment between locally-based markets and an
emergent national grain market — a transition accompanied
by sudden fluctuations of price, by the export of grain from
areas affected by dearth, and ruptures of the customary
channels of communication. He also suggests that, at least in
the short term, riot was successful, in terms of its own
objectives.[1] What this may suggest is that riot is functional,
and may be expected to show itself at the same transitional
moment in many national histories.

Why, then, does it not assert itself in Irish history? There
were severe episodes of famine in Ireland in the eighteenth
and early nineteenth century, long before the "Great
Hunger". But the Irish case is not as clear as it has sometimes been made to seem. It is often stated that there is not a
tradition of food rioting in Ireland.[2] Yet during the serious
famine of 1740-1, the Dublin paper, *Pue's Occurrences*,
reported bakers' and mealmen's shops broken open by the
Dublin mob, and the boarding of a ship on the Liffey (June
1740), an anti-export riot in Galway quelled by the army
(August), anti-export and price-setting riots in Youghal and
generally in Munster (December), shops in Limerick broken
into (March 1741), and a boat loaded with oats for Waterford stopped on the river at Carrick-on-Suir, with troops
firing on the crowd (April 1741).[3] That does not sound like a
nation with no food riot tradition. Women were reported as
rioters in Wexford in 1757[4] and in 1758 John Wesley found
"the mob" busy in Sligo harbour, unloading a Dutch ship of
corn bought up by forestallers "to starve the poor" — the
mob brought it all to the market and "sold it for the owners
at the common price. And this they did with all the calmness
and composure imaginable, and without striking or hurting
anyone".[5]

Thus the "classical" food riot was certainly known to the

[1] David Arnold, "Looting, Grain Riots and Government Policy in
South India, 1918", *Past and Present*, 84 (1979).
[2] See for example George Rudé, *Protest and Punishment* (Oxford,
1978), p. 57, who says that food riot "played little part" before 1829-31.
[3] These examples were collected in a pamphlet published by the
Foreign Office and Irish Office, *Famine in Ireland, 1740-41* (1847).
[4] *Gentleman's Magazine*, May (1757).
[5] Wesley's *Journal*, 27 May 1758.

eighteenth-century Irish, and it may be under-reported in general histories. If food riot failed to prevent exports and to relieve famine (as in 1740-1) this might account for a weakening of the tradition as the century wore on.[1] And one can only speculate as to the reasons for the divergent national traditions. Perhaps food rioters had less "political" clout in Ireland, since they did not threaten in the same direct way the stability and "face" of a resident governing gentry. Nor (in the absence of poor laws) did they stimulate in the same way an apparatus of relief, nor even (despite some examples) of gentry charity.[2]

Thus in Ireland food riots did not "work", partly because there was no political space (as in England) within which the plebs could exert pressure on their rulers. Arguing backwards from these cases we may pass the English evidence under review once more. Twenty years ago the notion that food riots could have served any positive function could scarcely gain the attention of historians. Smithian doctrine saw them as examples of social malfunction, while also postulating harvest short-fall (FAD) as sufficient explanation for most surges in the price of grain. What one scholar has called "an anachronistic reading of early modern society as a market society marked by the triumph of economic individualism", has given credibility to "a Malthusian model of social and economic change", which proposes an unproblematic and un-mediated relationship between harvest, price, and (until the seventeenth century) mortality.[3]

But recent advances in historical demography are now showing us a more complex set of events. A. B. Appleby clearly identified regional famine in the north-west in 1596-7 and 1622-3, and raised in interesting ways the question as to

[1] But food riots are reported in 1792, Samuel Clark and J. S. Donnelly (eds.), *Irish Peasants* (Manchester, 1983), p. 55; and in 1793, C. H. E. Philpin (ed.), *Nationalism and Popular Protest in Ireland* (Cambridge, 1987), p. 196 (counties Cork and Waterford).

[2] See L. M. Cullen and T. C. Smout, *Comparative Aspects of Scottish and Irish Economic and Social History* (Edinburgh, 1977), p. 10 and ch. 2.

[3] John Walter, "The Social Economy of Dearth in Early Modern England", in John Walter and Roger Schofield (eds.), *Famine, Disease, and the Social Order in Early Modern Society* (Cambridge, 1989), pp. 82, 121.

why the rest of England had managed to escape starvation. Several cogent reasons have been proposed for the difference in the "ecology of famine" between the north-west and the south. And to these may be added the differential effectiveness of measures of relief, which ensured that what little surplus grain was available was brought to market or transferred at subsidised rates to those in most need. The *Book of Orders* may have had more than symbolic functions and (with the aid of poor relief and charities) have mitigated the effects of dearth in the south, whereas the north-western region was not only pastoral and corn-poor, it also lacked the administrative and financial structures to set the *Book of Orders* in motion.[1]

Wrigley and Schofield's important *Population History of England* enables us to pursue these arguments further. While it is usually argued that the threat of famine had passed from England by 1650, a weak relation between grain prices and mortality can be shown until 1745. A weak relation (when generalised across the nation) might mask sharp local crises, or differential mortality in which the excess deaths fell chiefly among "the poor", or certain exposed groups. Moreover, the threat of famine had not moved far away. Wrigley and Schofield examine a sample of 404 parishes between 1541 and 1871 for years in which the death rate in many parishes was markedly above trend; 1727-9 and 1741-2, which are dearth and riot years, appear high on the table (with death rates from 30 to 40 per cent above trend), although other riot years — 1709, 1757, and 1795 — do not.[2] But these cannot be confidently identified as local subsistence crises, since epidemics may have caused the high mortality.[3]

These are complex questions. For the purposes of our argument it is sufficient to note that local crises persist into the eighteenth century, that harvest shortfall or high prices have a differential impact upon different (even neighbouring) communities, and that insignificant movements in national

[1] John Walter and Roger Schofield, "Famine, Disease and Crisis Mortality in Early Modern Society", in *ibid.*, p. 47.

[2] E. A. Wrigley and R. S. Schofield, *The Population of England, 1541-1871* (Cambridge, Mass., 1981), p. 653. The riot years 1766-7 show a death rate 10.4% above trend.

[3] See *ibid.*, pp. 668-9.

statistical series may mask very sharp local suffering. Moreover, "by far the highest overall incidence of [local] crisis
mortality occurred in the south-west, in an area extending
from south Gloucestershire and west Wiltshire through
Dorset to Devon": i.e. precisely one of the strongest food riot
areas in the eighteenth century.[1]

This suggests that rioters had good reasons for concern,
and for actions in self-defence. And that in high-price years
they were pressed close to a margin, so that even small
modifications of their market situation might make a mortal
difference. There were many ways of obtaining subsistence,
not all of which depended upon the market,[2] and in
emergency "the poor" were not altogether without resources.
A correspondent writing from "a manufacturing neighbourhood" in the West at a time of low employment and high
prices (1741), concluded:

> The poor every month grow poorer, for their clothes apparently wear
> into rags and they are in no capacity of buying new ones. They have sold
> almost all their little superfluities already, or perhaps one had a gold
> ring, another two or three pewter dishes, a third a brass pot or kettle;
> these they have been disposing of to buy bread for themselves and
> families. . .[3]

That is not (yet) a crisis of subsistence, but it is the context for
chronic malnutrition.

One should not misread "entitlement theory" to conclude
that there were no such things as failures of grain supply, and
that every dearth is man-made. What Sen shows is that, given
a shortfall in harvest, the way in which the supply is distributed between social groups is decidedly man-made, and
depends upon choices between means of allocation, of which
market price is only one among many. Even in times of
dearth there was always some supply, and the problem was
how to squeeze this surplus out of granaries and barns and

---

[1] *Ibid.*, p. 692.
[2] See John Walter, "The Social Economy of Dearth", a good deal of
which still applies in the early eighteenth century.
[3] "Philo-Georgius" to duke of Newcastle, 7 Dec. 1741, Brit. Lib. Add
MS 32, 698, f. 496.

direct it to those in most need.[1] The measures comprised in the *Book of Orders* worked reasonably well, and it is not clear why they lapsed after 1630. In a clearly-argued essay, Dr Outhwaite has suggested that the complexity and inefficiency of their operation resulted in "disenchantment".[2] But interest and ideology might also be awarded a role, as the market oriented, cereal-growing landed classes became more influential in the state. For long periods after 1660 the problem was not dearth but abundant production, low prices and rent arrears, and mercantilist theory was preoccupied with cereal export (and bounties). In such conditions the Tudor measures of provision lay dormant, although they were not forgotten in high-price years. In 1693 in Oxfordshire the crowd took the corn "as it was carrying away by the ingrossers, saying they were resolved to put the law in execution since the magistrates neglected it".[3] "Some of our rioters" (a dealer wrote in 1766) "have been so infatuated as to think they were only assisting the execution of wholesome laws. . ."[4]

What may have eased the abrogation of the *Book of Orders* was the growing effectiveness of the poor laws in providing an institutional safety-net for those with a settlement. The responsibility which the central authorities refused was taken back to the parish or to the urban corporation. And alongside this limited relief, in times of dearth the local traditions of charity had more vitality than they are sometimes credited with. In a sense the Tudor practices of "housekeeping" and of hospitality were extended into the eighteenth-century landed gentleman's contest, through large

---

[1] Professor Sen continues to lay great stress on the *political* context of famine in the twentieth century. Governments which are accountable to public opinion are more likely to exert themselves in relief measures than those which are not, and "it is hard to find a case in which a famine has occurred in a country with a free press and an active opposition within a democratic system": Amartya Sen, "Individual Freedom as a Social Commitment", *New York Review of Books*, 14 June, 1990.

[2] Outhwaite, "Dearth and Government Intervention", p. 404.

[3] "The Life and Times of Anthony Wood, Antiquary of Oxford, 1632-95", ed. A. Clark, cited in W. Thwaites, "The Corn Market and Economic Change: Oxford in the 18th Century", *Midland History* (forthcoming).

[4] *Reflections on the Present High Price of Provisions*, p. 27.

gestures of "liberality", for local influence.[1]

In every high-price year — at least until the 1760s — substantial landowners came forward in most parts of the country, sending corn at reduced rates to market as an example to others, selling off cheap grain at their gates, ordering their tenants to supply the market at moderate rates, entering into county agreements to reduce prices and to prosecute those who sold by sample, forestallers, etc., and so on. (By the 1780s and 1790s opinion was more divided, and those — like the earl of Warwick — who continued the old charitable gestures, tended to mark themselves out as traditional "Tory" paternalists.) This tradition of highly-visible charity may in part be ascribed to humanitarian motives and to an approved self-image of the gentry as protectors of the poor against heartless employers, mean parish overseers and grasping middlemen. But it was also a calculated stance in the culturally-constructed alliance between patricians and plebs against the middling orders, and it distracted attention from the landowners' prosperity to point to prominent Dissenters and Quakers among the pro-fiteering food dealers.[2]

Viewed from this aspect, poor laws and emergency charities were constituent components of the system of property and power. Indeed, subsidies and subscriptions can often be seen as direct moves to buy off riot, or even as a reward for not rioting.[3] John Bohstedt has warned us:

[1] Much of what John Walter writes about seventeenth-century charities in time of dearth applies equally to the first seven decades of the eighteenth century: Walter, "Social Economy of Dearth".

[2] So widespread was the abuse of Quaker dealers that the Friends issued a public statement in 1800: "The Society of Friends. . . having been for some time calumniated as oppressors of the laborious and indigent classes of the community, by combining to monopolize those necessary articles of life, Corn and Flour, think themselves called upon to vindicate their own innocence and integrity. . .": *Meetings for Sufferings*, xl, pp. 404-6, 6 October 1800 (Friends House Library, London). My thanks to the Librarian, Malcolm Thomas.

[3] In 1766 local gentry raised a subscription in Melksham "in consideration of the poor not having joined in the late riots which occurred all round the town", and beef was distributed to over 1,600 poor persons. But the beef was given in November, months after the height of the crisis had passed. Dr Randall suggests that the riotous poor of Chippenham,

It is not historically useful to separate the undoubted humanitarianism of these charities from their function in preserving class rule. Plebeian misery assaulted the conscience of the wealthy and challenged their capacity for remedy, just as it threatened to assault their property and challenge the legitimacy of their political monopoly.

In the 1790s "a waning 'paternalism'. . . was merely thinly-disguised self-preservation".[1]

From the 1790s this was the case, and the supposed threat of "Jacobinism" provided an additional spur. But in earlier decades one can perceive a kind of social bargain, less calculating and more unconscious — a kind of obligatory dues paid for the everyday exercise of hegemony. It gave a character of liberality to some country gentry which allows one to forgive them other sins. "In this sense", John Walter has written, "years of dearth continued to provide an arena in which the nature of social responsibilities between the poor and their betters could be continually re-negotiated". But over the longer course, what had been once perceived as reciprocal duties (and by the labourers as rights) became re-defined as "discriminatory and discretionary charity". If "the poor" escaped "vulnerability to crises of sub-subsistence" it was at the cost of becoming "enmeshed in a web of deference and dependence".[2] Yet if this is true of rural England — and perhaps of some towns — the record of food riot shows an alternative.

In any case, relief measures cannot be shrugged off as only a matter of gestures or as an exercise in social control. There is reason to suppose that they may have mitigated crises of subsistence. If the margin between a poor subsistence and (for groups at risk) famine was small, then marginal

---

Stroud, Frome or Bradford (Wiltshire) might have done better: A. J. Randall, "Labour and the Industrial Revolution in the West of England Woollen Industry" (Univ. of Birmingham Ph.D. thesis, 1979), p. 166.

[1] Bohstedt, *op. cit.*, pp. 96-7, 48. See also Peter Mandler's discussion of the conversion of the landed gentry in these years from a weak paternalism which acknowledged the customary rights of the poor to a language of the "natural order" (as defined by Smith and by Malthus) in which "the only true natural right" is that of property: "The Making of the New Poor Law *Redivivus*", *Past and Present*, 117 (November 1987).

[2] Walter, "Social Economy of Dearth", pp. 127-8; Walter and Schofield, "Famine, Disease and Crisis Mortality", p. 48.

redistribution to those in most need may have mattered enough to have shifted a demographic digit. Even between neighbouring towns the different profile of riot/relief might have influenced mortality. The patchwork of poor laws, charities, subsidies — even petty measures like limits upon malting, banning hair-powder, or commending austere diets to the deferential middling orders — might have added their mite to someone's survival.

This is simply to rehearse that food supply (and indeed demography) have their own kind of politics, in which riot may be seen as a rational and effective agent. If there had been no food riots then this whole elaborate patchwork of protection might never have come into being. If we say, with Roger Wells, that "staving off starvation in the most vulnerable locations necessitated the speediest suppression of riot", then we are taking a short-term view of the need, in emergency, to force the traffic in grain through a popular blockade. Over the longer-term view of two centuries and more, riot and the threat of riot may have staved off starvation, sometimes by actually forcing prices down, and more generally by forcing Government to attend to the plight of the poor, and by stimulating parish relief and local charity. The thesis then must be that the solidarities and collective actions of the urban working people, and in the manufacturing and mining districts, did something to bring the crisis of subsistence to an end. And conversely — but as a more tentative hypothesis — it might be that the comparative *absence* of riot in nineteenth-century Ireland and India was one factor (among others) which allowed dearth to pass into famine. And if this is the case, then the best thing that we, in our affluence, can do to help the hungry nations is to send them experts in the promotion of riot.[1]

---

[1] Wendy Thwaites, who kindly read these pages in manuscript, has very sensibly rebuked me for even making this joke. She points out that the resources of modernised hungry nations have advanced since the eighteenth century, and (citing Nigel Twose, *Cultivating Hunger* (Oxfam, 1984)) describes a vehicle developed to deter food rioters in the Dominican Republic of Haiti: "the AMAC-1 has nineteen weapon points, four multiple grenade launchers, a water canon, an infra-red video camera for surveillance, and its bodywork can be electrified with a 7,000 volt charge". She concludes that for riot to work there "have to be certain constraints on

I say this only partly in jest, for what are at issue are the community defences and the political influence of the working people. At the very least, rulers are likely to be more busy with the relief of the poor if they fear that otherwise their rule may be endangered by riot. I don't, of course, suppose that there was (and is) one alternative and universal set of remedies, "the moral economy", for the successful overcoming of dearth and the prevention of famine. It is exactly against such universalist dogma (the "free market") that I have been arguing. Perhaps all that can be expected in times of crisis is energetic improvisation, using whatever resources and options lie to hand. If political economy rests upon persuasive but misleading metaphors (such as "rationing"), the moral economy nourished its own irrationalisms and superstitions, such as the popular conviction that every dearth was the consequence of hoarding and speculation, "artificial scarcity", or even some malevolent *pacte de famine*.

A case can always be made on both sides of the question. The exemplary punishment of profiteers[1] or fraudulent dealers has sometimes had a beneficent effect upon prices, but the draconian imposition of price maximums has on occasion summoned forth a black market or a producers' strike (the peasants withholding supply) with consequences

---

how far the authorities will go in repression". I have left my jest in because it enables me also to include her thoughtful caution.

[1] Adam Smith in his digression took a benign view of profiteers, since (a) the high profits of years of scarcity compensated dealers for the modest returns of normal years, and (b) the excessive profits of a few might be the inevitable price to pay for the market's functions for the general public. In any case, hoarders and profiteers (if they misjudged the market) would be caught out when prices fell. No-one has as yet succeeded in finding a way to study systematically the question of hoarding and profiteering in eighteenth-century high-price years, nor is it easy to see how it could be done. But that is no reason for the widely-held dogma that its effect (if it happened at all) was insignificant, and that no case can be made for excessive prices (in a seller's market, shored up by Corn Laws) which transferred wealth from the petty consumers to the grain-growing interests. Some scholars show great expertise in such matters as the behaviour of rats and fleas, or in the ratios of seed-corn to available harvest surplus, while stubbornly refusing to acknowledge rather large factors such as human greed.

no less baneful than those of doctrinaire *laissez-faire*. The mentality of urban revolutionaries has sometimes been profoundly hostile to the peasantry, and in the twentieth century collectivist states have precipitated famines as appalling as those presided over by complacent political economy. Some theorists today are interested in remembering the first, and in forgetting the second, which are tidied away as unmentionable in little exercises of political thought. For that reason I have redressed the account, to show that rioters had their reasons.

And (in conclusion) more caution might be proper in the use of the term, "market". I return to my earlier question: is market an actual market or is it a metaphor? One hears on every side these days talk of "a market economy". When this is contrasted with the centralised direction of old-style collectivist states one understands what is being described. And, very certainly, the "market" here is beneficial and can also be democratic, in stimulating variety and in expressing consumer choice. But I cannot clearly say what was "a market economy" in eighteenth-century England; or, rather, I cannot find a non-market-economy to contrast it with. One cannot think of an economy without a market; and even the most zealous food rioters, such as Cornish tinners or Kingswood miners or West of England clothing workers,[1] were inextricably committed to the market, both as producers and as consumers. How could they have existed for a month or a week without it? What we can find are different ways of regulating the market or of manipulating exchanges between producers and consumers, to the advantage of one party or the other. It is with the special case of the marketing of "necessities" in time of dearth that we have been concerned,

[1] We are fortunate in having excellent studies of these groups of workers, both in their capacities as (hard-bargaining) producers and (riotous) consumers. Even "custom" was not pre-market or non-market but a particular community consensus as to the regulation of wages and prices. See J. G. Rule, "The Labouring Miner in Cornwall, c. 1740-1820", (Univ. of Warwick Ph.D. thesis, 1971), esp. pp. 116-80; R. W. Malcolmson, "A Set of Ungovernable People", in J. Brewer and J. Styles (eds.), *An Ungovernable People* (1980) (the mining population of Kingswood); A. J. Randall, "Labour and the Industrial Revolution in the West of England Woollen Industry" (Univ. of Birmingham Ph.D. thesis, 1979).

and the crowd's preferred model was precisely the "open market" in which the petty producers freely competed, rather than the closed market when large dealers conducted private bargains over samples in the back parlours of inns.[1]

The "market economy", I suspect, is often a metaphor (or mask) for capitalist process. It may even be employed as myth. The most ideologically-compelling form of the myth lies in the notion of the market as some supposedly-neutral but (by accident) beneficent entity; or, if not an entity (since it can be found in no space but the head) then an energising spirit — of differentiation, social mobility, individualisation, innovation, growth, freedom — like a kind of postal sorting-station with magical magnifying powers, which transforms each letter into a package and each package into a parcel. This "market" may be projected as a benign consensual force, which involuntarily maximises the best interests of the nation. It may even seem that it is the "market system" which has "produced" the nation's wealth — perhaps "the market" grew all that grain?

Market is indeed a superb and mystifying metaphor for the energies released and the new needs (and choices) opened up by capitalist forms of exchange, with all conflicts and contradictions withdrawn from view. Market is (when viewed from this aspect) a mask worn by particular interests, which are not coincident with those of "the nation" or "the community", but which are interested, above all, in being mistaken to be so. Historians who suppose that such a market really could be found must show it to us in the records. A metaphor, no matter how grand its intellectual pedigree, is not enough.

III

Let us next take the question of the role of women in food riots. In 1982 Jennifer Grimmett and M. I. Thomis published a helpful chapter on the theme,[2] in which they raised but left

---

[1] *Mist's Weekly Journal*, 12 March 1726 reported that the mob rose on market days in Northampton, Kettering, Oundle, Wellingborough, Stony Stratford, because farmers would not bring corn to the market-place "but kept it in the Inns". At Towcester a riot was prevented by the Cryer giving notice that corn must be brought "into open market".

[2] Malcolm I. Thomis and Jennifer Grimmett, *Women in Protest, 1800-1850* (1982), ch. 2. This is based on a survey of published sources and some use of newspapers in 1800 and 1812.

unanswered the question as to which sex was the more
prominent. Kenneth Logue, in a study of "meal mobs" in
Scotland found that women were very active, although they
comprised only 28 per cent of those charged before the
courts. But this was possibly because "they were less likely to
be prosecuted than their male colleagues", so that, again, the
question is left open.[1] In 1988 John Bohstedt sought to bring
a conclusive answer in a substantial article which purports to
demolish "the myth of the feminine food riot".[2]

Bohstedt's conclusions are as follows:

> Women did not dominate food riots; food riots were not a distinctly
> feminine province. . . Women typically joined men in food riots. . .
> Women's co-operation with men is much more significant than the
> monopoly suggested by the older view. Women were significant partners
> to men as bread rioters partly because they were essential partners as
> bread-winners in the household economies of pre-industrial society and
> partly because bread riots were still effective politics in stable small-to-
> medium-sized traditional towns.

These conclusions are sustained in two ways. First, John
Bohstedt presents what purport to be refined statistics of all
riots in England and Wales between 1790 and 1810. Second,
he introduces some pages of speculation as to gender roles in
the proto-industrial household economy.

I have already expressed my admiration for Bohstedt's
major study of riot. And there is interesting material in this
new article. But the piece obscures as much as it reveals. The
first difficulty is that there is no "myth of the feminine food
riot" to demolish. No-one, no historian, has ever suggested
that food riots were a "monopoly" of women or were predominantly feminine, and Bohstedt can show none. The best
that he can do is hold up to censure Barbara and J. L.
Hammond for writing (in 1911) of the crisis year of 1795 as
the year of "the revolt of the housewives", because of "the
conspicuous part taken by women" in the food riots.[3] That

[1] Kenneth J. Logue, *Popular Disturbances in Scotland, 1780-1815*
(Edinburgh, 1979), pp. 199, 202-3.
[2] John Bohstedt, "Gender, Household and Community Politics:
Women in English Riots, 1790-1810", *Past and Present*, no. 120 (August
1988), pp. 88-122. The claim to have demolished "the myth of the feminine
food riot" is at pp. 90, 93.
[3] *Ibid.*, p. 88. J. L. and B. Hammond, *The Village Labourer* (1911;
reprint 1966), pp. 116-8.

does not constitute a "myth", so that we are being led into a spurious polemic. Previous historians have, perhaps, not always given enough attention to women's part in riots, but most have agreed that women were highly visible rioters and were frequently involved. Since all historians show riots in which men also were highly visible, or in which men and women acted together, no-one has suggested that food riots were "a distinctly feminine province".

In his eagerness to drive this mythical opponent from the field, Bohstedt introduces his tables. He has with great industry assembled a "sample" of 617 riots between 1790 and 1810 and he drills this sample through various statistical manoeuvres. Now I don't know what to say to this. There are times when his figures are helpful — for example, in showing a rough division between different occasions for riot. And Bohstedt is a careful scholar who sometimes remembers the limitations of his evidence. But in general his history becomes less credible the more he surrenders to his own figures and the further he gets away from "literary" and contextual sources. This is because much of the evidence is too "soft" to be introduced to the hard definitions of a table. And when one looks at some of John Bohstedt's counting, the points at issue may seem absurd. Of his 617 riots he is able to identify 240 as food riots. These are further refined as:

A. Women dominant	B. Women and men	C. Men only	D. Gender unknown
35	42	81	82

If one deducts D, and puts A and B together, then 77 out of 158, or 49 per cent of these food riots had female participation and 51 per cent did not. So that if one wished to claim that women took part in "most" food riots, one would be at fault by 2 per cent. But, putting B and C together, one would discover that 123 out of 158, or 78 per cent had male participation — which could be a step on the way to a myth of a male food riot, to be demolished by a subsequent generation of computers.

When Bohstedt offers to drill these figures through more refined manoeuvres (such as violence and disorder quotients), he must make anyone laugh who is familiar with the source material which he is using. Let me explain some of the difficulties. There are, first of all, the difficulties in gathering any reliable count. These are familiar, and have often been discussed.[1] Bohstedt's sample is drawn from the *Annual Register*, two London newspapers, and the in-letters to the Home Office concerning disorders (HO 42). This is a wide survey, but the provincial coverage of the London press was patchy, JPs might not always wish to report their local affairs to the central authorities, the sample tends to over-report dramatic or violent affrays and under-report quieter episodes (hence possibly under-reporting women's participation), and so on. When compared to regional studies which draw upon local sources, Bohstedt's sample shows a serious under-count. A most thorough study, by Alan Booth, of food riots in the north-west of England in the same years, lists forty-six disturbances of which only twelve are in Bohstedt's sample. Booth adds that "in most riots where sexual composition was recorded women appear to have been both more numerous and particularly active", and he goes on to cite thirteen examples. Hence Booth's examples (which he does not suggest are exhaustive) exceed the total of Bohstedt's count of food riots in all categories, which *must* undercount the feminine presence.[2]

Next, we must consider the nature of the evidence which is being used. How does it come about that in eighty-two cases (or more than one third of the sample) the sex of the rioters is unknown, and how hard or soft is the evidence in the eighty-one cases of men only? The evidence often comes in a sexually-indeterminate vocabulary: "rioters", "the mob", "the poor", "the inhabitants", "the populace". Let us take a letter of 12 July 1740 from Norwich, published in the *Ipswich Journal*, which describes a riot by "the common People", "the meanest of the People", "the Multitude,":

> About Eight in the Evening the Mayor committed three of four dis-
> orderly Fellows to Prison; which Act so incens'd the Mob, that they
> broke open the Prison, releas'd their Companions, and have scarce left

---

[1] The best comment is Roger Wells, "Counting riots in eighteenth-century England", *Bulletin of Lab. Hist. Soc.*, 37 (1978), pp. 68-72. Alan Booth discusses successive errors in estimates in his excellent and dense study, "Food Riots in the North-West of England, 1790-1801", *Past and Present*, 77 (1977), esp. pp. 89-90.

[2] Bohstedt, *Riots and Community Politics*, pp. 11-14, 230-1; Booth, *op. cit.*, pp. 98-9.

a Pane of Glass in the whole Prison. . . Upon this Outrage of the Mob, an unthinking Gentleman is said to have taken a Musket out of the Hands of a Dragoon, and shot a Man thro' the Head. You will imagine how this enrag'd the Populace; and the Consequence of that Evening's Work was, three Men, a Boy, and two Women, were shot. . .[1]

This report commences as indeterminate (D), becomes male (C) at "disorderly Fellows", and moves sharply across to (B) — women and men — only when the dragoons, by firing point-blank into the crowd, take a random sample. Amongst all the indeterminate ("mob", "populace") and male vocabulary, the first mention of women, in a long report, is when two of them are shot. A similar sexually-indeterminate crowd, in 1757, descended on a Hereford miller, and insisted on searching his house and mill for grain. The miller refused:

Yet they persisted in having another search, saying that if he had no grain he had some money, upon which declaration there was necessity for fireing on them in which four women and two men were wounded, which occasioned the rest to disperse.[2]

Again and again reports of "mobs" leave them sexually indeterminate until the moment of some action or arrests make individuals visible. Nor is this any indication of sexist bias in the reporter. The bias (if there is one) is more likely to be in the mind of the twentieth-century historian or reader whose expectations, when he reads of "mobs", are of crowds composed of men, and who reads the accounts accordingly. Perhaps, in the later nineteenth century, "the mob" became a male noun? But the image called to the eighteenth-century mind by these collective nouns was very different — for them a "mob" suggested women, men and (often) older children, especially boys. I think it probable that Bohstedt's table is misleading, and that many riots in column (D) (gender unknown) and some in (C) (men only) were mixed affairs.

Moreover, these figures which enter the tables, whether derived from the press or from a letter to the Home Office, normally report a particular moment of riot — perhaps its

[1] *Ipswich Journal*, 26 July 1740. I am indebted to Robert Malcolmson for this.
[2] *Bristol Journal*, 11 June 1757, cited in Jeremy N. Caple, "Popular Protest and Public Order in 18th-century England: the Food Riots of 1756-7" (Queens Univ. Ontario, M.A. thesis, 1978), p. 102.

crisis — and they rarely describe its evolution. Yet a riot may pass through phases, for example it might commence with actions by women, be joined by men, and end with men alone. In my view there are two situations in which we may expect to find a predominantly male crowd. First, when disciplined male working groups, accustomed to acting together, spearhead the riot: such may be the case with coal miners, keelmen, Cornish tinners, and seamen. In the second case, when heavy conflict is expected with the authorities, the women sometimes seem to fall back — or perhaps are asked by the men to do so.

Yet the evidence is not as tidy as that. Miners and tinners were archetypical male rioters, yet also it is notorious that the whole communities shared in their movements. The Kingswood "mob" is usually thought of as masculine, for example in its destruction of turnpikes and toll-gates. But on occasion its resistance to authority was more like a rising of the whole district. During riots against the cider tax of 1738 the excise officers were "resisted by that savage Crew by Fire Armes": "there are now in the Forest not less than 1000 Men, Women and Boys in Armes, destroying all before them. . .".[1] In 1740 the Kingswood colliers marched into Bristol and demonstrated against the price of corn at the Council House, leaving behind "their usual Armour of Clubs and Staffs", but accompanied by "some weavers, colliers' wives and abundance of other women".[2] Both the absence of "armour" and the presence of women suggests (on that occasion) a commitment to peaceable courses.

In 1740 the north-east was swept with food riots, which culminated in the sacking of the Newcastle Guildhall. (See above p. 70 & p. 231.) Pitmen and keelmen were prominent in this, and at a superficial view this might appear as a male riot. But a longer and closer view will show an alternation of male and female presence. The regional actions against export were first raised in Stockton by "a Lady with a Stick and a horn". (See above p. 233.) Women as well as men took part in boarding vessels loaded with corn, and forcing them

[1] G. Blenkinsop, 14 Oct. 1738 in PRO, T 1/299(15).
[2] *Northampton Mercury*, 6 Oct. 1740; R. Malcolmson in Brewer and Styles, *op. cit.*, p. 117.

to off-load to the crowd on shore.[1] When — after three weeks of popular export embargo — the Sheriff raised the *posse comitatus* against them, the people of Stockton, to the number of three thousand, "sent for the Colliers of Ederly and Caterhorn".[2] Meanwhile there had been small disturbances in Newcastle-on-Tyne, involving a group of women "incited by a leader calling herself 'General' or Jane Bogey, ringing bells and impeding the passage of horses carrying grain through the town".[3] After five women had been committed,[4] the troubles in Newcastle died down, only to resume on a much greater scale in mid-June, with the involvement of keelmen and pitmen (who struck their pits). In the first phase, "a body of 3 or 4 hundred men women and children" came into the city and demanded corn at a low rate; granaries were broken into, and the crowd marched about the streets in triumph, huzzaing and blowing horns. The magistrates then summoned and armed the Watch and Ward and seized some prisoners; the crowd then appears in accounts as increasingly male, with "Colliers, Wagoners, Smiths and other common workmen", well armed with cudgels, breaking open the keep and releasing the prisoners, and marching in great discipline through the town with drum, bagpipes and mock colours.[5]

Other episodes were to follow, including the firing on the crowd and the attack on the Guildhall. My point is to illustrate the evolution of a food rioting crowd, which may now be incited by women, may then become of assorted sexes and ages, and may then (when rescue and confrontation are the object) become predominantly male. But none of this should be stereotyped. The most careful historian of the affair observes that the role of women and children was under-

[1] Edward Goddard, 24 May 1740 in PRO, SP 36/50/431 and miscellaneous depositions in SP 36/51.

[2] J. J. Williamson, Sheriff of Durham, 10 June 1740 in PRO, SP 36/51.

[3] Joyce Ellis, "Urban Conflict and Popular Violence: the Guildhall Riots of 1740 in Newcastle-upon-Tyne", *Int. Rev. Social Hist.*, xxv, 3 (1980).

[4] They were discharged at the Sessions a few days later.

[5] "Account of the Riots" by Alderman Ridley in Northumberland CRO, 2R1 27/8.

stated in subsequent investigations, and that of pitmen over-stated. Women contributed to both physical and verbal episodes of violence, breaking into granaries and one woman going down on her knees in front of the magistrates and crying out "Blood for blood!".[1] The authorities came down most heavily upon the women who had unloaded wheat from a boat at Stockton,[2] whereas in Newcastle they selected the pitmen for indictment and passed over the women.

This shows whole communities in action, with one sex or the other coming into prominence as each assumes a different part. The episode might fall into any one of John Bohstedt's categories according to the moment at which it was reported. It also shows that the crowd might be made up of different elements, consciously playing different parts in co-operation with each other. There are other occasions when it is reported that the "people" sent for the miners to help them. In anti-export riots in St Asaph (Flint) in 1740 it was said that "men, women and boys" were joined by "Severall Colliers and Miners"; not only so, but it was alleged that the colliers "belonging" to Sir Thomas Mostyn were deliberately laid off, given cudgels, and encouraged to take part. In the event they completely dominated the affair, marching together under Mostyn colours and crying out "a Mostyn!".[3] In Coventry (1756) the poor — presumably of both sexes — "patted the colliers on the back and urged them to go thro with what they had begun".[4] And at Nottingham in the same year, the colliers negotiated an agreement with the mayor, and then, as they were leaving the town "a number of women. . . gave them money to come back, and showed them to a Wind-mill. . . having French stones". The colliers obligingly destroyed several mills in the vicinity.[5] In the anti-export

[1] Ellis, *op. cit.*, pp. 341-6.

[2] At Durham Assizes Anne Withy, Hannah Crone and William Young were transported for seven years for taking a large quantity of wheat out of a ship at Stockton. Three more women and one man were tried and acquitted: *Newcastle Journal*, 9 Aug. 1740. My thanks to Robert Malcolmson again.

[3] William Price, 13 June 1740 in PRO, SP 36/51, and various depositions in SP 36/50 and 36/51.

[4] PRO, SP 36/135.

[5] Caple, *op. cit.*, p. 82.

riots in Poole (Dorset) in 1737 (by contrast) the women took action, with the men supporting them and swearing that "if any one offers to molest any of the Women in their Proceedings" they would raise a great number of men and destroy both ships and cargoes" (above p. 233). [1]

Two unusual examples of supportive gender actions come from Scotland. In January 1813 in Montrose the magistrates tried to bully the town carters into loading grain onto ships, and the carters reluctantly promised to do so; but (surprise!) on their return to their homes they found that they could not, because their wives had locked the stables or sent the horses away. In 1801 in Errol the Volunteers were called out for possible action against a "meal mob". "As they were going to parade, some of the women, mainly the wives and mothers of the Volunteers, took their guns from them, but immediately gave them back." The crowd then stoned an inn with impunity, and, Kenneth Logue suggests, "It may be that women simply removed part of the firing mechanisms, rendering the weapons useless and relieving the Volunteers of the unhappy task of shooting at their own townspeople". [2]

A more elaborate series of actions was described in Exeter in 1757:

Last Market-Day some Farmers demanded 11s. per Bushel for Wheat, and were agreeing among themselves to bring it to 15s. and then make a stand. But the Graecians (as the Inhabitants of St. Sidwell's are called) hearing of this Complot, sent their wives in great Numbers to Market, resolving to give no more than 6s. per Bushel, and, if they would not sell it at that Price, to take it by Force; and such wives, as did not stand by this Agreement, were to be well flogg'd by their Comrades. Having thus determined, they marched to the Corn-Market, and harangued the Farmers in such a Manner, that they lowered their price to 8s. 6d. The Bakers came, and would have carried off all at that Price, but the Amazonians swore, that they would carry the first man who attempted it before the Mayor, upon which the Farmers swore they would bring no more to Market; and the sanguine Females threatened the Farmers, that, if they did not, they would come and take it by Force out of their

[1] Holles Newcastle to Secretary at War, 26 May 1737, PRO, SP 41/10.
[2] Logue, *op. cit.*, pp. 21. 44.

Ricks. The Farmers submitted and sold it for 6s. on which the poor weavers and woolcombers were content.[1]

One doubts whether the male "Graecians" could have "sent their wives" on such a skilfully exercised sequence of actions, unless they had mutually agreed upon their gender roles: which (in this case) left the action and the thinking to the women, and only the eating to the men.

A further (and insurmountable) difficulty is that evidence taken from the years 1790-1810, however skilfully it is counted, cannot support generalisations as to the feminine presence in food riots which extended over a period of well over two hundred years. After 1812 food riots in most parts of the country gave way to other kinds of (political, trade union) protest. So that John Bohstedt's quantities are taken from the last stages of the traditional riot, in which — as he himself argues — the role of women may have been changing. At the least, generalisations would have to be supported by a review of the evidence across the seventeenth and eighteenth centuries.[2]

Instead of attempting this, John Bohstedt leaps across to another line of argument altogether. He raises doubts as to whether women had a significant place in the market at all. Indeed, pursuing the rather fashionable ploy in the Western academy of offering oneself as more-feminist-than-thou, he suggests that those who offer women as marketers are pedlars of sexist stereotypes. I am one target of his scorn, since in my essay I had, while drawing particular attention to the very active part played by women, suggested that one reason for this might be that they were "those most involved in face-to-face marketing, most sensitive to price significancies, most experienced in detecting short-weight or inferior quality" (p. 234). Bohstedt challenges this: "It is an anachronistic mistake to assume that women's role in food riots grew out of some special female role as the shopper of the family. Nowhere is there evidence for the frequent assumption that in

[1] R. W. Malcolmson, *Life and Labour in England, 1700-1780* (1981), p. 118.
[2] Wendy Thwaites has found women present in Oxfordshire food riots in 1693, 1713, 1757, 1766 and 1795: Thwaites, thesis, table p. 472 (for 1795), pp. 485-6.

this period women were the primary shoppers. . .". "Plebeian women were income producers and earners, not unwaged housewives and shoppers confined by gender to the more modern role of 'home-making'."[1] Indeed, he waxes indignant at the stereotype of his own invention: "Women were not simply housewife furies, drying their hands and heading off to the market or igniting there as a crowd of shoppers". He does not attempt to show who did the purchasing of provisions, or how,[2] but he develops instead hypotheses as to the "nearly coequal" relations between women and men in the proto-industrial household economy.

I agree that "housewives" and "shopping" are (in their current usage) anachronistic terms, although I used neither of them. I have a little difficulty, in that I don't regard skills in marketing or home-making as unimportant and inferior, although it is true that male-dominated cultures may make them seem so, and may then try to confine women to "inferior" roles. But there are really two questions here: an empirical question — who did the marketing and how? — and a theoretical question about the proto-industrial household economy, and we will take them in that order.

There is no single source to which one can go to establish gender roles in the market-place. Women were certainly present as sellers of food, although few were licensed dealers.[3] One might expect to find, in a market-town, a large throng of sellers of poultry, eggs, butter, vegetables, fruit and other locally-grown produce, and most of these were women: the wives, daughters and servants of local farmers,

[1] Thomas and Grimmett, op. cit., p. 10, also accuse me, on the same grounds, of placing women "firmly in the market-place, if not exactly beside the kitchen sink"; and they also throw no light on how marketing was done.
[2] Bohstedt is strangely inconsistent. He suggests that men did the marketing (p. 116). But women (who did not normally do so and hence were confined to the household?) were nevertheless somehow knitting the networks of neighbourhood, and he commends a French study for noting that housework "overflowed into communal co-operation" in "fetching water and *provisions*, for example" (p. 98, my italics).
[3] See Wendy Thwaites' excellent study, "Women in the Market Place: Oxfordshire c. 1690-1800", *Midland History*, ix (1984), pp. 23-42, and, for the earlier tradition, Rodney Hilton, "Women Traders in Medieval England", in *Class Conflict and the Crisis of Feudalism* (1985), p. 213.

while others would be petty dealers from the labouring class. In a strictly governed market some of these might pay toll for stands — for example, at the Butter Cross (see Plate XVIIa) — but more commonly they would set out their wares on the periphery.[1] In 1816 a local historian described Bicester market —

> I have heard many of the aged inhabitants say that they have formerly seen the whole market-hill covered with sacks of corn etc; the avenues leading to it crowded by the farmers' wives with their baskets of butter, eggs and poultry. . .[2]

In fact the poultry, fruit and vegetable market was sometimes known as "the women's market". An experienced dealer, looking back to the 1760s, described the prosperous tourist market of Bath, where "the farmer, his wife, daughter, or servant", trudged there with "the best milk butter, whey butter, cheeses. . . roasting pigs. . . fattened bacon. . . black and white pudding, abundance of lard, chitterlings nicely cleaned, and made up by the hand of a neat dairy maid; variety of poultry. . . fresh eggs. . . fruits, flowers, herbs, honey, and the honey combs, &c, &c, &c.".[3] By the 1790s this trade was being taken over by "jobbers, higlers, &c.",[4] and as farmers became more prosperous it was the common complaint that farmers were "purchasing piano fortes for their daughters, instead of bringing their butter and eggs to market".[5]

It is less easy to identify the purchasers, although they were certainly of both sexes. Oxford, a well-regulated corn market

[1] In the early eighteenth century Lord of the Market of Woodbridge (Suffolk) was threatening to prosecute "persons who come to this town with fish, fowl, fruits, butter, cheese, eggs" on market days, and who carry these things from house to house, instead of taking a stand or stall in the market: Ipswich and East Suffolk CRO, V 5/9/6 - 3 (3). Perhaps similar attempts at control were behind a rash of prosecutions of petty dealers (garden stuff, fruit, fish) for regrating in Oxford in 1712: of 24 persons prosecuted, 21 were women: Thwaites, p. 30.

[2] J. Dunkin cited in *ibid.*, p. 29.

[3] J. Mathews, *Remarks on the Cause and Progress of the Scarcity and Dearness of Cattle. . .* (1797), pp. 9-10.

[4] *Ibid.*, pp. 70-71.

[5] J. Malham (Vicar of Helton, Dorset, and Ordinary of the Wiltshire County Gaol), *The Scarcity of Grain Considered* (Salisbury, 1800), p. 43.

in the eighteenth century, has very little record of petty purchases, and the records show the main buyers to be bakers, millers and dealers. But petty purchases may have gone unrecorded. Or perhaps working people did not often buy a sack of wheat of a bushel of flour.[1] An inquest on Ruth Pierce, who died in bizarre circumstances in Devizes market in 1753, shows that she had clubbed together with three other women to buy one sack of wheat from a farmer.[2] Regions had differing practices, but by the mid-century in many parts of the South and Midlands working people were buying flour or bread, not wheat.[3] Five cases involving Assize of Bread offences (short-weight, etc.) came up at Oxfordshire Quarter Sessions, Epiphany 1758, from Ploughley Hundred, and four of the purchasers whose oaths were taken were women.[4] The Crown brief in 1766 against Hester Pitt and Jane Pitt shows that they stopped Mary Cooke in Ruscombe, near Stroud, as she was on horseback loaded with sixteen dozen of bread, pushed her off the horse and took the bread.[5] This reminds us that in the second half of the century, bakers' and hucksters' shops were increasingly common, that bread might be brought around by horse, or horse-and-cart, and that riot could be by women against women.

The evidence suggests to me that working people were not, by the 1790s, buying wheat, flour or bread in the market on market day, but getting it elsewhere, at inns, shops, or bakeries. Catherine Phillips tells us in 1792 that "it was formerly the custom of the wives of labourers and artificers to purchase, on market days, two or three gallons of malt, which would perhaps brew tolerable good table beer for the week", but they were now ceasing to do so since the malt tax

---

[1] Thwaites, thesis, i, pp. 208-21, discusses the question with care.

[2] "Inquisition on Ruth Pierce", *Wiltshire Archaeological and Natural History Magazine*, xii (1870), pp. 256-7. My thanks to Mary Prior.

[3] "A Person in Business", *Two Letters on the Flour Trade* (London, 1757, 1766), pp. 7-8; the author is writing from Hampshire. See also Wendy Thwaites, "Dearth and the Marketing of Agricultural Produce: Oxfordshire", *Agric. Hist. Rev.*, xxxiii (1985), p. 121.

[4] Thwaites, "Women in the Market Place", p. 37.

[5] PRO, TS 11/1138/5956: Special Commission, Gloucester, 14 Nov. 1766, Crown Brief.

had raised the price too high.[1] Where people came in to the urban market from a little distance, they perhaps got hold of some transport, and women, men and older children piled on together; no doubt husband and wife often went round the market together. An observer in 1800 noted a man and wife coming to an inn to buy a peck of wheat, and "after the wheat was measured, the woman says to her husband, 'John I want some money to go to the grocer's for some tea, sugar, butter' ".[2] In this division of gender roles, hers was to finish off the shopping and his (no doubt) was to stay at the inn and drink.

All ages, shapes, sizes and sexes would throng together in a busy market. The genteel were falling away as the century wore on; they did not like to be squashed in the plebeian press and they sent their servants instead. (They are more likely to have sent the cook or kitchen maid to buy provisions than the footman.) The wives and daughters of cottagers might stay on to spend their small takings from selling eggs or cherries on cloth or ribbons or houseware. (Money earned from such produce belonged to "the distaff side" of the family budget.) Some farmers would stay on, get drunk, and have to be collected by their wives.[3] There would be carters and ostlers, ballad-mongers, perhaps a fiddler or two, and a card-sharper. There would be wide-eyed children, hoping to scrump an apple. There would be courting couples, on the only day out when they saw each other. Bakers and millers, higglers and jobbers, market officials. And a throng of purchasers, very many of whom were women. As a rule it was the woman's role to bake, brew and cook — Mary Collier, the washer-woman, eloquently disclosed woman's dual roles as wage-earner and house-worker, in 1739[4] — and it has long been assumed that women had the major role in purchasing provisions. The point has not been fully proven,

[1] Catherine Phillips, *Considerations on the Causes of the High Price of Grain. . .* (1792), p. 7.
[2] William Brooks, *The True Causes of our present Distress for Provisions* (1800), pp. 29-30. My thanks to Dr Thwaites.
[3] F. W. Steer (ed.), "The Memoirs of James Spershott", *The Chichester Papers*, 30 (Chichester, 1962).
[4] See Mary Collier, *The Woman's Labour*, ed. Marian Sugden and E. P. Thompson (1989).

but if research is directed at it then I have little doubt as to its results.

The market was, in any case, a great occasion of sociability. Dare one suggest that market day could actually be fun? If women played so important a part in networking households into a community how could it happen that they should not take part in so important an occasion for community social-ising (and gossip) as the market? Bohstedt offers us no evidence, but suggests that both the family income and necessary purchases were "probably collected by the man on the weekly trip to the warehouse and the market". He is thinking of a "proto-industrial" clothing worker or nail-maker, who works in his own household economy, but must collect raw materials and deliver the finished product to the putter-out. But the day for delivering his "piece" was not often the same as market day. And in a majority of house-holds spinning was the mainstay of women's work until the 1790s or later, and the women (wives or spinsters) would have to visit their own putter-out, or the shopkeeper who acted as agent, as frequently. A 1741 pamphlet shows women in Hampshire, Wiltshire and Dorset coming in to market on farmers' wagons, taking their spun yarn to the clothiers: "then they get the few things they want, and return to the Inn to be carried home again". (There might be as many as three or four hundred poor people, chiefly women, in the market doing this.[1]) A well-informed observer, in 1794, wrote of the dismay of a labourer, "whose wife and children return home from the next market town with the sad tidings that the Wool-man puts out no more handwork. . .".[2]

If women usually did the cooking in the household economy and if some (but not all) women's food riots had targets in the market-place, common-sense suggests that women knew a lot about food marketing. It often seems so from the reports. In 1740 in Newport Pagnell (at a time when the crowd was blocking exports) farmers sold two wagons of wheat to factors. The wheat was disguised by being packed

[1] Alice Clark, *Working Life of Women in the Seventeenth Century* (1919; reprint 1982), pp. 108-9.
[2] "A.B.", *Observations on the detriment that is supposed must arise to the family of every cottager. . . from the loss of woollen spinning. . .* (1794).

like cheese, but "some cunning old women" suspected the deception, stopped the wagons, and (joined by three hundred more women) entered into a long and successful engagement with the farmers.[1] John Bohstedt wishes to play down this female role in the market because he wants to emphasise the productive role of women in the proto-industrial household, which made them "virtually equal to men in the communal economy and polity". Women took part in riots, "not as housewives but as full-fledged contributors to the family income". "They should be seen as proto-citizens and constituents of the local polity and economy, nearly coequal to men in claiming their rights to affordable bread."

I don't wish to dispute the importance of the women's labour in the clothing or metal-working household. But there is no reason why they should not also have been the main food marketers just as the men may have dealt most often with the tools and materials of the trade. What may be misleading are the notions of "equality" and status brought to bear upon them from our own status-conscious and contractual society. These women (and these men) were for themselves and not for us: they were proto-nothing. They were not bugged by notions of equality, in a competitive sense, since they were deeply habituated to the acceptance that men's and women's roles were different, and that neither was the more nor the less for that. There were certainly places of overlap, and also occasions when each sex (the women more often than the men) would take part in the other's work. But Bohstedt goes too far, in his commendable attempt to emphasise the women's independent position, in suggesting that the roles of men and women in the household or cottage economy were almost indistinguishable.[2]

On the contrary, different gender roles were firmly demarked, perhaps the more firmly in that each sex's sphere of responsibility held the other's respect. One emphatically

---

[1] *Ipswich Journal*, 7 June 1740.
[2] Bohstedt may be drawing too far upon the suggestions of Hans Medick on "The proto-industrial family economy", in Peter Kriedte, H. Medick and Schlumbohm, *Industrialization before Industrialization* (Cambridge, 1987), pp. 60-3.

literary source is the poem "descriptive of the manners of the clothiers" in the West Riding of Yorkshire, *circa* 1730. It is, exactly, a comedy of manners about gender roles in a "proto-industrial" household, although one of small master rather than journeyman status. In this the food is certainly cooked by the Mistress, with the help of "prentice Bess": in includes broth, oaten cakes, mutton, bread (home baked), "dumplins", and home-brewed ale. The "Maister" oversees the needs of the weaving trade; he or his sons (or apprentices) will get wool from the Wolds, take it out to the spinners, get size, dye, and so on. The Mistress must oversee getting yeast (perhaps from a neighbour), malt and hops for brewing, soap and "blue". She and Bess must also "sit at t'bobbin wheel", dye, do the washing (and washing-up), get the children to and from school, and oversee the work folk when the master is away. And a dozen other things.[1]

It was exactly the extent and manifest importance of the woman's role, and her manifold responsibilities, each calling for specialised skills, which gave to her authority in the household and respect in the community. Her work was indispensible and she well knew it. It is pointless to try to grade the feminine and masculine spheres of work in terms of degrees of "near equality". Certainly in the public sphere of law and religion and property the woman was in a subject position. But in the household economy the terms which we need are "authority", "worth" and "respect": perhaps the parity and mutual interdependence of unlikes.[2]

If women were especially prominent in food riots in regions where the manufacturing household economy was strong, such as clothing districts, this was in part because their role in this economy gave them authority and self-confidence. But this was not because gender roles were almost indistinguishable. The female sphere of authority probably took in most marketing for provisions, and within

[1] The full text is in *Publications of the Thoresby Society*, xli, pt. 3, p. 95 (1947). Extracts are in H. Heaton, *Yorkshire Woollen and Worsted Industries* (1920), pp. 344-7; Thompson, *The Making of the English Working Class*, pp. 300-1.

[2] See Dorothy Thompson, "Women, Work and Politics in Nineteenth-Century England: the Problem of Authority", in Jane Randall (ed.), *Equal or Different* (Oxford, 1987), pp. 61-3.

the household the women had responsibility for baking, brewing, and seeing that the household was fed. They were therefore especially sensitive to price and quality, and were the first to have to work out economies and strategies of survival when dearth threatened. This role made them as much guardians of the household's survival as were the men, who might earn the greater part of the family income. They would discuss their problems, anger or anxieties with other women, not only on market day but daily on their neighbour-hood occasions. This favoured — Alice Clarke wrote long ago — "the formation of a feminine public opinion on current events". Thus households would be bonded and the nucleus for direct actions prepared.[1]

By downplaying this role and by fastening his analysis upon women's role as income-earners in the manufacturing household, Bohstedt — quite against his own intentions — gives an almost patronising account of women as rioters: "Women typically *joined* men in food riots" (above p. 306, my italics). The suggestion is conveyed that women expressed their solidarity *with* men, as their "near coequals". But the evidence does not feel like that. On these matters the women were often the leaders of community opinion, and the initiators of actions; sometimes they were the sole executors of actions, and the men joined in in solidarity with them as often as they joined the men.

In 1766 and afterwards there were fewer spontaneous crowd actions in the market-place because less grain was being sold there. Sales were removing to inns, and the open market was in some places coming to an end. Working people in the south and midlands were increasingly buying bread. This might fluctuate in price, or (if the priced loaf remained steady) in weight, which was more difficult to judge. In the high-price years of the 1790s, the huge quartern or half-quartern loaves normally baked in many towns went out of reach of "the poor", who "were obliged to buy fragments of bread, with several surfaces exposed to the sun, air, flies,

[1] Clark, *op. cit.*, p. 51. See also Maxine Berg's suggestion as to networks in *The Age of Manufactures* (1985), pp. 164-7, and the excellent survey of women's work in the family economy in Bridget Hill, *Women, Work, and Sexual Politics in Eighteenth-Century England* (Oxford, 1989), chapters 3 and 4.

dust, and all the contingencies of a huckster's shop".[1] But the end product in a huckster's shop was a futile target for those who wished to bring down the price of grain. Hence the crowd had to plan more carefully, and to select targets, often outside the market-place, such as inns, canals, wharfs, granaries, farms, mills, wagons on the road. These actions around wheat or flour must have followed upon discussions (and rumours of hoarding or speculation) within the working community.

Spontaneous actions by women in the market-place were more frequent in the first half of the century, because wheat and flour were still in the open market. Thus in Oxford in 1693 we find women in the market "pelting millers, mealmen, bakers etc with stones";[2] in 1740 most of the riots were against export, but market-place riots are also reported, such as that at Peterborough where "a number of women rose in a tumultous manner on the market day, rioted the farmers out of their sacks & strow'd their corn in the street".[3] Similar market-place actions by women are reported in 1757 in Bewdley, Worcester, Taunton, Newcastle-under-Lyme, and Salisbury, while in 1766 in Kidderminster, when some poor women were bidding in the corn market for a bag of wheat, and a baker offered more, "the people immediately became riotous".[4] If that sort of affair then fell away, women might (and did) still initiate spontaneous actions in the market-place about other foodstuffs, such as potatoes or meat. In Ashby-de-la-Zouche in 1766, when a farmer put up his butter by 2d. a pound, "an old woman clapped one hand around the nape of his neck and with the other smeared his face with butter".[5]

It is not a significant matter whether women took part in

[1] Thomas Parsons, *Letters to an M.P. on the absurdity of popular prejudices. . .* (Bath, 1800).

[2] Thwaites, thesis, ii, pp. 468-9.

[3] *Gloucester Journal*, 24 June 1740.

[4] Bewdley — *Northampton Mercury*, 6 June 1757; Worcester — *Worcester Journal*, 19 May 1757; Taunton, Newcastle-under-Lyme, Salisbury, Kidderminster — all in R. W. Malcolmson, *Life and Labour in England, 1700-1780* (1981), pp. 117-8.

[5] Dale E. Williams, "Midland Hunger Riots in 1766", *Midland History*, iii, 4 (1976).

more or less than 50 per cent of the recorded riots. What
remains significant — and indeed remarkable — is the extensive evidence of women's active part in food riots over a
period of more than two hundred years, and in many parts of
Great Britain.[1] No other issue commanded women's
support so wholeheartedly and consistently, at least in
England.[2] On a review of indictments in the Western and
Oxford Assize circuits in the second half of the eighteenth
century, there are a few cases of what appear to be the
community's defence of trade practices (but not of formal
trade unionism), of resistance to enclosures, of rough music,
and of civic politics in old clothing towns, all of which appear
to have significant female involvement. But food riots are the
indictments where the women are most often to be found.
There are some all-male indictments,[3] just as there are some
all-female ones.[4] There are indictments where there seems
to be the selection of a token woman,[5] just as there seem to
be token men.[6] There are other cases where the prosecution

[1] John Walter in Charlesworth (ed.), *An Atlas of Rural Protest* (1983),
shows women present in riots in Kent (1595), Essex (1596), and unloading a
ship at Southampton (1608).

[2] In Scotland at the end of the eighteenth century, the issue which
occasioned the highest participation of women in direct action "was
opposition to the exercise of church patronage by lay patrons against the
popular wishes of the congregation". Food riots came second. Logue,
op. cit., pp. 199-204.

[3] PRO, Assi 24/42, Devon, Winter 1767: 21 men (17 weavers, 2 woolcombers, 2 labourers, 1 cordwainer) for attacking a boulting mill; *ibid.*, 9
men of Ottery St Mary for pulling down a water mill (and the two following
cases); *ibid.*, Somerset 1766, cheese riot, Wellington (13 woolcombers,
weavers, etc. indicted); *ibid.*, Somerset, Summer 1767, cheese riot, 7
labourers of Trowbridge indicted (but no true bill found); *ibid.*, Wiltshire,
Winter 1767, 8 men indicted (5 broadweavers, 2 scribblers, 1 labourer).

[4] PRO, Assi 4/22, Shropshire, Summer 1767, 5 women of Culmington,
for cutting sacks and throwing grain on the floor. Assi 4/20, Worcestershire, Summer 1768, 7 women for carrying away 60 bushels of wheat. Assi
4/21, Worcestershire, Lent 1775, 7 women from Old Swinford (1 widow, 2
spinsters, 2 colliers' wives and 2 labourers' wives) for a flour riot in which
200 took part. Assi 24/43, Somerset, Lent 1801, 4 women for compelling
the sale of bread under market price.

[5] PRO, Assi 24/43, Devon, Summer 1801, 5 labourers and 1 single-
woman, for compelling the sale of barley under the market price.

[6] PRO, Assi 24/42, Somerset, Summer 1767, butter riot, 5 women and
1 labourer indicted.

appears to be even-handed in serving out indictments.[1] But the indictments testify to the vigorous presence of women.

There is room for further research into this, for as yet no-one appears to have interrogated the legal records systematically over a long period of time. Nor should we expect that uniform answers will be forthcoming. John Bohstedt notes that of fifty-four rioters committed for trial in Devon in 1795 and 1801, only seven were women; but that at Manchester in 1795, of twelve persons charged for food rioting, nine were women.[2] My own searches into Assize records show a similar discrepancy between the Western circuit (taking in Devon, Wiltshire, Dorset and Somerset riots in 1765-72) with 114 men and only fourteen women indicted; and the Oxford circuit (taking in food rioters indicted in Herefordshire, Worcestershire and Shropshire in 1767 to 1774), where there are twenty women and only five men.[3] Do these figures indicate differential gender behaviour or differential practices in policing and prosecution?[4]

We do not know how far the authorities were as willing to prosecute women as men, or whether women must have committed particular "outrages" before they were indicted.[5] There is a little evidence to suggest that in the deeply traditional West of England, where food rioting was almost a tolerated mode of "negotiation", the authorities found the indictment of female rioters to be distasteful. In 1765

[1] For a Bicester (Oxfordshire) wheat riot in 1757, 4 men and 4 women were tried, of whom 1 man and 1 woman were sentenced to 7 years transportation; for a riot involving beans, 2 men were transported, and 1 woman was branded: Thwaites, thesis, pp. 471, 473.

[2] Bohstedt, "Gender, Household and Community Politics", p. 120, note 116.

[3] PRO, Assi 24/42, 24/43, 4/20, 4/21, 4/22. I have only counted cases of riot related explicitly to food.

[4] Douglas Hay has found women leading food riots in Staffordshire in 1740, 1757, 1783 and 1800: "Crime, Authority and the Criminal Laws in Staffordshire 1750-1800" (Univ. of Warwick Ph.D. thesis, 1975), p. 265, and private communication.

[5] In 1795 miners from the Forest of Dean searched a trow at Awre on the Severn. Finding wheat and flour, 100 men, women and children came down from the Forest with horses and asses and carried off 500 bushels. According to a witness "the women were more riotous than the men". But 5 miners were arrested, of whom 2 were hanged for stealing flour; PRO, Assi 5/116; London Chronicle, 17-19 Nov. 1795.

Tiverton was convulsed by community-and-trade riots
against the Mayor and Corporation, in which (according to
literary evidence) the women were most prominent, dashing
in upon the Mayor through the windows of an inn, pulling
off his wig and threatening to kill him if he did not sign a
paper. But of twenty-six indicted for these riots, only six were
women.[1] But, then, what was the function of prosecution?
In the Western circuit the prosecution of food rioters seems
to have been a haphazard and often a lenient process. It was
often difficult to persuade the grand jury to find a true bill
against food rioters, and (once found) the petty jury might
not convict. For a Devon attack on a bolting-mill in 1767,
twenty-one were discharged and in two cases a bill could "not
be found" by the grand jury, and for another attack on a mill
all of eighteen indicted in Ottery St Mary were "not to be
found".[2] And so on. A little more zeal was shown in 1795
and 1800-1, but a Devon forced sale in 1801 resulted in the
acquittal of five men charged and no process against the only
woman, while the prosecution was abandoned of two men
indicted for terrorising a farmer (with a rope about his neck)
to sign a paper. On the other hand four women from
Montacute (Somerset) were indicted for grand larceny for
compelling Elizabeth Hopkins to sell seventy-two loaves at a
lower rate than she was willing, and Mary Gard and Sarah
Baker were convicted.[3]

In several other cases in both Western and Oxford circuits
the offenders were bound over with one shilling fine, or were
discharged as "paupers".[4] This suggests that the function of
prosecution was to inspire momentary terror until order
could be restored, and that the accused would be brought to a
due state of contrition by the anxiety and nuisance of the trial

[1] PRO, Assi 24/42, Devon, Summer 1765; F. J. Snell, *The Chronicles
of Twyford* (Tiverton, 1893), pp. 192-201.
[2] PRO, Assi 24/42. Those whose indictments were "not to be found"
by the grand jury in Ottery St Mary included 4 carpenters, 4 woolcombers,
3 husbandmen, 2 tailors, 2 labourers, 2 cordwainers, 1 thatcher.
[3] PRO, Assi 24/43.
[4] In a Taunton cheese riot, 11 men and 6 women were indicted. All
were found "paupers" and discharged. The "paupers" included 3 woolcombers, 2 serge weavers, 2 cordwainers, 2 labourers, 1 whitesmith,
1 fuller: and 3 spinsters, the wives of a cordwainer, a labourer and a serge
weaver; PRO, Assi 24/42, Somerset, Winter 1767.

itself. Prosecution was attended with difficulties — the selection of offenders, the drilling of reluctant witnesses, the odium attaching to the prosecutor — and local magistrates (notoriously in the West) were reluctant to set the process in motion.[1] Since prosecution was both selective and uncertain — that is, it was undertaken to provide an "example" but had no necessary direct relation to the incidence of riot — it cannot be assumed that it was gender-blind. Except in cases where women were manifestly predominant in riots, the authorities might have found it to be more convenient to make an example of men.

There might even have been a hierarchy of levels of prosecution, with differing gender ratios at each level. At the top of the hierarchy would be the Special Commissions of Oyer and Terminer which government instituted in late 1766 with the aim of making "examples" in the disturbed districts. Those brought to trial here were predominantly male: thirteen men in Berkshire, and no women; fifteen men in Wiltshire, and four women; and in Gloucestershire fifty-four men and twelve women.[2] There may have been some reluctance to launch women into a process which might end in their execution,[3] but once so launched it is difficult to say whether they received any preferential treatment from the courts.[4] Of the Wiltshire women, Priscilla Jenkins was sentenced to death for stealing in a dwelling-house (commuted to life transportation), Elizabeth Moody and Mary

[1] See Wells, *Wretched Faces*, ch. 16, "The Role of the Courts".

[2] These are the formal returns in Baga de Secretis, *G.B. Deputy Keeper of Public Records, 5th Report* (1844), Appendix II, pp. 198-204. But some prisoners were held over for subsequent trial or their cases were dismissed. The *Gloucester Journal*, 15 Dec. 1766, reported that 96 rioters were then in prison, of whom 16 were women: see also Williams, thesis, pp. 162-3. But other records suggest that as many as 22 women were committed: cases against one or two were dropped, and another turned evidence against her fellows; crown brief, PRO, TS 11/1188/5956, and "A Calendar of the Criminal Prisoners in the Castle Gaol of Gloucester", 13 Dec. 1766 (annotated) in TS 11/995/3707.

[3] This is suggested by John Beattie in his authoritative article, "The Criminality of Women in Eighteenth-Century England", *Journal of Soc. Hist.*, viii, (1975), p. 113, note 57. Also Beattie, *Crime and the Courts in England, 1660-1800* (Oxford, 1986), pp. 436-9.

[4] Booth, *op. cit.*, p. 106 finds that in the courts in Lancashire 1790-1801 "no differentiation seems to have been made between the sexes".

Nash were transported for seven years for stealing to the value of 1s. 7d. in a dwelling-house, and Sarah Pane, a widow, found guilty of stealing flour to the value of 6d., was privately whipped and discharged. This seems severe enough. But these were the counts upon which juries had been willing to convict. On a closer view it seems that they had been selected for trial because all except Sarah Pane, went beyond "food riot" to theft from the homes of farmers or traders. Priscilla Jenkins was supposed to have taken off a gammon of bacon, a pair of boots, a bundle of things on her head tied up in a handkerchief. . . and a gun. Elizabeth Moody and Mary Nash were not such desperate felons, but they were accused of breaking into a house, smashing the windows and some of the furniture, and carrying off the family's clothes. [1]

A little more can be worked out about the Gloucestershire accused. [2] The Special Commission at Gloucester was restrained by a grand jury which refused to act as a rubber-stamp and perhaps by a reluctant petty jury. Of twenty-one women who were being prepared for trial, one was not indicted, presumably as *feme couvert*. More than one-half of the remainder were either acquitted (eight) or the grand jury found "ignoramus" (three). Of seventy-five male prisoners, about the same proportion got off, with eighteen acquittals and twenty "no true bills". And there is no great difference in the conviction rate: seven out of twenty-one women as against thirty-five out of seventy-five men. The marked difference is in the severity of the convictions and sentencing. Sixteen of the men were convicted of felonies, nineteen of misdemeanours, whereas only two of the women were found felons and five were found guilty of misdemeanours. Nine rioters were sentenced to death — all men, although in six cases the condemned were reprieved — and nine were

---

[1] Crown briefs in PRO, TS 11/1116/5728. Elizabeth Moody and Mary Nash were both pregnant, giving birth immediately after their trials, Mary Nash with twins: it is not clear whether their sentences were enforced. See Williams, *op. cit.*, pp. 167, 170.

[2] Some of the following deductions depend upon rough annotations to the Gaol Calendar in PRO, TS 11/995/3707, but these are difficult to decipher and not always accurate. Also TS 11/1188/5956; Williams, *op. cit.*; *Gloucester Journal*, 22 Dec. 1766; Gloucester CRO, Q/SG 1767-70, Gloucester Gaol Calendar, 13 Jan. 1767.

sentenced to seven years' transportation, of whom two were women.

A closer view of the cases does not tell us much. Six of the female acquittals were for a cheese riot at Farmer Collett's, for which one man was also acquitted and one other man convicted. Mary Hillier ran after the mob in Minchin-hampton and "told them Mr Butt was come home & had fired a gun and killed 2 children and desired them to come back and pull down the House". The grand jury found no true bill. Elizabeth Rackley and Elizabeth Witts, both sentenced to transportation, were convicted of stealing 10d. worth of flour, but as part of several night-time break-ins of the mill of Richard Norris. It was the night-time breaking and entering which made the offence felony.[1] The clearest case of gender discrimination concerned John Franklyn and Sarah Franklyn, his wife, jointly committed for entering a shop in Stroud and carrying off in their laps soap, glue and other things. But Sarah was not indicted, presumably because while acting with her husband she was, according to the legal doctrine of *feme couvert*, not responsible for her actions. That was fortunate for her, since John Franklyn was found guilty of grand larceny and was transported for seven years.[2]

This suggests that the heavier exercises of the courts might fall a little less heavily on women. But the lighter exercises need not show the same gender inflection. Summary committals to Bridewells or convictions for minor public order offences were used by magistrates to cool off a crowd, without respect for differences of sex. For example, a letter from Lincolnshire in 1740 notes that "we have had a Disturbance by the Mobb at Bourn they Cutt Some Sacks of Wheat in the Boat & Obstructed its passage to Spalding for a time, but was Quel'd seasonably by the Officers of the Town & 5 Women Committed to the House of Correction".[3] Such episodes are unlikely to have left traces in national records,

[1] Elizabeth Rackley was later pardoned.
[2] Gaol Calendar in PRO, TS 11/995/3707. On *feme couvert*, see Blackstone, *op. cit.*, iv, pp. 26-7 and John Beattie, *op. cit.*, p. 238, note 71.
[3] Letter of John Halford, 1 July 1740, in Lincs., Archives Office, 3 Anc. 7/4/14.

although after the 1760s they were more likely to be brought to Quarter Sessions.[1]

John Bohstedt tells us that "repression did not know gender", and he is right that troops were frequently ordered to fire into mixed crowds. From Anne Carter of Maldon, Essex, in 1629 to Hannah Smith of Manchester in 1812, a trickle of victims or heroines were sent to the gallows, while others were sentenced to transportation.[2] Yet I am undecided; it remains possible that, while "examples" were made from time to time, the examples made of women were fewer, that they sometimes enjoyed the "privilege of their sex", and that much depended upon place, time and the temper of the authorities.

If the central authorities insisted that examples had to be made, then gender did not matter. In 1766 government and law officers were pressing hard for capital offenders to be selected, and the Treasury Solicitor regretted that "at Leicester, the Evidence is very slight, against a Woman for throwing Cheese out of a Waggon to the Mob, which if not a Highway Robbery, is not Capital".[3] (Hannah Smith was convicted of highway robbery nearly fifty years later, for selling off butter cheaply to the crowd.) In the end, no women were hanged for the riots of 1766, although Sarah Hemmings was capitally convicted for her part in a riot in Wolverhampton: the town petitioned for her life, and the sentence was commuted to life transportation.[4] In 1800 *The Times* correspondent lamented from Nottingham and its environs that "there is not even a prospect of the riot

[1] Ann Welford and Barbara Mason were sentenced to six months hard labour at Northampton Quarter Sessions in 1796 for trying, with a great number of persons, "principally women", to stop a market wagon: *Northampton Mercury*, 9 Apr. 1796. My thanks to Jeanette Neeson.

[2] For Anne Carter, see John Walter, "Grain Riots and Popular Attitudes to the Law: Maldon and the Crisis of 1629", in Brewer and Styles (eds.), *An Ungovernable People*, pp. 47-84, an excellent study which follows the rioters back into the local records. For Hannah Smith, see Thomis and Grimmett, *op. cit.*, pp. 43-44.

[3] Memorandum as to the state of evidence against food rioters (1766) from Treasury Solicitor in Shelburne Papers, Vol. 132, William L. Clements Library, University of Michigan, Ann Arbor; see also PRO, SP Dom 44/141.

[4] Williams, "Midland Hunger Riots in 1766", p. 277.

subsiding", owing to the non-arrest of the women, who were "the principal aggressors".[1] In the sixteenth and early seventeenth centuries, women rioters had been liminal people with an "ambivalent legal status at the margins of the law's competence". They claimed, in enclosure riots, "that women were lawlesse, and not subject to the lawes of the realme as men are but might. . . offend without drede or punishment of law".[2] If the sex had been disabused of that illusion in the eighteenth century, yet perhaps some notion of "privilege", both among offenders and prosecutors, lingered on in such regions as the West.

Were there other peculiarities of the feminine input into food riots? I doubt the value of tabulating disorder and violence according to gender, partly because of the imperfect nature of the evidence, partly because all riot must involve disorder and violence of some kind. When an affair involved outright confrontation, with cudgels against fire-arms — the attack on a mill, the break-in to a keep to rescue prisoners — the predominant sex would be male. The women are more commonly reported as throwing missiles — stones or potatoes — and on one occasion, in the Midlands in 1766 "planted in rows five or six deep", defending a bridge with stones and brickbats against horsemen.[3] Whatever conclusions we reach as to the gender reciprocities and respect between women and men in these communities, it would be foolish to suppose that these dissolved sexual differences. Without doubt the physical confrontation of men and women, of soldiers and crowd, aroused sexual tensions, perhaps expressed by the women in robust ribaldry, by the male forces of "order" in a contest between the inhibition of violence and sexually-excited aggression.[4] On occasion the military affected contempt for the women. The commander of troops sent to deal with a riot in Bromsgrove in 1795

[1] Wells, op. cit., p. 121.
[2] John Walter in An Ungovernable People, p. 63; see also Roger B. Manning, Village Revolts (Oxford, 1988), pp. 96, 116.
[3] Williams, op. cit., pp. 273-4.
[4] After "repeated solicitations" from a Captain of marines, the constable of Brentwood reluctantly arrested two women, in "The Ship" alehouse, who had been "singing a song in Brentwood Street reflecting on the military": Essex CRO, Q/SBb 352/55 (Aug. 1793).

complained loftily that they found the cause was "a parcel of old women. . . as in all pretended riots in this part of the country". But this parcel of women (not all of whom were old) had given a good account of themselves, some seventy of them stopping a wagon and six horses, and carrying off twenty-nine sacks of wheaten flour.[1]

When women rioted they made no attempt to disguise their sex or to apologise for it. In my view there was very little cross-dressing in food riots, although once or twice there are unconfirmed reports of men in women's clothes.[2] These "rites of inversion" or, maybe, simple exercises in the most available disguise, were more commonly encountered in turn-pike riots, in "carnival" protests, and, later, in Luddism.[3] But inversion, whether intentional or not, was exactly what the women did *not* wish to achieve. So far from wishing to present an ominous androgynous image, they sought to present their particular right, according to tradition and gender role, as guardians of the children, of the household, of the livelihood of the community. That symbolism — the blood-stained loaves on poles, the banging of kitchen ware — belonged especially to the women's protests. They evinced what Temma Kaplan has called "female consciousness" rather than feminist, which rested upon "their acceptance of the sexual division of labor" which is one which "assigns women the responsibility of preserving life". "Experiencing reciprocity among themselves and competence in preserving

[1] PRO, WO 1/1091, 5 and 8 Aug. 1795; Assi 2/26 and 5/116.

[2] *Jackson's Oxford Journal*, 28 May 1757 reports a wagon of wheat taken away in Bath by a mob in women's clothes. I have not found any eighteenth-century indictment for such an offence in a food riot.

[3] See Natalie Davis, "Women on Top", in *Society and Culture in Early Modern France* (Stanford, 1975). I think Professor Davis overlooks the fact that a woman's gown was the most readily-available garment to disguise a collier or a cottager. Some of the upside-down symbolic effects (which she describes so well) were consequence rather than intention. Attacks on turnpikes had more military symbolism: "Deponent saith. . . they heard the Noise of Horns blowing. . . and soon after a great Number of Persons armed with Guns & Axes, some of them disguised with black'd faces and Womens Cloathes. . .". This was an attack on a turnpike gate in Ledbury, Herefordshire. James Baylis, labourer, who was apprehended said that he had blacked his face with a burnt cork, and that the gown, apron and straw hat which he wore were his wife's: informations in PRO, TS 11/1122/5824, 4 Nov. 1735.

life instills women with a sense of their collective right to administer daily life, even if they must confront authority to do so.[1]

Nothing pleased female rioters more than the humiliation of pompous male "aggro". In a Tiverton riot in 1754 a certain Lieutenant Suttie attracted the crowd's notice by his zeal; he was heard to say to a JP, "Give me leave sir, to order the men to fire, and you shall see the fellows hop like peas". The troopers were unleashed upon the crowd and they "rode through the streets hacking with their broad-swords and stabbing with their bayonets":

> While the troopers were dashing about in the execution of their orders, some women seized Lieutenant Suttie by the collar and took away his sword, which he never recovered. This was a sore blow to his pride, and a favourite subject of banter on the part of his friends, who, very cruelly, would not allow him to forget his skirmish with the women and the inglorious loss of his weapon.[2]

Not for the first or last time, disarming symbolised emasculation.

Men in authority still feared the violence and the incitement of the female tongue (see below pp. 501-2), and women could sometimes attain their ends by mockery, insult, or by shaming farmers or dealers by their expostulations. Susannah Soons was convicted in Norwich in 1767 for "uttering several scandalous and inflammatory speeches", and Mary Watts in Leicester for "assaulting" the magistrates "with indecent and opprobrious Language and Gestures".[3] In Montrose in 1812, when the Riot Act was being read and the military were deployed to disperse the crowd, Elizabeth Beattie called out, "Will no person take that paper out of his hand?" and tried to snatch the Act from the magistrate.[4]

Elizabeth Beattie knew what she was doing. But so did Anne Carter, in 1629. She clearly despised the pomp of the local authorities, calling one of Maldon's chief magistrates in 1622 "bloud sucker and. . . many other unseemely tearmes".

[1] Temma Kaplan, "Female Consciousness and Collective Action: The Case of Barcelona, 1910-1918", *Signs*, vii, 3 (1982), pp. 545, 560, 565.

[2] Snell, *The Chronicles of Twyford*, pp. 194-5. This was an election riot.

[3] Williams, thesis, pp. 203, note 2, and p. 279.

[4] Logue, *op. cit.*, p. 22.

When the bailiff had questioned her about her absence from church, she had answered back: "that yf he woold prouid [provide] wone to doe hir worke shee would goe". In the riots she described herself as "Captain", calling out: "Come, my brave lads of Maldon, I will be your leader for we will not starve." [1] "General Jane Bogey" in Newcastle in 1740 knew what she was doing, and so did "Lady Ludd", the title claimed by leaders of riots in 1812 in both Nottingham and Leeds. [2] So too did fifty-four-year-old Hannah Smith who "headed up the mob" for some days in Manchester in the same year, bringing down the prices of potatoes, butter and milk, and boasting that she could raise a crowd in a minute. [3] It was lack of deference as much as rioting which got Anne Carter and Hannah Smith hanged. What clergyman was likely to give a character reference, what nobleman to intercede, on behalf of such viragos?

The women's riots may not have been precisely of the same violence quotient as the men's, but they were not shrinking, demure affairs. Frequently they came to a climax when women led off the fore-horses, climbed aboard the wagons and threw down the sacks to their fellows, sometimes took the horses out of the shafts and pulled the wagon back themselves to a place for convenient distribution of its load. [4] In the engagement at Newport Pagnell in 1740 (above pp. 319-20), the women fought with the farmers for a considerable time, declaring that they were "unwilling that so much Wheat should go out of the Kingdom, while they wanted bread, [and] swore they would lose their lives before they would part with it". At length "with great acclamations of joy the waggons were unloaded". The reporter of the *Northampton Mercury* found that the affair merited a little comment:

[1] Walter, *op. cit.*, pp. 58, 72.
[2] Ellis, *op. cit.*, p. 340; Thomis and Grimmett, *op. cit.*, p. 31.
[3] *Ibid.*, pp. 43-5.
[4] For examples, see *Derby Mercury*, 10 July 1740 (Derby 1740). Elizabeth Beer and Elizabeth Bell were each sentenced to 7 years transportation for their part in this riot. Information of Thos. Higgins against Ann Burdon, who stopped his wagon in Long Handborough in August 1795, took the horse out of the shafts, and got into the shafts to prevent the horses being put back in: PRO, Assi 5/116.

The Conquerors are now holding a Grand Council to consider what to do with it among themselves. Such uncommon Bravery and Resolution appearing in the soft & tender Sex is a Matter of Surprize to those who stile themselves their despotick Sovereigns, & the Lords of Creation.[1]

Such bravery was not uncommon. Repeatedly women faced troops and were fired upon. In one of the only letters that survives from a food rioter, he wrote of a great riot in Nottingham (1800): "your hearts would have ached to have seen the women Calling for Bread and Declaring they would fight till they died Before they would be used so any longer. . . the conduct of the people. . . who stood the fire from the yeomanry with such undaunted courage that astonished the gentlemen for they poured such showers of stones on them in all directions that they could load their pieces no more after they had fired them. . .".[2]

Perhaps the poor of both sexes partnered each other better in bad times than we suppose. Maybe men were more prominent in food riots than women, and maybe not.[3] But if one adds up all that is already known (and there is much still to find out) there were an awful lot of women involved in food riots, sometimes on their own, more often in mixed affairs in which there was a loyal gender partnership.

For two hundred and more years these food riots were the most visible and public expressions of working women's lack of deference and their contestation with authority. As such these evidences contest, in their turn, the stereotypes of feminine submission, timidity, or confinement to the private world of the household. Robert Southey (p. 234) may not have been so silly after all. Indeed, when once aroused the women may have been more passionate than men in their eloquence, less heedful of the consequences, and, in their role

---

[1] *Northampton Mercury*, 2 June 1740; *Ipswich Journal*, 7 June 1740.

[2] Intercepted letter of J. and L. Golby to "Dear Brother and Sister", dated Nottingham 7 Sept. 1800, in PRO, HO 42/51. Extracts of the letter are in Quinault and Stevenson (eds.), *op. cit.*, pp. 58-9 and in Wells, *Wretched Faces*, pp. 120-2.

[3] Or maybe the answer differed according to place and time. Walter, *op. cit.*, p. 62 writes that "women were present in almost every food riot in the period [i.e. early seventeenth century] and some riots were exclusively feminine affairs".

as guardians of the family, more determined to get quick results.[1] Perhaps — as John Bohstedt suggests — many women were more immersed than were men "in the moral, less in the market, economy", and they were among the last to give the practices of the moral economy up.[2]

That is not the whole truth about women and authority, but food riots provide an important and weighty chunk of evidence, which must not be tidied away. It may enlarge our sense of the possibilities of feminine "nature". The more difficult question may be, not why women sometimes rioted, but why, in the mid nineteenth century, the tradition of public protest became so much weaker and women's presence retreated into a serial world of private households.[3] Perhaps (in contrast to what came after) a "myth of the feminine food riot" should be rehabilitated after all?

IV

I do not know how far back one must go to find the origin of the term, "moral economy". I think that it comes from the late eighteenth century, but I cannot now find references. It

[1] Tom Wedgwood wrote to his father, Josiah, describing "the mob" in the Potteries in March 1783: "The women were much worse than the men, as for example, Parson Sneyd got about 30 men to follow him. . . but a woman cried: 'Nay, nay, that wunna do, that wunna do', and so they turned back again, and it was agreed that the corn taken [in] the boat should be sold at a fair price": *The Wedgwood Letters*, ed. Ann Finer and G. Savage (1965), p. 268. My thanks to Douglas Hay.

[2] Women and miners were prominent in traditional price-setting in south-west England in 1847, and women and fishermen in north-east Scotland: A. Rowe, "Food Riots of the Forties in Cornwall", *Royal Cornwall Polytechnic Society* (1942); E. Richards, *The Last Scottish Food Riots, Past and Present Supplement* (1981). See also Roger E. Swift, "Food Riots in Mid-Victorian Exeter, 1847-67", *Southern History*, 2 (1980). Robert Storch, in a most interesting study, shows how in 1867 in Devon and Oxfordshire, traditions of food riot, of rough music, and of "Guy Fawkes" carnival came together, with the women and the disguised "bonfire boys" playing the leading roles: "Popular Festivity and Consumer Protest: Food Price Disturbances in the Southwest and Oxfordshire in 1867", *Albion*, 14, 3-4 (1982). Although women were often the most active in these events, few of the women were arrested or brought to trial. See Storch, p. 233, note 41.

[3] Dorothy Thompson, "Women and Nineteenth-Century Radical Politics: a Lost Dimension", in Juliet Mitchell and Ann Oakley (eds.), *The Rights and Wrongs of Women* (Harmondsworth, 1976), pp. 112-138.

was certainly around in the 1830s,[1] and it was used by
Bronterre O'Brien, the Chartist, in 1837 in a polemic against
political economists:

> True political economy is like true domestic economy; it does not
> consist solely in slaving and saving; there is a moral economy as well as
> political. . . These quacks would make wreck of the affections, in
> exchange for incessant production and accumulation. . . It is, indeed,
> the MORAL ECONOMY that they always keep out of sight. When they
> talk about the tendency of large masses of capital, and the division of
> labour, to increase production and cheapen commodities, they do not
> tell us of the inferior human being which a single and fixed occupation
> must necessarily produce.[2]

This directly anti-capitalist usage is close to that which I
introduce into *The Making of the English Working Class*,
when I referred to food riots as being "legitimized by the
assumptions of an older moral economy, which taught the
immorality of. . . profiteering upon the necessities of the
people". And I went on to describe the food riots of 1795 as
"a last desperate effort" to re-impose the "old paternalist
moral economy" as against the economy of the free
market.[3]

I subsequently defined more carefully the term, the
practices associated with it, and the contradictory components of paternalist control and crowd rebellion. The
reason for this retrospective enquiry is that the theory of a
moral economy has now taken off in more than one direction
and in several fields of specialist study, and my essay is sometimes cited as authority. But while the term is available for
every development which can be justified, my own usage has
in general been confined to confrontations in the market-
place over access (or entitlement) to "necessities" —
essential food. It is not only that there is an identifiable

[1] Thus Robert Southey was claiming to espouse "MORAL versus
political economy", see David Eastwood, "Robert Southey and the
Intellectual Origins of Romantic Conservatism", *Eng. Hist. Rev.*, civ
(1989), p. 323. The "moral economy of the factory system" was employed
in a very different sense by Dr Andrew Ure in *The Philosophy of
Manufactures* (1835).
[2] *Bronterre's National Reformer*, 21 Jan. 1837. I am indebted to
Dorothy Thompson for this reference.
[3] (Penguin, 1968), pp. 67-73.

CUSTOMS IN COMMON

bundle of beliefs, usages and forms associated with the marketing of food in time of dearth, which it is convenient to bind together in a common term, but the deep emotions stirred by dearth, the claims which the crowd made upon the authorities in such crises, and the outrage provoked by profiteering in life-threatening emergencies, imparted a particular "moral" charge to protest. All of this, taken together, is what I understand by moral economy.[1]

If the term is to be extended to other contexts, then it must be redefined or there will be some loss of focus. Adrian Randall has so redefined it, in applying it to "The Industrial Moral Economy of the Gloucestershire Weavers" in the eighteenth century.[2] The same weaving communities that were involved in food riots (1766) were involved in industrial actions (1756); these were informed by the same values, showed the same community solidarities and sanctions (such as rough music against those who broke the norms of the trade), a similar appeal to custom and to Tudor and Stuart statute law (when this protected their own interests), and a similar insistence that, where the community's economic well-being was concerned, market forces and the profits of individuals should be subdued to custom. Moreover, Randall

---

[1] Similar "moral economy" themes have been examined in different national histories — notably (France) Louise Tilly, "The Food Riot as a Form of Political Conflict in France", *Journal of Interdisciplinary History*, i (1971), pp. 23-57, and Cynthia A. Bouton, "L' 'économie morale' et la Guerre des farines de 1775", and also the editors' "Introduction" in Florence Gauthier and Guy-Robert Ikni (eds.), *La Guerre du Blé au XVIIIe Siécle* (Paris, 1988); Laura Rodriguez, "The Spanish Riots of 1766", *Past and Present*, 59 (1973); Barbara Clark Smith, "Food Rioters in the American Revolution", in Alfred F. Young, (ed.), *Beyond the American Revolution* (Urbana, forthcoming); John Rogers, "The 1866 Grain Riots in Sri Lanka", *Comparative Studies in Society and History*, xxix, 3 (1987).

[2] A. J. Randall in John Rule (ed.), *British Trade Unionism, 1750-1850* (1988), pp. 29-51. See also Charlesworth and Randall, "Morals, Markets and the English Crowd", pp. 206-9. Professor Charles Tilly, in a private communication, has suggested a further definition: "The term 'moral economy' makes sense when claimants to a commodity can invoke non-monetary rights to that commodity, and third parties will act to support *these* claims — when, for example, community membership supersedes price as a basis of entitlement. To the extent that moral economy comes merely to mean tradition, custom, or exchange outside the established market, it loses its conceptual force.".

shows that the industrial crowd also would seek to press the gentry into the role of conciliators and arbitrators, so that "the moral economy was the obverse of the paternalist model".

I am more than half persuaded by this argument. In those West of England clothing towns there was a dense texture of trade rituals and customary usages, endorsed by community sanctions, which may be seen as the stubborn plebeian under-side to mercantilist industry. Of course these workers were habituated to an economy with markets, but markets conducted within customary norms; in times of conflict they affirmed the priorities of "the Trade", or they elevated the defence of the interests of the working community above those of the profits of the few, and if the term "moral economy" helps us to identify these norms and practices, then let it be used. It certainly helps us to see the strongly defensive, and, in that sense, conservative nature of this plebeian culture.

But where are we to draw the line? Pirates had strongly-transmitted usages and customs: did they have a moral economy.[1] Keith Snell suggests that the poor's right to a settlement "formed a consistent part of those 'moral economy' values" which I have analysed. And he extends the list of candidates for inclusion in this moral economy to the poor laws generally, to yearly hirings and "fair wages", and even to "popular consumption, fashion [and] leisure activities". *Then* he turns around and gives me a dressing-down for "the amorphous character" of my moral economy.[2]

I admire Dr Snell's work, but on this occasion I am perplexed, because I can see little evidence that he knows much about the tensions around the nexus of food in time of dearth. What is "amorphous" is his own extension of the term's use, and this stems from the error of supposing that what are at issue are "moral economy *values*". But if values, on their own, make a moral *economy* then we will be turning up moral economies everywhere. My own notion of the moral

---

[1] Marcus Rediker, *Between the Devil and the Deep Blue Sea* (Cambridge, 1987), ch. 6.

[2] K. D. M. Snell, *Annals of the Labouring Poor* (Cambridge, 1985), pp. 99-199, 103.

economy of the crowd in the food market includes ideal models or ideology (just as political economy does), which assigns economic roles and which endorses customary practices (an alternative "economics"), in a particular balance of class or social forces. It is by taking "values" or "moral attitudes" out of the context of a particular historical formation that Snell gets his amorphous results.

However, I have no right to patent the term. Some historians prefer a more descriptive and looser use. No other term seems to offer itself to describe the way in which, in peasant and in early industrial communities, many "economic" relations are regulated according to non-monetary norms. These exist as a tissue of customs and usages until they are theatened by monetary rationalisations and are made self-conscious *as* a "moral economy". In this sense, the moral economy is summoned into being in resistance to the economy of the "free market".[1] As Charlesworth and Randall have argued, "The basis of the moral economy was that very sense of community which a common experience of capitalist industry generated".[2] The rationalisations or "modernisations" of the capitalist market offended against community norms and continually called into being a "moral" antagonist.

This is an extension which is further generalised by William Reddy in *The Rise of Market Culture*, for whom the moral economy is "a set of values and moral standards that were violated by technical and commercial change":

Defence of such moral standards need not have been motivated by memory of the past. The inadequacy of market language was constantly being brought to the laborer's attention by the very conditions of work.

And Reddy concludes that "something like a moral economy is bound to surface anywhere that industrial capitalism

[1] The great British miners' strike of 1984 was a late example of such a confrontation, although "free market" forces appeared in the guise of every resource of the State.

[2] Charlesworth and Randall, "Morals, Markets and the English Crowd", p. 213.

spreads".[1] This has the advantage of discarding the notion that "moral economy" must always be traditional, "backward-looking", etc.; on the contrary, it is continuously regenerating itself as anti-capitalist critique, as a resistance movement.[2] We are close to the language of Bronterre O'Brien. But what this gains in breadth it loses in focus, and in inexpert hands may bleed off the edge into uncontextual moralistic rhetoric.[3]

There is less danger of this in the alert theoretical discussions in the field of peasant studies, where a "moral economy theory" is now at the centre of controversy. This is thanks to James C. Scott whose *The Moral Economy of the Peasant* (1976) generalised an argument derived from studies in Lower Burma and Vietnam. The term is drawn from my own essay but it is now brought to bear upon "peasant conceptions of social justice, of rights and obligations, of reciprocity". But what distinguishes Scott's use is that it goes much further than descriptive accounts of "values" or "moral attitudes". Since for the peasantry, subsistence depends upon access to land, customs of land use and of entitlement to its produce are now at the centre of analysis rather than the marketing of food. And custom is seen (against a background of memories of famine) as perpetuating subsistence imperatives, and usages which insure the community against risk. These imperatives are also expressed in protective landlord-tenant (or patron-client) relations, and in resistances to technical innovations and to market rationalisations, where these might entail risks in the event of crisis. Scott analyses village redistributive institutions and religious charitable obligations, and shows that "there is good reason for viewing both the norm of reciprocity and the

[1] William Reddy, *The Rise of Market Culture* (Cambridge, Mass., 1984), pp. 331-4.

[2] Carl Gersuny and Gladys Kaufman, "Seniority and the Moral Economy of U.S. Automobile Workers, 1934-46", *Journal of Social History*, xviii (1985), extend the notion into non-"economic" trade union defences.

[3] A danger which Reddy himself does not wholly avoid in his sequel, *Money and Liberty in Modern Europe* (Cambridge, 1987), in which "asymmetrical monetary exchange" is made the key to all modern history, wherein "honour" and "money" enact an unequal contest.

right to subsistence as genuine moral components of the
'little tradition'. . ." — that is, in peasant culture universally.
The threat to these institutions and norms associated with
European expansion and with market rationalisations has
often provoked the peasantry to participation in revolutionary movements.[1]

There is some likeness here to the moral economy of the
eighteenth-century English crowd, although Scott does not
elaborate the comparison and he is in fact more interested in
patron-client relations in the village rather than in those
confrontations or negotiations which mark the European
tradition of food riot.[2] Predictably his theories have been
vigorously contested by protagonists of "market forces", and
Samuel L Popkin delivered a polemic against what were
presented as "the moral economists" in *The Rational
Peasant* (1979). This offered the characteristic peasant as a
rational actor, shrewdly adjusting to the market economy in a
satisfactorily self-interested and normless manner. So that
the old debate between moral and political economists
seemed likely to re-enact itself over the paddy fields of South-
East Asia — a debate into which it would be foolish for me to
enter, although my sympathies are certainly with James
Scott.

However, Professor Scott has moved the debate forwards
(and sideways) in his *Weapons of the Weak*, and onto
territory where comparisons may be explored with advantage. This territory is not only that of the tenacious forms of
resistance to power of the weak and of the poor: "in
ridicule, in truculence, in irony, in petty acts of non-
compliance, in dissimulation. . . in the disbelief in elite
homilies, in the steady and grinding efforts to hold one's own

---

[1] James C. Scott, *The Moral Economy of the Peasant: Rebellion and
Subsistence in Southeast Asia* (New Haven, 1976). See also James M.
Polachek, "The Moral Economy of the Kiangsi Soviet", *Journal of Asian
Studies*, xlii, 4 (1983), p. 825.

[2] For constructive criticism, see David Hunt, "From the Millenium to
the Everyday: James Scott's Search for the Essence of Peasant Politics",
Radical Hist. Rev., 42 (1988), pp. 155-72; Michael Adas, " 'Moral
Economy' or 'Contest State'?", *Journal of Social History*, xiii, 4 (1980).

against overwhelming odds".[1] It is also, and at the same time, into the limits which the weak can impose upon power. As Barrington Moore has argued in *Injustice*:

> In any stratified society. . . there is a set of limits on what both rulers and subjects, dominant and subordinate groups can do. There is also a set of mutual obligations that bind the two together. Such limits and obligations are not set down in formal written constitutions or contracts. . .

There is (rather) "an unverbalized set of mutual understandings", and "what takes place is a continual probing on the part of rulers and subjects to find out what they can get away with, to test and *discover* the limits of obedience and disobedience". This takes us, by way of the concept of social reciprocity, or, as Moore prefers, mutual obligation ("a term that does *not* imply equality of burdens or obligations"),[2] back to the "moral economy", in the sense of the equilibrium or "field of force" which I examined in Chapter I and in the bargaining between unequal social forces in which the weaker still has acknowledged claims upon the greater. Of those who have recently developed these ideas I find a particular sympathy with Michael Watts, whose *Silent Violence* examines food and famine among the Hausa in northern Nigeria. He sees the norms and practices of an imperative collective subsistence ethic as permeating the peasant universe, but he sees this without sentimentality:

> The moral economy was not especially moral and the Caliphate was certainly no Rousseauian universe of peasant welfare and benevolent patrons. Rather, the moral economy was necessary to the survival of ruler and ruled, and the price was paid by prevailing power blocs for the maintenance and reproduction of the social relations of production replete with its exploitative relations and class struggles.

[1] James C. Scott, *Weapons of the Weak: Everyday Forms of Peasant Resistance* (New Haven, 1985), p. 350. See also the editors' contributions in Andrew Turton and Shigeharu Tanabe (eds.), *History and Peasant Consciousness in South East Asia* (Osaka, 1984), and the special issue of the *Journals of Peasant Studies*, xiii, 2 (1986).

[2] Barrington Moore Jr, *Injustice: The Social Bases of Obedience and Revolt* (1978), pp. 18, 506.

"There is no need to saddle the moral economy with the legacy of Durkheim, Rousseau, and Ruskin."[1]

Much of the very interesting discussion which is now extending under the rubric of "moral economy" from African and Asian to Latin American[2] or to Irish studies has little to do with my (1971) usage but is concerned with the social dialectic of unequal mutuality (need and obligation) which lies at the centre of most societies. The term "moral economy" has won acceptance because it is less cumbersome than other terms (such as "dialectical asymmetrical reciprocity") which we might otherwise be clobbered with. When an Irish historian writes of "moral economy", he is writing of eighteenth-century paternalism, deference, and non-economic (i.e. unprofitable) "easygoing farming practices" such as low rents and tolerance of arrears.[3] A scholar (Paul Greenough) writing on the Bengal famine of 1943-44 has an even more extended definition:

> By 'moral economy' I mean the cluster of relations of exchange between social groups, and between persons, in which the welfare and the merit of both parties to the exchange takes precedence over other considerations such as the profit of the one or the other.[4]

These capacious definitions will certainly allow in most things we might wish to introduce, and if the term will encourage historians to discover and write about all those areas of human exchange to which orthodox economics was once blind, then this is a gain.

If we employ the terminology of class, then "moral economy" in this definition may be concerned with the way in which class relations are negotiated. It shows how

[1] Michael Watts, *Silent Violence: Food, Famine and Peasantry in Northern Nigeria* (Berkeley, 1983), pp. 106, 146.

[2] Leslie Anderson, "From Quiescence to Rebellion: Peasant Political Activity in Costa Rica and Pre-Revolutionary Nicaragua" (Univ. of Michigan Ph.D. thesis, 1987; Erick D. Langer, "Labor Strikes and Reciprocity on Chuquisaca Haciendas", *Hispanic American History Review*, lxv, 2, 1985.

[3] Thomas Bartlett, "An End to Moral Economy: The Irish Militia Disturbances of 1793", in C. H. E. Philpin (ed.), *Nationalism and Popular Protest in Ireland* (Cambridge, 1987).

[4] Paul R. Greenough, "Indian Famines and Peasant Victims: The Case of Bengal in 1943-44", *Modern Asian Studies*, xiv, 2 (1980), p. 207.

hegemony is not just imposed (or contested) but is articulated in the everyday intercourse of a community, and can be sustained only by concession and patronage (in good times), by at least the gestures of protection in bad.[1] Of the two parts of the term, the "economy" can probably now look after itself, since it will be defined in each scholar's practice. It is the "moral" part which may now require more attention. One benefit that has accrued from the term's transportation into peasant studies is that it can be viewed in operation within cultures whose moral premises are not identical with those of a Judeo-Christian inheritance.[2]

No-one has made this more explicit than has Professor Greenough in his study of Bengal famine, and he has done this on the directly comparative ground of the crisis of subsistence. Greenough presents a conspectus of the Bengali peasants' value-system,[3] and he derives this, not (as does Scott) from remembered scarcity and from risk-avoiding strategies, but, on the contrary, from a Bengal tradition of abundance. At the centre of this value-system is *Laksmi*, both a conception of order and abundance and a benevolent goddess of prosperity. Prosperity flows down from above, from *Laksmi*, or from "kings", patrons or parents. In its simplest form there are two situations only: the givers and the receivers of rice, and in time of crisis the peasant's reflex is to seek refuge in the patron-client relationship, to search for new patrons, or to wait in patience for *Laksmi's* gifts to be restored. Greenough also finds "an unyielding Bengali antipathy to individual assertion":

> Temple art, learned texts, and folk apothegms reiterate that whatever success one has comes only through a superior's benevolence. . . There is no widely accepted creed of commercial accumulation.[4]

[1] See Scott, *Weapons of the Weak*, ch. 8 — an excellent discussion of "hegemony" in this everyday sense.

[2] See also Charles F. Keyes, "Economic Action and Buddhist Morality in a Thai Village", *Journal of Asian Studies*, xlii, 4 (1983).

[3] Paul R. Greenough, *Prosperity and Misery in Modern Bengal* (Oxford, 1982), esp. ch. 1. Greenough derives his account from Hindu cosmology and is silent as to any differences between Hindu and Moslem villagers.

[4] Paul R. Greenough, "Indulgence and Abundance as Asian Peasant Values: a Bengali Case in Point", *Journal of Asian Studies*, xlii, 4 (1983), p. 842.

This brief summary will serve if it leaves us with the expectation that "giving" and beseeching "protection" are critical to the peasantry's discourse of crisis, rather than "duties" or "rights". Greenough finds in this an explanation for the Bengali response to famine. In the appalling conditions of 1943-44 attacks on granaries or shops were rare. "Food of all sorts lay before their eyes", while people were starving on the streets of Calcutta, "but no one attempted to seize it by force". The attitude of the people was one of "complete resignation", and "they attribute their misery to fate or *karma* alone. . .". An English medical officer contrasted this with the Punjab or the United Provinces where "you would have had terrific riots", and:

> The husbands and brothers would have had those food shops opened,
> but in Bengal they died in front of bulging food shops.
> Q. Bulging with grain?
> A. Yes, they died in the streets in front of shops bulging with grain.
> Q. Because they could not buy?
> A. Yes, and it was due to the passive, fatalistic attitude of those people
> that there were no riots. . .[1]

A leading Bengali Communist wrote with admiration of these villagers, "saturated with the love of peace and honesty", turning away from the path of looting, and with "unbounded fortitude. . . standing in the queue of death".[2] And regarding this evidence, Greenough concludes that this behaviour represented "the continued acceptance in a crisis of the very values which hitherto had sustained the victims"

> Abandoned victims could do no more than to dramatize their helpless-
> ness in the hope of re-stimulating a flow of benevolence. Mendicancy,
> cries and wails, imploring gestures, the exhibition of dead or dying
> children — all were part of the destitutes' attempts to evoke charity
> and to transfer responsibility for their nurture to new 'destined
> providers'.[3]

Professor Greenough's intervention is most welcome. But it does present certain difficulties. One set of difficulties arises from his interpretation of complex evidence. His reconstruction of the value-system of Bengali peasants bear

[1] Greenough, *Prosperity and Misery*, pp. 266-7.
[2] *Ibid.*, p. 268.
[3] *Ibid.*, p. 271.

the mark of a certain school of holistic anthropology and allows no space for variety and contradiction. This is most evident in his discussion of the demoralisation induced by prolonged dearth, the break-up of families, and the abandonment of wives and children by the father. Greenough concludes that "familial disintegration did not occur randomly but seems to have been a result of the intentional exclusion of less-valued family members from domestic subsistence". Such exclusion was "desperate but not reprehensible" and was "explicable in terms of Bengali moral conceptions". The most favoured member of the family (in this account) is the male family head, who might — even if he should be the only survivor — reconstitute the familial lineage. So deeply are these patriarchal values internalised that the abandoned passively assent to their own abandonment.[1]

This may be true, or may be part of the truth.[2] But Greenough hangs his interpretive apparatus upon slender evidence — a few accounts of the "banishment" of wives or desertion of families — and alternative interpretations are not tested.[3] And he affirms his conclusions in increasingly confident form, as if they were incontestible findings. What were "desperate" measures on one page becomes, fifty pages

[1] *Ibid.*, pp. 215-25 and "Indian Famines and Peasant Victims", pp. 225-33.

[2] Megan Vaughan in "Famine Analysis and Family Relations: 1949 in Nyasaland", *Past and Present*, 108 (1985), has similar disturbing evidence of the aged, the young and the disabled being abandoned, and of husbands abandoning their families: and M. Vaughan, *The Story of an African Famine. Gender and Famine in Twentieth-Century Malawi* (1987).

[3] Some men may have left their families in the hope of finding work (and sending remittances) or in the expectation that in their absence the wife's kin or village charities would support the family. Wives might have been encouraged to go begging as the ultimate recourse against starvation. Similarly, the sale of children may have been an ultimate strategy to secure their survival. (Greenough assumes that "the dominant motive" for selling children was to secure cash for the parents' food, or else to "relieve themselves of the intolerable clamoring of their children for food"! *Prosperity and Misery*, p. 221.) Greenough's account of age-differential mortality during famine (*ibid.*, ch. 6) makes no attempt to relate this to the findings of historical demography as to trends commonly encountered during subsistence crisis. Indeed his treatment of historical and demographic studies is cavalier: see David Arnold, *Famine*, pp. 89-90.

later, the sweeping assertion that "authority figures in
peasant households abandoned numerous dependents
deemed inessential for the reconstitution of family and
society in the post-crisis period".[1] What is found in extremity
is now offered as if it were the norm: "husbands and heads of
families appropriated domestic assets and abandoned their
spouses, and parents sold children for cash".[2]

We must leave these questions to specialists in Bengali
culture. But they strongly influence Greenough's comparative findings as to riot:

> This pattern of victimization has nothing in common with European
> traditions of rage and revolt. In Europe famine violence was turned
> 'outward' and 'upward' against offending landlords, merchants, and
> officials; in Bengal the tradition was to turn violence 'inward' and
> 'downward' against clients and dependents. This was the cold
> violence of abandonment, of ceasing to nourish, rather than the hot
> violence of bloodshed and tumult.[3]

The comparison would be more convincing if Greenough had
not misread the European evidence in such a way as to
accentuate the violence of that tradition. He prefers an
exciteable letter from the Abbé Raynal, in which European
food rioters in the 1780s are shown as pursuing each other
with daggers in their hands, "massacring each other", "tear-
ing and devouring their own limbs", etc., to the less sensational conclusions of historians of riot.[4] This rigging of the
evidence, in which submissive sufferers are contrasted with
"enraged looters", devalues his comparative study.

There remains, however, the significant interrogation of
"moral" premises, in relation to subsistence, in differing
cultures. In criticising *The Moral Economy of the Peasant*,
Greenough argues that:

> Scott's model of the moral economy. . . is essentially legal in nature.
> Scott says that peasants everywhere assert a *right* to subsistence, that

[1] *Prosperity and Misery*, pp. 215 and 264. Cf. Greenough,
"Indulgence and Abundance", pp. 832-3: heads of households "coolly
abandon" their dependents; in "an extreme realization of core patriarchal
values. . . it becomes acceptable to channel threats of extinction toward less
essential actors like clients, women and children".

[2] "Indulgence and Abundance", p. 847.

[3] *Ibid.*, p. 847; *Prosperity and Misery*, pp. 270-1.

[4] *Ibid.*, p. 268.

this assertion is felt to be *just*, and that it arises from a *norm* of reciprocity; further, it is the *duty* of elites to subsist their peasants, and any failure to do so entails a loss of their *legitimacy*. This Latinate terminology is derived from study of the numerous food riots that erupted in Western Europe in the seventeenth through nineteenth centuries; its appropriateness in explaining Bengali conditions is doubtful. Bengalis in crisis have spoken of their needs for "boons" (*bar*), "help" (*sahajya*), and "gifts" (*dan*), but rarely of their "rights"; of "indulgence" rather than "reciprocity"; of kingly *dharma*. . . but rarely of an enforceable class "duty".

This is not just "a narrow matter of terminology, but of the cognitive structures and customary paths for action that are conjured by the use of such terms".[1]

This is partly an academic language-game which, unfortunately, is rigged once more in order to score points off Scott. For Greenough has confused the language (and cognitive structures) of the historical subjects and of the academic interpreter. Neither English food rioters nor Burmese peasants acted with a vocabulary of "norms", "reciprocity" or "legitimacy" on their lips, and, equally, Professor Greenough's interpretive terminology ("cosmology", "hierarchical", "anthropomorphized") can be as Latinate (or Hellenic), as Scott's and, perhaps, even less likely to be found on the lips of a Bengal peasant.

But let us forgive him his polemical zeal. For he has reminded us of two important things. The first is that even extreme hunger, and even the simplest act of preparing food, may have differential cultural expression: "to cultivate, cook, share, and eat rice in Bengal is to perform a series of rituals. . . To dissect out an area of economic activity and label it 'subsistence' is to sever the social, sacral and even cosmic links" that food preparation and commensality may represent. For these reasons Greenough suspects that "the moral economy of rice in much of Asia is more truly moral, more pregnant with implication, than economic and political historians have been ready to admit".[2] But there is no reason to confine these thoughts to Asia or to rice. Bread, which is "the staff of life", features in the Lord's Prayer, bread and salt are the gifts with which European peasants

---

[1] "Indulgence and Abundance", p. 846.
[2] *Ibid.*, p. 848.

once welcomed visitors, and the wafer of the sacrament of Eucharist was unleavened bread.

We are also reminded that we are always in danger of confusing the historical evidence with the terms of interpretation which we have ourselves introduced. Food rioters did sometimes appeal to justice (or "fair" prices) and they certainly protested against unfair practices; but the language of "duties", "obligations", "reciprocity" and even of "rights" is mostly our own. Rioters abused those accused of sharp practices in marketing as "rogues", and, in the theatre of confrontation, anonymous letter-writers elaborated a rhetoric of threat — murder, arson, even revolt.[1] Yet if we were to find ways of interrogating the cognitive structure of food rioters, we might find certain essential premises, whether expressed in the simplest biblical terms of "love" and "charity", or whether in terms of notions of what humans "owe" to each other in time of need, notions which may have little to do with any Christian instruction but which arise from the elementary exchanges of material life.

There was a plebeian "discourse" here, almost beneath the level of articulacy, appealing to solidarities so deeply assumed that they were almost nameless, and only occasionally finding expression in the (very imperfect) record which we have. Walter Stephens, indicted for riot before the Gloucestershire Special Commission in December 1766, was alleged to have declared that "what the Mob had done was right and justifiable, and that for all the Justices' acting they would have it all on a Level before it were long".[2] That certainly is not reputable political thought, and it will not be allowed to pass by King's College, Cambridge. But Walter Stephens said this at a time when he stood in danger of being tried for his life for these opinions (which, at the present moment, is not

[1] See my essay, "The Crime of Anonymity", in Hay, Linebaugh and Thompson, *Albion's Fatal Tree*, esp. the "Sampler of Letters", pp. 326-43. But even these letters are studied and "literary" productions.

[2] Crown brief in PRO, TS 11/1188/5956. I cannot find out what happened to Walter Stephens. His name does not appear on the Calendar of Prisoners in TS 11/995/3707. The case against him may have been dropped, or he might have been the Thomas Stephens committed for riot and diverse outrages and felonies, who appears in the Calendar with an annotation "acquitted".

— so far as I know — the case with any Fellow of King's) and his meanings deserve our respect.

Comparative enquiry into what is "the moral" (whether as norm or as cognitive structure) will help us to understand these meanings. It is an agenda for forward research. It would be a shame to leave future historians with nothing to do. In any case, if I did father the term "moral economy" upon current academic discourse, the term has long forgotten its paternity. I will not disown it, but it has come of age and I am no longer answerable for its actions. It will be interesting to see how it goes on.

Chapter Six

Time, Work-Discipline and Industrial Capitalism

We kept an old Servant whose name was *Wright*, in constant Work, though paid by the Week, he was a Wheel-wright by Trade. . . It happen'd one Morning that a Cart being Broken-down upon the Road. . . the old Man was fetch'd to repair it where it lay; while he was busy at his Work, comes by a Countryman that knew him, and salutes him with the usual Compliment, *Good-Morrow Father Wright, God speed your Labour*; the old Fellow looks up at him. . . and with a kind of pleasant Surlyness, answer'd, *I don't care whether he does or no, 'tis Day-Work.*
> D. Defoe, *The Great Law of Subordination Considered; or the Insolence and Insufferable Behaviour of SERVANTS in England duly enquired into* (1724)

To the upper Part of Mankind Time is an Enemy, and. . . their chief Labour is to kill it; whereas with the others, Time and Money are almost synonymous.
> Henry Fielding, *An Enquiry into the Causes of the late Increase of Robbers* (1751)

Tess. . . started on her way up the dark and crooked lane or street not made for hasty progress; a street laid out before inches of land had value, and when one-handed clocks sufficiently subdivided the day.
> *Thomas Hardy*

I

It is commonplace that the years between 1300 and 1650 saw within the intellectual culture of Western Europe important changes in the apprehension of time.[1] In the *Canterbury*

[1] Lewis Mumford makes suggestive claims in *Technics and Civilization* (1934), esp. pp. 12-18, 196-9: see also S. de Grazia, *Of Time, Work, and Leisure* (New York, 1962), Carlo M. Cipolla, *Clocks and Culture 1300-1700* (1967), and Edward T. Hall, *The Silent Language* (New York, 1959).

Tales the cock still figures in his immemorial role as nature's timepiece: Chauntecleer —

> Caste up his eyen to the brighte sonne,
> That in the signe of Taurus hadde yronne
> Twenty degrees and oon, and somwhat moore,
> He knew by kynde, and by noon oother loore
> That it was pryme, and crew with blisful stevene. . .

But although "By nature knew he ech ascensioun/Of the equynoxial in thilke toun", the contrast between "nature's" time and clock time is pointed in the image —

> Wel sikerer was his crowyng in his logge
> Than is a clokke, or an abbey orlogge.

This is a very early clock: Chaucer (unlike Chauntecleer) was a Londoner, and was aware of the times of Court, of urban organisation and of that "merchant's time" which Jacques Le Goff, in a suggestive article in *Annales*, has opposed to the time of the medieval church.[1]

I do not wish to argue how far the change was due to the spread of clocks from the fourteenth century onwards, how far this was itself a symptom of a new Puritan discipline and bourgeois exactitude. However we see it, the change is certainly there. The clock steps on to the Elizabethan stage, turning Faustus's last soliloquy into a dialogue with time: "the stars move still, time runs, the clock will strike". Sidereal time, which has been present since literature began, has now moved at one step from the heavens into the home. Mortality and love are both felt to be more poignant as the "Snayly motion of the mooving hand"[2] crosses the dial. When the watch is worn about the neck it lies in proximity to the less regular beating of the heart. The conventional Elizabethan images of time as a devourer, a defacer, a bloody

[1] J. Le Goff, "Au Moyen Age: Temps de L'Eglise et temps du marchand", *Annals E.S.C.*, xv (1960); and the same author's "Le temps du travail dans le 'crise' du XIVe Siècle: du temps médiéval au temps moderne", *Le Moyen Age*, lxix (1963).
[2] M. Drayton, "Of his Ladies not Comming to London", *Works*, ed. J. W. Hebel (Oxford, 1932), iii, p. 204.

tyrant, a scytheman, are old enough, but there is a new immediacy and insistence.[1]

As the seventeenth century moves on the image of clock-work extends, until, with Newton, it has engrossed the universe. And by the middle of the eighteenth century (if we are to trust Sterne) the clock had penetrated to more intimate levels. For Tristram Shandy's father — "one of the most regular men in everything he did. . . that ever lived" — "had made it a rule for many years of his life, — on the first Sunday night of every month. . . to wind up a large house-clock, which we had standing on the back-stairs head". "He had likewise gradually brought some other little family concernments to the same period", and this enabled Tristram to date his conception very exactly. It also provoked *The Clockmakers Outcry against the Author*:

> The directions I had for making several clocks for the country are countermanded; because no modest lady now dares to mention a word about winding-up a clock, without exposing herself to the sly leers and jokes of the family. . . Nay, the common expression of street-walkers is, "Sir, will you have your clock wound up?"

Virtuous matrons (the "clockmaker" complained) are consigning their clocks to lumber rooms as "exciting to acts of carnality".[2]

However, this gross impressionism is unlikely to advance the present enquiry: how far, and in what ways, did this shift in time-sense affect labour discipline, and how far did it influence the inward apprehension of time of working people? If the transition to mature industrial society entailed a severe restructuring of working habits — new disciplines, new incentives, and a new human nature upon which these incentives could bite effectively — how far is this related to changes in the inward notation of time?

[1] The change is discussed in Cipolla, *op. cit.*; Erwin Sturzl, "Der Zeitbegriff in der Elisabethanischen Literatur", *Wiener Beiträge zur Englischen Philologie*, lxix (1965); Alberto Tenenti, *Il Senso della Morte e l'amore della vita nel rinanscimento* (Milan, 1957).

[2] Anon., *The Clockmaker's Outcry against the Author of. . . Tristram Shandy* (1760), pp. 42-3.

II

It is well known that among primitive peoples the measurement of time is commonly related to familiar processes in the cycle of work or of domestic chores. Evans-Pritchard has analysed the time-sense of the Nuer:

> The daily timepiece is the cattle clock, the round of pastoral tasks, and the time of day and the passage of time through a day are to a Nuer primarily the succession of these tasks and their relation to one another.

Among the Nandi an occupational definition of time evolved covering not only each hour, but half hours of the day — at 5.30 in the morning the oxen have gone to the grazing-ground, at 6 the sheep have been unfastened, at 6.30 the sun has grown, at 7 it has become warm, at 7.30 the goats have gone to the grazing-ground, etc. — an uncommonly well-regulated economy. In a similar way terms evolve for the measurement of time intervals. In Madagascar time might be measured by "a rice-cooking" (about half an hour) or "the frying of a locust" (a moment). The Cross River natives were reported as saying "the man died in less than the time in which maize is not yet completely roasted" (less than fifteen minutes).[1]

It is not difficult to find examples of this nearer to us in cultural time. Thus in seventeenth-century Chile time was often measured in "credos": an earthquake was described in 1647 as lasting for the period of two credos; while the cooking time of an egg could be judged by an Ave Maria said aloud. In Burma in recent times monks rose at daybreak

---

[1] E. E. Evans-Pritchard, *The Nuer* (Oxford, 1940), pp. 100-4; M. P. Nilsson, *Primitive Time Reckoning* (Lund, 1920), pp. 32-3; P. A. Sorokin and R. K. Merton, "Social Time: a Methodological and Functional Analysis", *Amer. Jl. Sociol.*, xlii (1937); A. I. Hallowell, "Temporal Orientation in Western Civilization and in a Pre-Literate Society", *Amer. Anthrop.*, new series, xxxix (1937). Other sources for primitive time reckoning are cited in H. G. Alexander, *Time as Dimension and History* (Albuquerque, 1945), p. 26, and Beate R. Salz, "The Human Element in Industrialization", *Econ. Devel. and Cult. Change*, iv (1955), esp. pp. 94-114.

"when there is light enough to see the veins in the hand".[1] The Oxford English Dictionary gives us English examples — "pater noster wyle", "miserere whyle" (1450), and (in the New English Dictionary but not the Oxford English Dictionary) "pissing while" — a somewhat arbitrary measurement.

Pierre Bourdieu has explored more closely the attitudes towards time of the Kaabyle peasant (in Algeria) in recent years: "An attitude of submission and of nonchalant indifference to the passage of time which no one dreams of mastering, using up, or saving. . . Haste is seen as a lack of decorum combined with diabolical ambition". The clock is sometimes known as "the devil's mill"; there are no precise meal-times; "the notion of an exact appointment is unknown; they agree only to meet 'at the next market' ". A popular song runs:

> It is useless to pursue the world, No one will ever overtake it.[2]

Synge, in his well-observed account of the Aran Islands, gives us a classic example:

> While I am walking with Michael someone often comes to me to ask the time of day. Few of the people, however, are sufficiently used to modern time to understand in more than a vague way the convention of the hours and when I tell them what o'clock it is by my watch they are not satisfied, and ask how long is left them before the twilight.[3]

> The general knowledge of time on the island depends, curiously enough, upon the direction of the wind. Nearly all the cottages are built. . . with two doors opposite each other, the more sheltered of which lies open all day to give light to the interior. If the wind is northerly the south door is opened, and the shadow of the door-post moving across the kitchen floor indicates the hour; as soon, however, as the wind changes to the

---

[1] E. P. Salas, "L'Evolution de la notion du temps et les horlogers à l'époque coloniale au Chili", *Annales E.S.C.*, xxi (1966), p. 146; *Cultural Patterns and Technical Change*, ed. M. Mead (New York, UNESCO, 1953), p. 75.

[2] P. Bourdieu, "The attitude of the Algerian peasant toward time", in *Mediterranean Countrymen*, ed. J. Pitt-Rivers (Paris, 1963), pp. 55-72.

[3] Cf. *ibid.*, p. 179: "Spanish Americans do not regulate their lives by the clock as Anglos do. Both rural and urban people, when asked when they plan to do something, gives answers like: 'Right now, about two or four o'clock' ".

south the other door is opened, and the people, who never think of putting up a primitive dial, are at a loss. . .

When the wind is from the north the old woman manages my meals with fair regularity; but on the other days she often makes my tea at three o'clock instead of six. . .[1]

Such a disregard for clock time could of course only be possible in a crofting and fishing community whose framework of marketing and administration is minimal, and in which the day's tasks (which might vary from fishing to farming, building, mending of nets, thatching, making a cradle or a coffin) seem to disclose themselves, by the logic of need, before the crofter's eyes.[2] But his account will serve to emphasise the essential conditioning in differing notations of time provided by different work-situations and their relation to "natural" rhythms. Clearly hunters must employ certain hours of the night to set their snares. Fishing and seafaring people must integrate their lives with the tides. A petition from Sunderland in 1800 includes the words "considering that this is a seaport in which many people are obliged to be up at all hours of the night to attend the tides and their affairs upon the river".[3] The operative phrase is "attend the tides": the patterning of social time in the seaport follows *upon* the rhythms of the sea; and this appears to be natural and comprehensible to fishermen or seamen: the compulsion is nature's own.

In a similar way labour from dawn to dusk can appear to be "natural" in a farming community, especially in the harvest months: nature demands that the grain be harvested

[1] J. M. Synge, *Plays, Poems, and Prose* (Everyman edn., 1941), p. 257.

[2] The most important event in the relation of the islands to an external economy in Synge's time was the arrival of the steamer, whose times might be greatly affected by tide and weather. See Synge, *The Aran Islands* (Dublin, 1907), pp. 115-6.

[3] PRO, WO 40/17. It is of interest to note other examples of the recognition that seafaring time conflicted with urban routines: the Court of Admiralty was held to be always open, "for strangers and merchants, and sea-faring men, must take the opportunity of tides and winds, and cannot, without ruin and great prejudice attend the solemnity of courts and dilatory pleadings", see E. Vansittart Neale, *Feasts and Fasts* (1845), p. 249, while in some Sabbatarian legislation an exception was made for fishermen who sighted a shoal off-shore on the Sabbath day.

before the thunderstorms set in. And we may note similar "natural" work-rhythms which attend other rural or industrial occupations: sheep must be attended at lambing time and guarded from predators; cows must be milked; the charcoal fire must be attended and not burn away through the turfs (and the charcoal burners must sleep beside it); once iron is in the making, the furnaces must not be allowed to fail.

The notation of time which arises in such contexts has been described as task-orientation. It is perhaps the most effective orientation in peasant societies, and it remains important in village and domestic industries. It has by no means lost all relevance in rural parts of Britain today. Three points may be proposed about task-orientation. First, there is a sense in which it is more humanly comprehensible than timed labour. The peasant or labourer appears to attend upon what is an observed necessity. Second, a community in which task-orientation is common appears to show least demarcation between "work" and "life". Social intercourse and labour are intermingled — the working day lengthens or contracts according to the task — and there is no great sense of conflict between labour and "passing the time of day". Third, to men accustomed to labour timed by the clock, this attitude to labour appears to be wasteful and lacking in urgency.[1]

Such a clear distinction supposes, of course, the independent peasant or craftsman as referent. But the question of task-orientation becomes greatly more complex at the point where labour is employed. The entire family economy of the small farmer may be task-orientated; but within it there may be a division of labour, and allocation of roles, and the discipline of an employer-employed relationship between the farmer and his children. Even here time is beginning to become money, the employer's money. As soon as actual

[1] Henri Lefebvre, *Critique de la Vie Quotidienne* (Paris, 1958), ii, pp. 52-6, prefers a distinction between "cyclical time" — arising from changing seasonal occupations in agriculture — and the "linear time" of urban, industrial organisation. More suggestive is Lucien Febvre's distinction between "Le temps vécu et le temps-mesure", *La Problème de L'Incroyance en XVIᵉ Siècle* (Paris, 1947), p. 431. A somewhat schematic examination of the organisation of tasks in primitive economies is in Stanley H. Udy, *Organisation of Work* (New Haven, 1959), ch. 2.

hands are employed the shift from task-orientation to timed labour is marked. It is true that the timing of work can be done independently of any time-piece — and indeed precedes the diffusion of the clock. Still, in the mid seventeenth century substantial farmers calculated their expectations of employed labour (as did Henry Best) in "dayworks" — "the Cunnigarth, with its bottomes, is 4 large dayworkes for a good mower", "the Spellowe is 4 indifferent dayworkes", etc.;[1] and what Best did for his own farm, Markham attempted to present in general form:

> A man. . . may mow of Corn, as Barley and Oats, if it be thick, loggy and beaten down to the earth, making fair work, and not cutting off the heads of the ears, and leaving the straw still growing one acre and a half in a day: but if it be good thick and fair standing corn, then he may mow two acres, or two acres and a half in a day; but if the corn be short and thin, then he may mow three, and sometimes four Acres in a day, and not be overlaboured. . .[2]

The computation is difficult, and dependent upon many variables. Clearly, a straightforward time-measurement was more convenient.[3]

This measurement embodies a simple relationship. Those who are employed experience a distinction between their employer's time and their "own" time. And the employer must *use* the time of his labour, and see it is not wasted: not the task but the value of time when reduced to money is dominant. Time is now currency: it is not passed but spent.

---

[1] *Rural Economy in Yorkshire in 1641. . . Farming and Account Books of Henry Best*, ed. C. B. Robinson (Surtees Society, xxxiii, 1857), pp. 38-9.

[2] G.M., *The Inrichment of the Weald of Kent*, 10th edn. (1660), ch. xii: "A generall computation of men, and cattel's labours: what each may do without hurt daily", pp. 112-8.

[3] Wage-assessments still, of course, assumed the statute dawn-to-dusk day, defined, as late as 1725, in a Lancashire assessment: "They shall work from five in the morning till betwixt seven and eight at the night, from the midst of March to the middle of September" — and thereafter "from the spring of day till night", with two half hours for drinking, and one hour for dinner and (in summer only) one half hour for sleep: "else, for every hour's absence to defaulk a penny": *Annals of Agriculture*, xxv (1796).

We may observe something of this contrast, in attitudes
towards both time and work, in two passages from Stephen
Duck's poem, "The Thresher's Labour".[1] The first describes
a work-situation which we have come to regard as the norm
in the nineteenth and twentieth centuries:

> From the strong Planks our Crab-Tree Staves rebound,
> And echoing Barns return the rattling Sound.
> Now in the Air our knotty Weapons Fly;
> And now with equal Force descend from high:
> Down one, one up, so well they keep the Time,
> The *Cyclops* Hammers could not truer chime. . .
> In briny Streams our Sweat descends apace,
> Drops from our Locks, or trickles down our Face.
> No intermission in our Works we know;
> The noisy Threshall must for ever go.
> Their Master absent, others safely play;
> The sleeping Threshall doth itself betray.
> Nor yet the tedious Labour to beguile,
> And make the passing Minutes sweetly smile,
> Can we, like Shepherds, tell a merry Tale?
> The Voice is lost, drown'd by the noisy Flail. . .
>
> Week after Week we this dull Task pursue,
> Unless when winnowing Days produce a new;
> A new indeed, but frequently a worse,
> The Threshall yields but to the Master's Curse:
> He counts the Bushels, counts how much a Day,
> Then swears we've idled half our Time away.
> Why look ye, Rogues! D'ye think that this will do?
> Your Neighbours thresh as much again as you.

This would appear to describe the monotony, alienation from
pleasure in labour, and antagonism of interests commonly
ascribed to the factory system. The second passage describes
the harvesting:

> At length in Rows stands up the well-dry'd Corn,
> A grateful Scene, and ready for the Barn.
> Our well-pleas'd Master views the Sight with joy,
> And we for carrying all our Force employ.
> Confusion soon o'er all the Field appears,
> And stunning Clamours fill the Workmens Ears;
> The Bells, and clashing Whips, alternate sound,
> And rattling Waggons thunder o'er the Ground.

[1] "The Threshers Labour", ed. E. P. Thompson and Marian Sugden
(1989).

The Wheat got in, the Pease, and other Grain,
Share the same Fate, and soon leave bare the Plain:
In noisy Triumph the last Load moves on,
And loud Huzza's proclaim the Harvest done.

This is, of course, an obligatory set-piece in eighteenth-century farming poetry. And it is also true that the good morale of the labourers was sustained by their high harvest earnings. But it would be an error to see the harvest situation in terms of direct responses to economic stimuli. It is also a moment at which the older collective rhythms break through the new, and a weight of folklore and of rural custom could be called as supporting evidence as to the psychic satisfaction and ritual functions — for example, the momentary obliteration of social distinctions — of the harvest-home. "How few now know", M. K. Ashby writes, "what it was ninety years ago to get in a harvest! Though the disinherited had no great part of the fruits, still they shared in the achievement, the deep involvement and joy of it".[1]

III

It is by no means clear how far the availability of precise clock time extended at the time of the industrial revolution. From the fourteenth century onwards church clocks and public clocks were erected in the cities and large market towns. The majority of English parishes must have possessed church clocks by the end of the sixteenth century.[2] But the accuracy of these clocks is a matter of dispute; and the sundial remained in use (partly to set the clock) in the seventeenth, eighteenth and nineteenth centuries.[3]

[1] M. K. Ashby, *Joseph Ashby of Tysoe* (Cambridge, 1961), p. 24.

[2] For the early evolution of clocks, see Cipolla, *op. cit., passim*; A. P. Usher, *A History of Mechanical Inventions*, rev. edn. (Cambridge, Mass., 1962), ch. vii; Charles Singer *et al* (eds.), *A History of Technology* (Oxford, 1956), iii, ch. xxiv; R. W. Symonds, *A History of English Clocks* (Penguin, 1947), pp. 10-16, 33; E. L. Edwards, *Weight-driven Chamber Clocks of the Middle Ages and Renaissance* (Alrincham, 1965).

[3] See M. Gatty, *The Book of Sun-diales*, rev. edn. (1900). For an example of a treatise explaining in detail how to set time-pieces by the sundial, see John Smith, *Horological Dialogues* (1675). For examples of benefactions for sundials, see C. J. C. Beeson, *Clockmaking in Oxfordshire* (Banbury Hist. Assn., 1962), pp. 76-8; A. J. Hawkes, *The Clockmakers and Watchmakers of Wigan, 1650-1850* (Wigan, 1950), p. 27.

Charitable donations continued to be made in the seventeenth century (sometimes laid out in "clockland", "ding dong land", or "curfew bell land") for the ringing of early morning bells and curfew bells.[1] Thus Richard Palmer of Wokingham (Berkshire) gave, in 1664, lands in trust to pay the sexton to ring the great bell for half an hour every evening at eight o'clock and every morning at four o'clock, or as near to those hours as might be, from the 10th September to the 11th March in each year

> not only that as many as might live within the sound might be thereby induced to a timely going to rest in the evening, and early arising in the morning to the labours and duties of their several callings, (things ordinarily attended and rewarded with thrift and proficiency). . .

but also so that strangers and others within sound of the bell on winter nights "might be informed of the time of night, and receive some guidance into their right way". These "rational ends", he conceived, "could not but be well liked by any discreet person, the same being done and well approved of in most of the cities and market-towns, and many other places in the kingdom. . .". The bell would also remind men of their passing, and of resurrection and judgement.[2] Sound served better than sight, especially in growing manufacturing districts. In the clothing districts of the West Riding, in the Potteries, (and probably in other districts) the horn was still used to awaken people in the mornings.[3] The farmer aroused his own labourers, on occasion, from their cottages; and no doubt the knocker-up will have started with the earliest mills.

---

[1] Since many early church clocks did not strike the hour, they were supplemented by a bell-ringer.

[2] *Charity Commissioners Reports* (1837/8), xxxii, pt. 1, p. 224; see also H. Edwards, *A Collection of Old English Customs* (1842), esp. pp. 223-7; S. O. Addy, *Household Tales* (1895), pp. 129-39; *County Folk-lore, East Riding of Yorkshire*, ed. Mrs Gutch (1912), pp. 150-1; *Leicestershire and Rutland*, ed. C. J. Bilson (1895), pp. 120-1; C. J. C. Beeson, *op. cit.*, p. 36; A. Gatty, *The Bell* (1848), p. 20; P. H. Ditchfield, *Old English Customs* (1896), pp. 232-41.

[3] H. Heaton, *The Yorkshire Woollen and Worsted Industries* (Oxford, 1965), p. 347. Wedgwood seems to have been the first to replace the horn by the bell in the Potteries: E. Meteyard, *Life of Josiah Wedgwood* (1865), i, pp. 329-30.

A great advance in the accuracy of household clocks came with the application of the pendulum after 1658. Grandfather clocks began to spread more widely from the 1660s, but clocks with minute hands (as well as hour hands) only became common well after this time.[1] As regards more portable time, the pocket watch was of dubious accuracy until improvements were made in the escapement and the spiral balance-spring was applied after 1674.[2] Ornate and rich design was still preferred to plain serviceability. A Sussex diarist notes in 1688:

> bought. . . a silver-cased watch, w[eh] cost me *3Ii*. . . This watch shewes ye hour of ye day, ye month of ye year, ye age of ye moon, and ye ebbing and flowing of ye water; and will goe 30 hours with one winding up.[3]

Professor Cipolla suggests 1680 as the date at which English clock- and watch-making took precedence (for nearly a century) over European competitors.[4] Clock-making had emerged from the skills of the blacksmith,[5] and the affinity can still be seen in the many hundreds of independent clock-makers, working to local orders in their own shops, dispersed through the market-towns and even the large villages of England, Scotland and Wales in the eighteenth century.[6]

[1] W. I. Milham, *Time and Timekeepers* (1923), pp. 142-9; F. J. Britten, *Old Clocks and Watches and Their Makers*, 6th edn. (1932), p. 543; E. Burton, *The Longcase Clock* (1964), ch. ix.

[2] Milham, *op. cit.*, pp. 214-26; C. Clutton and G. Daniels, *Watches* (1965); F. A. B. Ward, *Handbook of the Collections illustrating Time Measurement* (1947), p. 29; Cipolla, *op. cit.*, p. 139.

[3] Edward Turner, "Extracts from the Diary of Richard Stapley", *Sussex Archaeol. Coll.*, ii (1899), p. 113.

[4] See the admirable survey of the origin of the English industry in Cipolla, *op. cit.*, pp. 65-9.

[5] As late as 1697 in London the Blacksmith's Company was contesting the monopoly of the Clockmakers (founded in 1631) on the grounds that "it is well known that they are the originall and proper makers of clocks &c. and have full skill and knowledge therein. . .": S. E. Atkins and W. H. Overall, *Some Account of the Worshipful Company of Clockmakers of the City of London* (1881), p. 118. For a village blacksmith/clock-maker see J. A. Daniell, "The Making of Clocks and Watches in Leicestershire and Rutland", *Trans. Leics. Archaeol. Soc.*, xxvii (1951), p. 32.

[6] Lists of such clock-makers are in Britten, *op. cit.*; John Smith, *Old Scottish Clockmakers* (Edinburgh, 1921); and I. C. Peate, *Clock and Watch Makers in Wales* (Cardiff, 1945).

While many of these aspired to nothing more fancy than the work-a-day farmhouse longcase clock, craftsmen of genius were among their numbers. Thus John Harrison, clock-maker and former carpenter of Barton-on-Humber (Lincoln-shire), perfected a marine chronometer, and in 1730 could claim to have

> brought a Clock to go nearer the truth, than can be well imagin'd, considering the vast Number of seconds of Time there is in a Month, in which space of time it does not vary above one second. . . I am sure I can bring it to the nicety of 2 or 3 seconds in a year.[1]

And John Tibbot, a clock-maker in Newtown (Montgomery-shire), had perfected a clock in 1810 which (he claimed) seldom varied more than a second over two years.[2] In between these extremes were those numerous, shrewd, and highly-capable craftsmen who played a critically important role in technical innovation in the early stages of the industrial revolution. The point, indeed, was not left for historians to discover: it was argued forcibly in petitions of the clock- and watch-makers against the assessed taxes in February 1798. Thus the petition from Carlisle:

> . . . the cotton and woollen manufactories are entirely indebted for the state of perfection to which the machinery used therein is now brought to the clock and watch makers, great numbers of whom have, for several years past. . . been employed in inventing and constructing as well as superintending such machinery. . .[3]

Small-town clock-making survived into the eighteenth century, although from the early years of that century it became common for the local clock-maker to buy his parts ready-made from Birmingham, and to assemble these in his own workshop. By contrast, watch-making, from the early years of the eighteenth century, was concentrated in a few centres, of which the most important were London,

---

[1] Records of the Clockmaker's Company, London Guildhall Archives, 6026/1. See (for Harrison's chronometer) Ward, *op. cit.*, p. 32.

[2] I. C. Peate, "John Tibbot, Clock and Watch Maker", *Montgomery-shire Collections*, xlviii, pt. 2 (Welshpool, 1944), p. 178.

[3] *Commons Journals*, liii, p. 251. The witnesses from Lancashire and Derby gave similar testimonies: *ibid.*, pp. 331, 335.

Coventry, Prescot and Liverpool.[1] A minute subdivision of labour took place in the industry early, facilitating large-scale production and a reduction in prices: the annual output of the industry at its peak (1796) was variously estimated at 120,000 and 191,678, a substantial part of which was for the export market.[2] Pitt's ill-judged attempt to tax clocks and watches, although it lasted only from July 1797 to March 1798, marked a turning-point in the fortunes of the industry. Already, in 1796, the trade was complaining at the competition of French and Swiss watches; the complaints continue to grow in the early years of the nineteenth century. The Clockmakers' Company alleged in 1813 that the smuggling of cheap gold watches had assumed major proportions, and that these were sold by jewellers, haberdashers, milliners, dressmakers, French toy-shops, perfumers, etc., "almost entirely for the use of *the upper classes of society*". At the same time, some cheap smuggled goods, sold by pawnbrokers or travelling salesmen, must have been reaching the poorer classes.[3]

It is clear that there were plenty of watches and clocks around by 1800. But it is not so clear who owned them.

[1] Centres of the clock- and watch-making trade petitioning against the tax in 1798 were: London, Bristol, Coventry, Leicester, Prescot, Newcastle, Edinburgh, Liverpool, Carlisle, and Derby: *Commons Journals*, liii, pp. 158, 167, 174, 178, 230, 232, 239, 247, 251, 316. It was claimed that 20,000 were engaged in the trade in London alone, 7,000 of these in Clerkenwell. But in Bristol only 150 to 200 were engaged. For London, see M. D. George, *London Life in the Eighteenth Century* (1925), pp. 173-6; Atkins and Overall, *op. cit.*, p. 269; *Morning Chronicle*, 19 Dec. 1797; *Commons Journals*, liii, p. 158. For Bristol, *ibid.*, p. 332. For Lancashire, *Victoria County History, Lancashire*.

[2] The lower estimate was given by a witness before the committee on watch-makers' petitions (1798): *Commons Journals*, liii, p. 328 — estimated annual home consumption 50,000, export 70,000. See also a similar estimate (clocks and watches) for 1813, Atkins and Overall, *op. cit.*, p. 276. The higher estimate is for watch-cases marked at Goldsmiths Hall — silver cases, 185,102 in 1796, declining to 91,346 in 1816 — and is in the *Report of the Select Committee on the Petitions of Watchmakers, PP*, 1817, vi and 1818, ix, p. 1, 12.

[3] Atkins and Overall, *op. cit.*, pp. 302, 308 — estimating (excessively?) 25,000 gold and 10,000 silver watches imported, mostly illegally, per annum; and Anon., *Observations on the Art and Trade of Clock and Watchmaking* (1812), pp. 16-20.

Dr Dorothy George, writing of the mid eighteenth century, suggests that "labouring men, as well as artisans, frequently possessed silver watches", but the statement is indefinite as to date and only slightly documented.[1] The average price of plain longcase clocks made locally in Wrexham between 1755 and 1774 ran between £2 and £2 15s. 0d.; a Leicester price-list for new clocks, without cases, in 1795 runs between £3 and £5. A well-made watch would certainly cost no less.[2] On the face of it, no labourer whose budget was recorded by Eden or David Davies could have meditated such prices, and only the best-paid urban artisan. Recorded time (one suspects) belonged in the mid-century still to the gentry, the masters, the farmers and the tradesmen; and perhaps the intricacy of design, and the preference for precious metal, were in deliberate accentuation of their symbolism of status.

But, equally, it would appear that the situation was changing in the last decades of the century. The debate provoked by the attempt to impose a tax on all clocks and watches in 1797-8 offers a little evidence. It was perhaps the most unpopular and it was certainly the most unsuccessful of all of Pitt's assessed taxes:

> If your Money he take — why your Breeches remain;
> And the flaps of your Shirts, if your Breeches he gain;
> And your Skin, if your Shirts; and if Shoes, your bare feet.
> Then, never mind TAXES — *We've beat the Dutch fleet!*[3]

The taxes were of 2s. 6d. upon each silver or metal watch; 10s. upon each gold one; and 5s. upon each clock. In debates upon the tax, the statements of ministers were remarkable only for their contradictions. Pitt declared that he expected the tax to produce £200,000 per annum:

[1] George, *op. cit.*, p. 70. Various means of time-telling were of course employed without clocks: the engraving of the wool-comber in *The Book of English Trades* (1818), p. 438 shows him with an hour-glass on his bench; threshers measured time as the light from the door moved across the barn floor; and Cornish tinners measured it underground by candles (information from J. G. Rule).

[2] I. C. Peate, "Two Montgomeryshire Craftsmen", *Montgomeryshire Collections*, xlviii, pt. 1 (Welshpool, 1944), p. 5; Daniell, *op. cit.*, p. 39. The average price of watches exported in 1792 was £4: *PP*, 1818, ix, p. 1.

[3] "A loyal Song", *Morning Chronicle*, 18 Dec. 1797.

In fact, he thought, that as the number of houses paying taxes is 700,000 and that in every house there is probably one person who wears a watch, the tax upon watches only would produce that sum.

At the same time, in response to criticism, ministers maintained that the ownership of clocks and watches was a mark of luxury. The Chancellor of the Exchequer faced both ways: watches and clocks "were certainly articles of convenience, but they were also articles of luxury. . . generally kept by persons who would be pretty well able to pay. . .". "He meant, however, to exempt Clocks of the meaner sort that were most commonly kept by the poorer classes."[1] The Chancellor clearly regarded the tax as a sort of Lucky Bag; his guess was more than three times that of the Pilot:

GUESSWORK TABLE

Articles	Tax	Chancellor's estimate	Would mean
Silver and metal watches	2s. 6d.	£100,000	800,000 watches
Gold watches	10s. 0d.	£200,000	400,000 watches
Clocks	5s. 0d.	£3 or £400,000	c. 1,400,000 clocks

His eyes glittering at the prospect of enhanced revenue, Pitt revised his definitions: a *single* watch (or dog) might be owned as an article of convenience — more than this were "tests of affluence".[2]

Unfortunately for the quantifiers of economic growth, one matter was left out of account. The tax was impossible to collect.[3] All householders were ordered, upon dire pains, to return lists of clocks and watches within their houses. Assessments were to be quarterly:

[1] The exemptions in the Act (37 Geo. III, c. 108, cl., xii, xxii and xxiv) were (a) for one clock or watch for any householder exempted from window and house tax (i.e. cottager), (b) for clocks "made of wood, or fixed upon wood, and which clocks are usually sold by the respective makers thereof at a price not exceeding the sum of 20s. . .", (c) Servants in husbandry.

[2] *Morning Chronicle*, 1 July 1797; *Craftsman*, 8 July 1779; *Parl. Hist.*, xxxiii, *passim*.

[3] In the year ending 5 April 1798 (three weeks after repeal) the tax had raised £2,600: *PP*, ciii, Accounts and Papers (1797-98), xlv, pp. 933 (2) and 933 (3).

Mr. Pitt has very proper ideas of the remaining finances of the country. The *half-crown* tax upon watches is appointed to be collected *quarterly*. This is grand and dignified. It gives a man an air of consequence to pay *sevenpence halfpenny* to support *religion, property*, and *social order*.[1]

In fact, the tax was regarded as folly; as setting up a system of espionage; and as a blow against the middle class.[2] There was a buyer's strike. Owners of gold watches melted down the covers and exchanged them for silver or metal.[3] The centres of the trade were plunged into crisis and depression.[4] Repealing the Act in March 1798, Pitt said sadly that the tax *would* have been productive much beyond the calculation originally made; but it is not clear whether it was his own calculation (£200,000) or the Chancellor of the Exchequer's (£700,000) which he had in mind.[5]

We remain (but in the best of company) in ignorance. There were a lot of timepieces about in the 1790s: emphasis is shifting from "luxury" to "convenience"; even cottagers may have wooden clocks costing less than twenty shillings. Indeed, a general diffusion of clocks and watches is occurring (as one would expect) at the exact moment when the industrial revolution demanded a greater synchronisation of labour.

Although some very cheap — and shoddy — time-pieces were beginning to appear, the prices of efficient ones remained for several decades beyond the normal reach of the artisan.[6] But we should not allow normal economic

[1] *Morning Chronicle*, 26 July, 1797.

[2] One indication may be seen in the sluggardly collection of arrears. Taxes imposed, July 1797: receipts, year ending Jan. 1798 — £300. Taxes repealed, March 1798: arrears received, year ending Jan. 1799, £35,420; year ending Jan. 1800, £14,966. *PP*, cix, Accounts and Papers (1799-1800), li, pp. 1009 (2) and 1013 (2).

[3] *Morning Chronicle*, 16 Mar. 1798; *Commons Journals*, liii, p. 328.

[4] See petitions, cited in note 1 on p. 365; *Commons Journals*, liii, pp. 327-33; *Morning Chronicle*, 13 Mar. 1798. Two-thirds of Coventry watchmakers were said to be unemployed: *ibid.*, 8 Dec. 1797.

[5] *Craftsman*, 17 Mar. 1798. The one achievement of the Act was to bring into existence — in taverns and public places — the "Act of Parliament Clock".

[6] Imported watches were quoted at a price as low as 5s. in 1813: Atkins and Overall, *op. cit.*, p. 292. See also note 1 on p. 367. The price of an efficient British silver pocket watch was quoted in 1817 (*Committee on*

preferences to mislead us. The small instrument which regulated the new rhythms of industrial life was at the same time one of the more urgent of the new needs which industrial capitalism called forth to energise its advance. A clock or watch was not only useful; it conferred prestige upon its owner, and a man might be willing to stretch his resources to obtain one. There were various sources, various occasions. For decades a trickle of sound but cheap watches found their way from the pickpocket to the receiver, the pawnbroker, the public house.[1] Even labourers, once or twice in their lives, might have an unexpected windfall, and blow it on a watch: the militia bounty,[2] harvest earnings, or the yearly wages of the servant.[3] In some parts of the country Clock and Watch Clubs were set up — collective hire-purchase.[4] Moreover, the time-piece was the poor man's bank, an investment of

Petitions of Watchmakers, PP, 1817, vi) at two to three guineas; by the 1830s an effective metal watch could be had for £1: D. Lardner, *Cabinet Cyclopaedia* (1834), iii, p. 297.

[1] Many watches must have changed hands in London's underworld: legislation in 1754 (27 Geo. II, c. 7) was directed at receivers of stolen watches. The pickpockets of course continued their trade undeterred: see, e.g. *Minutes of Select Committee to Inquire into the State of the Police of the Metropolis* (1816), p. 437 — "take watches could get rid of them as readily as anything else. . . It must be a very good patent silver watch that fetched £2; a gold one £5 or £6". Receivers of stolen watches in Glasgow are said to have sold them in quantities in country districts in Ireland (1834): see J. E. Handley, *The Irish in Scotland, 1798-1845* (Cork, 1943), p. 253.

[2] "Winchester being one of the general rendezvous for the militia volunteers, has been a scene of riot, dissipation and absurd extravagence. It is supposed that nine-tenths of the bounties paid to these men, amounting to at least £20,000 were all spent on the spot among the public houses, milliners, watch-makers, hatters, &c. In mere wantonness Bank notes were actually eaten between slices of bread and butter": *Monthly Magazine*, Sept. 1799.

[3] Witnesses before the Select Committee of 1817 complained that inferior wares (sometimes known as "Jew watches") were touted in country fairs and sold to the gullible at mock auctions: *PP*, 1817, vi, pp. 15-16.

[4] Benjamin Smith, *Twenty-four Letters from Labourers in America to their Friends in England* (1829), p. 48: the reference is to parts of Sussex — twenty people clubbed together (as in a Cow Club) paying 5s. each for twenty successive weeks, drawing lots each for one £5 time-piece.

savings: it could, in bad times, be sold or put in hock.[1] "This 'ere ticker", said one Cockney compositor in the 1820s, "cost me but a five-pun note ven I bort it fust, and I've popped it more than twenty times, and had more than forty poun' on it altogether. It's a garjian haingel to a fellar, is a good votch, ven you're hard up".[2]

Whenever any group of workers passed into a phase of improving living standards, the acquisition of time-pieces was one of the first things noted by observers. In Radcliffe's well-known account of the golden age of the Lancashire hand-loom weavers in the 1790s the men had "each a watch in his pocket" and every house was "well furnished with a clock in elegant mahogany or fancy case".[3] In Manchester fifty years later the same point caught a reporter's eye:

> No Manchester operative will be without one a moment longer than he can help. You see, here and there, in the better class of houses, one of the old-fashioned, metallic-faced eight-day clocks; but by far the most common article is the little Dutch machine, with its busy pendulum swinging openly and candidly before all the world.[4]

Thirty years later again it was the gold double watch-chain which was the symbol of the successful Lib-Lab trade union leader; and for fifty years of disciplined servitude to work, the enlightened employer gave to his employee an engraved gold watch.

IV

Let us return from the time-piece to the task. Attention to time in labour depends in large degree upon the need for the synchronisation of labour. But in so far as manufacturing industry remained conducted upon a domestic or small workshop scale, without intricate subdivision of processes,

[1] *PP*, 1817, vi, pp. 19, 22.

[2] [C. M. Smith], *The Working Man's Way in the World* (1853), pp. 67-8.

[3] W. Radcliffe, *The Origin of Power Loom Weaving* (Stockport, 1828), p. 167.

[4] *Morning Chronicle*, 25 Oct. 1849. But J. R. Porter, *The Progress of the Nation* (1843), iii, p. 5 still saw the possession of a clock as "the certain indication of prosperity and of personal respectability on the part of the working man".

the degree of synchronisation demanded was slight, and task-orientation was still prevalent.[1] The putting-out system demanded much fetching, carrying, waiting for materials. Bad weather could disrupt not only agriculture, building and transport, but also weaving, where the finished pieces had to be stretched on the tenters to dry. As we get closer to each task, we are surprised to find the multiplicity of subsidiary tasks which the same worker or family group must do in one cottage or workshop. Even in larger workshops men sometimes continued to work at distinct tasks at their own benches or looms, and — except where the fear of the embezzlement of materials imposed stricter supervision — could show some flexibility in coming and going.

Hence we get the characteristic irregularity of labour patterns before the coming of large-scale machine-powered industry. Within the general demands of the week's or fortnight's tasks — the piece of cloth, so many nails or pairs of shoes — the working day might be lengthened or shortened. Moreover, in the early development of manufacturing industry, and of mining, many mixed occupations survived: Cornish tinners who also took a hand in the pilchard fishing; Northern lead-miners who were also smallholders; the village craftsmen who turned their hands to various jobs, in building, carting, joining; the domestic workers who left their work for the harvest; the Pennine small-farmer/weaver.

It is in the nature of such work that accurate and representative time-budgets will not survive. But some extracts from the diary of one methodical farming weaver in 1782-83

---

[1] For some of the problems discussed in this and the following section, see especially Keith Thomas, "Work and Leisure in Pre-Industrial Societies", *Past and Present*, 29 (1964). Also C. Hill, "The Uses of Sabbatarianism", in *Society and Puritanism in Pre-Revolutionary England* (1964); E. S. Furniss, *The Position of the Laborer in a System of Nationalism* (Boston, 1920; reprint 1965); D. C. Coleman, "Labour in the English Economy of the Seventeenth Century", *Econ. Hist. Rev.*, 2nd series, viii (1955-6); S. Pollard, "Factory Discipline in the Industrial Revolution", *Econ. Hist. Rev.*, 2nd series, xvi (1963-4); T. S. Ashton, *An Economic History of England in the Eighteenth Century* (1955), ch. vii; W. E. Moore, *Industrialization and Labor* (New York, 1952); and B. F. Hoselitz and W. E. Moore, *Industrialization and Society* (UNESCO, 1963).

may give us an indication of the variety of tasks. In October 1782 he was still employed in harvesting, and threshing, alongside his weaving. On a rainy day he might weave $8\frac{1}{2}$ or 9 yards; on October 14th he carried his finished piece, and so wove only $4\frac{3}{4}$ yards; on the 23rd he "worked out" till 3 o'clock, wove two yards before sunset, "clouted [mended] my coat in the evening". On December 24th "wove 2 yards before 11 o'clock. I was laying up the coal heap, sweeping the roof and walls of the kitchen and laying the muck [midden?] till 10 o'clock at night." Apart from harvesting and threshing, churning, ditching and gardening, we have these entries:

January 18, 1783:	"I was employed in preparing a Calf stall & Fetching the Tops of three Plain Trees home which grew in the Lane and was that day cut down & sold to john Blagbrough."
January 21st:	"Wove $2\frac{3}{4}$ yards the Cow having calved she required much attendance." (On the next day he walked to Halifax to buy medicine for the cow.)

On January 25th he wove 2 yards, walked to a nearby village, and did "sundry jobs about the lathe and in the yard & wrote a letter in the evening". Other occupations include jobbing with a horse and cart, picking cherries, working on a mill dam, attending a Baptist association and a public hanging.[1]

This general irregularity must be placed within the irregular cycle of the working week (and indeed of the working year) which provoked so much lament from moralists and mercantilists in the seventeenth centuries. A

[1] MS diaries of Cornelius Ashworth of Wheatley, in Halifax Ref. Lib.; see also T. W. Hanson, "The Diary of a Grandfather", *Trans. Halifax Antiq. Soc.* (1916). M. Sturge Henderson, *Three Centuries in North Oxfordshire* (Oxford, 1902), pp. 133-46, 103, quotes similar passages (weaving, pig-killing, felling wood, marketing) from the diary of a Charlbury weaver, 1784. It is interesting to compare time-budgets from more primitive peasant economies, e.g. Sol Tax, *Penny Capitalism — a Guatemalan Indian Economy* (Washington, 1953), pp. 104-5; George M. Foster, *A Primitive Mexican Economy* (New York, 1942), pp. 35-8; M. J. Herskovits, *The Economic Life of Primitive Peoples* (New York, 1940), pp. 72-9; Raymond Firth, *Malay Fishermen* (1946), pp. 93-7.

rhyme printed in 1639 gives us a satirical version:

> You know that Munday is Sundayes brother;
> Tuesday is such another;
> Wednesday you must go to Church and pray;
> Thursday is half-holiday;
> On Friday it is too late to begin to spin;
> The Saturday is half-holiday again.[1]

John Houghton, in 1681, gives us the indignant version:

> When the framework knitters or makers of silk stockings had a great price for their work, they have been observed seldom to work on Mondays and Tuesdays but to spend most of their time at the ale-house or nine-pins. . . The weavers, 'tis common with them to be drunk on Monday, have their head-ache on Tuesday, and their tools out of order on Wednesday. As for the shoemakers, they'll rather be hanged than not remember St. Crispin on Monday. . . and it commonly holds as long as they have a penny of money or pennyworth of credit.[2]

The work pattern was one of alternate bouts of intense labour and of idleness, wherever men were in control of their own working lives. (The pattern persists among some self-employed — artists, writers, small farmers, and perhaps also with students — today, and provokes the question whether it is not a "natural" human work-rhythm.) On Monday or Tuesday, according to tradition, the hand-loom went to the slow chant of *Plen-ty of Time, Plen-ty of Time*: On Thursday and Friday, *A day t'lat, A day t'lat.*[3] The temptation to lie in an extra hour in the morning pushed work into the evening, candle-lit hours.[4] There are few trades which are not described as honouring Saint Monday: shoemakers, tailors, colliers, printing workers, potters, weavers, hosiery workers, cutlers, all Cockneys. Despite the full employment

---

[1] *Divers Crab-Tree Lectures* (1639), p. 126, cited in John Brand, *Observations on Popular Antiquities* (1813), i, pp. 459-60. H. Bourne, *Antiquitates Vulgares* (Newcastle, 1725), pp. 115 ff. declares that on Saturday afternoons in country places and villages "the Labours of the Plough Ceast, and Refreshment and Ease are over all the Village".

[2] J. Houghton, *Collection of Letters* (1683), p. 177, cited in Furniss, *op. cit.*, p. 121.

[3] Hanson, *op. cit.*, p. 234.

[4] J. Clayton, *Friendly Advice to the Poor* (Manchester, 1755), p. 36.

of many London trades during the Napoleonic Wars, a
witness complained that "we see Saint Monday so religiously
kept in this great city. . . in general followed by a Saint
Tuesday also".[1] If we are to believe "The Jovial Cutlers", a
Sheffield song of the late eighteenth century, its observance
was not without domestic tension:

> How upon a good Saint Monday,
> Sitting by the smithy fire,
> Telling what's been done o't Sunday,
> And in cheerful mirth conspire,
>> Soon I hear the trap-door rise up,
>> On the ladder stands my wife:
>> "Damn thee, Jack, I'll dust they eyes up,
>> Thou leads a plaguy drunken life;
>> Here thou sits instead of working,
>> Wi' thy pitcher on thy knee;
>> Curse thee, thou'd be always lurking.
>> And I may slave myself for thee".

The wife proceeds, speaking "with motion quicker/Than my
boring stick at a Friday's pace", to demonstrate effective
consumer demand:

> "See thee, look what stays I've gotten,
> See thee, what a pair o' shoes;
> Gown and petticoat half rotten,
> Ne'er a whole stitch in my hose. . ."

and to serve notice of a general strike:

> "Thou knows I hate to broil and quarrel,
> But I've neither soap nor tea;
> Od burn thee, Jack, forsake thy barrel,
> Or nevermore thou'st lie wi' me".[2]

[1] *Report of the Trial of Alexander Wadsworth against Peter Laurie* (1811), p. 21. The complaint is particularly directed against the Saddlers.

[2] *The Songs of Joseph Mather* (Sheffield, 1862), pp. 88-90. The theme appears to have been popular with ballad-makers. A Birmingham example, "Fuddling Day, or Saint Monday" (for which I am indebted to the late Charles Parker) runs:

> Saint Monday brings more ills about,
>> For when the money's spent,
> The children's clothes go up the spout,
>> Which causes discontent;
> And when at night he staggers home,
>> He knows not what to say,
> A fool is more a man than he
>> Upon a fuddling day.

Saint Monday, indeed, appears to have been honoured almost universally wherever small-scale, domestic, and out-work industries existed; was generally found in the pits; and sometimes continued in manufacturing and heavy industry.[1] It was perpetuated, in England, into the nineteenth — and, indeed, into the twentieth[2] — century for complex economic and social reasons. In some trades, the small masters themselves accepted the institution, and employed Monday in taking-in or giving-out work. In Sheffield, where the cutlers had for centuries tenaciously honoured the Saint, it had become "a settled habit and custom" which the steel-mills themselves honoured (1874):

> This Monday idleness is, in some cases, enforced by the fact that Monday is the day that is taken for repairs to the machinery of the great steelworks.[3]

Where the custom was deeply-established, Monday was the day set aside for marketing and personal business. Also, as Duveau suggests of French workers, "le dimanche est le jour de la famille, le lundi celui de l'amitié"; and as the

---

[1] It was honoured by Mexican weavers in 1800: see Jan Bazant, "Evolution of the textile industry of Puebla, 1544-1845", *Comparative Studies in Society and History*, viii (1964), p. 65. Valuable accounts of the custom in France in the 1850s and 1860s are in George Duveau, *La Vie Ouvrière en France sous le Second Empire* (Paris, 1946), pp. 242-8, and P. Pierrard, *La Vie Ouvrière à Lille sous le Second Empire* (Paris, 1965), pp. 165-6. Edward Young, conducting a survey of labour conditions in Europe, with the assistance of U.S. consuls, mentions the custom in France, Belgium, Prussia, Stockholm, etc. in the 1870s: E. Young, *Labour in Europe and America* (Washington, 1875), pp. 576, 661, 674, 685, etc.

[2] Notably in the pits. An old Yorkshire miner informs me that in his youth it was a custom on a bright Monday morning to toss a coin in order to decide whether or not to work. I have also been told that "Saint Monday" is still honoured in its pristine purity by a few coopers in Burton-on-Trent.

[3] E. Young, *op. cit.*, pp. 408-9 (Report of U.S. Consul). Similarly, in some mining districts, "Pay Monday" was recognised by the employers and the pits were only kept open for repairs: on Monday, only "dead work is going on", *Report of the Select Committee on the Scarcity and Dearness of Coal, PP*, 1873, x, QQ 177, 201-7.

nineteenth century advanced, its celebration was something
of a privilege of status of the better-paid artisan.[1]

It is, in fact, in an account by "An Old Potter" published
as late as 1903 that we have some of the most perceptive
observations on the irregular work-rhythms which continued
on the older pot-banks until the mid-century. The potters (in
the 1830s and 1840s) "had a devout regard for Saint
Monday". Although the custom of annual hiring prevailed,
the actual weekly earnings were at piece-rates, the skilled
male potters employing the children, and working, with little
supervision, at their own pace. The children and women came
to work on Monday and Tuesday, but a "holiday feeling"
prevailed and the day's work was shorter than usual, since the
potters were away a good part of the time, drinking their
earnings of the previous week. The children, however, had to
prepare work for the potter (for example, handles for pots
which he would throw), and all suffered from the exception-
ally long hours (fourteen and sometimes sixteen hours a day)
which were worked from Wednesday to Saturday:

> I have since thought that but for the reliefs at the beginning of the week
> for the women and boys all through the pot-works, the deadly stress of
> the last four days could not have been maintained.

"An Old Potter", a Methodist lay preacher of Liberal-
Radical views, saw these customs (which he deplored) as a
consequence of the lack of mechanisation of the pot-banks;
and he urged that the same indiscipline in daily work
influenced the entire way of life and the working-class
organisations of the Potteries. "Machinery means discipline
in industrial operations":

> If a steam-engine had started every Monday morning at six o'clock, the
> workers would have been disciplined to the habit of regular and
> continuous industry. . . I have noticed, too, that machinery seems to
> lead to habits of calculation. The Pottery workers were woefully
> deficient in this matter; they lived like children, without any

[1]Duveau, *op. cit.*, p. 247. "A Journeyman Engineer" (T. Wright)
devotes a whole chapter to "Saint Monday" in his *Some Habits and
Customs of the Working Classes* (1867), esp. pp. 112-6, under the mistaken
impression that the institution was "comparatively recent", and conse-
quent upon steam power giving rise to "a numerous body of highly skilled
and highly paid workmen" — notably engineers!

calculating forecast of their work or its result. In some of the more northern counties this habit of calculation has made them keenly shrewd in many conspicuous ways. Their great co-operative societies would never have arisen to such immense and fruitful development but for the calculating induced by the use of machinery. A machine worked so many hours in the week would produce so much length of yarn or cloth. Minutes were felt to be factors in these results, whereas in the Potteries hours, or even days at times, were hardly felt to be such factors. There were always the mornings and nights of the last days of the week, and these were always trusted to make up the loss of the week's early neglect.[1]

This irregular working rhythm is commonly associated with heavy week-end drinking: Saint Monday is a target in many Victorian temperance tracts. But even the most sober and self-disciplined artisan might feel the necessity for such alternations. "I know not how to describe the sickening aversion which at times steals over the working man and utterly disables him for a longer or shorter period, from following his usual occupation", Francis Place wrote in 1829; and he added a footnote of personal testimony:

For nearly six years, whilst working, when I had work to do, from twelve to eighteen hours a day, when no longer able, from the cause mentioned, to continue working, I used to run from it, and go as rapidly as I could to Highgate, Hampstead, Muswell-hill, or Norwood, and then "return to my vomit". . . This is the case with every workman I have ever known; and in proportion as a man's case is hopeless will such fits more frequently occur and be of longer duration.[2]

We may, finally, note that the irregularity of working day and week were framed, until the first decades of the

[1] "An Old Potter", *When I was a Child* (1903), pp. 16, 47-9, 52-4, 57-8, 71, 74-5, 81, 185-6, 191. Mr W. Sokol, of the University of Wisconsin, has directed my attention to many cases reported in the *Staffordshire Potteries Telegraph* in 1853-4, where the employers succeeded in fining or imprisoning workers who neglected work, often on Mondays and Tuesdays. These actions were taken on the pretext of breach of contract (the annual hiring), for which see Daphne Simon, "Master and Servant", in *Democracy and the Labour Movement*, ed. J. Saville (1954). Despite this campaign of prosecutions, the custom of keeping Saint Monday is still noted in the *Report of the Children's Employment Commission, PP*, 1863, xviii, pp. xxvii-xxviii.
[2] F. Place, *Improvement of the Working People* (1834), pp. 13-15: Brit. Mus. Add MS 27825. See also John Wade, *History of the Middle and Working Classes*, 3rd edn. (1835), pp. 124-5.

nineteenth century, within the larger irregularity of the working year, punctuated by its traditional holidays, and fairs. Still, despite the triumph of the Sabbath over the ancient saints' days in the seventeenth century,[1] the people clung tenaciously to their customary wakes and feasts, and may even have enlarged them both in vigour and extent.[2]

How far can this argument be extended from manufacturing industry to the rural labourers? On the face of it, there would seem to be unrelenting daily and weekly labour here: the field labourer had no Saint Monday. But a close discrimination of different work-situations is still required. The eighteenth- (and nineteenth-) century village had its own self-employed artisans, as well as many employed on irregular task work.[3] Moreover, in the unenclosed countryside, the classical case against open field and common was in its inefficiency and wastefulness of time, for the small farmer or cottager:

> . . . if you offer them work, they will tell you that they must go to look up their sheep, cut furzes, get their cow out of the pound, or, perhaps, say they must take their horse to be shod, that he may carry them to a horse-race or cricket-match (Arbuthnot, 1773.)

> In sauntering after his cattle, he acquires a habit of indolence. Quarter, half, and occasionally whole days are imperceptibly lost. Day labour becomes disgusting. . . (Report on Somerset, 1795.)

> Whenalabourerbecomespossessedofmorelandthanheandhis family can cultivate in the evenings. . . the farmer can no longer depend on him for constant work. . . (*Commercial & Agricultural Magazine*, 1800.)[4]

[1] See Hill, *op. cit.*

[2] Clayton, *op. cit.*, p. 13, claimed that "common custom has established so many Holy-days, that few of our manufacturing work-folks are closely and regularly employed above two-third parts of their time". See also Furniss, *op. cit.*, pp. 44-5, and the abstract of my paper in the *Bulletin of the Society for the Study of Labour History*, 9 (1964).

[3] "We have four or five little farmers. . . we have a bricklayer, a carpenter, a blacksmith, and a miller, all of whom. . . are in a very frequent habit of drinking the King's health. . . Their employment is unequal; sometimes they are full of business, and sometimes they have none; generally they have many leisure hours, because. . . the hardest part [of their work] devolves to some men whom they hire. . .", "A Farmer", describing his own village (see note 3 on p. 380), in 1798.

[4] Cited in J. L. and B. Hammond, *The Village Labourer* (1920), p. 13; E. P. Thompson, *The Making of the English Working Class* (1963), p. 220.

To this we should add the frequent complaints of agricultural improvers as to the time wasted, both at seasonal fairs, and (before the arrival of the village shop) on weekly market days.[1]

The farm servant, or the regular wage-earning field labourer, who worked, unremittingly, the full statute hours or longer, who had no common rights or land, and who (if not living-in) lived in a tied cottage, was undoubtedly subject to an intense labour discipline, whether in the seventeenth or the nineteenth century. The day of a ploughman (living-in) was described with relish by Markham in 1636:

> ... the Plowman shall rise before four of the clock in the morning, and after thanks given to God for his rest, & prayer for the success of his labours, he shall go into his stable. . .

After cleansing the stable, grooming his horses, feeding them, and preparing his tackle, he might breakfast (6-6.30 a.m.), he should plough until 2 p.m. or 3 p.m., take half an hour for dinner; attend to his horses etc. until 6.30 p.m., when he might come in for supper:

> ... and after supper, hee shall either by the fire side mend shooes both for himselfe and their Family, or beat and knock Hemp or Flax, or picke and stamp Apples or Crabs, for Cyder or Verdjuyce, or else grind malt on the quernes, pick candle rushes, or doe some Husbandly office within doors till it be full eight a clock. . .

Then he must once again attend to his cattle and ("giving God thanks for benefits received that day") he might retire.[2]

Even so, we are entitled to show a certain scepticism. There are obvious difficulties in the nature of the occupation. Ploughing is not an all-the-year-round task. Hours and tasks must fluctuate with the weather. The horses (if not the men) must be rested. There is the difficulty of supervision: Robert Loder's accounts indicate that servants (when out of sight) were not always employed upon their knees thanking God for their benefits: "men can worke yf they list & soe they can

---

[1] See e.g. *Annals of Agriculture*, xxvi (1796), p. 370 n.
[2] G. Markham, *The Inrichment of the Weald of Kent*, 10th edn. (1660), pp. 115-7.

loyter".[1] The farmer himself must work exceptional hours if he was to keep all his labourers always employed.[2] And the farm servant could assert his annual right to move on if he disliked his employment.

Thus enclosure and agricultural improvement were both, in some sense, concerned with the efficient husbandry of the time of the labour-force. Enclosure and the growing labour-surplus at the end of the eighteenth century tightened the screw for those who were in regular employment; they were faced with the alternatives of partial employment and the poor law, or submission to a more exacting labour discipline. It is a question, not of new techniques, but of a greater sense of time-thrift among the improving capitalist employers. This reveals itself in the debate between advocates of regularly-employed wage-labour and advocates of "taken-work" (i.e. labourers employed for particular tasks at piece-rates). In the 1790s Sir Mordaunt Martin censured recourse to taken-work

> which people agree to, to save themselves the trouble of watching their workmen: the consequence is, the work is ill done, the workmen boast at the ale-house what they can spend in "a waste against the wall", and make men at moderate wages discontented.

"A Farmer" countered with the argument that taken-work and regular wage-labour might be judiciously intermixed:

> Two labourers engage to cut down a piece of grass at two shillings or half-a-crown an acre; I send, with their scythes, two of my domestic farm-servants into the field; I can depend upon it, that their companions will keep them up to their work; and thus I gain. . . the same additional hours of labour from my domestic servants, which are voluntarily devoted to it by my hired servants.[3]

---

[1] Attempting to account for a deficiency in his stocks of wheat in 1617, Loder notes: "What should be the cause herof I know not, but it was in that yeare when R. Pearce & Alce were my servants, & then in great love (as it appeared too well) whether he gave it my horses. . . or how it went away, God onely knoweth". *Robert Loder's Farm Accounts*, ed. G. E. Fussell (Camden Society, 3rd series, liii, 1936), pp. 59, 127.

[2] For an account of an active farmer's day, see William Howitt, *Rural Life of England* (1862), pp. 110-1.

[3] Sir Mordaunt Martin in *Bath and West and Southern Counties Society, Letters and Papers* (Bath, 1795), vii, p. 109; "A Farmer", "Observations on Taken-Work and Labour", *Monthly Magazine*, Sept. 1798, May 1799.

In the nineteenth century the debate was largely resolved in favour of weekly wage-labour, supplemented by task-work as occasion rose. The Wiltshire labourer's day, as described by Richard Jefferies in the 1870s, was scarcely less long than that described by Markham. Perhaps in resistance to this unremitting toil he was distinguished by the "clumsiness of his walk" and "the deadened slowness which seems to pervade everything he does".[1]

The most arduous and prolonged work of all was that of the labourer's wife in the rural economy. One part of this — especially the care of infants — was the most task-orientated of all. Another part was in the fields, from which she must return to renewed domestic tasks. As Mary Collier complained in a sharp rejoinder to Stephen Duck:

> . . . when we Home are come,
> Alas! we find our Work but just begun;
> So many Things for our Attendance call,
> Has we ten Hands, we could employ them all.
> Our Children put to Bed, with greatest Care
> We all Things for your coming Home prepare:
> You sup, and go to Bed without delay,
> And rest yourselves till the ensuing day;
> While we, alas! but little Sleep can have,
> Because our froward Children cry and rave. . .
>
> In ev'ry Work (we) take our proper Share;
> And from the Time that Harvest doth begin
> Until the Corn be cut and carry'd in,
> Our Toil and Labour's daily so extreme,
> That we have hardly ever *Time to dream*.[2]

Such hours were endurable only because one part of the work, with the children and in the home, disclosed itself as necessary and inevitable, rather than as an external imposition. This remains true to this day, and, despite school times and television times, the rhythms of women's work in the home are not wholly attuned to the measurement of the clock. The mother of young children has an imperfect sense

[1] J. R. Jefferies, *The Toilers of the Field* (1892), pp. 84-8, 211-2.

[2] Mary Collier, now a Washer-woman, at Petersfield in Hampshire, *The Woman's Labour: an Epistle to Mr. Stephen Duck; in Answer to his late Poem, called The Thresher's Labour* (1739), pp. 10-11, reprinted (1989).

of time and attends to other human tides. She has not yet altogether moved out of the conventions of "pre-industrial" society.

V

I have placed "pre-industrial" in inverted commas: and for a reason. It is true that the transition to mature industrial society demands analysis in sociological as well as economic terms. Concepts such as "time-preference" and the "backward sloping labour supply curve" are, too often, cumbersome attempts to find economic terms to describe sociological problems. But, equally, the attempt to provide simple models for one single, supposedly-neutral, technologically-determined, process known as "industrialisation" is also suspect.[1] It is not only that the highly-developed and technically-alert manufacturing industries (and the way of life supported by them) of France or England in the eighteenth century can only by semantic torture be described as "pre-industrial". (And such a description opens the door to endless false analogies between societies at greatly differing economic levels.) It is also that there has never been any single type of "the transition". The stress of the transition falls upon the whole culture: resistance to change and assent to change arise from the whole culture. And this culture expresses the systems of power, property-relations, religious institutions, etc., inattention to which merely flattens phenomena and trivialises analysis. Above all, the transition is not to "industrialism" *tout court* but to industrial capitalism or (in the twentieth century) to alternative systems whose features are still indistinct. What we are examining here are not only changes in manufacturing technique which demand greater synchronisation of labour and a greater exactitude in time-routines in *any* society; but also these changes as they were lived through in the society of nascent industrial capitalism. We are concerned simultaneously with time-sense in its technological conditioning, and with time-measurement as a means of labour exploitation.

[1] See the valuable critique by André Gunder Frank, "Sociology of Development and Underdevelopment of Sociology", *Catalyst* (Buffalo, Summer 1967).

There are reasons why the transition was peculiarly protracted and fraught with conflict in England: among those which are often noted, England's was the first industrial revolution, and there were no Cadillacs, steel mills, or television sets to serve as demonstrations as to the object of the operation. Moreover, the preliminaries to the industrial revolution were so long that, in the manufacturing districts in the early eighteenth century, a vigorous and licensed popular culture had evolved, which the propagandists of discipline regarded with dismay. Josiah Tucker, the dean of Gloucester, declared in 1745 that "the *lower* class of people" were utterly degenerated. Foreigners (he sermonised) found "the *common people* of our *populous cities* to be the most *abandoned*, and *licentious* wretches on earth":

> Such brutality and insolence, such debauchery and extravagance, such idleness, irreligion, cursing and swearing, and contempt of all rule and authority. . . Our people are *drunk with the cup of liberty.*[1]

The irregular labour rhythms described in the previous section help us to understand the severity of mercantilist doctrines as to the necessity for holding down wages as a preventative against idleness, and it would seem to be not until the second half of the eighteenth century that "normal" capitalist wage incentives begin to become widely effective.[2] The confrontations over discipline have already been examined by others.[3] My intention here is to touch upon several points which concern time-discipline more particularly. The first is found in the extraordinary Law Book of the Crowley Iron Works. Here, at the very birth of the large-scale unit in manufacturing industry, the old autocrat, Crowley, found it necessary to design an entire civil and penal code, running to more than 100,000 words, to govern and regulate his refractory labour-force. The preambles to Orders Number 40

---

[1] J. Tucker, *Six Sermons* (Bristol, 1772), pp. 70-1.

[2] The change is perhaps signalled at the same time in the ideology of the more enlightened employers: see A. W. Coats, "Changing attitudes to labour in the mid-eighteenth century", *Econ. Hist. Rev.*, 2nd series, xi (1958-9).

[3] See Pollard, *op. cit.*; N. McKendrick, "Josiah Wedgwood and Factory Discipline", *Hist. Journal*, iv (1961); also Thompson, *op. cit.*, pp. 356-74.

(the Warden at the Mill) and 103 (Monitor) strike the prevailing note of morally-righteous invigilation. From Order 40:

> I having by sundry people working by the day with the connivence of the clerks been horribly cheated and paid for much more time than in good conscience I ought and such hath been the baseness & treachery of sundry clerks that they have concealed the sloath & negligence of those paid by the day. . .

And from Order 103:

> Some have pretended a sort of right to loyter, thinking by their readiness and ability to do sufficient in less time than others. Others have been so foolish to think bare attendance without being employed in business is sufficient. . . Others so impudent as to glory in their villany and upbrade others for their diligence. . .

> To the end that sloath and villany should be detected and the just and diligent rewarded, I have thought meet to create an account of time by a Monitor, and do order and it is hereby ordered and declared from 5 to 8 and from 7 to 10 is fifteen hours, out of which take $1\frac{1}{2}$ for breakfast, dinner, etc. There will then be thirteen hours and a half neat service. . .

This service must be calculated "after all deductions for being at taverns, alehouses, coffee houses, breakfast, dinner, playing, sleeping, smoaking, singing, reading of news history, quarelling, contention, disputes or anything foreign to my business, any way loytering".

The Monitor and Warden of the Mill were ordered to keep for each day employee a time-sheet, entered to the minute, with "Come" and "Run". In the Monitor's Order, verse 31 (a later addition) declares:

> And whereas I have been informed that sundry clerks have been so unjust as to reckon by clocks going the fastest and the bell ringing before the hour for their going from business, and clocks going too slow and the bell ringing after the hour for their coming to business, and those two black traitors Fowell and Skellerne have knowingly allowed the same; it is therefore ordered that no person upon the account doth reckon by any other clock, bell, watch or dyall but the Monitor's, which clock is never to be altered but by the clock-keeper. . .

The Warden of the Mill was ordered to keep the watch "so locked up that it may not be in the power of any person to alter the same". His duties also were defined in verse 8:

Every morning at 5 a clock the Warden is to ring the bell for beginning to work, at eight a clock for breakfast, at half an hour after for work again, at twelve a clock for dinner, at one to work and at eight to ring for leaving work and all to be lock'd up.

His book of the account of time was to be delivered in every Tuesday with the following affidavit:

This account of time is done without favour or affection, ill-will or hatred, & do really believe the persons above mentioned have worked in the service of John Crowley Esq the hours above charged.[1]

We are entering here, already in 1700, the familiar landscape of disciplined industrial capitalism, with the time-sheet, the time-keeper, the informers and the fines. Some seventy years later the same discipline was to be imposed in the early cotton mills (although the machinery itself was a powerful supplement to the time-keeper). Lacking the aid of machinery to regulate the pace of work on the pot-bank, that supposedly-formidable disciplinarian, Josiah Wedgwood, was reduced to enforcing discipline upon the potters in surprisingly muted terms. The duties of the Clerk of the Manufactory were:

To be at the works the first in the morning, & settle the people to their business as they come in, — to encourage those who come regularly to their time, letting them know that their regularity is properly noticed, & distinguishing them by repeated marks of approbation, from the less orderly part of the workpeople, by presents or other marks suitable to their ages, &c.

Those who come later than the hour appointed should be noticed, and if after repeated marks of disapprobation they do not come in due time, an account of the time they are deficient in should be taken, and so much of their wages stopt as the time comes to if they work by wages, and if they work by the piece they should after frequent notice be sent back to breakfast-time.[2]

[1] Order 103 is reproduced in full in *The Law Book of the Crowley Ironworks*, ed. M. W. Flinn (Surtees Society, clxvii, 1957). See also Law Number 16, "Reckonings". Order Number 40 is in the "Law Book", Brit. Lib. Add MS 34555.
[2] MS instructions, *circa* 1780, in Wedgwood MSS (Barlaston), 26.19114.

These regulations were later tightened somewhat:

> Any of the workmen forceing their way through the Lodge after the time alow'd by the Master forfeits 2/-d.[1]

and McKendrick has shown how Wedgwood wrestled with the problem of Etruria and introduced the first recorded system of clocking-in.[2] But it would seem that once the strong presence of Josiah himself was withdrawn the incorrigible potters returned to many of their older ways.

It is too easy, however, to see this only as a matter of factory or workshop discipline, and we may glance briefly at the attempt to impose "time-thrift" in the domestic manufacturing districts, and its impingement upon social and domestic life. Almost all that the masters *wished* to see imposed may be found in the bounds of a single pamphlet, the Rev. J. Clayton's *Friendly Advice to the Poor*, "written and publish'd at the Request of the late and present Officers of the Town of Manchester" in 1755. "If the *sluggard hides his hands* in his bosom, rather than applies them to work; if he spends his Time in sauntring, impairs his Constitution by Laziness, and dulls his Spirit by Indolence. . ." then he can expect only poverty as his reward. The labourer must not loiter idly in the market-place or waste time in marketing. Clayton complains that "the Churches and Streets [are] crowded with Numbers of Spectators" at weddings and funerals, "who in spight of the Miseries of their Starving Condition. . . make no Scruple of wasting the best Hours in the Day, for the sake of gazing. . .". The tea-table is "this shameful devourer of Time and Money". So also are wakes and holidays and the annual feasts of friendly societies. So also is "that slothful spending the Morning in Bed":

[1] "Some regulations and rules for this manufactory more than 30 years back", dated *circa* 1810, in Wedgwood MSS (Keele University), 4045.5.

[2] A "tell-tale" clock is preserved at Barlaston, but these "tell-tales" (manufactured by John Whitehurst of Derby from about 1750) served only to ensure the regular patrol and attendance of night-watchmen, etc. The first printing time-recorders were made by Bundy in the U.S.A. in 1885. Ward, *op. cit.*, p. 49; also T. Thomson's *Annals of Philosophy*, vi (1815), pp. 418-9 and vii (1816), p. 160; Charles Babbage, *On the Economy of Machinery and Manufacturers* (1835), pp. 28, 40; Bruton, *op. cit.*, pp. 95-6.

> The necessity of early rising would reduce the poor to a necessity of going to Bed betime; and thereby prevent the Danger of Midnight revels.

Early rising would also "introduce an exact Regularity into their Families, a wonderful Order into their Oeconomy".

The catalogue is familiar, and might equally well be taken from Baxter in the previous century. If we can trust Bamford's *Early Days*, Clayton failed to make many converts from their old way of life among the weavers. Nevertheless, the long dawn chorus of moralists is prelude to the quite sharp attack upon popular customs, sports, and holidays which was made in the last years of the eighteenth century and the first years of the nineteenth.

One other non-industrial institution lay to hand which might be used to inculcate "time-thrift": the school. Clayton complained that the streets of Manchester were full of "idle ragged children; who are not only losing their Time, but learning habits of gaming", etc. He praised charity schools as teaching Industry, Frugality, Order and Regularity: "the Scholars here are obliged to rise betimes and to observe Hours with great Punctuality".[1] William Temple, when advocating, in 1770, that poor children be sent at the age of four to work-houses where they should be employed in manufactures and given two hours' schooling a day, was explicit about the socialising influence of the process:

> There is considerable use in their being, somehow or other, constantly employed at least twelve hours a day, whether they earn their living or not; for by these means, we hope that the rising generation will be so habituated to constant employment that it would at length prove agreeable and entertaining to them. . .[2]

Powell, in 1772, also saw education as a training in the "habit of industry"; by the time the child reached six or seven it should become "habituated, not to say naturalized to Labour and Fatigue".[3] The Rev. William Turner, writing from Newcastle in 1786, recommended Raikes' schools as "a spectacle of order and regularity", and quoted a manufacturer of hemp and flax in Gloucester as affirming that the

[1] Clayton, *loc. cit.*, pp. 19, 42-3.
[2] Cited in Furniss, *op. cit.*, p. 114.
[3] Anon. [Powell], *A View of Real Grievances* (1772), p. 90.

schools had effected an extraordinary change: "they are. . . become more tractable and obedient, and less quarrelsome and revengeful".[1] Exhortations to punctuality and regularity are written into the rules of all the early schools:

> Every scholar must be in the school-room on Sundays, at nine o'clock in the morning, and at half-past one in the afternoon, or she shall lose her place the next Sunday, and walk last.[2]

Once within the school gates, the child entered the new universe of disciplined time. At the Methodist Sunday Schools in York the teachers were fined for unpunctuality. The first rule to be learned by the scholars was:

> I am to be present at the School. . . a few minutes before half-past nine o'clock. . .

Once in attendance, they were under military rule:

> The Superintendent shall again ring, — when, on a motion of his hand, the whole School rise at once from their seats; — on a second motion, the Scholars turn; — on a third, slowly and silently move to the place appointed to repeat their lessons, — he then pronounces the word "Begin". . .[3]

The onslaught, from so many directions, upon the people's old working habits was not, of course, uncontested. In the first stage, we find simple resistance.[4] But, in the next stage, as the new time-discipline is imposed, so the workers begin to fight, not against time, but about it. The evidence here is not wholly clear. But in the better-organised artisan trades, especially in London, there is no doubt that hours were progressively shortened in the eighteenth century as combination advanced. Lipson cites the case of the London tailors

---

[1] W. Turner, *Sunday Schools Recommended* (Newcastle, 1786), pp. 23, 42.

[2] *Rules for the Methodist School of Industry at Pocklington, for the instruction of Poor Girls in Reading, Sewing, Knitting, and Marking* (York, 1819), p. 12.

[3] *Rules for the Government, Superintendence, and Teaching of the Wesleyan Methodist Sunday Schools* (York, 1833). See also Harold Silver, *The Concept of Popular Education* (1965), pp. 32-42; David Owen, *English Philanthrophy, 1660-1960* (Cambridge, Mass., 1965), pp. 23-7.

[4] The best account of the employers' problem is in S. Pollard, *The Genesis of Modern Management* (1965), ch. v, "The Adaptation of the Labour Force".

whose hours were shortened in 1721, and again in 1768: on both occasions the mid-day intervals allowed for dinner and drinking were also shortened — the day was compressed.[1] By the end of the eighteenth century there is some evidence that some favoured trades had gained something like a ten-hour day.

Such a situation could only persist in exceptional trades and in a favourable labour market. A reference in a pamphlet of 1827 to "the English system of working from 6 o'clock in the morning to 6 in the evening"[2] may be a more reliable indication of the general expectation as to hours of the mechanic and artisan outside London in the 1820s. In the dishonourable trades and outwork industries hours (when work was available) were probably moving the other way.

It was exactly in those industries — the textile mills and the engineering workshops — where the new time-discipline was most rigorously imposed that the contest over time became more intense. At first some of the worst masters attempted to expropriate the workers of all knowledge of time. "I worked at Mr. Braid's mill", declared one witness:

> There we worked as long as we could see in summer time, and I could not say at what hour it was that we stopped. There was nobody but the master and the master's son who had a watch, and we did not know the time. There was one man who had a watch. . . It was taken from him and given into the master's custody because he had told the men the time of day. . .[3]

A Dundee witness offers much the same evidence:

> . . . in reality there were no regular hours: masters and managers did with us as they liked. The clocks at the factories were often put forward in the morning and back at night, and instead of being instruments for the measurement of time, they were used as cloaks for cheatery and oppression. Though this was known amongst the hands, all were afraid

[1] E. Lipson, *The Economic History of England*, 6th edn. (1956), iii, pp. 404-6. See e.g. J. L. Ferri, *Londres et les Anglais* (Paris, An xii), pp. 163-4. Some of the evidence as to hours is discussed in G. Langenfelt, *The Historic Origin of the Eight Hours Day* (Stockholm, 1954).

[2] *A Letter on the Present State of the Labouring Classes in America*, by an intelligent Emigrant at Philadelphia (Bury, 1827).

[3] Alfred [S. Kydd], *History of the Factory Movement.* . . (1857), i, p. 283, quoted in P. Mantoux, *The Industrial Revolution in the Eighteenth Century* (1948), p. 427.

to speak, and a workman then was afraid to carry a watch, as it was no uncommon event to dismiss any one who presumed to know too much about the science of horology.[1]

Petty devices were used to shorten the dinner hour and to lengthen the day. "Every manufacturer wants to be a gentleman at once", said a witness before Sadler's Committee:

> and they want to nip every corner that they can, so that the bell will ring to leave off when it is half a minute past time, and they will have them in about two minutes before time. . . If the clock is as it used to be, the minute hand is at the weight, so that as soon as it passes the point of gravity, it drops three minutes all at once, so that it leaves them only twenty-seven minutes, instead of thirty.[2]

A strike-placard of about the same period from Todmorden put it more bluntly: "if that piece of dirty suet, 'old Robertshaw's engine-tenter', do not mind his own business, and let ours alone, we will shortly ask him how long it is since he received a gill of ale for running 10 minutes over time".[3] The first generation of factory workers were taught by their masters the importance of time; the second generation formed their short-time committees in the ten-hour movement; the third generation struck for overtime or time-and-a-half. They had accepted the categories of their employers and learned to fight back within them. They had learned their lesson, that time is money, only too well.[4]

VI

We have seen, so far, something of the external pressures which enforced this discipline. But what of the internalisation of this discipline? How far was it imposed, how far assumed? We should, perhaps, turn the problem around once again, and place it within the evolution of the Puritan ethic. One cannot claim that there was anything radically new in the

[1] Anon., *Chapters in the Life of a Dundee Factory Boy* (Dundee, 1887), p. 10.

[2] *PP*, 1831-32, xv, pp. 177-8. See also the example from the Factory Commission (1833), in Mantoux, *op. cit.*, p. 427.

[3] Placard in my possession.

[4] For a discussion of the next stage, when the workers had learned "the rules of the game", see E. J. Hobsbawm, *Labouring Men* (1964), ch. xvii, "Custom, Wages and Work-load".

preaching of industry or in the moral critique of idleness. But there is perhaps a new insistence, a firmer accent, as those moralists who had accepted this new discipline for themselves enjoined it upon the working people. Long before the pocket watch had come within the reach of the artisan, Baxter and his fellows were offering to each man his own interior moral time-piece.[1] Thus Baxter, in his *Christian Directory*, plays many variations on the theme of Redeeming the Time: "use wholly in the way of duty". The imagery of time as currency is strongly marked, but Baxter would seem to have an audience of merchants and of tradesmen in his mind's eye:

> Remember how gainful the Redeeming of Time is. . . in Merchandize, or any trading; in husbandry or any gaining course, we use to say of a man that hath grown rich by it, that he hath made use of his Time.[2]

Oliver Heywood, in *Youth's Monitor* (1689), is addressing the same audience:

> Observe exchange-time, look to your markets; there are some special seasons, that will favour you in expediting your business with facility and success; there are nicks of time, in which, if your actions fall, they may set you forward apace: seasons of doing or receiving good last not always; the fair continues not all the year. . .[3]

The moral rhetoric passes swiftly between two poles. On the one hand, apostrophes to the brevity of the mortal span, when placed beside the certainty of Judgement. Thus Heywood's *Meetness for Heaven* (1690):

> Time lasts not, but floats away apace; but what is everlasting depends upon it. In this world we either win or lose eternal felicity. The great weight of eternity hangs on the small and brittle thread of life. . . This is our working day, our market time. . . O Sirs, sleep now, and awake in hell, whence there is no redemption.

---

[1] John Preston used the image of clock-work in 1628: "In this curious clocke-worke of religion, every pin and wheel that is amise distempers all": *Sermons Preached before His Majestie* (1630), p. 18. Cf. R. Baxter, *A Christian Directory* (1673), i, p. 285: "A wise and well skilled Christian should bring his matters into such order, that every ordinary duty should know his place, and all should be. . . as the parts of a Clock or other Engine, which must be all conjunct, and each right placed".

[2] *Ibid.*, i, pp. 274-5, 277.

[3] *The Whole Works of the Rev., Oliver Heywood* (Idle, 1826), v, p. 575.

Or, from *Youth's Monitor* again: time "is too precious a commodity to be undervalued. . . This is the golden chain on which hangs a massy eternity; the loss of time is unsufferable, because irrecoverable".[1] Or from Baxter's *Directory*:

> O where are the brains of those men, and of what metal are their hardened hearts made, that can idle and play away that Time, that little Time, that only Time, which is given them for the everlasting saving of their souls?[2]

On the other hand, we have the bluntest and most mundane admonitions on the husbandry of time. Thus Baxter, in *The Poor Man's Family Book* advises: "Let the time of your Sleep be so much only as health requireth; For precious time is not to be wasted in unnecessary sluggishness": "quickly dress you"; "and follow your labours with constant diligence".[3] Both traditions were extended, by way of Law's *Serious Call*, to John Wesley. The very name of "the Methodists" emphasises this husbandry of time. In Wesley also we have these two extremes — the jabbing at the nerve of mortality, the practical homily. It was the first (and not hell-fire terrors) which sometimes gave an hysterical edge to his sermons, and brought converts to a sudden sense of sin. He also continues the time-as-currency imagery, but less explicitly as merchant or market-time:

> See that ye walk circumspectly, says the Apostle. . . redeeming the time; saving all the time you can for the best purposes; buying up every fleeting moment out of the hands of sin and Satan, out of the hands of sloth, ease, pleasure, worldly business. . .

Wesley, who never spared himself, and until the age of eighty rose every day at 4 a.m. (he ordered that the boys at Kingswood School must do the same), published in 1786 as a tract his sermon on *The Duty and Advantage of Early Rising*: "By *soaking*. . . so long between warm sheets, the flesh is as it were parboiled, and becomes soft and flabby. The nerves, in the mean time, are quite unstrung". This reminds us of the voice of Isaac Watts' Sluggard. Wherever Watts looked in nature, the "busy little bee" or the sun rising at his "proper

---

[1] *Ibid.*, v, pp. 386-7; see also p. 562.
[2] Baxter, *op. cit.*, i, p. 276.
[3] R. Baxter, *The Poor Man's Family Book*, 6th edn. (1697), pp. 290-1;

hour", he read the same lesson for unregenerate man.[1] Alongside the Methodists, the Evangelicals took up the theme. Hannah More contributed her own imperishable lines on "Early Rising":

> Thou silent murderer, Sloth, no more
>   My mind imprison'd keep;
> Nor let me waste another hour
>   With thee, thou felon Sleep.[2]

In one of her tracts, *The Two Wealthy Farmers*, she succeeds in bringing the imagery of time-as-currency into the labour-market:

> When I call in my labourers on a Saturday night to pay them, it often brings to my mind the great and general day of account, when I, and you, and all of us, shall be called to our grand and awful reckoning. . . When I see that one of my men has failed of the wages he should have received, because he has been idling at a fair; another has lost a day by a drinking-bout. . . I cannot help saying to myself, Night is come; Saturday night is come. No repentance or diligence on the part of these poor men can now make a bad week's work good. This week is gone into eternity.[3]

Long before the time of Hannah More, however, the theme of the zealous husbandry of time had ceased to be particular to the Puritan, Wesleyan, or Evangelical traditions. It was Benjamin Franklin, who had a life-long technical interest in clocks and who numbered among his acquaintances John Whitehurst of Derby, the inventor of the "tell-tale" clock, who gave it its most unambiguous secular expression:

> Since our Time is reduced to a Standard, and the Bullion of the Day minted out into Hours, the Industrious know how to employ every Piece of Time to a real Advantage in their different Professions: And he that is prodigal of his Hours, is, in effct, a Squanderer of Money. I remember a notable Woman, who was fully sensible of the intrinsic Value of *Time*. Her Husband was a Shoemaker, and an excellent Craftsman, but never minded how the Minutes passed. In vain did she inculcate to him, *That Time is Money*. He had too much Wit to

[1] *Poetical Works of Isaac Watts, D.D.* (Cooke's Pocket Edn., [1802]), pp. 224, 227, 232. The theme is not new, of course: Chaucer's Parson said. "Sleepinge longe in quiete is eek a great norice to Lecherie".
[2] H. More, *Works* (1830), ii, p. 42. See also p. 35, "Time".
[3] *Ibid.*, iii, p. 167.

apprehend her, and it prov'd his Ruin. When at the Alehouse among his idle Companions, if one remark'd that the Clock struck Eleven, *What is that,* says he, *among us all?* If she sent him Word by the Boy, that it had struck Twelve; *Tell her to be easy, it can never be more.* If, that it had struck One, *Bid her be comforted, for it can never be less.*[1]

The reminiscence comes directly out of London (one suspects) where Franklin worked as a printer in the 1720s — but never, he reassures us in his *Autobiography*, following the example of his fellow-workers in keeping Saint Monday. It is, in some sense, appropriate that the ideologist who provided Weber with his central text in illustration of the capitalist ethic[2] should come, not from that Old World, but from the New — the world which was to invent the time-recorder, was to pioneer time-and-motion study, and was to reach its apogee with Henry Ford.[3]

VII

In all these ways — by the division of labour; the supervision of labour; fines; bells and clocks; money incentives; preachings and schoolings; the suppression of fairs and sports — new labour habits were formed, and a new time-discipline was imposed. It sometimes took several generations (as in the Potteries), and we may doubt how far it was ever fully accomplished: irregular labour rhythms were perpetuated (and even institutionalised) into the present century, notably in London and in the great ports.[4]

[1] *Poor Richard's Almanac,* Jan. 1751, in *The Papers of Benjamin Franklin,* ed. L. W. Labaree and W. J. Bell (New Haven, 1961), iv, pp. 86-7.

[2] Max Weber, *The Protestant Ethic and the Spirit of Capitalism* (1930), pp. 48-50 and *passim.*

[3] Ford commenced his career repairing watches: since there was a difference between local time and standard railroad time, he made a watch, with two dials, which kept both times — an ominous beginning: H. Ford, *My Life and Work* (1923), p. 24.

[4] There is an abundant literature of nineteenth-century dockland which illustrates this. However, in recent years the casual labourer in the ports has ceased to be a "casualty" of the labour market (as Mayhew saw him) and is marked by his preference for high earnings over security: see K. J. W. Alexander, "Casual Labour and Labour Casualties", *Trans. Inst. of Engineers and Shipbuilders in Scotland* (Glasgow, 1964). I have not touched in this paper on the new occupational time-tables introduced in

Throughout the nineteenth century the propaganda of time-thrift continued to be directed at the working people, the rhetoric becoming more debased, the apostrophes to eternity becoming more shop-soiled, the homilies more mean and banal. In early Victorian tracts and reading-matter aimed at the masses one is choked by the quantity of the stuff. But eternity has become those never-ending accounts of pious death-beds (or sinners struck by lightning), while the homilies have become little Smilesian snippets about humble men who by early rising and diligence made good. The leisured classes began to discover the "problem" (about which we hear a good deal today) of the leisure of the masses. A considerable proportion of manual workers (one moralist was alarmed to discover) after concluding their work were left with

> several hours in the day to be spent nearly as they please. And in what manner. . . is this precious time expended by those of no mental cultivation?. . . We shall often see them just simply annihilating those portions of time. They will for an hour, or for hours together. . . sit on a bench, or lie down on a bank or hillock. . . yielded up to utter vacancy and torpor. . . or collected in groups by the road side, in readiness to find in whatever passes there occasions for gross jocularity; practising some impertinence, or uttering some jeering scurrility, at the expense of persons going by. . .[1]

This, clearly, was worse than Bingo: non-productivity, compounded with impertinence. In mature capitalist society all time must be consumed, marketed, put to *use*; it is offensive for the labour force merely to "pass the time".

But how far did this propaganda really succeed? How far are we entitled to speak of any radical restructuring of man's social nature and working habits? I have given elsewhere some reasons for supposing that this discipline was indeed internalised, and that we may see in the Methodist sects of the early nineteenth century a figuration of the psychic crisis

---

industrial society — notably night-shift workers (pits, railways, etc.): see the observations by "A Journeyman Engineer" [T. Wright], *The Great Unwashed* (1868), pp. 188-200; M. A. Pollock (ed.), *Working Days* (1926), pp. 17-28; Tom Nairn, *New Left Review* 34 (1965), p. 38.

[1] John Foster, *An Essay on the Evils of Popular Ignorance* (1821), pp. 180-5.

entailed.[1] Just as the new time-sense of the merchants and
gentry in the Renaisance appears to find one expression in the
heightened awareness of mortality, so, one might argue, the
extension of this sense to the working people during the
industrial revolution (together with the hazard and high
mortality of the time) helps to explain the obsessive emphasis
upon death in sermons and tracts whose consumers were
among the working-class. Or (from a positive stand-point)
one may note that as the industrial revolution proceeds, wage
incentives and expanding consumer drives — the palpable
rewards for the productive consumption of time and the
evidence of new "predictive" attitudes to the future[2] are
evidently effective. By the 1830s and 1840s it was commonly
observed that the English industrial worker was marked off
from his fellow Irish worker, not by a greater capacity for
hard work, but by his regularity, his methodical paying-out
of energy, and perhaps also by a repression, not of enjoy-
ments, but of the capacity to relax in the old, uninhibited
ways.

There is no way in which we can quantify the time-sense of
one, or of a million, workers. But it is possible to offer one
check of a comparative kind. For what was said by the
mercantilist moralists as to the failures of the eighteenth-
century English poor to respond to incentives and disciplines
is often repeated, by observers and by theorists of economic
growth, of the peoples of developing countries today. Thus
Mexican paeons in the early years of this century were regarded as an "indolent and child-like people". The Mexican
mineworker had the custom of returning to his village for
corn planting and harvest:

> His lack of initiative, inability to save, absences while celebrating too
> many holidays, willingness to work only three or four days a week if
> that paid for necessities, insatiable desire for alchohol — all were
> pointed out as proof of a natural inferiority.

[1] Thompson, *op. cit.*, chs. xi and xii.
[2] See the important discussion of forecasting and predictive attitudes
and their influence upon social and economic behaviour, in Bourdieu,
op. cit.

He failed to respond to direct day-wage incentives, and (like the eighteenth-century English collier or tinner) responded better to contract and sub-contract systems:

> Given a contract and the assurance that he will get so much money for each ton he mines, and that it doesn't matter how long he makes doing it, or how often he sits down to contemplate life, he will work with a vigour which is remarkable.[1]

In generalisations supported by another study of Mexican labour conditions, Wilbert Moore remarks: "Work is almost always task-orientated in non-industrial societies. . . and. . . it may be appropriate to tie wages to tasks and not directly to time in newly developing areas".[2]

The problem recurs in a dozen forms in the literature of "industrialisation". For the engineer of economic growth, it may appear as the problem of absenteeism — how is the Company to deal with the unrepentant labourer on the Cameroons plantation who declares: "How man fit work so, any day, any day, weh'e no take absen'? No be 'e go die?" ("How could a man work like that, day after day, without being absent? Would he not die?")[3]

> . . . the whole mores of African life, make a high and sustained level of effort in a given length of working day a greater burden both physically and psychologically than in Europe.[4]

> Time commitments in the Middle East or in Latin America are often treated somewhat casually by European standards; new industrial workers only gradually become accustomed to regular hours, regular attendance, and a regular pace of work; transportation schedules or the delivery of materials are not always reliable. . .[5]

The problem may appear as one of adapting the seasonal rhythms of the countryside, with its festivals and religious holidays, to the needs of industrial production:

[1] Cited in M. D. Bernstein, *The Mexican Mining Industry, 1890-1950* (New York, 1964), ch. vii; see also Mead, *op. cit.*, pp. 179-82.

[2] W. E. Moore, *Industrialization and Labor* (Ithaca, 1951), p. 310, and pp. 44-7, 114-22.

[3] F. A. Wells and W. A. Warmington, *Studies in Industrialization: Nigeria and the Cameroons* (1962), p. 128.

[4] *Ibid.*, p. 170. See also pp. 183, 198, 214.

[5] Edwin J. Cohn, "Social and Cultural Factors affecting the Emergence of Innovations", in *Social Aspects of Economic Development* (Economic and Social Studies Conference, Istanbul, 1964), pp. 105-6.

The work year of the factory is necessarily in accord with the workers' demands, rather than an ideal one from the point of view of most efficient production. Several attempts by the managers to alter the work pattern have come to nil. The factory comes back to a schedule acceptable to the Cantelano.[1]

Or it may appear as it did in the early years of the Bombay cotton-mills, as one of maintaining a labour force at the cost of perpetuating inefficient methods of production — elastic time-schedules, irregular breaks and meal-times, etc. Most commonly, in countries where the link between the new factory proletariat and their relatives (and perhaps land-holdings or rights to land) in the villages are much closer — and are maintained for much longer — than in the English experience, it appears as one of disciplining a labour force which is only partially and temporarily "committed" to the industrial way of life.[2]

The evidence is plentiful, and, by the method of contrast, it reminds us how far we have become habituated to different disciplines. Mature industrial societies of all varieties are marked by time-thrift and by a clear demarcation between

[1] Manning Nash, "The Recruitment of Wage Labor in the Development of New Skills", *Annals of the American Academy*, cccv (1956), pp. 27-8. See also Manning Nash, "The Reaction of a Civil-Religious Hierarchy to a Factory in Guatemala", *Human Organization*, xiii (1955), pp. 26-8, and Salz, *op. cit.*, (note 1 on p. 355), pp. 94-114.

[2] W. E. Moore and A. S. Feldman (eds.), *Labor Commitment and Social Change in Developing Areas* (New York, 1960). Useful studies of adaptation and of absenteeism include W. Elkan, *An African Labour Force* (Kampala, 1956), esp. chs. ii and iii; and F. H. Harbison and I. A. Ibrahim, "Some Labor Problems of Industrialization in Egypt", *Annals of the American Academy*, cccv (1956), pp. 114-29. M. D. Morris, *The Emergence of an Industrial Labor Force in India* (Berkeley, 1965) discounts the seriousness of the problems of discipline, absenteeism, seasonal fluctuations in employment, etc. in the Bombay cotton-mills in the late nineteenth century, but at many points his arguments appear to be at odds with his own evidence: see pp. 85, 97, 102; see also C. A. Myers, *Labour Problems in the Industrialization of India* (Cambridge, Mass., 1958), ch. iii, and S. D. Mehta, "Professor Morris on Textile Labour Supply", *Indian Economic Journal*, i, 3 (1954), pp. 333-40. Useful studies of an only partially "committed" labour force are G. V. Rimlinger, "Autocracy and the early Rusian Factory System", *Jl. Econ. Hist.*, xx (1960) and T. V. von Laue, "Russian Peasants in the Factory", *ibid.*, xxi (1961).

"work" and "life".[1] But, having taken the problem so far, we may be permitted to moralise a little, in the eighteenth-century manner, ourselves. The point at issue is not that of the "standard-of-living". If the theorists of growth wish us to say so, then we may agree that the older popular culture was in many ways otiose, intellectually vacant, devoid of quickening, and plain bloody poor. Without time-discipline we could not have the insistent energies of industrial man; and whether this discipline comes in the forms of Methodism, or of Stalinism, or of nationalism, it will come to the developing world.

What needs to be said is not that one way of life is better than the other, but this is a place of the most far-reaching conflict; that the historical record is not a simple one of neutral and inevitable technological change, but is also one of exploitation and of resistance to exploitation; and that values stand to be lost as well as gained. The rapidly-growing literature of the sociology of industrialisation is like a landscape which has been blasted by years of moral drought: one must travel through many tens of thousands of words of parched a-historical abstraction between each oasis of human actuality. Too many of the Western engineers of growth appear altogether too smug as to the gifts of character-formation which they bring in their hands to their backward brethren. The "structuring of a labour force", Kerr and Siegel tell us:

> . . . involves the setting of rules on times to work and not work, on method and amount of pay, on movement into and out of work and from one position to another. It involves rules pertaining to the maintenance of continuity in the work process. . . the attempted minimization of individual or organized revolt, the provision of view of the world, of ideological orientations, of beliefs. . .[2]

Wilbert Moore has even drawn up a shopping-list of the "pervasive values and normative orientations of high relevance to the goal of social development" — "these

[1] See G. Friedmann, "Leisure and Technological Civilization", *Int. Soc. Science Jour.*, xii (1960), pp. 509-21.
[2] C. Kerr and A. Siegel, "The Structuring of the Labor Force in Industrial Society: New Dimensions and New Questions", *Industrial and Labor Relations Review*, ii (1955), p. 163.

changes in attitude and belief are 'necessary' if rapid economic and social development is to be achieved":

Impersonality: judgement of merit and performance, not social background or irrelevant qualities.

Specificity of relations in terms of both context and limits of interaction.

Rationality and problem-solving.

Punctuality.

Recognition of individually limited but systematically linked inter-dependence.

Discipline, deference to legitimate authority.

Respect for property rights. . .

These, with "achievement and mobility aspirations", are not, Professor Moore reassures us,

suggested as a comprehensive list of the merits of modern man. . . The "whole man" will also love his family, worship his God, and express his aesthetic capacities, But he will keep each of these other orientations "in their place".[1]

It need cause no surprise that such "provision of ideological orientations" by the Baxters of the twentieth century should have been welcome to the Ford Foundation. That they should so often have appeared in publications sponsored by UNESCO is less easily explained.

VIII

It is a problem which the peoples of the developing world must live through and grow through. One hopes that they will be wary of pat, manipulative models, which present the working masses only as an inert labour force. And there is a sense, also, within the advanced industrial countries, in which this has ceased to be a problem placed in the past. For we are now at a point where sociologists are discussing the "problem" of leisure. And a part of the problem is: how did it come to be a problem? Puritanism, in its marriage of convenience with industrial capitalism, was the agent which converted people to new valuations of time; which taught children even in their infancy to improve each shining hour; and which saturated peoples' minds with the equation, time is

---

[1] E. de Vries and J. M. Echavarria (eds.), *Social Aspects of Economic Development in Latin America* (UNESCO, 1963), p. 237.

money.[1] One recurrent form of revolt within Western industrial capitalism, whether bohemian or beatnik, has often taken the form of flouting the urgency of respectable time-values. And the interesting question arises: if Puritanism was a necessary part of the work-ethos which enabled the industrialised world to break out of the poverty-stricken economies of the past, will the Puritan valuation of time begin to decompose as the pressures of poverty relax? Is it decomposing already? Will people begin to lose that restless urgency, that desire to consume time purposively, which most people carry just as they carry a watch on their wrists?

If we are to have enlarged leisure, in an automated future, the problem is not "how are people going to be able to *consume* all these additional time-units of leisure?" but "what will be the capacity of experience of the people who have this undirected time to live?" If we maintain a Puritan time-valuation, a commodity-valuation, then it is a question of how this time is put to *use*, or how it is exploited by the leisure industries. But if the purposive notation of time-use becomes less compulsive, then people might have to re-learn some of the arts of living lost in the industrial revolution: how to fill the interstices of their day with enriched, more leisurely, personal and social relations; how to break down once more the barriers between work and life. And hence would stem a novel dialectic in which some of the old aggressive energies and disciplines migrate to the newly-industrialising nations, while the old industrialised nations seek to rediscover modes of experience forgotten before written history begins:

> . . . the Nuer have no expression equivalent to "time" in our language, and they cannot, therefore, as we can, speak of time as though it were something actual, which passes, can be wasted, can be saved, and so forth. I do not think that they ever experience the same feeling of fighting against time or of having to co-ordinate activities with an abstract passage of time because their points of reference are mainly the activities themselves, which are generally of a leisurely character. Events

[1]Suggestive comments on this equation are in Lewis Mumford and S. de Grazia, cited note 1 on p. 352; Paul Diesing, *Reason in Society* (Urbana, 1962), pp. 24-8; Hans Meyerhoff, *Time in Literature* (Univ. of California, 1955), pp. 106-19.

follow a logical order, but they are not controlled by an abstract system,
there being no autonomous points of reference to which activities have
to conform with precision. Nuer are fortunate.[1]

Of course, no culture re-appears in the same form. If
people are to meet both the demands of a highly-
synchronised automated industry, and of greatly enlarged
areas of "free time", they must somehow combine in a new
synthesis elements of the old and of the new, finding an
imagery based neither upon the seasons nor upon the market
but upon human occasions. Punctuality in working hours
would express respect for one's fellow workers. And
unpurposive passing of time would be behaviour which the
culture approved.

It can scarcely find approval among those who see the
history of "industrialisation" in seemingly-neutral but, in
fact, profoundly value-loaded terms, as one of increasing
rationalisation in the service of economic growth. The
argument is at least as old as the industrial revolution.
Dickens saw the emblem of Thomas Gradgrind ("ready to
weigh and measure any parcel of human nature, and tell you
exactly what it comes to") as the "deadly statistical clock" in
his observatory, "which measured every second with a beat
like a rap upon a coffin-lid". But rationalism has grown new
sociological dimensions since Gradgrind's time. It was
Werner Sombart who — using the same favourite image
of the Clockmaker — replaced the God of mechanical
materialism by the Entrepreneur:

> If modern economic rationalism is like the mechanism of a clock,
> someone must be there to wind it up.[2]

The universities of the West are today thronged with
academic clocksmiths, anxious to patent new keys. But few
have, as yet, advanced as far as Thomas Wedgwood, the son
of Josiah, who designed a plan for taking the time and work-
discipline of Etruria into the very workshops of the child's
formative consciousness:

---

[1] Evans-Pritchard, *op. cit.*, p. 103.
[2] "Capitalism", *Encyclopaedia of the Social Sciences* (New York,
1953), iii, p. 205.

My aim is high — I have been endeavouring some master stroke which should anticipate a century or two upon the large-paced progress of human improvement. Almost every prior step of its advance may be traced to the influence of superior characters. Now, it is my opinion, that in the education of the greatest of these characters, not more than one hour in ten has been made to contribute to the formation of those qualities upon which this influence has depended. Let us suppose ourselves in possession of a detailed statement of the first twenty years of the life of some extraordinary genius; what a chaos of perceptions!. . . How many hours, days, months have been prodigally wasted in unproductive occupations! What a host of half formed impressions & abortive conceptions blended into a mass of confusion. . .

In the best regulated mind of the present day, had not there been, & is not there some hours every day passed in reverie, thought ungoverned, undirected?[1]

Wedgwood's plan was to design a new, rigorous, rational, closeted system of education: Wordsworth was proposed as one possible superintendent. His response was to write *The Prelude* — an essay in the growth of a poet's consciousness which was, at the same time, a polemic against —

> The Guides, the Wardens of our faculties,
> And Stewards of our labour, watchful men
> And skilful in the usury of time,
> Sages, who in their prescience would controul
> All accidents, and to the very road
> Which they have fashion'd would confine us down,
> Like engines. . .[2]

For there is no such thing as economic growth which is not, at the same time, growth or change of a culture; and the growth of social consciousness, like the growth of a poet's mind, can never, in the last analysis, be planned.

[1] Thomas Wedgwood to William Godwin, 31 July 1797, published in David Erdman's important article, "Coleridge, Wordsworth and the Wedgwood Fund", *Bulletin of the New York Public Library*, lx (1956).
[2] *The Prelude* (1805), book v, lines 377-83. See also draft in *Poetical Works of William Wordsworth*, ed. E. de Selincourt and Helen Darbishire (Oxford, 1959), v, p. 346.

Chapter Seven

The Sale of Wives

I

Until a few years ago the historical memory of the sale of wives in England might better be described as amnesia. Who would want to remember practices of such barbarity? By the 1850s nearly all commentators were committed to the view that the practice was (a) exceedingly rare, and (b) utterly offensive to morality (although some folklorists began to toy apologetically with the notion of pagan survival).

The tone of Chambers's *The Book of Days* (1878) is representative. The picture "is simply an outrage upon decency. . . It can only be considered as a proof of the besotted ignorance and brutal feelings of a portion of our rural population". And it was the more important to disclaim and denounce the practice because Britain's "continental neighbours" had noticed the "occasional instances of wife-sale" and they "seriously believe that it is a habit of all classes of our people, and constantly cite it as evidence of our low civilization".[1] The French, with their habitual rancorous levity, were the worst offenders in this: Milord John Bull was portrayed, booted and spurred, in Smithfield Market, crying *"à quinze livres ma femme!"*, while Milady stood haltered in a pen.[2]

[1] *The Book of Days*, ed. R. Chambers (1878), i, pp. 487-8.
[2] Interesting comments on the practice appear as early as 1776, *Courrier de L'Europe* (26 Nov.). Thereafter the French press often carried examples with appropriate comment. See also [J. E. Jouy], *L'Hermite de Londres* (Paris, 1821), ii, p. 324; Anon., *Six mois à Londres* (Paris, 1817); and Piliet, note 1, p. 438 below. Many examples are cited in J. W. von Achenholtz, *Annals*, v (1790), pp. 329-30, ix (1796), pp. 187-8.

The Book of Days was able to gather only eight cases, between 1815 and 1839, and these cases, with three or four more, were circulated with little further enquiry for fifty or more years in antiquarian or journalistic accounts. As enlightenment waxed, so curiosity waned. For the first half of this century historical memory was generally satisfied with occasional throwaway references in popular accounts of eighteenth-century popular mores. These were commonly offered as a colourful element within an antithetical liturgy contrasting the animalistic culture of the poor (Gin Lane, Tyburn and Mother Proctor's Pews, bull-baiting, fireworks tied to animals, pugilism with nailed boots, naked races, wife sales) with whatever forms of enlightenment was supposed to have displaced these.[1]

Against this indifference, one powerful influence was asserted: the careful reconstruction of the sale of a wife, in a credible human context, taking a significant place in the structure of the plot of a major novel, *The Mayor of Casterbridge*. Thomas Hardy was a superbly perceptive observer of folk customs, and his touch is rarely more sure than in this novel. But in the episode of Michael Henchard's sale of his wife, Susan, in a wayside fair to a passing sailor, Hardy appears to have relied, not upon observation (or direct oral tradition) but on newspaper sources. These sources (as we shall see) are usually enigmatic and opaque. And the episode, as drawn in the novel, in its seemingly casual provenance and in its brutal expression, does not conform to more "typical" evidence. The auction of Susan Henchard lacks ritual features; the purchaser arrives fortuitously and bids on impulse. Hardy succeeds admirably, in his reconstruction of the episode and in his disclosure of its consequences, in presenting the general popular consensus as to the legitimacy of the transaction and as to its irrevocable character — a conviction certainly shared by Susan

---

[1] Thus wife sales find mention in J. Wesley Bready, *England Before and After Wesley* (1938), under a section headed: "Immorality as Sport".

Henchard.[1] But in the last analysis Hardy's presentation still
fell within the same stereotype as that of *The Book of Days*.
"For my part", the drunken Henchard says,

> I don't see why men who have got wives and don't want 'em, shouldn't
> get rid of 'em as these gipsey fellows do their old horses. . . Why
> shouldn't they put 'em up and sell 'em by auction to men who are in
> need of such articles?

The assumption underlying both accounts is that the wife
sale was a direct chattel purchase. And once this stereotype
has become established, it is only too easy to read the
evidence through it. It can then be assumed that the wife was
auctioned like a beast or chattel, perhaps against her will,
either because the husband wished to be rid of her or for
merely mercenary motives. As such, the custom disallowed
any scrupulous examination. It could be taken as a
melancholy example of abject feminine oppression, or an
illustration of the levity with which marriage was regarded
among the male poor.

But it is this stereotype — and not the fact that wives were
on occasion sold — which requires interrogation. In any case,
it seemed advisable to collect some evidence before offering
confident explanations. In the 1960s I commenced — with
much assistance from friends and correspondents — to build
up files on "ritual" sales in the eighteenth and nineteenth
centuries; and in the late 1960s and through the 1970s I
inflicted drafts of this chapter upon many seminars and
audiences in Britain and the United States. By 1977 I had
some three hundred cases on my index cards, although at
least fifty of these are too vague or dubious to be taken as
evidence. Meanwhile I delayed publication of my findings,
although these were briefly reported in other scholars' work.[2]
Further delay resulted in my research being overtaken, and in

---

[1] Hardy attributes Susan's conviction to "the extreme simplicity of her
intellect": by the sale, her purchaser "had acquired a morally real and
justifiable right to her. . . though the exact bearings and legal limits of that
right were vague".

[2] I reported some conclusions in "Folklore, Anthropology, and Social
History", *Indian Historical Review*, iii, 2 (1978). For other reports, see
J. Weeks, *Sex, Politics and Society* (1981) and Robert W. Malcolmson,
Life and Labour in England, 1700-1780 (1981), pp. 103-4.

1981 there was published a substantial volume, *Wives for Sale*, by Samuel Pyeatt Menefee.

Mr Menefee's ethnographic study was undertaken as a dissertation in the Department of Social Anthropology at Oxford University, and the subject had perhaps come to the notice of this Department when I gave a paper on this theme to one of its seminars. I could claim no proprietorship in the topic, and, indeed, my intention had been to arouse historical and anthropological interest. Nevertheless, my first response was to regard my own work as having been made redundant. Mr Menefee had pursued the theme with great industry; had circulated many libraries and record offices; had assembled much curious and some relevant material; and had over-passed my own count, with an Appendix of 387 cases. More-over, he shared my redefinition of the ritual by subtitling his volume, "An Ethnographic Study of British Popular Divorce". With a little sadness — for the theme had preoccupied me for some years — I laid my paper aside.

It is revived now, and presented tardily to the public, because I do not think, after all, that Mr Menefee and I duplicate each other or are pursuing the same questions. Mr Menefee wrote as an apprentice ethnographer, and his knowledge of British social history and its disciplines was elementary. As a result he has little understanding of social context, few criteria for distinguishing between sound and corrupt evidence, and his fascinating examples appear in a jumble of irrelevant material and contradictory inter-pretations. We may be grateful for his book, which is immensely painstaking and carefully documented. But it cannot be taken as the final word on the sale of wives.

The ritual may be of only marginal interest, and may have little general relevance to sexual behaviour or marital norms. It offers only a small window upon these questions. Yet there are not many such windows, and we will never have a full view until every window is uncurtained and the perspectives intersect. From this fragmentary and enigmatic evidence we must tease out what insights we can into the norms and sensibility of a lost culture, and into the interior crises of the poor.

II

The quantitative evidence as to wife sales and their frequency
is, in most respects, the least satisfactory to be offered in this
chapter, so we will commence with this. I have collected some
three hundred cases, of which I have disallowed fifty as
dubious. Menefee lists 387 cases, but this includes many
vague and dubious cases, frequent double-counting of the
same case, and cases which are not "true" ritual sales. Let us
say that I have two hundred and fifty authentic cases and
Menefee has three hundred. But about one hundred and fifty
cases appear in both lists — cases collected from such obvious
sources as *Notes and Queries*, the indexes to *The Times*,
folklore collections, etc. Thus together we have collected
some four hundred examples.

Even so, I have felt it necessary to prune this material,
especially in the earlier (pre-1760) years and those later than
1880. The sale or exchange of a wife, for sexual or domestic
services, appears to have taken place, on occasion, in most
places and at most times. It may be only an aberrant transaction, with or without a pretended contractual basis — it is
recorded sometimes today. Unfortunately, some of the
earlier examples afford almost no evidence as to the nature of
the practice recorded. Thus a local historian's record "from
an old document relating to Bilston" — "November, 1692.
John, ye son of Nathan Whitehouse, of Tipton, sold his wife
to Mr. Bracegirdle", cannot arise, without further evidence
to the dignity of being counted as a ritual wife sale.[1] But
some of the later examples, although better documented, also
present difficulties. Thus a young married woman gave
evidence in a Leeds police court in 1913 (in a maintenance
case) that she had been sold for £1 by her husband to a work-
mate who lived in the next street. Her child was fathered by
the second man: he acknowledged it for six weeks and then
told her to drown it. But this man was already married, and
he subsequently returned to his wife.[2] If this was a wife sale
then the custom was in an advanced stage of decomposition
and the practice departs from previously-accepted usage.

[1] F. W. Hackwood, *Staffordshire Customs, Superstititions and Folklore* (1924), p. 70.
[2] *Leeds Weekly Citizen*, 6 June 1913.

There are some cases before 1760 and after 1880 which provide better evidence. But for the purpose of counting I decided to leave pre-1760 cases to historians better qualified to read the evidence, and to ignore those after 1880. This reduced me to 218 cases which I can accept as authentic between 1760 and 1880:[1]

Wife Sales: Visible Cases

1760-1800	42
1800-1840	121
1840-1880	55

Cases have come to hand from every region of England, but I have only one case in this period from Scotland and very few cases from Wales. Counties with ten or more examples are: Derbyshire (10), Devon (12), Kent (10), Lancashire (12), Lincolnshire (14), Middlesex and London (19), Nottinghamshire (13), Staffordshire (16), Warwickshire (10), and (high at the top of the table) Yorkshire (44).

These figures show little, except that the practice certainly occurred, and in most parts of England. The numbers are of *visible* cases, and visibility must be taken in at least three senses. First, these are events whose trace happens to have become visible to me. While Menefee and I offer the same general profile, we have both been dependent in some degree on what caught the notice of folklorists or was copied by metropolitan newspapers. There are no sources from which one could extract a systematic sample, and only a scanning of provincial newspapers in every region could pretend to such a sample.[2] Second, these were events which had to acquire a certain notoriety to leave any traces in the records at all. A ritual sale in the market-place of a large town might do this, but a private sale in a public house might not, unless some unusual circumstance attended it. Since the second form was

[1] The quantities reported here are based upon my study as it stood in 1977. I have not attempted the difficult task of checking and conflating with the examples in the Appendix of S. P. Menefee, *Wives for Sale* (Oxford, 1981), (cited hereafter as Menefee), nor have I added cases which have come to hand since its publication.

[2] My collection probably gives too much weight to Yorkshire (where I used to live and where A. J. Peacock kindly collected samples) and to Lincolnshire (where Rex Russell kindly did the same), and it may give too little weight to the West of England.

favoured in some districts, and displaced the first form generally after 1830 or 1840, we can never hope to recover any accurate quantities.

But it is visibility in a third sense which is of most importance, which offers the largest qualification to any quantities, and which illustrates the slippery nature of the evidence which we must handle. For when did a wife sale become visible to a genteel or middle-class public and hence become worthy of a note in public print? The answer must relate to indistinct changes in social awareness, in moral standards, and in news values. The practice became a matter for more frequent report and comment early in the nineteenth century. But through much of the eighteenth century newspapers were not vehicles for social or domestic comment of this kind. There is good reason to suppose that wife sales were widely practised well before 1790. The custom was little reported because it was not considered worthy of report, unless some additional circumstance (humorous, dramatic, tragic, scandalous) gave it interest. This silence might have been for several reasons: polite ignorance (the distance between the cultures of the newspaper public and of the poor), indifference to a custom so commonplace that it required no comment, or distaste. Wife sales became newsworthy contemporaneously with the evangelical revival, which, by raising the threshold of middle-class tolerance, redefined a matter of popular "ignorance" into one of public scandal.

This has unfortunate consequences. For although the practice is reported after 1790 on occasion as comedy or human interest, it is more often reported in a tone of moral disapproval so strong as to obliterate that evidence which only objectivity could have brought. Wife sales showed that a "system of trading in human flesh" was "not confined to the shores of Africa"; the rope in which the wife was haltered might be better employed in hanging or whipping the parties to the transaction; and (commonly) it was "a most disgusting and disgraceful scene" (Smithfield, 1832), "one of those disgusting scenes which are a disgrace to civilized society" (Norwich, 1823), "an indecent and degrading transaction" (York, 1820). The husband who sold his wife was "a brute in human shape" (Nottingham, 1844), and the wife herself was either an "impudent hussy" or an object of maudlin pity.

This makes enquiry difficult. A decadal count of visible cases between 1800-60 shows: 1800-09, 22; 1810-19, 32; 1820-29, 33; 1830-39, 47; 1840-49, 22; 1850-59, 14.[1] If plotted on a graph this would show a rising curve of sales, reaching a peak in the early 1830s (9 sales in 1833) and then falling off sharply. But a graph of actual sales might run counter to a graph of visible sales. For the latter graph is not one of sales but of the moral outrage provoked by sales. This outrage was accompanied by increasing action against sales by magistrates, constables, market officials and moralists. It was also associated with a rising current of disapproval within the popular culture itself, fed from evangelical, rationalist and radical or trade unionist sources. It is quite possible that actual sales could have come to a peak at some point in the eighteenth or very early nineteenth century, and publicity given to sales between 1820 and 1850 may have been given to late and somewhat shame-faced survivals of a practice already in decline. This publicity, in its turn, may have helped to drive the wife sale out of the public market-place and into more secretive forms.

Some literary evidence supports this suggestion. Thus there is a clear description of ritual wife sale, with public auction and with delivery in a halter, in a workmanlike legal treatise on *The Laws Respecting Women As They Regard Their Natural Rights*, published in 1777. Neither I nor Menefee have many cases before 1777 which clearly indicate a ritual sale, yet the author of this practical treatise can have had no motive for inventing the matter. John Brand also, in his *Observations on Popular Antiquities*, reports the practice in terms which suggest survival from a more vigorous tradition:

> A remarkable Superstition still prevails among the lowest of our Vulgar, that a Man may lawfully sell his Wife to another, provided he deliver her over with a Halter about her Neck.[2]

---

[1] Menefee (Appendix) has: 1800-09, 32; 1810-19, 45; 1820-29, 47; 1830-39, 48; 1840-49, 20; 1850-59, 18.

[2] John Brand, *Observations on Popular Antiquities*, arranged and revised by Henry Ellis (1813), ii, p. 37, which adds: "It is painful to observe that instances of this occur frequently in our Newspapers".

From these references we might assume that the ritual wife sale was commonplace in 1777, and scarcely worthy of comment, and had been so for a century or more. I think this improbable, and the tone of reports in the press suggests a different evolution. Thus an Oxford case in 1789 is noted as "the vulgar mode of *Divorce* lately adopted"; in 1790 a Derbyshire report noted the delivery of the wife in a halter "in the usual way which has been lately practised", and in the same year newspapers in both Derby and Birmingham found it necessary to note that, "as instances of the sale of wives have of late frequently occurred among the lower class of people", such sales were "illegal and void".[1] This could suggest that the wife sale, in its ritual form of market-place auction and halter, while prevalent in some parts of the country in 1777 was only slowly spreading to others.[2] By the 1800s newspapers can refer to sales "in the usual style" and to "disgraceful scenes which have of late become too common".[3] But the evidence as to this evolution is uncertain, and the question must be left open.

It is always uncertain whether the cases reported are the tip of an iceberg or a true index of frequency.[4] At any time before

[1] *Jackson's Oxford Journal*, 12 Dec. 1789; *Northampton Mercury*, 19 Dec. 1789; *Derby Mercury*, 4 and 25 Feb. 1790; *Birmingham Gazette*, 1 Mar. 1790.

[2] Cornwall may have been slow to adopt a practice widespread in Devon. A sale in 1819 in Redruth was reported as "the first of its kind" there: *West Briton*, 17 Dec. 1819.

[3] For examples, *Norfolk Chronicle*, 9 Feb. 1805; W. Andrews, *Bygone England* (1892), p. 203.

[4] Lawrence Stone is over-confident when he concludes (*Road to Divorce*, Oxford 1990, p. 148) that "fewer than three hundred cases of wife-sale occurred in all England during the peak seventy years from 1780 to 1850". If this were so, it would be highly improbable that both Menefee and I should have recovered almost that number from a somewhat random sample of printed sources. In my view many sales, especially before 1820, will not have been recorded at all. Professor Stone underestimates the opacity of the plebeian culture to polite inspection (including his own): he is right, however, to say that wife sales were "very infrequent" as compared with the number of (male) desertions and of elopements: see *ibid.*, pp. 142, 148.

1790 and 1830 visibility cannot be taken to indicate the exceptional nature of the event. When the rector of Clipsham in Rutland indicted a parishioner in 1819 for purchasing a wife, it was noted that "the purchaser was selected for punishment, as the most opulent, and fittest to make an example of" — yet Clipsham at that time contained only 33 houses and 173 inhabitants.[1] By the 1830s and 1840s, however, there is more suggestion that the visible cases were regarded as unusual or as survivals. In 1839 a sale at Witney was noted as "one of those disgraceful occurrences, happily not. . . frequent"; while a sale at Bridlington in the previous year was compared to "a similar transaction" in the same town ten years before.[2]

The consensus of mid nineteenth-century enlightened opinion was that the practice existed only amongst the lowest stratum of the labourers, especially in the remote countryside: as Brand had expressed it, "the lowest of our Vulgar". This may be tested against occupations attributed to either the husband or the purchaser in my sample. While the nature of the reports is not such as to ensure accuracy, attributions of occupation are given in 158 cases:

Wife Sales: Attributed Occupation of Husband or Purchaser

15 Labourers
8 Colliers (including pitmen and miners)
7 Navvies (including ditchers and bankers)
6 Coachmen (including postillions and ostlers)
5 Blacksmiths : Farmers : Farm labourers or "countrymen" : Shoemakers : Soldiers : Tailors
4 Chimney-sweeps : Gardeners
3 Bricklayers : Brickmakers : Butchers : Carpenters or joiners : Factory workers : Horse or cattle dealers : Nailmakers : Tinkers
2 Bakers : Clerks : Donkey-drivers : Dustmen : Gentlemen : Graziers : Grinders : Ironworkers : Sailors : Stockingers : Watermen : Weavers

[1] *The Times*, 2 Feb. 1819. The case from Rutland Quarter Sessions (Oakham) and perhaps an example was being looked for from the whole county? See also Roy Palmer, *The Folklore of Leicestershire and Rutland* (Wymondham, 1985), pp. 58-9.

[2] *Jackson's Oxford Journal*, 4 May 1839; *York Herald & General Advertiser*, 27 Oct. 1838; *Hull Advertiser*, cited in *Operative*, 4 Nov. 1838.

1 Basket-maker : Blanket-hawker : Breeches-maker : Button-maker :
  Carter : Cinder-burner : Cloth worker : Coal dealer : Delver : Fell-
  monger : Gingerbread Hawker : Hatter : Hay salesman : Hog driver :
  Lighterman : Mason : Mattress-maker : Officer : Painter : Publican :
  Rag merchant : Sand carrier : Sawyer : Steel-burner : Stone-cutter :
  Straw-cutter : Tradesman : Woodward
  Designated by office, circumstance, etc., rather than by occupation:
  Pauper (2) : Pensioner (2) : Returned from transportation (2) : Poacher
  (1) : and Henry Brydges, 2nd duke of Chandos.

One should add to this general (but imprecise) suggestions that wife selling was prevalent among certain occupational groups, such as railway navvies, bargees, and tinkers or travellers. But highly picaresque occupations, with great mobility and many accidents of fortune, seem — as with sailors and soldiers — to have encouraged different notations of "marriage", which was seen on both sides to be a more transient arrangement.

This table of occupations carries (the duke of Chandos apart) few surprises.[1] There is a large group (19) engaged in some way in the livestock and transport trades, and likely to frequent cattle markets. Another group (14) come from the building trades, which shared with navvying a high mobility. The odd men out are those of higher social status. Of the two reputed gentlemen, one purchased the wife of a clothworker in Midsomer Norton, Somerset, in 1766 for six guineas: no public ritual is mentioned, the sale was by private contract, and, by her own account, the wife was not consulted (see below p. 431). In the other case, at Plymouth in 1822, the gentleman was the husband and intending seller: we will return to this unusually well-documented case (below pp. 440-1). A further case, at Smithfield in 1815, attracted

---

[1] It is probable that the duke of Chandos did buy his second wife, Maria, from an ostler in Newbury *circa* 1740, since the story clung to him persistently with circumstantial additions. But I am not convinced that Maria was sold in an inn-yard in a halter, nor that Chandos's presence at the sale was a matter of chance: this detail rests on oral transmission across 130 years, see *N & Q*, 4th series, vi (1870), p. 179. See also Menefee, p. 214 (Case 15).

attention precisely because of the wealth and status of the parties: the husband was a cattle grazier, the purchaser a "celebrated horse-dealer", the purchase price high (fifty guineas and "a valuable horse upon which the purchaser was mounted"), and "the lady (the object of the sale), young, beautiful, and elegantly dressed, was brought to market in a coach, and exposed to the view of her purchaser with a silk halter round her shoulders, which were covered with a rich white lace veil". It was noted reprovingly in the press that "hitherto we have only seen those moving in the lowest classes of society thus degrading themselves".[1]

The occupational profile suggested by this sample is not that of the luxury trades nor of the skilled artisans, but of the older plebeian culture that preceded these and long co-existed with them. Workers in the staple productive industry, textiles, are greatly under-represented; although Yorkshire provides more examples than any other county, it shows colliers and unskilled trades, but no croppers or wool-combers, and only two weavers. In the sample there are blacksmiths but no engineers or instrument-makers; navvies but no shipwrights; and only three mill-hands or factory operatives. The women, being wives, are described by their looks, deportment or supposed moral conduct, but very rarely by occupation. But we do know that there were two pit-lasses; at least two were paupers sold off to save parish poor rates; one was a factory operative and another a winder in a mill.

It would be futile (for reasons that will become apparent) to quantify the rising or falling cost of buying wives. At the top of the list (an unsatisfactory case) a Wolverhampton coal-dealer was supposed to have sold his wife in 1865 to an American sailor at £100, plus £25 each for two children.[2] At the other extreme wives were given free, or for a glass of ale; the lowest sum of money exchanged was three-farthings. Perhaps two shillings and sixpence to five shillings was the median range, although many examples fall above or below this. But the husband frequently exacted a bowl of punch or a

[1] John Ashton, *Social England under the Regency* (1890), i, pp. 374-5.
[2] *Wolverhampton Chronicle* cited in *Yorkshire Gazette*, 28 Jan. 1865.

gallon of beer on top of the purchase price, and sometimes
some other article — a watch, some cloth, some tobacco. A
Westminster donkey-driver sold his wife to another driver for
thirteen shillings and a donkey. In a much-cited case in
Carlisle (1832) a farmer, renting 42 acres, sold his wife to a
pensioner for twenty shillings and a large Newfoundland dog.
He slipped the straw-halter, in which he had led his wife to
market, off her neck and put it around the neck of his new
acquisition, betaking himself to the nearest inn.[1]

III

This is all very well for those who enjoy quantitative gossip,
but we must now get to serious work and enquire: what is the
significance of the form of behaviour which we have been
trying to count? The material appears in the press, most
often, in an abbreviated — or occasionally a sensational —
form, opaque to investigation. The report may be of the
briefest:

> On Tuesday, February 25th, one Hudson brought his wife into Stafford
> market-place and disposed of her by public auction, after many
> biddings, at five shillings and five pence.[2]

> A fellow named Jackson sold his wife for 10s. 6d. at Retford, last week,
> in the public market.[3]

Or a report may carry a more jocular tone:

> Monday last Jonathan Heard, gardener at Witham, sold his wife and
> child, a fowl and eleven pigs, for six guineas to a bricklayer of the same
> place. He this day made a demand of them and received them with open
> arms amidst a prodigious concourse of people. The knowing ones think
> the bricklayer has a very hard bargain.[4]

Or the report may be somewhat fuller. The *Derby Mercury*
in 1841 described a "disgraceful scene" in Stafford market:

---

[1] This much-reprinted example seems to derive from the *Lancaster
Herald*, reaching *The Times*, 26 Apr. 1832, and the *Annual Register* for
1832. The colourful report was perhaps dressed up by the reporter: see
Chambers's Journal, 19 Oct. 1861.
[2] *Monthly Magazine*, ix (1800), p. 304.
[3] *Derby Mercury*, 18 Aug. 1841.
[4] *Chelmsford Chronicle*, 18 July 1777, in A. J. Brown (ed.), *English
History from Essex Sources* (Chelmsford, 1952), p. 203.

A labouring man, of idle and dissolute habits, called Rodney Hall, residing at Dunstone Heath near Penkridge led his wife into the town with a halter round her body, for the purpose of disposing of her in the public market to the best bidder. Having taken her into the market-place and paid toll he led her twice round the market, when he was met by a man named Barlow, of the same class of life, who purchased her for eighteen pence and a quart of ale, and she was formally delivered over to the purchaser. The parties then went to the 'Blue Posts Inn' to ratify the transfer. . .[1]

A further example concerns Barton-upon-Humber (Lincolnshire), 1847:

On Wednesday. . . it was announced by the cryer that the wife of Geo. Wray, of Barrow. . . would be offered for sale by auction in the Barton market-place at 11 o'clock;. . . punctually to the time the salesman made his appearance with the lady, the latter having a new halter tied round her waist. Amidst the shouts of the lookers on, the lot was put up, and. . . knocked down to Wm. Harwood, waterman, for the sum of one shilling, three-halfpence to be returned 'for luck'. Harwood walked off arm in arm with his smiling bargain, with as much coolness as if he had purchased a new coat or hat.[2]

This is, usually, all the material that we have. Only in a very few cases — for example, when some case arises in the courts — do we obtain more information. But the material is not worthless, and as one works over it certain patterns emerge. The sale of a wife was by no means a casual, and rarely a comic, affair. It was highly ritualised; it should be performed in public and with accepted ceremony. It is possible that there were two forms of wife sale, favoured in different parts of the country, which overlapped with each other and which confuse the picture: 1) a form requiring publicity in the market-place and the use of the halter; I call this the "true" ritual wife sale; 2) a form involving a paper contract of sale, with witnesses, and some abbreviated ritual of "delivery" in a public bar. Of my 218 cases, a market-place

[1] *Derby Mercury*, 18 Aug. 1841.
[2] *Stamford Mercury*, 12 Mar. 1847. For a sequel, see *ibid.*, 25 May 1849: Harwood refused to acknowledge (in county court) a debt contracted by his "wife" before purchase, "inasmuch as at the time he bought the woman, he did not take her debts along with her. The Judge (with astonishment): 'What do you mean by buying the woman?' The lady alluded to here stepped forward, and said she was purchased in the usual way. . . His Honour seemed to be dumfounded".

sale is indicated in 121, a sale inside an inn (before witnesses) in 10 cases, and a private paper contract (with no mention of an inn) in 5 cases. The halter is mentioned in 108 cases, usually in the market-place but on occasion inside the inn. There is no evidence as to the form (market, inn or halter) in the remaining 82 cases.

In the true wife sale, ritual prescribed some of the following forms, although there were regional variations and not every one of the forms discussed below need, in any one case, be observed.

a) The sale must take place in an acknowledged market-place or similar nexus of exchange. Antiquity or familiarity influenced the choice. Frequently the parties took their station before the old market "cross" or some outstanding feature: at Preston (1817) the obelisk, at Bolton (1835) the new "gas pillar".[1] If the sale took place in a large village without a market, then the parties would perform the ceremony in front of the main inn or wherever public transactions customarily took place. But such village sales seem to have been rare, and even from large villages the parties usually proceeded to the market-town, walking miles to their objective.[2]

On occasion the scene of the sale was some other public mart or exchange: at Dartmouth (1817) the public quay,[3] or, as in Hardy's novel, a fair. Popular opinion seems to have been uncertain as to the legitimacy of such transactions. In a confusing case in Bath market-place (1833) a "dashingly attired" lady in a silk halter was put up for sale, although she had been sold earlier in the week, for 2s. 6d., at Lansdown Fair, "but the bargain was not considered legal; first because the sale was not held in a public market-place, and secondly because the purchaser had a wife already".[4] The second reason was probably the more weighty of the two, since sales

---

[1] *Preston Chronicle*, 3 May 1817; *Bolton Chronicle*, cited in *British Whig* (Kingston, Ontario), 8 May 1835.

[2] "This day a woman sold in the Market for 4/- the parties came from Stoke Golding": Anon., "Memorandum Book of Occurences at Nuneaton" (typescript in Warwicks. CRO of original in Nuneaton Public Library), entry for 1 June 1816.

[3] *The Times*, 12 Apr. 1817.

[4] *Ibid.*, 27 Aug. 1833 and *Man*, 1 Sept. 1833, citing *Bath Chronicle*.

at other fairs certainly took place.[1]

b) The sale was sometimes preceded by some public announcement or advertisement. The town cryer or bell-man might be employed, or the husband might carry a notice of intending sale through the market. Baring-Gould records the story of a Devonshire publican who posted a —

NOTICE

This here be to hinform the publick as how James Cole be dispozed to sell his wife by Auction. Her be a dacent, clanely woman, and be of age twenty-five ears. The sale be to take place in the New Inn, Thursday next, at seven o'clock.

One is unhappy with this story (and its self-consciously comic orthography), even though Baring-Gould insisted upon it and claimed that the woman was still living at the time of writing (1908).[2] But undoubtedly some advance announcements took place.

c) The halter was central to the ritual. The wife was brought to market in a halter, usually around her neck, sometimes around her waist. It was usually of rope and was new (costing about 6d.), but there were silk halters, halters decorated with ribbons, straw plaitings and mere "penny slips".

The symbolism of the halter may have undergone some evolution. The critical term may be "delivery". Some early reports suggest that on occasion the husband and the purchaser first came to an agreement of sale (which might then be drawn up as a paper) and that the wife was then, on the next day or following week, publicly "delivered" to the purchaser in a halter. In a late example (Stockport, 1831) we have the actual form of words. The husband made an agreement to sell his wife to a butcher, Booth Milward:

[1] For example, Market Drayton Fair, *Shrewsbury Chronicle*, 27 June 1817; Bakewell Fair, *Derby and Chesterfield Reporter*, 14 June 1838; Horsham colt fair, 1820, 1825, and 1844, Henry Burstow, *Reminiscences of Horsham* (1911), pp. 73-4; Headley fair, W. W. Capes, *Scenes of Rural Life in Hampshire* (1901), p. 302. Also Menefee, ch. 3.

[2] Sabine Baring-Gould, *Devonshire Characters and Strange Events* (1908), p. 61.

> I, Booth Milward, bought of William Clayton, his wife for five shillings, to be delivered on the 25th of March, 1831, to be delivered in a alter, at Mr. Jn. Lomax's house.

The agreement, drawn in a beershop, was signed by the husband and three witnesses.[1]

But "delivered" had not yet acquired the casual sense of delivering groceries or a message. In its common usage before 1800 it signified more "to free, to give up entirely, to surrender, to hand over to another's possession or keeping" (OED). Hence delivery in a halter symbolised the surrender of the wife into another's possession, and the importance of the ritual lay exactly in its public demonstration that the husband was a willing (or resigned) party to the surrender. This publicity was also essential because it displayed the wife's consent — or enabled her to repudiate a contract entered into between her husband and another without her consent.

However and whenever the ritual of the halter originated, by the end of the eighteenth century it was regarded in many parts of the country as an essential constituent of a "lawful" transfer. At Thame the re-sale of a wife took place in 1789: a man who had sold his wife two or three years before for half a guinea was told by his neighbours that "the bargain would not stand good, as she was not sold in public Market". He therefore "led her seven Miles in a String to Thame Market, and there sold her for Two Shillings and Six Pence, and paid *Four-Pence Toll*".[2]

The wife might be led into market in a halter, or the halter could be produced at the moment of sale. (If the woman was bashful, she might prefer to be haltered beneath her clothes, around her waist, keeping the spare rope in her pocket: when the auction commenced the husband took hold of the halter's end.) And ritual of this kind tends to breed its own local refinements and superstitions. In some cases it was held necessary to lead her around the market a magical three times.[3] In other cases the wife was led in a halter all the way

[1] *The Times*, 6 Apr. 1831.
[2] *Northampton Mercury*, 2 Jan. 1790.
[3] At a sale in Witney in 1839 it was reported that the woman was led three times around the market-place followed by hundreds of people, "the

to market from her home, and then led back in the same way to her new home.[1] The symbolism was obviously derived from the beast market, and here and there more elaborate forms were devised to sustain the pretence that the wife was a beast. Perhaps this was, in an old folk mode, a play at out-witting the devil (or God)? The most frequent additional business was to tie the wife to market railings, to fasten her in a sheep-pen, to take her through turnpike gates (sometimes again the magical three), and, most often, to pay to the market officials the toll for a beast sale. And it seems to have been accepted practice in some markets — including, for a time, Smithfield — for the officials to receive the toll.[2]

d) In the market someone must perform the office of auctioneer, and there must be at least the semblance of an open auction. In most cases the husband auctioned his own wife, but on occasion someone of official status — a market official, poor law officer, auctioneer or drover — performed the part.

Considerable ingenuity was shown in adopting the style of a qualified auctioneer. At its most dismal we have the recollections of an old Gloucester annalist who, when a boy in 1838, was hanging around the beast market when he and his companions saw a countryman leading a "fatigued, dust-covered woman by a halter":

A facetious old pig dealer exclaimed, 'Hallo, old 'un. What's up? What bist a gwain to do wee the old ooman, to drown her, hang her, or what?' 'No, I be gwain to sell her,' was the reply. There was a chorus of laughter at this. 'Who be her?' the pig dealer asked. 'Her be my wife,' the countryman answered, soberly, 'and as tidy, sober, industrious, hard-working a creetur as was ever meyud. Her be as clean and tidy as a pink, and wud skin a flint to save a saxpuns; but her a got such a tongue, and kips on nagging from monnin' to midnite. I can't have a moment's peace for her tongue, so we have agreed to part, and her have agreed to go to the highest bidder in the Market. . .' 'Be you willin' to be

woman waving a blue handkerchief" and exhibiting "a most barefaced and disgusting effrontery": *Jackson's Oxford Journal*, 4 May 1839.

[1] A husband took his wife one mile out of town before bringing her back in a halter to Arundel market, "he having been told that he must put the rope on at that distance, or the sale would not be legal": *The Times*, 25 Dec. 1824.

[2] I have at least 14 cases of tolls paid and accepted, and other cases of commissions to auctioneers or drovers, Menefee has others.

sold, missus?' enquired one. 'Iss, I be,' she replied very tartly. 'Now then', said the man, 'how much for her?' There was a pause, when an old cow-banger, with a ground-ash stick, bawled out 'Saxpuns for her!' The husband, holding the halter in one hand and raising the other, cried out in the stereotyped style 'Gwain at saxpuns; who ses a shillin?' There was another prolonged pause, when I, a vivacious youth. . . imprudently exclaimed 'A shilling!' 'Gwain, gwain at a shillin. Have ee all done?' called the husband. . . The bystanders laughed and chaffed, one exclaiming 'Here's a go, youngster! Her'll be knocked down to thee!' I perspired with apprehension. . . With renewed earnestness the vendor again cried: 'Who'll bid eighteen pence, vor her be a capital ooman as ever baked a batch o' bread or made a happle dumplin.' To my intense relief a tidy, respectable-looking man made the bid, and the husband, striking his hands together, exclaimed, 'Her be thine, man. Thee'st got a bargain and a good ooman, all but her tongue. Be good to her.' The vendee took the end of the halter, having paid the eighteen pence, and led the woman away.[1]

The account arouses suspicions, with its verbatim recall of fifty-years-past conversations. No doubt it is embellished in the telling. But the episode does include ritual features found in most sales: the wife's public consent ("Be you willin' to be sold, missus?", "Iss, I be"), the formal auction, the transfer of the halter. The husband passes over the frivolous bid from the boy, but closes instantly with a serious bid (which may possibly have come from an expected quarter).

The auctioneer's elaborate encomiums on the desirability of the article for sale ("her be as clean and tidy as a pink") was also expected by the crowd. It is a highly-theatrical transaction, and the husband sometimes acted up to this with jocular bravado, entertaining the audience with a patter which was in part traditional, in part carefully rehearsed. (This was, perhaps, one way of braving through a situation of public exposure.) Little reliance can be placed on newspaper accounts embellished for the readers,[2] and less on the wife

---

[1] Frank W. Sterry, *"H.Y.J.T."* [H. Y. J. Taylor] (Gloucester, 1909).

[2] Most often cited is the supposed patter of a small farmer, Joseph Thompson, at Carlisle in 1832, who is supposed to have cautioned the crowd against "troublesome wives. . . Avoid them the same as you would a mad dog, a roaring lion, a loaded pistol, cholera morbus, Mount Etna", etc. But then he went on to recommend Mary Anne — "she can read novels, and milk cows. . . make butter and scold the maid; she can sing Moore's Melodies, and plait her frills and caps; she cannot make rum, gin or whiskey, but she is a good judge of the quality from long experience in

sale ballads and broadsheets, which were standard printers' stock.[1] But 'Samuel Lett', a ballad from Bilston (Staffordshire), gives at least an authentic sense of the humorous expectations — a jocular alternation of praise and denigration — provoked by an auction:

> This is ter gie notice
> That bandy legged Lett
> Will sell his wife Sally
> For what he can get.
>
> At 12 o'clock sertin
> The sale'll begin.
> So all yer gay fellers
> Be there wi' yur tin.
>
> For Sally's good lookin'
> And sound as a bell,
> If you'n ony once heerd her
> You'n know that quite well.
>
> Her bakes bread quite handy
> An' eats it all up;
> Brews beer, like a good 'un,
> An' drinks every cup.[2]

A public auction, then, was central to the ritual, but the form allowed for improvisations and variety. And it was by no means always good-humoured. It could be degrading for all parties and most of all for the wife.

e) Ritual demanded the passage of some money. This was generally one shilling or above, although less was sometimes given. The purchaser commonly agreed to pay for a quantity of drink in addition to the purchase price, and sometimes an additional sum was added for the halter. The husband

---

tasting them" etc. (See below p. 416, note 1.) I think this speech (but not the sale) is a journalist's invention.

[1] Roy Palmer, with great generosity, has passed on to me many examples of these. Some are spurious or are mere excuses for sexual innuendo (listing the tools of each trade — "the cobbler bristled up his wife with two big balls of wax"). See also Menefee, ch. 11.

[2] Jon Raven found this ballad in G. T. Lawley's notes in Bilston Central Library. He recorded it to his own tune on his record *Kate of Coalbrookdale* (Argo ZFB29). See also Jon Raven, *The Urban and Industrial Songs of the Black Country and Birmingham* (Wolverhampton, 1977), pp. 143-4, 253.

frequently returned a small portion of the purchase money to the purchaser "for luck": in this the parties followed the old — and still vigorous — form of the horse and cattle markets, the return of "luck money".

f) The actual moment of the transfer of the halter was sometimes solemnised by an exchange of pledges analogous to a marriage ceremony: " 'Be you willing Missis to have me, and take me for better or worse?' 'I be willing,' says she. 'And be you willing to sell her for what I bid maister?' 'I be,' said he, 'and will give you the rope into the bargain'." [1] On occasion the report notes that the wife returned her old ring to her husband and received a new one from her purchaser. The passing of the end of the rope from seller to purchaser might also be accompanied by a public declaration by the former that he was renouncing his wife, and would no longer be responsible for her debts or actions. It could also be a moment for sentimental adieus, as in a record from Spalding (Lincolnshire) in 1786:

> Hand [took] a halter and put [it] upon her, and delivered her to Hardy, pronouncing the following words: — 'I now, my dear, deliver you into the hands of Thomas Hardy, praying the blessings of God to attend you both, with all happiness.' Hardy replied: 'I now, my dear, receive you with the blessings of God, praying for happiness,' Etc. and took off the halter, saying, 'Come, my dear, I receive you with a kiss; and you, Hand, shall have a kiss at parting. [2]

The transfer and exchange might be the end of the matter, the newly-linked couple departing hurriedly from the scene. But the ceremony was also sometimes followed by the adjournment of all three parties, with witnesses and friends, to the nearest inn, where the sale might be "ratified" by the signing of papers. It would also, of course, be pledged in drink (which, as we have seen, was sometimes included in the purchase money or returned by the seller for "luck").

Where the exchange was pre-arranged this part of the proceedings would presumably depend on the amount of good-will or ill-will in the air. Where bad feeling was

[1] Recollections of a "Nonagenarian" in *Hereford Times*, 21 May 1876; E. M. Leather, *The Folk-Lore of Herefordshire* (Hereford, 1912; reprint 1970), p. 118.
[2] Menefee, p. 100.

dominant, but a "paper" was required, this might be drawn prior to the public auction and at the sale the parties would split up for ever. Where goodwill was ascendant all parties would drink and draw up a paper together. A number of examples of such "contracts" survive, the most frequently cited being an entry in the toll-book at the Bell Inn, Edgbaston Street, Birmingham:

> August 31, 1773. Samuel Whitehouse, of the parish of Willenhall. . . this day sold his wife, Mary Whitehouse, in open market, to Thomas Griffiths, of Birmingham, value, one shilling. To take her with all her faults.

The signature of Samuel and Mary Whitehouse and of a witness followed.[1] Some eighty years later we have a Worcester example:

> Thomas Middleton delivered up his wife Mary Middleton to Philip Rostins for one shilling and a quart of ale; and parted wholly and solely for life, never to trouble one another.

Witness.	Thomas **X** Middleton, his mark
Witness.	Mary Middleton, his wife
Witness.	Philip **X** Rostins, his mark
Witness.	S. H. Stone, Crown Inn, Friar St.[2]

Presumably S. H. Stone was the publican where the paper was drawn up. It is of interest that of the three parties only Mary Middleton could sign her name.

Such papers were safeguarded, like "marriage lines", as a proof of respectability. Thus a Mrs Dunn of Ripon was quoted in 1881 as saying: "Yes, I *was* married to another man, but he sold me to Dunn for 25 shillings, and I have it to show in black and white, with a receipt stamp on it, as I did not want people to say I was living in adultery".[3] So convinced were people as to the legality of the procedure that they would attempt to secure an attorney's aid in drawing such papers, or would endorse them with official stamps. In Bolton (1833), after the market-place auction had taken place, the three parties adjourned to the "One Horse Shoe" where "the purchase money was paid after a stamped receipt

---

[1] *Annual Register*, 1773.
[2] *Worcester Chronicle*, 22 July 1857.
[3] *N & Q*, 6th series, iv (1881), p. 133.

had been given" and the wife was then "duly delivered". "The party afterwards partook of beefsteaks together, as a parting meal, and paid for two quarts of ale. . ."[1] Husband and wife had come into Bolton from a village five miles away, and the purchaser was a neighbour from the same place. What might have seemed, from a briefer or more sensational report, to be an unstructured and open auction can now be seen to have been carefully arranged.

This covers the main features of the "true" ritual wife sale: the open market, publicity, the halter, the form of auction, the passage of money, the solemn transfer, and on occasion ratification by paper. Elaborations or more exotic forms (such as literally stepping into the first husband's shoes) are sometimes found.[2] But the only significant alternative form which has left clear evidence was that of a more private transaction in the public bar of an inn. Although this took place before witnesses it was a form which avoided the full glare of publicity of the open market sale, and hence it may be seriously under-reported.[3] Cases most often came to light when some other matter (poor law settlement or custody of children) brought them before the authorities.

In 1828 the three parties to such a sale were brought before the West Kent Quarter Sessions, charged with a misdemeanour, and the court proceedings throw a little light on the form and how it was regarded. The three shared a parish (poor law) cottage in Speldhurst, and they agreed to meet at the "George and Dragon" in nearby Tonbridge. The publican deposed:

Skinner came first, and asked for a pot of beer; he sat in the kitchen; his wife then came in, and shortly after Savage entered; they all drank together, and in a little time Savage went out; he soon returned, and Skinner then said to him, "Will you buy my wife?" He replied, "What will you have for her?" Skinner said, "A shilling and a pot of beer." Savage then tendered him half a crown, and Skinner delivered his wife to him; they drank together, and then went away; there were about four persons present; before they went, the woman took a handkerchief

[1] *Bolton Chronicle*, cited in *British Whig*, 8 May 1835.
[2] *Birmingham Daily Mail*, 29 Mar. 1871.
[3] It may have been the form most favoured in Kent, where I have several examples; and for a sale outside a pub in East London, see below, p. 455.

from her pocket-hole, which appeared to have been round her waist, and Skinner taking it, said, "I've now nothing more to do with you, and you may go with Savage."

We also know, on this occasion, a little about the reasons for the sale. Rumour was rife in the village that Mrs Skinner had taken Savage as her lover. As a result the overseers of the poor (who owned the cottage) ordered Skinner to turn Savage out, or he would be turned out as well. In their simplicity the three seem to have supposed that by a sale (or act of divorce and re-marriage) the parish authorities would permit Savage and the new Mrs Savage to remain in undisturbed tenancy of the cottage. But the Tonbridge Vestry was not so easily placated. Perhaps all three were evicted as soon as the sale came to light. Or perhaps Skinner took his solitary way from the "George and Dragon" to the parish workhouse, where he was resident at the time of the court proceedings.

Passing sentence on all three the "very learned" Chairman of the Bench allowed himself to indulge in a little dry wit ("the lady certainly did not rate her own value very highly, for a pot of beer and a shilling was the only consideration given for that valuable commodity") before passing on to higher levels of invigilatory moral exhortation. The practice of wife sales was "highly immoral and illegal" and "had a tendency to bring the holy estate of matrimony into contempt". But "the crime" would have been greater if it had been committed in open market. Taking also into consideration the fact that the offence was committed "in a state of ignorance", he thought a sentence of one month's imprisonment for each of them was sufficient. It is not recorded whether the accommodation at the local gaol was more, or less, salubrious than that at the local workhouse. The convicted felons had almost nothing to offer in their defence. Mrs Skinner said, "My husband did not go on to my wishes, and that was the reason I wished to part" [a laugh]. [1]

IV

It is now clear — although it was not so in the 1960s when I commenced to collect this evidence — that we must remove the wife sale from the category of brutal chattel purchase and

[1] *Morning Chronicle*, 25 July 1828.

place it within that of divorce and re-marriage. This still may arouse inappropriate expectations, since what is involved is the exchange of a woman between two men in a ritual which humiliates the woman as a beast. Yet the symbolism cannot be read only in that way, for the importance of the publicity of the public market-place and of "delivery" in a halter lay also in the evidence thus provided that all three parties concurred in the exchange. The consent of the wife is a necessary condition for the sale. This is not to say that her consent may not have been extracted under duress — after all, a husband who wanted (or threatened) to sell a wife was not much of a consort. A wife who was sold in Redruth (1820) and who was brought, with her purchaser, before the Quarter Sessions in Truro, "stated her husband had ill-treated her so frequently and expressed his determination of selling her, that she was induced to submit to the exposure to get rid of him". This must have been true of some cases. But not, perhaps, the whole truth in this Redruth case, for the wife went on to admit "that she had lived with. . . her purchaser before she was publicly sold to him".[1] In many sales, even where there was a semblance of an open auction and public bidding, the purchaser was pre-arranged and was already the wife's lover.

To recover the "truth" about any marital history is not easy: to attempt to recover it, from newspaper snippets, after 150 years have passed is to go on a fool's errand. Even where direct assertions are made as to the wife's "misconduct" prior to the sale, all that we are given is the evidence of gossip or scandal. Yet this evidence does not tell us exactly nothing — let us take three cases, all from the year 1837.

The first concerns a sale in the butter market at Bradford (West Yorkshire). The report notes: "The alleged ground of the separation was the incontinence of the wife, whose affections were stated to have been alienated by an old delver, who had occasionally got his dinner at their house." When the husband commenced the auction "the first and only *bona fide* bid" was a sovereign from the delver. This "was immediately accepted, and, the money being paid, the couple

---

[1] *West Briton*, 14 Apr. 1820.

walked off amidst the execrations of the crowd".[1]

The second took place in Walsall market. Here a man led in his wife by a halter from a village eight or nine miles away, and sold her in a few minutes for 2s. 6d. The purchaser was a nailer, who had come in from the same village. All parties were reported to be satisfied. The wife had in fact been living with the purchaser for the previous three years.[2]

The third case took place in Wirksworth, Derbyshire. The wife of John Allen had eloped with James Taylor the previous summer. The "injured husband", learning that the couple were at Whaley Bridge, went and found them together in lodgings. "He demanded £3 for her clothes, which Taylor said he would pay on condition that he would accompany them to Wirksworth on the market day, and deliver her, as he called it, according to the law." Here we have a clear case of "delivery": Allen passed over the end of the halter to Taylor, and made a formal statement.

'I, John Allen, was bereaved of my wife by James Taylor, of Shottle, on the 11th of July last. I have brought her here to sell her for 3s 6d. Will you buy her, James?' James answered: 'I will, here is the money, and you are witness, Thomas Riley' — calling to a potman who was appointed for the purpose.
The ring was delivered to Allen with three sovereigns and 3s 6d, when he shook hands with his wife and her paramour, wishing them all the good luck in the world.[3]

It could be argued that the first example offers no more than gossip; but the second and third cannot be passed over so easily. A purchaser does not happen to arrive from the same village, eight miles away, at the moment of sale: this was pre-arranged. Nor is a reporter likely to have invented the story of prior elopement and co-habitation. Indeed, the frequency of cases in which the wife was sold to a man with whom she was living already — and had been so living in some cases for three, four or five years[4] — raises a quite different question: why, if elopement and desertion was

[1] *Halifax Express*, cited in *The Times*, 9 Feb. 1837.

[2] *Wolverhampton Chronicle*, cited in *Globe*, 27 Oct. 1837.

[3] *Derbyshire Courier*, cited in *The Times*, 22 Aug. 1837.

[4] *See e.g. Derby Mercury*, 3 Jan. 1844; Nottingham case in *The Times*, 23 Sept. 1834; Menefee, p. 279 note 32; *London City Mission Magazine*, Aug. 1861, p. 189.

possible, on occasion, on the wife's part as well as on the husband's, did the parties still feel it necessary to undergo the public (and shaming) ritual of a sale?

I will come back to this searching question, although the answer may in the end be found only in the inaccessible personal history of each case. The difficulty with this material is not only that the evidence is so unsatisfactory but also that one can not conclusively show any one case to be "representative". Today's obligatory methodological imperative is to quantify, but the complexities of personal relationships are especially resistant to this exercise. And the "typical" short newspaper report gives no information at all on the motives of the parties — it is no more than a bleak report of a sale.

However, I have attempted to press the evidence into rude classifications, with this result:

Sales and Attempted Sales, 1760-1880: Consent of Wife

No information	123
Wife consenting	41
Wife sold to lover	40
Arranged divorce	10
Wife not consenting	4
	218

Since "no information" means no information on the point whatsoever, this shows 91 cases which signify the wife's assent or active participation as against 4 non-consents. If we look at sales between 1831 and 1850 (at which time the news reports tend to be fullest), we find:

Sales, 1831-50: Consent of Wife

No information	27
Wife consenting	10
Wife sold to lover	19
Arranged divorce	4
Wife not consenting	—
	60

I regard these quantities as literary and impressionistic evidence, as contrasted with the "hard" evidence in this chapter, which is the close interrogation of texts and contexts. The classifications are not finely-aimed. Let us examine each in its turn.

Wife not consenting. Moralistic notices at the time, as well as much subsequent historical commentary, imply that the wife was a passive chattel or unwilling party to the transaction. In fact, three of the four cases in the first table did not result in sales. In each of these cases we are told that a bargain was made privately between the husband and a purchaser, but was subsequently disowned by the wife.

The exception rests upon a letter addressed by Ann Parsons to a Somerset magistrate, 9 January 1768:

> I am the daughter of Ann Collier that lived at the bottom of Rush Hill and in the Early part of Life to my Great Mortification I was Married to a Man who had no Regard for himself or for the Support of Me and My Children. At the Commencement of the last Warr he Entered into the Kings service and Sir I Can't relate to you the tenth part of the abuses that I received from Him before his admission and Since his Return from the Army, at last for the Support of his Extravagancy He made Sale of me and Sold me for Six pound and Six Shillings and I was not in the least acquainted until he told me what he had done. At the same time He requested of me to keep the younges child. . .

In support of this account she enclosed a bill of sale drawn between her husband, John Parsons of Midsomer Norton, clothworker, and John Tooker of the same parish, gentleman: this asigned and set over Ann Parsons "with all right Property Claim Services and demand whatsoever" to John Tooker.

This is clear enough. But Ann Parsons went on to complain — not that the sale had taken place — but that her husband had not honoured the treaty. Three months after the sale (which took place on 24 October 1766) her husband "Visited me and Demanded Mor Money and abused me and the Man that he sold me too violently forcing open the door Swearing he would be Death to us both", and continuing this harassment until she applied for protection to a magistrate, who committed John Parsons to the Bridewell in Shepton Mallet. Committal had taken place the previous Michaelmas, and Ann Parsons was now afraid of the vengeance he might take when set at liberty. Her reason for petitioning the magistrate was to ensure her husband's continued detention.

It is not easy to know what to make of this story. Ann Parsons may (as she testified) have been sold without her knowledge and consent; or she may have thought this to be the best story to tell to the JP from whom she was seeking protection. Once sold — and (note) to a man of higher social status — it is certain that she wished the contract to be honoured, and she was pursuing her ex-marital revenge with skill and success.[1]

In the other cases of non-consent there is less to go on. In one case (North Bovey, Devon, *circa* 1866) it is said that the husband made a private agreement with a purchaser to sell his wife for a quart of beer. She repudiated the agreement, took her two children to Exeter, and returned to North Bovey only for her husband's funeral.[2] Another case came to light in a trial for bigamy in Birmingham in 1823. John Homer, an ex-soldier, was alleged to have treated his wife brutally and to have finally sold her against her will in a halter in the market. But the purchaser was her own brother, who for three shillings was "buying her out" of the marriage or "redeeming" her. (One does not know whether this case should be classified as non-consent or as an arranged divorce.) Homer then supposed that he was free to marry again and made the error of going through a formal church ceremony. He was convicted of bigamy and sentenced to seven years transportation.[3] In the other case, at Swindon Fair in 1775, it was said that an "eminent shoemaker" of Wootton Bassett came to a formal agreement with a cattle dealer to sell his wife to him for £50, and to "deliver her upon demand the next morning" —

> Agreeable to this bargain the purchaser set out in a post-chaise accompanied by many of his friends, decked in white cockades, in order to demand his purchase, when to their disappointment neither Crispin nor Crispiana. . . were to be met with.[4]

These cases do not contradict the rule, which was noted by some contemporaries, that the wife's consent was essential.

[1] Brit. Lib. Add MSS 32, 084 ff. pp. 14-15. My thanks to Douglas Hay for the transcription.
[2] *Devon N & Q*, iv (1906-7), p. 54.
[3] *Birmingham Chronicle*, 7 Aug. 1823.
[4] *Jackson's Oxford Journal*, 23 Dec. 1775.

This is confirmed by occasions when the wife repudiated with vigour an attempted sale. A visitor to Smithfield market in 1817 saw a man struggling to place a halter around the neck of a young woman of remarkable beauty. In the midst of a large and growing crowd, the wife resisted the attempt with all her strength. Crowd and constables intervened and the couple were taken before a magistrate. The husband explained that his wife had been unfaithful and he was therefore asserting a right to sell her. [1] In the wife's resistance to the halter we have confirmation that both halter and her consent were essential to confer legitimacy on the transaction. Even where the purchaser was not pre-arranged and where there was a genuine auction with open bidding, the wife was able to exercise a veto. Thus a report from Manchester (1824) says that "after several biddings she was knocked down for 5s; but not liking the purchaser, she was put up again for 3s and a quart of ale". [2] In a more dubious Bristol case (1823) the wife was "quite satisfied" with her purchaser, who, however, then re-sold her to another; "the lady. . . not liking the transfer, made off with her mother" and refused to be claimed by the second purchaser unless "by order of a magistrate, who dismissed the case". [3]

There must have been cases of forcible wife sale, in which the wife was terrified into consent or was too simple-minded or friendless to resist. [4] And there must have been other affairs in taverns which were drunken muddles. William Hutton, in a poem, "The Pleasures of Matrimony", reconstructed one of these which might have been a model

---

[1] *L'Hermite de Londres, ou Observations sur les Moeurs et Usages des Anglais au Commencement du XIX Siècle* (Paris, 1821), ii, pp. 318 ff.

[2] *The Times*, 29 June 1824.

[3] See Menefee, p. 68.

[4] Menefee, pp. 115 and 117 suggests examples, but those I have consulted are inconclusive. In a Grassington case, 1807, the wife "refused to be delivered": *Annual Register*, 1807, p. 378. In the case of a woman supposedly sold in the Grass Market, Edinburgh (1828), a broadside gives a lurid account of seven hundred women stoning and attacking the husband "in consequence of the insult the fair sex had received": W. Boag, printer, Newcastle, *Bibliotheca Lindesiana* (1898), no. 1656. However an identical story, with the same seven hundred women, is found in a broadside in the Madden Collection (no. 1872), but is there attributed not to Edinburgh but to Liverpool. See also Menefee, Case 215, p. 239.

for the sale in *The Mayor of Casterbridge*. The wife called into the ale-house to get her husband to come home to help with "the infant flock"; the husband was beside himself with anger (even though "he spent the money which she earn'd") and sold her to a fellow-drinker — William Martin, a young stockinger — for a pint of ale:

> The pint was order'd, bargain struck,
> And nothing back return'd for luck.
> The parties of a halter thought,
> But this they found would cost a groat.
>
> The halter scheme was instant lost,
> As being twice what Hannah cost,
> For that same reason neither would
> Pay fourpence that she might be toll'd.

But a deed of sale was drawn and signed between the two men, with the two children of the marriage divided — the child on its feet to the father, the babe-in-arms to the mother. Throughout all this the wife is described as a non-consenting party. But she does go off with the young stockinger, tramps with him from Hinckley to Loughborough: they fall in love with each other, live happily for a year, and are devastated when the husband repents and sends the Hinckley overseers to bring her back —

> She follow'd, but in anguish cried,
> O that the knot could be untied![1]

The poem is not evidence, but it is not altogether fiction either, since it was based on the poet's own experiences as a stockinger's apprentice in the 1740s, and the purchaser, William Martin, was his own friend. Yet the poem had been written (or re-written) in 1793, and was no doubt reinvented from distant recollections.[2] I am suggesting, not that wives

---

[1] William Hutton, *Poems: chiefly Tales* (1804). Menefee, pp. 194-5 is quoting Hutton by way of a cutting of an article by G. T. Lawley (possibly "In the Good Old Days", *County Advertiser for Staffordshire and Worcestershire*, 7 Aug. 1921): both get the poem a bit wrong and delete Hannah's opposition to the sale (which she subsequently accepts).

[2] Hutton's *Poems* were in part reconstituted from manuscripts of thirty or more years earlier, burned with his premises in the Birmingham Riots of 1791. For William Martin, see Llewellyn Jowitt, *The Life of William*

were not sometimes sold under duress, but that if they distinctly repudiated the transaction then the sale was not held to be good according to customary lore and sanction. The alternative view, of the wife sale as a chattel purchase against the wife's will, presents very serious difficulties. For that would have offended against law on a number of counts, and very probably an action could lie for rape. Some wives might be too ignorant to take recourse to law and have no kin to come to their defence. But even in the eighteenth-century village people knew how to make their way to the magistrate's, parson's or parish officer's door; and it is beyond all probability that no such case should ever have occurred. If any such case had ever come before the courts, then the courts — at any time after 1815 — would have administered exemplary punishment and with the maximum of publicity, for polite opinion had come to abhor the practice, and JPs and constables often sought to intervene and prevent it. But no record of any action of that kind, on the wife's application, or on the part of her kin or friends, has come to light.

Wife Consenting. This is the least satisfactory category. The evidence is derived from some explicit reference to consent in the source, or else to some such phrase as the wife departed with her purchaser "in high glee", seemed "very happy", "much pleased", or "eager". A few other cases are included in which the indications of consent are so strong that they allow of no other inference: as, for example, where the first marriage was in common law only and where the sale was followed immediately by a second marriage in church or registry, or cases where the husband immediately regretted the sale, tried to get his wife to return to him, but she refused.

No Information. In these cases the sources afford no information as to the wife's consent. But the reading has been strict. In a number of cases it could be possible to infer her assent from circumstantial evidence: thus, when all three parties come to a market-town from a village several miles

---

Hutton (1872), pp. 144-6; Catherine Hutton, *The Life of William Hutton* (1817), p. 128.

distant; where the wife is a signatory to a paper sale; where the wife is sold to a lodger or neighbour; cases where the husband sells (or gives) his stock or implements of trade with his wife (thus implying that he is leaving the new couple in possession of his livelihood); cases where the husband evinces acute jealousy, or where he evinces a show of unusual generosity to the new couple; or a handful of cases recorded by local historians who go on to add that the second marriage was happy and long-lasting. I am satisfied in my own mind that in many of these cases the wife was an active party to the exchange, but, since the evidence is slender, I have resisted the temptation to remove them from this group.

Arranged Divorce. This small group includes four cases in which the wife was sold to her own kin — to her brother, to her mother, and (two cases) to her brother-in-law. What this indicates is that a sale might not only be an exchange between husbands; it might also be a device by means of which a wife could annul or be "bought out of" her existing marriage. Both parties might then feel free to take a new consort. If the husband was making life unbearable for the wife she might agree to a sale and make her own arrangements for her "purchase".[1] In at least one case she is named as her own purchaser, and how this could be possible we will see in a notorious case at Plymouth (below p. 440). It also seems that the purchaser (in open auction) need not be the man whom the wife expected to end up living with, for the sale could be made to an "agent" acting on that man's behalf (or even on her own behalf).[2] Finally, this group includes two cases in which we are simply told that the sale was by a "previous

[1] See e.g. *Yorkshire Gazette*, 3 Aug. 1833 (Halifax case of sale to own mother); *Derby & Chesterfield Reporter*, 12 Feb. 1835; *Birmingham Chronicle*, 7 Aug. 1823 (wife sold to her own mother).

[2] Macclesfield case, reported in *Lincoln, Rutford & Stamford Mercury*, 7 Nov. 1817. Also Oxford case in J. R. Green, "Oxford During the Eighteenth Century", in C. L. Stainer (ed.), *Studies in Oxford History*, xl (1901), pp. 218-9, which suggests that the purchaser may have been acting as agent for the Woodward of Bagley. In the only oral record of a wife sale which I have collected, the family tradition — as recounted by the wife's grandson — is that the husband married her to get hold of her house, and then tried to sell her off. But "neighbours bought her in" and took her back to her parents' home: account of the late Bob Hiscox (then aged 84) of Pilton, Somerset, given to me in 1975; the sale was in Shepton Mallet

arrangement". And in three cases the wife was sold off by poor law officials.[1]

In one of these cases, which was brought to light in the *Second Annual Report of the Poor Law Commissioners* (1836) one sees official institutions (workhouse, overseers of the poor, vestry, church) co-existing with unofficial rites. In 1814 Henry Cook, a pauper whose settlement was in Effingham, Surrey, was "apprehended by the parish officers of Slinford, in Sussex, as the father of an illegitimate child" of a Slinford woman. "In accordance with the old system, a forced marriage was contracted", but one infers that the couple did not live together, for six months later Mrs Cook and her child were in Effingham workhouse. The master of the workhouse, who farmed his office for a fixed annual sum, complained at the expense of the newcomers. The overseers of the poor accordingly told the workhouse master to take Mrs Cook (with Henry Cook's agreement) to Croydon, where she was duly sold in the market in a halter to John Earl, from the parish of Dorking, Surrey. It is not said whether Earl was Mrs Cook's lover or not, nor how and why he came into the picture; all that we know is that the one shilling purchase price paid by Earl was given to him by the Effingham workhouse master, who was evidently most anxious to get these charges off his hands. A receipt was drawn up over a 5s. stamp and the workhouse master was a witness to the document. The new couple were then brought back to Effingham workhouse for the first night of their honeymoon, before being sent on the next day to Dorking where (after due publication of banns) they went through the marriage ceremony in church: "the parish officers of Effingham on this occasion provided them with a leg of mutton as a wedding dinner". All the expenses of these transactions were entered in the parish accounts and "regularly passed at a parish vestry". The story, which

---

and was perhaps the case reported in the *Castle Cary Visitor* of September or October 1848 in which the husband was roughly handled by the crowd (information from John Fletcher, who introduced me to Bob Hiscox).

[1] A young woman of Swadlincote whose husband had "some time since absconded" leaving her chargeable on the parish, sold in market by parish officer: *Derby Mercury*, 4 Feb. 1790.

started unhappily, ended in the same way, with Mrs Earl (now with seven or eight children) deserted by Earl (who had "ascertained" that his marriage was "not valid", presumably because Mrs Cook-Earl had been forced by these august conspirators — overseers, workhouse master and vestry — into bigamy?) and removed back to Effingham and the mercies of its poor law officials.

One really can not make out anything of the inwardness of this affair. Was Cook falsely sworn as father of the first child? Was Earl Mrs Cook's lover? All that is certain is that the marital history of the three was heavily influenced by economy-minded officials; and that, in 1814-15, the legitimacy of ritual wife sale went unquestioned in the parishes of Effingham and Dorking.

Wife sold to lover. None have been included in this group unless there is an explicit allegation to this effect in the source. No doubt many more could be added from the categories of "consent" and "no information". This can be supported by some literary evidence. One of the fullest accounts of the custom is from a Major-General Pillet, who travelled widely in England as a prisoner-of-war (on parole of honour) during the French Wars. His chapter on the subject is entitled "Divorces among the common people", and in his account the sale was always with the wife's consent, and generally followed upon her "misconduct". The purchaser must be single, and "is generally a lover of the commodity sold, and is well acquainted with it. She is only brought into the market place for the sake of form." [1] In any case, the sale only took place — as a Devon folklorist noted — "when the course of matrimony has arrived at a crisis". [2]

[1] R. Pillet, *L'Angleterre vue à Londres et dans ses provinces* (Paris, 1815), translated as *Views of England, during a Residence of 10 Years, 6 of them as a Prisoner-of-War* (Boston, Mass., 1818), ch. 33.

[2] *Devon N & Q*, iv (1906-7), p. 54. "Generally the affair was a pre-arranged one between the buyer, the seller, and the sold, who seem to have salved their consciences by going through the ceremony of a mock-auction": "Better-Half Barter", *Chambers's Journal*, 19 Feb. 1870. *The Laws Respecting Women, as they regard their Natural Rights* (1777), p. 55, described sale as "a method of dissolving marriage" among the common people, when "a husband and wife find themselves heartily tired of each other, and agree to part, if the man has a mind to authenticate the intended

How such crises arrived. . . at this point we must abandon all search for the typical. I have not come upon any case in which the evidence allows us to reconstruct a detailed marital history. But there are two cases in which, for accidental reasons, some information survives. In the first, there was a settlement dispute between the Somerset parishes of Spaxton and Stogumber. In 1745, when he was fifteen, William Bacon obtained a settlement in Stogumber by hiring himself for a year's service. Three years later (1748) he was "taken up" as the father of a bastard child with which Mary Gadd, of the same parish, was then pregnant. The couple were forced into marriage, although William Bacon later testified that he knew of his own marriage only by hearsay since he was "carried to Stogumber Church by the officers of the parish", and "being very high in Liquor he doesn't know whether he was married or not". The couple never lived together: William left Mary in Stogumber and found work in Bridgewater, a few miles away. Mary gave birth to their child, Betty, in December 1748 (in William's absence); several years later she was living with Robert Jones, with whom she had ten more children between 1757 and 1775. In the years that followed, William lived with another woman, by whom he had several children.

All this had gone on without any ritual of wife sale until 1784, when both William and Mary will have been in their early fifties. Then the Stogumber poor law officers intervened in their marital (or extra-marital) affairs once more. William Bacon had improved his position a little, becoming the lessee of some grist mills in the parish of Spaxton, at sixteen guineas a year. Thus this became his parish of settlement. Meanwhile Mary and her four youngest children looked as if they might at some time in the future become paupers, and one of them — young Mary — was "big with child". She was about twenty, and her pregnancy was the reason for the parish officers of Stogumber applying for a removal order, "not to suffer her to have Child in the parish, which would have been a Bastard". On the 18th December 1784 William Bacon was hauled in and examined as to his

---

separation by making it a matter of public notoriety". "A purchaser is generally provided beforehand on these occasions."

settlement before two magistrates. The removal order had
been drawn, not only for young Mary, but also for her
mother and three siblings, although none of them were then
chargeable. The administrative despotism of the poor laws
was about to fall upon both families. Mary (the mother) and
her four younger children were to be separated from Robert
Jones (the children's father) and sent off to be supported by
the miller and his family in Spaxton — and this after the
passage of thirty-six years! Two days later (20th December)
William Bacon came to Stogumber market-place to sell Mary
and the children; he asked five shillings for them (that is, one
shilling a-piece) and Robert Jones "accepted them at the
price". This happened on the same day as the removal order
— to expel all five to Spaxton — had been made, and the sale
was used by both families as a device to defy the move.[1]

That case is typical of nothing, unless of the exceeding
meanness of which poor law officials were capable. It seems
that neither William nor Mary had felt any need for any ritual
"divorce" until the overseers tried to break up their actual (if
not legal) homes. (Possibly the wife sale was a fairly recent
innovation in Somerset?) The other case comes from
Plymouth in 1822 and it attracted unusual attention owing to
the wealth and status of the parties. Here we are able to add a
few details, as to which the husband and wife corroborated
— or did not contradict — each other. Notice was given that
a young and handsome lady, who would soon succeed to
£600, would ride to town on her own horse, for sale in the
cattle market. She arrived punctually, accompanied by the
ostler of the "Lord Exmouth" inn, was met by her husband,
and the auction had reached the sum of £3 (a bid from the
ostler) when constables intervened, and husband and wife
were taken to the Guildhall before the mayor.

Interrogated, the husband said he did not think there was
"any harm" in doing it. He and his wife had not lived
together for a considerable time; they had been married
about two and a half years, and she brought him a child three

[1] Somerset CRO, D/P/Stogm, 13/3/6 (Settlement appeals). My thanks
to Dr Polly Morris, and to Mr R. J. E. Bush, Somerset Deputy County
Archivist. See also L. G. Mead, "What am I bid?", *The Greenwood Tree*,
vol. 10, Autumn 1985 for a careful inspection of parish registers.

weeks after marriage, a child which (the innocence suggested
here is surprising) "until after it was born he never knew
anything about". The baby died shortly afterwards —

> He got a coffin for it, paid the expenses of the funeral, and put it
> comfortably out of the way, without ever reproaching his wife with her
> conduct; but all would not do. She soon deserted him. . .

— went to live with another man, by whom she had had one
child since and was expecting another. The sale had been
arranged at her instance: she said that someone was ready to
give £20 for her — £3 in hand and £17 at Christmas. He had
advertised the sale in Modbury on three separate market
days, and had come to Plymouth by her appointment. The
wife confirmed his account, adding that, since she had some
doubt as to whether her lover would honour his promise to
buy her at the auction, she had employed the ostler of the
"Lord Exmouth" to buy her out of the marriage with her
own money, provided that the price did not exceed £20. Both
assumed the legitimacy of the ritual. The husband said
"many people in the country told him he could do it", and
the wife added "she had been told by different persons that
the thing could be done, by public sale in the market place on
a market day". "There was nothing below board in it", said
the husband. [1]

The case is quite untypical. The vocabulary of ritual sale
could be turned to many purposes. But the case illustrates the
vocabulary clearly, and the general popular endorsement of
its legitimacy. It is an interesting example of the disassociation of co-existing cultures, which allowed many
people to accede to some of the forms and sanctions of Law
and Church, but nevertheless to endorse customs which on
occasion over-rode them. "Lor' bless yer honours", a West
Country man said to the Reverend Baring-Gould, "you may
ask any one if that ain't marriage, good, sound, and
Christian, and everyone will tell you it is". [2]

[1] *Public Ledger*, 23 Dec. 1822; *The Times*, 23 Dec. 1822; H. F.
Whitfield, *Plymouth and Devonport* (Plymouth, 1900), pp. 296-7.
[2] Baring-Gould, *op. cit.*, pp. 59-60. In some cases the actors may have
genuinely assimilated their ritual sale and Christian marriage forms. The
Glouster Journal, 24 Nov. 1766, reported that a husband in Thorne
(Yorkshire) had sold his "old" wife in a halter for 5s. to a neighbour. Both

V

The ritual wife sale was probably an "invented traditon".[1] It may not have been invented until the late seventeenth century and possibly even later. Certainly there were instances of wives being sold before 1660, but I know of none before the eighteenth century which affords clear evidence of the public auction and the halter.[2]

The symbolism was derived from the market, but not necessarily (at first) from the beast market. Several early cases are of sale by weight, the best-documented (which rests on churchwardens' presentments) being from Chinnor (Oxfordshire) in 1696, where Thomas Heath, a maltster, was presented (and did penance) for selling his wife at "2d.q." the lb.[3] This suggests that the transaction at first borrowed the forms of the malt, cheese or butter market, and subsequently (halter, auction, turnpike gates, tolls, the pens) those of the cattle market or horse fair.

This suggests, not an ancient custom of forgotten origin transmitted down the centuries, but the pressure of new needs seeking for a ritual as outlet. An explanation suggested by nineteenth-century observers was that wife selling was a

---

men then went to Doncaster for a marriage licence, and at the ceremony the first husband gave the bride away to her new husband. (The minister officiating knew nothing of the circumstances.)

[1] See Eric Hobsbawm's introduction to Eric Hobsbawm and Terence Ranger (eds.), *The Invention of Tradition* (Cambridge, 1983).

[2] Sir Keith Thomas, Martin Ingram and other correspondents have with great kindness passed on to me early examples of allegations of the sale of a wife. These appear to be private transactions which follow no one particular form. Dr Ingram, who is an authority on sixteenth- and seventeenth-century church court records, has encouraged me in my view that wife selling in its ritual fform is a creation of the very late seventeenth and the eighteenth centuries: see Martin Ingram, *Church Courts, Sex and Marriage in England, 1570-1640* (Cambridge, 1987), p. 207.

[3] S. A. Peyton, *The Churchwarden's Presentments in the Oxfordshire Peculiars of Dorchester, Thame and Banbury* (Oxford, 1928), pp. 184-5. Other cases: Wife sold for 3/4d. a lb (but in fact by "guess" at 7s. 6d.), *Aris's Birmingham Gazette*, 11 Mar. 1745; wife sold at Rowley (Staffordshire) for 1 lb 6 oz of bread by husband who is now "gone for a soldier", *ibid.*, 18 Mar. 1745; Case 33 in Menefee, p. 216, from Newmarket, 1770 of wife sold at 5½d. a lb.

consequence of wars, with the separations and the new attachments that resulted. This was especially noted at the end of the French Wars:

> In the manufacturing districts in 1815 and 1816 hardly a market day passed without such sales month after month. The authorities shut their eyes at the time, and the people were confirmed in the perfect legality of the proceedings.[1]

There is some evidence as to sales of this kind, when a long-absent (or supposedly-dead) husband returned from the sea or from the wars to find his wife with a new husband and family.[2] The French Wars, when multitudes were uprooted from their parishes, will have multiplied these occasions. Many wives, like Margaret in Wordsworth's "The Ruined Cottage", will have been left behind without news —

> She had learned
> No tidings of her husband; if he lived,
> She knew not that he lived; if he were dead,
> She knew not he was dead.[3]

But such cases count for only a small minority of our collection. The majority of wife sales were not occasioned by wars.

They were occasioned by the breakdown of marriages, and were a device to enable a public divorce and re-marriage by the exchange of a wife (not any woman) between two men. For such a device to be effective required certain conditions: the decline in the punitive invigilation over sexual conduct of the church and its courts: the assent of the community, and a measure of autonomy of plebeian culture from the polite: a distanced, inattentive or tolerant civil authority. These

[1] *N & Q*, 3rd series, iv (1863), p. 450.
[2] E.g. *Sherborne Mercury*, 13 Sept. 1784 and *Aris's Birmingham Gazette*, 6 Sept. 1784 (Worcester case of husband returning from "some years abroad"); *Jackson's Oxford Journal*, 20 Aug. 1785 (returned sailor, Liverpool); *Independent Whig*, 28 May 1815 (soldier returned after ten years); *The Times*, 10 Nov. 1838 (Dulverton, Devon — husband returned from transportation). In a famous Halifax case, the returned soldier sold his wife to the father of her three children, who was able to marry her only 25 years later, when the first husband had died. She was given away by her grandson: William Andrews, *Curiosities of the Church* (1890), pp. 177-8.
[3] W. Wordsworth, *Poetical Works* (Oxford, 1959), v, p. 35.

conditions were met in England through much of the eighteenth century, in which the ritual struck root and became established.

One scarcely needs to explain that marriages break down and that some form of divorce is a convenience. There was, of course, no such divorce available to the English or Welsh people at this time. The alternative might be informal exchanges and cohabitations. In practice the absence of forms had usually favoured the male partner, who could — as poor law and Sessional records testify — far more easily desert his wife and children than she could desert them. The man might be able to take with him some trade; once hidden in the city from the pursuit of the overseers of the poor he might set up with a new "common law" partner. The wife's outlet from an impossible or violent marriage was normally to the home of her parents or kin — unless she had already found herself a new lover.

There were suggestions among historians of fifty years ago that a great part of the labouring people in the eighteenth century lived in normless and formless animal promiscuity, and although this lampoon has been a good deal revised, some echoes of it still survive. The wife sale has sometimes been offered as an exemplar of this brutalism. But, of course, this is exactly what it is not. If sexual behaviour and marital norms were unstructured, where would have been the need for this high-profile public rite of exchange? The wife sale was invented in a plebeian culture which was sometimes credulous or superstitious, but which had a high regard for rituals and forms.

We have noted already the strongholds of this kind of culture — those communities, sometimes described as proto-industrial, tightly-knit by bonds of both kinship and economic activity: colliers, cutlers, framework knitters and stockingers, the iron workers of the Black Country, weavers, those who served the markets and transport. It does not matter much whether church or common-law marriages were most in favour in this community or that,[1] nor whether

---

[1] The best overview is John R. Gillis, *For Better, For Worse: British Marriages, 1600 to the Present* (Oxford, 1985); also R. B. Outhwaite (ed.), *Marriage and Society* (1981).

bastardy and pre-nuptial conception rates were rising. These indices do not tell us all that we might wish to know about the marital norms, expectations, reciprocities and roles of couples when once committed to a household and to children. A marriage (whether formal or common law) engages compulsions of kin, of neighbours, of work-fellows; it involves far more emotional interests than those of the two persons primarily concerned. We shall see, when we come to consider "rough music", that the expectations of the community penetrated into the family home, directing and sometimes constraining marital conduct. The watchful eyes of kin and of neighbours meant that marital offences were unlikely to go unknown in the wider community. Marital disputes were often taken out of doors and acted out as street-theatre, with a voluble appeal to the neighbours as an audience of jurors.

This was not a Puritan culture, and Methodists and evangelical reformers were shocked by the licence which they imputed to it, and especially by the sexual laxity of the young and unmarried. But there is abundant evidence that the consensus of such communities was such as to impose certain proprieties and norms, and to defend the institution of marriage itself, or of the family household.

This household was an "economic" as well as a domestic unit; indeed, it is impossible to show where "economic" relations ended and "personal" relations began, for both were imbricated in the same total context. When lovers courted each other they were "sweethearts", but when they were settled in the new unit they were each others' "help-meets", a word which carries sentiment and domestic function or economic role in equal measure. It is wrong to suppose that, because men and women had a need for each other's economic support, or for the support of their children in the daily work of the home, this necessarily excluded affection and gave rise to a callous instrumentalism. "Feeling may be more, rather than less, tender or intense because relations are 'economic' and critical to mutual survival".[1]

[1] See my "Happy Families", *New Society*, 8 Sept. 1977; H. Medick and D. Sabean, *Interest and Emotion* (Cambridge, 1984), pp. 9-27.

Within such communities it was impossible to change marriage partners — and to move into a new household in the next street or the next village — without it being a cause for daily, continuing scandal. Separation, especially if children were involved, made a rent in the kinship netting and disturbed the working neighbourhood.[1] It might seem to threaten other households. But the new couple might not be able to take the easy way out, by migrating to the nearest city and its more tolerant "anonymity", simply because it was not easy. The trade (nail-making, frame-work knitting, colliery) might be local, no other employer might be on offer, no other cottage to rent. If they stayed in their own community, some ritual which acknowledged the transaction must be found.

I concur with the most careful historian of British popular marriage — John Gillis — that the wife sale was most strongly supported in these plebeian or proto-industrial communities; that in general it was not a peasant custom and "the rite itself was not meant to deal with marriages in which property was involved";[2] and that it declined in frequency in the large cities, "where people could separate and remarry without anyone knowing or caring" — an overstatement, since in any urban street people knew or made it their business to find out. In short, we have moved from a land-usage to a money economy: a marriage with household is set up from the joint savings of bride and bridegroom (perhaps as servants or apprentices) and not from dower or land-rights. But we are still in a communal world of a known working neighbourhood with its market nexus. And if the community is knit together by kinship and common work it also has strands of common culture, made up of strong oral traditions (which are essential to transmit folk rituals) and an inheritance of custom and anecdote which is often encoded in the dialect speech of the people.

One further reason why, in such communities, a rite which signalled divorce might have been necessary could lead us

---

[1] When children are mentioned in reports of wife sales, it is generally assumed that babies-in-arms and toddlers stay with the mother: occasionally a family is split, and the older (working age?) children go with the father.

[2] Gillis, op. cit., p. 218.

further into the psychic resources of those men and women than we are able to follow. But one may hazard that even when a couple had changed partners and removed to some other district, the more "simple" minded (as Hardy described Susan Henchard) would continue to feel acute mental discomfort if there had been no rite which unloosed them from their previous allegiance or oath. An oath could have a terrifying sanction, an inexorable obligation, upon men and women of this time; and the marriage vow carried with it a whole freight of traditional lore.

All this argues the need for some rite, and the rite itself has been sufficiently described. It can be seen as a bleak transaction, or as street-theatre, or as a shaming ritual. The nearest that we can get to a thick description of the whole affair is in a reconstitution by an observant journalist, who saw it as a comedy of manners of the Black Country (Appendix pp. 463-6). But the form was flexible enough to carry many different messages, according to the cases involved and the judgement of the public.

This can be illustrated by the function of money paid in the exchange. The sum passed varied from the merest formality to substantial damages. Here are some examples as they arise from my notes. In Stowmarket in 1787 a farmer sold his wife for five guineas. Then he presented her with a guinea to buy a new gown, and ordered the bells to be rung for the occasion.[1] At Sheffield in 1796 a husband sold his wife for 6d. He then paid a guinea for a coach to take her and her purchaser to Manchester.[2] In Hull in 1806 a man sold his wife for twenty guineas to a man who had lodged with them for four years: this looks like punitive damages.[3] At Smithfield in 1832 the wife was sold for 10s. with 2s. commission to the drover. The wife was then released from the pens opposite to the "Half Moon" public house, which the three parties then entered, where the late husband spent the greater part of the purchase money in brandy and water.[4]

---

[1] *Ipswich Journal*, 28 Jan. 1787, cited in J. Glyde, *New Suffolk Garland* (Ipswich, 1866), p. 286.

[2] *The Times*, 30 Mar. 1796, citing *Sheffield Register*.

[3] *Annual Register*, 1806.

[4] *The Times*, 25 Feb. 1832.

At Boston (Lincolnshire), 1821, a price of 1s., the husband returning 11d. to the purchaser "for luck".[1] But at the same place in 1817 a wife had been sold for three-farthings, and the husband "delivered into the bargain her paraphernalia, a shoulder of mutton, basket, &c.".[2]

That it was a shaming ritual for the wife is explicit in the symbolism. Most wives (like "Rough Moey's" in the Appendix) were at some point in tears. But because a wife is reported as "scarcely to be sustained from fainting" as she was being "dragged" in a halter to sale (Dartmouth, 1817) we cannot necessarily infer that she was an unwilling party to the exchange; we know, in this case, that she was sold to "her first sweetheart", and her reluctance might equally have come from the shame of the public exposure.[3] The humiliation might also extend to the husband who was acknowledging that he had been cuckolded. If the report can be trusted, Jonathan Jowett, a farmer near Rotherham (1775), braved his way through the transaction with a "ludicrous piece of business". He agreed to sell his wife for twenty-one guineas to William Taylor, a potter, whom he suspected of being her lover, and he duly delivered her in a "regular procession":

Jowett went first, having his head ornamented, by his own desire, with a large pair of ram's horns gilded, on the front of which the following sentence was wrote in gold letters, 'cornuted by William Taylor'; a broad collar was fixed about his neck by which a ring and a cord being fastened thereto, one of his neighbours led him. And the wife with a halter about her neck was led by her husband to the place appointed amidst the shouts of upwards of one thousand spectators — Jowett returned the purchaser a guinea for luck and both sides seemed pleased with the bargain.[4]

The affair was being performed in the public eye. Just as the condemned before execution, the parties were acting up to expected roles. But they were given licence to improvise their own lines. For the husband the theatre provided opportunities for saving face. He could ridicule and humiliate

[1] *Hull Advertiser*, 2 Feb. and 23 Mar. 1821.
[2] *Stamford Mercury*, 7 Nov. 1817.
[3] *The Times*, 12 Apr. 1817.
[4] *Sherborne Journal*, 24 Aug. 1775. It was reported of a sale in Witney in 1848 that the wife was led by a halter to the market by her husband who wore a huge pair of horns: *Gazette des Tribunaux*, 22 June 1848.

his wife in the patter of an auctioneer; or he could suggest good-riddance by asking a derisory price; or he could court a reputation for generosity, showing his goodwill by causing the bells to be rung, showering gifts on the new couple, or hiring a coach; or he could, like "Rough Moey", signify a comic resignation — "We all on us know how the matter stands. It cawn't be helped, so we needn't be so savige about it."

Not all partings were smooth. In a few cases the husband is reported as evincing anger or jealousy towards his rival. In other cases he "repented" the sale and harassed the new couple. A stocking-weaver in Ansty (Leicestershire) in 1829 sold his wife to another stockinger. A few weeks later he passed the new couple's house and "saw her at work in a stocking frame, apparently very contentedly". This sight of his former helpmeet now helping his rival enraged his jealousy, he came back with a loaded gun and was aiming it at her through the window when a passer-by intervened.[1] Another case which ended in an unhappy parting took place in Goole market (1849). Here a waterman named Ashton had been an in-patient in Hull Infirmary with an infected knee; meanwhile (according to the report) his wife eloped with a paramour, taking with them a great part of the husband's effects. On his release from the Infirmary Ashton tracked the couple down and a sale was agreed. The wife was made to mount a chair in the market-place with a halter around her waist. After a little "spirited" bidding,

The woman was eventually knocked down to her paramour for five and ninepence, when, snapping her fingers in her husband's face, she exclaimed: 'There, good for nought, that's more than thee would fetch,' and departed, apparently in high glee, with her new lord and master, the husband as they were passing him holding out his hand to her and saying, 'Give us a wag of thy hand, old lass, before we part'.[2]

But that is not all that "savige", and by no means as savage as things which commonly have gone on in twentieth-century divorce courts. Indeed, it is the language of moralistic reporters which sometimes seems more savage than the behaviour reported. As an instance here is a Yorkshire

[1] *Morning Chronicle*, 9 Feb. 1828.
[2] *Doncaster, Nottingham & Lincoln Gazette*, 14 Dec. 1849.

newspaper in 1829:

> According to the usual custom [the husband] purchased a new halter, for which he gave sixpence, and having tied it round his wife's neck, paraded her along the street, the impudent hussey being nothing loth to this public display of her attractions. A purchaser soon appeared, who bid eighteen pence for the woman and the rope, and her husband soon came to terms. A bargain was struck and the shameless parties retired amid the jeers of the assembled crowd, to a public house, where the money was spent, and the former owner of the slut drank to the luck of the purchaser, and the jade declared she was quite satisfied with the transfer, for she had 'got the lad she loved'.[1]

Beneath this crippled language one can detect humour, generosity and independent minds.

When this was street-theatre, what was the role of the audience? The crowds were sometimes large — sometimes "many hundreds" were reported — but more commonly the usual market day throng. So far as one can infer the response of the crowd was dictated by their views as to the rights and wrongs of the particular marital case enacted before them. Where the husband was known to have ill-treated his wife, the new couple might be cheered on their way; where the husband was popular and it was thought that he had been betrayed by his wife and her lover, they might witness the scene with hisses and execrations. At Ferrybridge (Yorkshire) in 1815 the purchaser and wife were pelted with snow and mud.[2] A North Yorkshire case, where an old man was held to have been betrayed by his young wife, resulted in the new couple being burned in effigy on the village green.[3] And there are other cases of the rough musicking of the new

[1] *York Courant*, 30 June 1829

[2] *N & Q*, 2nd series, i (1856), pp. 420-1. In Norwich when it was learned that the purchaser was already married and that he had turned his own wife out of door, he was hustled by the crowd: *Norfolk Chronicle*, 3 May 1823. Another pelting at Glastonbury, *Sherborne & Yeovil Mercury*, 21 Oct. 1833; *Western Flying Post*, 21 Oct. 1833.

[3] *N & Q*, 6th series, v (1882), signed A.J.M. —. This is A. J. Munby, whose MS Diary (Trinity College Library, Cambridge), iv, 27 February 1860, has the original story as told to him by "J.W. & Rev. J.S.". Munby ends the account in his diary: "Such is the influence of modern refinement that the whole village are indignant, and have even burnt the pair in effigy on the Green. Poor things!". (My thanks to Anna Davin for this reference.)

couple, most of them after 1850, when the rite was falling into disuse.[1] On other occasions the crowd appears to have defended the right of the parties to proceed with a sale. General Pillet witnessed an occasion at Ashburn (Derbyshire) during the French Wars, when a JP tried to prevent a sale and the constables were mobbed and pelted by the crowd. The crowd protected the sale from intervention in a similar way at Bolton (1835).[2]

It is one's impression that, until the early nineteenth century, neither lay nor clerical authorities were over-zealous in rebuking any of the parties. Some rural clergy and magistrates were well aware of the practice, and entries in baptismal registers can be found: "Amie Daughter of Moses Stebbing by a bought wife delivered to him in a Halter" (Perleigh, Essex, 1782).[3] The magistrate who tried, unsuccessfully, to intervene at Ashburn, confessed to General Pillet that the grounds of his action were uncertain. He could act against the parties for disturbing the peace ("coming to the market in a sort of tumult"), but "as to the act of selling itself, I do not think I have a right to prevent it. . . because it rests upon a custom preserved by the people, of which perhaps it would be dangerous to deprive them".[4] A disciplinary tone becomes more evident after the Wars, with heavy and indignant censures from the courts and press, the break-up of sales by constables, and the parties haled into

---

[1] For an angry episode, see *Bury Times*, 12 Nov. 1870. The wife had "transferred her affections" to a neighbour on the other side of the street, whose own wife died five weeks before the sale. The wife had eight children, four of whom ("in the receipt of wages") she took with her on her sale. After the sale first the wife was burnt in effigy in front of her new home, and the next day her purchaser; the report implies that women took the leading part in this rough music. Menefee has other good examples, pp. 117, 126.

[2] *Preston Pilot*, 7 Feb. 1835, citing *Bolton Chronicle*.

[3] See Menefee, Case 47, and pp. 270 and 198 note 16. Also entry in Formby Catholic Register for 9 April 1799 of birth of a child to James Wright and Mary Johnson: "This Mary Johnson was sold by her husband at formby Cross and purchased by Jas Wright for 15s and a crown bowl of Punch", Lancs. CRO, RCFO I (1799), p. 7. My thanks to Robert Malcolmson.

[4] See note 1 on p. 438.

court.[1] But it was not altogether clear what the courts could
do with them.[2] For in the eyes of the law the rite of wife sale
was a non-event. (If it had been accepted as an event, this
would have entailed bigamy.) Legally, the parties might have
been taking part in a pantomime. Indeed, when a dispute
between two parishes about the maintenance of three
children came before the sessions at Boston (Lincolnshire) in
1819, it was held that at law the paternity *must* be with the
wife's lawful husband, John Forman, even though he had
sold her to another man, Joseph Holmes, seventeen years
before, had ceased then to cohabit with her, and two of the
three children (the eldest of which was twelve) had been
entered in the baptismal register as sons of Joseph and
Prudence Holmes. Counsel argued that the sale of a wife was
"a scandalous action", that children born in wedlock must be
taken to be those of their legal parents, and that "it would be
monstrous to admit of a husband's coming forward to
bastardize the issue of his own wife". The court upheld
these views.[3]

Since all agreed that wife sales were "monstrous" and
"scandalous" the courts could proceed for misdemeanours,
although not felonies. We have already followed the fate of
the unfortunate Charles and Mary Skinner and John Savage,
as they took their way from poor law cottage or workhouse
via the tap-room of the "George and Dragon" at Tonbridge
to prison (above pp. 426-7). They were conducted there by a
very grand indictment, drawn (*vi et armis*) in the manner of
Kings Bench —

Being persons of wicked and depraved minds, and wholly lost to a due
sense of decency, morality, and religion. . . did, with force of arms, at

[1] A man was sentenced at Manchester to three months imprisonment
and to the pillory in 1815 for selling his wife: *Derby Mercury*, 3 Aug. 1815.
Judge Edward Christian in his *Charges to Grand Juries* (1819), p. 93, called
for prosecutions against the "shameful and scandalous practice" then so
prevalent, and suggested that seller and purchaser might be sent to the
pillory. Since the pillory was abolished in 1816 (Geo. III, c. 178) this
charge was presumably delivered in 1815 or before.
[2] The practices were described as "mere pretences to sanction the
crime of adultery" in the *Birmingham Gazette*, 1 Mar. 1790.
[3] *Stamford Mercury*, 12 Feb. 1819. For a similar decision at
Warwick Quarter Sessions, see *Warwick Advertiser*, 15 Apr. 1809.

combine, confederate and agree together to bring into contempt the holy estate of matrimony. . . and to corrupt the morals of his Majesty's liege subjects, and to encourage a state of adultery, wickedness and debauchery. . . di da di da di da. . . sold all his marital rights. . . di da di da. . . for a certain valuable consideration, (to wit,) the sum of one shilling and a pot of beer. . . di da tiddely pom. . . to the great displeasure of Almighty God, to the great scandal and subversion of the holy estate of matrimony, and of religion, morality, decency and good order, in contempt of our Lord the King, &c.[1]

These monstrous miscreants were especially privileged in their indictment. A Rutland purchaser had to be content with being indicted as "a person of most wicked lewd lascivious depraved and abandoned mind and disposition and wholly lost to all sense of decency Morality and Religion", for which he was fined one shilling.[2] It was less common for the wives to be harrassed by the courts, since the law supposed them to be acting under the cover or control of their husbands. As Menefee has shown, the matter only entered the standard magistrates' reference books in the 1830s, at which time sentences of imprisonment (one, three, and even six months) were imposed.[3]

This may have done something to "put wife sales down", although it is more likely to have driven them out of the market-place and into the pub. More influential, in the decline of the ritual, will have been the decline in its legitimacy within the popular consensus — the old plebeian culture was fast losing its hold, faced with criticism from within, and uncertainty as to its own sanctions and codes. The Radical and Chartist press viewed the practice as scandalous.[4] Even Eliza Sharples, the "moral" (i.e. common-law) wife of Richard Carlile, who acknowledged the sale's function as divorce, found the practice offensive and brutal: "How much better would a quiet separation have

[1] *Sunday Herald*, 27 July 1828.
[2] Palmer, *The Folklore of Leicestershire and Rutland*, p. 58.
[3] See Menefee, ch. 8, and (for sentences) p. 299, note 24 and p. 300, notes 25 and 27.
[4] See e.g. *Northern Star*, 3 Mar. 1838. But the *Destructive and Poor Man's Conservative*, 13 July 1833, while finding wife sales "an outrage", added that "there should be some immediate cheap method of separation provided by the Legislature for the humbler classes. . .". Such a law would "put an end to such scenes".

been, and each left to a new and free choice. While women will consent to be treated as inferior to men, so long may we expect men to be brutes."[1]

By the mid-century, in the agitation which led up to the Matrimonial Causes Act of 1857 (which first established secular divorce procedures) there were more frequent comments on the double standards which permitted a difficult and costly divorce procedure to the rich, through the Ecclesiastical Courts and the House of Lords, but which denied these to the poor. Although — as *Punch* pointed out — the same procedure was free to the poor also:

> At the Central Court, one Stephen Cummins, painter, is found guilty of bigamy. He sells his wife for six shillings, and 'one shilling to drink health.' That the transaction may be in due form, Cummins gives a receipt. The Recorder, sentencing Cummins to imprisonment and hard labour for one year, says, 'Under any circumstances, it were a great public offence for a man to go through the ceremony of marriage with another woman, while his wife was living.' But then the poor are so depraved — are so illiterate! They will *not* go to the Ecclesiastical Court — they will *not* appeal to the House of Lords. A legal separation, conveying the right of future marriage, is always to be had on proper evidence given, — and yet the poor will not purchase their remedy.[2]

Caroline Norton made the same point in equally angry terms: since the time of Henry VIII, the English method of divorce "has remained an indulgence sacred to the aristocracy":

> The poorer classes have no form of divorce amongst them. The rich man makes a new marriage, having divorced his wife in the House of Lords: his new marriage is legal; his children are legitimate. . . The poor man makes a new marriage, *not* having divorced his wife in the House of Lords; his new marriage is null; his children are bastards; and he himself is liable to be put on his trial for bigamy. . . Not always offending knowingly, — for nothing can exceed the ignorance of the poor on this subject; they believe a Magistrate can divorce them; that an absence of seven years constitutes a nullity of the marriage tie; or that they can give each other reciprocal permission to divorce: and among some of the rural populations, the grosser belief prevails, that a man may legally *sell* his wife, and so break the bond of union! They believe anything, rather than what is the fact, — viz. that *they* cannot do legally that which they know is done legally in the classes above them. . .[3]

[1] *Isis*, 5 May 1832.
[2] *Punch*, xvii (1849), p. 129.
[3] The Hon. Mrs Norton, *A Letter to the Queen on Lord Chancellor Cranworth's Marriage and Divorce Bill* (1855), pp. 14-15.

By the 1850s the wife sale was a survival, in pockets where the old "plebeian" culture still endured. There is a late case, in Bradford (Yorkshire) in 1858, which suggests a moment of cultural insecurity, as the oral transmission of the forms is breaking down. Hartley Thompson offered his wife, "of prepossessing appearance", for sale in front of a beerhouse in a Bradford suburb. By one account the couple, both factory workers, "had become mutually tired of each other, and, it is said, had been mutually unfaithful to their marriage vow". A sale had taken place (it is not explained in what form) to the wife's lover, Ike Duncan, also a factory worker. "However, it was afterwards discovered that some formality, considered essential, had been overlooked." On the present occasion every possible formality was carried through. The bell-man was sent around to announce the sale. The wife appeared in a new halter, decorated with red, white, and blue streamers. An auctioneer was prepared on horseback. A large crowd assembled. But the owners of the factory in which they were employed prevented the sale by threatening to sack anyone who took part. Ike Duncan was kept in at work and the wife declared that "she would not be sold to any person. . . but Ike". The sale was called off.[1]

From the 1850s onwards the practice retreated into the more secretive forms of paper contracts witnessed in the public bar. The latest case in my collection which specifically mentions a halter is Hucknall Torkard, near Sheffield, 1889, where "a leading member of the Salvation Army" sold his wife to a friend for a shilling and led her by a halter to his house.[2] Paper contracts come to light more frequently: one Lincolnshire villager called at the Barton-on-Humber stamp-office to get a stamp on his.[3] The exchanges were sad and sometimes furtive affairs, outside or inside the pubs. One witness recalled a sale outside a pub in Whitechapel: the husband "a wretched-looking fellow", the wife "a respectably dressed woman, aged about thirty"; the landlord as auctioneer, and a young man who "it was understood would be the highest bidder". The newly-united pair walked

---

[1] *Bradford Observer*, 25 Nov. 1858; *Stamford Mercury*, 26 Nov. 1858.
[2] *Yorkshire Gazette*, 11 May 1889.
[3] *Stamford Mercury*, 22 Aug. 1856.

off, "the man with an air of bravado, and the woman with a sniff in the air", while the ex-husband "looked glum, and [his] neighbours manifested neither sympathy nor approval".[1] In the Midlands and the North it was said that sales took place among navvies, some colliers, bargees, some labourers. All that ritual now seemed to demand was publicity. The press reported (1882) a woman sold by her husband for a glass of ale in a pub in Alfreton on a Saturday night. "Before a room full of men he offered to sell her for a glass of ale, and the offer being accepted by the young man, she readily agreed, took off her wedding-ring, and from that time considered herself the property of the purchaser.[2]

Folklorists and journalists in the 1870s and 1880s indicate that the sense of the legitimacy of the practice endured. The *Standard* in a leading article in 1881 claimed that sales still took place in pubs in the Potteries, in certain mining districts, and in Sheffield amongst steel workers. The halter was rarely used. "The seller", wrote the editorialist, "the 'chattel', and the buyer all firmly believe that they are taking part in a strictly legal act of divorce and re-marriage".[3] On the same day the Home Secretary, Sir William Harcourt, was questioned about the matter in the House of Commons by an Irish Nationalist MP. His reply was curt:

> Everyone knows that no such practice exists. ["Oh!"] Well, Sir, if hon. Gentlemen from Ireland know the case to be different with reference to that country, I have nothing to say. . .

But in the view of the Home Secretary in England the practice was "unknown".[4]

VI

Wife sales have served to inspire eloquent exercises in moralism. In the nineteenth century the French, and other Continental neighbours, used them against the English in

---

[1] S. C. Hall, *Retrospect of a Long Life* (1883), i, pp. 43-4. This could, however, refer to a sale before 1850. Menefee (Case 245) suggests 1833.

[2] *South Wales Daily News*, 2 May 1882.

[3] *Standard*, 30 May 1881. Later cases are cited in *Daily Mail*, 1 Mar. 1899, *Globe*, 16 Nov. 1903, and A. R. Wright, *English Folklore* (1928).

[4] *Parliamentary Debates*, 261, col. 1646-7, 30 May 1881.

indignation or in jest. Americans also (wrote the feminist, Caroline Dall) "are anxious to understand this outrage. Is it possible that a government which forbids the sale of a negro cannot forbid the sale of a Saxon wife?". [1] Even the Anglo-Indian or "Eurasian" community, resentful of their twilight racial status, brought the matter up accusingly. [2] The polite classes in England — as we have seen abundantly — in their turn accused the brutalised labouring poor.

Since the scanty evidence did not exactly "feel" like that, I commenced my research, and in due course took the makings of this chapter around as an occasional lecture. By the late 1970s I was regretting my choice, and I would have stopped giving it as a lecture anyway, even if I had not been distracted by other matters. For it was decided by some feminists that my lecture was a male reading of the evidence and was offensive to correct views of "women's history". American feminists in the tradition of Caroline Dall voiced this criticism most strongly. At one university which has a little reputation (Yale) a faculty member shouted out as I left the lecture-room that my lecture had been "a con trick". On another occasion I was taken to task very forcibly by a scholar whom I greatly respect for suppressing the fact that the wife, when sold, was being cheated of her dower and attendant rights. But the evidence for this has not yet come my way. [3]

In short, it got about that I was taking around an anti-feminist lecture, and welcome parties were prepared. While British audiences were more good-humoured, I became weary

[1] Caroline H. Dall, *"Woman's Right to Labour" or Low Wages and Hard Work* (Boston, Mass., 1860), pp. 44-6.

[2] Herbert Alick Stark, *Hostages to India* (Calcutta, 1936), p. 78.

[3] We know too little about the decline of dower among working people, although see Alan Macfarlane, *Marriage and Love in England, 1300-1840* (Oxford, 1986), ch. 12. In a few cases wives sold in rural districts might have lost cottage property with common rights: see Bob Hiscox, above p. 436, note 2. J. F. Howson, rector of Guisely and Archdeacon of Craven (Yorkshire) recalled in the 1930s talking with an old man in his parish, who said: "A grandmother o' mine wur sold that road, she were that. 'Ave 'eered my father tell abaht it many a time. They put an 'alter rahnd 'er neck, tha' knaws, 'appen to maake it legal like. . . And worst of it wur. . . 'at we lost two cottages along of it, we did an' all". (Private communication to me from E. R. Yarham.)

of the hostile tone of questions — as if I was trying to pass some fraud over on the audience — and also a little hurt, since I had supposed myself to be on the side of women's rights (a supposition as to which my questioners were anxious to disabuse me). So I put the lecture away. This kind of intellectual charivari is only to be expected after generations of masculine-inflected history; it is merited; and it is a small price to pay for the rapid advance in feminine readings and definitions.

What I had done was to arouse certain expectations and then disappoint them. My title, "The Sale of Wives", had led the audience to expect a scholarly disquisition on yet one more example of the miserable oppression of women. But my matter did not (and does not) exactly conform to that stereotype. Indeed, my intention was to decode behaviour (and even inter-personal relationships) which had been stereotyped by middle-class moralists (mostly male). The matter of feminine oppression was a subordinate theme.

Perhaps too much so. Perhaps in this chapter it has been too much taken for granted. One cannot always be reiterating the elemental organisation of a society and its gender relations, just as, if one is always parsing the parts of speech, one cannot listen to what a sentence is saying. If all that one can find in the relations between men and women is patriarchy, then one may be missing something else of importance — and of importance to women as well as to men. The wife sale is certainly telling us something about male-domination, but something which we already know. What we could not know, without research, is the small space for personal assertion which it might afford to the wife.

Let us agree, without any reservation, that the wife sale took place in a society in which the law, the church, economy and custom placed women in an inferior or (formally) powerless position. We may call this patriarchy if we wish, although a man did not have to be head of a household to be privileged over most women (of his own class). Men of all classes used a vocabulary of authority, and of ownership, with respect to their wives and children, and church and law encouraged this. The wife sale, then, appears as an extreme instance of the general case. The wife is sold like a chattel and the ritual, which casts her as a mare or cow, is degrading and was intended to degrade. She was exposed, in her sexual nature, to the inspection and coarse jests of a casual crowd. Although sold with her own assent, it was a profoundly humiliating experience which sometimes provoked her fellow women to anger[1] and sometimes called forth their sympathy: "Neer mind, Sal, keep yer pecker up, and never say die!" (below, p. 464).

Even if we redefine the wife sale as divorce-with-consent it was an exchange of a woman between two men[2] and not of a man between two women. (There are, in fact, records of husband sales, but they could be counted on the fingers of one hand.)[3] The fact that the ritual took place within the forms and vocabulary of a society in which gender relations were structured in superordinate/subordinate ways is not in doubt.

Yet there was something at work within the form, which sometimes contradicted its intention. Sales need not take place to the husband's advantage. Nor should we suppose that the norms of these working people were identical to those prescribed by church and law — that gives rise to serious mis-readings. In these "proto-industrial" working communities the relations between the sexes were undergoing some change. It is not yet appropriate to use a vocabulary of "rights"; perhaps "worth" or "respect" are the terms we need. The worth of women in these hard-working households was substantial, as was their responsibility, and it brought an area of corresponding authority and independence. I shall suggest, when we come to consider rough music, that male

[1] See Menefee, p. 124.

[2] Even this must be qualified, since (as anthropologists warn us) what is exchanged is not "a woman" but rights over a woman: see J. R. Goody, "Marriage Prestations, Inheritance and Descent in Pre-Industrial Societies", *Journal of Comparative Family Studies*, p. 40.

[3] There is a cryptic report of the sale of a husband in a halter at Dewsbury market cross, *Cambridge Gazette*, 26 Aug. 1815, *Warwick Advertiser*, 19 Aug. 1815. Another (1814?) in Drogheda was widely cited: e.g. Pillet, *op. cit.*, p. 185. A broadside (*Bibliotheca Lindesiana*, no. 1631) has a circumstantial account of the sale of a shoemaker by his wife in Totnes, Devon, 1824, but I doubt this case, which looks like confected printer's copy. There are a few *bona fide* cases of private contractual sales, for example of a husband who had left his wife to go to Australia: *Birmingham Daily Post*, 12 Jan. 1888.

insecurity in the face of this growing independence may
explain some of the "skimmingtons" in the traditional West,
with their obsession with cuckoldry and fear of women "on
top". And the robust women whom we have seen in the front
of food riots scarcely fall into the role of abject victims — a
role ascribed to them a few years ago in the orthodoxy of
certain campus feminists.

To read the history of women as one of unrelieved victim-
hood, as if anything before 1970 was feminine pre-history,
can make for good polemics. But it is scarcely flattering to
women. I was disabused of this early in my career as an adult
tutor when I was talking to a Workers' Educational Association day school in a market-town in North Lincolnshire, and
was waxing into condescending eloquence about women's
oppression. An elderly self-educated villager, with a keen
weather-beaten face, became tense, and at length burst out:
"We women knew our rights, you know. We knew what was
our due". And I realised with embarrassment that my callow
emphasis on feminine victim-hood had been received by her
and other members of the audience as an insult. They
instructed me that working women had made their own
cultural spaces, had means of enforcing their norms, and saw
to it that they received their "dues". Their dues might not
have been today's "rights", but they were not history's
passive subjects.

Many years later I was at a conference somewhere in New
England, when a speaker had been denouncing with great
vivacity, and much applause, the sins of the author of *The
Making of the English Working Class* "brackets male" and
was indicating my omissions. It was all fair stuff, but my
friend, the late Herbert Gutman, felt I needed some
reassurance and whispered into my ear: "You know, these
people are making the same mistake as some of the historians
of the blacks did. They always wanted to show their subjects
as victims. They denied them their self-activity."[1] Since
Herb's whisper was more like a growl, his comment upset five
or six rows before and behind us. Never mind, he was right.

[1] In one sense Herbert G. Gutman, *The Black Family in Slavery &
Freedom* (New York, 1976), is a massive correction of acounts of slavery
which have understated the slaves' cultural identity.

The wife sale was one possible (if extreme) move available in the politics of the personal of eighteenth-century working people. Yes, the rules of these politics were male-dominative, although the women in the community were the particular guardians of the institutions of the family. But it would seem that the women had the skill, on occasion, to turn the moves to their own advantage. I can see no reason why anyone should have supposed this to be an "anti-feminist" conclusion.

There are certainly victims among those sold wives,[1] but far more often the reports suggest their independence and their sexual vitality. The women are described as "fine-looking", "buxom", "of good appearance", "a comely-looking country girl", or as "enjoying the fun and frolic heartily".[2] Sally, in the Bilston ballad of "Samuel Lett", gives us the folk type of the sort of wife who might get sold:

> Her wears men's breeches
> So all the folks say;
> But Lett shouldna let her
> Have all her own way.
>
> Her swears like a trooper
> And fights like a cock,
> And has gin her old feller
> Many a hard knock.[3]

And we may identify at least one wife sold (in Hereford market very early in the nineteenth century) who lives up to this type —

That was the woman who carried the bloody loaf in the bread riots. I saw it all. I saw her head the women to seize the load of grain. Old Dr Symonds told her to take the garter off her right leg and tie it to the

---

[1] One wife who was sold at Spilsby (Lincolnshire) in 1821 was committed to the house of correction the next week for threatening to set fire to her former husband's premises: *Stamford Mercury*, 7 Dec. 1821. There is a fierce denunciation of the husband who had sold her, published by Martha Barnard in a wall poster in Cambridge, July 1841: reproduced in Philip Ward, *Cambridge Street Literature* (Cambridge, 1978), p. 48.

[2] Among many examples, *British Whig*, 8 May 1835; *Leeds Times*, 10 Aug. 1844; *Derby Mercury*, 11 Oct. 1848; John Hewitt, *History and Topography of the Parish of Wakefield* (1963). Also Menefee, p. 276 note 10.

[3] See p. 423, note 2.

fore horse, and let the team go, and they did. . . They made a fine song about them all, beginning with —

> Have you not heard of our Herefordshire women?
> How they ran and left their spinning —
> How they ran without 'hat or feather
> To fight for bread, 'twas through all weather —
> Oh, our brave Herefordshire women![1]

We are not told whether she was sold before or after this affray.[2] But she does not sound like someone who could have been sold unless she had wanted that.

Another wife, who was sold in Wenlock market for 2s. 6d. in the 1830s, was quite decided about the matter. When her husband got to "market-place 'e turned shy, and tried to get out of the business, but Mattie mad' un stick to it. 'Er flipt her apern in 'er gude man's face, and said, 'Let be, yer rogue. I wull be sold. I wants a change' ".[3]

[1] "Nonagenarian" in *Hereford Times*, 15 Apr. 1876.
[2] The food riots were probably those of 1800. A wife was reported as being sold in Hereford in 1802 by a butcher for £1. 4s. and a bowl of punch: *Morning Herald*, 16 Apr. 1802.
[3] C. M. Gaskell, "Old Wenlock and its Folklore", *Nineteenth Century*, (1894).

APPENDIX

The account below is from Frederick W. Hackwood, *Staffordshire Customs, Superstitions and Folklore* (Lichfield, 1924), pp. 71-3. He describes it as "a descriptive account of a wife sale at Wednesbury, upwards of a century ago, written and published by a spectator", but no further details are given of the source.

"The town-crier, taking his stand before a low tavern, rings his bell to attract attention, and then gives notice in slow, deliberate phrases, that 'a woman —and her little baby — will be offered — for sale — in the Market Place — this afternoon — at four o'clock — by her husband — Moses Maggs'."

The announcement was received by roars of laughter, followed by loud "hurrahs," for the worthy named was one of the most notorious characters in the town, and commonly known as Rough Moey. He was a stout, burly fellow of about forty-five; his face had once been deeply pitted by smallpox, but the impress of the disease had been literally ploughed out by deep-blue furrows, the result of a pit explosion. He had lost one eye, and the place of one leg was supplied by a wooden stump. Neither in feature nor in figure was he prepossessing.

Shopkeepers came to their doors to pass remarks on the bell-man's announcement, and women with arms akimbo stood about the street in groups of two or three to gossip on the same subject. Other interested loafers adjourned the discussion to the nearest taproom. The crier moved away to repeat his announcement elsewhere, followed by a crowd of ragged urchins.

Just before the specified time a crowd gathered in the Market Place, in front of the White Lion, a well-frequented tavern, where four tall fellows, armed with cudgels, cleared a space, and kept back the eager sightseers from crushing upon a man, a woman, and an infant — the lions of the day.

The woman was younger than the man, probably about twenty-three, with as many good looks as was compatible with her situation in life, married, or "leased" to such a man as her mate. In her arms she carried a child about twelve months old, which was quite undisturbed by the uproar around. The woman was evidently in her best attire, her face was freshly washed, her hair was gathered behind in a bob and tied by a bit of blue ribbon, the ends of which floated behind in gallant streamers, no doubt in honour of the occasion.

Though a common hempen halter hung loosely round her neck, the end of which was held by her husband and master, she did not — to judge by her appearance — find the situation trying or unpleasant; and to such encouraging cries as "Ne'er mind, Sal, keep yer pecker up, and never say die!" she replied with a merry laugh, and such remarks as assured her hearers that she'd be glad to get rid of the old rascal, and that it served her right for marrying such an old vagabond.

Then some sort of order having been obtained, some ale was sent for, two tubs were brought out into the space and up-ended by the four stout fellows, on one of which the woman and her child were mounted, and on the other the man took his stand. While the ale was being consumed by the principals, a fiddler was brought in to enliven the proceedings with a merry tune or two.

During the interlude, inquiries among the crowd by the recording inspector, elicited these facts. That Rough Moey had given a sturdy pit wench, about half his own age, a new gown and other articles of dress, with a fortnight's treat, to marry him. That after a time she had transferred her affections to a good looking young collier; upon which the husband naturally became jealous and took to beating her. This, instead of curing her, only awakened thoughts of retaliation; and, as Moey often came home at night in a state of helpless intoxication, she would gently unstrap the wooden leg of the sleeping drunkard and thrash him with it to her heart's content. At last, tiring of this state of affairs, the discomfited husband had resolved to put an end to it by the only means known to him, that of making a "lawful" transfer of an undesired wife, by selling her to her admirer in open market.

The fiddling having ceased, the attention of the crowd was concentrated on the principal actors in the scene. The man, holding the halter in his left hand, raised aloft a quart jug full of ale in the other, and with a sly wink of his single eye, said in a loud throaty voice, "Laerdies an' gentlemin, 'ere's all yoar good 'ealths!" — and taking a long, long draught, finished with a long sigh of satisfaction, "Ah-h-h!" while inverting the jug to show that it was empty. A number of his friends (or "butties", as he called them) responded with "Thank thee, Moey"; while some of the women shouted at him, "Well done, old lad!"

Near to the woman stood a stalwart young fellow, evidently the intending purchaser, who supplied her with ale. She was keeping up a running fire of wordy exchanges with the women around; but notwithstanding this attitude of bravado, her eyes were seen presently to fill with tears, and her bosom began to heave as if her heart were beating fiercely under the strain of suppressed excitement. Then her voice faltered, and hurriedly handing the child to the young man, she sat down on the tub, buried her face in her hands, and wept bitterly. Instantly all laughing ceased, the clamour was hushed, and a look of indignation spread over every woman's countenance. Even some of the men seemed unable to suppress a sense of outrage, expression to which was given by the expectant purchaser, who hissed out in a savage voice, "Come, now, o'l chap, ha' done with this foolery; and get on wi' it!"

So old Rough Moey got on in this strain: "Laerdies an' gentlemin," he said, "we all on us know how the matter stands. It cawn't be helped, so we needn't be so savige about it." Then fortifying himself with another drink, and winking hideously with his remaining eye, he continued: "Laerdies an' gentlemin, I ax lafe to oppose to yer notice, a very handsome young ooman, and a nice little baby wot either belongs to me or to somebody else." Here there was a general laugh, good humour again gaining the ascendant among the onlookers.

"Her's a good cratur," went on the amateur auctioneer, "an' goos pritty well in harness, wi' a little flogging. Her con cook a sheep's yed like a Christian, and mak broth as good as Lord Dartmouth. Her con carry a hundred and a 'alf o' coals from the pit for three good miles; her con sell it well, and put it down her throat in less ner three minits."

This sally raised another laugh, and the orator was rewarded with more drink. Thus refreshed, Moey proceeded: "Now, my lads, roll up, and bid spirited. It's all right, accordin' to law. I brought her through the turnpike, and paid the mon the toll for her. I brought her wi' a halter, and had her cried; so everythin's right accordin' to law, and there's nothin' to pay. Come on wi' yer bids, and if yer gies me a good price fer the ooman, I'll gie yer the young kid inter the bargain. Now, gentlemin, who bids? Gooin', gooin', gooin'! I cawn't delay — as the octioneer sez, I cawn't dwell on this lot!"

The orator ceased, and a cheer rewarded his efforts. A voice from the crowd shouted "Eighteenpence".

"Eighteenpence," repeated Moey, "on'y eighteenpence for a strong and full-growed young ooman! Why, yo'd ha' to pay the parson seven and six for marryin' yer, an' here's a wife ready made to yer honds — an' on'y eighteenpence bid!"

"I'll gie thee half-a-crown, o'd Rough Un," came from the young man whom all knew would be the purchaser.

"I'll tell thee wot, Jack," said Moey, "if thee't mak it up three gallons o' drink, her's thine, I'll ax thee naught fer the babby, an' the halter's worth a quart. Come, say six shillins!"

After a little chaffering the young man agreed to pay for three gallons of ale, which it was stipulated should be forthcoming at once, so that his newly-bought wife, himself, and a few chosen "butties", not forgetting the obliging fiddler, should participate in the ratifying pledge-cup.

The bargain being thus concluded, the halter was placed in the young man's hand, and the young woman received the congratulations of numerous dingy matrons. She wiped her eyes and smiled cheerfully; her new husband planted a sharp barking kiss on her rounded cheek by way of ratification, and as the new wedding party moved away the crowd broke up and slowly dispersed. The tragi-comedy of rude Black Country life was terminated.

Chapter Eight

Rough Music

I

"Rough music" is the term which has been generally used in England since the end of the seventeenth century to denote a rude cacophony, with or without more elaborate ritual, which usually directed mockery or hostility against individuals who offended against certain community norms. [1]

It appears to correspond, on the whole, to *charivari* in France, to the Italian *scampanate*, and to several German customs — *haberfeld-treiben, thierjagen* and *katzenmusik*. [2] There is, indeed, a family of ritual forms here, which is European-wide, and of great antiquity, but the degree of kinship within this family is open to enquiry. [3]

In international scholarship *charivari* has won acceptance as the term descriptive of the whole genus. In 1972 I followed this example by entitling a study published in

[1] OED offers an early use of "rough music" in 1708, but it is noted as "the harmony of tinging kettles and frying pans" in R. Cotgrove, *A Dictionarie of the French and English Tongues* (1611). Regional terms such as "skimmington", "lowbelling", "hussiting" and "riding the stang" were probably more generally used, for which see Joseph Wright, *The English Dialect Dictionary*, 6 vols. (1896-1905).

[2] For French sources see the bibliography in Jacques le Goff and Jean Claude Schmitt (eds.), *Le Charivari* (École des Hautes Études en Sciences Sociales, Paris, 1981), pp. 435-42. This is cited hereafter as *Le Charivari*. For Italy, A. del Vecchio, *Le Seconde Nozze* (Firenze, 1885), esp. pp. 290-301. For Germany, E. Hoffman-Krayer and H. Bachtold-Staubli, *Handworterbuch des Deutschen Aberglaubens* (Berlin, 1931-2), entries under "Katzenmusik", "Haberfeldtreiben", "Thierjagen", etc; George Phillips, *Ueber den Ursprung der Katzenmusiken* (Freiburg im Breisgau, 1849), and the contributions of Ian Farr and Ernst Hinrichs in *Le Charivari*.

[3] See Violet Alford, "Rough Music or Charivari", *Folklore*, lxx (1959), p. 507; H. Usener, "Italische Volksjustiz", *Rheinisches Museum für Philologie*, lxi (1901), and the section of contributions in *Le Charivari* on

France " 'Rough Music': Le Charivari anglais".[1] The difficulty of this assimilation soon became apparent. For the very term "charivari" arouses inapposite expectations and constructs the subject according to a French problematic, with its strong emphasis upon charivari as occasioned by second marriages, and also upon the role of unmarried youths. When a learned round table on charivari was convened in Paris in 1977, some visitors from Britain, Germany and Italy had reason to feel that the terms of discourse were "francocentric" and inapposite to their own national evidence. Yet there is no other generic term of international scope, and to say that a French typology has become dominant outside of France's own borders — and is exported with the word — is also to pay tribute to France's strong traditions in folklore, ethnology and anthropology.[2] One could not imagine, in the 1970s, a round table of international scholars convening in a British university to discuss rough music, and one should applaud the French intellectual initiative.

But, while applauding, one should resist inappropriate constructions. Perhaps one should resist, for most purposes, the term "charivari" altogether (unless one is working on French materials), and should stick to "rough music" for English materials?

"Rough music" is also a generic term, and even within the British islands, the ritual forms were so various that it is possible to view them as distinct species. Yet beneath all the

---

ancient and medieval Europe. P. Saintyves, "Le charivari de l'adultère et les courses à corps nus", *L'Ethnographie* (1935), pp. 7-36 offers a wide-ranging survey of penalties and humiliations for adultery, but one must agree with Lévi-Strauss that, so far as the rituals of charivari are concerned, most of his examples are not relevant. There are, however, striking similarities in rituals cited in Persia and Northern India (Saintyves pp. 22 and 28), and also in the brutally-sadistic ritual witnessed by Gorki in the Crimea: see A. Bricteux, "Le Châtiment Populaire de l'infidélité conjugale", *Revue Anthropologique*, xxxii (1922), pp. 323-8. For Hungary, see Tekle Dömötör in *Acta Ethnographica Academice Scientarum Hungaricae*, (Pest, 1958), pp. 73-89.

[1] *Annales E.S.C.*, (1972). Some passages in that article reappear in this chapter.

[2] See the summary of discussion in *Le Charivari*, pp. 401-3.

elaborations of ritual certain basic human properties can be found: raucous, ear-shattering noise, unpitying laughter, and the mimicking of obscenities. It was supported, in Thomas Hardy's description, by "the din of cleavers, tongs, tambourines, kits, crouds, humstrums, serpents, ram's horns, and other historical kinds of music".[1] But if such "historical" instruments were not to hand, the rolling of stones in a tin kettle — or any improvisation of draw-tins and shovels — would do. In a Lincolnshire dialect glossary (1877) the definition runs: "Clashing of pots and pans. Sometimes played when any very unpopular person is leaving the village or being sent to prison."[2]

It is not *just* the noise, however, although satiric noise (whether light or savage) is always present. The noise formed part of a ritualised expression of hostility, even if in the (perhaps debased?) forms recorded in late nineteenth-century examples the ritual was attenuated to a few scraps of doggerel or to the repetition of the "music" on successive nights. In other cases the ritual could be elaborate, and might include the riding of the victim (or a proxy) upon a pole or a donkey; masking and dancing; elaborate recitatives; rough mime or street drama upon a cart or platform; the miming of a ritual hunt; or (frequently) the parading and burning of effigies; or, indeed, various combinations of all of these.

In Britain the rituals extended across the spectrum from the good-humoured chaffing of the newly-wed to satire of the greatest brutality. Cornish "shallals" might only be a light

---

[1] See Thomas Hardy's admirably-observed novel, *The Mayor of Casterbridge* (1884). A Leicestershire dialect dictionary adds: "Pokers and tongs, marrow-bones and cleavers, warming-pans and tin kettles, cherry-clacks and whistles, constables' rattles, and bladders with peas in them, cow's horns and tea-trays" as well as "yells and hisses": A. B. and S. Evans, *Leicestershire Words, Phrases and Proverbs* (1881). Compare Diderot et d'Alambert, *Encyclopédie* (Paris, 1753), p. 208: "bruit de dérision, qu'on fait le nuit avec des poëles, des bassins, des chauderons, &c."; A. Van Gennep, *Manuel de Folklore Francais Contemporain* (Paris, 1946), i, pt. 2, p. 616: "chaudrons, casseroles, sonnettes, cloches à vaches, grelots de cheveaux ou de mulets, faux, morceaux de fer et de zinc, trompes en corne", etc. Compare for Italy, G. Gabrieli, "La 'Scampanata' o 'Cocciata' nelle nozze della Vedova", *Lares*, ii (1931), pp. 58-61.

[2] E. Peacock, *A Glossary of Words used in. . . Manley and Corringham, Lincs.* (English Dialect Society, 1887), p. 208.

community comment on bride or bridegroom — on their
previous sexual reputation, and on whether they were held to
be well- or ill-assorted.[1] Such affairs, not unlike Saxony
polter-abends,[2] migrated across the Atlantic, and long
survived in parts of the United States in the form of
"shivarees".[3]

At the other end of the spectrum, perhaps one of the most
psychologically-brutal rituals was that of the Devon stag-
hunt. In this, a youth dressed in horns (and sometimes skins)
would act as proxy for the victim. He would, by pre-
arrangement, be "discovered", perhaps in a wood near the
village, and be hunted by the "hounds" (the village youths)
through the streets, backyards, across the gardens, run to
earth and flushed out of alleys and stables. The hunt would
continue for an hour or more, and, with a sadistic
psychological refinement, the "stag" would avoid, until a
final kill, approaching too close to the house of the intended
victim. Eventually the kill took place — slow, brutal, and
realistic. The "stag" was run to earth on the door-step of the
victim, and a bladder of bullock's blood which he carried on

[1] See M. A. Courtney, "Cornish Folk-Lore", *Folk-lore Journal*, v
(1887), pp. 216-7; A. L. Rowse, *A Cornish Childhood* (1942), pp. 8-9.

[2] For a good description of this ritual, when crockery was smashed
against the door of newly-weds, see Henry Mayhew, *German Life and
Manners as Seen in Saxony at the Present Day* (1864), i, p. 457.

[3] See Alice T. Chase in *American Notes and Queries*, i, p. 263,
(September 1888); W. S. Walsh, *Curiosities of Popular Custom*
(Philadelphia, 1914). "Shivarees" were reported as widely distributed in
Ohio, Indiana, Illinois, Kansas and Nebraska. All married couples might
expect a "shivaree", which could be bought off only by drink and
hospitality to the crowd. For this, and also for more robust (and sometimes
violent) affairs, see Bryan Palmer's fine study of "Discordant Music:
Charivaris and Whitecapping in Nineteenth-Century North America",
Labour/Le Travailleur, iii (1978); Alfred D. Young, "English Plebeian
Culture and Eighteenth-Century American Radicalism", in Margaret and
James Jacobs (eds.), *The Origins of Anglo-American Radicalism* (1984);
and Bertram Wyatt-Brown, "Charivari and Lynch Law", in his *South
Honor: Ethics and Behaviour in the Old South* (New York, 1982), ch. 16.
Good-humoured rough music to celebrate weddings also migrated to New
Zealand, in the form of "tin-canning", and is occasionally practised at this
day. I was kindly shown much oral reminiscence of "tin-kettling" when
lecturing at the University of Auckland in 1988. This material is now held
by Professor R. C. J. Stone.

his breast was pierced by a hunter's knife and spilled upon the stones outside the victim's house.[1]

One notes here the ritual hunt with diabolic under-tones.[2] The manifestation of "wooset-hunting" still to be found in nineteenth-century Wiltshire carried a similar symbolism. An observer in a Wiltshire village in the 1830s encountered a procession, accompanied by the beating of frying-pans, the shaking of kettles with stones, the blowing of sheeps' horns and the sounding of sheep bells. Four men carried on long sticks hollowed turnips, with candles inside:

> Those were followed by a person bearing a cross of wood. . . seven feet high; on the arms of which was placed a chemise, and on the head of it a horse's skull, to the sides of which were fixed a pair of deer's horns, as if they grew there; and to the lower part of the horse's skull the under jaw bones were so affixed, that by pulling a string, the jaws knocked together as if the skull were champing the bit; and this was done to make a snapping noise during pauses in the music.

The procession, "got up by the village lads", went past the house or houses of the victims for three successive nights, on three successive occasions, with intermissions between each triplet: that is, for nine nights in all. It was (says the observer) employed against "conjugal infidelity".[3]

Other refined regional rituals could be cited. But we may say that most of the other forms fall into four groups, although these may overlap and borrow features from each other. These groups are: a) the *ceffyl pren* (Welsh for "wooden horse") associated with "Rebecca riots" in several parts of Wales); b) "riding the stang", widely distributed in

---

[1] Sabine Baring-Gould, *The Red Spider* (1887), ii, pp. 78, 109; Theo Brown, "The 'Stag-Hunt' in Devon", *Folklore*, xliii (1952), pp. 104-9. Cf. Carlo Ginzburg on "Charivari, associations juveniles, chasse sauvage" in *Le Charivari*, pp. 131-40.

[2] Until recently a frightening and diabolic horned mask used in such rituals survived in Dorset: see H. S. L. Dewar, "The Dorset Ooser" (Dorchester, 1968). (Plate XXVI).

[3] F. A. Carrington, "Of Certain Wiltshire Customs", *Wilts. Archaeological Magazine*, i (1854), pp. 88-9.

the Scottish Lowlands and northern England; c) "skimmington" or "skimmety" riding, entrenched still, in the
nineteenth century, in the West Country, but surviving
elsewhere in the South; and d) plain rough music, un-
accompanied by any riding, although very often accompanied by the burning of the victims in effigy, found almost
everywhere, and commonly in the Midlands and the South.
Indeed, it is not clear whether unadorned rough music is a
distinct form, or is simply the vestigial ritual still surviving
into the nineteenth and early twentieth centuries after the
elaborations of older ritual had fallen away. Thus in
Cambridgeshire in the first decade of this century, the
banging of tins and shaking of kettles is all of the ritual that
is left.[1]

We will return to the *ceffyl pren*. The forms of plain
rough music (d) will become sufficiently evident when we
describe particular occasions. "Riding the stang" (b) and the
"skimmington" (c) require some formal description.

In "riding the stang" either the offender, or a proxy
(sometimes a near neighbour, sometimes a youth) repre-
senting him, was carried on a long pole, or stang, attended by
a rough band, or a "swarm of children, huzzaing and throwing all manner of filth".[2] If the victim was ridden in person,
the procession might end by tipping him into a duck-pond or
watery ditch.[3] Sometimes a ladder or a donkey might be
substituted for the "stang"; more often an effigy in a cart.[4]
If the riding was by proxy, a traditional recitative or
"nominy" was shouted at different parts of the town or
village:

[1] Enid Porter, *Cambridgeshire Customs and Folklore* (1969), pp. 9-10.
[2] J. T. Brockett, *A Glossary of North Country Words in Use*
(Newcastle-on-Tyne, 1829).
[3] S. O. Addy, *A Glossary of Words Used in the Neighbourhood of
Sheffield* (1888), pp. 185-6; Thomas Wright, *The Archaeological Album*
(1845), pp. 54-6.
[4] W. E. A. Axon, *Cheshire Gleanings* (Manchester, 1884), pp. 300-1;
Mrs Gutch, *County Folk-lore: East Riding of Yorkshire* (1912),
pp. 130-3.

Here we cum, wiv a ran a dan dan;
It's neather fo' mah cause nor tha cause
    that Ah ride this stang
But it is fo' Jack Nelson, that Roman-nooased man.
Cum all you good people that live i' this raw,
Ah'd he' ya tak wahnin, for this is oor law;
If onny o' you husbans your gud wives do bang
Let em cum to uz, an we'll ride em the stang.
He beat her, he bang'd her, he bang'd her indeed;
He bang'd her afooar sha ivver stood need.
He bang'd her wi neather stick, steean, iron nor
    stower,
But he up wiv a three-legged stool an knockt her
    backwards ower.
        Upstairs aback o' bed
        Sike a racket there they led.
        Doon stairs, aback o' door
        He buncht her whahl he meead her sweear.
Noo if this good man dizzant mend his manners,
The skin of his hide sal gan ti the tanner's,
An if the tanner dizzant tan it well,
He sal ride upon a gate spell;
An if the spell sud happen to crack,
He sal ride upon the devil's back;
An if the devil sud happen ti run,
We'll shut him wiv a wahld-goose gun;
An if the gun sud happen ti missfire,
Ah'll bid y good neet, for Ah's ommast tired.[1]

The procedure was repeated, sometimes in several parishes, sometimes on three nights. If an effigy was carried, it was shot at, buried, or, most commonly burned.

This rhyme or "nominy" — the example is from Hedon in

---

[1]Mrs Gutch, *op. cit.* Other examples of such recitatives or "nominys" are in A. Easther and T. Lees, *A Glossary of the Dialect of Almondbury and Huddersfield* (1883), pp. 128-9; R. Blakeborough, *Character, Folklore and Custom of the North Riding of Yorkshire* (1898), p. 89; George Ratcliffe, *Sixty Years of It* (London and Hull, n.d. [*c.* 1935]), p. 2; G. Oliver, *Y Byrde of Gryme* (Grimsby, 1866), pp. 207-8; Thomas Miller, *Our Old Town* (1857), p. 198; Axon, *op. cit.*, p. 301; E. Cooper, *Muker: the Story of a Yorkshire Parish* (Clapham, 1948), p. 84; *Yorkshire Notes and Queries*, ed. C. F. Forshaw (Bradford, i, 1905), p. 209; *N & Q*, 9th series, i (11 June 1898), p. 479; *Folk-lore Journal*, i (1883), pp. 394-6.

the East Riding of Yorkshire — allowed for improvisations to
be added, to suit the victim and the occasion.[1] The name of
the offender might be shouted, although in some regions it
was concealed to avoid an action for defamation,[2] or lightly
disguised in a pun. When a husband called Lamb was beaten
by his wife, he was ridden by proxy with a "nominy"
similar to Hedon's, whose third line ran "But it is for the
awde Yowe that threshest poor Lamb".[3] Variants of the
rhymes have a wide geographic dispersal over the North and
the Midlands. In Grassington,

> He neither took stick staff nor stoure
> But he up with his fist and he knocked her owre
> He struck so hard and it sank so deep
> The blood ran down like a new sticked sheep.[4]

The essentials of the "nominy" seem to have been as
indelibly memorised as children's rhymes, and collectors have
found elderly informants to be word-perfect in them. The
words preserved in printed folklore collections may perhaps
be a little bowdlerised, either by collectors or by their
informants. An American collector, fifty years ago,
preserved a version of the last two lines which is more
credible (and also rhymes better) than the Hedon version
preserved by that excellent collector, Mrs Gutch:

> If the gun should happen to miss,
> We'll scale him to death with a barrel o' red-hot piss.[5]

[1] The "nominy" (traditional doggerel accompanying the riding) is not
the same as lampoons or rhymes made for the occasion, which Martin
Ingram treats together with rough music in "Riding, Rough Music and
Mocking Rhymes in Early Modern England", in Barry Reay (ed.), *Popular
Culture in Seventeenth-Century England* (1985).

[2] Edwin Grey, *Cottage Life in a Hertfordshire Village* (St. Albans,
n.d.), pp. 160-2.

[3] James Hardy (ed.), *The Denham Tracts* (1895), ii, p. 5.

[4] Robert White Collection, Newcastle University Library, Bell/White 3.
My thanks to Dave Harker.

[5] James M. Carpenter was collecting in the late 1920s and early
1930s. My thanks to Roy Palmer and to Malcolm Taylor (librarian) for
copies of records at Cecil Sharp House: the originals are in the
Library of Congress. For the late Victorian and Edwardian collectors'
censorship of the bawdy from folksong, see Vic Gamman, "Folk Song
Collecting in Sussex and Surrey, 1843-1914", *History Workshop Journal*,
10 (1980), and "Song, Sex and Society in England, 1600-1850", *Folk Music
Journal* (1982), pp. 219-20.

When a friend of mine, a village schoolmistress in North Yorkshire, recorded an account of the "stang", her informant — a man of about sixty — refused to repeat the words to her, and would only put them on her typewriter when she had left the room.

The "stang" merges its form almost imperceptibly with the "skimmington", and in parts of the Midlands it is scarcely useful to distinguish between the two. The "nominys" used in the East Riding "stang" (above) and in a West Somerset "skimmity" are clearly of common derivation:

> Now Jimsy Hart, if thee disn mend thy manners,
> The skin of thy ass we'll send to the tanner's;
> And if the tanner, he on't tan un well,
> We'll hang un 'pon a naail in hell;
> And if the naail beginth to crack,
> We'll hang un 'pon the devil's back;
> And if the devil urnth away,
> We'll hang un there another day.[1]

Some folklore accounts of the "stang" seem much like "skimmingtons", such as this one from Northenden in Cheshire. In about 1790 Alice Evans the wife of a weaver, and a powerful athletic woman "chastised her own lord and master for some act of intemperance and neglect of work" —

This conduct (of hers) the neighbouring lords of creation were determined to punish, fearing their own spouses might assume the same authority. They therefore mounted one of their body, dressed in female apparel, on the back of an old donkey, the man holding a spinning wheel on his lap, and his back towards the donkey's head. Two men led the animal through the neighbourhood, followed by scores of boys and idle men, tinkling kettles and frying pans, roaring with cows' horns, and making a most hideous hullabaloo, stopping every now and then while the exhibitioner on the donkey made the following proclamation:
> Ran a dan, ran a dan, ran a dan,
> Mrs Alice Evans has beat her good man;
> It was neither with sword, spear, pistol, or knife
> But with a pair of tongs she vowed to take his life. . .[2]

The "skimmington", as it survived into the nineteenth century in the West Country, was distinguished by two

[1] Joseph Wright, *English Dialect Dictionary* (1903), v, entry under "Skimmington".
[2] Axon, *op. cit.*, pp. 330-1, citing Charles Hulbert, *History and Description of the County of Salop* (1828).

features: the elaboration of the ritual, and the frequency with which the victims satirised remained (as had been the case two or three centuries earlier)[1] the woman at odds with the values of a patriarchal society: the scold, the husband-beater, the shrew. Wiltshire Quarter Sessions records of 1618 give us an idea of the possible elaboration:

> About noon came again from Calne to Quemerford another drummer. . . and with him three or four hundred men, some like soldiers armed with pieces and other weapons, and a man riding upon a horse, having a white night cap upon his head, two shoeing horns hanging by his ears, a counterfeit beard upon his chin made of a deer's tail, a smock upon the top of his garments, and he rode upon a red horse with a pair of pots under him, and in them some quantity of brewing grains. . .

Coming to the victims' house (Thomas Mills, a cutler, and his wife, Agnes), the gunners shot off their pieces, "pipes and horns were sounded, together with lowbells and other smaller bells. . . and rams' horns and bucks' horns. . .". The doors and windows of the house were stoned, Agnes was dragged out of her chamber, thrown in the mud, beaten, and threatened with being carried off to Calne to the cuckingstool.[2]

Two centuries and more after this, "skimmingtons" were still being recorded in the West Country, if not on the same scale yet requiring elaborate preparation. In Uphill (Somerset) in 1888, 270 years after Agnes Mills was victimised in Quemerford, a wagon was drawn through the streets at dusk:

> Preceding it was a band of motley musicians, beating a fearsome tattoo on old buckets, frying pans, kettles, and tin cans. Mounted on horses, and riding with mock solemnity beside the waggon, was a bodyguard of six grotesquely attired cavaliers. Erected on a platform on the waggon were two effigies.

[1] See especially Martin Ingram, "Ridings, Rough Music and the 'Reform of Popular Culture' in Early Modern England", *Past and Present*, 105 (1984), and David Underdown, *Revel, Riot and Rebellion* (Oxford, 1985), *passim*.

[2] See Ingram, "Ridings", p. 82, whose transcription corrects that in *Folklore*, xli (1930), pp. 287-90.

The procession went round the village, and then turned into a field where the effigies were burned to the accompaniment of the "Dead March".[1]

The ritual had many variants and allowed for much improvisation, invention and dressing-up. Where the victim satirised was a masterful woman or a husband-beater, two proxy performers might be seated in a cart or face-to-face on a donkey, beating each other furiously with culinary weapons, or back-to-back, with the man holding the beast's tail.[2] Where the reputed infidelity of the wife was the occasion, a petticoat or shift would be carried in the procession, along with horns, brewing grains and other symbols of cuckoldry. (Plate XXIII.)[3] On one occasion, recorded in Dorset as late as 1884, three character were satirised, one male, two female: both the females rode on donkey-back, while one of them "was represented as having an extraordinarily long tongue, which was tied back to the neck, whilst in one hand she held some note-paper, and in the other pen and holder".[4]

So much for the forms. More could be said. And more has been said. Unfortunately, those nineteenth-century folk-lorists to whom we are indebted for many of the best accounts of these rituals were interested, in the main, in the forms themselves; and, if they went further, it was most often to speculate upon their origin and relationship, to classify the forms according to a sort of human botany. Admirably-observed accounts of the form may include only the most casual, throw-away, allusion to the occasion for the event: the status of the victims, their supposed offence, the consequence of the rough music.

Nevertheless, before proceeding, let us see what evidence is offered to us from the forms themselves.

[1] *Somerset County Herald*, 24 Aug. 1946; also 23, 30 Aug. 1952. My thanks to John Fletcher for directing me to this and other sources.

[2] G. Roberts, *The History and Antiquities of Lyme Regis and Charmouth* (1834), pp. 256-61.

[3] See e.g. *N & Q*, 4th series, xi (1873), p. 455, referring to an occasion in Bermondsey (London) "about thirty years ago".

[4] J. S. Udal, *Dorsetshire Folklore* (Hertford, 1922), pp. 195-6, citing the *Bridport News*, Nov. 1884.

1) The forms are dramatic: they are a kind of "street theatre". As such, they are immediately adapted to the function of publicising scandal. Moreover, the dramatic forms are usually processional. Perhaps one should say, indeed, that they are *anti*-processional, in the sense that horsemen, drummers, banners, lantern-carriers, effigies in carts, etc., mock, in a kind of conscious antiphony, the ceremonial of the processionals of state, of law, of civic ceremonial, of the guild and of the church.

But they do not *only* mock. The relationship between the satirical forms of rough music and the dignified forms of the host society is by no means simple. In one sense the processional may seek to assert the legitimacy of authority. And in certain cases this reminder may be remarkably direct. For the forms of rough music and of charivari are part of the expressive symbolic vocabulary of a certain kind of society — a vocabulary available to all and in which many different sentences may be pronounced. It is a discourse which (while often coincident with literacy) derives its resources from oral transmission, within a society which regulates many of its occasions — of authority and moral conduct — through such theatrical forms as the solemn procession, the pageant, the public exhibition of justice or of charity, public punishment, the display of emblems and favours, etc.[1]

The formal continuities are sometimes startling. The naked parade or "carting" of lewd women or of prostitutes was a punishment which had once been imposed by ecclesiastical and civil authorities. Thus, in the Lincoln diocese in 1556 Emma Kerkebie, found guilty of adultery, was sentenced to the public penance: "That the said Emme shal ride through the city and market in a cart, and be ronge out with basons": i.e. rough musicked.[2] A similar punishment was inflicted by officers of the Parliamentary forces in 1642 upon "a whore,

---

[1] See C. Phythian-Adams, "Ceremony and the Citizen: the Communal Year at Coventry, 1500-1700", in Peter Clark and Paul Slack (eds.), *Crisis and Order in English Towns, 1500-1700* (1972).

[2] J. Strype, *Ecclesiastical Memorials relating chiefly to Religion and the Reformation* (1822), iii, p. 409. Riding backwards with the face to the horse's tail was a punishment inflicted for perjury, corruption, etc. by courts in London and by the Star Chamber in the sixteenth and early seventeenth centuries: see Ingram, "Riding, Rough Music and Mocking Rhymes".

which had followed our camp from London". She was "first led about the city, then set in the pillory, after in the cage, then duckt in a river, and at the last banisht the City".[1] And riding upon a pole or a "wooden horse" was a recognised military punishment, and was inflicted upon soldiers whose behaviour (assaults, petty thefts) endangered relations with the civil populace. Thus in 1686 a court martial sentenced an offending soldier accused of the theft of two silver cups "to ride the wooden horse the next market day in the public market place. . . for the space of two hours with a paper on his breast signifying his offence".[2] The punishment humiliated the offender in front of the populace, and hence it supposedly repaired the damage done to military-civil relations.[3]

The punishment could still be inflicted under Army regulations until the early nineteenth century. In 1845, at Yeovil, the same punishment had become an informal institution, it being reported that —

> The almost obsolete punishment of "riding the stang", or wooden horse, was revived in this town last Thursday by a number of builders who, suspecting that one of their number had made free with his comrades' dinners, pinioned him and paraded him through the streets upon a piece of wood with the words "the thif" chalked on his back. The Lynchers had contrived to refine the cruelty of the punishment by sharpening to a point the rafter on which the unfortunate fellow rode, and by jagging it in several places. He was taken home to Bradford Abbas in a cart on Friday, being so much injured as to be unable to walk.[4]

[1] Letters of Nehemiah Wharton, *Archaeologia*, xxxv (1853), pp. 310-34.

[2] PRO, WO 30/17, pp. 68-9. See also Young, *op. cit.*, p. 190 for the use of this military punishment at Louisbourg (1746) and Boston Common (1764). Black soldiers still received this punishment in the American Civil War: Bell I. Wiley, *Southern Negroes 1861-1865* (New Haven, 1965), pp. 317-8.

[3] The wooden horse may have been a permanent civil piece of punitive machinery in some places, along with pillory and stocks. An action in Newcastle-under-Tyne in 1654 turned on a man libelling another as "a base beggarly rascal, and hath cozened the Parliament a hundred times, and deserves to ride the wooden horse, standing on the Sandhill": *Tompkins v Clark* (1654), Style 422, ER 82, p. 829.

[4] *Sherborne, Dorchester and Taunton Journal* (1845) reported in *Somerset County Herald*, 23 Aug. 1952.

I do not know whether the formal (legal) and the informal (customary) infliction of such punishments coincided in late medieval and early modern times or whether popular, self-regulating forms (which were often initiated independently of any persons in authority, and which were sometimes conducted in such a way as to ridicule them) took over to new uses forms which the authorities were ceasing to employ. The answer may be "both". Until the early nineteenth century, publicity was of the essence of punishment. It was intended, for lesser offences, to humiliate the offender before her or his neighbours, and in more serious offences to serve as example. The symbolism of public execution irradiated popular culture in the eighteenth century and contributed much to the vocabulary of rough music.[1] The elaborate effigies of the offenders which were carted or ridden through the community always ended up with a hanging or a burning — which recalled the burning of heretics. In extreme cases a mock funeral service was conducted over the effigy before a "burial". One would be mistaken to see this as only a grotesque jest. To burn, bury or read the funeral service over someone still living was a terrible community judgement, in which the victim was made into an outcast, one considered to be already dead.[2] It was the ultimate in excommunication.

Effigy burning does not belong only with rough music. It can often be found in Britain and in North America detached from other forms of rough music and of course it has been

[1] See Douglas Hay, Peter Linebaugh and E. P. Thompson, *Albion's Fatal Tree* (1975). Compare Natalie Z. Davis, "The Rites of Violence", *Society and Culture in Early Modern France* (Stanford, 1975).

[2] Among examples of burial: *Leicester Herald*, 17 Apr. 1833 (an unpopular employer is rough musicked by framework knitters, his effigy is carried around on a gallows, executed by gunfire, placed in a grave, and then burned); *Hampshire and Berkshire Gazette*, 4 Feb. 1882 (a man who has jilted a woman whom he has been courting for several years — his effigy is carried through the village, the funeral knell is tolled, the effigy is hanged, cut down, shot at and burned); *Gloucester Standard*, 8 Oct. 1892 (the "Dead March" is played during the rough musicking of "scabs" in a boot and shoemakers dispute).

and remains central to Guy Fawkes Day.[1] November 5th was a day when effigy burning and rough music ran into each other, and local or public scores were often paid off.[2] And effigies were appropriated to every kind of political and religious demonstration. They were simply one (effective and enduring) component of the available symbolic vocabulary, which could be employed in combination with other components (noise, lampoons, obscenities), or could be detached from these altogether. Innumerable examples — political, industrial, private grievances — can be found in any locality.

With growing literacy, effigies, verse lampoon and anonymous letters or papers posted on the church doors or gates could all be used together. The Reverend Charles Jeffrys Cottrell, JP, the Rector of Hadley in Middlesex, was driven in 1800 to take legal action when he received in the post a portrait of a gibbeted parson with his genitals exposed, inscribed "O what a miserable Shitting Stinking Dogmatick Prig of an April fool I do appear". (Plate VI.) It seems, from the accompanying depositions, that the prime mover in the campaign against him was Isaac Emmerton, a nursery-man and seedsman, who had also erected on his own land, overlooking the Great North Road, a ten-foot-high gibbet from which was suspended an effigy in a black coat which he had got from a local undertaker. Cottrell was chairman of the local Commissioners of Tax against whom Emmerton had a grievance. But clearly this "Parson and Just Ass" was generally unpopular and people in nearby Barnet were enjoying similar "ludicrous drawings", which were being

---

[1] Alfred Young, "Pope's Day, Tar and Feathers and Cornet Joyce, Jun", (forthcoming), discusses both American and English sources; C. S. Burne, "Guy Fawkes Day", *Folk-lore*, xxiii, 4 (1912).

[2] Rough music often flourished on November 5th, when it was the custom to make effigies of "any evil doer, bad liver, or unpopular person" in the village and burn these before their homes (example, an unmarried couple): *Trans. Devon Assoc.*, lxvi (1934). See the excellent essay " 'Please to Remember the Fifth of November': Conflict, Solidarity and Public Order in Southern England, 1815-1900", in Robert E. Storch, *Popular Culture and Custom in Nineteenth-Century England* (1982), esp. pp. 82-4. John Fletcher, a famous wizard in Pilton, has collected many examples of Guy Fawkes rough musickings in nineteenth-century Somerset, Glastonbury, Wells and Bridgewater being especially ebullient.

passed around. Isaac Emmerton explained, very reasonably, that the effigy was a scarecrow to protect some "curious seeds" and that for this purpose "none but a black coat would answer".[1]

This has taken us a little out of our way. But the consideration of even such a commonplace part of the symbolic vocabulary as the effigy enforces the point that the symbolism owes much to authority's pomp of awe and justice, and that rough music may be ambivalent and move between the mockery of authority and its endorsement, the appeal to tradition and the threat of rebellion. By the eighteenth century rough music was normally — but not always — initiated independently of any persons in authority or of gentry status, and was sometimes conducted in opposition to them. Since the church courts in England were in decline from the late seventeenth century, and were exercising less effectively their powers to inflict penalties for domestic and sexual offences, it is tempting to suggest that the vigour of eighteenth-century rough music indicated a shift from ecclesiastical regulation to community self-regulation in such cases. But this hypothesis has not been seriously tested. Or, if one sees an antiphony between the forms of authority and of the populace, one might ask whether, as ritual and processional declined in Protestant England, so the satiric anti-processional element in popular forms declined in ratio? In Catholic societies which maintained the processions and festivals of church and state with more vigour, did the mock processionals of charivari maintain for longer their elaboration?

2) The forms are pliant. Indeed, they have great flexibility. Even in the same region similar forms can be used to express a good-humoured jest or to invoke inexorable community antagonism. "Skimmingtons" of great elaboration were sometimes mounted as community jokes — for example, in Exeter in 1817 a riding with horsemen, a band, twenty-four donkeys, and much paraphernalia was laid on to ridicule the second marriage of a local saddler who had made himself

[1] Depositions and letter in PRO, King's Bench Affidavits, KB 1.30 (Easter 40 Geo. III, no. 2). For anonymous threatening letters, see my "The Crime of Anonymity", in Hay, Linebaugh and Thompson, *op. cit.*

obnoxious as a braggart and ostentatious patriot during the French Wars.[1] In Barnsley in 1844 the marriage of two local characters thought for some reason to be comic was "published" by an elaborate procession of power-loom weavers. Two led, one dressed in a skin, the other with a flag "Haste to the Wedding"; next a cart drawn by a mule with a fiddler astride it, and with whistles and tin cans played by the cart's occupants.[2] Jests of this kind might easily turn sour. When a butcher on the Isle of Wight, at Newport, married "an elderly maiden lady of good fortune" (1782) his fellow butchers attended to celebrate the event with marrowbones and cleavers. The bridegroom lost his temper and ordered them to go away:

> They had been expecting to be treated instead of being threatened with prison as a riotous mob. They returned, each with a pair of rams' horns fixed on their heads, and a drummer which they had hired. . . beating the cuckolds march. Outraged, the bridegroom fired at them, killing one and wounding two.[3]

The "skimmington" could also, in one variant, be used to establish what was known as a "horn fair" — in Devon if a "skimmington" or "skivetton" rode uncontested through a town, and nailed a pair of horns to the church door, then the claim to establish a cattle fair was made (and upheld).[4] "In consequence of some Woman in Calstock having beat her Husband", a correspondent wrote to the duke of Portland in 1800, "the Miners have made a Procession thro' the Neighbourhood & several Market Towns, in order, as they say, to establish an Horn or Cuckold's Fair at Calstock Town; the first of which Fairs is to be held there on Tuesday next". "Riotous Consequences" were apprehended, as "several very notorious bad Fellows" were among them.[5] The most famous Horn Fair might have had some such origin, and was held at Charlton on the Kentish edge of

[1] *Exeter Flying Post*, 2 Oct. 1817; U. Radford, "The Loyal Saddler of Exeter", *Trans. Devon Assoc.*, lxv (1933), pp. 227-35.
[2] *Halifax Guardian*, 20 Jan. 1844. Thanks to Dorothy Thompson.
[3] *Hampshire Chronicle*, 11 Feb. 1782. Thanks to John Rule.
[4] J. R. Chanter, "North Devon Customs", *Trans. Devon Assoc.*, ii (1867-8), pp. 38-42.
[5] J. P. Carpenter to Portland, 22 June 1800, PRO, HO 42.50.

London. By the seventeenth century it had become an annual carnival, held on St. Luke's day. In the eighteenth century it was proclaimed by printed summonses (Plate XXIV), and consisted of "a riotous mob, who. . . meet at Cuckold's Point, near Deptford, and march from thence in procession, through the town and Greenwich, to Charlton, with horns of different kinds upon their heads; and at the fair. . . even the gingerbread figures have horns".[1] Attendance at this supposedly licentious and bacchanalian event was not confined to the plebs — young patricians also might come, masked and in transvestite disguise — and all the symbolic vocabulary of "skimmingtons" and cuckoldry was kept vigorously alive (Plate XV).[2]

The more one examines the diversity of the evidence, the more difficult it is to define exactly what a rough music was. Sometimes we have nothing more than a boozy, jocular row outside the cottage on a couple's first wedding-night — although rarely without a satirical accent — by the unmarried young men of the community.[3] Some forms were also employed as games on festivals or as initiations into trades.[4] In the North-East in the eighteenth and early nineteenth centuries when a pitman married he was made to "ride the

[1] Francis Grose, *A Classical Dictionary of the Vulgar Tongue*, 2nd edn. (1788).

[2] John Brand, *Observations on Popular Antiquities* (1813), ii, p. 112; William Hone, *The Every-Day Book* (1826), i, cols. 1386-8; Robert W. Malcolmson, *Popular Recreations in English Society* (Cambridge, 1973), pp. 77-8.

[3] The late Mr G Ewart Evans kindly loaned to me a tape of an account given to him by Mrs Flack of Depden Green, near Bury St Edmunds in 1964, who described such "music" as very common until 1920 at weddings. People of "all sorts" gathered, and were asked in for drinks. She recalled only one occasion where it was used against supposed offenders. In London and elsewhere butchers' men made up bands, with marrowbones beating on cleavers (ground to the production of notes like a peal of bells), and attended wedding parties until paid off with money or beer: R. Chambers, *The Book of Days* (1878), i, p. 360.

[4] See Ingram, "Riding, Rough Music and Mocking Rhymes", pp. 94-6. "Wooset" or "hooset" hunting seems to be a cousin to Christmas and animal-guising customs, such as the hooden horse in East Kent and souling in Cheshire: see P. Maylam, *The Hooden Horse, an East Kent Christmas Custom* (Canterbury, 1909), ch. 4; Violet Alford, *The Hobby Horse and other Animal Masks* (1978).

stang", and was carried on a pole by his fellow pitmen to a pub where he was expected to treat his mates to drinks:

> They myed me ride the stang, as suin
> As aw show'd fyece at wark agyen.[1]

This was a good-humoured custom whose only function was as a ransom for drink. But in the same region in the same period "riding the stang" was a severe, and on occasion mutilating, punishment inflicted by pitmen and seamen upon blacklegs during a strike or upon informers or crimps.[2]

3) Even when rough music was expressive of the most absolute community hostility, and its intention was to ostracise or drive out an offender, the ritual element may be seen as channelling and controlling this hostility. There seems to have been a progressive distancing from direct physical violence, although the evidence is inconclusive. Dr Martin Ingram shows us seventeenth-century next-door-neighbours serving as proxies for the ridings, just as proxies are frequently found in the nineteenth century. But just as Agnes Mills of Quemerford was physically assaulted and thrown in the mud in 1618, so examples of such assaults — or of "stang ridings" ending in the midden or the duck-pond — can be found two hundred years later.[3] And the "stang", as we

---

[1] Thomas Wilson, *The Pitman's Pay, and other poems* (Gateshead, 1843), pp. 56-63.

[2] *Newcastle Chronicle*, 7 and 21 May 1785, 4 Nov. 1792; *Sunderland Herald*, 12 Feb. 1851; W. Henderson, *Notes on the Folk-lore of the Northern Counties of England and the Borders* (1879), p. 30. In February 1783 at the close of the first American war sailors got shore leave and revenged themselves upon informers who had betrayed them to the press-gang by "stanging" them through the streets: the women "bedaubed them plentifully with rotten eggs, soap suds, mud, &c.". One was treated so severely on the "stang" that he subsequently died: "The Press Gang in the Northern Counties", *Monthly Chronicle of North Country Lore and Legend*, v, 47 (1891).

[3] This was especially the case with blacklegs, and also with sexual offenders if taken *flagrante delicto*: W. Woodman, "Old Customs of Morpeth", *History of the Berwickshire Naturalists' Club*, xiv (1894), p. 127. There are infrequent cases of running a victim out of town in nineteenth-century England (e.g. R. L. Tongue, *Somerset Folklore* (1965), p. 181 for a "wicked" old woman run out on a hurdle with tin cans tied round it accompanied by a rough band — a practice more common in the New World).

have seen, could be employed as a mutilating instrument. In Galloway wife-beaters were ridden to a "nominy",

> Ocht yt's richt'll no be wrang,
> Lick the wife an ride the stang.
> At the words 'wife' and 'stang' they liftit it as heich as they could, an then loot it suddenly fa' again; and he cam doon wi' a thud every time on some o' the ens o' the brenches yt had been left sticking oot for his benefit, an the scraichs o' him wus fearfu.
> The stang wus through atween his legs, ye ken.[1]

So any generalisation must be qualified. A "skimming-ton" or "stang riding" could get out of hand, and if the person victimised offered resistance, or was so unwise as to rush out of the house when a proxy or effigy was displayed before it, some violence was likely to ensue. But at the same time a rough music was a licensed way of releasing hostilities which might otherwise have burst beyond any bounds of control. A scholar who has studied both charivaris and lynchings in the Old South of the United States suggests that "ritual only half-loosens social controls; it circumscribes just how far the participants should go, thus upholding stability and order".[2] In contrast to a lynching party this may be so, although the Ku Klux Klan ritualised lynching as well.

The argument that rough music rituals were a form of *displacement* of violence — its acting out, not upon the person of the victim, but in symbolic form — has some truth. It is my impression that in nineteenth-century England the proxy and the effigy usually stood in for the offender.[3] Rough music did not only give expression to a conflict within a community, it also regulated that conflict within forms which established limits and imposed restraints. It is (again) my impression that where the ritual forms still had a vigorous life in oral tradition, the disorder of rough music was most "orderly", whereas when they migrated across the Atlantic and were re-enacted with uncertainty in a society with general

---

[1] R. de B. Trotter, *Galloway Gossip: the Stewartry* (Dumfries, 1901), p. 442. My thanks to Roy Palmer.

[2] Wyatt-Brown, *op. cit.*, p. 447.

[3] Firmer law enforcement and heavier policing may have contributed to this.

access to firearms, the outcome was more often violent.[1]
Even the softened "shivaree", which in Canada may have
owed more to French than to British influence, and which
was frequently employed on the occasion of re-marriage,
could with little change of form assume a more brutal
expression. One author described a charivari supported by
"some of the young gentlemen in the town" on the occasion
of the marriage of a runaway negro (a barber) to an Irish
woman. Clearly, racism added a vicious tone to the ritual.
The young man was dragged from his bed and ridden on a
rail, almost naked, on a winter night, and he died under this
treatment.[2]

4) What is announced — when the stag collapses with his
pierced bladder of blood on the doorstep, when the effigies
are burned before the cottage, when the rough band parades
night after night while the victim listens within — is the total
publicity of disgrace. It is true that the forms of rough music
are sometimes ritualised to the point of anonymity or
impersonality: occasionally the performers are masked or
disguised: more often they come at night. But this does not
mitigate in any way the disgrace: indeed, it announces
disgrace, not as a contingent quarrel with neighbours, but as
judgement of the community. What had before been gossip
or hostile glances becomes common, overt, stripped of the
disguises which, however flimsy and artificial, are part of the
currency of everyday intercourse.

Perhaps we are sheltered from each other more by artifice
than we realise. Two parties to a social pretence, even when
each knows perfectly well that the other is pretending, are
none the less enabled by that artifice to co-exist. Even

---

[1] See Palmer, *op. cit.*, and Wyatt-Brown. Canada had vigorous
traditions of charivari, derived from both English and French traditions
and applied to many purposes. See also Bryan Palmer, *Working-Class
Experience* (Toronto, 1983), pp. 41-5. Charivaris accompanied the
rebellion in Lower Canada in 1837, and they were often supported by
patrician young men, with elaborate masking and masquerading. As late
as 1846 the first by-law passed by the city of Kingston, Ontario, was to
"suppress the useless and foolish custom, called the Charivari"
(Minutes in Kingston City Archives).
[2] Susanna Moodie, *Roughing It in the Bush; or Life in Canada*
(1852), i, pp. 230-1. My thanks to Robert Malcolmson.

hypocrisy is a kind of mist which blurs the hard radiance of mutual hostility. But rough music is a public naming of what has been named before only in private. After that, there is no more mist. The victim must go out into the community the next morning, knowing that in the eyes of every neighbour and of every child he or she is seen as a person disgraced.

It is therefore not surprising that rough music, except in its lightest forms, attached to the victim a lasting stigma. Observers often noted this. The intention of rough music, especially when it was repeated night after night, was, exactly, to "drum out" the victim(s) from the neighbourhood. "A Skimmington riding makes many laugh," an observer noted, "but the parties for whom they ride never lose the ridicule and disgrace which it attaches."[1] "As a rule", noted another observer of "riding the stang", "the guilty parties could not afterwards endure the odium thus cast upon them, but made a 'moonlight flit', i.e. left the neighbourhood clandestinely".[2] Of rough music at Woking (Surrey) it was noted that it "carried with it local ostracism":

> In more than one case the culprit was refused regular employment, and it was not unusual for shopkeepers and others to decline their business.[3]

On occasion, rough music could lead on to death, through humiliation (as Hardy suggests in the *Mayor of Casterbridge*) or from suicide.[4]

Not all, and perhaps not the majority of cases suffered from rough music as brutal as this; common nineteenth-century targets, the quarrelsome couple or the wife-beater, were usually treated somewhat more lightly. For some offences, once the offenders had paid the penalty of being humiliated they might be held to have expiated their

[1] Roberts, *op. cit.*, p. 260.

[2] *N & Q*, 5th series, v (1876).

[3] A. C. Bickley, "Some Notes on a Custom at Woking Surrey", *Home Counties Magazine*, iv (1902), p. 28.

[4] For suicide resulting from rough music, see *Caledonian Mercury*, 29 Mar. 1736 (occasion: wife-beating); *Northampton Herald*, 16 Apr. 1853 — attempted suicide of married labourer who had fathered the child of an unmarried young woman.

offence and subsequently be left alone.[1] But some kinds of sexual offenders were not forgiven; and for these one must suggest that they were subjected to a hostility of magical dimensions, a ritual hunt. The community defined the boundaries of permitted behaviour by expelling the hunted from its protection.

One is thinking here of the village or small town community or the compact urban neighbourhood. For not only individuals or families but also communities have reputations to maintain. There are villages or streets which acquire the reputation of being "rough".[2] Neighbours within a community may be rebuked for their behaviour — "They'll think we're all savages." Such a community may meet any enquiry from outsiders with extreme reticence, protecting its "own". Even intolerable behaviour is tolerated, or kept hidden from outside view,[3] — until and unless the offence is so grave that it is signalled by rough music, which signifies that the offenders are extruded and their neighbours (and perhaps even their kin) don't "own" them any more.[4]

5) There is a suggestion in some accounts that rough music was performed in the execution of some actual deliberative judgement, however shadowy, in the local community. "The *Vehm-Gericht* is self-constituted, sits in the tavern, and passes its sentence without summons and hearing of the accused" — thus an observer on the Devon stag-hunt.[5] At a Staffordshire village "a committee is formed to examine into the case. Then the village poet is employed to give a history of the occurrence in verse".[6] In

[1] Cf. Nicole Belmont, "Fonction de la derision et symbolisme du bruit dans le charivari", *Le Charivari*, p. 18.

[2] See M. K. Ashby, *Joseph Ashby of Tysoe* (1974), pp. 150-1.

[3] Folklore collectors often found this reticence quite impenetrable, especially on sexual matters. They were not only outsiders geographically but also (being genteel or middle class) socially. I have been asked by informants not to mention names or details of persons rough musicked fifty or more years ago, because children or grandchildren still live in the village. Other enquirers have told me of the same resistance.

[4] "Own" still has this meaning in Yorkshire. See Wright's *English Dialect Dictionary* for "own-born parish" and for the meaning of "own" as "to recognize, identify; to acknowledge an acquaintanceship".

[5] Baring-Gould, *op. cit.*, ii, p. 78.

[6] *N & Q*, 1st series, ix, 17 June (1854), p. 578.

parts of South Wales there was a "Coolstrin" court, which sometimes summoned offenders before it, and whose chairman was crowned with the collar-bone of a horse. At Woking (Surrey), where rough music appears to have been institutionalised in unusual strength, there was known to be a village "court" that was "put into shape at an alehouse. . . but when, who by, and how, was kept a profound secret".[1] Thomas Hardy suggests such a court in the "Peter's Finger" inn, where "ex-poachers and ex-gamekeepers, whom squires had persecuted without a cause, sat elbowing each other".[2] In less formal senses, the support of the community was assumed: the women loaned their kitchen utensils, the men clubbed together their pennies for beer for the band.[3]

Even where no "court" of judgement existed, the essential attribute of rough music appears to be that it only works *if* it works: that is, if (first) the victim is sufficiently "of" the community to be vulnerable to disgrace, to *suffer* from it: and (second) if the music does indeed express the consensus of the community[4] — or at least of a sufficiently large and dominant part of the community (supported, as was nearly always the case, by the boys who found in a riding a superb occasion for legitimised excitement and aggression, directed

---

[1] Bickley, *op. cit.* The same author, in a novel, *Midst Surrey Hills: a Rural Stay* (1890), devotes a chapter to a reconstruction of such a tavern "court". For a consultation at the smithy, see Hardy (ed.), *The Denham Tracts*, ii, p. 4. For the "Coolstrin" court in South Wales, see W. Sikes, *British Goblins: Welsh folklore &c* (1880) and John Gillis, *For Better, For Worse* (Oxford, 1985), p. 133.

[2] See Hardy, *The Mayor of Casterbridge*, ch. 36.

[3] See e.g. *N & Q*, 2nd series, x (1860), p. 477. An elderly informant, Mr Gustavus Pettit of Leamington Spa, who witnessed a rough music when he was a child in the last years of the last century, told me that he overheard adult labourers planning the affair in a communal wash-house attached to a group of cottages: see also *Coventry Evening Telegraph*, 10 Sept. 1970.

[4] Some categorise a charivari as a "ritual of degradation" or reversal. To be effective it must carry the force of an impersonal or community judgement: "The denouncer must so identify himself to the witnesses that during the denunciation they regard him not as a private but as a publicly known person. He must not portray himself as acting according to his personal, unique experience. He must rather be regarded as acting in his capacity as a public figure, drawing upon communally entertained and verified experience." H. Garfinkel, "Conditions of Successful Degradation Ceremonies", *Amer. Jour. of Sociology*, vol. 61, March 1965, p. 423.

against adults) to cow or to silence those others who — while perhaps disapproving of the ritual — shared in some degree the same disapproval of its victim.

Hardy shows this point superbly in the *Mayor of Caster-bridge* .There are some, like Longways, who hearing rumours of the impending "skimmety" feel "'tis too rough a joke, and apt to wake riots in towns". But no energetic steps are taken to prevent it, and, on the day, the authorities are not fore-warned, the constables hide from the crowd in an alley and stuff their staves into a water-pipe, discreet citizens stay indoors. When authority at length arrives on the scene, no-one has seen the "skimmety", no-one will inform on any other who has taken part. In the street, where only minutes before the procession had blared its raucous way, "the lamp flames waved, the Walk trees soughed, a few loungers stood about with their hands in their pockets. . . Effigies, donkey, lanterns, band, all had disappeared like the crew of *Comus*".

II

And, like the crew of *Comus*, they disappeared also from written British history in the twentieth century, to return only in the past decade.[1] If we are to interrogate rough music and its functions, we must turn back to nineteenth-century folk-lorists and observers, who themselves may have been pater-nalists, observing the "popular antiquities" of an alien culture across a wide social distance.

Their comments on rough music were often reticent and contradictory. Thus, of the Devon stag-hunt, one observer

---

[1] In Britain some interest continued among folklorists. However, English academic disciplines have shown until recently considerable hostility towards folklore, as "a mixture of scholarly curio-collecting and crack-pot fantasy": *TLS*, 16 Sept. 1969. Even Keith Thomas's path-breaking *Religion and the Decline of Magic* (1971) has only one passing reference to rough music. The revival of scholarly interest came from across the Channel, with Claude Lévi-Strauss, *Mythologiques I. Le Cru et le Cuit* (Paris, 1964), and with Natalie Z. Davis's important article, "The Reasons of Misrule", *Past and Present*, 50 (1971). My own first attempt at this chapter appeared in France but not in Britain, in *Annales E.S.C.* in 1972. The phenomena have since been visible in more and more studies, on both sides of the Atlantic, and became momentarily fashionable: see Edward Shorter, *The Making of the Modern Family* (New York, 1975), pp. 218-27.

tells us that it could be held "only when *two married* people were known to be guilty". In another part of Devon it "did not apply to married people" but to youths "guilty of grave moral offence"; in yet another the victim was "a male pervert". A further witness gives us yet another definition:

> The stag hunt takes place either on the wedding-night of a man who has married a girl of light character, or when a wife is suspected of having played her husband false. [1]

A similar conflict of evidence arises with the "skimmington" and "riding the stang". Some observers assumed that the "skimmington" had one target only: "to put to shame households where the mistress had got the whip-hand of the master"; others emphasise adultery as the occasion; yet others discriminate between two variant forms — the "skimmington" and "skimmerton" — applied to different purposes. [2]

The most helpful definitions are, perhaps, those which are least exact and which suggest a fluidity of function. Thus Roberts identified several occasions for "riding the skimmerton": 1) when a man and his wife quarrel, and he gives up to her; 2) when a woman is unfaithful to her husband, and he submits patiently, without resenting her conduct; 3) any grossly licentious conduct on the part of married persons. [3] With "riding the stang", where there is a similar conflict of evidence, Brockett's observation is useful: the ritual was —

> inflicted upon fornicators, adulterers, severe husbands, and such persons as follow their occupations during particular festivals or holidays, or at prohibited times, when there is a stand or combination among workmen. [4]

Another account is equally flexible: the ritual "set forth the public reprobation of certain disgraceful actions, e.g. sins against the seventh commandment, cruelty to women, especially the beating of wives by their husbands,

[1] Brown, *op. cit.*, pp. 104-7; Baring-Gould, *op. cit.*, ii, p. 78; Baring-Gould, *A Book of Folklore* (1913), pp. 251-2.

[2] *N & Q*, 4th series, iii, 26 June (1868), p. 608; *ibid.*, 4th series, xi, 15 March (1873), p. 225; *ibid.*, 4th series, iii, 5 June (1869), p. 529; Tongue, *op. cit.*, p. 181.

[3] Roberts, *op. cit.*, pp. 256-7.

[4] Brockett, *op. cit.*, entry for "Riding the Stang".

unfaithfulness of workmen to their fellows when on strike, and dishonest tricks in trade". [1]

It is useful, if arbitrary, to divide these occasions into two groups, which may be described as "domestic" and "public", and to examine each separately. We will examine the "public" group later. Of the "domestic" group, from many occasions, we may attempt a preliminary sub-division of the offences which occasioned rough music.

1) Specific offences against a patriarchal notation of marital roles. These include wives who beat or assault their husbands; the virago, or scold, or the "masterful" or nagging wife and the submissive husband; notorious quarrelsomeness in a married couple; and the complaisant cuckold or *mari complaisant*. In all these cases, although the woman may have occasioned the offence, both parties were satirised in the public disgrace, since the husband had failed to establish his patriarchal authority.

2) Rough music — although sometimes of a somewhat lighter character — might be enacted against the re-marriage of widows or widowers; and against marriages held by the community to be in some sense ill-assorted, grotesque, founded upon avarice, displaying a great disparity in ages, or even sizes or in which at least one party to the marriage had a lively pre-marital sexual reputation.

3) A number of sexual offences could occasion rough music. Unfortunately contemporary definition of the offence is usually evasive and lacking in specificity. Most often, the occasion appears to have been adultery between two married persons. A noted seducer of young women (especially if himself married) could be victimised. On occasion homosexuality or other "nameless" behaviour, regarded as perversion, was the object. A broken marriage or the sale of a wife could (but usually did not) bring rough music as a sequel.

4) Wife-beating or other ill-treatment of the wife by the husband; and cruelty to children.

Before examining these occasions further, it will be of interest to note the findings of other studies, based not upon

[1] W. Henderson, *Notes of the Folk-lore of the Northern Counties of England and the Borders* (1879), p. 29.

British but upon French and European materials. Violet
Alford, who claimed to have more than 250 examples of
charivari "under her hand" offered this break-down:

77   The re-marriage of widows or widowers.
49   Wives beating husbands.
35   Adultery.
24   For newly-married couples.
89   "Other causes" (some of which might be in my category of
      "public").

Her examples are of interest, but since they are derived from
South, Central, and Western Europe, and are culled from
perhaps eight centuries, they necessarily lack specificity
of context.[1]

The learned French folklorist, Arnold Van Gennep,
attempted no tabulation of his findings, but suggested that
the main occasion for charivari in France over several
centuries was for the marriage of widow or widower.
Charivari has been directed also —

> aux maris battus par leur femme; aux avares, notamment dès la
> période enfantine, aux parrains et marraines chiches de dregées et de
> sous; aux étrangers qui, venus s'installer aux même de passage, ne
> paient pas le *bienvenue*; aux filles folles de leur corps; aux femmes
> adultères; aux ivrognes invétérés, brutaux et tapageurs; aux
> dénonciateurs et calomnieteurs; aux maris qui courent trop le guilledon;
> bref, à tous ceux qui, d'une manière ou d'une autre, excitent contre eux
> l'opinion publique de la communiaute locale.[2]

To the sexual occasions may be added girls who turn down a
suitor of repute in the community for another who is richer,
too old, or foreign; pregnant brides who marry in white; a
youth who "sells" himself to a woman for her money;
marriages which do not respect the prohibited degrees of kinship; girls who take a married man as their lover; *maris
complaisants*, or husbands who "se conduisant dans leur
ménage d'une manière plutôt féminine que masculine".[3] All
these offenders (if we except certain cases which might fall
into the "public" category) appear to fall within my divisions

[1] Alford, "Rough Music or Charivari", *op. cit.*
[2] Van Gennep, *op. cit.*, i, p. 202.
[3] *Ibid.*, i, pt. 2, pp. 614-28.

1), 2) and 3). Van Gennep appears to cite only one case of wife-beating.[1]

Lévi-Strauss, on the basis of unpublished findings by P. Fortier-Beaulieu, affirmed that 92.5 per cent of the cases under examination are occasioned by re-marriage, accompanied by disparity in age or wealth; or between individuals who are old; or after improper conduct during widowhood.[2] Unfortunately, these findings were based on a survey conducted in 1937, into (precisely) manifestations on the occasion of the re-marriage of a widow or widower, and hence had an inbuilt tendency to endorse Lévi-Strauss's theorisation of charivari as signalling a fracture in "la continuité idéale de la chaîne des alliances matrimoniales".[3]

In her important study Natalie Davis examined some aspects of charivari in sixteenth-century France. Her findings suggest that the overwhelming majority of cases fell within categories 1) and 2), and that re-marriage was a primary target for the rituals. The most frequent occasion for charivari in villages (she writes):

> was in connection with second marriages, especially when there was a gross disparity in age between the bride and groom. Then the masked youth with their pots, tambourines, bells, rattles and horns might make their clamor for a week outside the house of their victims, until they settled and paid a fine.

In an urban context she detects a shift; second marriages receive less attention, while the husband-beating wife and the beaten husband receive more, "for according to the provision of divine and civil law, the wife is subject to the husband; and if husbands suffer themselves to be governed by their wives, they might as well be led out to pasture". Adulteries, it would seem, received attention, and miscellaneous "faits vicieux" —

---

[1] A case is cited in Franche-Comté, *ibid.*, p. 619, note 2. In Diderot et d'Alambert, *Encyclopédie* (Paris, 1753, edn.), p. 208, it is assumed that charivari is occasioned by "personnes qui convolent en secondes, en troisièmes noces; & meme de celles qui épousent des personnes d'un âge fort inégal au leur".

[2] Lévi-Strauss, *op. cit.*, pp. 293-5. See also P. Fortier-Beaulieu, *Mariages et Noces Campagnardes dans. . . le Department de la Loire* (Paris, 1937).

[3] See Appendix II.

thefts, murders, bizarre marriages, seductions; but wife-
beating scarcely at all.[1]

Subsequent research, by Davis and others, has refined
these views and has added new occasions, but has not
seriously revised them.[2] Martin Ingram's work on rough
music in early modern England suggests both parallels and
divergences. The institutional or quasi-institutional role of
young unmarried men, or of the French youth "abbeys", has
not yet been proved to have been found in England.[3] Ingram
finds that "domestic situations, especially female domination, were the most usual occasions for charivaris in early
modern England", just as they could occasion charivaris in
seventeenth-century Lyons or Geneva.[4] An impression is
formed that British rough music, over several centuries, may
have been more abrasive and retributive than French
charivari; although it is not impossible that, until recently,
charivari has been a little softened and made picturesque in
the French *folklorique* tradition.[5] Nineteenth- and
twentieth-century collectors had been familiar with colourful
parties investing a wedding and serenading the couple until
paid off with money or drinks:

[1] N. Z. Davis, "The Reasons of Misrule: Youth Groups and
Charivaris in Sixteenth-Century France", *Past and Present*, 50 (1971). The
author cites one case only occasioned by wife-beating, at Dijon in the
month of May, 1583: see p. 45, note 13.

[2] See especially the contributions of André Burguière and Nicole
Castan in *Le Charivari*.

[3] However Bernard Capp, "English Youth Groups and *The Pinder of
Wakefield*", in Paul Slack (ed.), *Rebellion, Popular Protest and the Social
Order in Early Modern England* (Cambridge, 1984) offers some suggestive
evidence.

[4] Ingram, "Riding, Rough Music and Mocking Rhymes", p. 169 and
"Ridings", pp. 90-91; Natalie Zemon Davis, "Charivari, honneur et
communauté à Lyon et à Genève au XVIIᵉ siecle", *Le Charivari*, pp. 221-8.

[5] The account of suicides and vendettas associated with charivari which
is hinted at by Alford, "Rough Music or Charivari", pp. 510 and 513-4
contrasts with more romantic accounts by some popular authors. Compare
the psychic violence of the "el vito" as described by J. A. Pitt Rivers, *The
People of the Sierra* (1954), pp. 169 ff.

Dis donc vielle carcasse
Veux-tu pas nous payer
La dime de tes noces
Aux enfants du quartier.
Si tu fais la rebelle
On vient t'avertir,
Que pendant la semaine
On battre Charivari![1]

This had become, in expectation, what a charivari *was* and the ritual was theorised accordingly. And the paradigm of charivari was seen to be in the serenading of the re-marriage of the widow or the widower.

But the evidence available from Germany, some parts of Central and Eastern Europe, and North America does not give the same priority to second marriages. In Bavaria the punitive *haberfeldtreiben* passed through phases, but was primarily directed at offenders against sexual norms,[2] while the occasions for *katzenmusik* in Western Germany seem to have been as various as occasions for "skimmingtons" and "stangs".[3] Re-marriage rarely is mentioned among these, nor does it feature in Roumania, where other attributes of rough music — noisy, masked demonstrations with effigies and obscene verses — are found.[4] Nor, indeed, in Hungary, which had, until recently, a group of colourful, and sometimes vindictive, practices involving rough music (with ploughshares tied together and caterwauling), animal guising, mock marriage ceremonies, shadowy courts of popular law (as in Bavaria) and lampoons.[5] Re-marriage does turn up as an occasion for charivaris in North America, especially in regions of strong French influence, but the evidence is as various as the British.[6]

Let us content ourselves, for the moment, with saying that the evidence is untidy, and does not even show us whether

[1] Musée national des Arts et Traditions populaires, Paris, MS B 19, song from Thônes (Haute Savoie). See Shorter, *op. cit.*, p. 221 for a variant.

[2] See Ian Farr and Ernst Hinrichs in *Le Charivari*.

[3] Hoffman-Krayer and Bachtold-Staubli, *op. cit.*, entry under "Katzenmusik".

[4] See Dominique Lesourd in *Le Charivari*.

[5] Tekle Dömötör, *op. cit.*

[6] See especially Bryan Palmer, "Discordant Music".

French charivari or English rough music is the mutant from
some common European stock; or, indeed, whether in their
simplest components of noise and ridicule, both may not
be universal.

Re-marriage of a widow or widower may have occasioned
rough music in England, if accompanied by other circumstances, such as a disparity of ages or the imputed avarice of a
young bride for a wealthy old widower. But examples are
few. Rough music — and especially the "skimmington" —
was directed until the nineteenth century against those who
had offended against male-dominative norms and imperatives (group 1). A "skimmington" —

> Is but a riding, used of course
> When the grey mare's the better horse;
> When o'er the breeches greedy women
> Fight, to extend their vast dominion.[1]

Or in Andrew Marvell's *Last Instructions to a Painter*:

> A Punishment invented first to awe
> Masculine Wives, transgressing Natures Law.
> Where when the brawny Female disobeys,
> And beats the Husband till for peace he prays;
> No concern'd *Jury* for him Damage finds,
> No partial *Justice* her Behaviour binds;
> But the just Street does the next House invade,
> Mounting the neighbour Couple on lean Jade.
> The Distaff knocks, the Grains from Kettle fly,
> And Boys and Girls in Troops run houting by. . .

---

[1] From the fullest literary account of a "skimmington riding", in
Samuel Butler, *Hudibras*, Second Part, Canto II, ed. J. Wilders
(Oxford, 1967), pp. 142-9. The Second Part of this poem was first
published in 1663. This section continues:

> When *Wives* their Sexes shift, like *Hares*,
> And ride their *Husbands*, like *Night-mares*,
> And they in mortal *Battle* vanquish'd,
> Are of their *Charter* dis-enfranchizd,
> And by the Right of *War* like *Gills* (a)
> Condemn'd to *Distaff, Horns* (b), and *Wheels* (c);
> For when Men by their *Wives* are Cow'd,
> Their *Horns* of course are understood.

(a) *Gills* — wenches, girls; (b) *Horns* — the symbol of the cuckold;
(c) *Wheels* — spinning-wheels (like distaffs) are symbols of women's work
and feminine roles.

Still, in the eighteenth century and, in some regions, in the
nineteenth, the "patriarchal" humiliation of unruly women
remains a predominant theme; or of those families in which
(as the phrase is) "the grey mare is the better horse".[1] When
Henri Misson met in the London streets a woman carrying a
straw effigy crowned with a fine pair of horns, "preceded by
a Drum, and follow'd by a Mob, making a most grating
Noise with Tongs, Grid-irons, Frying-pans, &c.", he was told
that "a Woman had given her Husband a sound beating for
accusing her of making him a Cuckold, and that upon such
Occasions some kind Neighbour of the *poor innocent injur'd
Creature* [la pauvre Calomniéel] generally perform'd this
Ceremony".[2] This was, presumably, London's attenuated
"skimmington", and the mockery was being directed quite as
much against the husband as the wife. But as late as 1838
Mrs Gaskell (a reliable observer) was writing to Mary
Howitt of "Riding Stang" as "a custom all over Cheshire",
and in its older male-dominative form:

> When any woman, a wife more particularly, has been scolding, beating
> or otherwise abusing the other sex, and is publicly known, she is made
> to ride stang. A crowd of people assemble towards evening after work
> hours, with an old, shabby, broken down horse. They hunt out the
> delinquent. . . and mount her on their Rozinante. . . astride with her
> face to the tail. So they parade her through the nearest village or town;
> drowning her scolding and clamour with the noise of frying pans &c,
> just as you would scare a swarm of bees. And though I have known this
> done in many instances, I never knew the woman seek any redress, or
> the avengers proceed to any more disorderly conduct after they had
> once made the guilty one "ride stang".[3]

I have placed "patriarchal" in inverted commas, because
the term can involve us in difficulties. Feminist theorists, who
allocate a central place to patriarchy, are rarely historians and
they are sometimes impatient with historians' objections. As
a result "patriarchy" is invoked indiscriminately, to cover

[1] Robert W. Malcolmson, *Life and Labour in England, 1700-1780*
(1981), p. 105.
[2] Henri Misson de Valbourg, *Memoirs et Observations Faites par un
Voyageur en Angleterre* (Paris, 1698), p. 70, and H. Misson, *Memoirs and
Observations in his Travels over England* (1719), p. 129.
[3] J. A. V. Chappel and Arthur Pollard (eds.), *The Letters of
Mrs. Gaskell* (Manchester, 1966), pp. 29-31. My thanks to David
Englander.

every situation and institution of male-domination. The "trouble with patriarchy" (as Sheila Rowbotham warned long ago) is not only that it generalises a very specific set of theories and institutions where the monarch or the head of the household commanded authority over subjects, wife, children, apprentices, servants, etc. — theories and institutions under challenge in the seventeenth century and beginning to decompose — but also that the term is so undiscriminating that it offers no vocabulary to express differences in degree and even in quality of male-domination. As Rowbotham warned:

> "Patriarchy" implies a structure which is fixed, rather than the kaleidoscope of forms within which women and men have encountered one another. It does not carry any notion of how women might act to transform their situation as a sex. Nor does it even convey a sense of how women have resolutely manoeuvred for a better position within the general context of subordination. . .

Moreover, "some aspects of male-female relationships are evidently not simply oppressive, but include varying degrees of mutual aid. The concept of 'patriarchy' has no room for such subtleties." " 'Patriarchy' suggests a fatalistic submission which allows no space for the complexities of women's defiance",[1] and if this is so — and in widespread ideological usage it is so — it does not illuminate women's history but obscures and even confiscates some part of it.

Male-domination is not at issue, but this may take place through brothers, neighbours, employers, the structures of law or of religion, as much as through the household-head implicit in Filmer's patriarchal theory.[2] Moreover, "patriarchy" gives us a poor vocabulary to express large modifications in the forms of male-domination and control, gender alienation or (on occasion) gender partnership. Both sexes might find themselves committed to the house of correction for no more explicit an offence than being "loose

---

[1] Sheila Rowbotham, "The Trouble with 'Patriarchy' ", *New Statesman*, 21-28 Dec. 1979, reprinted in Rowbotham, *Dreams and Dilemmas* (1983), pp. 207-14.
[2] See G. Schochet, *Patriarchalism in Political Thought* (New York, 1975).

and disorderly persons".[1] But in backward or "traditional" areas, women might be presumed to be "loose and disorderly" if they were working people and if they had no male structure of control and protection. These assumptions find clear expression in an affidavit (1704) by Thomas Sexton, a Suffolk husbandman, who was defending himself against a charge of assault brought by Joanna Box, spinster:

> The said Joanna & Mary Box are two lusty young wenches & fare well & plentifully, & will not go to service, but live with their said mother, in a little house & occupy no land, nor having any visible estate or stock to live upon in an honest way, except Spining wch is a miserable trade now since the wars; no man nor woman living with them, except when some men of no very good fame haunt & frequent their company.[2]

Joanna and Mary's mother was married to a chimney sweep but they had split up. This Suffolk husbandman presumed that he could insinuate that any such masterless women were whores.

Such truly "patriarchal" attitudes persist into the nineteenth (and indeed twentieth) centuries. The ducking-stool is still employed against scolds (almost always against the feminine tongue) in the eighteenth century,[3] and there are even instances of the use of the vicious scold's bridle in the early nineteenth century. There is a remarkable

---

[1] Examples can be found in most CROs, especially in the committals to bridewells or houses of correction. For plentiful "loose and disorderly" committals (both sexes) see e.g. Hants. CRO, QS B/xvib/2/5, Calendars of prisoners in House of Correction, April, July and October 1723. Or in the 1760s an unusually zealous magistrate in Cirencester (Thomas Bush) was frequently committing persons for swearing (usually men), for disobedience to their masters (apprentices), for being "rogues and vagabonds" and (Ann Rundle, committed 28 July 1766) for "Being a Very Lewd Idle and Disorderly Person and Refusing to Give Security for her Good Behaviour". Gloucester CRO, Q/SG 1763-6. All this was normal; see Joanna Innes, "Prisons for the poor: English bridewells, 1555-1800", in Francis Snyder and Dougla Hay, *Labour and Crime* (1987), esp. pp. 84-5, 99, 114 n 21.

[2] PRO, KB 2.1 (Part One), Affidavits, Anne (Misc.): *Regina v William Copsey.*

[3] "Mary the wife of John Morris of Gosport being convicted upon her own Confession & pleading guilty to. . . being a comon scold & disturber of the peace of her neighbours doe undergo the punishment of the ducking Stoole at the city of Winchester. . ." Hants. CRO, QM/5, Minute Book, 6 October 1724.

reminiscence of this from the deeply-traditional little town of
Wenlock in Shropshire. Public punishments — whippings,
the stocks, the shrew's bridle — were inflicted on Mondays,
which were market days:

> Often have I seen poor Judy Cookson walked round the town in the
> shrew's bridle. 'Er was said to be the best abuser in the borough, and 'er
> wud go and curse anybody for three-ha'pence — that was the fee.

The bridle "punished a Christian terrible", "the poor
Creature's face streamed with blood" and two teeth fell out
in removing the bridle:

> Judy used to abuse Sir Watkins agent something terrible, 'im as they
> called 'King Collins', for 'e did what 'e listed and none durst say 'im
> nay. She was a fearsome pelrollick, it is true, was Judy, but I never
> knowed the bridle did 'er any good. It makes me swimmy-headed. . .
> only to think of those Mondays, with the relatives all cursing and crying,
> the lads laughing and jesting, and lawyer men looking on to see as *their*
> law was carried out.[1]

I could not restrain myself from working in this remarkable reminiscence, which throws new light on the functions of
scolding and cursing — an intrepid "pelrollick" such as Judy
was assuming a function as advocate of the intimidated
majority. From the same source I must also cite another
reminiscence, which illustrates how the traditional controls
on sexual conduct could (indeed, always did) bear most
hardly on women. Until well into the nineteenth century the
most traditionalist clergy inflicted upon members of the
congregation accused of sexual offences (including the
conception of children in advance of marriage) the penance
of standing in the church porch in a white sheet. In Wenlock
this was inflicted especially upon girls who "lost their good
name". One day a neighbour met Betty Beaman at the village
pump:

> As I was holding the pail, she was a-pumping in. 'Er burst into tears, for
> 'er was a-thinking, poor crittur, of 'er young days. 'Er said, "Sally I
> bain't what I was, and never shall be, afore I paid penance. That's many
> a year agone, but standing' up in that there white sheet a' took

---

[1] C. M. Gaskell, "Old Wenlock and its Folklore", *The Nineteenth Century* (Feb. 1894).

something out of me that'll never come back. The spirit left me, and even sin', though I can eat my wittles regler, somehow I 'ave a-lived like in the dust.[1]

The punishment for bastardy was always more flagrantly sexist. Unmarried mothers, especially if they were "repeaters", could be confined to a house of correction for a year, on a diet of bread and water. A reforming magistrate reported that —

> A woman. . . committed. . . on account of her first child within a month after it was born — asked me pertinently, 'Why the man who had seduced her was not to be imprisoned as well as herself?' I could only answer, 'Because women were not legislators and men were parish officers.'[2]

I am happy to call these controls "patriarchal", although the term is unhelpful: these offences and humiliations were inflicted, not by "patriarchs", but by neighbours, magistrates, poor law officials, estate bailiffs, officious clergy. But one was unlikely to find such practices as the scold's bridle, the ducking-stool and the penance surviving in eighteenth-century Manchester or Leeds or Gloucester.[3] And this can be of real significance if we are to interpret the meaning of rough music and of "skimmingtons". In an important essay David Underdown has drawn attention to a general sense of insecurity in gender relations between 1560 and 1660, finding expression in witchcraft accusations, in the

[1] *Ibid.* See also John Gillis, *op. cit.*, p. 131.
[2] Sir G. O. Paul, *Address to His Majesty's Justices of the Peace for the County of Gloucester, Epiphany General Quarter Sessions 1809* (Gloucester, 1809), pp. 129, 135. However, although form and theory allowed this sexist discrimination, late eighteenth-century practice was more lenient. Paul collected figures to show the number of "criminal offenders" in county gaols and bridewells in the sixteen years ending in 1807: these showed 241 males imprisoned for "bastardy" (presumably for failing to pay the affiliation orders sworn against them) and 39 females. There were also 213 imprisoned for leaving their families chargeable on the parish (presumably all male). The sexist laws remained available to vindictive magistrates and poor law officials, but were being used less often. It had also been accepted that the public whipping of women was "an offence against the common decency" and by 32 Geo. III, c. 45 (1792) this could no longer be inflicted on women convicted as rogues and vagabonds: see *ibid.*, pp. 8, 35.
[3] Or so I suppose. The matter has not yet been fully researched.

more vigorous punishment of the scold, and in the elaboration and practice of forms of rough music.[1] And he has noted that these phenomena are to be found, in the West of England, not so much in the arable farming villages as in the woodland and pasture districts — the regions in which dairying and the clothing industry were based. Both industries afforded employment and (with dairying) responsible roles for women, and Underdown suggests that the harassment of the "women on top" (by both official shaming rituals — ducking-stool and scold's bridle — and unofficial ones — "skimmingtons") need not simply be ascribed to the "traditionalism" of the West Country, but may, rather, be expressive of growing male insecurity as women in fact were becoming more independent and assertive.[2] This may have been found, precisely, in those "communities most subject to the destabilising effects of economic change".[3] And when we come to the later seventeenth century and eighteenth century we must also take account of the supposed move towards more egalitarian gender relations in proto-industrial regions (of which the West Country woollen industry was one). We have already discussed this in relation to women's role in food riots (above p. 320-2). Certainly we need a vocabulary more flexible than "patriarchy" to explore the contradictions and to analyse the fluctuations and modifications in gender relations in changing occupations and

[1] See Keith Thomas, *op. cit.*, pp. 528-31; D. E. Underdown, "The Taming of the Scold: the Enforcement of Patriarchal Authority in Early Modern England", in Anthony Fletcher and John Stevenson (eds.), *Order and Disorder in Early Modern England* (Cambridge, 1985).

[2] An example of this feminine presence and self-confidence may be taken from Coronation Day celebrations for Queen Anne in the lace-making and clothing town of Honiton (23 April 1702): three hundred women and girls in good order, two and two, with three women drummers, and a guard of twenty-five young men on horseback, marched up and down the town from 10 a.m. to 8 p.m., hurrahing and weaving long white rods with tassels of white and blue ribbon (the Queen's colours) and bone lace: F. N. Poynter (ed.), *The Journal of James Yonge* (1962), p. 210. Similar processionals with wands sometimes marked the anniversaries of female benefit societies, and Thomas Hardy, in the second chapter of *Tess of the D'Urbervilles*, may have been right to say that the club "had walked for hundreds of years".

[3] Underdown, *op. cit.*, p. 135. See also David Underdown, *Revel, Riot and Rebellion* (Oxford, 1985), esp. pp. 102-3.

communities. Rough music against wife-beaters was enforcing different norms and values than were "skimmingtons" against women who "wore the breeches". If we try to bring both within the categories of patriarchy, then we are still left with everything to be explained.

Many examples could be given of rough music occasioned by offences in groups 2) and 3). Satire upon ill-assorted marriages is recorded. The marriage of a man in his seventies to a girl of eighteen occasioned at Charing Cross in London in 1737 "a grand Hudibrastic Skymmington, composed of the chairmen and others of that class".[1] Rough music is still from time to time recorded in the nineteenth century against scolds as well as against husband-beaters.[2] And against adulterers, seducers of young women, and other kinds of (usually nameless) sexual offenders, it continues.[3] Ironical rough musics welcome back runaway couples or married partners who have split up and come back together, and wife sales, when they affront neighbourhood opinion in some particular way, can ensue in effigy burning and ran-tanning (above p. 450).[4] There is, however, one significant shift in occasions in the early years of the nineteenth century: the rapid rise to predominance of offenders in group 4), the wife-beaters. If a similar rise took place in other parts of Europe, it has not yet been recorded.

So large was this shift that the majority of contributors to *Notes and Queries* from the 1850s, and of commentators and editors of regional folklore collections and dialect glossaries

[1] *Read's Weekly Journal*, 16 Apr. 1737.

[2] *N & Q*, 4th series, iv (1869), p. 105 (Somerset, 1826); *ibid.*, 5th series, v (1876), p. 253 (Lancashire, late eighteenth century?); *ibid.*, 2nd series, x (1860), p. 363.

[3] Conjugal infidelity — both parties tied back to back on a donkey, W. H. K. Wright (ed.), *The Western Antiquary* (Plymouth, 1882), p. 31; against a coal-dealer with "loose notions on the privileges of married life" at Market Rasen, Lincolnshire, 1872, *Stamford Mercury*, 19 Jan. 1872; against an ostler who had proved unfaithful to his newly-wedded bride at Northallerton (Yorkshire) in 1887, *York Herald*, 1 Mar. 1887; against a young man who had jilted his mistress in a Hampshire village in 1882, *Hants and Berks Gazette*, 4 Feb. 1882; and many others.

[4] S. P. Menefee, *Wives for Sale* (Oxford, 1981), pp. 117, 126-7, 183; *Northern Standard*, 4 Nov. 1882; *Bury Times*, 12 Nov. 1870; Katharine M. Briggs, *The Folklore of the Cotswolds* (1974), pp. 116-7.

in the same years, assume that the inhibition of wife-beating is the primary function of rough music. There is ample evidence to assure us that this was not an invention of folklorists; and some of their accounts suggest accurate observation. From a village in Surrey or Sussex (1840s?):

> As soon as it was dark a procession was formed. First came two men with huge cow horns; then another with a large old fish-kettle round his neck. . . Then came the orator of the party, and then a motley assembly with hand-bells, gongs, cow horns, whistles, tin kettles, rattles, bones, frying pans. . . At a given signal they halted, and the orator began to recite a lot of doggerel verses. . . beginning:
>
> 'There is a man in this place
> Has beat his wife!! (*forte*: a pause)
> Has beat his wife!! (*fortissimo*)
> It is a very great shame and disgrace
> To all who live in this place,
> It is indeed upon my life!!'

The rough band then broke out with every instrument, accompanied by howling and hooting. "A bonfire was then lighted, round which the whole party danced as if they were crazy." The noise could be heard two miles away. After half an hour, silence was proclaimed, and the orator advanced once more towards the house, and expressed the hope that he would not have to return, urging upon the husband a moral reformation.[1]

Newspaper reports or legal documents enable one to look a little more closely into such incidents. At a substantial rough musicking at Waddesdon (Buckinghamshire) in 1878, when more than two hundred men, women, and children serenaded one Joseph Fowler on at least two occasions, Fowler explained (in court) that "the cause of the row was that he had an illegitimate child, and he did not think it was well used, and in consequence gave his wife three stripes".[2] One should note that this suggests not just an event (wife-beating), but an event with a *history*, well-known to the community. The victim (Fowler) appears to be a man who was held to have mis-used his wife in more than one way, and over a period; although she had accepted his illegitimate child into

[1] *N & Q*, 2nd series, x (1860), p. 477.
[2] *Bucks Herald*, 27 July 1878. It was a tenaciously held popular belief that the husband had the right to chastise his wife with three blows, and no more, and with a stick no thicker than his own thumb.

the home, he continued to abuse her.

In a Berkshire case of 1839 we have rather more detail. The immediate history of the event is as follows. The victim, William Goble, was a small farmer, occupying a cottage and a few acres; he was a tenant of Mr John Walter, but his farm lay in the midst of the estate of a neighbouring landowner, Mr Simmonds. On Saturday August 17th he and his wife had a quarrel, which "ended in blows". On Monday, the 19th, Mrs Goble was "very unwell", and a surgeon was called in from Wokingham. That evening there was the first occasion of rough music, with sixteen or eighteen men and boys with flags, horns, etc., parading before his house. The music was repeated, by larger numbers, on no fewer than eight occasions. On the sixth occasion Mr Walter's son (that is, the landlord's son), his gardener, and several other servants, came to Goble's aid, and there was a scuffle between the parties, which resulted in legal action.

In most respects this appears as characteristic rough musicking. The adults most frequently involved included eight labourers, two carpenters, one sawyer, one blacksmith, one shoemaker, one bricklayer, as well as the groom, coachman, gamekeeper and miller to Mr Simmonds. The unusual element in the case is the involvement in the affair of the households of two rival landowners' estates; and in subsequent litigation it appeared plausible that Mr Simmonds was aiding and encouraging the rough music (protracted over an unusual number of days) in the hope of driving Goble (whose lands intruded inconveniently into his estate) out of his tenancy. And beneath the rivalry of the two gentlemen we find a further layer of rivalry again, between the households and the young men attached to the Walter estate (Bearwood) and the Simmonds estate (Aborfield). During the course of the affair the Bearwood gardener (who was among the party which came to Goble's aid) received an anonymous letter, accusing the Bearwood men of being "licktrenchers", and comparing the Bearwood butler to "a tom tit upon a round of Beef". The letter concluded: "If I was your wife you should not have a bit of Sugar in your tea I would put a turd in to see if that would sweeten it. . .".[1]

[1] Miscellaneous documents in Berks. CRO, D/EW1, L.3. My thanks to John Fine who directed me to them.

An unsatisfactory case; but if one knew more of any case, it might well prove to be equally unsatisfactory. It emphasises that context is generally thicker and more complex than is disclosed by any superficial view. Wife-beating is a simple explanation: but in any community both wife and husband, and their marital history, are known to the neighbours; and even the most "domestic" of incidents takes place within the context of other tensions and allegiances. Thus in this case we appear to have a marital episode provoking the traditional response among some, and serving as a pretext for others. The victim is, in a sense, an "alien" on a boundary: his lands lie within another estate. And his offence touches off a rivalry between two neighbouring gentry, and also between the households and youth of two adjacent rural communities.

A third example must suffice: from Cambridgeshire in 1904. In this case rough music was directed against a man whom a girl of the local village had married when she was in service in London:

> The marriage had not been a success, so the girl had returned to her home, to which she was, after a time, traced by her husband, a heavy drinker. Rumours began to spread that he was ill-treating his wife, who often appeared in the village with a black eye or a cut on her face. Then, one winter's night, he came home drunk, dragged her out of bed and threw her out of the house.

Two neighbours came to her aid, beat up the husband and trussed him with rope. For some time after this he was quiet. Then he resumed his drinking, and his ill usage of his wife. Finally, the rough music took place: two hours of hubbub on tin kettles and pans, with shouts of "clear out! clear out!". On the next morning the husband left for London.[1] The incident, once again, emphasises that we are dealing not with an isolated episode but with an event whose history was well-known; and, once again, we have the element of a local community closing against an "alien".

It is not as simple to decipher the significance of these rough musics as may at first appear. Even classic charivari on re-marriage continues to inspire conflicting (but persuasive) explanations. The diversity of the forms and occasions for rough music should discourage any attempt to propose any

[1] Porter, *op. cit.*, pp. 9-10.

single function as *the* function for the "skimmington" or
"stang". These forms were, as I have suggested, part of the
symbolic vocabulary of the time, capable of being expressed
in sentences with different meanings. But it was not just *any*
vocabulary, for each symbol was evocative of meaning in its
own right: the man sitting mutely with a distaff in his hands,
being belaboured by a man in woman's clothes; the
symbolism of effigies and gallows; the metaphors of the
hunt. If we are right to resist a structuralist analysis in which
the mythic constituents from which charivari may have been
derived assume ascendancy over the social process and
replace it by formal logic, so also we must guard against
disintegrating the mythic properties into a plastic empiricism
of one case after another, defined only by their manifest
functions. Between myth, on one hand, and function, on the
other, there is — Carlo Ginzburg has reminded us — the
intermediacy of rehearsed and transmitted *rites*.[1] Those
who enact these rites may have long forgotten their mythic
origins. Yet the rites themselves powerfully evoke mythic
meanings, even if only fragmentarily and half-consciously
understood. Rough music is a vocabulary which brushes the
carnival at one extreme and the gallows at the other; which is
about crossing forbidden frontiers or mixing alien categories;
which traffics in transvestism and inversion; whose flaring
bonfires may recall heretics or even hell whose horned master
brings to mind the cuckold who is mocked. Still, in the early
years of this century, a boy (whom I later knew as a vigorous
man) witnessed a rough music in industrial Yorkshire, and
said it was "like devil's madjic". (See p. 532.)

But this vocabulary was not re-enacted involuntarily by
village yokels as if they were somnambulists in the possession
of a "folk memory". If we are always to discard the meanings
given to an event by the participants themselves, and search
instead for an ulterior meaning more in conformity to the

---

[1] See Carlo Ginzburg, "Charivari, associations juveniles, chasse
sauvage", in *Le Charivari*. In my article in *Annales E.S.C.* I took issue with
the formalist structuralism of Lévi-Strauss's interpretation of charivari in
Le Cru et le Cuit. Ginzburg criticises me in turn for formless empiricism
and obsession with manifest functions, and seeks to show common ground
between our positions in the forms *and* functions of rites. I can accept his
correction.

structure of myth, then this is to diminish the rationality and
stature of the actors and underestimate the self-awareness of
illiterate people. They may not have read *Mythologiques*, but
they had their own notions as to what they were turning
out about.

This "folk" was not perfect nor pretty nor was it empty of
all norms. They employed the inherited vocabulary selective-
ly, for their own reasons. The importance of rough music to
the historian may lie not in any single function or group of
functions, but in the fact that the episodes are — if only we
can get inside the motives of the actors — a most sensitive
indicator of changing notations of sexual norms or marital
roles. It is evidence, also, of the ways in which even the most
private or "personal" relationship is conditioned by norms
and roles imposed by the society in which the couple acts,
quarrels, or loves. The society is the host, but the couple are
hostages to its opinion. The wife who is beaten, or whose
husband is faithless, is perhaps also a daughter, a niece, a
sister, a cousin, to others in the community. The wife who
scolds and brow-beats her husband, who takes his financial
and business affairs into her hands, threatens by her un-
reproved example the marital equilibrium of her neighbours.
A participant in a riding in Suffolk in 1604, directed against a
wife who had beaten her husband, explained that the object
was that "not only the woman which had offended might be
shamed. . . but other women also by her shame might be
admonished [not] to offend in like sort".[1] The rites may be
less interesting in themselves than as tools to prize open the
secrets of a community's moral code. For vigorous rough
music can show us the border between the tolerated and the
intolerable.

The shift to wife-beaters as prime targets for rough music
in Britain in the nineteenth century could be an index of
profound changes in gender relations. It suggests, with the
corresponding dying-away of "skimmingtons", some
decomposition of the older "patriarchal" framework. And
while such rough musics were generally led by men or

[1] Cited by Ingram, "Riding, Rough Music and Mocking Rhymes",
p. 174.

youths,[1] with children (often of both sexes) as followers,
there are a few pieces of evidence to suggest that women were
on occasion leading the actions or turning them to their
own account.[2]

In Glamorgan in the early nineteenth century there is
an account of the women in one community refusing to
support a rough music procession aimed at a couple where
the wife had beaten her husband. They remained indoors
and "mocked at [the men] through the windows", while
some "collected to scoff" at the house of the victims and
"poured out a din of hoots and yells" to drown the rough
music band.[3] One wonders if other communities witnessed
a similar turning of the tide? In one (half-remembered?)
Lincolnshire variant on the "stang nominy", the women
are incited to deal with the husband-beater in their own
way:

[1] The evidence as to who took part is inconclusive, and varied
according to the offence. While men would carry a "stang" or "ride
skimmington", women often turned out to hoot and bang pans (see Plate
XXIII). When cases came to the courts, those indicted were nearly always
male: thus a case at Burton (Oxfordshire) in 1803, where 15 labourers were
indicted and 5 imprisoned: Oxfordshire CRO, QSM I/7; in a Warwickshire
case, 1811, those indicted were two wheelwrights, one husbandman, one
farmer, one labourer, one shoemaker, and one tallow chandler:
Warwicks. CRO, QS 32/3, bundle 3.

[2] Women sometimes led rough musics in the eighteenth century: in
1747 at Billingshurst a husband who was ill-treating and starving his wife
was rung out of his house by women, who put him in a blanket and ducked
him in the pond (cited in *Sussex Agricultural Express*, 28 Oct. 1848). An
Islington tradesman in 1748 whipped his wife with rods "till the Blood ran
down her Heels": she "had a Warrant against him, and carrying him to a
Justice of the Peace, he was. . . sent to Prison, to which Place he was
conducted through the Pelting, and Hissing, and Blows of two Thirds of
the Women in the Town": *Northampton Mercury*, 11 July 1748. In parts
of the Scottish Lowlands it was reported that women "rode the stang" on
wife-beaters, seizing the offender with their own hands: R. Forsyth, *The
Beauties of Scotland* (Edinburgh, 1806), iii, p. 157.

[3] Charles Redwood, *The Vale of Glamorgan* (1839), p. 289-95,
cited in Gillis, *op. cit.*, esp. pp. 133-4. But "patriarchal" rough music long
continued in parts of mid and North Wales: see Julius Rodenberg,
An Autumn in Wales (1856), translated and ed. by William Linnard
(Cowbridge, 1985).

Ran, tan, tan!
The sign of the old tin kettle, and the old tin pan.

Old Abram Higback has been paying his good woman;
But he neither paid her for what or for why,
But he up with his fist, and blacked her eye.

Now all ye old women, and old women kind,
Get together, and be in a mind;
Collar him, and take him to the shit-house,
And shove him over head.

Now if that does not mend his manners,
The skin of his arse must go to the tanners;
And if that does not mend his manners,
Take him and hing him on a nail in Hell.

And if the nail happens to crack,
Down with your flaps, and at him piss.[1]

We can see in these charming verses the evidence of refinement and "modernisation".

So it is possible that the rough musicking of wife-beaters indicates some "reform" of popular manners or amelioration of the lot of wives. But I cannot share the confidence of Edward Shorter, who, citing my own earlier article, argued that the evidence confirms "the early modernization of domestic relationships in England":

> As egalitarian relationships between husband and wife diffused, the community began to perceive as intolerable such vestiges of earlier patriarchal authority as the right to slam one's wife about; and so it moved to rebuke wife-beaters.[2]

I do not know firm evidence that "egalitarian relationships" between husband and wife were becoming diffused in England by 1850. Some historians have noted a decline in the respect afforded to women during the industrial revolution. I repeat my earlier warning: the increase in rough music against wife-beaters could with equal reason be read as an index to the increasing brutality with which some wives were being treated, or as to their loss of other "traditional" defences in this situation. It is not even clear that "patriarchal authority" in the older tradition included approval for

[1] From Sturton by Stowe, in the James M. Carpenter collection in Cecil Sharp House.
[2] Shorter, *op. cit.*, p. 235.

husbands who "slammed their wives about", for, in an older masculine code of honour and shame, women could be sheltered from male violence by the notion that such assaults were "unmanly". In most traditional societies, the defence of the maltreated wife is the responsibility of her male kin, and in the first place of her brothers. This defence might be supplemented by the intervention of the priest. In England, between 1800 and 1850, various factors could have operated to bring about a new kind of crisis. Geographic mobility could have removed more wives from the protection of their kin. The English clergy had no confessional and rather little pastoral role — they were not frequent visitors to labourers' homes. The law afforded little protection to the wife treated with brutality. Is it possible that there were more frequent instances of the inhibitions upon male marital violence — inhibitions which in the older community would have been upheld by neighbourhood opinion or kin — breaking down? In such circumstances the community may have turned the old forms of rough music to new account.

In any case, rough music was not automatic and was not always visited upon an offence. We do not have a "pre-industrial society" in which "community norms imposed themselves with steely force", as if acting out an inherited cultural programming, until "modernization" brought enlightenment.[1] Not all wife-beaters were ran-tanned or burned in effigy, and in certain cases rough music may have been an excuse for "a little innocent amusement" or a pretext to "satiate. . . personal malice or revenge" arising from a history of conflicts:

> Some perhaps may entertain a notion that they are rendering their aid to protect the weak and defenceless. . . [but] it too frequently happens that they are unconsciously lending themselves as the instruments of gratifying private pique. . .[2]

It is the same when sexual offenders are the target. Because certain adulterers were rough musicked, it cannot be assumed that we are observing a community of pagan puritans, for whom marital fidelity was an imperative. To be sure, the

[1] *Ibid.*, p. 218.
[2] This is from a brief on behalf of a victim of rough music, Berks. CRO, D/EW1.L3.

rituals emphasise that the working people did not live in casual, unstructured promiscuity. Even where the marriage rites of the church were ignored, or where there was a large tolerance of pre-marital intercourse, the society maintained distinct norms of sexual behaviour.

These norms, however, should not be set up as absolutes. On the contrary, I suspect that each occasion when adulterers and similar offenders were subjected to rough music had a known history; that more evidence would lead us to particular aggravations of an offence which, in other cases, might pass unnoticed — or noticed only by gossip. It need not have been adultery as such which invoked public disgrace, but the way in which particular adulterers (perhaps already unpopular for other reasons) "carried on".

Where adultery was the evident target, it is possible that the community was incensed to this degree, not so much by the fact, as by the "flagrancy" with which it was committed and which might threaten the institution of marriage itself, as when a married person eloped with another married partner,[1] or when two couples (or two partners) attempted to change spouses and to remain living within the same small community.[2] or a *ménage-à-trois*.[3] In the village of "Lark Rise" illegitimate children were accepted, but adultery between a labourer's wife and a lodger, in the labourer's own house, called down rough music which expelled all three from the parish.[4]

The rites of rough music were part of the resources of what it is now obligatory to call the "discourse" of a society. They were employed with intelligence and wit on occasion, and on other occasions with prejudice (against innovators, "deviants", outsiders) and rancour.[5] The rites are like a

---

[1] *N & Q*, 6th series, vi (1882); *ibid.*, 5th series, v (1876).

[2] See Appendix I.

[3] At Gorton, Manchester, "riding the stang" was administered when "it was discovered that a painter was living harmoniously with two women in one house", *N & Q*, 5th series, v (1876).

[4] Flora Thompson, *Lark Rise to Candleford* (Oxford, 1954), pp. 145-6.

[5] A vindictive "skimmerton riding" was visited on a gardener and his wife and the wife's brother in Oakhill (Somerset) in 1900: the wife and her brother were German, and the villagers refused to believe that he was her brother: *Shepton Mallet Journal*, 31 Aug. 1900.

keyboard that can be played lightly, satirically, or struck brutally. Rough music may be employed in factional conflicts in a community. There is nothing automatic about the process; much depends on the balance of forces within a community, the family networks, personal histories, the wit or stupidity of natural leaders.

The decisive factor may be whether offenders are already unpopular for other reasons. I was told by an informant in Somerset of a man who had been rough musicked because he had been detected in keeping a very young woman (whom he had met at a fair) as his secret mistress. But this did not demonstrate that all such liaisons, in this industrial village, called forth rough music. For this offender was unpopular for other reasons: he lived in an isolated cottage, and was a professing Methodist and teetotaller, who earned his living by delivering cider to public houses. He was held to be an outsider and a censorious hypocrite. No doubt the rough music was planned in the local pub, whose customers enjoyed publicising their teetotal opponent's scandal. [1]

Hence the compilation of occasions for rough music is not enough. We need, even more, a detailed inner history of even a few particular incidents, and the recovery of their contexts. That is why David Rollison's remarkable study of a "groaning" in the Gloucestershire village of Westonbirt in 1716 is such an important addition to our understanding. [2] This "groaning" was a piece of street theatre, to which all and sundry were invited, savagely mocking a substantial farmer and bailiff accused of sodomy; it employed elements in rough music's vocabulary — transvestism, blasphemy, obscenity and drama. But it does not prove that all homosexuals were visited with rough music. In Rollison's recovery of the episode he is aided by an unusually rich archive of letters passing between the village and its absentee (but vigilant)

[1] Information of the late Bob Hiscox of Pilton, Somerset, given to me in 1975 and referring to events *circa* 1910.

[2] David Rollison, "Property, Ideology and Popular Culture in a Gloucestershire Village, 1660-1740", *Past and Present*, 93 (1981), reprinted in Slack (ed.), *op. cit.* For another well-documented (but enigmatic) case, see Jean R. Kent, "Folk Justice and Royal Justice in early 17th-century England: a 'Charivari' in the Midlands", *Midland History*, viii (1983).

landowner, who felt himself to be scandalised, and good order and established religion to be mocked in the insult to his bailiff. The episode arose out of a history, and the supposed offender was decisively unpopular for other reasons. The "groaning" enlarges in meaning and is enriched in complexity when placed in this context, and at the same time it floods this context with its eccentric and eerie light. It is an exemplary study, which may be set beside the "skimmington" in Hardy's *Mayor of Casterbridge* — which also acquired its meaning in a context and from a history.

III

Plastic in "domestic" contexts, the forms could be adapted also to "public occasions — and perhaps always had been: a leader of the "Rising in the West" in 1628-31 was supposed to go under the name of "Lady Skimmington".[1] Rough music was applied to a score of purposes. Petty theft from one's neighbours appears to have been one occasion. In 1691 in a Warwickshire village two offenders were musicked by the smith (dressed as an old woman) and a farmer (wearing buck's horns) at the head of a hundred others who "tumultuously and riotously led a dance forwards and backwards across the town. . . for the space of three hours", shouting in chorus outside the victims' house: 'Pay for the timber, you rogue, you cuckoldy dog, you stole', and 'pay for the clocking [chickens] and ducks, you whore".[2] But it could, equally be used in a different direction altogether, "to mark disapproval of a magisterial decision",[3] or of an officious or severe prosecution. The prosecutor of a boy (who had been stealing eggs) at Iver (Buckinghamshire) in 1878 brought rough music down upon his own head: his effigy was burned to the accompaniment of shouts of "quack,

[1] D. G. Allan, "The Rising in the West, 1628-31", *Econ. Hist. Rev.*, 2nd series, v, i (1952-3); Buchanan Sharp, *In Contempt of All Authority* (Univ. of California, 1980), who argues (p. 105) that there was never any one "leader" who was "Skimmington", just as there was never any General Ludd or Rebecca.

[2] *Warwickshire Quarter-Sessions Proceedings*, ed. H. C. Johnson and N. J. Williams (Warwick, 1964), pp. xiii-xiv.

[3] J. H. Bloom, *Folklore, Old Customs and Superstitions in Shakespeare Land* (1930), p. 53.

quack".[1] More serious and sustained was an outbreak at Ampthill (Bedfordshire) in 1817, following upon the conviction and execution of a local man for rape. As many as two hundred people assembled on successive nights before the house of the prosecutrix, exhibiting obscene effigies of herself and of her father and mother, stoning the house, and "hallooing and charging the family with having hung the man". The trouble was ended only when four of the actors were imprisoned.[2]

Rough music was also employed against unpopular officials. In 1797 a tallow chandler, a yeoman and five labourers were indicted for their part in an affair at Belchamp St. Paul's (Essex); they had mounted the effigy of a resident excise officer on an ass, paraded it before his house, fired guns at it, and burned the effigy at a stake on the green — on three occasions.[3] Instances can be found of rough music employed against the police;[4] against informers;[5] against body snatchers;[6] against crimps; against unpopular preachers[7] and Mormons;[8] against the unfair dismissal of a servant, eviction from a tied cottage, and against game-keepers. In a well-reported cast at Chilton (Buckingham-shire) in 1878 a crowd of some twenty or thirty men and

[1] *Bucks Herald*, 13 July 1878. A Warwickshire woman was rough musicked for prosecuting her own son for taking 6s. 9d. from her purse: *Leamington Chronicle*, 16 July 1870. My thanks to Chris Ryan.

[2] Bedfordshire CRO, QSR 23, 1817, pp. 230-1.

[3] PRO, KB 11.59.

[4] See e.g. W. E. Haigh, *A New Glossary of the Dialect of the Huddersfield District* (Oxford, 1928), p. 118; John Bland, *Bygone Days in Market Harborough* (Market Harborough, 1924), pp. 102-3.

[5] A. Boyer, *Political State of Great Britain*, LIII, 1737, p. 116.

[6] See, for example, Ruth Richardson, *Death, Dissection and the Destitute* (1987), p. 138.

[7] Against a "cobler" preaching at Towcester, 1767, Northants. CRO, Quarter Sessions Grand File, 1767. Early Methodist history provides many examples of the rough musicking of preachers and noted members: information from John Walsh. The rector of Fillingham was ran-tanned and his effigy was "ridden the stang" before being burned: *Stamford Mercury*, 23 May 1884.

[8] In Soham (Cambridgeshire) on April Fool's Day, 1853, there were mock Mormon weddings outside the homes of local believers, in which seven "brides" on donkeys were married to a single "husband": *Millenial Star*, xv (1853), p. 269. My thanks to J. F. C. Harrison.

boys rough musicked (for the third time) Mr Augustus Campbell of Chilton House, his gamekeeper, and his coachman. It is clear that the villagers believed that the gamekeeper, on Campbell's orders, was shooting or poisoning their dogs if they strayed onto the estate. The music had been got up on this occasion by a farmer whose land was adjacent to Campbell's and two of whose puppies had been involved in an incident the previous day. But the landowner and his servants may have been unpopular for other reasons. Campbell was an in-comer from Berkshire, and the crowd sang before his door: "the meanest, measliest, lowest man that e'er in Berkshire stood". Outside the coachman's house they shouted, "Who stole the dogs?" and "Blackbird!". Outside the gamekeeper's they called "go home, gipsy keeper" and "gipsy king!".[1]

Still, in the nineteenth century, rough music and forms of ridicule could be employed by people of substance against each other, sometimes putting up more humble people to do the actual business and hiding behind them. In 1805 a carter in Tewkesbury was employed to carry certain ridiculous effigies in a "procession" through the town in a cart; he claimed that he didn't realise that the figures represented the surveyor and inspector of the taxes.[2] In the 1790s a long and bitter feud developed between two neighbouring landowners near Handsworth (Staffordshire). The hostilities, which involved disputes about game but which extended to a dozen other issues, also drew in the brother-in-law of one landowner, the Rev. Thomas Lane, the rector of Handsworth. He was clearly unpopular, since he had been involved in pulling down cottages and closing down alehouses. His opponent visited him with the vocabulary of rough music, persuading his own tenants in Handsworth to display offensive effigies and handbills. (See Plate V.)[3] But gentry involvement was

[1] *Bucks. Herald*, 19 Oct. 1878.
[2] PRO, KB 1.33 (Part One), *Rex v James Attwood, John Sashand and Henry Rickett*: affidavit of James Attwood.
[3] Handbill in KB 1.30 (Part Two), Mich. 41 Geo. III, no. 1: affidavit of Joseph Storrer (1800), and papers in file 41. For the background to this case, see Douglas Hay, "Crime, Authority and the Criminal Laws in Staffordshire, 1750-1800" (Univ. of Warwick Ph.D. thesis, 1975), pp. 309-14.

now becoming uncommon and rough music was regarded as plebeian and, for that reason, potentially subversive.

In Woking rough music was used for upholding common rights, and employed against those who overstocked the common or cut excessive turfs and faggots.[1] And if we are to assume that effigy burnings belong to the same family of rituals (and most of them were accompanied by raucous noise and processional) the list could be extended indefinitely: against a tithe-proctor for herrings, against a landlord over-zealous to extend his fishing rights, against enclosure, and against any person riding rough-shod over local custom. Parson Woodforde records a dispute between Justice Creed and his churchwardens about the gallery in the church, which the justice wanted to take down and which the singers wanted to keep. The dispute escalated by way of a brawl in church to a court case, and the magistrate's effigy,

Was had through the streets of Castle Cary. . . upon the Engine, and then had into the Park and burnt in a bonfire immediately before the Justice's house. . . The whole Parish are against the Justice.[2]

Any historians with full notebooks could compile their own lists. Rough music was commonly adapted to industrial conflict. The "cool-staffing" (or cowl-staffing) of blacklegs by West Country weavers was a riding of them to a duck pond on a pole,[3] just as the "stang" was used in the same way by pitmen and seamen in the North-East. The usage was especially widespread in the West, the heartland of the "skimmington", and the ritual vocabulary was also employed

[1] See Bickley, op. cit.

[2] James Woodforde, The Diary of a Country Parson (1949), p. 53. For an Oxfordshire case arising from a church dispute, see J. C. Cox, Churchwardens' Accounts (1913), p. 53.

[3] W. E. Minchinton, "The Beginnings of Trade Unionism in the Gloucestershire Woollen Industry", Trans. Bristol & Gloucs. Arch. Soc. (1951), pp. 134-5; Adrian Randall, "Labour and the Industrial Revolution in the West of England Woollen Industry" (Univ. of Birmingham Ph.D. thesis, 1979), esp. pp. 300-1, 541; F. J. Snell, The Chronicles of Twyford (Tiverton, 1893), pp. 186-7, 191-2, 232-2. For Banbury shag-weavers, see John Money, Experience and Identity, Birmingham and the West Midlands, 1760-1800 (Manchester, 1977), pp. 240-1; Robert Spillman, 25/26 August 1793 in PRO, HO 42/26.

in actions against workhouses and turnpikes.[1] In London a wheel-barrow could take the place of a "stang": it was used in this way in 1696 against a journeyman hatter working beneath the rates.[2] Southwark hat-dyers, in 1770 —

> took one of their brother journeymen into custody, whom they charged with working over hours without any more pay, and for taking under price. They obliged him to mount an ass, and ride through all the parts of the Borough where hatters were employed. . . a label was carried on a pole before him, denoting his offence; and a number of boys attended with shovels, playing the rough music. At all shops they came to in their way of business, they obliged the men to strike, in order to have their wages raised.[3]

A similar case of "donkeying" took place in Coventry in 1818, during a strike of ribbon-weavers, but on this occasion the victim on parade was an elderly ribbon manufacturer.[4] Rough music on various occasions was being employed in London — notably Kentish London — until the end of the nineteenth century. It was employed in Woolwich in 1870 with great ceremony against a waterman convicted of carrying more fares than he was licensed to carry; in this case, his effigy was paraded by fellow watermen accompanied by a rough band, placed in a barge, set to float on the Thames, fired at, and ultimately burned.[5]

One might cite many other examples. These were commonplace of industrial conflict, at least until the early nineteenth century, and the "ran-tanning" of blacklegs

---

[1] In May 1725 over a hundred men and women (broadweavers?) assembled in Stroud to pull down the workhouse, carried an overseer around the parish on a stick, and threatened to put one of "the gentlemen" on the stick if they met him: PRO, Assi 5.44 (i). For a turnpike episode, also in Stroud, see SP 36.32.

[2] S. and B. Webb, *The History of Trade Unionism* (1920), p. 28. A case was reported in 1743 of an unapprenticed hatter being "stanged" with such violence in Southwark that he died: *Sherborne Mercury*, 18 Oct. 1743.

[3] *Annual Register* (1770), p. 74.

[4] "Donkeying" was vigorous in the Coventry silk industry, and was used against both workers and employers who defied the regulations of "the Trade"; *The Times*, 20 Aug. 1819; *Report of the Trial of the Prisoners Charged with Rioting and Destroying the Machinery of Josiah Beck* (Coventry, 1832), p. 3; *PP*, 1835, xxv, p. 1834; information from Peter Searby.

[5] *Greenwich & Deptford Chronicle*, 12 Mar. 1870. My thanks to Geoffrey Crossick.

continues into the twentieth century. But there appears to have been only one occasion in Britain when ritual forms were deeply involved with activity of mass dimensions. These occur in the early nineteenth century in Wales, and are associated with the *ceffyl pren.*

The form of this ritual corresponded closely to that of "riding the stang":

> a figure of a horse is carried at night in the midst of a mob with their faces blackened, and torches in their hands, to the door of any person whose domestic conduct may have exposed him to the censure of his neighbours, or who may have rendered himself unpopular by informing against another, and by contributing to enforce the law. On the horse is mounted some-one who, when the procession makes a halt opposite the residence. . . addresses the mob on the cause of their assembling. . .

When the exhibition was directed against "domestic" offenders it was accompanied "with the grossest indecency". In the 1820s and 1830s in parts of South Wales the *ceffyl pren* was increasingly brought into use against "public" offenders — in agrarian grievances, against prosecutors in cases of petty theft, against unpopular municipal officials, etc. The translation of the ritual from the private to the public domain was viewed by the authorities with anxiety:

> The right which is thus arrogated of judging. . . another man's domestic conduct, is certainly characteristic of a rude state of society; when the same measures are applied to. . . thwarting the operation of the laws of the land, they become of much more serious import. The principle is perfectly Irish, and. . . contains the germ of resistance to legal order.[1]

This last observation was borne out by the use of the *ceffyl pren* in the "Rebecca riots" against the turnpike tolls in South Wales in the 1840s. The "Scotch Cattle" disturbances in the mining areas of the early 1820s (mainly in Monmouthshire) had already evinced ritualistic elements: men, with blackened faces, dressed as women; animal-guising with horns, skins, and masks; the blowing of horns, lowing,

---

[1] *First Report of the Constabulary Commissioners* (1839), pp. 83-4; PRO 52.35 and 73.4 (memorandum of Sir E. Head); J. C. Davies, *Folk-lore of West and Mid-Wales* (Aberystwyth, 1911), p. 85.

rattling of chains, and firing of guns outside the homes of blacklegs or informers.[1]

In the 1830s and into the 1840s the practices of the *ceffyl pren* extended through Carmarthenshire, until the "laws of the land" gave way to the law of "Rebecca", the mythical leader (as well as the *nom-de-plume*) of the agrarian rebels.[2] At the height of the disturbances, "Rebecca" extended her authority simultaneously over the private and public realms. Her followers delivered children to the doors of their putative fathers, threatened young men who refused to marry the girls they had "betrayed", warned husbands to stop beating their wives, and forcibly reconciled the astonished vicar of Bangor Teify to his separated wife, while at the same time pursuing the campaign against turnpikes, articulating agrarian grievances, and intimidating informers against her rule.

Some of her actions were curious, but also deeply revealing. Some three years earlier a young labourer, returning in a "drunken frolic" from a wedding, had met an unmarried lady landowner in the road and had kissed her. For this offence — far more against status than honour — he had been fined twenty shillings. Now the followers of "Rebecca" demanded the return of the fine; when the money was refused they damaged the plantations of both the offending magistrate who had inflicted the fine and of the offended lady. "This shows", commented another local gentleman,

> that the public is perverted in its notions of justice, which in a political point of view is a thing much more difficult to be dealt with than a mere marauding Banditti.

It shows, one would add, the fuel on which popular grievances were fed, and the length of time that the embers could burn. It shows also that for a brief few months even the poorest and most despised of the people of Carmarthenshire had a glimpse of an ideal of truly popular justice. Two weeks later the same gentleman wrote that "a poor idiotic girl" had

[1] See D. V. J. Jones, "Popular Disturbances in Wales, 1792-1832" (Univ. of Wales, Aberystwyth, Ph.D. thesis, 1965), esp. pp. 217, 195ff.

[2] See D. Williams, *The Rebecca Riots* (Cardiff, 1955). Professor Williams writes (p. 56): "it can. . . be said with complete certainty that the Rebecca Riots were an extension of the practice of the *ceffyl pren*"; See also D. J. V. Jones, *Rebecca's Children* (Oxford, 1989), esp. ch. 6.

come to his door begging. When he refused her, and told her to go to the hated officials of the poor law, "she quietly said she would tell 'Becca":

> I told her that if she did not behave well & continued to use that threat she wd be sent to prison — her only reply was murmured out (in Welsh) "I'll tell 'Becca." [1]

In the end "Rebecca" ceded her temporal authority, but undoubtedly her spiritual dictatorship survived for much longer, and in ways which only a Welsh-speaking historian will be able to disclose. There is a report as late as 1898 from Llanbister in Radnorshire, describing the descent of a "Rebecca" gang, with blackened faces, upon the (separate) houses of a man and woman who had made some "breach of the laws of morality". Both in a nearly naked state (it was January) were forced to walk backwards and forwards in a stream for twenty minutes, and then to run up and down the fields while they were beaten with straps and sticks. They were then taken back to the man's house, where "Rebecca" sat in judgement. They were condemned to undergo further flogging, and to march up and down the fields hand in hand. Their hair was cut off, and they were threatened with tar and feathers (which was not in the end used). [2] The incident reminds us that the rituals of rough music and charivari, transposed across the Atlantic, contributed not only to the good-humoured "shivaree" but may also have given something to lynch law and the Ku Klux Klan. [3] And it suggests, finally, that we might look again at certain

---

[1] These accounts are based on PRO, HO 45.454 (i) and (ii), and especially the reports of Edward Lloyd Hall, the gentleman cited above, in (ii), fos. 521-3, 664ff; H. T. Evans, *Rebecca and Her Daughters* (Cardiff, 1910); "Rebecca in West Wales", *West Wales Hist. Records*, VII (1917-18).

[2] *Hull and North Lincs. Times*, 15 Jan. 1898.

[3] See Wyatt-Brown, *op. cit.*, pp. 435-561. "Carting", tarring and feathering, and riding on a pole were frequent in eighteenth- and nineteenth-century North America, and were sometimes used against "public" offenders, sometimes against domestic offenders, including wife-beaters: see J. E. Cutler, *Lynch-Law: an Investigation into the History of Lynching in the United States* (1905), esp. pp. 46-7, 60-71, 63-7, 92, 103; R. B. Morris, *Government and Labor in Early America* (New York, 1965), p. 147; H. D. Graham and T. R. Gurr (eds.), *The History of Violence in America* (New York, 1969), p. 70.

manifestations of popular retribution in the twentieth
century, to see whether similar ritual elements might not be
present also in these: to the public humiliation after the
liberation of European countries of women who had kept
company with members of the occupying forces during
World War II, or to the rites of public humiliation
practised during the Cultural Revolution in China.

IV

"Public" rough music presents few analytical problems. In its
industrial forms it is clear enough what offences blacklegs
had committed and whose popular "law" was being
enforced. As more becomes known about the popular dimension of eighteenth-century politics in London and the cities,
so elements in the vocabulary of rough music — mocking,
obscenities and the emblems of cuckoldry — turn out to be
everywhere. They are employed by Tories, Whigs, the
followers of Wilkes, and the ungoverned "mob" alike. It
would be foolish even to begin to cite examples, since such
symbols were the medium of discourse, and sometimes of
negotiation, between the plebs and the patricians. Crowd
actions were sometimes little other than the manipulation of
these symbols, in the endeavour to demystify authority or to
ridicule political opponents (see pp. 68-9 and Plate XXI).[1]

One doubts whether it is useful to debate whether rough
music belonged to a plebeian, as contrasted with a
consensual, tradition. Certainly, until late in the eighteenth
century the vocabulary was well enough understood among
all social classes. Domestic rough music was socially
conservative, in the sense that it defended custom and male-
dominative tradition, and Ingram has argued that the élite
saw little threat in it and were casual in their attempts to put
the practices down. On the other hand, rough music was
always potentially subversive, with its rites of inversion, its
blasphemies and obscenities, and, as Rollison has shown in

---

[1] See Nicholas Rogers, "Popular Protest in Early Hanoverian
London", in Slack (ed.), *op. cit.*; Peter Burke, "Popular Culture in
Seventeenth-Century London", in Reay (ed.), *op. cit.*; John Brewer, *Party
Ideology and Popular Politics at the Accession of George III* (Cambridge,
1976), *passim.*

his study of the "groaning" at Westonbirt, it could rapidly acquire a polemical social meaning. In the eighteenth century, as the distance widened between the culture of the patricians and that of the plebs, so rough music became more distinctively a plebeian form. It thrived, as a means of self-regulation, above all in certain kinds of "peasant" and of proto-industrial community.[1] Yet rough music cannot be claimed as a "working-class" tradition, for the forms were imperfectly integrated into the early organised labour movement. Luddism depended for its success upon the swift movements of small groups of men in silence; the oaths and ceremonies of illegal trade unions grew out of a different group of rituals. And thereafter it appears to be true that the more sophisticated, organised, and politically-conscious the movement, the less indebtedness it shows to traditional forms of folk violence. The Chartists of Monmouthshire put behind them the forms of the "Scotch Cattle".[2]

The burning of effigies, accompanied by tumult or processional, might appear to offer an exception to this generalisation. This continued in vigorous use into the present century (it is by no means extinct today), and it was often employed by the "radicals". It was employed (among many examples) by the English "Jacobin" reformers of the 1790s; against the magistrates and yeomanry after "Peterloo" in 1819; during the agitations for the Reform Bill of 1832; and against unpopular landowners or farmers during the labourers' agitation of the 1870s in the Eastern Counties.

But effigy burning is not a noted method of the Chartists, nor of reform and trade union agitations generally. This may have been because reformers sensed, in the very forms, a disposition to favour the traditional — or even atavistic — mood of the people. For it was a form which was used, very consciously, by traditionalists against reformers or out-groups. After Guy Fawkes, the most burned-in-effigy man in

[1] Gerald M. Sider argues convincingly that groups which maintained the self-regulation of their working economy also upheld certain rituals: "Christmas Mumming in Outport Newfoundland", *Past and Present*, 71 (1976).

[2] On the decline of folk violence, see Dorothy Thompson, *The Early Chartists* (1971), pp. 16-17, and "Chartism as a Historical Subject", *Bull. Soc. Lab. Hist.*, 20 (1970), p. 12.

British history was without any doubt Tom Paine. The number and distribution of the officially-inspired "Church and King" Paine-burnings, especially in 1790-93, has never been counted. But it was immense, taking in almost every township and many villages in England. Undoubtedly many of these affairs drew upon the rituals of rough music. In Heckmondwike (Yorkshire) a man impersonating Tom Paine was "discovered" among some coal-pits, reading *Rights of Man*. He was seized, his face was covered with a frightful mask, and he was led by a rope through the market place. The mask was then deftly transferred to a straw effigy, which was placed against a lamp-post and shot at, to the accompaniment of tremendous hootings and cries of "Church and King".[1]

There were a few cities where the reformers were strong enough to respond in kind. Bishop Horsley received a well-merited burning-in-effigy in his own cathedral city of Rochester after he had said, in the House of Lords, that "the mass of the people have nothing to do with the laws, but to obey them".[2] But reformers were more often the targets of such affairs, and they formed a dislike for their "mob" characteristics. Where the rites of rough music survive after 1815 they appear to have an increasingly socially-conservative character.

So much is easy to set down: and it may mean less than it seems to mean. For it is by no means easy to identify the kind of nineteenth-century community in which rough music survived longest. While the elaborated forms of the ritual were clearly a folklorist's delight, while such forms as "wooset-hunting" and the stag-hunt were recorded in isolated West Country villages with names like Ogburne St. George, Whitechurch Canonicorum and Okeford Fitzpaine, and can be seen as animated ethnological vestiges, exotic

[1] Frank Peel, *Spen Valley: Past and Present* (Heckmondwike, 1893), pp. 307-8.

[2] *Parliamentary Register*, xliii, pp. 351-4. The duke of Brunswick (in effigy) was given a ceremonial hanging and burning on Kensington Common on November 5th, 1792: letter from London in *Pittsburgh Gazette*, 2 Feb. 1793. In Norwich in 1796 bonfires were preceded by a mock procession in which effigies of Pitt, Windham and the bishop of Rochester were carted with ropes around their necks.

blow-flies in rural amber, at the same time good old-fashioned rough music continued vigorously in an urban and industrial context. We have noted it in Kentish London; it was vigorous in mid nineteenth-century Huddersfield or Pudsey in the West Yorkshire industrial belt;[1] and in Gorton, near Manchester, when a married surgeon who had eloped with a patient's wife was the object, Gorton cotton mills were closed for half a day in order that eight hundred factory hands could take part.[2]

There is, even in such cases, a sense that rough music belonged in some way to the "older", "rougher" parts of the town; but it is difficult to detect exactly what such descriptions imply, unless the tautology that where rough music persisted must be rough. Thomas Hardy suggests that his "skimmington" emerged from the district of Mixen Lane —

> the Adullam of all the surrounding villages. It was the hiding-place of those who were in distress, and in debt, and trouble of every kind. Farm-labourers and other peasants, who combined a little poaching with farming, and a little brawling and bibbing with their poaching, found themselves sooner or later in Mixen Lane. Rural mechanics too idle to mechanize, rural servants too rebellious to serve, drifted or were forced into Mixen Lane.

But the evidence does not altogether confirm Hardy's characterisation. The vigorous rough music described in Appendix 1 took place early in this century in Siddal, a district of Halifax dominated by one large woollen mill, and with some mining, quarrying and brick-making. Decidedly working-class and traditional, yet Siddal was also one of the first places where (in 1892) I.L.P. councillors were elected. It is clear that the "old culture" of rough music could survive with great tenacity alongside more "modern" forms, and could co-exist with these. Yet this does not happen everywhere, and one must look for additional explanations for this co-existence. Munby found, in the 1860s, old forms surviving as a set in the Surrey of Ripley:

---

[1] See e.g. Easther and Lees, *op. cit.*, pp. 128-9; J. Lawson, *Letters to the Young on Progress in Pudsey* (Stanningley, 1887), p. 66.
[2] *N & Q*, 5th series, v (1876), p. 253.

They still play football in the street on Shrove Tuesday, and turn out on
Guy Faux Day in a long procession of masks and mummers: they still
pursue every cruel husband with the Nemesis of marrowbones and
cleavers.

On May Day young girls in muslin still carried little
Maypoles wreathed with flowers from house to house. But
Munby could suggest no reason for these survivals other
than the village's isolation — six miles from a railway and
no intercourse with London other than a weekly carrier's
cart.[1]

In the same year that Munby visited Ripley, rough music
was a little discouraged by a legal decision that a stag-hunt
was "a game" within the meaning of 5 & 6 Will. IV, c. 50,
and hence prohibited in the streets.[2] It was widely argued
thereafter that all rough music in the streets were prohibited
"games". It is doubtful whether this had much influence on
rough music's decline, which was inexorable but very slow. In
1930 it was reported in the *Evening Standard* that —

> Grey-haired women, their hair streaming in the breeze, clasped hands
> and danced solemnly round a bonfire where the effigies of three people
> were in flames. No smile was on their faces, and from their lips fell
> curses on a young husband. All around them were a host of men,
> women and children, chanting monotonously and beating tin cans, old
> kettles and cracked bells.

This "hussitting" in the Berkshire village of Woodley was
directed at a man who had been summoned by his wife for
cruelty, and against his mother and sister who had sided
against the wife: "It is 30 years since we gave anyone 'rough
music' ", one of the oldest villagers said. "Then it was a
married man who had been annoying girls."[3]

I would hazard that there may be a relation between the
continuity of rough music and the continuity of local dialect.
(The *ceffyl pren* persisted most vigorously in Welsh-speaking
regions, such as Carmarthen.) The rites belong in an orally-

[1] Munby diaries in Trinity College, Cambridge, vols. xvii, p. 241,
4 March 1863; xix, pp. 4-5, 7, 13, 2 May 1863. My thanks to Anna Davin.

[2] See *Pappin v Maynard*, in *Law Times*, 21 Nov. 1863. Decisions in
King's Bench in the late seventeenth century had defined "riding
skimmington" as riot, see Ingram, *op. cit.*, p. 101.

[3] *Evening Standard*, 3 Oct. 1930.

transmitted culture, and the strength of dialect signals also
the tenacity of a traditional consciousness, upheld (perhaps)
in such villages as Ripley and Woodley by closely-knitted kinship. Both dialect and customs can reproduce themselves
together, and can long persist into mature industrial society.
But at a certain point those engines of cultural acceleration,
literacy and schooling, combine with increasing in-migration
and general mobility, to "saturate" the old culture, to
disperse it as a living practice, to break down the old
sensibility, leaving nothing but antiquarian survivals.

What then may survive, in pockets in urban districts and,
more often, in the remote countryside, are certain old
traditions maintained sometimes by particular occupational
groups who are at odds with the politer modern norms and
who are seen by their neighbours as "rough" or "ruffians"
(i.e. "rough 'uns"). In the North Yorkshire village of
Kirkby Malzeard "stang riding" still was being practised at
the end of the last century, with a variant of the old
"nominy". It always originated in the pub. "Everything
originated in the pub in them days. They'd all be 'leaders' ",
recalled an informant in 1971. The initiators were a small
group of men: building workers, a blacksmith, itinerant
labourers who worked at various jobs, working on estates, at
fair grounds, hedging and dyking in the winter; "they were
rough types", poachers, heavy drinkers — "if they thought
they could get a glass of beer they'd bray owt". But they were
also the people who kept alive the "Plough Stots" and the
complex Sword Dance of Kirkby Malzeard, and who
performed it for money or drink at fairs and at flower shows:

> These sort used to go sword dancing — but they always used to spend
> the money on beer, and sleep out in the woods. . . But the Stang was
> different. They did that because working class people are more faithful
> to their wives than are t'nobs. And anyone as beats 'is wife or a child
> is a bad 'un. They really had to feel very, very strongly about this carry-
> on. Then it was a big disgrace, it brought it out in the open. They didn't
> do it just for a lark.

The last time the "stang" was ridden in Kirkby Malzeard was
because a labourer had been beating his wife:

> He'd a houseful of kids — ten or a dozen children. It had got out that
> he'd been braying his wife — coming home from the pub, she'd be there
> with a houseful of kids, and then he'd start in and bashed her about.

They got a big effigy which they fastened on a hand-cart, "and these big brawling chaps they went to the house and bumped on the door". As they went down the village street they rang a big bell and reeled off "the ditty". "They used to make such a din and commotion people would pay anything to get them away."[1]

This sounds folksy and even reassuring. But rough music could also be an excuse for a drunken orgy or for blackmail. It could legitimise the aggression of youths, and (if one may whisper it) youths are not always, in every historical context, protagonists of rationality or of change. I make the point strongly, arguing in a sense with part of myself, for I find much that attracts me in rough music. It is a property of a society in which justice is not wholly delegated or bureau-criticised, but is enacted by and within the community. Where it is enacted upon an evident malefactor — some officious public figure or a brutal wife-beater — one is tempted to lament the passing of the rites. But the victims were not all of this order. They might equally be some lonely sexual non-conformist, some Sue Bridehead and Jude Fawley living together out of holy wedlock. And the psychic terrorism which could be brought to bear upon them was truly terrifying: the flaring and lifelike effigies, with their ancient associations with heretic-burning and the maiming of images — the magical or daemonic suggestiveness of masking and of animal-guising — the flaunting of obscenities — the driving out of evil spirits with noise.

Rough music belongs to a mode of life in which some part of the law belongs still to the community and is theirs to enforce. To this one may assent. It indicates modes of social self-control and the disciplining of certain kinds of violence and anti-social offence (insults to women, child abuse, wife-beating) which in today's cities may be breaking down. But, when we consider the societies which have been under our examination, one must add a rider. Because law belongs to people, and is not alienated, or delegated, it is not thereby made necessarily more "nice" and tolerant, more cosy and folksy. It is only as nice and as tolerant as the prejudices and norms of the folk allow. Some forms of rough music

---

[1] Accounts collected by the late Kathleen Bumstead in 1971.

disappeared from history in shadowy complicity with bigotry, jingoism and worse. In Sussex rough music was visited upon "pro-Boers", including William Morris's close friend, Georgie Burne-Jones. In Bavaria the last manifestations of *haberfeldtreiben* were linked to mafia-like blackmail, anti-semitism and, in the final stage, to ascendant Nazism.[1] For some of its victims, the coming of a distanced (if alienated) Law and a bureaucratised police must have been felt as a liberation from the tyranny of one's "own".

[1] See *Le Charivari*, pp. 294, 306.

APPENDIX I

The late Mr Hanson Halstead was born in Siddal, Halifax at the end of the last century. He was for some years an engineer, active trade unionist and socialist, and member of the NCLC; but he seemed more like a countryman, was a strong dialect speaker, and in his later years took on a smallholding with pig-keeping. At the end of his life, in the early 1960s, he started jotting down reminiscences in a Boots diary (which he gave to me). The episode below is undated, but probably dates from the earliest years of the present century.

The Burning of the Shrew

When Mary came hoam from her wark she war full o news. She said, 'Has ta heard, Bill, 'at Jack so and so has gorn a living wi Misis so and so in Jubilee Road?' 'Well, I'll be damned. Them 'at haven't trouble seem to make some for the'sens.' 'Aye, but I haven't told thee all yet.' 'Well, what else is ther to tell?' 'Well, to-morn neet they are goin to burn them up.' 'So there is goin to be some fun, eh?' 'Aye, sum on 'em is making two big dummies, stuffed wi' sawdust, and pariffin oil, and they are going to be facing one another on a long pole, and there is going to be a procession around the village and to end in Jubilee Road.'

A lott were all looking for'ard to it, a lott 'at wor no better theirselves. On the night, as it became dusk they went and fetched out the dummies, and it was like some devil's madjic. They sett off around the village, and the procession grew and grew — folk wi' bells and draw tins, cake tins, owt 'at would make a noise; and it was nearly as good a noise as a jazz band ont wireless reckons to make with £2,000 worth of instruments. It went around the village, and landed in Jubilee Road. Talk about advertising! The police was there, and, Hell, they had to get a lott to break a way through, for the dummeys. There were a lott more people packed in Jubilee Road than lived in Siddal and no advertising. Well, the dummeys went through. The police tried to get it, but women danced in front of them and sat down in the street in front of them to stop them. But it went on, and up Scarhall stepps and back darn Backhold Lane around to Jubilee Road. Then they sett them on fire, and when they got in front of the house, and it was blazing like hell, the police was protecting the door. Then it was thrown on top of them. Two days later they removed, and they drummed them out unceremoniously with cake-tins and draw-tins. But that crowd! you could have walked on their heads. There will never be a crowd like that in Jubilee Road again, and no advertising. (A little bit of savagery.) Don't think I am making out Siddal to be a reight good moral place: I am not. It was like any other place, as the Parson's egg.

(One or two modifications to spelling and also to punctuation.)

APPENDIX II

It has been noted (see p. 495 above) that Lévi-Strauss cited in *Mythologiques I. Le Cru et le Cuit* an unpublished survey of the practice of charivari carried out by P. Fortier-Beaulieu, from which he derived the conclusion that in 92.5 per cent of the examined cases, the occasion for charivari was re-marriage.

Some extracts from Fortier-Beaulieu's survey were published in *Revue de folklore francaise et de folklore colonial*, xi (1940). The original replies to his questionnaire remain in the archives of the Musée National des Arts et Traditions Populaires (see MS B 19, 1 a 620, et MS 44,390) and I am greatly indebted to M. le Conservateur, and to the staff of the Musée for their courtesy and assistance in permitting me to consult these archives.

The survey took place between June and August 1937, and took the form of a questionnaire submitted to Mairies by P. Fortier-Beaulieu, at that time Secrétaire à la Propaganda of the Folklore Society. The questionnaire, in fact, makes no reference to charivari, but is headed simply "Manifestation à l'occasion du remariage d'un veuf ou d'une veuve"; a reply was called for urgently, to enable Fortier-Beaulieu to prepare a report on "Veuvage et le Remariage" at the forthcoming International Congress of Folklore.

Thus the enquiry was not conducted into the practice of charivari as such, but into any type of manifestation at re-marriage. It is therefore surprising, not that 92.5 per cent of the responses cite re-marriage as the occasion for charivari, but that the number falls short of 100 per cent. But the responses are not, in any case, of a kind which may be submitted to a serious exercise in quantification. Of 307 responses, 123 signalled manifestations of some kind upon re-marriage (usually charivari), 113 signalled no manifestations, 42 signalled that such manifestations no longer occurred, and 29 signalled "néant". Of the 123 affirmative replies, perhaps one half were perfunctory and completed in haste ("oui", "non"), while some thirty or forty were answered scrupulously and in detail. Except in a few cases, where the mayor passed the questionnaire over to a local folklorist or historian, the respondents had no special qualifications to answer the questions. One deduces that often the form was passed over to a secretary in the Mairie, while on a few fortunate occasions the mayor was a man of wide local knowledge and observation, and took pleasure in a task unfamiliar among routine business.

Thus the value of the survey lies not in any quantitative deductions, of even the most elementary kind, but in the materials presented in some thirty of the more conscientious replies. Before attending to these, we must offer a caution. The survey, in 1937, is dealing not with a custom in its vigour, but with vestiges and survivals. Hence we may not properly deduce from it functions which belong to the custom in its maturity. "A l'heure actuelle cette coutume qui n'existe que dans les campagnes est une plaisantrie et un divertissement pour la jeunese" (Rodez, Aveyron); it survived, if at all, as a good-humoured form of blackmail, to raise a few sous *pour boire.*

Insofar as such vestiges can offer evidence, there are replies which give support to most of the hypotheses debated by students of charivari. From Brive (Corrèze): "La veuve qui se remarie n'est guère bien considérée comme devenant infidèle à la mémoire du mari défunt"; or, again, "parce que le mariage est considéré comme un sacrement et que les conjoints n'ont pas moralement le droit de le rompre même après la mort" (Castillon, Ariège). A few replies indicate in some manner the representation of the spirit of the dead spouse at the charivari: "on évoque la vie passée des époux, leurs moeurs, leur vie galante, quelquefois c'est bien corsé" (Donzers, Drôme). Sexual ridicule of the aged, and in particular of disparity of ages, is frequently mentioned. An explanation which is offered only once is "pour chasser les mauvais esprits" (Aups, Var). The theory of a limited "pool of eligibles" also appears — if the second marriage should "enlève une possibilité du moins du choix pour les autres" (Séez, Savoie). The jealousy of friends, neighbours, parents (or of the parents of the dead spouse), and of children is more often mentioned. A charivari at Hyères (Var) had been organised by the grown-up son of the widower. The function was to protect "les intérêts des enfants du premier lit" (Remiremont, Vosges); "les enfants d'un premier lit ayant souvent à pâtir du second mariage — d'où le péjoratif:

marâtre" (Cahors, Lot). The relationship of charivari to differing inheritance customs is not a question which, to my knowledge, has yet been adequately pursued.

While most of the responses assume that the promoters of charivari were "des jeunes gens", a few replies suggest more particularity: the initiators are described, in one, as "les voisins ennemis et plus particulièrement les parents mécontents par l'union" (Uzès, Gard). Whoever were the initiators, the charivari was supported — as most replies make clear — by "un peu tout le monde de la basse classe" (Burzet, Ardèche); although in some regions there was some distinction among the actors:

> Dans certains cas où la différence d'âge est trop accentuée (vieillard contractant union avec jeune fille) les femmes manifestant plus que les hommes — Dégoût, peut-être, plus souvent jalousie si l'homme est fortuné.
>
> (Castillon, Ariège)

It is clear that re-marriage *as such* rarely provoked charivari; there was normally some other attendant circumstance. In certain regions, it is true, there was a marked disposition to disapprove of re-marriage and (correspondingly) to honour widowhood:

> La veuve qui respecte son veuvage est très bien vue dans le village. Les voisins l'aident dans son ménage et les hommes font le Dimanche matin les corvées volontaires pour lui couper son bois, lui faucher ses prés et labourer ses champs.
>
> (Castillon, Ariège).

In other regions, on the contrary, as one perceptive respondent noted, re-marriage was made essential by the economic nature of the household. Thus there were no manifestations against re-marriage in Nibelle-St. Sauveur (Loiret), a commune —

> composée pour sa grande majorité de petits propriétaires ruraux exploitant eux-mêmes, la vie en ménage est une nécessité. En conséquence, les veufs et veuves. . . se remarient généralement en un court délai. . .

Perhaps the most thoughtful reply came from Dax (Landes).* "Calhibari" was occasioned frequently by

---

*From Dr Aparisi-Serres, secrétaire général de la Société de "Borda": See *Revue de folklore.* . ., xi (1940), pp. 17-19.

remarriage, "mais il faut en outre une circonstance qui rende le remariage grotesque, odieux ou antipathique". Such a circumstance might be in 1) the difference in ages of the couple, 2) the difference in their social position, as when "un propriétaire 'monsieur' qui épouse une jeune paysanne", 3) a difference in fortune which suggested that one of the spouses was marrying for money, 4) the infirmity of the widow or widower, "ce qui suppose toujours la *vente* de soi-même", 5) the antecedent sexual conduct of either party, as for example "si l'on soupconne qu'ils étaient *bien* ensemble du vivant du mort ou de la morte" (this could occasion the bravest charivaris), 6) if both parties were old.

The suggestion that some aggravation of circumstances was necessary is present in many replies: "quand elle s'ajoute à la disproportion d'âge" (Moulins, Allier); "quand les futurs époux — veufs ou veuves — prêtent un peu le flanc à la critique et au ridicule" (Burzet, Ardèche); "plutôt à la veuve de mauvaise conduite qui se remarie" (Ruffec, Charente); "un vieux riche épousant une jeunesse pauvre. . . surtout s'il y a des enfants déjà grands d'un premier lit" (Brioude, Haute Loire). Without such aggravation, it was possible for the re-married to avoid the compliment of charivari even in a district where it was endemic. The respondent from Vico (Corse) replied in an unexpectedly personal sense:

> On tient plutôt compte de situations particulières: l'auteur de ces renseignements est un veuf remarié qui n'a pas eu l'honneur du campanaccio [charivari] parce que Instituteur dans la Commune, épousant une Institutrice.

One reply afforded a valuable case-history of such particularity. The most recent charivari in Abzac (Gironde) "s'adressait à un homme d'âge mûr qui allait épouser une jeune fille que l'on savait enceinte et qui avait une conduite plus que douteuse". A procession was held, in which were three wagons drawn by donkeys. In the first was a goat, with the slogan: "Viande à bas prix", in the second "un vieillard complètement perclus"; in the third, "un jeune homme déguisé en nourrice faisait le simulacre d'allaiter un énorme poupon et au moyen d'une paille de seigle fendue imitait les cris du nouveau-né". When charivari could attain such heights in the 1930s, there is no cause for surprise that its

occasional outcome in violence was signalled in some 16 per
cent of the replies: e.g. Dax (Landes), Thèze (Basses
Pyrénées), Conques (Aveyron), Remiremont (Vosges). One
wonders what the percentage would have been in 1837?

So much for re-marriage. What of the 7.5 per cent of
cases which (it would seem) fell outside this category? This
must indicate simply that handful of replies where the
respondent went beyond the enquiries of the questionnaire,
and added unsolicited information. From Conques: "quand
une femme a blessé son mari au visage, on conduit tous les
ânes ou mulets de la contrée, en procession dans les rues de la
localité". Charivaris had been held in Echire (Deux-Sèvres)
when one of the engaged "avait eu certaines atteintes au point
de vue galanteries, enfant naturel, etc.". From Dampniet
(Corrèze) there came a valuable case-history:

> Au village de la Jubertie une famille composée du père, de la mère et du
> fils, vivait dans une petite aisance. Une femme sexagénaire survint qui
> troubla ce bonheur paisible. Le père en devint toqué. Mais ne pouvant
> lui-même épouser 'la belle' il voulut la donner pour femme à son propre
> fils âgé de 26 ans et d'esprit un peu simple. Celui-ci accepte d'épouser la
> sexagénaire.

This charivari had violent and tragic tones: the father tried to
drown himself, and (failing) committed arson against one of
its organisers. The matter no doubt forced itself upon the
page, although not falling within the terms of the questionnaire, since it had occurred only two months previously — in
April 1937 — and had caused the mayor much concern.

One further reply deserves quotation — a reply thrown in,
perhaps, as an afterthought:

> Le 'callabari' se fait quelquefois à d'autres personnes que des veufs et
> des veuves — par exemple à des curés, des maîtres d'école, des
> fonctionnaires en résidence dans les villages lorsque la population devait
> se plaindre d'eux.
>
> (Tarbes, Hautes Pyrénées).

This evidence demolishes the supposed statistic of "92.5
per cent".

Index of Names and Places

Ireland 264, 295-6
Italy 467-8
Iver (Bucks.) 516-7

Jacobins 248-9, 292, 301
Jacobites 27, 68, 75-6, 80-1, 92
James II, king 246
Jefferies, Richard 381
Jeffreys, Judge 105
Jenkins, Priscilla 327-8
Jones, Robert 439
Jonson, Ben 222-3
Jowett, Jonathan 448

Kaira 280
Kaplan, Temma 332
Kemp, Thomas 116n
Kent 409, 426
Kenyon, Lloyd, lord chief-justice
    200, 270
Kerkebie, Emma 478
Kerridge, Eric 128-9, 137-8
Kettering 234, 305n
Kidderminster 61, 247, 323
King, Peter 141, 144, 169-70
Kingston (Surrey) 64
Kingswinford (Staffs.) 119n
Kingswood 304, 310
Kirkby Malzeard (Yorks.) 529-30
Ku Klux Klan 486, 523

Lancashire 409
Lane, Rev. Thomas 518
Langhorne, John 23, 44
Lansdown Fair 418
Laqueur, Thomas 48n
"Lark Rise" 514
Lascelles, Henry, second earl of
    Harewood 82
Laslett, Peter 19, 22-3
Le Goff, Jacques 353
Leake (Notts.) 146
Ledbury 332n
Leeds 82, 198, 333, 408, 503
Leicester 124, 290, 330, 333, 336,
    469n
Leigh, Lady 254
Lévi-Strauss, Claude 495, 534
Lewes 248

Lewis, John 111-13, 118-19
Limerick 295
Lincolnshire 409, 460, 478, 511-12
Liverpool 365
Llanbister (Radnorshire) 523
Lloft, Capel 141
Lloyd, Sir Richard 112
Locke, John 160-1, 164-5, 170
Loder, Robert 379-80
Logue, Kenneth 306, 313
Lomax, John 419
London 32, 67, 88, 125, 142-3,
    195, 211, 215, 223, 364, 365n,
    369n, 388, 394, 409, 479, 484,
    499, 505, 508, 520, 527
Loughborough 434
Loughborough, first baron, chief-
    justice common pleas 139-41,
    163
Loughton (Essex) 102, 142
Lowther, Sir William 110
"Ludd, Lady" 334
Ludham Waste (Norfolk) 132
Lyford, John 229
Lyndhurst (Hants.) 108
Lyons 496

Macpherson, C. B. 161
Macaulay, T. B. 28n, 29
Madras 174, 280, 294
Malcolmson, Robert 52
Maldon (Essex) 248, 330, 333-4
Malinowski, Bronislaw 187
Malthus, T. R. 276, 281-2, 287,
    296
Malvern 116n
Manchester 60-1, 195n, 209n, 211,
    220-1, 325, 330, 334, 370, 387,
    433, 447, 451n, 503
Mandeville, Bernard 3, 31, 55,
    270
Manning, Dr 211
Mansfield, first earl, lord chief-
    justice 112, 118n, 139
Maoris 166-7
March (Cambs.) 177-8
Mark (Som.) 131
Markham, G. 359, 379
Marlborough, duke of 280

Penkridge 416
Penryn (Cornwall) 231, 241
Perkin, Harold 22
Peterborough 123
Phillips, Catherine 317
Pickard, Edward 290-1
Pierce, Ruth 317
Pillet, Maj-Gen. R. 438, 450-1
Pilton (Som.) 436n
Pitt, Hester 317
Pitt, Jane 317
Pitt, William (the elder) 28n
Pitt, William (the younger) 276, 366-7
Place, Francis 377
Ploughley Hundred (Oxon.) 317
Plumb, Sir John 93
Plymouth 257, 436, 440-1
Poole (Dorset) 233, 313
Popkin, Samuel L. 342
Porlock (Som.) 119
Port Isaac (Cornwall) 231
Portland, duke of 250-1, 279-80, 483
Portsea (Hants.) 231
Potter, John 48
Poulett, earl 80-81
Prescot 365
Preston 194-5, 418
Priestley Riots 91

Quakers 209, 300n
Quemerford (Wilts.) 476, 485

Rackley, Elizabeth 329
Ramsbury (Wilts.) 248
Randall, Adrian 266, 337-8, 340
Raynal, Abbé 348
Reading 243
"Rebecca" 471, 521-3
Reddy, William 340-1
Redruth 427-8
Reigate 192
Retford 416
Richmond, duke of 243
Richmond Park 63-4, 99, 111-13
Riland, Rev. John 158
Ripley (Surrey) 527-9
Ripon 425

Rockingham Forest 98-9
Rogers, Nicholas 94
Rollison, David 515, 524
Ropley Commons 109
Rostins, Philip 425
Rostow, W. W. 187
Rotherham 448
Rowbotham, Sheila 500
Rudé, George 67, 237, 260n
Rutland 452-3
Ryton - upon - Dunsmore (Warwks.) 145-6

Saffron Walden 236
St Asaph 312
St Austell 71
Saint Monday 373-8, 394
Salcey Forest 106-7
Salisbury 216
Sampford Peverell (Devon) 237
Savage, John 426-7, 452
Schofield, R. S. 297
Scott, James C. 341-2, 345, 348-9
Scray, Lathe of (Kent) 227
Seaford 136
Sen, Amartya 284-7, 298, 299n
Severn, river 214, 325n
Sexton, Thomas 501
Sharples, Eliza 453
Sheffield 125, 374-5, 447, 455
Shelburne, earl of 197
Shepton Mallet 431, 436n
Sherborne (Dorset) 244-5
Shorter, Edward 512
Siddal (Yorks.) 527, 532-3
Simmonds, Mr 507
"Skimmington, Lady" 516
Skinner, Charles 426-7, 452
Skinner, Mary 426-7, 452
Sligo 295
Slinford (Surrey) 437
Smiles, Samuel 395
Smith, Adam 162, 201, 203-4, 207-8n, 261, 268-71, 273-84, 287, 288n, 296, 303n
Smith, Baird 281
Smith, Betty 229
Smith, Charles 189, 201, 222, 277